# ANCIENT ROME

# AN ANTHOLOGY OF SOURCES

# ANCIENT ROME

## AN ANTHOLOGY OF SOURCES

*Edited and Translated, with an Introduction, by*

CHRISTOPHER FRANCESE AND R. SCOTT SMITH

Hackett Publishing Company, Inc.
Indianapolis/Cambridge

22 21 20    3 4 5 6 7

For further information, please address
  Hackett Publishing Company, Inc.
  P.O. Box 44937
  Indianapolis, Indiana 46244-0937

  www.hackettpublishing.com

Cover design by Abigail Coyle
Composition by Graphic Composition, Inc., Bogart, Georgia


**Library of Congress Cataloging-in-Publication Data**

Ancient Rome : an anthology of sources / edited and translated, with an
introduction, by R. Scott Smith and Christopher Francese.
     pages cm.
  Includes bibliographical references and index.
  ISBN 978-1-62466-000-9 (pbk.) — ISBN 978-1-62466-001-6 (cloth)
  1. Rome—Civilization—Sources. 2. Politics and culture—Rome—History.
3. Politics and literature—Rome—History. 4. Civilization, Classical—Literary
collections. 5. Latin literature—Translations into English. 6. Rome—Social life
and customs. 7. Rome—Intellectual life. 8. Rome—History. I. Smith, R. Scott,
1971– translator, editor. II. Francese, Christopher, translator, editor.
  DG77.A585 2014
  937—dc23                                              2013036580

# CONTENTS

## LITERARY TEXTS

# DOCUMENTARY SECTION

# ACKNOWLEDGMENTS

Our sincere gratitude goes to all those scholars who graciously looked over our work and offered suggestions for improvement. Two anonymous referees for Hackett gave close and thoughtful readings to the proposal and helped refine the concept at an early stage. Eric Casey read and commented on the whole manuscript with great acumen, made many detailed improvements, and saved us from countless errors. Rolando Ferri gave close and expert attention to our translation of the difficult *Colloquia Monacensia*. Adrienne Su helpfully critiqued the Catullus translations. Stephen Trzaskoma translated the *Laudatio Turiae*, and offered strategic suggestions about the composition of the whole volume.

Here too we have the pleasure of thanking all the instructors—too many to name— who kindly sent us their syllabuses so that we could get a sense of what is going on in the front lines, so to speak, of classes in Roman civilization and history.

Four translations found in this volume are taken from other books in Hackett's excellent catalog, and we here thank the following scholars for allowing us to use their work: Sarah Ruden (Petronius), Martin Ferguson Smith (Lucretius), Henry John Walker (Valerius Maximus), and Valerie Warrior (Livy). We heartily thank our editor at Hackett Publishing, Rick Todhunter, for his steadfast support and encouragement, and also Hackett's crack production squad, led by Liz Wilson, for making the final stages go so smoothly. Derek Frymark did excellent work on the index, funded by generous grants from the Dickinson College Research and Development Committee and from the University of New Hampshire Center for the Humanities. Finally, we would like to acknowledge the Dean's Office at University of New Hampshire College of the Liberal Arts, whose summer fellowship allowed Smith the time to complete part of this book. To all our friends and colleagues who contributed in various ways, let the fact that this book finally saw the light of day be a source of pride for you, as it is for us.

# INTRODUCTION

This book contains writings by twenty-three ancient Roman authors, newly translated and equipped with brief introductions and explanatory notes. It includes some well-known classical works, intriguing texts by lesser-known figures, the words of ordinary people on epitaphs and other inscriptions, and some anonymous graffiti and utilitarian documents. The earliest texts included here, the Laws of the Twelve Tables, date in substance to the 5th century BC, the latest to around AD 250. A number of different genres appear: history, satire, philosophy, poetry, biography, and letters. The subjects range from early Roman legends to political history, slavery, the practice of religion, and many other topics.

## Selection and Arrangement

We have aimed to include works that are not only representative of different types of Roman writings and revealing of various aspects of Roman culture, but also readily discussable. We looked for whole texts and substantial passages that can be considered from more than one point of view, that reasonable people might see differently, that were likely to provoke some debate or controversy, and that could be applicable or relevant in different ways to the modern world. These texts should inspire conversation. They illustrate not so much what "the Romans" did or thought as how this or that particular Roman saw things within the context of more general Roman controversies, obsessions, and (sometimes conflicting) priorities. They can all be used to examine critically both ancient Roman and more recent practices and ideas.

Our alphabetical organization by author is meant to encourage readers to encounter the authors as distinct personalities, not merely as vehicles for information about the Romans. This book differs from most such sourcebooks in that it does not give small excerpts to illustrate some particular point, or categorize material based on a series of concepts that we wanted to exemplify, or restrict it to focus solely on a particular kind of history, whether political, military, social, or cultural. Of course, no one would want to read the book straight through in alphabetical order by author, and we give advice below on where to begin exploring specific topics.

For reasons of space we decided early on that we would not include Roman comedy or tragedy, extended historical texts, epic, and biography. In the last category we made two exceptions (all of Plutarch's *Life of Cato* and a significant excerpt from his *Life of Aemilius Paullus*) because they embody so well the values and customs that many Romans themselves thought were characteristic of their own culture. In any case, authors such as Plautus, Tacitus, and Vergil are readily available in good, inexpensive editions.

We realize and admit outright that with so many choices an element of subjectivity or even idiosyncrasy has crept in. As one of our early readers put it, "every instructor will have his or her own wish list," and to a degree this book represents ours, based on our own experience as teachers in consultation with as many others as was practicable. Yet not even all of our own favorite authors and texts made the cut, and some simply had to be left out to keep the volume at a reasonable size.

# Where to Start

The main body of the anthology is arranged alphabetically by author; there follows a second "Documentary" section for anonymous texts, inscriptions, and other non-literary material. For those readers interested in a particular topic rather than an author, we suggest the following as good places to begin. A full index in the back of the book has more complete lists of references.

1.  **Roman History.** The myths and legends of early Rome in Livy's *History of Rome*, though not "historical" in the full sense of the word, are nonetheless a good, and traditional, starting point. The *Laws of the Twelve Tables* give a somewhat more documentary glimpse of early Rome. Book 6 of Polybius' *Histories* provides a good overview of the traditional constitution of the middle Republic and the structure that was torn apart in the civil wars of the late Republic, as described by Appian in his *Civil Wars*. The selection of Cicero's letters included here chronicles the death throes of the Republic, and finishes up with a few letters that deal specifically with the young Octavian, who would emerge as the first emperor of Rome. This makes a natural segue to Octavian/Augustus' description of his own career in the *Accomplishments of the Deified Augustus* (*Res Gestae*), which reflects the political and cultural sea-change represented by establishment of the Principate under a single emperor. This story can be followed further in the Documentary Section through the inscriptions relating to emperors and the imperial cult (nos. 57–63).

2.  **Roman Values.** Traditional Roman values and ideals are explored by Livy through the medium of legend and mythology, and are given critical discussion by Plutarch in his *Life of Cato the Elder*. The latter presents an emblematic Roman senator, a conservative traditionalist of the Republic whose combative and controversial career exposes many of the enduring tensions of Roman culture and values. Polybius' description of aristocratic Roman funerals, in turn, shows how public rituals during the Republic encouraged young Romans to achieve greatness by emulating their forefathers. Pliny the Younger is a successful senator from a different era—the early Principate—a gentler figure who nonetheless shares Cato's drive for distinction through state service, public speaking, and writing.

3.  **The Structure of Roman Society.** The Documentary Section includes a selection of Roman epitaphs arranged according to class distinctions that will give a rough idea of the different sorts of legal and social statuses into which Romans divided each other, from senator to slave (nos. 1–56). Quintus Cicero's *Running for Office: A Handbook* contains advice on how to appeal to

each section of the Roman electorate, and other authors (especially Juvenal, Martial, and Petronius) deal with class tensions and status anxiety from a variety of perspectives.

4. **Patrons and Clients**. This key aspect of Roman social relations, politics, and morality can be seen at work in Horace's *Satires* 1.6 and 1.9, from the perspective of a successful client: the upwardly mobile son of a freedman. The *Epigrams* of Martial and Juvenal's third *Satire* give a more satirical view of the client's predicament. The letters of Cicero and Pliny often deal with the duties, privileges, and dilemmas of being a patron.

5. **The Roman Family**. Roman ideals of behavior and sentiment within the family emerge well from the epitaphs and related texts collected in the Documentary Section (nos. 1–56). The inscription honoring Turia (no. 1 in our collection) is especially notable. A variety of relationships between parents and children and husbands and wives can be glimpsed in the letters of Cicero (especially those to and about his wife Terentia and his daughter Tullia, nos. 2, 7, 8, 11, and 16), and Pliny (especially nos. 12, 13, 20, and 31); in Perpetua's account of the desperate conflict between her and her father in the *Passion of Perpetua and Felicitas*; and in Plutarch's discussion of Cato the Elder's approach to raising his son (*Life of Cato the Elder* ch. 20).

6. **Roman Women**. Two female authors are included: the love poet Sulpicia and the Christian martyr Perpetua. There are a number of inscriptions that were probably or certainly authored by women (nos. 6, 40, 43, 71, 80, 82, 84), and many that honor women and girls. Several of Pliny's letters discuss women of his circle (nos. 6, 12, 13, 18, and 20). The remarkable Lesbia—probably a fictionalized version of a prominent socialite of the late Republic—figures unforgettably in the poetry of Catullus.

7. **Education**. An outline of Roman aims and methods in upper-class education is given in our selection from Quintilian's *The Instruction of an Orator*. Seneca (*Letters* 10 in this volume, "On the Liberal Arts") subjects this system to caustic critique from a philosophical perspective. In the Documentary section we provide the rarely read late antique schoolbook, the so-called *Colloquia Monacensia*, which, besides shedding light on educational methods, runs interestingly through the day of a "typical Roman boy."

8. **Freedmen and Slaves**. The Documentary section includes epitaphs of slaves (nos. 51–55) and freedmen (nos. 47–50), as well as an evocative collection of inscribed slave collars (many translated here for the first time; no. 56). "Trimalchio's Dinner Party," a substantial section from Petronius' novel *Satyricon*, features a satirical portrayal of some freedmen who have become rich, and has several descriptions of urban slaves at work. Roughly contemporary to Petronius, Seneca's letter on slaves (no. 4 in this volume) offers a philosophical view on the institution of slavery, suggesting that all of humanity are in a sense "slaves." Pliny's *Letters* also deal frequently with his attitudes toward slaves and freedmen (nos. 10, 14, 21, 29–32). The *Handbook of Stoic Philosophy* was written by a former slave, Epictetus.

9. **Religion**. Inscribed prayers and dedications in the Documentary section give a sense of official Roman state cults (nos. 89–92), as well as the sheer diversity of gods available to individuals (seen especially clearly in the collection of altars found at Carvoran, along Hadrian's Wall, no. 93). Valerius Maximus provides anecdotes that reveal a Roman sense of what it meant to be pious, as well as giving a good overview of the kinds of rituals and officials associated with Roman state religion. An excerpt from Ovid's *Fasti* illustrates the central role of festivals and fun in Roman religion, and the calendar from Praeneste gives a sense of the rhythm of the year. The curse tablets in the Documentary Section (Inscriptions nos. 94–97) reveal practices that, while widespread, were by no means accepted by the Roman authorities (see also below no. 20, "Christians").

10. **Poetry**. Catullus is perhaps the most beloved of Roman poets by modern audiences, and we give a representative sample of his poems. Horace is Latin poetry's great craftsman, and we have translated several poems from his most famous collection, the *Odes*. Vergil's great epic, the *Aeneid*, could not be included for reasons of space, but we give the first and fourth of his highly influential collection of pastoral poems, the *Eclogues*. Other important poetic works included are Lucretius' *On the Nature of Things* (excerpts), Ovid's *The Art of Love* (Book 1), and all six surviving love elegies by Sulpicia. Cicero's speech *In Defense of Archias* and Juvenal's first *Satire* are revealing in different ways about Roman literary culture more generally.

11. **Love and Sexuality**. The Romans have a reputation as sexual libertines, but even a cursory reading of their literature shows complex and contradictory attitudes. The eroticism of love poets like Catullus and Ovid in his *Art of Love* needs to be set beside the extremely conservative attitudes about women's sexuality embodied in the story of Lucretia as told by Livy (chs. 57–58). Martial's poems on sexual topics (*Epigrams* nos. 11, 14, 18, 27, 32, 36, 45, 50) are sometimes shockingly obscene, but, as he tells us, that is a traditional part of the genre of epigram in which he writes. Some epitaphs in the Documentary section, too, give us insight into the relationships of husbands and wives; contrary to a common misconception, not all Roman marriages—in fact, very few—were politically arranged, loveless unions.

12. **Daily Life**. The school-exercise dialogues of the *Colloquia Monacensia* give a schematic run-through of a day in the life of a Roman town dweller, including a visit to the baths, the law courts, the money-lenders, and an evening meal with lists of typical foods. Juvenal's third *Satire* rails against the hazards of city life and contrasts them with an idealized picture of life in the country. Seneca (*Letters* 7 in this volume) gives an amusing account of what it was like to live over a Roman bath. Several of Martial's *Epigrams* deal with living conditions and life in the city (nos. 13, 28, 30, 37, 42, and 48) or in the country (no. 31). Pliny's letters about his tenant-farmers (nos. 10 and 25) give a rare glimpse into the plight of free Italian peasants in the early Principate.

13. **Meals and Food**. Petronius' *Trimalchio's Dinner Party* centers on a ridiculously lavish banquet thrown by a rich and tasteless freedman. The Roman schoolbook *Colloquia Monacensia* includes lists of more typical foods. Dinner

parties were the main venue for social gathering among friends, and are the settings of anecdotes in letters of Pliny (nos. 3, 24) and Cicero (no. 17), as well as the object of satirical jabs from Martial (*Epigrams* 25, 39).

14. **Land and Economics**. Plutarch's *Life of Cato* contains many references to land management, farming, and other entrepreneurial activities. Appian's account of the origins of the Roman civil wars and the rebellion of the slave Spartacus puts justified emphasis on the problems of land and land reform in the genesis of those conflicts. Two of Pliny's *Letters* discuss the economics of tenant farming and slavery in Roman Italy (nos. 10 and 25).

15. **Government and Politics**. Book 6 of the *Histories* by Polybius provides an overview of the constitution of the middle Republic. This adds an eyewitness account to the system described as the "Servian Constitution" by Livy (chs. 42–43) two centuries later. The treatise *Running for Office: A Handbook*, which purports to be by Marcus Cicero's brother Quintus, gives a vivid picture of the rough and tumble world of Roman elections, with more than a few correspondences with modern politics. The selection of electoral graffiti from Pompeii (Inscriptions no. 13) gives a sense of how vibrant political culture was in municipalities as well. The major political transformation represented by the Principate comes through in the inscriptions honoring emperors (especially the *Law on the Powers of the Emperor Vespasian*, no. 60). The inscriptions dealing with public works (nos. 65–71) reveal the importance of municipal elites in adorning cities and making them run.

16. **The Emperors**. Texts authored by emperors include Augustus' *Accomplishments*, Claudius' speech on the expansion of the citizen body (Inscriptions no. 59), and Hadrian's speech to the soldiers at Lambaesis (no. 63). Other inscriptions (nos. 57 and 58) show the participation of townships in supporting the emperor through loyalty oaths, while no. 60 gives a picture of the wide constitutional powers of the Emperor Vespasian. Seneca's *The Ascension of the Pumpkinhead Claudius into Heaven* is a satirical treatment of that emperor written after his death by one of the next emperor's courtiers. The correspondence between Pliny and the Emperor Trajan (Pliny, *Letters* 27–34) is revealing of the kinds of administrative and legal issues confronting Roman emperors.

17. **The Army**. Book 6 of Polybius' *Histories* gives a classic description of the Roman army of the middle Republic. Plutarch describes Cato's military service at some length in his *Life of Cato the Elder*, and we include a number of epitaphs for soldiers of various ranks (Inscriptions nos. 19–33). A remarkable inscription from Lambaesis in North Africa (no. 63) is Hadrian's address to the soldiers based there, the only surviving address by an emperor to the troops.

18. **Games and Shows**. The first eight pieces by Martial included here come from *On the Spectacles*, a set of short poems about the shows at the dedicatory games at the Colosseum. The political importance of theater emerges clearly from one of Cicero's letters (no. 5). The set of inscriptions relating to games and shows (nos. 72–88) includes epitaphs of gladiators, charioteers, dancers, actors, and other theater people, as well as inscriptions honoring sponsors that make clear how the games and shows were paid for. A letter of Seneca (no. 2

in this volume) explores the allegedly negative effects of games on spectators. Novatian's *On the Spectacles* (a shorter and more coherent discussion of some of the same themes in the more commonly read work of the same name by Tertullian) provides a thoroughly Christian critique that nonetheless reveals the extraordinary variety and popularity of public entertainments available.

19. **Philosophy**. Of the two major schools of Greek philosophy that gained substantial footholds among Roman writers, the Epicureans and Stoics, the first is represented by the poet Lucretius, whose *On the Nature of Things* dates to the mid-1st century BC. As for the Stoics, Seneca's *Letters* approach their doctrines in a conversational way, in words of friendly advice to a certain Lucilius. More rigorous and more challenging of conventional Roman attitudes is the famous *Handbook of Stoic Philosophy* by Epictetus, which in short order sets out the basic principles by which a Stoic must live.

20. **Christians**. Two of Pliny's *Letters* (nos. 33 and 34 in this volume) concern trials of Christians in the province of Bithynia around AD 110. *The Passion of Perpetua and Felicitas* is an extraordinary text, not least for being the sole surviving intimate journal written by a woman in antiquity. We include three *libelli*, or papyrus certificates of sacrifice, from the widespread but short-lived persecution of Christians carried out by the Emperor Decius in AD 250 (Inscriptions nos. 98–100).

# The Translations

The translations are our own work and created for this volume, except for the selections from Livy, Petronius, Lucretius, and Valerius Maximus, which are recent translations by others. At every turn we aimed to ensure that our translations were simultaneously accurate and readable. Our goal has been to represent clearly the sense of the original, while being faithful to contemporary (American) English idiom and style. At the same time, we tried to avoid gratuitous modernizing that would sound anachronistic and soon dated as well. Details on the original Latin and Greek texts that we used may be found in "Notes on Texts and Translations" at the end of the book.

# Reading the Romans: Some Rules of Thumb

For those encountering Roman writers for the first time, it may be helpful to articulate a few rough guidelines which, though partly a matter of common sense, also reflect some peculiar features of Roman literate culture, and will allow the reader to better appreciate what these texts have to offer.

1. **Consider the perspective of the author.** Each author will have his or her own viewpoint and aims in a particular instance, which will be shaped by circumstances, status, family, education, life experiences, and so forth. It helps to keep certain questions in mind: Is the writer attempting to persuade, entertain, praise, inform, impress, draw some pertinent moral, or some combination of these aims? Is he talking about contemporary events

or some remote period? Does he wholeheartedly endorse the views presented or propose them merely for the sake of argument or as something to think about? Is the author speaking in his own voice or through the persona of some particular character? Does he have any motive to be less than truthful or honest? Does his social position or economic circumstances or other factors predispose him to think in a certain way? Is he attempting to challenge received views or reporting what seems like a consensus? Is he attempting to shock his audience? The conventional wisdom is that Roman writing is less confessional and more influenced by models, personae, and what needs to be said on a particular occasion than is writing in more modern eras—though this generalization is debatable.

2.  **Consider the audience.** Is the intended receiver a single individual, a friend, an enemy, a student, a group, or a god? A good deal of Roman writing is persuasive or hortatory (urging people to do something), and this includes poetry. Consider what a particular argument implies about the predisposition of the audience and its expected views.

3.  **What is extraordinary is not typical.** We tend to remark on things that are not obvious or ordinary. What is surprising or noteworthy implies by contrast what is normal or average. Beware of inferring that, because some individual Roman is said to have done things in a certain way, or that somebody says that people *should* do things a certain way, that most people in fact did do it that way. The opposite is often more likely to be the case. By the same token, things that are said as if they had no special importance are often good evidence for common practices. All of this is especially relevant for anything to do with sexuality.

4.  **Ideas reflect controversies.** Like any group of people, the Romans disagreed strenuously among themselves about many things. What counterarguments are stated or implied in the positions taken by a given author? Are the terms of the debate familiar from modern controversies, or do they seem to reflect peculiar Roman institutions, customs, blind spots, or preoccupations? What do the positions taken imply about values and priorities of the author and the audience?

5.  **Look for the evaluation.** Roman authors, no less than modern ones, rarely describe things simply for the sake of describing them. Usually there is an expressed or implied evaluation, a position being taken that a particular fact or behavior is good or bad, right or wrong, or somewhere in between. These evaluations are key to the interpretation and assessment of what is being said, and are often foregrounded—something that has given Roman authors a well-earned reputation for being moralistic. But evaluations are often unstated, especially in historiography and letters. Attempt to figure out the implied position on what is being described.

6.  **Consider the genre.** Put very simply, Roman love poetry is meant to evoke desire, pastoral to conjure up an idyllic landscape, oratory to stir the mind and emotions, and satire to attack vice. Every genre has its traditional goals and parameters, which can be followed or subverted by individual authors, and which are usually not coextensive with their modern relatives. Roman and Greek

biographers were primarily interested in illustrating and evaluating character, rather than simply describing the facts and circumstances of the subject's life (see further the introduction to Plutarch). Similarly, historical writing tends to be more exemplary (that is, offering a model for behavior) and moralizing than its modern counterpart. Philosophy can be cast as poetry (as with Lucretius) or as letters (as with Seneca). Epigram, a genre perfected by Martial but now rare, will always be short and have a sting in the tail. Try to get a sense of what genre an author is writing in, and what that implies about the kinds of things he is likely to say, and how he innovates. Roman authors were fond of playing with genre, as when Ovid humorously adopts the conventions of instructional literature in *The Art of Love*. The introductions in this book offer some guidance on this matter.

7. **Consider what is not said.** Many types of documents we would like to have either do not survive or were not written in the first place. We do not have personal diaries, church and municipal archives, or journalism of the sort historians of more recent eras take for granted. And there are many other gaps, due both to the vagaries of what was preserved in the Middle Ages, as well as to who could write, who chose to write, and what they chose to write about. A figure like Cicero looms large because he was so prolific and his Latin style so beloved in later ages. But the thoughts of even some very influential Romans, like Marius, Sulla, or Nero—not to mention countless ordinary people—are relatively or entirely inaccessible to us. One would like to have the memoirs of Roman priestesses, engineers, magicians, slaves, soldiers on the frontiers, or Gallic tribesmen who adopted Roman ways, but we do not. And even within the documents we do possess, many issues we would like to hear about are simply not discussed. These silences are themselves often significant.

# Advice to the Reader

The following conventions have been adopted as aids to enjoyment of, and navigation within, the book.

- **Introductions.** For each author we provide a short general introduction, and if there is more than one text for that author, separate introductory remarks for each text. These are intended to provide orientation for reading and understanding the text at hand, so we urge readers to consult them before diving into the texts themselves.

- **Editorial Additions.** Introductory matter and explanatory notes on the main part of the page are set in a different font to distinguish them from the words of the texts themselves. Footnotes are always editorial, never by the Roman authors.

- **Special Terms.** Peculiar Roman terms that have no simple and unambiguous English equivalents, such as *lictor* or *pontifex*, are explained in the Glossary or in footnotes. Many other culturally specific terms can be found in the Glossary as well.

- **Titles.** Titles that we have added for individual sections of ancient works and particular letters or poems are printed in bold to make it clear that they are editorial, not originating with the Roman authors. We have added them to make it easier to find individual passages.

- **References.** There are standard ways for scholars to reference ancient texts, and we have provided these traditional references. These normally include a "book" number (each "book" of a Roman work typically being what would fit on a single roll of papyrus), then a number that represents a specific section, chapter, paragraph, poem, letter, or line within that book, as appropriate (e.g., "Ovid, *The Art of Love* 1.44" means Book 1 of Ovid's *The Art of Love* line 44). Works that are mentioned in the notes but not included here can be followed up in modern editions and translations, which almost always use the standard numberings. Many of these can be easily accessed on the web.

- **Our Numberings.** In some cases we created our own numberings for discrete poems and letters written by a single author, but in those cases we give the standard references as well. Cross-references to items in this book will use our numbering system, not the standard references. The goal here was to make it easier for instructors to refer to individual sections or groups of texts.

- **Place Names.** Places are normally designated by the ancient names used by the authors themselves, but with the equivalent modern name (if any) given in parentheses, or in a note. Some Roman geographical names, such as Asia and Africa, are superficially identical to modern names but completely different in what they represent. These are explained as they come up, and most of the important places can be found in our collection of maps.

- **Appendices.** Following the literary and documentary sections, we include several appendices to help orient the reader: A) Roman Naming Conventions; B) Roman Time Reckoning; C) Roman Currency, Weights, and Measures; D) A List of Roman Emperors to AD 337.

# Chronology of Authors and Texts

Republican Texts

Note: Twelve Tables, according to tradition, composed in 451–450 BC.

| (BC) | 210 | 180 | 150 | 120 | 90 | 60 | 30 |
|------|-----|-----|-----|-----|-----|-----|-----|

Polybius
M. Cicero
Q. Cicero
Lucretius
Catullus

Late Republic–Augustan Period

| 70 | 60 | 50 | 40 | 30 | 20 | 10 | 0 | 10 | 20 |
|----|----|----|----|----|----|----|----|----|----|

Vergil
Horace
Augustus
Livy
Sulpicia
Ovid
Fasti P.

Early Empire

| | 0 | 20 | 40 | 60 | 80 | 100 | 120 | 130 | 140 | 150 | 160 |
|---|---|---|---|---|---|---|---|---|---|---|---|

Val. Max.
Seneca
Petronius
Quintilian
Martial
Plutarch
Epictetus
Pliny
Juvenal
Appian

Late Empire

| | 180 | 200 | 220 | 240 | 260 | 280 | 300 |
|---|---|---|---|---|---|---|---|

Perpetua
Novatian
Roman School Book

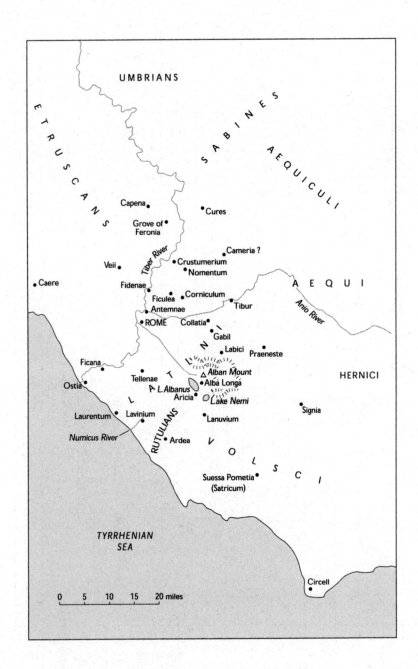

UMBRIANS

ETRUSCANS

SABINES

AEQUICULI

AEQUI

HERNICI

• Capena

Grove of •
Feronia

• Cures

• Cameria ?

Veii •

• Crustumerium
• Nomentum

• Caere

Fidenae •

Ficulea •
• Antemnae

• Corniculum

• Tibur

Anio River

• ROME

Collatia •

L A T I N I

Ficana •

• Gabii

• Labici

Praeneste •

Tellenae •

Alban Mount

• Alba Longa

Ostia •

L. Albanus

Aricia

Lake Nemi

Signia •

Laurentum •

• Lavinium

RUTULIANS

• Lanuvium

Numicus River

• Ardea

V O L S C I

Suessa Pometia •
(Satricum)

TYRRHENIAN
SEA

Tiber River

0    5    10    15    20 miles

Circeii •

Latium in the Period of the Kings

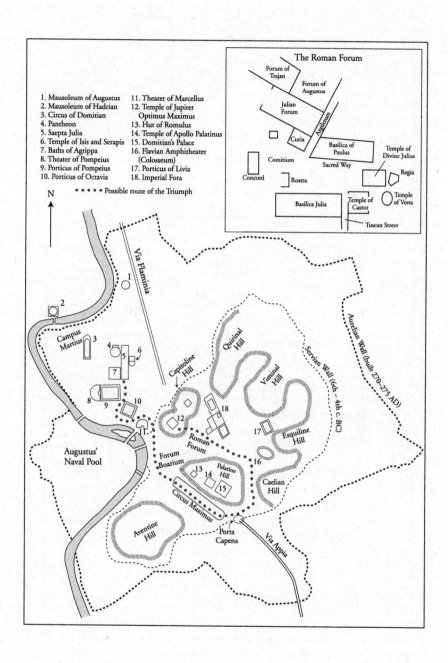

1. Mausoleum of Augustus
2. Mausoleum of Hadrian
3. Circus of Domitian
4. Pantheon
5. Saepta Julia
6. Temple of Isis and Serapis
7. Baths of Agrippa
8. Theater of Pompeius
9. Porticus of Pompeius
10. Porticus of Octavia
11. Theater of Marcellus
12. Temple of Jupiter
    Optimus Maximus
13. Hut of Romulus
14. Temple of Apollo Palatinus
15. Domitian's Palace
16. Flavian Amphitheater
    (Colosseum)
17. Porticus of Livia
18. Imperial Fora

• • • • • Possible route of the Triumph

N

**The Roman Forum**

Forum of Trajan
Forum of Augustus
Julian Forum
Argiletum
Curia
Basilica of Paulus
Temple of Divine Julius
Comitium
Sacred Way
Concord
Rostra
Regia
Basilica Julia
Temple of Castor
Temple of Vesta
Tuscan Street

Via Flaminia

Campus Martius

Capitoline Hill

Quirinal Hill

Viminal Hill

Servian Wall (6th – 4th c. BC)

Aurelian Wall (built 270–275 AD)

Augustus' Naval Pool

Roman Forum

Forum Boarium

Esquiline Hill

Palatine Hill

Caelian Hill

Circus Maximus

Aventine Hill

Porta Capena

Via Appia

The City of Rome and the Forum

The Roman World

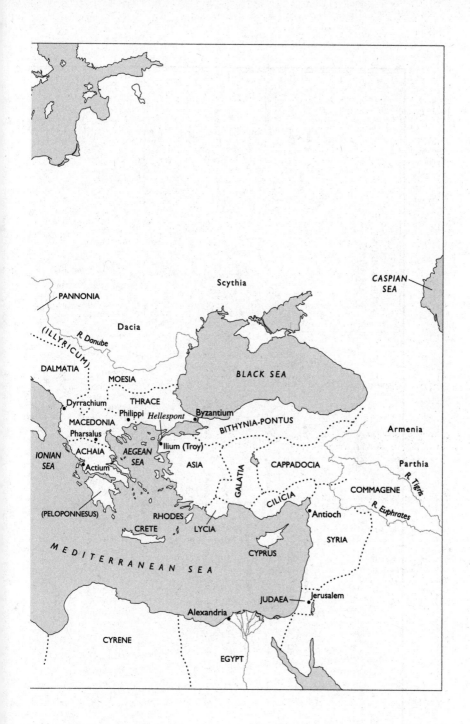

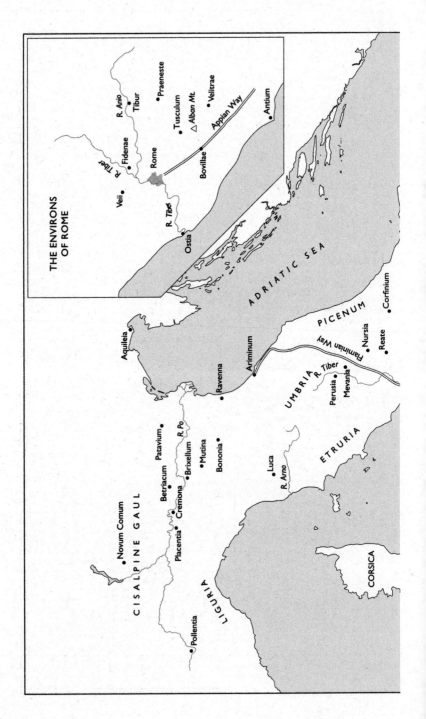

THE ENVIRONS
OF ROME

R. Anio
Tibur
Praeneste
Fidenae
Tusculum
Rome
△ Alban Mt.
Velitrae
Appian Way
Antium
Bovillae
R. Tiber
Veii
R. Tiber
Ostia

ADRIATIC SEA

Aquileia
Ariminum
Ravenna
PICENUM
Corfinium
Flaminian Way
Nursia
Reate
UMBRIA
R. Tiber
Perusia
Mevania
Patavium
R. Po
Betriacum
Brixellum
Mutina
Bononia
Cremona
ETRURIA
Luca
R. Arno
Novum Comum
CISALPINE GAUL
Placentia
LIGURIA
CORSICA
Pollentia

Italy

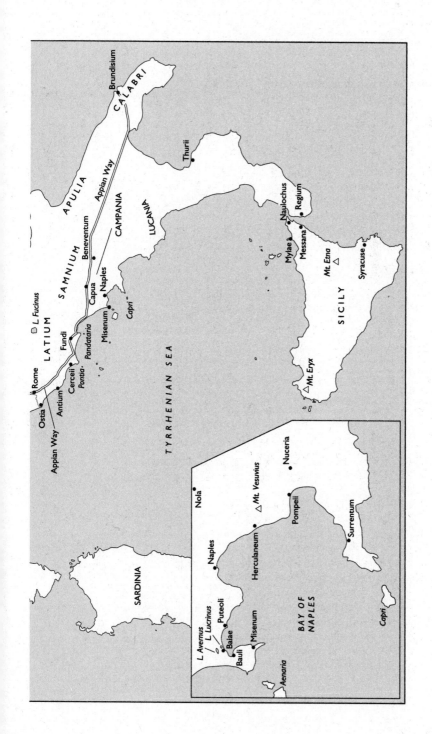

# APPIAN

(ca. AD 90–160, wrote in Greek)

## Introduction

Appian was born in Alexandria, Egypt, but later moved to Rome and was active there as an attorney before rising to a high administrative position as an imperial financial officer. He is best known for writing a comprehensive history of the world from the foundation of Rome to the reign of Trajan, organized for the most part geographically, by peoples (Samnites, Celts, Iberians, Carthaginians, Egyptians, etc.). Much of that is lost, but five books on the Roman civil wars survive, and it is from this section that the excerpts below derive. Appian's *Civil Wars* are concerned with the internal strife that afflicted Rome from 133–30 BC and ultimately brought down the mixed republican constitution (see Polybius in this volume), and yielded one headed by an emperor (*princeps*, hence the name for the following period, "Principate"). Appian wrote to explain how this change from endemic civil strife to stability and monarchy came about, a tale, he says, that "should make compelling reading for those who want to know the infinite ambition of men, their destructive lust for power, their relentless perseverance, and the countless forms of evil" (1.6). Appian clearly admired the constitution of the Republic a great deal, even as he looked back in horror at the convulsions that gave birth to the stable imperial order he knew.

Appian is the only extant ancient source to treat this period in a comprehensive and detailed way. Though not always reliable, Appian's account of the causes leading up to the crisis is generally regarded as coherent and accurate. We provide three excerpts from the first book: (A) Appian's overview of the crisis of the late Republic; (B) his account of the death of the revolutionary Tiberius Gracchus; and (C) the uprising of the charismatic slave Spartacus. The first two show Appian's flair for economic and political analysis as he traces the roots of the crisis and the failed reform efforts of Tiberius Gracchus (1.1–16). The third shows his gift for suspenseful narrative, as he tells the tale of Spartacus and the massive Italian slave revolt of 73–71 BC (1.116–120), events which highlight the dangers of the massive slave population—an issue, in fact, that had been central to Tiberius Gracchus' arguments for reform as described in excerpt A.

## The Civil Wars

### A     The Crisis of the Late Republic

At Rome the people and Senate were frequently at odds over the establishment of laws, the cancellation of debts, the distribution of land, and the election of magistrates. These internal conflicts did not result in physical violence, but were merely disagreements and quarrels within the confines of the law, and these they settled with great restraint and by making mutual concessions. At one point the people even fell into such a quarrel during a military campaign, but even so, they did not employ the weapons at their fingertips. Instead, they took refuge on the hill that has been called the Sacred Mount ever since.[1] Even then there was no recourse to violence. Instead, they created a public official, called the tribune of the people, to champion their interests generally. But their primary tasks were to curb the power of the consuls, who were chosen from the Senate, and to ensure that their power within the constitution was not unlimited. From that time forward these two magistracies became ever more hostile and antagonistic toward each other, with the Senate and the people taking sides. Each believed that they could dominate the other by increasing the powers of their own magistrate. In fact, it was amidst this sort of conflict that Marcius Coriolanus was unjustly banished from Rome, went into exile among the Volsci, and declared war against his own country.[2]

[2] This is the only example of armed civil conflict you will find in the early history of Rome, and it is worth pointing out that it was initiated by a deserter. No one ever brought a sword into the Senate, nor was there ever a case of civil bloodshed. This all changed, however, with Tiberius Gracchus, who, while he was trying to pass new laws as tribune of the people, became the first man to be killed in civil unrest. A great crowd of his supporters, too, were killed as they huddled around him beside the temple on the Capitoline Hill [133 BC].

But the civil unrest did not end with this heinous act. At every opportunity the two factions openly faced off against each other, frequently with daggers in their hands. Occasionally, a magistrate—be it a tribune, praetor, consul, a candidate for those offices, or some other distinguished person—would be killed in a temple, in the assembly, or in the Forum. Chaos and violence were the order of the day, as was shameful contempt for law and justice. The crisis got increasingly worse. People openly revolted against the government. Exiles and convicts, as well as all those people who were vying with each other over some office or military command, waged large and violent cam-

---

1. According to Livy (2.30–33), in 494 BC the plebeians, still under arms from battles against neighboring peoples, retired to the Sacred Mount in protest over their lack of rights compared to the aristocracy. A compromise was reached through the creation of the office of tribune of the people (*tribunus plebis*; see Glossary).

2. Livy reports the story (2.34–41): during the famine of 491 BC Coriolanus argued that, in return for low grain prices, the people should relinquish their recent political gains, including the office of tribune. The plebeians protested, and Coriolanus was forced into exile; he found refuge with the Volscians, Rome's enemy, and led them against his former city. He relented only when his mother and wife begged him to do so.

paigns against their own country. Power was frequently seized by juntas and individuals aiming for a kingship. Some refused to disband the armies entrusted to them by the state, while others even went so far as to enlist mercenaries on their own, without authorization of the state, to fight against each other. When one party took possession of the city, the other side took to war, claiming that their fight was against the opposing faction, when in reality it was against their own country. They would attack Rome as if it were an enemy city, ruthlessly slaughtering all those that got in their way. Some were put on proscription lists, were exiled, or lost their property. Others were tortured horrifically.

[3] Every conceivable horror was perpetrated up until the rule of Cornelius Sulla, one of the party leaders, some fifty years after Gracchus.[3] But his cure was worse than the disease. He made himself monarch for quite a long time, reinstating the office of "dictator," which was originally a six-month position employed by the early Romans in times of great crisis, but one that had long fallen out of use. Technically, Sulla was "elected," but in reality he used violence to force his way into becoming dictator for life. Yet, when he became sated with his absolute power, he had the courage to lay it down willingly—the first man, as far as I know, to have done so. He also made a public declaration that he was prepared to defend his actions as dictator against anyone who found fault with them. For a long time he, now but a private citizen, could walk down to the Forum in front of the whole population and return home without being subjected to violence or abuse—a sign of the deep fear that the onlookers still felt for his former position. Or perhaps it was due to the astonishment caused by his laying it down, or to their reluctance to call him to account for his actions. Perhaps they felt some compassion for the man. Or maybe they all just reckoned that his dictatorship had done some good.

Be that as it may, there was a brief respite from the civil unrest so long as Sulla lived—compensation, as it were, for all the ills that he himself had wrought while in power. [4] But after Sulla died, the factious strife blew up again, no less than before, and continued until Gaius Caesar. This man was voted into power and held a long-term command in Gaul.[4] But when the Senate demanded that he give up the command, he did not think that the Senate actually wanted this, but that it was just doing the bidding of Pompeius, who was his personal enemy and had control of an army in Italy. Caesar charged him with scheming to deprive him of his command, and proposed either that both he and Pompeius should keep possession of their armies, eliminating the fear of reprisals by the other; or that Pompeius too should disband his army and become a private citizen obedient to the laws like himself.

---

3. L. Cornelius Sulla (ca. 138–78 BC), the leader of the aristocratic party (*optimates*, see Glossary), invaded Italy and marched on Rome twice, once in 88 BC against Marius, the leader of the people's party (*populares*, see Glossary), and again in 83. In 82 he declared himself dictator in order to restore the republican constitution, but resorted to proscriptions—public bounties—to eliminate political opponents and confiscate their property and wealth. He gave up the position and retired to Campania in 79.

4. C. Julius Caesar (100–44 BC) was elected consul in 59 BC and received the province of Gaul from 58–49. After marching on Rome and defeating Pompeius, he assumed the dictatorship until his death.

Neither proposal was adopted, so Caesar marched against Pompeius.[5] He left Gaul and invaded Italy, pursuing his enemy all the way to Thessaly, where he had fled, and secured a brilliant victory in a massive battle.[6] Pompeius fled to Egypt, and Caesar followed him. After Pompeius was killed by Egyptian men, Caesar stayed in Egypt until he could put its affairs in order and settle the dynastic struggle there.[7] Then he returned to Rome. Now that he had eliminated, through victory in war, his chief adversary—the man who had been dubbed "The Great" because of his own remarkable military achievements—there was no one left to dispute him on any matter, and he was chosen, just as Sulla had been before him, dictator for life.

For a second time there was a break in the civil unrest until Brutus and Cassius, jealous of Caesar's great power and desirous of restoring the ancestral republican constitution, killed him during a meeting of the Senate,[8] even though Caesar was extremely popular with the people and excelled at governing. And it was the general public who missed him most of all. They combed the city in search of his assassins, buried his body in the middle of the Forum, built a temple over the ashes of the pyre, and made sacrifice to him as a god.[9]

[5] It was at precisely this moment that the civil unrest broke out again and increased to monstrous proportions: there were murders, exiles, and proscriptions of both senators and the members of the so-called equestrian class in vast numbers. Party leaders cooperated with one another by surrendering one another's enemies into their adversaries' hands, without regard for the ties of friendship or even of blood.[10] Their hostility toward their adversaries was so great that it overpowered any feelings of love they had for their kin. Three men came to the fore: Antonius, Lepidus, and Octavian, who later assumed the name Caesar because he was related to the other Caesar and was named as his adopted heir in his will. These three men divided up the Roman empire among themselves as if it were their private possession. Almost immediately after they had divvied up their realms they clashed, as was only natural. Octavian's intelligence and experience proved far superior. He first removed Lepidus from his allotted portion, Africa, and then took over Antonius' realm, which stretched from Syria to the entrance of the Adriatic, after defeating him in battle at Actium.[11] After these events, which were truly monumental and shocked the whole Roman world, Caesar sailed to Egypt and took possession of that territory, too. Egypt, the most ancient power of that day, and the strongest of the kingdoms that arose after Alexander's death, was the last

---

5. See Cicero, *Letters* 12 in this volume.

6. At Pharsalus (in Greece) in 48 BC.

7. Ptolemy XII and his daughter (and coregent) Cleopatra VII were embroiled in a power struggle after the death of Pompeius. Captivated by Cleopatra, Caesar not only reinstalled her on the throne, but also fathered by her a son, Caesarion.

8. March 15, 44 BC.

9. Caesar was formally deified by a vote of the Senate, who established a priesthood to oversee the cult worship of this newly created "god."

10. Appian reports (*Civil Wars* 4.12) that Lepidus' brother and Antonius' uncle (L. Caesar) were on top of the proscription list.

11. In 36 and 31 BC, respectively.

remaining piece to complete the Roman empire as it still stands today. And so imme-diately, while he was still alive, Octavian earned the unprecedented name Augustus ("Revered") because of his achievements, for that was how he was seen and what he was called by the Romans. He declared himself ruler of Rome and all nations subject to it, an autocrat like Gaius Caesar before him, but taking it to even greater extremes—he disposed of all elections and voting on public issues, and did not even keep up the charade that the nation was democratic.[12] His rule proved to be both long-lived and temperate, and he himself, a formidable man, found success in all of his endeavors. He bequeathed this autocratic power as a legacy to his descendants and successors, who, like him, ruled with complete authority.

[6] To summarize: out of many complex internal conflicts there evolved a Roman state that was a harmonious monarchy. I have synthesized multiple sources to produce this narrative in order to show how this state of affairs came to be. It should make compelling reading for those who want to know the infinite ambition of men, their destructive lust for power, their relentless perseverance, and the countless forms of evil. . . .[13]

# B    The Problem of Land and Tiberius Gracchus (1.7–16)

[7] As the Romans conquered Italy little by little through war, they would take part of the land and either found new cities or enlist colonists from their ranks to settle preexisting ones. They intended these settlements to act as outposts in lieu of military forts. Now, as for the land that they acquired in each war, the farmland they would immediately distribute to the colonists, or else they would sell or lease it. But as for the uncultivated countryside gained through war (and there happened to be a great deal of this), since they did not have the time to distribute it fully, they made the following proclamation: those who wished could work the land for the time being at a rent of one-tenth of the yearly produce in the case of sown crops and one-fifth for orchards. A similar system was devised for those who raised livestock, both the larger and the smaller animals. Their aim in this was to increase the population of Italians—in their view the most hardworking of all peoples—so as to have allied manpower close to home.

But this plan failed to pan out, and in fact the opposite happened. The wealthy, as it turned out, gobbled up the majority of this unassigned land, and over time gained confidence that it would never be taken away from them. They annexed all of the poor people's small lots around them—convincing some to sell, taking the rest by force—and began large-scale production on giant estates, eliminating the small farms. These owners bought slaves at auction to work the fields and pasture the animals, so that they could avoid the very real possibility of having their freeborn employees pulled from working the land to serve in the army. The possession of slaves also brought them great profit, since their slaves continually produced slave children who were not liable for military service. The outcome? The rich got spectacularly rich, the number of slaves

---

12. An overstatement. See *The Accomplishments of the Deified Augustus* chs. 4 and 34 in this volume.

13. The rest of chapter 6, which outlines the contents of this book, is omitted here.

ballooned across the countryside, and there was a severe shortage of military-eligible men in Italy, since they had been worn out by poverty, taxation, and military service. Those that happened to avoid these oppressive conditions would pass the time idly with nothing to do. After all, the land lay in the hands of the wealthy, and they chose to use slaves as workers instead of free men.

[8] These conditions made the Romans anxious for two reasons. First, there was no longer an abundance of allied manpower in Italy from which they could draw, and second, their sovereignty was now at risk because of the enormous number of slaves.[14] The way to correct these problems was not immediately apparent to them. It would not be easy, nor would it be entirely fair, to take away from so many men such a large amount of property that they had held for so long: private gardens and orchards, buildings, and other such fixtures. Eventually the tribunes were able, though not without difficulty, to push through a measure which was ratified by the people: no one could have more than 300 acres[15] of this land, and could not raise more than 100 large and 500 small heads of livestock. It was also required that they had to employ a number of free men, who were to watch over the land and report back to Rome.

When they passed this comprehensive law, they swore oaths to uphold it and established penalties for failure to do so. They believed that the excess land would be sold off to the poor small plot by small plot. But there was not the slightest consideration for the laws and oaths, and those who did follow the law (or rather, *seemed* to) only did so for outward appearances and distributed the land to their relatives. The vast majority simply scorned the laws altogether.

[9] That is, until Tiberius Sempronius Gracchus arrived on the scene.[16] He was a man of distinction, ambitious for honors and recognition, and an extremely compelling speaker. For all of these reasons he was the talk of the whole town. As tribune he gave a very moving speech concerning the Italian peoples, how they were both excellent fighting men and the Romans' kinsmen but were slowly being reduced to small numbers—and those few had been reduced to utter poverty. Worst of all, they had lost all hope for change. Tiberius also unleashed his bile against the slave population. They were useless in war and never loyal to their masters. He brought up the recent horrors that slaves had wrought against their masters in Sicily, where the number of slaves had spiked because of agricultural production. He noted that the war that the Romans had waged against them had been neither easy nor short. No, it was a protracted war, one in which the Romans had to overcome countless dangerous situations.[17]

After this speech, he resuscitated the law: no one could have more than 300 acres of public land. Then he added a further provision to the old law, namely, that the landholder's children could each have an additional 150 acres. A committee of three

---

14. Appian here implies the threat of slave revolts, which were rare, but in fact materialized in 135 BC (in Sicily), and again in 73 BC under the leadership of Spartacus (see section C below).

15. Five hundred *iugera* (see Appendix "Roman Currency, Weights, and Measures"). For comparison, the Roman farms on the periphery of Cologne, Germany, averaged between three and ten *iugera* (two and seven acres).

16. Born around 163 BC, Tiberius Gracchus became tribune of the people in 133 BC.

17. In 135 BC the slave population revolted in Sicily, with an estimated army of some 60,000 fighters. After several losses, the Romans finally prevailed in 132.

elected officials, the composition of which would change every year, would distribute the remaining land to the poor.

[10] This last point is what troubled the wealthy most of all. Because there was official oversight, they could no longer ignore the law as before, or purchase land from those poor who had received a plot. (Gracchus had foreseen that this might happen and forestalled it by forbidding anyone to sell their apportioned plots.) So the wealthy came together in groups to protest, saying that the poor were getting their ancient farmlands, orchards, and homes. Some claimed that they had already made payments to their neighbors for their land—would they lose their investment along with the land? Others asked what was to happen to their ancestors' graves, which lay on their land, land that had been given to them as if by inheritance. Still others complained that they had spent their wives' dowries on the purchase of land, or had given the land to their daughters to use as dowries. Creditors pointed out that some land was being used as collateral for debts. Generally speaking, there was a riotous mixture of complaint and outrage.

The poor, for their part, responded to the complaints of the wealthy with their own. They claimed that they were being prevented from making a living wage and thrust into abject poverty. Their lack of money made it impossible to have children since they could not support them. They recounted all the military campaigns that they had participated in, campaigns that had won for the Romans the land now under dispute, and they made it clear that they were incensed at the possibility of being deprived of access to this public land. At the same time they reproached those wealthy men who chose to employ slaves over men who were free, citizens, and soldiers, even though slaves were always an untrustworthy and hostile bunch and for that reason completely useless in war.

While these two groups were voicing their complaints and criticizing each other, there arrived yet another crowd with similar fears—people from colonies or free municipalities, and those with a vested interest in what was to happen to the land. They were split among both factions. Encouraged by their swelling numbers, each side grew more and more intransigent. They ignited continuous disturbances in the days leading up to the vote, with one side firmly committed to defeating the law, the other committed to seeing it passed at any price. Besides their own vested interests, each side was seized with a passion to win, and preparations were made on both sides for the appointed day.

[11] Gracchus' main intention was not to increase wealth, but manpower. He was so incredibly enthusiastic about the good that his work would do (he firmly believed that nothing greater or more glorious could be done for Italy) that he did not consider any of the difficulties the law might cause. When the vote was about to take place, Gracchus made many compelling arguments, going into great detail, and asked the following questions: isn't it right that public land be allotted to the public? Shouldn't a citizen always get more consideration than a slave? Isn't a soldier more useful than someone who knows nothing of war? Wouldn't someone be more concerned with the public good if he had some stake in it? He did not linger on the contrast between free and slave—there were more glorious topics to discuss—so he quickly turned to giving an account of the country's hopes and fears. Had they not become the master of most of their land through the violence of war, and did they not have hopes set on conquering the rest of the world? And here they were, at a critical juncture where everything hinged on what they did next: either they were going to acquire the rest of

the world with throngs of fighting men, or lose what they already had at the hands of their enemies because of their weakness caused by mutual jealousy.[18]

After he had exaggerated Rome's glories and successes on the one hand, and the threats and fears on the other, he urged the wealthy to consider his words carefully and to bestow this land, freely if necessary, to men who would raise children—only then would their hopes become reality. The wealthy had to make sure that they, while they were fighting over smaller issues, did not overlook the greater good. After all, they were getting, as compensation for their hard work in cultivating the land, undisputed ownership of 300 acres of the choicest land, without cost and in perpetuity, and those who had children were eligible to receive an additional 150 acres for each son. With these and many other similar arguments he kindled the passions of the poor, as well as those who thought about the situation from a logical point of view and not from the perspective of greed. Then he asked the clerk to read out the law.

[12] But there was another tribune, Marcus Octavius, who had been prompted by the landowners to oppose Tiberius' measures. He ordered the clerk to stop speaking (according to Roman law, the tribune who interceded to block a measure always trumped the one proposing it). Gracchus, after roundly criticizing Octavius, postponed the assembly until the following day. The next day Gracchus surrounded himself with an armed guard big enough to compel Octavius if he should object again, and then ordered the clerk, under threat of violence, to read out the law to the people. But when he started reading it, Octavius forbade him from continuing, and the clerk stopped. The tribunes started hurling insults at each other, and the crowd raised quite an uproar. Influential men asked the tribunes to take their differences to the Senate, and Gracchus seized on the suggestion. He thought that this law would surely appeal to all reasonable people—and marched directly to the Senate house. When he got there, however, he was outnumbered and abused by the wealthy, and so he ran back to the Forum. He announced to the people that he would put two matters to a vote on the next day, the law itself *and* Octavius' position: should a tribune who acts contrary to the interests of the people be allowed to retain his office? And Gracchus did just this. When Octavius, refusing to be bullied, again blocked the measure, Gracchus initiated a vote whether Octavius should retain his position.

After the first tribe voted that Octavius should remove himself from office, Gracchus turned to him and begged him to change his mind. When Octavius refused to budge, Gracchus let the voting continue. At that time there were thirty-five tribes;[19] the first seventeen vehemently and unanimously voted against Octavius. As the eighteenth tribe was about to cast the deciding vote, Gracchus once again, in full view of the people, passionately pleaded with Octavius, who at that moment was risking his whole career, not to thwart a measure that was not only righteous but extremely beneficial to all of Italy, nor to invalidate the people's clearly expressed desires. After all, it was right for a tribune to yield to the wishes of the people and not to stand by and watch as his office was stripped from him and he himself suffered disgrace in public. After this plea, he

---

18. In accordance with the conventions of Greek and Roman historical writing, these arguments represent Appian's summary and analysis of what he believed Gracchus was likely to have said, rather than a documentary account of what Gracchus actually said.

19. On these geographically based "tribes," and Roman voting procedures generally, see the Introduction to Q. Cicero, *Running for Office: A Handbook* in this volume.

called the gods to witness that he was being forced, against his will, to disenfranchise his fellow tribune since the latter refused to listen, and he let the vote continue. Octavius, immediately reduced to a common citizen, discreetly fled the scene. Q. Mummius was chosen to replace him as tribune, and the law concerning the land was passed.

[13] The first men elected to distribute the land were Gracchus himself, the author of the law, his like-named brother, and his father-in-law Appius Claudius. The people were, even after the passage of the law, quite afraid that it would not be implemented fully unless Gracchus and his family took the lead. Gracchus for his part received great acclaim because of the law; he was escorted home by the masses as if he were the restorer not just of a single city or one people, but of all the nations of Italy. After this, those who had just won a victory returned to their farms, which they had left because of the vote, while those who had just suffered defeat remained in Rome in a state of despondency. They told themselves that Gracchus would not be so exultant once he became a private citizen, since he had not only abused a hallowed and sacred office, but had also planted in Italy the seeds that would surely lead to massive civil unrest.

[14] Soon it was summer, and the candidates for the tribunate had been posted. As the election drew closer, it became completely clear that the wealthy had put their energies into supporting those candidates that were particularly hostile to Gracchus. Meanwhile, Gracchus saw that things would turn out ugly for him if he was not elected tribune for the following year, and so he called upon the farmers in the fields to come to Rome to vote. But it was summer, and they were busy, so at the last minute he was compelled to make an appeal to the urban population. He made the rounds, begging them to elect him tribune since, after all, he was assuming great risks on their account. As the voting got underway and the first two tribes declared their votes for Gracchus, the wealthy objected. Was it not illegal for the same man to hold the same office in consecutive years? Since Rubrius, the tribune presiding over this particular assembly, was uncertain about the whole matter, Mummius (he was the one chosen to replace Octavius as tribune) told him to hand over control of the assembly to him. Rubrius did just that, but the other tribunes protested. They thought that the presidency of the assembly should be determined randomly by lot; their argument was that when Rubrius, who had been chosen by lot, stepped down, they should redo the process completely and open it up to all of them. A great quarrel erupted over this issue, and Gracchus, realizing that it was going against him, postponed the election to the following day. Thinking that all was lost, Gracchus wore black—though he was still in office—and for the rest of the day he led his son around the Forum, commending him to everyone he met and entrusting him to their care, as if he himself were being destroyed by his enemies right then and there.

[15] As the poor reflected on these developments, they were wracked with great worry not only for themselves, but also for Gracchus. For their own part, they worried that they would no longer have equal civil rights and would be reduced to being slaves to the rich. They also felt bad that Gracchus had suffered such maltreatment and had been reduced to such a state of fear on their behalf, and so the whole population, wailing and in tears, escorted him home in the evening,[20] giving him words of

---

20. For a prominent figure to be escorted home from the Forum by clients and supporters was normal; the crowd would swell on special occasions. See Cicero, *Letters* 4.5 and Plutarch, *Life of Cato* 24 in this volume.

encouragement for the next day. This gave Gracchus courage; he assembled his supporters while it was still night, issued the secret signal to start fighting, if it should come to that, and took possession of the temple on the Capitoline Hill, which would be centrally located in the middle of the assembly when the voting took place.

Harassed the next day by the tribunes and the wealthy, who refused to let the vote concerning his candidacy continue, he gave the signal to fight. Suddenly a shout went up from Gracchus' conspirators and violence erupted on the spot. Some of Gracchus' supporters circled around him like bodyguards. Others hitched up their cloaks, grabbed rods and staves that were carried by the lictors, and broke them into pieces.[21] They drove the wealthy from the assembly with such an uproar and with so many violent blows that the tribunes left their positions in the middle of the assembly in fear and the priests closed the doors of the temple. The scene was chaotic, with many people running in every direction trying to escape, unaware of what was really going on. Rumors spread. Some said Gracchus had deprived all the other tribunes of their office (at least it *seemed* that way since they were nowhere to be found). Others reported that he had declared himself tribune-elect for the following year without a vote.

[16] These events prompted the Senate to assemble in the temple of Fides ("Trust"). I'm deeply surprised that they did not think of appointing a dictator, even though they had frequently been rescued from similar crises by appointing this officer with supreme power. In fact, even though appointing a dictator had in the past proven to be extremely beneficial, that apparently never occurred to the people, neither at that point nor later in the crisis. Instead, the Senate made up their minds and proceeded up the Capitoline, led by the chief priest (called the Pontifex Maximus), Cornelius Scipio Nasica. He let out a great cry: "Follow me if you want to save your country!" Then he drew the border of his toga up over his head, either because he thought he could entice more people to join him by the distinctiveness of his appearance, or because he wanted to symbolize to onlookers that he was helmeted, as it were, and so prepared for war, or else because he felt shame before the gods for what he was about to do.

As he approached the temple and the supporters of Gracchus, the people made way for him as was right in the presence of such an outstanding man, not to mention the fact that they also saw that the Senate was following in his trail. Some of the senators snatched the bats right out of the hands of Gracchus' supporters, or broke apart the chairs and other equipment that had been brought in for the assembly, and set to beating them. They drove Gracchus' supporters to the cliff face and started throwing them over. In the midst of this commotion, Gracchus and many of his supporters were killed as they huddled near the temple beside its doors and alongside the statues of the kings. The bodies of all these men were cast into the river at night.

This is how Gracchus, the son of Gracchus, twice consul, and of Cornelia, the daughter of the Scipio who had once destroyed the Carthaginian empire, was killed on the Capitoline Hill even though he was still tribune. He died as a consequence of a most noble cause—one, however, that he pursued too vehemently. This was the first heinous act perpetrated during an assembly, but it was hardly the last. No, this was the first in a long line of similar horrific acts. The city was divided in its reaction to Gracchus' death. Some felt sadness, others joy. Some grieved over their own lot,

---

21. For "lictors," see Glossary. The act of breaking the *fasces* (the rods and staves) was a gesture of defiance toward the Senate and its magistrates.

Gracchus' death, and the miserable state of affairs, how there was no longer a constitutional government, only the rule of force and violence. Everyone else, however, thought that their wildest dreams had come true.

## C    Spartacus and the Great Slave Revolt (1.116–20)

Another development was taking place in Italy about the same time.[22] Gladiators were being trained at Capua for upcoming shows. One of these was Spartacus, a Thracian man who had once served in the Roman army but had subsequently been taken captive and sold to a school of gladiators. This Spartacus convinced seventy or so of his brethren that if they were going to risk their lives, they should do it for their own freedom rather than for the entertainment of spectators. Convinced, these men overpowered the guards and escaped. Arming themselves with clubs and daggers that they took from travelers, they took refuge on Mount Vesuvius. They were joined by fugitive slaves and a few free men from the countryside and began raiding the nearby areas under the leadership of Oenomaus and Krixus, once gladiators, now Spartacus' lieutenants. Since he divided the spoils equally among all his men, Spartacus quickly attracted a great number of men to his side.

The first man sent against him was Claudius Glaber, the second, Publius Varinius. Neither of these men commanded a regular army, but a militia comprised of men levied hastily and haphazardly. The Romans did not believe, after all, that they were facing a real war; they thought that they were dealing with some kind of raiding or banditry. Both Roman leaders attacked Spartacus and lost. In fact, Spartacus himself stole Varinius' horse right from under him—that is how close the Roman praetor came to being taken prisoner by a mere gladiator. After these engagements, even more men joined Spartacus. His army now numbered 70,000, and he started producing his own weapons and armor and assembling the necessary equipment for a full-fledged war.

The Romans then dispatched the consuls with two legions. [117] One of these defeated Krixus, who led 30,000 men around Mount Garganus, killing him and two-thirds of his troops. For his part, Spartacus tried to make a break for the Alps in an attempt to join the Celts on the other side by tracking along the Apennine mountains, but one of the consuls anticipated the move and blocked his path, while the other consul pursued him from the rear. But Spartacus turned against them in successive strikes and defeated each in turn. The Romans beat a hasty and confused retreat from the spot. Meanwhile, Spartacus sacrificed 300 Roman prisoners of war as an offering to Krixus' departed spirit, then marched on Rome with 120,000 infantry. So that they could travel more quickly, he burned all inessential equipment, killed the prisoners of war, and slaughtered the beasts of burden. Many deserters tried to defect to his side, but he did not accept them. The consuls once again met him in battle near Picenum. A second great battle arose, and the Romans suffered a second great defeat.

Spartacus changed his mind about heading toward Rome. He did not think he was yet a match for her might, and his army was not fully outfitted for war. No city had joined them in their revolt, only slaves, deserters, and washouts. So Spartacus headed

22. In 73 BC; Appian has just given an account of Pompeius' victory over the rebel Sertorius in Iberia (Spain).

south toward Thurium, where he took control of the city itself and the mountains around it. He prohibited merchants from bringing gold and silver into the city and his men from possessing them. They instead bought large quantities of iron and bronze, allowing importers of those metals free access to his men. Because of this, Spartacus' men abounded in resources for war, outfitted themselves properly, and went on frequent raids in the surrounding areas. When they were again confronted by the Romans in war, they came away victorious and left the battle weighed down with spoils.

[118] This war, which was laughable and contemptible at the outset because, well, they were *gladiators* after all, was now in its third year and was making the Romans very fearful. When they held the election for the next praetors, everyone was hesitant because of fear, and no one put himself up as a candidate. Finally Licinius Crassus,[23] distinguished among the Romans because of both his family and his wealth, accepted the praetorship and marched out against Spartacus with six additional legions. When he arrived on the scene, he took control of the two consular legions as well. Since these latter two legions had been defeated so many times, he randomly chose by lot a tenth of them and put them to death.[24] Some think it happened differently, that after Crassus engaged Spartacus with his whole army and lost, he randomly chose by lot a tenth from all eight legions and, unconcerned with the large number, put to death upwards of 4,000 soldiers. However it happened, Crassus made it clear that the soldiers should fear him more than defeat at the hands of the enemy, and he immediately overpowered 10,000 followers of Spartacus who were encamped nearby, killing nearly two-thirds of them. He then pressed on against Spartacus himself, with nothing but contempt for him and his men. He defeated him soundly and pursued him all the way to the sea. Spartacus was heading there in the hope of sailing across to Sicily, but Crassus beat him to the punch and fenced him in with a ditch, a wall, and a palisade of stakes.

[119] Spartacus was compelled to try to break through the line and make for Samnite country, but Crassus slaughtered nearly 6,000 of his men in the morning and just as many in the evening. Roman casualties: three dead, seven injured. This shows just how much Crassus' punishment of the troops changed their commitment to victory. Spartacus, waiting for cavalry reinforcements to arrive from some quarter, avoided a pitched battle with his whole army and contented himself with harassing his besiegers with separate, localized sallies. He would ambush them incessantly, throwing flaming bundles of wood into the Romans' entrenchments, and generally making their work much harder. He hanged a Roman prisoner in no-man's land between the armies and pointed out to his own men that this is what awaited them if they allowed themselves to be defeated.

When those back in Rome learned about the siege, they thought that it would be shameful if the war against a bunch of gladiators dragged on endlessly, so they voted to send Pompeius, who had just returned from Spain, to help out with the war effort—they had finally realized that eliminating Spartacus was a difficult and enormous task.

[120] When Crassus heard about the vote back in Rome, he pressed the issue from every possible angle and tried to engage with Spartacus' troops so that the glory of

---

23. M. Licinius Crassus (consul in 70 and 55 BC) received proconsular imperium to suppress the slave revolt in 72 BC.

24. This was a recognized punishment in the Roman army. See Polybius, *Histories* chapter 38 in this volume.

defeating him in war would not fall to Pompeius. Spartacus, for his part, thinking it best to act before Pompeius arrived, invited Crassus to negotiate terms of a treaty. When Crassus ignored this offer, Spartacus decided it was time to put everything on the line, and now that his cavalry reinforcements had arrived, he broke through siege works with his whole army and made for Brundisium with Crassus in hot pursuit. But Lucullus had just arrived at Brundisium fresh from his victory over Mithridates,[25] and when Spartacus learned of this, he, in complete desperation, met Crassus in battle with his forces, which were even then still quite numerous. It was a long and hard-fought battle—not unexpected given that there were tens of thousands of men with nothing to lose. Spartacus was wounded in the thigh by a spear. He fell to one knee, but held his shield up against his attackers, trying to fight back until he and the crowd with him were surrounded and killed. The rest of his army, now in disarray, was massacred in great numbers. The slaughter was so great that one could not get an accurate count. The Romans lost about 1,000 men.

Spartacus' body was never found. A fairly large number of his troops survived the battle and fled to the mountains, and Crassus followed up after them. They fought back, having divided themselves into four units, until all but 6,000 perished. The survivors were taken captive and put up on crosses all along the road from Capua to Rome.[26]

---

25. Appian is mistaken. It was not L. Licinius Lucullus (who successfully put an end to Mithridates' offensive in 73–70 BC) but his younger brother M. Terentius Varro Lucullus (consul in 73 BC), who arrived in Brundisium in 71 BC.

26. This extreme form of punishment was reserved for slaves and other outlaws, so in this case it would have been thought quite appropriate. Doing it along the Appian Way ensured maximum visibility.

# AUGUSTUS

(63 BC–AD 14, wrote in Latin)

## Introduction

The Emperor Augustus, born C. Octavius in 63 BC, was adopted by his great-uncle Julius Caesar in his will, thus gaining the name Octavianus (modern "Octavian"). Although a relative unknown, he asserted his claim as Caesar's heir by raising an army, hunting down Caesar's murderers, and ultimately making himself sole master of the Roman state, as Caesar had done (see Appian A, ch. 5, for a brief sketch). In order to commemorate his accomplishments Augustus composed, apparently late in life, this official version, which was set up after his death in massive inscriptions both in Rome and the provinces. The copy inscribed on bronze tablets and set up at the entrance of his dynastic Mausoleum in Rome does not survive, but a copy is preserved on an inscription on the temple of Rome and Augustus at Ancyra (modern Ankara, Turkey), as well as on two other more fragmentary inscriptions. In addition to the Latin original, which is translated here, a Greek paraphrase was included on the inscription in Ancyra, for the benefit of the native Greek-speaking population in the East.

The *Res Gestae* (literally "Things Done"), as the original document is commonly called after its Latin title, contains the information that Augustus wished to be memorialized about his life. As one might expect, it passes lightly over the controversial beginning of his career, his ruthless and bloody rise to power, and his participation in the creation of proscription lists (see Glossary) that marked for death many senators, among them Cicero. The boastful tone of the document derives partly from the Roman tradition of epitaphs and funeral eulogies, which were supposed to celebrate the services to the state and military achievements of the deceased (see Polybius chs. 53–54 in this volume and Inscriptions, esp. nos. 1–4), and partly from the unique and truly astonishing accomplishments of Augustus himself. There is plenty of propaganda in this account, but Augustus did bring an end to over a century of chronic civil wars and founded a new, stable political order that lasted for over 200 years and brought relative peace and prosperity—the so-called *Pax Romana* ("Roman Peace"). There is also a note of defensiveness, as Augustus repeatedly stresses the legal, legitimate, traditional, and consensual nature of his extraordinary powers. These powers technically preserved, but fundamentally subverted, the old republican constitution and the traditional dominance of the Senate. Besides being a priceless historical source, the *Res Gestae* shows a crucial step in the formation of Roman imperial ideology.

---

# The Accomplishments of the Deified Augustus

The following is a copy of the *Accomplishments of the Deified Augustus*, a record of the deeds by which he subjected the whole world to the power of the Roman people, and of the expenditures he made for the benefit of the Republic and the people of Rome. The original is inscribed on two bronze pillars set up in Rome.

[1] At the age of nineteen [44–43 BC] I raised an army on my own initiative and at my own expense, and with it I freed the state from the oppression and domination of one particular faction.[1] For this reason in the consulship of C. Pansa and A. Hirtius [43 BC] the Senate enrolled me into its ranks with honorific decrees, bestowed upon me the right to express my opinion in the Senate with those of consular rank, and granted me the legal power to command an army. It also instructed me as propraetor to work with the consuls to ensure that the state would not suffer any harm.[2] In that same year, when both consuls died in battle, the people elected me consul and triumvir for the purpose of restoring the state.

[2] I drove into exile the men who butchered my father, and punished their crime through legally established tribunals. Later, I defeated them in battle twice when they made war against the state.[3]

[3] I waged many wars, both civil and foreign, the whole world over, on land and at sea. When victorious I spared all citizens who asked for mercy; as for foreign nations, I preferred to preserve rather than exterminate them so long as this could be done without danger. Approximately 500,000 Roman citizens took the soldier's oath of loyalty and served under me. I settled well over 300,000 of these in new colonies or sent them back to their own communities after their period of service was done, and to all of them I assigned lands or awarded money as compensation for their military service. I captured 600 ships, not including those ships smaller than the class of triremes.

[4] I celebrated two ovations and three full triumphs and was hailed as victorious general twenty-one times. The Senate voted more triumphs for me, all of which I declined to celebrate. I deposited the laurel wreaths that graced my *fasces* in the temple of Capitoline Jupiter after I fulfilled the vows I had made during each war. Fifty-five times the Senate decreed that public thanksgivings should be made to the immortal gods because of successful operations on land and sea conducted either by me or by

---

1. The "faction" is that of M. Antonius (Mark Antony), consul at the time and hence the legally established authority. Antonius was perceived as a would-be tyrant by many, who welcomed Octavian's intervention against him. In a turnabout typical of the period, Octavian joined forces with Antonius in the following year to hunt down Caesar's murderers; see Cicero, *Letters* 18–23 in this volume. The unwillingness to name Antonius is typical of the document as a whole, in which Augustus names only his own family members, not counting the consuls who are named only for the purpose of specifying dates.

2. "That the state would not suffer any harm" echoes the language of a formal declaration of a state of emergency that granted magistrates extraordinary powers to protect the state.

3. M. Brutus and C. Cassius were the ringleaders of C. Julius Caesar's assassination in 44 BC and were defeated in the two battles of Philippi in 42 BC by Octavian and Antonius.

my lieutenants acting under my auspices. The total number of days of thanksgiving decreed by order of the Senate was 890. During my triumphal processions nine kings or children of kings were led before my chariot. When I composed this document [AD 14], I had been consul thirteen times and was holding the tribunician power for the thirty-seventh year.[4]

[5] In the consulship of M. Marcellus and L. Arruntius [22 BC], the people and the Senate offered me the dictatorship first in my absence and then when I was in Rome itself. I did not accept it, but I did take responsibility for the grain supply, since Rome was suffering a great grain shortage. At my own expense and with concentrated effort I managed to free the whole city from imminent danger and fear within a few days. At that time I was also offered the chance to hold the annual consulship in perpetuity, but I did not accept it.

[6] In the consulship of M. Vinicius and Q. Lucretius [19 BC], again in that of P. Lentulus and Cn. Lentulus [18 BC], and for a third time in that of Paullus Fabius Maximus and Q. Tubero [11 BC], the Senate and the people of Rome unanimously agreed that I should be made overseer of laws and morality, with no colleague and with unlimited power, but I did not accept any position offered to me that went against the traditions of our ancestors.[5] The job that the Senate wished me to carry out at that time I performed by the power vested in me as tribune. Five times I personally requested from the Senate and was granted a colleague with tribunician power.

[7] I was triumvir for the purpose of restoring the state for ten continuous years. At the time I wrote this document, I had been leader of the Senate for forty years, and was Pontifex Maximus, an augur, one of the Board of Fifteen in charge of performing sacrifice, one of the Board of Seven in charge of banquets, an Arval Brother, a member of the society of the Titii, and a fetial priest.

[8] When I was consul for the fifth time [29 BC], I increased the number of patricians as directed by the people and the Senate, and I revised the membership of the Senate three times. In my sixth consulate [28 BC], I conducted a census of the people with Marcus Agrippa as my colleague. I performed a *lustrum*; it had been forty-two years since the last.[6] At the time of the *lustrum*, 4,063,000 Roman citizens were recorded. I performed a *lustrum* for a second time in the consulship of C. Censorinus and C. Asinius [8 BC], without a colleague and by virtue of my consular power; at the time of this *lustrum* 4,233,000 Roman citizens were recorded. I performed a third *lustrum* in the consulship of Sex. Pompeius and Sex. Appuleius [AD 14], with my son Tiberius Caesar as my colleague and again by virtue of my consular power; at the time

---

4. The republican government was based on the sharing and orderly transfer of power to different men every year. Though Augustus refers to himself discreetly as *princeps*, "first man" (chs. 13, 30, 32), his thirteen consulships and continuous tribunician power reflect the establishment of a new monarchy imposed upon the structure of the old republican institutions, which he shrewdly—and visibly—left largely intact. See below, ch. 34.

5. Augustus did in fact take over the duties traditionally assigned to the office of censor (see Glossary).

6. For *lustrum*, which marks the end of a census, see Glossary. The last census had been taken in 70 BC, at which time 910,000 had been counted (Cicero, *In Defense of Archias* 11, in this volume). The apparent "explosion" of population is probably explained by the inclusion of women and children in the Augustan censuses.

of this *lustrum* 4,937,000 Roman citizens were recorded. Through new laws passed under my sponsorship, I resurrected many commendable traditional practices which were already dying out in our generation, and I myself passed down many commendable practices which posterity would do well to imitate.

[9] The Senate decreed that vows were to be made by the consuls and priests every four years for my wellbeing. In accordance with these vows, games have frequently been celebrated, sometimes by the four most distinguished colleges of priests,[7] sometimes by the consuls. In addition, the whole citizen body, both as private citizens and as communities, has unanimously and continuously offered entreaties for my wellbeing at all the sacred banquets for the gods.

[10] By senatorial decree my name was added to the Hymn of the Salii[8] and it was sanctioned by law that I would be inviolable in perpetuity and that, for as long as I should live, I would hold the tribunician power. I refused to become Pontifex Maximus in the place of my colleague while he was still alive, although the people conferred upon me this priesthood that my father had held. Some years later, after the man who had taken the opportunity presented by civil disturbance to seize this priesthood passed away,[9] a great multitude poured in from all over Italy to my election—such as had never been documented in Rome before that time—and I became Pontifex Maximus; this took place in the consulship of P. Sulpicius and C. Valgius [12 BC].

[11] The Senate consecrated the Altar of Fortune the Returner in front of the temples of Honor and Valor at the Capena Gate on account of my safe return home. The Senate also ordered that the *pontifices* and the Vestal Virgins were to make annual sacrifice on the altar on the anniversary of my return from Syria in the consulship of Q. Lucretius and M. Vinicius [19 BC]. The Senate named the day [October 12] "Augustalia" after my cognomen.[10]

[12] In accordance with the will of the Senate, some of the praetors and the tribunes of the people, along with the consul Q. Lucretius and some leading men of the state, were sent to Campania to meet me—a distinction that has not been conferred on anyone else but me up to this present time. When I returned to Rome after successful campaigns in the provinces of Spain and Gaul, the Senate decreed that an Altar of the Augustan Peace was to be consecrated on account of my safe return home. This occurred in the consulship of Ti. Nero and P. Quintilius [13 BC].[11]

[13] Our elders deemed that the temple of Janus Quirinus should be closed when

---

7. The *pontifices*, augurs, the Board of Fifteen, and Board of Seven (see Glossary).

8. Including Augustus in this ancient hymn suggests that the welfare of Rome was intimately bound up with his safety and is also a quasi-divine honor, the only one which Augustus mentions in this document.

9. Lepidus, one of the triumvirs, became Pontifex Maximus after Caesar's assassination, a position he held until he died in 12 BC.

10. Augustus was absent 22–19 BC, touring Sicily, Greece, Asia Minor, and Syria, and engaging in diplomacy with the Parthians; in his absence Rome suffered from chronic political rioting over the election of consuls, and other disturbances. The honors listed here symbolized the relief felt by the citizens at his return.

11. Augustus was absent from Rome again 16–13 BC on military campaigns in Gaul, Germany, and the Alps, extending the empire west to the Danube. The altar mentioned here, the *Ara Pacis*, survives in Rome and is the most important artistic expression of Augustan ideals.

by our military victories peace had been achieved throughout the empire of the Roman people on land and sea. According to tradition, the temple had been closed only twice from the foundation of the city up to my birth. Three times while I was *princeps* the Senate decreed its closure.

[14] My sons, Gaius and Lucius Caesar, whom Fortune stole from me when they were but young men, were in my honor designated as consuls at the age of fourteen by the Senate and the people of Rome, with the stipulation that they were to assume the magistracy after a period of five years. The Senate decreed that from the day that they were led into the Forum they would be able to take part in state deliberations. The entire class of Roman *equites* designated them as "Leaders of the Youth" and bestowed upon each of them silver shields and spears.[12]

[15] To each member of the Roman plebs I paid 300 sesterces as directed in my father's last will and testament. In my fifth consulship [29 BC] I distributed in my own name 400 sesterces to each man from war-profits. Again in my tenth consulship [24 BC] I disbursed a gift of 400 sesterces from my personal estate to each man. In my eleventh consulship [23 BC] I purchased grain at personal expense and distributed twelve shares to each man. And in my twelfth year of tribunician power [11 BC] I doled out to each man 400 sesterces in my third distribution of this kind. My donations never reached fewer than 250,000 people. In the eighteenth year of my tribunician power and my twelfth consulship [5 BC] I gave 240 sesterces apiece to 320,000 of the urban poor. When consul for the fifth time [29 BC] I gave to each one of my soldiers living in colonies 1,000 sesterces from war-profits; somewhere around 120,000 colonists received this donative made in honor of my triumph. When I was consul for the thirteenth time [2 BC] I gave 240 sesterces to those members of the plebs who were on public grain assistance at that time, helping a little more than 200,000 persons.

[16] Twice I paid townships (*municipia*) cash for the land that I distributed to soldiers, first in my fourth consulship [30 BC] and a second time in the consulship of M. Crassus and Cn. Lentulus [14 BC]. The total sum I paid out for Italian property was about 600,000,000 sesterces, and for provincial lands about 260,000,000. Of all those generals who established military colonies in Italy or the provinces, I was the first and only person in living memory to pay for the land.[13] Later, in the consulship of Ti. Nero and Cn. Piso [7 BC], and again in that of C. Antistius and D. Laelius [6 BC], that of C. Calvisius and L. Pasienus [4 BC], that of L. Lentulus and M. Messalla [3 BC], and that of L. Caninius and Q. Fabricius [2 BC], I paid out monetary compensation to soldiers whom I resettled in their own townships after their period of service was completed; expenditures on this amounted to 400,000,000 sesterces.

[17] On four occasions I subsidized the public treasury with my own monies, transferring 150,000,000 sesterces to those in charge of the treasury. In the consulship

---

12. Augustus stresses the broad support from both the Senate and the equestrian class for the new and now hereditary monarchy. Gaius and Lucius, Augustus' grandsons by his only child, Julia, and Agrippa, were adopted as his sons in order to provide him with heirs and successors, hence "sons" here. For "Leaders of the Youth," see Glossary.

13. Augustus omits discussion of the settlement of veterans in 41–40 and 36 BC, presumably because these settlements involved widespread confiscations of land. See Vergil, *Eclogue* 1 in this volume.

of M. Lepidus and L. Arruntius [AD 6] the military treasury, the function of which was to provide compensation to soldiers who had completed twenty or more years of service, was established at my suggestion. From my personal funds I transferred 170,000,000 sesterces to this treasury.

[18] Beginning with the consulship of Cn. and P. Lentulus [18 BC], whenever the tax revenues were insufficient, I provided disbursements of grain and cash from my own storehouses and my own funds, sometimes reaching 100,000 people, sometimes many more.

[19] I built the following: the Curia and the Chalcidicum adjoining it; the temple of Apollo on the Palatine, along with its porticoes; the temple of the deified Julius; the Lupercal; the portico at the Flaminian Circus, which I allowed to retain the name of the man who had built the earlier portico in the same place, Octavius; the imperial box at the Circus Maximus; the temples of Jupiter the Striker and Jupiter the Thunderer on the Capitoline; the temple of Quirinus; the temples of Minerva, Juno the Queen, and Freedom Jupiter on the Aventine; the temple of the Lares on the upper Via Sacra; the temple of the Di Penates on the Velia; the temple to Youth; and the temple of the Great Mother on the Palatine.

[20] I restored the Capitolium and the Theater of Pompey, each at considerable expense, without having my name inscribed on either. I restored in a great many places aqueduct conduits that were in bad condition because of their age, and I doubled the volume of the Aqua Marcia by directing a new source into it. I completed the Julian Forum and the basilica[14] that stood between the temples of Castor and Saturn, works that my father had begun and nearly finished. When that basilica was consumed by fire [AD 12], I enlarged the site and began construction on another basilica in the name of my two sons, and I gave orders that my heirs should finish the work if I did not complete it before my death. When I was consul for the sixth time [28 BC], I restored eighty-two temples of the gods in the city on the Senate's authority, missing none of those that needed repair at that time. When I was consul for the seventh time [27 BC], I repaired the Flaminian Road up to Rimini and all of its bridges except for the Mulvian and the Minucian.

[21] On private land I built the temple of Mars the Avenger and the Augustan Forum from war-profits. I built the theater next to the temple of Apollo on land largely bought from private owners, which was to bear the name of my son-in-law Marcellus. I consecrated offerings to the gods from war-profits in the temple of Capitoline Jupiter, in the temple of the deified Julius, in the temple of Apollo, in the temple of Vesta, and in the temple of Mars the Avenger, on which I spent approximately 100,000,000 sesterces. During my fifth consulship [29 BC] I returned 35,000 pounds of crown-gold[15] which the townships and colonies in Italy donated for my triumphs; after this, whenever I was hailed as victorious general, I refused to accept the crown-gold whenever townships and colonies voted to donate it as generously as they had before.

[22] I presented gladiatorial games three times in my own name, five times in the name of my sons or grandsons; at these games around 10,000 men fought in the arena.

---

14. A type of general-purpose public building (see Glossary).

15. Contributions in the form of gold offered to rulers by communities, a custom that originated in the East and was adopted by the Greeks and later the Romans.

Three times, twice in my own name and a third time in that of my grandson, I put on public exhibitions of athletes summoned from every quarter of the empire. Four times I produced shows in my own name, twenty-three times in the names of other magistrates. As the head and on behalf of the Board of the Fifteen I, along with my colleague Marcus Agrippa, put on the Secular Games in the consulship of C. Furnius and C. Silanus [17 BC]. As consul for the thirteenth time [2 BC] I put on the first annual Festival of Mars, which consuls have put on annually since that time in accordance with senatorial decree and established law. Twenty-six times in my own name or in that of my sons or grandsons I staged public animal hunts featuring wild African beasts. These were staged in the Circus, in the Forum, and in amphitheaters, and all together some 3,500 animals were killed.

[23] I staged a naval battle as a spectacle for the people across the Tiber where the Grove of the Caesars now stands. There a site 1,800 feet long and 1,200 feet across was hollowed out so that thirty beaked triremes and biremes, plus many more smaller ships, could engage in battle. Approximately 3,000 men, excluding the rowers, fought amidst these fleets.

[24] After gaining victory over my rival in battle,[16] I replaced in the temples of every city of the province of Asia the ornaments which he had appropriated as private possessions when he plundered them. There once stood in the city eighty silver statues of me on foot, on horseback, and in chariots; I myself had these taken down, and from the monies these statues supplied I made offerings of gold in the temple of Apollo, both in my own name and in the name of those who had honored me with those statues.

[25] I cleared the sea of pirates and made it safe. In the course of this war I captured some 30,000 slaves who had escaped from their masters and had taken up arms against the state, and I sent them back to their masters to receive their punishment.[17] All of Italy voluntarily swore an oath of allegiance to me and demanded me as its leader in the war which I successfully brought to a close at Actium. The provinces of Gaul, Spain, Africa, Sicily, and Sardinia also swore the same oath of allegiance to me.[18] Serving under my standards at that time were more than 700 senators. In that group were eighty-three men who either had been or later became consuls up to the time of writing, and about 170 who had been or would become priests.

[26] I increased the territory of every province of the Roman people that bordered on nations who were not subject to our authority. I pacified the provinces of Gaul and Spain and also Germany—all the area that Ocean encloses from Cadiz to the Elbe River. I pacified the Alps from the area adjacent to the Adriatic Sea west to the Tuscan Sea, while waging no war against any nation without just cause. My fleet sailed through Ocean from the mouth of the Rhine eastward all the way to the land of the Cimbri, a point which no Roman had reached before, either by land or by sea. The Cimbri, the Charydes, the Semnones, and other Germanic peoples in that region sent representatives to seek an alliance with me and the Roman people. On my orders and under my auspices two armies were led on campaign into Ethiopia and Arabia, which is called

---

16. Antonius, at the battle of Actium in Greece, 31 BC.

17. This refers to Octavian's triumph in 36 BC over Sextus Pompeius, the son of Cn. Pompeius (the Great), who had employed a great number of slaves in his navy.

18. For a loyalty oath to Augustus, see Inscriptions no. 57 in this volume.

*Eudaimon* ("Blessed"), virtually at the same time. Great enemy armies of both nations were cut down in battle, and a great many towns were captured. In Ethiopia they went as far as the town Nabata, which is right next to Meroë; in Arabia the army penetrated all the way to the town of Mariba in the territory of the Sabaeans.

[27] I added Egypt to the empire of the Roman people.[19] As for greater Armenia, although I could have made it a province after the murder of its king, Artaxes, I preferred to follow the traditional practice of our ancestors and handed the kingdom over to Tigranes, the son of king Artavasdes and the grandson of king Tigranes; the transfer of power was handled by my step-son at the time, Tiberius Nero. When this same nation rebelled in open war, my son Gaius quelled the insurrection, and I entrusted the kingdom to king Ariobarzanes, the son of Artabazus king of the Medes, and when he died, to his son Artavasdes. When he was murdered I sent Tigranes, descendant of the royal family of Armenia, to rule over that kingdom. I recovered all the eastern provinces across the Adriatic Sea, together with Cyrene—most of them at the time controlled by kings. Earlier I had recovered Sicily and Sardinia which had been seized during the slave war.

[28] I established soldier-colonies in Africa, Sicily, Macedonia, both Spanish provinces, Achaea, Asia, Syria, Gallia Narbonensis, and Pisidia. In Italy twenty-eight colonies were founded on my authority, and these became densely populated and booming during my lifetime.

[29] I defeated enemy forces and recovered a great many military standards that had been lost by other leaders in Spain, Gaul, and Dalmatia. I compelled the Parthians to return the spoils and standards of three Roman armies to me and to beg for an alliance with the Roman people. These standards I placed in the innermost and most sacred room of the temple of Mars the Avenger.

[30] I subjected to the rule of the Roman people the nations of Pannonia, whom no Roman army had ever engaged before I became *princeps*. Tiberius Caesar, at the time my son-in-law and lieutenant, carried out the campaign and defeated them, and with this victory I extended the boundaries of Illyricum to the banks of the Danube. When an army of Dacians crossed this river it was conquered in a decisive defeat under my auspices. Afterwards my army was led across the Danube and compelled the Dacian nations to submit to the authority of the Roman people.

[31] Kings of India on many occasions sent ambassadors to me, something which no Roman leader had experienced until my time. Other nations sought alliances with Rome through ambassadors: the Bastarnae, the Scythians, the kings of the Sarmatians on both sides of the River Don, as well as the kings of the Albani, the Iberi, and the Medes.

[32] These kings took refuge with me as suppliants: Tiridates, and later Phraates son of King Phraates, both kings of the Parthians; Artavasdes, the king of the Medes; Artaxares, the king of the Adiabeni; Dumnobellaunus and Tincommius, kings of the Britons; Maelo, the king of the Sugambri, and [*unintelligible name*]. Phraates son of Orodes, king of the Parthians, sent to me all of his sons and grandsons, not because he had been conquered in war, but because he was seeking an alliance with Rome by surrendering his children as pledges of good faith. A great many other nations which had

---

19. After defeating Antonius and Cleopatra at Actium in 31 BC.

not previously been in diplomatic contact or had an alliance with the Roman people experienced the good faith of the Roman people during my time as *princeps*.

[33] When the Parthians and the Medes sent noblemen as ambassadors to ask that I choose their kings for them, I granted their request. The Parthians received Vonones, the son of King Phraates and grandson of King Orodes; the Medes received Ariobarzanes, the son of King Artavazdes and grandson of King Ariobarzanes.

[34] In my sixth and seventh consulships [28–27 BC], after I had brought the civil wars to a close and was the undisputed master of all things, I transferred the state from my control to the authority of the Senate and people of Rome. In return for this worthy deed of mine, by senatorial decree I was named "Augustus," laurel wreaths were draped over my door-posts at public expense, a civic crown was fastened above my door, and a golden shield was placed in the Curia Julia. The inscription on this last item bears witness that the Senate and people of Rome gave it to me on account of my valor, clemency, fairness, and sense of duty. Subsequently, although I excelled everyone in influence, when it came to official power, I had no more of it than all my others colleagues in each of the offices I held.

[35] During my thirteenth consulship [2 BC], the Senate, the class of the *equites*, and the people of Rome unanimously gave me the title Father of the Fatherland (*pater patriae*), and they ruled that this title was to be inscribed on the entrance of my house, in the Senate House, and in the Augustan Forum beneath the chariot which had been set up there in my honor by senatorial decree.

I was seventy-six years of age when I wrote this document.[20]

# Appendix[21]

[1] The total sum of money that he gave to the treasury, the Roman plebs, or discharged soldiers came to 600,000,000 denarii. [2] His new construction projects: the temples of Mars, Jupiter the Thunderer, Jupiter the Striker, Apollo, deified Julius, Quirinus, Minerva, Juno the Queen, Freedom Jupiter, the Lares, the Di Penates, Youth, the Great Mother, the Lupercal, the imperial box at the Circus Maximus, the Senate House along with the Chalcidicum adjacent to it, the Augustan Forum, the Julian Basilica, the Theater of Marcellus, the Octavian Portico, and the Grove of the Caesars across the Tiber. [3] He rebuilt the Capitolium, eighty-two sacred temples, the Theater of Pompey, the conduits of aqueducts, and the Flaminian Road. [4] The expenditures that he paid out for dramatic performances, gladiatorial games, athletes, animal hunts, mock naval battles, and the monies he gave to colonies, townships, and towns devastated by earthquake and fire, or individually to friends and senators who did not have enough money to qualify for the Senate, are incalculable.

---

20. Augustus turned seventy-six on September 23, AD 13.

21. This summary is evidently an addition, not contained in the original document by Augustus.

# CATULLUS

(ca. 84–54 BC, wrote in Latin)

## Introduction

C. Valerius Catullus was of equestrian status and came from Verona, a Romanized town in an area of northern Italy beyond the Po River. Though without serious political ambitions, he did serve in a semi-official capacity in the entourage (*cohors*) of the governor of the province of Bithynia (modern northwest Turkey). This governor, C. Memmius, was praetor in 58 BC, and his term as governor was probably from spring 57 to spring 56. Poem 10 is set shortly after Catullus' return from Bithynia. Poem 11 mentions Caesar's expedition to Britain in 55, and another mentions Pompeius' second consulship, also in 55. These are the last datable events in his preserved works.

Catullus' poems are studded with names and allusions to people we know from other sources: Julius Caesar, Pompeius, Cicero, and above all his tempestuous mistress, Lesbia (a pseudonym chosen in honor of the great lyric poet of the 6th century BC, Sappho, who came from the island of Lesbos). This "Lesbia" is a literary creation, but also likely a pseudonym for Clodia, a sister of Cicero's nemesis, Clodius Pulcher (see Cicero, *Letters* 3–5 in this volume), and the woman attacked for immoral conduct in Cicero's speech *In Defense of Caelius* (*Pro Caelio*).

The poems in the surviving collection bear no titles and are conventionally given numbers from 1 to 116. There is evidently some order to the collection as we have it, but the connections between poems or groups of poems are not always clear, and we do not know if Catullus himself was responsible for the arrangement or if someone else gathered and published his poems after his death. In any case, the range of subjects in Catullus' oeuvre is remarkable. Alongside the better known love poetry to Lesbia, we encounter (to touch only on those selected here) sardonic attacks on public figures (no. 29); a hymn to the goddess Diana, imagined as being recited at a public occasion by a chorus of young girls and boys (no. 34); letters to his literary friends (nos. 1, 49, and 50); adaptations of Greek poems (no. 51 is a version of one of Sappho's poems); anecdotes from daily life (no. 10); a moving poem set at the grave of his brother, who died prematurely and away from home in Asia Minor (no. 101); and love poems addressed to a boy named Juventius, which echo the sentiments he addressed to Lesbia (no. 48).

---

*Selected Poems*

**1**

Here it is, my neat new collection
polished at the roll-ends with dry
pumice—but on whom to bestow it?
You, Cornelius.[1] For you always said
my foolishness amounted to something,
even as you were chronicling
the whole of history (in three books!),
the only Italian with the courage to do it.
Gods, the learning and labor in that work.
So here, accept this, for what it's worth.
Patron Muse, I pray, may it endure
for more than one generation.

**5**

Let us live, my Lesbia, and let us love.
And as for all those old curmudgeons
and their gossip, who gives a penny for it?
The sun—it rises and sets, and rises again.
Once *our* brief light has sunk in dusk
we must sleep a single, eternal night.
Give me a thousand kisses, then a hundred,
then a thousand again, a second hundred,
another thousand (no stopping), then a hundred.
When we have made many thousands,
we'll jumble the accounts.
We must never know the correct amount.
None must fix on us an evil eye,
knowing exactly how many kisses there are.

**7**

You ask, my Lesbia, just how many
of your smooches would be enough
and more than enough for me.
Think about all the sands in Libya,
the countless grains that lie around

---

1. Cornelius Nepos, a fellow northern Italian, an intimate friend of Cicero, and a distinguished
author in his own right.

Cyrene, silphium-bearer, between
the oracle of sweltering Jupiter
and the tomb of old Battus—
that would be about the right number,
or the countless stars, when night grows still,
that look upon the furtive transit of lovers.
To kiss you that many kisses is ample
enough for your madman Catullus,
and enough to ensure that nosy folk
can't count them up and use their
wicked tongues to cast a spiteful spell.

**8**

Poor, poor Catullus, stop being a fool.
Just let go of what you see is lost.
Once, you were bathed in sunlight,
when you followed wherever the girl led.
You loved her then as no other shall ever
be loved. And things happened, many
playful things, things you wanted,
Catullus, and the girl never refused.
You were truly bathed in sunlight then.
Now she is unwilling. You, too, must stop
wanting. Try to find some self-control.
Stop chasing the woman who runs from you.
Stop living in wretchedness. Endure,
toughen up, steel your mind.
Farewell, girl, now Catullus is tough.
He will not try to track you down, will make
no advances, since you are unwilling.
You will suffer when no one asks at all.
To hell with you, cruel bitch.
What sort of life awaits you now?
Who will come to you? Who will think you
lovely? Whom will you love, whose
girl will you be said to be? Whom
will you kiss? Whose lips will you bite?
As for you, Catullus: be resolute, be tough.

**10**

My friend Varus saw me lounging in the Forum
and hauled me off to visit his new
girlfriend—a little whore, as I immediately saw,

but not disagreeable, not without charm.
We got there, and talked of various things,
such as, what's up in Bithynia, and did I
make any cash while in the province?
I told the truth: the locals were broke;
neither praetor nor entourage came back
with a palm even slightly greased—
unsurprising, since our praetor was a
cocksucker who cared not a bit for his staff.[2]
"But come now," they all chimed, "surely
you managed to acquire some slaves
to carry your litter—they say that's
the prime Bithynian export." And I,
to make the girl think I was quite the success:
"It wasn't so grim. Just because I drew
a lousy province, that doesn't mean
I couldn't get eight straight-backed men."
The fact is, I had nothing of the kind,
not here, not there, not one slave who could
bear the creaky frame of an old cot on his neck.
Now, like the shameless wench she is,
that girl decided to ask, "Dear Catullus,
won't you please let me borrow them
for a bit? I want to ride down to Serapis."[3]
"Wait, actually," I said to the girl, "I
misspoke. My friend—Gaius Cinna?—
*he* bought them. But his or mine, what's
the difference? I use them just the same.
But you're a drag, and quite annoying.
With you, one can't make even a tiny slip!"

## 11

Furius and Aurelius: you're Catullus'
companions, whether he ventures to India,
far off where the eastern waves collide
    on a booming shore,
or visits the Hyrcani, or the soft-living
Arabs, the Sacae, or the Parthian archers,
or the sea that is colored seven times over

---

2. For the perspective of a governor faced with the monetary demands of his staff, see the nearly contemporary letter of Cicero, *Letters* 10 in this volume.

3. To the temple of Serapis in the Campus Martius. Serapis was a god created by the first Hellenistic king of Egypt, Ptolemy I, based on Egyptian gods of fertility and abundance, and his cult quickly spread throughout the Mediterranean.

by the silts of the Nile,
or crosses the lofty Alps to visit
great Caesar's monuments: Gaul,
the Rhine, the icy channel, the Briton
   at world's edge.
You would tackle all this with me,
and whatever the gods decide to send.
So bring a short message to my girl,
   not a pleasant one:
Tell her to live and be happy with her adulterers,
all three hundred, whom she embraces at once,
loving none truly, but over and over
   cracking their loins.
Tell her not to count on my love as before.
It's been cut down, thanks to her, like a flower
at the edge of a field, touched by the blade
   of a passing plow.

## 13

Fabullus, come over in a few days
and you will dine well, gods willing.
Just bring along a fine and ample
dinner, and don't forget a lovely girl.
Bring wine, wit, and all kinds of laughter.
Bring all this, my charming man,
and you will dine very well, I say,
for Catullus' purse has only cobwebs.
In return you will get pure, unmixed
love, or something even more elegant:
I'll give you a scent,[4] passed on to
my girl by Venus and Cupid themselves.
And when you smell *that*, dear Fabullus,
you will beg the gods on your knees
to turn you into one colossal nose.

## 16

Fuck you both up the ass. Suck my cock,
Furius, Aurelius, you asshole faggots.
You *dare* to infer from my verse—
a little risqué and soft, it is true—
that I do these lewd things myself?

---

4. It was customary on festive occasions to anoint the hair with aromatic oils.

A good and loyal poet must be pure
personally, but his verse need not be.
In fact, to have wit and a modicum of charm,
they *must* be a bit risqué and seductive,
just the trick to waken the prick,
and I don't mean only in callow lads,
but in those old, hairy bastards
who normally can't get it up.
You two, you read of many thousand
kisses, and think I'm less than a man?
Fuck you both up the ass. Suck my cock.


## 22

Varus, that friend of yours—you know him well,
Suffenus—he's elegant, he's witty, he's chic.
Yet, dear god, he writes endlessly long poems.
He's written, I think, a thousand, maybe ten thousand lines
or more, and not on any old recycled parchment,
but royal sheets, brand new rolls, fresh sticks,
exquisite red parchment jackets and strings,
text ruled with lead, ends all pumice-smoothed.
Read them, and suddenly this sharp, elegant
fellow Suffenus somehow becomes transformed
into a goat-milking, ditch-digging boor. That's how
inconsistent he is. What's to be made of this?
One minute a *scurra*,[5] or even more clever; the next,
more boring than the boring countryside itself.
Yet the moment he turns his hand to poetry, he's
*happy*, never more so than when writing. He looks
at himself and feels joy, pleasure, amazement.
No doubt we are all deceived in just this way.
Each of us, you know, is a Suffenus of something.
We are issued our own special flaws,
a knapsack that rides on our backs, unseen.


## 28

You're on Piso's staff, that governor's
empty-handed entourage, your packs
stripped down to basics, ready to march.
Dear Fabullus, my good man Veranius,
how's it going? Send me some word.

---

5. A type of entertainer, a sort of insult comic. See Pliny, *Letters* 24 in this volume and Glossary.

Had enough flat, cheap wine,
endured enough cold and hunger?
Noted any profit in your accounts?
Perhaps it's the kind I recorded
while following my praetor abroad.
Hey, Memmius, do you remember as I do,
how you fucked me well and long,
the whole shaft nice and slow?
But as far as I can see, my friends,
you're in much the same condition,
stuffed by a comparable dick.
"Seek noble friends!" they say, perfectly
fine advice. But all you so-called patrons,
here's hoping the goddesses and
gods fill your days with disaster.
You shame Romulus and Remus.


**29**

Who can look on this, who can bear it? (Well,
maybe a sex-addicted gluttonous gambler.)
*Mamurra* possesses what Long-haired Gaul
used to own, and all the wealth of farthest Britain.[6]
Romulus, you faggot, how can you watch?
And now, that arrogant, too-wealthy prick
will stroll through the bedrooms of all
like Venus' pet white dove or Adonis himself.
Romulus, you faggot, how can you watch?
You're a sex-addicted gluttonous gambler.
Peerless commander,[7] is this why
you went to that far-western isle,
so two or three hundred million could vanish
down the gullet of your oversexed minion?
Generosity has gone horribly wrong.
Hasn't this glutton squandered enough?
He butchered his own inheritance first,
then war-loot from Pontus, then more from Spain—

---

6. Mamurra was a Roman equestrian and Caesar's head engineer in Gaul from 58 BC. See Cicero *Letters* 17 in this volume, with note. Suetonius (*Life of Julius Caesar* 73), illustrating Caesar's magnanimity, says, "[Caesar] did not conceal the fact that some verses written by Valerius Catullus about Mamurra had placed an eternal stain on his reputation. And yet, when he apologized, Caesar invited him (Catullus) to dinner on the very same day, and continued to enjoy the hospitality of Catullus' father, as he had been accustomed to in the past."

7. Julius Caesar.

a tale the gold-bearing Tagus[8] could tell—
and now Gaul and Britain seem next on the list.
Why protect this villain? What are his skills,
apart from swallowing banquets of cash?
Can this be why, most loyal father- and son-in-law,
can this be why you wrecked the Republic?[9]

## 34

Diana, we sing to you, pure
girls and boys innocent
under your protection, Diana,
    we sing to you.
Daughter of Leto, great
offspring of greatest Jupiter,
your mother bore you on Delos
    beside the olive tree,
to be mistress of the mountains,
of the growing woodlands,
of the hidden forest glades,
    of roaring rivers.
Your title is Juno Lucina to
women in pangs of birth;
you're powerful Trivia, the Moon
    with light not your own.
You measure the course of the year
with your monthly path. You fill
the rustic farmer's dwelling
    with fine harvest.
May you be hallowed by whatever
name pleases you: we pray that you make
the race of Romulus prosper, as of old,
    with your good aid.

## 48

Your honeyed eyes, Juventius—
if I should be allowed a kiss,

---

8. A gold-bearing river (modern name Tajo) in what is now Spain and Portugal. Caesar conducted military campaigns in *Hispania ulterior* as propraetor in 61 BC.

9. "Father-in-law" and "Son-in-law" refer to Caesar and Pompeius respectively, since the latter had married the former's daughter, Julia. For more on the widespread criticism, especially among equestrians, of the perceived suspension of the constitution by the alliance of Caesar, Pompeius, and Crassus, see Cicero, *Letters* 5.3 in this volume.

I wouldn't stop till three hundred thousand.
No number, I think, would satisfy,
not if a waving field of dry
wheat were less thick on the ground
than the dense crop of my kissing.

## 49

Marcus Tullius, you're the finest,
most eloquent speaker of all
the grandsons of Romulus—those who
have gone before, those who are now,
and those who ever will be. Catullus
sends to you the greatest possible thanks,
though he himself is the rottenest
poet alive, just as much as you
are the greatest of all attorneys.

## 50

Licinius,[10] yesterday we played
and wrote much in my notebooks.
We had some time, and had agreed
to lavish it on our own pleasure:
each of us composed a few verses,
improvising, now in this meter,
now in that, capping each other,
all amid laughter and wine.
Licinius, I left so inflamed by
your charm and your brilliance,
that like a lover I could not eat,
nor would sleep cover my eyes.
No rest, I lay turning in bed,
thoroughly mastered by passion,
longing for the light of day, only
to speak and be with you again.
Still worn out with suffering, half-
dead from a night awake on my bed,
I made this poem for you, charmer,
so that you can understand my pain.
Careful, now, don't be mean.
Please, please, don't reject my request,
my darling, or you may pay the penalty

10. C. Licinius Calvus, a well-known orator and poet.

to Nemesis. A formidable goddess,
that one. Take care not to offend her.

## 51

Like a god, or even surpassing
(can I say it?) the gods, is he who
sits across from you. Again and again
   he listens and sees
you sweetly laughing. It robs me
of my senses. From the moment
I catch sight of you, Lesbia, I'm hopelessly,
   utterly helpless:
tongue immobile, a thin flame seeps
beneath my skin, strange tinnitus
muffles my ears, eyes enveloped
   by twin night.
Idleness, Catullus—it's bad for you.
Idle, you are restless, you run riot.
Idleness has toppled kings, ruined
   prosperous cities.

## 72

Lesbia, once you used to say that you knew only Catullus
   and that you'd prefer to hold me over Jupiter.
I adored you then, not as the mob loves its mistresses,
   but as a father adores his sons and sons-in-law.
Now, I know who you are. And that is why, though I burn more
   intensely, you seem far less worthwhile, more transitory.
How can this be, you ask? Such an injury forces the lover
   to love more, but to have less affection.

## 75

Lesbia, the wrong you have done me has so worked on my
   mind, so stopped its proper functioning,
it could no longer love you if you changed and were good,
   nor stop loving if you did all your worst.

## 83

Lesbia abuses me at length in front of her husband,
   a thing that gives the ass no end of pleasure.

Idiot, are you blind? If she were silent, as if I didn't matter,
   she'd be safe. But she snarls and vilifies me,
proof positive: she not only thinks of me, but more to the point,
   she's angry. Behold: she burns for me, and speaks.


**85**

I hate. And I love. How, you ask, can I manage to do both?
   No idea. But I feel it happen, and am tormented.


**93**

Caesar, I'm not much moved to make an effort to please you,
   nor really to know the first thing about you.


**101**

Across many lands and across many seas I have traveled,
   here now, brother, for your grim funeral rites.
I have come to bestow those final gifts we owe to death,
   and to speak, in vain, to unspeaking ash.
Fortune has deprived me of your living presence, oh my
   wretched brother, cruelly stolen from me.
So take these, at least for now, the dismal funeral gifts
   our ancestral custom has handed down.
Take them, wet with your brother's tears, and in eternity
   hail and farewell, brother, hail and farewell.

# MARCUS CICERO

(106–43 BC, wrote in Latin)

## General Introduction

M. Tullius Cicero, though not born into one of the old aristocratic families of Rome, rose to the consulship as a "new man" (like one of his heroes, Cato the Elder) thanks to his gifts as an orator and attorney. He came to prominence by prosecuting, among others, Verres, the corrupt governor of Sicily, in 70 BC. In the year of his consulship (63 BC) he thwarted an attempted coup by the indebted aristocrat Catiline, and had several of his supporters executed without trial, an act that ended up causing problems for Cicero later. Indeed, he spent a period in exile engineered by his archenemy Clodius (April 58–August 57 BC; see below, *Letters* 6–8), who used Cicero's illegal execution of Roman citizens in the Catilinarian conspiracy to win his case.

What could have been a brilliant political career ending in a senior position of influence like that of Cato the Elder was ultimately stymied by the collapse of the Republic that Cicero loved and idealized. Despite his substantial influence in the Senate, Cicero's political ideal of the "consensus of all good men" was ineffectual beside the vast resources of money and troops amassed by autocratic dynasts such as Crassus, Pompeius, and Julius Caesar, and (later) Marcus Antonius and Octavian. He supported but did not participate in the murder of Caesar. He became a vocal opponent of Caesar's successor Antonius, and initially supported the young Octavian, who had raised a private army in a wholly unconstitutional way, as a counterweight to Antonius. But when Antonius and Octavian became allies, they announced proscriptions (semi-legalized "hit lists" of political enemies in times of civil strife; see Glossary), and one of the first of many names on the list was Cicero's. He was executed in 43 BC.

Cicero was a prolific writer in many genres, and is considered the greatest of Roman prose stylists. His speeches, works on Greek philosophy, Roman politics, the history and theory of oratory, not to mention his fifty-eight surviving speeches themselves, set a standard for elegant, impressive Latin that was much emulated, especially in the European Renaissance. His many surviving letters reveal his more private thoughts and provide a vivid picture of the ups and downs both of his personal life and of the turbulent time in which he lived.

---

### Introduction to *In Defense of Archias*

The Greek poet Archias was prosecuted for exercising the rights of Roman citizenship without legal qualification to do so. At issue was not so much the right to vote as enhanced property rights, most importantly the ability to make a binding will according to Roman law, and hence the ability to acquire property through legacies from Roman citizens. These rights were not available to resident aliens, who also risked expulsion from Rome in certain circumstances. Thus citizenship had considerable legal and financial implications for Archias. The date of the trial was probably 62 BC, a year after Cicero's consulship.

In addition to discussing the matter at hand—Archias' citizenship status—Cicero defends the value and usefulness of poets and literature, and propounds an influential view of the purpose of education that he develops more fully elsewhere. For Cicero the study of literature, the arts, history, and public speaking are all linked and directed at both personal cultivation and leadership. These ideas are summed up by a word that appears frequently in this speech—*humanitas*, "civilization, culture"—a concept closely associated with Cicero's treatise on the ideal orator. The Ciceronian ideal of *humanitas*, in which literary and philosophical education makes us both better people and better citizens, was a powerful inspiration to Petrarch, Erasmus, and the other scholars whose devotion to classical learning shaped the European Renaissance, and who were called "Humanists" because of it. While the view of literature proposed here as directed mainly at serving the state is not one that many would share today, part of the value of this speech is that it prompts us to consider anew the proper relationship between education, the arts, and the public good.

## In Defense of Archias

Gentlemen of the jury. It is only fair that my client here, Aulus Licinius,[1] should claim the use of my services above practically all others. He has a legitimate right to them. If I have any talent, and I am aware how small it is, he has a right to it. If I have any experience in the art of speaking, on which I admit I have spent considerable time, he has a right to it. If I possess any skill in this craft born of training and the study of the fine arts, and I confess that I have avoided this at no time in my life, he has a pre-eminent claim upon it. As long as I can remember, as I look back over past time into the earliest recollections of my childhood, I see that this man has been my mentor. He led my initial engagement with and my further progress in the rigorous study of this discipline. My speaking voice has been shaped by this man's advice and teachings. If it has occasionally been the means of safety for some, then of course, as much as is in my power, I ought to bring assistance and safety to the very man from whom I have received the ability to assist and to save other men.

[2] I hope that no one is surprised to hear me say this simply because Archias has a different kind of talent, and is not trained in the art of oratory. I myself have never been exclusively devoted to this one pursuit. And in any case, all the humanistic arts share a kind of common bond and are connected by a certain kinship. [3] So please do

---

1. Cicero refers to Archias by the Roman names he adopted on becoming a citizen, rather than by his original Greek name, which he also kept as a cognomen. His full name was Aulus Licinius Archias. Frequently Cicero simply calls him "this man." The name Archias has been inserted as necessary for clarity.

not be surprised either if I employ this elevated style of speaking here in a criminal trial, in a court of law, when business is being done before a praetor[2] of the Roman people, a most worthy man, and in front of very serious judges, and with such a large audience in attendance. I know it is at odds not just with the custom of the courts but also with normal legal language. I ask that in this particular case you grant me an exception, one fitting for this defendant and not, I hope, bothersome to you. Allow me to speak a bit more freely about the humanities and literature. I do so on behalf of a great poet and a very learned man, in this assembly of very literate men, conscious of your civilized sensibilities and aware of which particular praetor administers this court. Permit me to use a somewhat new and unusual style of speaking, in a case concerning a figure of this type, who pursues his leisured studies out of the public eye, and for that reason has seldom been dealt with in the dangers of the court room.

[4] Do I sense that you have granted my wish and allowed me this license? Then I will convince you without delay that this man, Aulus Licinius, should not be severed from the citizen body, since he is indeed a citizen. In fact, when I am done you will think that if he were not a citizen, he ought to have been added to the rolls.

From the moment he left boyhood and completed the elementary studies that prepare the young for civilized culture, Archias applied himself to the writer's craft. He began at Antioch. That is where he was born, to a family of the high nobility. Even at Antioch, once a populous and wealthy city packed full with superb scholars of extremely refined literary tastes, he swiftly began to surpass them all in the fame acquired by his talent. Later he traveled throughout Asia Minor and all of mainland Greece in celebrated tours. His reputation there based on his writings was great. But that reputation was exceeded by the eager anticipation of a personal appearance. And that anticipation, immense as it was, was surpassed by the rapturous reception he received in person.

[5] At that time Italy was full of Greek culture and learning. Even up here in Latium these pursuits were appreciated more seriously than they are now in these same towns. And in Rome itself, thanks to the tranquility of the political situation, they were not neglected either. So it was natural that the people of Tarentum, Locri, Rhegium, and Naples bestowed on Archias their citizenship, and other rewards and privileges as well. Furthermore, everyone with any judgment about literary matters thought him worth meeting and inviting into his home. He arrived in Rome at the height of his fame, already well known here, though he had not yet visited. This was in the consulship of Marius and Catulus [102 BC].

At the beginning he met these excellent consuls, of whom Marius could provide great military achievements as material for his writings, while Catulus could offer not only his own deeds as subjects, but also enthusiasm and appreciation for his art. Soon after that, the family of the Luculli took him into their home, though Archias was still quite a young man. And this same family that fostered him in his youth is very friendly to him in his old age—an indication not just of his gifts but also of his sterling character and virtue. [6] In those early days he was on friendly terms also with the famous Quintus Metellus Numidicus, and his son Pius. Marcus Aemilius heard him perform. He lived with Quintus Catulus, both the father and son of the same name.

---

2. That is, "judge"; see Glossary, "praetor." According to an ancient commentator, Cicero's younger brother Quintus was the praetor in this trial.

Lucius Crassus cultivated his friendship. In fact he so captivated with the charm of his company men like the Luculli and Drusus and the Octavii and Cato, and the whole house of the Hortensii, that he received what I suppose is the highest possible tribute: he was courted not only by people who were eager to learn something and to listen, but also by those who merely wanted to appear so.

After a while he set off for Sicily in the company of Marcus Lucullus. On his journey from that province with the same Lucullus he visited Heraclea. Now Heraclea was a city federated with Rome, with full civic privileges under the law. So Archias decided he would like to be enrolled in its citizenship. This privilege he obtained from the Heracleans, both because he was thought worthy on his own merits, and also because of the considerable clout and influence of Lucullus. [7] By this act he became a citizen of Rome as well, in accordance with the law of Silvanus and Carbo, and I quote: "Citizens of federated states shall be Roman citizens if, at the time when the law was passed,[3] they had residence in Italy, and if they presented themselves before the praetor within sixty days." Since Archias had been resident at Rome for many years, he presented himself before the praetor, Quintus Metellus, his very good friend.

[8] Now, if this case is about nothing but citizenship, I need not go on. The case is closed. Tell me, Grattius, which piece of evidence can you refute? Will you deny that he was enrolled as a citizen of Heraclea? Well, a man of the utmost authority and rectitude and integrity, Marcus Lucullus himself, is here to testify to that. His testimony is not that he thinks this is the case, but that he knows; not that he heard about it, but that he saw it; not that he was involved in it, but that he made it happen. Delegates from Heraclea are here as well, leaders in their community. They have journeyed to Rome specifically for this case to provide official affidavits and depositions from the city government. These men testify that Archias was enrolled in the citizenship of Heraclea.

Come now, Grattius, are you seriously demanding the public records of the Heracleans, when we all know that they perished when the record house burned down during the Social War? It is ridiculous to say nothing about the evidence we have in front of us, and demand evidence we cannot possibly possess, to be silent about the memories of living men while insisting upon the memory of written records. You yourself often say that records can be tampered with. Why do you long for those, but spurn the solemn word of very important men, and the sworn oath and good faith of a most dependable allied city, things that cannot be corrupted?

[9] Or is your argument that Archias had not established residence at Rome? Really? A man who so many years earlier, even before he received the citizenship, had transferred all his effects and fortunes to Rome? Or maybe you maintain that he failed to present himself before the praetor? In fact, his declaration appears in the only records from that board of praetors involved in that registration that can still be trusted. As for the records of Appius, they are supposed to have been kept rather carelessly. Those of Gabinius, before his conviction, were undermined merely by the man's lack of seriousness. After his condemnation they lost what little credibility they had. But Metellus, the most scrupulous and honest of them all, was so diligent that he came before another praetor of that year, Lucius Lentulus, as he presided over a court, and said that he was

---

3. 89 BC, after the end of the Social War (see Glossary). This war resulted in the granting of full citizenship to all Italians through the Papirian Law, which outlined the process of enfranchisement.

disturbed about an erasure under a single name.[4] In Metellus' scrupulous records you see no erasure beneath the name of Aulus Licinius Archias. [10] Given this fact, how could you hold the slightest doubt about his citizenship status, especially since he was enrolled as a citizen of other states as well?

Among the Greeks in southern Italy it was customary to give out citizenship for the sheer fun of it to many men of moderate distinction, and some endowed with no skill at all or some humble art. So I'm to believe that the people of Rhegium or Locri or Naples or Tarentum would be unwilling to give to Archias, endowed as he is with the glory of a great talent, something they were accustomed to shower upon mere stage performers? In numerous other cases, dubious men have managed somehow or other to creep into the citizenship records of federated cities, not only after the granting of Roman citizenship to the allies, but even after the passage of the Papian law.[5] Shall we reject Archias, whose claim to Roman citizenship was based simply on being a citizen of Heraclea, and who doesn't even use the citizenship of all those cities in which he was legitimately enrolled? Surely not.

[11] You ask us to produce his name on the census lists of Roman citizens. No doubt! But it is clear that in the most recent census Archias was with the army under that very distinguished general, Lucius Lucullus. And during the one before that he was with the same man when he was quaestor in Asia. And in the one before that, in the censorship of Julius and Crassus, no part of the people was actually counted.[6] But in any case, the census is no guarantee of citizenship; it only indicates that any man counted was already acting as a citizen at the time. Archias frequently made a will in accordance with our laws, and accepted legacies from Roman citizens, and he was recommended to receive a reward from the war-spoils by Lucius Lucullus, the proconsul. Are these the actions of a man who, according to your charge, did not even himself believe he was entitled to partake in the privileges of Roman citizens? Search for arguments all you want. Archias will never be refuted based on his own actions or those of his friends.

[12] You ask, Grattius, why I take such delight in this man. Why? Because he furnishes me with the means to refresh my mind after the noise of the Forum. Thanks to him, my ears, worn out with verbal abuse, can at last have rest. How do you suppose I can find the words to speak every day on such a bewildering variety of affairs unless I develop my mind through study? How do you suppose I can find the energy to endure such strain if I cannot relax through that same study? I admit it. I am devoted to literature. Shame on those who have so buried themselves in literature that they can contribute nothing from it to the common good, nothing that they can bring out into public view. But why should I feel shame? I live, and have lived for so many years, gentlemen of the jury, in such a way that neither my own leisure, nor my own pleasure, nor even my sleep, has kept me from helping anyone in his time of need. [13] And so, who would criticize me? Who would justifiably be angry with me? I grant myself as much

---

4. This Lentulus seems to have been the praetor in charge of dealing with forgery cases in 89 BC. He is unknown outside this passage.

5. 65 BC. According to this law one who had used the privileges of Roman citizenship without legal qualification might be prosecuted. It was evidently the basis of Grattius' prosecution of Archias.

6. In 70, 86, and 89 BC, respectively.

time for cultivating these pursuits as other men spend looking after their fortunes or celebrating festivals. The time I spend on literature they spend on going to the games, or on other idle pleasures, or simply resting their minds and bodies. What I devote to the arts they devote to endless dinner parties, or gaming, or playing ball. And I feel all the more entitled to this license because my ability to speak, such as it is, derives from these very studies, and has never let my friends down in their time of danger.

But if this seems to anyone like a waste of time, I at least am conscious of the source from which I draw those things which are, indeed, most important. [14] Why have I thrown myself into so many great struggles and braved the daily attacks of corrupt men on behalf of your safety? Because from a young age I came to believe, on the basis of the teachings of many people and the reading of much literature, that nothing in life is particularly worth pursuing except glory and integrity. In the pursuit of these things every bodily pain and every risk of death and exile should be considered insignificant. Real examples of this kind of conduct are met everywhere in books, in the sayings of the wise, in our long and distinguished history. All of them would lie in darkness were it not for the illumination provided by literature.

How many portraits of the brave have Greek and Latin writers left to us, depicted not just for us to contemplate but also to imitate?[7] While governing the state I have always set these before myself and trained my heart and mind through the very process of thinking about excellent men. [15] Someone might ask, "Come now, Cicero. Those illustrious personages whose virtues have been passed down through literature, had *they* been educated by that study which you extol?" It is difficult to affirm this concerning all of them. But still, the response is clear. I admit that many people have developed excellent mental qualities and courage without the study of literature. They have become self-controlled and dignified on their own, because of the almost divine disposition of their inner nature. And I will also add that natural excellence without study has led to glory and merit more often than has literary study without natural excellence. But at the same time I maintain this, that when the system, as it were, and the discipline of literary study is added to an excellent and distinguished natural talent, then something truly outstanding and singular arises. [16] In this elite group I place that miraculous man, Scipio Africanus, seen by our fathers' generation. In this group I place Gaius Laelius and Lucius Furius, leaders of outstanding moderation and self-control. In this group I place Marcus Cato the Elder, who possessed great courage but was also the best scholar of his day. If such men were not helped at all by literature when it comes to acquiring and fostering excellence, they never would have spent their time studying it.

But leave this great practical benefit to one side. Suppose that pleasure alone were the goal of these studies. Even so, I believe, you should judge this kind of mental relaxation highly civilized and most worthy of a free man. Other types of recreation are appropriate neither to all times, nor to all stages of life, nor to all places. But these pursuits sharpen youth yet delight old age. They ornament success yet provide refuge and solace in adversity. They enchant us in private yet do not hinder us in public. They are with us at night, when we travel, and when we spend time in the country.

---

7. A manifestation of the idea of exemplary history, where models of great men become the enticement for the young to achieve greatness. See Livy's Preface, and Polybius chs. 52–53 in this volume.

[17] But even if we ourselves are not able to pursue the arts, or to experience them with our own faculties, still we ought to admire them even when we see them in others. Who among us has such a boorish and wooden heart that he was not deeply moved by the recent death of Roscius? He died an old man, it is true. But because of his amazing skill and elegance as an actor, it seemed that he ought never to have died at all. Roscius earned such great affection from all of us because of the movements of his body. Shouldn't we pay attention to the incredible movements of the mind and the agility of intellects as well?

[18] How many times have I seen this man Archias—judges, I appreciate your indulgence and thank you for paying such close attention as I employ this unfamiliar style of speaking—how many times have I seen Archias recite extemporaneously, without any kind of script, a huge number of excellent verses about actual current events? How many times have I seen him called back for an encore, only to describe the same events in new words and with new morals attached? Whatever he had written down carefully and deliberately was, as I myself witnessed, so acclaimed that it would approach the glory of the old masters. Shouldn't I love this man? Shouldn't I be amazed at him? Shouldn't I think that he ought to be defended in every way possible?

Great and learned men have said it before. Other fields of endeavor rely on theory and rules and acquired skill; the poet derives his strength from nature herself. He is impelled by pure mental power and is filled, as it were, by a kind of divine breath. And so with good reason our own Roman classic, Ennius, calls poets holy because they seem to be loaned to us, as it were, by a kind of gift of the gods. [19] Therefore, jurors, let this title of poet, which no barbarian race has ever treated with disrespect, remain holy among you highly civilized men. Inanimate rocks and deserts are said to respond to the human voice. Menacing beasts are soothed and stopped cold at the sound of singing. Shouldn't we, with our fine education, be moved by the voice of poets? The people of Colophon say that Homer is a citizen of their own state. The Chians claim him as their native son. The people of Salamis demand him back, while those of Smyrna say that he is their own, and have even dedicated a shrine to him in their city. And many others also fight and contend amongst themselves. Those cities press their claims on a foreigner even after his death, because he was a poet. Archias is still alive. He is ours by his own will and in accordance with the law. How can we reject him?

We should embrace him all the more since, for a long time now, Archias has dedicated all of his efforts and skill to celebrating and praising the glory of the Roman people. As a young man he took up the subject of the war with the Cimbri[8] and was friendly with the great Marius himself, though the general seemed rather ill-disposed to literary pursuits. [20] The fact is that no one is so uninterested in literature that he would prevent the permanent advertisement of his own labors being committed to verse. There is a story about Themistocles, the famous Athenian statesman. They say that when he was asked what entertainment, or whose voice he would most like to hear, his answer was the voice of the man by whom his own achievements were best proclaimed. It was for the same reason that Marius so loved Lucius Plotius: he thought that the great things he had done could be made famous by Plotius' literary gift.

---

8. A formidable Germanic tribe that invaded Italy from the north and were defeated by Marius in 101 BC.

[21] The Mithridatic War was a great and difficult one, prosecuted through many vicissitudes on land and sea.[9] Yet Archias wrote about all of it. These books glorify not just the commander Lucius Lucullus, an outstandingly brave and accomplished man, but also the name of the Roman people itself. How so? Under Lucullus as general, the Roman people opened up Pontus, a place formerly well protected by the wealth of King Mithridates and by the nature of the terrain itself. Under the same general, without a very great force, an army of the Roman people routed innumerable hordes of Armenians. It is to the credit of the Roman people that, thanks to the good generalship of the same man, the city of Cyzicus, our staunch ally, was saved and preserved from every attack of Mithridates and rescued from imminent destruction. And what about that amazing naval victory at Tenedos, also fought by Lucullus, when the enemy fleet was sunk, its admirals killed? This will always be spoken of and proclaimed as a Roman victory. The trophies are ours, the monuments ours, the triumphs ours. Those whose literary talents extol these events celebrate, in fact, the glory of the Roman people.

[22] Our own Roman poet Ennius was dear to the Scipio Africanus the Elder. A marble statue of him is even thought to have been set up in the tomb of the Scipios. But Ennius' hymns of praise certainly add luster not just to the man himself who is praised, but also to the name of the Roman people. Cato the Elder, ancestor of our contemporary Cato here, is praised to the skies in Ennius' works. But great honor attaches thereby to the achievements of the Roman people. In short, all those great men, the Maximi, the Marcelli, the Fulvii—when poets praise them they also add to the common glory of all of us. This is why our ancestors took the man from Rudiae who had accomplished these things, Ennius, and made him a Roman citizen. Are we to eject from our citizenship the man from Heraclea, one sought out by many states but established by law in this one? Surely not.

[23] Now, one might think that there is less to be gained from Greek poetry than from Latin. But he would be sorely mistaken. Greek literature is read in virtually every country, while Latin literature is confined to its own native territory, which is small indeed. So if Roman achievements are limited only by the extent of the earth, we ought to desire that our fame and glory penetrate everywhere our weapons have reached. On the one hand, such works do honor to the very peoples whose affairs are being written about. On the other hand, they provide a great incentive to those who are risking their lives for the sake of glory and undergoing dangerous and grueling work.

[24] They say that Alexander the Great kept with him countless writers to chronicle his own deeds. And yet, when he stood at the tomb of Achilles in Sigeum he said, "Oh, what a lucky young man you were to have found Homer as the herald of your valor." How right he was. If the *Iliad* had not been composed, the same tomb that covered Achilles' corpse would have buried his name. And what about our own general nicknamed "the Great"—Pompeius—a man whose good fortune equals his valor? Why, he granted citizenship to Theophanes of Mytilene, the chronicler of his own deeds, in the midst of an assembly of the soldiers. And those brave Roman men shouted their approval of the act. Mind you, these were simple country folk and soldiers. Yet they were moved, I think, by the sweet taste of fame, as if they shared in Pompeius' glory.

---

9. It had several phases, but Archias wrote about the campaigns led by his patron L. Licinius Lucullus from 73–68 BC, in the so-called Third Mithridatic War. Like the rest of his works, this one is lost.

[25] So come now, if Archias were not a Roman citizen by law, do you really think he could not have prevailed upon some general or other to bestow citizenship upon him? Take Sulla, for example. He used to give citizenship to Spaniards and Gauls. Do you really think he would have rejected this man's request? On one occasion a bad poet from among the common people slipped Sulla a little manuscript. We all watched as the dictator ordered a reward to be given to him out of the property he happened at the time to be auctioning off. Why did he do this? Simply because the fellow had written an epigram in his honor, a few ungainly couplets. Sulla gave the reward, but on one condition, that the man write nothing more in the future.

Sulla considered even the officiousness of a bad poet still worthy of some reward. Would he not have sought out Archias' talent, his excellence in writing, his expressive power? [26] And what about Quintus Metellus Pius, Archias' close friend, who gave citizenship to many? Would Archias not have obtained citizenship from him, either through his own efforts, or through the intervention of the Luculli? Absolutely. Metellus was so eager to have his achievements written about that he even lent his ears to the thick and foreign-sounding tones of poets born at Cordoba.

We ought not to disguise a fact that cannot be hidden; rather we ought to acknowledge it openly: we are all drawn by the desire for praise. And the best men are the ones most attracted by fame. Those very philosophers who write books about despising fame never seem to forget to affix their names on them. In the very act of despising self-advertisement and notability they advertise themselves and betray their desire to be noted.

[27] Now, Decimus Brutus, a great man and a great general, was close friends with the poet Accius, and inscribed his friend's words on the doorways to the temples and monuments he had built. Fulvius waged war with the Aetolians in the company of Ennius, then took the spoils of Mars and without hesitation built a holy temple to the Muses. In our city, generals, practically still in armor, have cultivated the name of poets and worshipped at the shrine of the Muses. You, judges, who wear the toga of civilians in this selfsame city, should not shrink from honoring the Muses and saving poets.

[28] I would like to make a confession to you, gentlemen of the jury, and to testify for a moment against myself, regarding my own love of fame, which I admit is perhaps too keen, but which is honorable nevertheless. I hope it will make you more willing to help Archias. Do you remember the things that I accomplished along with you during the time of my consulship, the measures I took on behalf of the safety of this city and of the empire, on behalf of the citizen body and the entire state?[10] Archias has started to write a poem on this subject. When I heard about this, I was of course pleased and flattered, and I furnished him with some material for completing the job. The fact is that merit requires no other reward for its labors and risks than that of glory and fame. But if this incentive is removed, gentlemen of the jury, what reason is there to wear ourselves out in so many labors during the ever so brief span of our lives? [29] Clearly if the human mind thought nothing of the future and limited all of its thoughts and aspirations to the circumscribed space of this life, it would never exhaust itself in so many labors; it would never allow itself to be afflicted by so many anxieties or sacrifice so much sleep; nor would it fight for its very life again and again.

In fact, a kind of inner voice of excellence lies within all the best men and spurs their

---

10. A reference to Cicero's victory over the revolutionary Catiline the year before (63 BC).

minds with the incentive of fame. It tells them that the end of life must not be the end of one's name—rather that it should last as long as there are people to remember it. [30] Are we so small minded, those of us who take part in service to the state, with all its attendant trials and risk to life and limb? Are we so small-minded as to believe that, when we have drawn not a single tranquil and leisurely breath throughout our entire careers, it will all die with us? Many great men have been keen to leave behind statues and portraits, images not of their minds but of their bodies. Should we not far prefer to leave behind representations of our ideas and our virtues, elegantly expressed by great writers? As for me, I thought that everything I was doing, at the very moment when I was doing it, was spreading my reputation abroad and disseminating it into the eternal memory of the world. It may be that after I die I will perceive nothing, and this fame will mean nothing to me then. Or perhaps, as the wisest men have supposed, it will reach some part of my consciousness. Be that as it may, here and now I certainly delight in the contemplation and hope of it.

[31] And so, judges, save this defendant, whose sterling character is vouched for, as you can see, by the status of his friends and the length of his friendships with them. Save this defendant, whose literary gifts (to the extent that it's proper to take that into account) are sought after by the judgment of all the best people. Save a defendant whose case is of a type that is buttressed by the law, by the authority of his home city, by the testimony of Lucullus, and by the records of Metellus. You see how the matter stands, gentlemen of the jury. If Archias' genius serves as any recommendation in the eyes not just of men but of the gods themselves, I ask you to take under your protection a man who has always showered fame on you, your generals, and on the achievements of the Roman people, and who promises that he will give eternal testimony to the glory won in these recent domestic dangers that you and I shared. He belongs to that class of men whom everyone has always considered and deemed holy. Take him under your protection. Let him be seen to be helped by your kindness, rather than injured by the cruelty of his enemies.

What I have said today about the case in a brief and simple fashion in accordance with my own custom—that much I am confident of having proven in the eyes of everyone. What I have said regarding the literary talent of Archias and about the arts in general, matters which are far from the normal business of the forum and the courts, I hope that these things, gentlemen of the jury, have been heard by you as sympathetically as I know for certain they have been by the praetor who presides over this court.

## Introduction to Cicero's *Letters*

Cicero's letters, which were not written for publication, provide vivid, personal, and sometimes poignant commentary on the dissolution of the Roman Republic, from the perspective of one of the major players in the events. The surviving letters, more than 900 of them, form a unique archive. The selection here includes some of the earliest surviving letters (65 BC), when Cicero was an ambitious "new man" and aspirant to the consulship (see also in this volume *Running for Office: A Handbook*, attributed to

Cicero's brother, Quintus), and extends through the period of the Bona Dea scandal and the trial of Clodius (61 BC); the "triumvirate" of Crassus, Caesar, and Cicero's friend Pompeius (60–59 BC); Cicero's exile (58 BC); the civil war between Caesar (whom Cicero knew and admired) and Pompeius (50–48 BC), in which he sided with the latter; Caesar's dictatorship and assassination (45–44 BC); and finally Cicero's unsuccessful crusade against M. Antonius, who ordered his murder in the proscriptions of late 43 BC.

## Letters

### 1    July 65 BC, On His Candidacy for the Consulship (Ad Atticum 1.1)

Cicero to Atticus, greetings.[11] I know that you take a great interest in my campaign, so here is the state of things, so far as anyone can guess at present. The only one currently campaigning is P. Galba. He is being met with a good old Roman "No," plain and simple. This premature entry of his into the field was, people suppose, a positive development for me. Generally speaking, those who say no to him tell him that they have pledged their support to me. So I hope I can make a little headway when word gets out that I do have quite a few friends. I was thinking of beginning my active campaigning on July 17, in the Campus Martius during the election of the tribunes (the very time when your slave is supposed to leave with this letter, according to Cincius). My rivals—to mention only those who seem certain to stand for election—are Galba, Antonius, and Q. Cornificius. I imagine this will make you laugh, or cry. Well, to make you positively slap your forehead, some people think Caesonius will run, too. I don't think Aquilius will; he says he won't and has given as excuses his health and his leading position in the law courts. Catiline will definitely run, as long as the verdict at his trial is that the sun does not shine at noon. As for Aufidius and Palicanus, I don't think you're waiting to hear about them from me.

[2] Of the candidates for this year's election, Caesar[12] is considered a shoo-in for consul. It looks like Thermus and Silanus will battle for the other spot. But they are so poor in both friends and popularity that I think it possible that Curius will sneak past them—but I'm the only one. By my reckoning the best thing for me would be if Thermus were elected with Caesar. None of the current crop of candidates, if left over to the following year, would be stronger than Thermus. He is commissioner in charge of repairing the *Via Flaminia*, and that will easily be done by then.[13] So I would much rather see him elected now, with Caesar.

That's my rough assessment of where things stand with the various candidates. I plan to work extremely hard at every aspect of the candidate's job. It seems to me that

---

11. T. Pomponius Atticus (110–32 BC), Cicero's lifelong friend and most frequent correspondent.

12. Lucius Caesar (consul in 64 BC), not C. Julius Caesar.

13. Hiring men to carry out the repairs would earn Thermus considerable popularity, as Cicero implies.

Gaul will have a lot of influence in the vote, so maybe when business cools down in the Forum here I will get a special appointment to go up and visit Piso in September.[14] That will get me back here in Rome by January. When I have figured out the leanings of the nobles, I will let you know. I hope the rest is plain sailing, at least when it comes to my rivals here in the city. As for the followers of my friend Pompeius, that contingent is your responsibility, since you are closer.[15] Tell him I will not be upset if he does not come to my election.

So that's the situation with that. [3] But there is something else, a matter on which I very much want your forgiveness. Your uncle Caecilius, having been cheated of a large sum of money by P. Varius, has sued Varius' cousin Caninius Satyrus for the property which (he alleges) Satyrus had received from Varius by a fraudulent sale. Others of Satyrus' creditors have joined in, including Lucullus and P. Scipio, as well as L. Pontius, the man whom they expect would be the official in charge of the auction if the property was put up for sale (though it is ridiculous to be talking about an official auctioneer). The point is this: Caecilius asked me to appear on his behalf against Satyrus. Now, scarcely a day passes without this Satyrus calling at my house.[16] L. Domitius comes first in his attention, I next. He has been of great service both to me and to my brother Quintus when we were candidates. [4] So I am put in an extremely awkward position because of my friendship with Satyrus, not to mention that with Domitius, on whom the success of my election depends more than on anyone else. I pointed out these facts to Caecilius, and I assured him that if it were just between him and Satyrus, I would have done what he asked. But with so many creditors involved—men of very high rank, who could easily win their case without the help of anyone specially retained by Caecilius—it was only fair that he should have consideration both for my obligation to Satyrus and my present situation. He seemed to take this refusal less graciously than I would have liked and than gentlemen normally do, and ever since, he has completely broken off the warm relationship that had begun only a few days before.

I am asking you to forgive me, and to understand that normal human kindness prevented me from attacking the reputation of a friend in great trouble, when the dutiful attention he had paid to me was unfailing. But if you want to take a less charitable view of my conduct, say the interests of my campaign prevented me. Even if that is the case, I still think you should forgive me, for as Homer would say, "it's no sacrificial victim or ox-hide shield we're fighting for."[17] You see the kind of contest I'm involved in, and how essential it is for me not just to hang on to the friends I have, but to make new ones. I hope I have proven my case to you—I am certainly anxious to do so.

[5] The Hermathena you sent is absolutely delightful. I found a perfect spot for it in the gymnasium,[18] so that the whole hall seems like an offering laid at its feet. Many thanks.

---

14. The governor of Gallia Narbonensis.

15. Pompeius was in the East, waging successful campaigns against Mithridates and Tigranes in Armenia. Atticus was in Greece.

16. For the morning *salutatio*. See Glossary.

17. That is, no trifle. Homer, *Iliad* 22.159.

18. A place for philosophical lectures, rather than athletics; the Hermathena was a bust of Athena (Minerva).

## 2     July 65 BC, On the Birth of His Son (*Ad Atticum* 1.2)

Cicero to Atticus, greetings. Important news! I have become the father of a baby boy, on the day of the election of L. Julius Caesar and C. Marcius Figulus as consuls. Terentia is doing well. It's been ages, and not a single letter from you! I already wrote to you in detail about what is going on with me. At the moment I am thinking about defending Catiline, who plans to run for consul like me. We have the jury we want, and the full consent of the prosecutor. My hope is that, if he is acquitted, Catiline will be more closely tied to me in the campaigning. But if it doesn't work out, I won't be too upset. [2] I need you to come back to Rome, and soon. The dominant opinion is that your aristocratic friends will be opposed to my election. I know that you can be extremely helpful in winning the nobles over to me. So make sure you are in Rome by January, as you arranged!

## 3     January 25, 61 BC, On the Bona Dea Scandal (*Ad Atticum* 1.13)

Cicero to Atticus, greetings. I got your three letters—one through M. Cornelius, which I think you gave him in the town of Three Taverns; a second which your host at Canusium delivered to me; and the third, which you said you sent from the boat just as you got underway. All three were sprinkled with the salt of learning, as they say in the schools, and also full of signs of your affection. In all three you urge me to reply, but the reason that I'm a bit slow is that I cannot find a trustworthy courier. Rare is the man who can carry a letter of any substance without lightening it by perusal. And I don't always know if someone setting out for Epirus will find you. For I suppose that once you performed a sacrifice at your Amalthea, you set off for the siege to Sicyon.[19] I'm also not sure when you are going to join Antonius,[20] and how long you plan to stay in Epirus. So I dare not entrust overly frank letters either to men from Achaea or Epirus. [2] Plenty of things worth writing about have happened since you left, but I could not risk that the letters might be lost, opened, or intercepted.

Well then, to begin with: I was not called upon to speak first in the Senate; rather the so-called pacifier of the Allobroges[21] was asked his opinion before me. The Senate murmured its disapproval, but I did not mind so much. It freed me of the need to kowtow to a certain crotchety individual, and allowed me to preserve some of my political dignity, since I was free to oppose his position. Besides, the second speaker carries almost as much weight as the first and isn't put under too much of an obligation to the consul. The third called on was Catulus; the fourth, if you are still interested, Hortensius. The consul himself is a petty, misguided man, the kind of sarcastic jokester who laughs even when nothing is funny.[22] People laugh at him for his face rather than

---

19. "Amalthea" refers to Atticus' villa in Epirus, Greece; Atticus wanted to collect some money he had loaned to the city of Sicyon in Greece.

20. C. Antonius Hybrida, Cicero's consular colleague in 63 BC (and uncle of M. Antonius), now governor of Macedonia.

21. C. Calpurnius Piso, consul in 67, had temporarily put down a rebellion among the Gallic tribe called the Allobroges, but they were already in revolt again.

22. M. Pupius Piso Frugi Calpurnianus, consul in 61 BC.

his wit. He does no actual state business, and stands aloof from the *optimates*.[23] You would never expect him to do the community any good, because he doesn't care, nor any harm, because he doesn't dare. His colleague,[24] on the other hand, is most complimentary to me, and an extremely energetic defender of the right side. [3] Their differences of opinion have been slight so far, but I am afraid that this minor infection may spread.

I suppose you have heard that when a state ritual was being conducted[25] at Caesar's home, a man[26] in woman's clothing got in; and that when the Vestals performed the rite again,[27] mention was made of the matter in the Senate by Q. Cornificius (he took the lead, in case you think it was one of us). Later, by decree of the Senate, the matter was referred to the Vestals and the Pontifices, and they decided that the occurrence constituted a sacrilege. [4] Then by senatorial decree the consuls promulgated a bill. Caesar divorced his wife. Piso, due to his friendship with Clodius, is working for the rejection of the proposal that he himself brought forward, in accordance with a decree of the Senate, and concerning sacrilege at that! Messalla is so far taking a very hard line. The honest men (*boni*)[28] are yielding to the pleas of Clodius and dropping out of the case. Hired gangs are being gotten together, and I myself, who was in the beginning as hardnosed as Lycurgus,[29] am daily losing enthusiasm. Cato is pursuing the case energetically. In short I am afraid that Clodius' acts, if ignored by the honest men and defended by those with no morals, will cause great mischief to the state. However, that friend of yours—do you know who I mean?[30]—who you said in your letter began to praise me when he no longer dared to criticize me: well, now he embraces me and ostentatiously flaunts his affection and love. Secretly he is jealous of me, but he does not hide it very well. No courtesy, no candor, no notable political action, no highmindedness, no bravery, no independence—but I will write to you about this in more detail later. I am still not quite fully informed, and I dare not entrust to any old messenger a letter about such important matters.

[5] The praetors have not yet drawn their lots for the provinces. The matter remains just as it was when you left. I will add to my speech a description of Misenum and Puteoli, as you suggest. I had already noticed that "December 3" was an error. The sections of the speeches that you liked were, you should know, my favorites as well, but I didn't dare say so before. Now that they have your approval, they seem even more "Attic" to me.[31]

---

23. See Glossary.

24. M. Valerius Messalla, mentioned below.

25. In honor of the Good Goddess (*Bona Dea*), held in December 62 BC; no men were allowed to be present. See Inscriptions no. 92.

26. P. Clodius Pulcher, an incendiary populist (tribune in 58 BC) who was Cicero's political archenemy. See letters 4, 5, and 9 below.

27. Standard in cases where a ritual had been disrupted.

28. Literally "the good men," essentially a synonym for *optimates* (see Glossary), men of Cicero's own political views.

29. The Spartan lawgiver.

30. Pompeius.

31. That is, having a simple and refined elegance, pure, classical.

I have added a little to my speech in reply to Metellus.[32] I'll send you the volume, since your affection for me has made you into a fan of rhetoric.

What news do I have for you? Let me see. Oh, yes! The consul Messalla has bought Autronius' house for 13,400,000 sesterces.[33] Why should you care, you ask? Only because due to that purchase people think that I made a good purchase as well, and they have started to realize that it's perfectly fine to make use of your friends' resources in buying a house, so as to reach to a certain level of status. The Teucris affair drags on, yet I have hopes. Just make sure to get your part finished. You shall have a less guarded letter soon.

January 25, in the consulship of M. Messalla and M. Piso.

## 4    Early July 61 BC, On the Trial of Clodius (*Ad Atticum* 1.16)

Cicero to Atticus, greetings. You ask me what happened at the trial to produce such an unexpected result,[34] and you also want to know why I was less full of fight than usual. I'll take the second one first, in the manner of Homer. As long as it was the Senate's authority that I had to defend, I fought so keenly and intensely that people were crowding around me and shouting my praises. If you ever thought I showed political courage before, you would have been amazed at me this time. Clodius took refuge in speaking at public rallies, and during them used my name to stir up ill will. Gods, how I came out fighting and wreaked havoc then. Oh, what assaults I made against Piso, Curio, that whole crowd. How I went after the old men for their cluelessness, the young for their recklessness. Dear gods! How I kept wishing you were not just my guide on the issues but also a spectator of those amazing battles of mine. [2] Later, however, Hortensius came up with the idea of having Fufius, a tribune of the people, put forward a law about the sacrilege, a measure that differed from the consular measure only in the type of jurors specified—though that was the key point. He fought hard to make this happen, because he had convinced himself and others that no conceivable jury would acquit Clodius. At that point, recognizing we had got a jury of paupers, I trimmed my sails and said nothing in my testimony at the trial itself that was not already so notorious and well-attested that I could not leave it out.

So if you want to know why Clodius was acquitted (to return now to the first question you asked), it was the poverty of the jurors and their lack of integrity. But it was Hortensius' miscalculation that made it all possible. He was afraid that Fufius would veto the law that was drafted on the basis of the Senate's decree. But he did not see that it would have been better to leave Clodius under a cloud of disgrace pending a trial rather than let him go to work on an unreliable jury. No, Hortensius was driven by sheer animosity to hurry the matter to trial, saying that a lead sword was sharp enough to cut Clodius' throat.

[3] If you want to know what happened at the trial itself, the result was so unbelievable that now, after the fact, Hortensius' plan is being criticized by others (though I

---

32. A tribune who had prevented Cicero from fulfilling one of his obligations as consul.

33. This number is extremely high, and possibly a mistake in the manuscripts. Cicero's similar house cost 3.5 million.

34. Clodius was acquitted.

disagreed from the start). The jury selection process went on amid deafening shouts, since the accuser, like a good censor, was rejecting all the most disreputable characters, but the defendant, like a kind-hearted trainer of gladiators, set aside all the most respectable people. As soon as the jury was seated the honest men began to have grave doubts, for there never was a seedier crew in any gambling den: scandal-hounded senators, bankrupt equestrians, tribunes on the take. Yet there were a few honest men on the panel, whom the accused had been unable to drive off in the selection process. They took their seats among their uncongenial comrades with gloomy looks, clearly disgusted at having to rub elbows with such filth. [4] In these circumstances it was amazing how uniformly stern the decisions were in the preliminary proceedings, as point after point was put before the jury. The defendant got nothing he wanted, the prosecutor more than he asked for. It goes without saying that Hortensius was crowing about his own foresight: who would have thought that such a defendant would not be condemned a thousand times over?

Then I was brought forward as a witness. Even *you*, I think, could have heard from the shouts of Clodius' supporters how the jury rose *en masse* and surrounded me when Clodius' supporters began to shout, and how they offered their throats to Clodius' sword in defense of me. To me this seemed a compliment even greater than the well-known occasion when your beloved Athenians stopped Xenocrates from taking an oath on the witness-stand, or when our Roman jurors refused to look at the account books of Metellus Numidicus when they were being handed around in the usual way[35]—yes indeed, this was a far greater gesture. [5] So the voices of the jury, defending me and proclaiming me as the savior of the state,[36] dealt a crushing blow to the defendant, and all of his advocates fell away. The crowd at my morning reception the next day was as big as the one that escorted me home from the Forum after the last day of my consulship.

At that point Clodius' eminent advocates exclaimed that they would not go into court unless a formal bodyguard were provided for them. The issue was referred to the tribunal, where there was just one vote that a bodyguard was unnecessary. The matter was referred to the Senate, which passed a solemn, elaborate decree commending the jury and assigning the protection of the court to the magistrates. No one thought that Clodius would defend his case.

"O Muses, tell me now how fire first fell upon the ships."[37] You know that bald fellow, the one who made a fortune on the proscriptions, the one who praised me? I wrote to you about his speech that was so complimentary toward me.[38] Well, he spent a mere two days taking care of the whole business. Using a single slave—and one from a gladiatorial school at that—he summoned each juror, made promises, advocated for Clodius, and paid money down. There is more. As a bonus some of the jurors (good gods, what a disgusting business!) were offered nights with certain women, and

---

35. Xenocrates was a pupil of Plato (4th century BC). Q. Metellus Numidicus was consul in 109 BC. Both were examples of incorruptible integrity.

36. A reference to Cicero's role in uncovering the revolutionary plot of Catiline in 63 BC, and his controversial execution of Catiline's supporters without trial, as consul in that year.

37. Homer, *Iliad* 16.112.

38. M. Licinius Crassus, the triumvir. He used his massive wealth to bribe the jury.

introductions to young men of noble status. Thus, after the vast majority of the good men had simply left, and the Forum was packed with slaves, there were still twenty-five jurors so brave as to risk their lives, preferring to die than to wreck everything. Thirty-one were influenced more by their bellies than their sense of shame. On seeing one of the latter Catulus said, "So why did you ask us for a guard? Were you afraid of being robbed of the money?"

[6] There you have it, as briefly as I could put it, the nature of the trial and the cause of the acquittal. You go on to ask about the current state of public affairs, and my own. As for the political situation, we thought we had a stable settlement—brought about, as you claimed, by my wisdom, but in my opinion by the wisdom of the gods. It seemed fixed and settled, thanks to the unity of all the honest men and the influence of my consulship. But you should know that, unless some god takes up our cause, it has slipped through our hands thanks to this one trial—if you can call it a trial when thirty of the most worthless and wicked citizens in all of Rome are bribed to destroy all justice and right, when Talna, Plautus, Spongia, and the rest of that riffraff look at the crime that every man—and dumb animal!—knows took place, and decide that nothing criminal happened at all.

[7] Still, the good news to console you about public affairs is that wickedness is not running riot in its triumph as quickly as the bad men had hoped, even though the state had received a grievous wound. For they clearly supposed that with the collapse of religion, clean living, the integrity of the courts, and the authority of the Senate, wickedness in her victory could openly take revenge on all the best men for the suffering that the severe justice of my consulship had imposed on the most vile of men.[39]

[8] It was I myself (and I don't think it's out of line to boast about myself to you, in a private letter, one which I don't want you to share with others), it was I myself, I say, who brought back the shattered courage of the honest men, encouraging each one of them, spurring them on. By attacking and harassing that corrupt jury I effectively stopped the unchallenged boasts of victory by that "winning side," and left the consul Piso with no firm ground to stand on. I took away Syria, which had already been informally promised to him as his province. I recalled the Senate to its former seriousness, and lifted its downcast spirits. In a Senate meeting I dominated Clodius in his presence in a set speech of impressive solemnity, then in informal debate. I'll give you just a taste of what happened, since most of it loses its force and wit once the heat of the struggle (or the *agon* as you Greeks put it) is past.

[9] At the meeting of the Senate on May 15 I was asked for my opinion and, after saying a great deal about the most important state matters of the day, I took the opportunity, by happy inspiration, to bring up my typical theme, how the Senate must not be crushed by a single blow; they must not be faint-hearted. I said it seemed to me that this was just the kind of wound that should be neither concealed nor excessively worried about. We don't want to look stupid for ignoring it, or weak for fearing it. First Lentulus was set free (twice), then Catiline (twice), and now a jury had let loose a third enemy on the state. "But you are wrong, Clodius. The jurors have not preserved

---

39. Cicero is talking in abstractions to avoid naming names. His point is that the *popularis* sympathizers of Catiline had hoped to take revenge on Cicero himself in the wake of the verdict. This in fact happened when Cicero was driven into exile.

you for the streets of Rome, but for the death-chamber.[40] Their intent was not to keep you in the political community, but to deprive you of the comfort of exile. So, senators, find your courage, keep your dignity. There still remains in this state a unified band of honest men; these good men have taken a hit, but their valor is undiminished. We haven't suffered any new damage. We have simply discovered the damage that was already there. At the trial of one wicked man we have simply learned that there are many more." [10] But what am I doing? I'm practically giving you the whole speech in this letter. Back to the informal debate. The pretty[41] little boy gets up and criticizes me for having been at Baiae. Untrue, but so what?

"It's as if you were accusing me of going there in secret,"[42] I said.

"Why does a hick from Arpinum need baths?"

"Tell that to your patron," I replied, "who wanted to take the waters of a man from Arpinum." (You know about Marius' baths, right?[43])

"How long are we going to listen to this man playing king?" said Clodius.

"Strange you mention me as king, when King made no mention of you." (He had been dying to inherit the money of Rex.[44])

"You purchased a house," he began.

"You say that like I purchased a jury," I put in.

"The jurors," he said, "did not credit your oath."

"Well, twenty-five of them credited my oath, but thirty-one did not give you credit, since they had to have their money in advance." At this point, assailed by loud hoots, he gave up and fell silent.

[11] My own position is this: with the honest men I hold the same place as when you left town. With the grimy dregs of the city I hold a much better one than at your departure. In that sense it is a good thing that my testimony seemed to carry no weight. This turned out to be a rather painless bloodletting of the ill will against me. What is more, all the supporters of that felonious proceeding confess that it was a perfectly clear-cut case whose verdict had been bought by bribing the jury. Besides, the wretched starveling mob that comes to rallies and sucks the treasury dry imagines me to be high in the favor of Pompeius the Great—and in fact we have been spending a great deal of pleasant time together, so much so that the young smart set with their little beards, who carouse and hatch intrigues, have nicknamed him Gnaeus Cicero. As a result, at both festivals and gladiatorial games, I have been getting surprisingly positive ovations—no hisses or cat-calls.

[12] Now everyone is looking forward to the elections. Our friend Pompeius the Great, to everyone's disgust, is pushing Aulus' son[45] and is fighting for him not by using

---

40. *Carcer*, a holding-cell where convicts were held prior to execution.

41. A play on Clodius' cognomen, Pulcher, which means "handsome."

42. As Clodius had done to get into the house where the rites of the Bona Dea were being performed.

43. C. Scribonius Curio the elder bought the villa of Marius at Baiae in the Sullan proscriptions. Curio was a patron of Clodius; Marius was, like Cicero, from Arpinum.

44. Q. Marcius Rex, Clodius' brother-in-law. *Rex* means "king" in Latin.

45. The Afranius mentioned in section 13 of this letter, just below.

his influence and powers of persuasion, but by employing the same means Philip[46] used to say could be employed to storm any fortified hill, provided that it could be climbed by a cash-laden ass. Meanwhile the consul Piso is rumored to have taken up the cause, like a supporting actor in a play, and to have hosted bribery agents in his own house. But I don't believe that. Nevertheless, the Senate has now passed two resolutions on the motion of Cato and Domitius, which are unpopular because they seem to be directed straight at the consul: one makes it legal to search the house of any magistrate, and another makes it a treasonable offense to have bribery agents in one's home.

[13] Lurco, the tribune of the people, proposed a law to combat electoral bribery. He was released from the requirements of the Aelian and Fufian laws <text uncertain> and so, despite being lame, he was able to make the proposal under favorable auspices.[47] As a result the elections have been postponed to July 27. The new feature of his bill is that someone who announces his intention to bribe a tribe is not liable if he does not actually render payment. But if he has actually given the money, he is to pay a fine of 3,000 sesterces per tribe, every year, as long as he lives. I remarked that Clodius had already been following this provision of the law, since it was his custom to promise but not to pay. But look here, if Afranius is elected, don't you see how the consulship, which Curio used to call a "deification," will have become an absolute farce? One will have to take up philosophy, I suppose, like you, and not give a damn about consulships.

[14] You mentioned in your letter that you have decided not to go to Asia Minor.[48] Personally I would prefer that you go, and I'm afraid that things might not go entirely well in that matter. Still, I'm in no position to criticize, especially since I myself have refused to go to a province.

[15] I will be happy with the few verses about me that you have placed under my statue in your shrine to Amalthea, especially since Thyillus has now abandoned me and Archias has written nothing about me. I am afraid that, now that he has finished his Greek poem about the Luculli, he is moving on to try his hand at some sort of drama about the Caecilii.[49]

[16] I have thanked Antonius on your behalf, and given that letter to Mallius. The reason I have not written many letters lately is that I have not had a suitable courier, nor did I know where to send them. I have sung your praises loudly. [17] If Cincius delegates any of your business to me I will take care of it; but at the moment he's got his own problems, in which I am ready to assist. And you, if you stay in one place, can expect frequent letters from me—but send back even more yourself. Write and tell me how your "Amalthea" is doing, its decoration and its plan, and send me any poems or

---

46. Of Macedon, father of Alexander the Great.

47. The Leges Aelia et Fufia (mid-2nd century BC) regulated the implementation of religious restraints against passing bills. Lurco was lame, which evidently would normally have created some religious problem with the auspices. But the passage is obscure.

48. As a member of the staff of Cicero's brother Quintus.

49. This letter dates to a couple of years after Cicero's defense of Archias in court (see In Defense of Archias in this volume). Cicero had evidently been hoping for a poem from Archias, and from the otherwise unknown Thyillus, on the subject of his own consulship.

tales you have about Amalthea herself.[50] I would love to build something similar at Arpinum. I will send you some of what I have been writing. Nothing is finished yet.

## 5     July 59 BC, On the First Triumvirate (*Ad Atticum* 2.19)

Cicero to Atticus, greetings. I have many worries, both from the great convulsions and disorders on the political scene, and also from the threats made against me personally, which are very numerous. But none of it bothers me more than the manumission of Statius.[51] As Terence would say, "To think that my authority counts for nothing—forget my authority, what about my displeasure?"[52] But there's nothing I can do, and the problem isn't so much the thing itself as what people are saying. For myself, I can never be angry with those I love deeply. I only feel sorrow, and very deep sorrow, too.

My other problems have to do with more significant things. Clodius' threats and the struggles in store for me do not bother me too much. I think I can either face them with honor or else avoid them with no trouble. Perhaps you will say, "Enough of honor. It's prehistoric. Please, look after your own safety." Ah, dear me, dear me, why are you not here? Nothing, certainly, would get by you, whereas I may be blind, too much affected by my love of high ideals. [2] Let me assure you that there has never been anything so disgraceful, so shameful, so equally offensive to people of all sorts, ranks, and ages, than the current political situation. It's a hell of a lot worse than I expected and worse than I would like. Those "friends of the people"[53] have taught even normally restrained men how to hiss. Bibulus is exalted to the skies, though I have no idea why. But to listen to his fans you would think he's Ennius' "one man who saved the state for us by delaying."[54] Pompeius—the man I loved—has, to my infinite sorrow, ruined his own reputation. The triumvirs keep no one's loyalty by good will, and I'm afraid they will be forced to resort to threats. I don't fight against the triumvirs because of my friendship with Pompeius. But I don't give them my support, either, else I would be going against everything I've stood for in the past. I go my own way.

[3] Popular sentiment is especially visible in the theater and at the spectacles. At the gladiatorial show both the master and his assistants were assailed by hisses. At the games for Apollo the tragic actor Diphilus attacked our dear Pompeius quite shamelessly, and the actor was compelled by the crowd to repeat the line "thanks to our misery you are Great" over and over. Another line, "the time will come when that very same power of yours will make you groan," was greeted with shouts from the whole theater. And there

---

50. Amalthea was a Cretan nymph by whose goat Zeus was suckled as an infant. Perhaps the reference is to a special statue in Atticus' villa that gave the villa its name?

51. The trusted slave, and now freedman, of his brother Quintus. Cicero was deeply upset at the influence that Statius wielded over his brother, and felt that it severely damaged Quintus' reputation to be seen as being under the thumb of a social inferior.

52. A quotation from a comedy, Terence, *Phormio* 232.

53. *Populares* (see Glossary), a bitter reference to the triumvirs: Pompeius, Crassus, and Caesar.

54. The epic poet Ennius' description of Q. Fabius Maximus, the general who defeated Hannibal by delaying engaging him in battle. Bibulus was obstructing the legislative efforts of the triumvirs at every opportunity.

was more of the same.[55] The line "if neither law nor custom can constrain" and others seemed as though they were written by an enemy of Pompeius for the occasion. They were received with tremendous shouting and clapping. When Caesar entered, applause was lifeless. But then the younger Curio entered, and he was applauded heartily, like Pompeius used to be, back when the constitution was still functioning.[56] Caesar took this hard. They say he dashed off a letter to Pompeius at Capua. The triumvirs despise the equestrian order, who stood up to applaud Curio, and are taking hostile measures against the whole community, threatening the Roscian law, and even the grain law.[57] Things are extremely unsettled. I used to think that it would be best to silently ignore what they do, but I am afraid that will no longer be possible. People cannot endure it, yet it appears we'll have to. All speak with one voice. But it's a unanimity that rests on pure hatred, rather than any effective means of resistance.

[4] Our man Clodius is threatening me and taking hostile actions. There is trouble ahead, which should bring you flying back to town. I feel well protected by that same army of all honest men (and the adequately honest) that stood beside me during my consulship. Pompeius is showing me considerable affection, and assures me that Clodius will not say a word about me. When he says that, he's not fooling me, but fooling himself. When Cosconius died I was invited to take his place,[58] to fill the dead man's shoes. But nothing would be more damaging to my reputation, or more inimical to that safety that you recommend. The Board of Twenty is unpopular with the honest men, I with the rascals, whose ill will I would retain while just adding more on. [5] Caesar wants to have me on his staff. That would be a more honorable way to avoid danger, but I have no desire to avoid danger. Why? Because I prefer to fight. But nothing is settled. I'll say it again, I wish you were here. But I'll send for you if it becomes essential. Anything else? One more thing, I think. Rome is finished, I am certain of that. Why pretend any longer?

But I'm writing this in haste and am really afraid of saying too much. I'll write everything to you later—openly, if I can find someone I trust completely to carry the letter, otherwise in cloaked terms that you will understand. In those sorts of letters I will refer to myself as Laelius, to you as Furius; the rest will be in veiled language. I am taking good care of Caecilius here, and keeping an eye on him. I hear that Bibulus' edicts have been sent to you. They make our dear Pompeius burn with rage and indignation.

## 6    April 3, 58 BC, On the Law Relating to His Exile (*Ad Atticum* 3.4)

Cicero to Atticus, greetings. I hope you'll understand that it was misery rather than inconstancy that made me leave Vibo suddenly after I had asked you to meet me there.

---

55. Roman audiences were quick to take up and reinterpret lines in the theater as a method of political commentary.

56. Curio was applauded on account of his well-known hostility to the triumvirate.

57. The Roscian law reserved special rows in the theater for the equestrians, and was central to their prestige. The grain law provided for the sale of wheat at certain fixed rates and was very popular.

58. As one of the twenty commissioners for the distribution of public land.

I received a copy of the bill relating to my ruin,[59] and found that the alteration I had heard about meant I am permitted to be 400 miles from Italy, but am not permitted to get there. I immediately headed for Brundisium so I would arrive before the bill became law, so as not to put the life of my host Sicca in jeopardy, and because I could not stay at Malta. Now hurry and join me, that is, if I can find anyone to take me in. At the moment I am receiving kind invitations, but I am afraid that won't last. Dear Pomponius, I am very sorry to be alive. You had a lot of influence with me on that score. But more of this when we meet. Just make sure you come.

## 7     April 6, 58 BC, On His Exile (*Ad Atticum* 3.5)

Cicero to Atticus, greetings. Terentia tells me often how very grateful she is to you, something which means the world to me. I am in a wretched state, worn down by a profound sadness. I do not know what to write to you. If you are in Rome you will be too late to catch me, but if you are on the way, when you reach me we can discuss in person what needs to be done. I only beg of you, because you have always loved me for my own sake, not to stop now. I am the same man. My enemies have robbed me of all I had, but not of what I am. Take care of your health. Dispatched April 6, Thurii.

## 8     April 30, 58 BC, To His Wife from Exile (*Ad Familiares* 14.4)

Tullius to his dear Terentia, Tullia, and Cicero, greetings.[60] It is true I don't write to you as often as I could. But it's because I am constantly miserable, and also because whenever I write to you or read a letter from you, I am in such floods of tears that I cannot stand it. Damn, if only I had been less attached to life! At least then I would never have known real sorrow, or at least not much of it. My mistake to keep on living will seem less awful if Fortune has kept me alive with even a glimmer of hope of regaining any vestige of my former life ever again. But if these evils are irrevocable I want to see you as soon as possible, my dearest one, and die in your embrace, since neither the gods whom you have worshipped with such pure devotion, nor men, whom I have always served, have shown us proper gratitude.

[2] I spent thirteen days at Brundisium in the house of M. Laenius Flaccus, an excellent man who has risked his fortunes and civil existence to keep me safe. The penalties laid down by a most wicked law[61] have not kept him from offering me hospitality and friendship, as is right and decent. I only hope that someday I can repay him. I

---

59. The decree sponsored by Clodius as tribune that led to Cicero's exile from Rome.

60. Terentia, of a prominent family, married Cicero between 80 and 77 BC. Their children were M. Tullius Cicero and Tullia. Terentia intervened in political life, e.g., in the trial of the supporters of Catiline in 63 BC, and in the proceedings against Clodius in 61 BC, which brought her difficulties during her husband's exile. Her personal fortune was not confiscated as her husband's was. Financial disagreements led to the breakdown of the marriage in 46 BC, and Cicero had to pay back the dowry of 400,000 *sestertii*. Terentia remarried and lived to the age of 103.

61. The one banishing Cicero beyond 400 miles from Italy. See *Letters* 6.

know I will always be grateful. [3] I set out from Brundisium on April 29, and plan to go through Macedonia to Cyzicus. What a fall, what a disaster! What can I say? Should I ask you to come—a woman of weak health and broken spirit? Should I refrain from asking you? Am I to be without you, then? This is the best plan, I think: if there is any hope of my restoration, stay to promote it and push the thing along. But if it's a done deal, as I fear, please come to me by any means in your power.

There is one thing you must understand: if I have you with me I won't seem to be so completely destroyed. But what will become of my darling Tullia? You must see to that now: I can think of nothing. But certainly, no matter what happens, we must look after the poor girl's marriage and reputation.[62] What about my little Cicero, what is he to do? I just want to hug him and hold him on my lap forever.[63] But I have to stop. I can't write because I am crying so much.

[4] I have no idea how you have been managing, whether you have held on to any of our property, or if you have been stripped of everything, as I fear. I hope that Piso will always be our friend, as you say. As to freeing the slaves, no need to worry.[64] To begin with, no promise was made to your slaves at all, except that you would treat each as he or she deserved. So far, Orpheus has behaved very well, but besides him none have shown themselves particularly deserving. In the case of my slaves, the arrangement made is as follows: if I lose my property,[65] they are to be considered my freedmen, provided that they can make good their title to that position.[66] But if my property remains in my ownership, they are to continue as slaves, with the exception of a very few.[67]

But these are minor matters. [5] You tell me to have courage, and not give up hope of coming back. I only wish that there were any good reason to entertain such a hope. Now what kills me is I do not know how I am going to get your letters. Who will deliver them? I was going to wait for them at Brundisium. But the sailors wouldn't have it, and refused to pass up the clear weather. All that's left to say is stay strong, and keep your dignity, as I know you can. I've had my life. I've had my moment in the sun. My downfall came not from my faults but from my virtues. I did nothing wrong, except that I did not let go of my life along with my honors. But if our children preferred to see me alive we must endure everything, however unendurable. But here I am encouraging you, though I cannot encourage myself.

I have sent home that loyal man Clodius Philhetaerus,[68] because he was suffering from an eye ailment. Sallustius is outdoing everybody. Pescennius has outdone

---

62. Tullia, now 21, had been married for at least four and a half years to C. Calpurnius Piso Frugi, quaestor of this year. Apparently her parents had not yet paid her dowry in full, and Cicero's property was now under forfeit to the state.

63. M. Cicero junior, born in 65 BC (see *Letters* 2) was six years old.

64. Terentia had heard that all their slaves had been given their freedom by Cicero.

65. By being sold at public auction.

66. Against the claims of those who might urge that the penalties of confiscation were being evaded.

67. To whom manumission had already been promised.

68. A freedman of Cicero's, like Sallustius, Pescennius, and Sicca, just below. Freedmen were expected to be loyal and helpful to their former masters, but obviously had more freedom of choice and movement than slaves.

everyone in his kindness toward me; and I have hopes that he will always be attentive to you. Sicca had said that he would accompany me, but has left Brundisium. Take the greatest possible care of your health, and believe me that I am more affected by your distress than by my own. My dear Terentia, most faithful and best of wives, and my darling little daughter, and that last hope of my lineage, Cicero, goodbye! April 30, Brundisium.

## 9    November 23, 57 BC, On the Gangs and Chaos in Rome[69]
(*Ad Atticum* 4.3)

Cicero to Atticus, greetings. You're dying to know what's going on here, I realize, and also to hear about it from me. Not that my reports about what is going on in plain view are any more reliable than what others will write or tell you. But from my letters I would like you to see my perspective on what is happening, my state of mind, and the whole status of my daily life. [2] Armed thugs came on November 3 and drove the workmen from the site of my house, then demolished the portico of Catulus, which was being rebuilt on a contract given out by the consuls in accordance with a decree of the Senate—a work that was all but complete! My brother Quintus' house was first smashed with volleys of stones thrown from my property, and then set on fire by order of Clodius. As the torches were hurled, the whole city watched, with loud complaints and groans, I will not say from the honest men—for I rather think there *are* none left—but of simply every human being.

That lunatic is running riot, and after this act of madness he is contemplating nothing less than the murder of his enemies. He's going from neighborhood to neighborhood, openly making offers of freedom to slaves.[70] Earlier, while he was trying to avoid trial, he had a case—a difficult case in which he was obviously guilty—but a case nevertheless.[71] He could have denied the facts, or blamed others, or defended this or that action as legitimate. But after this spree of wrecking, arson, and looting, his followers have left him. It's all he can do to hang on to Decius the undertaker, and Gellius. He takes slaves for his advisors. He sees that if he simply assassinates anyone he wants to out in the open, his legal case is not going to be one bit more difficult than it is right now.

[3] So on November 11, as I was coming down the Via Sacra, he stalked me with his men. Then shouting, stones, clubs, and swords. All this without a moment's notice. I darted into the vestibule of Tettius Damio's house. My companions were easily able to prevent his thugs from entering. It would have been possible to kill Clodius himself, but my current policy is that a diet is better than radical surgery, and I'm sick and tired of the latter. Now that he sees that everybody is calling not for his prosecution but his immediate execution, he has made all your Catilines seem like models of respectability. On November 12 he tried to storm and set fire to Milo's house, the one on the Palatine.

---

69. Cicero was recalled from exile by senatorial decree in August 57 BC (returning to Rome on September 4).

70. Presumably in exchange for service in his gangs. But the charge has the ring of slander.

71. Earlier in the year Clodius had been accused of inciting riots in protest of Cicero's recall.

Quite openly, at the fifth hour,[72] he led forth men armed with shields and with swords drawn, and others with lighted torches. Clodius himself had taken the house of P. Sulla as his staging area for the assault. Then Q. Flaccus led out some energetic men from Milo's other house (the Annianan one), and killed the most notorious of all Clodius' gang of bandits. Flaccus wanted to kill the man himself, but Clodius had taken refuge deep inside Sulla's house.

Next, the Senate met on the 14th. Clodius stayed at home. Marcellinus was excellent, and everyone backed him up energetically. Metellus, however, talked the business out with an obstructive speech, with help from Appius, and also, I must add, from your friend about whose consistency of conduct you wrote very truly in your letter. Sestius was beside himself. Later on Clodius vowed vengeance on the city if his elections were not held.[73] Marcellinus' resolution was posted, and he had it read out from a written copy. It called for a trial covering my entire case: my property, the arson, and the attack on me personally. And it was to take place *before* the elections. Milo published a written notice that he intended to watch the sky during all comitial days.[74]

[4] Then came public rallies, those organized by Metellus boisterous, those of Appius incendiary, and Clodius' absolutely insane. The upshot was this: the elections would go on unless Milo announced unfavorable omens in the Campus Martius. On November 19 Milo arrived on the Campus before midnight with a large following. Clodius, however, though he had a picked force of runaway slaves, did not venture into the Campus. Milo stayed there till noon, to the public's great delight and his own infinite credit: the campaign of the three brethren ended in their own disgrace. Their violence was crushed, their madness rendered moot. Metellus, however, demanded that on the next day religious objections be announced to him in the Forum, saying it was no good coming to the Campus before dawn: he would be ready in the Forum at daybreak.[75] So on the 20th Milo came to the Comitium[76] before sunrise. Meanwhile Metellus, at the first sign of dawn, was stealthily scurrying to the Campus through the alleys. Milo caught up with him on the way, and served his notice. Metellus retreated amidst Q. Flaccus' loud and insulting jeers. The 21st was a market day. For two days no public rallies.

[5] And now it's the ninth hour of the night on the 23rd.[77] Milo is already in position on the Campus. The candidate Marcellus is snoring so loudly that I can hear him next door. I am told that Clodius' vestibule is virtually deserted: there are a few ragged

---

72. Around 11:00 a.m. See Appendix "Roman Time Reckoning."

73. Clodius was running for the curule aedileship. The elections, which would normally have been held in July, had been delayed. Clodius was in fact elected in the following January.

74. Days on which assemblies could meet for legislation or election (see "A Roman Calendar: April" in this volume). Tribunes and other magistrates could announce that they intended to "watch the sky" for bad omens, an act that amounted to making it illegal for an assembly to vote, since the finding of bad omens was taken for granted.

75. Metellus' plan was to divert Milo's attention to the Forum, then hold the elections in the Campus at daybreak before Milo got there.

76. A place of assembly in the Forum. See map of the City of Rome and the Forum.

77. Around 3:00 a.m. See Appendix "Roman Time Reckoning."

hoodlums there with a shoddy lantern. His party complains that I am behind the whole business, unaware as they are of how heroically fearless and intelligent Milo is. His courage is astonishing. Some recent instances of his superhuman deeds I pass over, but the upshot is this: I don't think the elections will take place. I think Clodius will be brought to trial by Milo—unless Clodius is killed first. If he meets up with Milo in a riot, it's clear that Milo will kill him with his own hands. He advertises the fact that he would not hesitate to do it, unafraid of suffering the same fate of exile that I did. *He* will never listen to the advice of a jealous and faithless friend, nor trust a feeble aristocrat. [6] As for me, I'm as vigorous as I was in my heyday, mentally at least. Financially, however, I am crushed. I have repaid the generosity of my brother Quintus as best I could, in spite of his protests, with loans from my friends, so I won't be completely tapped out. With you absent I have no idea what plan to adopt with regard to my whole situation. So come back soon.

## 10      October 16, 50 BC, From Athens, On the Looming Conflict between Pompeius and Caesar (*Ad Atticum* 7.1)

Cicero to Atticus, greetings. I gave Saufeius a letter just for you, but only because I didn't want such a close friend of yours to arrive without a letter from me. I didn't have time at that moment to write a proper one. Given the speed at which philosophers move, I suppose this one will probably reach you first. But if you got the other one already you know that I arrived at Athens on October 14, and that when I disembarked in Piraeus I got your letter via our friend Acastus. I was disturbed to hear that you had arrived in Rome with a fever, but cheered up a bit because Acastus told me you were feeling better, which is exactly what I wanted to hear. I shuddered at the news in your letter regarding Caesar's legions, and urged you to make sure that a certain person's ambition does not do us harm.[78] I also explained briefly why I did not put my brother in charge of the province[79]—something about which I wrote to you a while back. But Turranius had misrepresented the matter to you at Brundisium, as I gathered from your letter I received from that excellent man Xeno. This was more or less the content of the letter that I sent you earlier.

[2] Now hear the rest. By our fortunes, by all the love you bear for me, by all that singular wisdom which I believe you possess in every sphere, I ask you: concentrate your attention on thinking from every angle about my position. It seems to me that a great conflict is looming, as great as history has ever known—unless some god takes pity on the state, the same god who freed us from a Parthian war in a manner better than I had dared to hope.[80] Well, that evil is one that I share with everybody else. I'm not asking you to solve that one, but please, put your mind to my own special dilemma. For you

---

78. Pompeius. Cicero was anxious to maintain good relations with both Caesar and Pompeius.

79. In 51 BC Cicero was persuaded to leave Rome to govern the province of Cilicia, in south Asia Minor, for a year.

80. The province of Cilicia, where Cicero was governor in 51 BC, had been expecting a Parthian invasion, but it never materialized—although Cicero did suppress some brigands on Mount Amanus (see below).

see, I plan to follow your advice about which one to embrace.[81] I wish I had listened to your friendly admonitions from the start. But "you never persuaded the heart in my chest."[82] Still, you finally convinced me to embrace the one because of all he had done for me, and the other because of his power. So I did, and by every kind of compliance and service I have earned a place in each of their good graces as high as any man's.

[3] That was our plan: as long as I was tied to Pompeius I would never have to commit any political misdeeds; on the other hand, as long as I supported Caesar it would not be necessary to fight against Pompeius—the two were so closely linked. Now, as you point out, and as I see, a massive conflict is brewing between them. Each counts me as his friend, unless one of them only pretends. Pompeius has no doubts, for he correctly believes that his current ideas on the government are very pleasing to me. I got letters from each of them at the same time yours arrived, of a tone suggesting that neither valued anyone more highly than me.

[4] But what am I supposed to do? I'm not asking about the ultimate decision—for if the thing is to be settled in warfare I see that it would be better to lose with one than to win with the other. What I'm concerned about is what's going to be happening when I arrive in Rome. I mean the effort to prevent Caesar running for the consulship *in absentia*, which would force him to give up his army. "Speak, Marcus Tullius!" What am I supposed to say, "Hold on, please, while I consult with Atticus"? There's no time for fence-sitting. Come out against Caesar? Ah, but "Where went that firm handshake?"[83] After all, *I* was the one who helped him obtain the privilege, as requested by the man himself at Ravenna in connection with Caelius who was tribune, and also by our friend Gnaeus in that oh-so-divine third consulship of his. Am I supposed to take a different line? "But I feel shame before the Trojan men and the Trojan women"—not just before Pompeius. "Polydamas will reproach me first of all."[84]
[5] Who's Polydamas? Why you, of course, who praise my deeds and my writings.

Having dodged this dilemma through two earlier consulships held by members of the Marcelli family,[85] when the matter of Caesar's province was raised, I am now falling into the thick of the trouble. The plan I like best is to start asking for a triumph.[86] That will give me an excellent reason to stay outside the city, so some other fool will have to give the first opinion in the Senate. Still, they will find a way to elicit my opinion.

This may make you laugh: how I wish I were still in my province! I would have stayed there if I knew this was coming, even though that position was intolerably awful. As an aside, let me tell you how it went. All those great beginnings, which even you

---

81. Caesar or Pompeius.

82. Homer, *Odyssey* 9.33.

83. Evidently a quotation from a lost play.

84. Homer, *Iliad* 6.442 and 22.100. The point is that his habitual optimate allies in the Senate would be shocked if he abandoned Pompeius, and Cicero could not endure that shame.

85. In 51–50 BC.

86. Cicero had conducted a modest military operation in Cilicia, suppressing brigands holed up on Mount Amanus (near Hatay, Turkey). The Senate granted a *supplicatio* (a period of public thanksgiving), although Cicero had hoped for a full triumph on his return to Rome. All admitted that he governed Cilicia with integrity.

were praising to the skies in your letters, were only veneer. [6] Integrity is not an easy thing to have; it is evidently even more difficult to keep up the false pretense of it on a daily basis. I thought the proper and creditable thing to do with the surplus left over from the year's expense money was to leave a year's worth to C. Cloelius the quaestor and return a million sesterces to the treasury. But my staff groaned and complained, supposing that all that money ought to be distributed among them, trying to make me treat the treasury of Rome less well than I had treated those of Phrygia and Cilicia! But I was unmoved. My own good reputation is more important to me, and besides, I had already bestowed honors on each of them at every possible opportunity. But let this be, as Thucydides says, a not unprofitable digression.

[7] Now you must think about my position: first, by what device I might keep Caesar's good will; second, about the triumph itself—which should be easy to obtain, barring political obstacles. This I conclude from letters from friends and from the positive vote for a public thanksgiving. Cato, who voted against it, voted for more compliments than if he had voted for all the triumphs in the world.[87] And among those who agreed with him were my friend Favonius and my current enemy Hirrus. Cato, however, did take part in the drafting of the decree and sent me a very pleasant letter about his vote. But Caesar, writing to congratulate me on the public thanksgiving, crows about Cato's vote. He writes nothing about what Cato said in the Senate, but only that he voted against the public thanksgiving.

[8] To come back to Hirrus. You had begun to reconcile him to me; accomplish it. You have Scrofa and Silius on your side. I wrote to them previously, and now I have written to Hirrus himself. He had told them that he could easily have prevented the decree, but did not want to—a statement calculated to his advantage. He merely agreed with Cato, my dear friend, when he spoke about me in the Senate in most honorific terms. And he says that I sent him no letter, though I was sending them to everybody. What he says is true. Hirrus and Crassipes were the only ones to whom I did not write.

[9] So much for public affairs. Let's return closer to home. I want to dissociate myself from that man Philotimus. He is an extremely shady character, a regular Lartidius. "But let us forget the past, grieved though we are."[88] We should rather deal with the remaining issues, and first of all an item that adds an element of anxiety to my hurt feelings: this sum, I mean, whatever it is, that comes from Precius. I don't want it mixed up in the accounts of mine that that man is handling. I wrote to Terentia and to Philotimus himself that I shall deposit with you any and all funds I may collect for my anticipated triumph. No one can criticize that, I think. But as they wish. Here is another matter for your consideration: how am I supposed to get free of this situation? You outlined a plan in a letter sent from Epirus or Athens, and I will support you in it.

---

87. When the proposal for a public thanksgiving (*supplicatio*) on account of Cicero's successes against the brigands at Mount Amanus came before the Senate at the end of April 50 BC, Cato spoke in opposition, but at the same time proposed a decree commending Cicero's administration in general. Hirrus and Favonius agreed with Cato, but otherwise support for the *supplicatio* was unanimous.

88. Homer, *Iliad* 18.112, that is, "let bygones be bygones."

**11    January 24, 49 BC, On Caesar's March on Rome** (*Ad Familiares* 14.18)

Tullius sends warm greetings to his wife, and Tullia's father to his sweetest daughter, and Cicero to his mother and sister. I think that you, my heart and soul, should carefully consider and reconsider what to do, whether to stay at Rome, or join me, or seek some place of safety. This is not a matter for my consideration alone, but for yours also. What occurs to me is this: you may be safe at Rome under Dolabella's[89] protection, and that may prove helpful to us in case any violence or looting starts. On the other hand, I am concerned because I see that all the honest men have left Rome and have their wives with them. The region where I am now consists of towns and estates that are in my *clientela*,[90] so you could be with me much of the time, and when we are apart you would be comfortable and among our own people. [2] I really can't decide which course is better. Have a look at what the other women of your social rank are doing, and take care that when it comes time to leave you still can. I would like you to consider all this carefully, and repeatedly, among yourselves and with our friends. Tell Philotimus to make sure that the house is protected by barricades and a guard. And I would like you to institute a system of regular messengers so I receive some letter from you every day. Most of all, take care that you stay well, if you want me to be well. January 24, at Formiae.

**12    January 29, 49 BC, On Caesar's March on Rome** (*Ad Familiares* 16.12)

Tullius to his dear Tiro, greetings.[91] You can assess the danger to my personal safety, to that of all the honest men, and to the whole state, from the fact that we have abandoned and given our homes and our very fatherland over to be looted and burned. Things have come to the point that unless some god or some accident comes to our aid we cannot possibly be saved.

[2] For my part, ever since I arrived in Rome[92] I have never stopped promoting in thought, word, and deed everything conducive to peace. But a strange mania for war has inflamed not only the rascals, but also those who are considered honest men, though I keep shouting that nothing can be more disastrous than a civil war. And so when Caesar, gripped by some sort of insanity and forgetting his good name and his

---

89. Tullia's husband, a partisan of Caesar.

90. That is, attached to him due to previous services on their behalf in Rome: for example, Capua and Atella.

91. M. Tullius Tiro (born 103 BC) was Cicero's trusted slave and (from 53 BC) freedman, and literary collaborator. He was a valuable help to his master in all possible ways, as the latter repeatedly emphasized. Tiro invented an ingenious shorthand system, *Notae Tironianae*, which was still in use up to the High Middle Ages. Tiro may have had a hand in publishing Cicero's letters, and also wrote, among much else, a treatise on Latin usage and style.

92. Cicero never in fact entered the city proper, since he was hoping to celebrate a triumph (see *Letters* 10.5).

honors, seized in turn Ariminum, Pisaurum, Ancona, and Arretium, I left the city.[93] Whether this was a wise or courageous step there is no point in discussing.

[3] You see what trouble we are in. The bottom line is this: proposals are coming from Caesar that Pompeius should go to Spain; that the troops we have enlisted so far and our garrisons should be disbanded; that he himself will hand over Further Gaul to Domitius, Nearer Gaul to Considius Nonianus (the men to whom these provinces have been allotted); that he will campaign for the consulship in person, and no longer wants to take advantage of his right to run *in absentia*; and that he will be in Rome as candidate for the statutory three Market Days.[94] We have accepted these terms, but on condition that he withdraw his garrisons from the places he has occupied, so a meeting of the Senate can be held at Rome to discuss these same proposals in an atmosphere of safety.

[4] If he does this, there is hope of peace—not an honorable one, since he is dictating terms to us. But anything is better than to be as we are now. If, on the other hand, he fails to abide by his own terms it will mean war, but of a kind that he cannot possibly endure, especially since he will have abandoned terms proposed by himself.[95] But all depends on keeping him from getting to Rome, which we hope can be done. We are recruiting troops on a large scale, and we think that he is afraid that if he begins a march on Rome, he may lose the Gallic provinces, both of which, with the exception of the Transpadani, are bitterly hostile to him. And in the direction of Spain there are six legions and a large force of auxiliaries under Afranius and Petreius on his rear. If he persists in his madness it seems possible to crush him—but it all depends on hanging on to Rome. He has taken a major hit in that Titus Labienus, who was extremely influential with Caesar's army, has declined to be his partner in crime. Labienus has abandoned him and is with us, and they say many others intend to do the same.

[5] So far I am in charge of the sea coast, based at Formiae. I refused any more important function. That way, my letters and calls for a peaceful resolution can have more credibility with Caesar. But if it's war I can see I will have to take command of an actual military camp and some legions.[96] Then there is the annoying fact that my son-in-law Dolabella is with Caesar.

I wanted you to know all this, but please don't let it upset you or impede your recovery. [6] I have recommended you with great earnestness to Aulus Varro, whom I know is warmly attached to me and very fond of you. I asked him to look after your health and your voyage, and generally to take you under his charge and look after you. I feel certain he will do all this. He promised to do so, and spoke to me in the kindest manner.

But you must not rush, or make the mistake of sailing when you are ill or when

---

93. Coming from Gaul, and after crossing the Rubicon, Caesar took a series of towns in north-central Italy on the way to Rome. See map of Italy.

94. A Market Day took place every eight days (see "A Roman Calendar: April" in this volume), and regulations required that a candidate had to be in residence for twenty-four days.

95. Resulting (as Cicero implies) in a loss of popular support.

96. He was not in fact asked to do so.

the weather is bad, just because you were prevented from being with me at that time when I most needed your help and your unswerving loyalty. To my mind, your arrival will never be late, so long as you arrive safe. So far I have seen no one who had seen you since M. Volusius, who handed me your letter. This wasn't surprising, and I don't suppose with this bad weather that my letters have reached you, either. But just take care to get well and, when you are well, and if you can travel safely by sea, then set sail. My son Cicero is at Formiae, Terentia and Tullia at Rome. Take care of yourself. January 29, Capua.

### 13    Around March 5, 49 BC, Julius Caesar to Cicero, Asking Cicero to Stay in Rome (*Ad Atticum* 9.6A)[97]

Caesar imperator to Cicero imperator, greetings. I saw our friend Furnius, but only that. I was unable to talk and listen to him at leisure, since I am in a rush and on the road—the legions have already been sent ahead. Still, I could not lose the opportunity to write to you and send him to you, and to give you thanks, even if I have done this often in the past and expect to do so even oftener—you give me so much cause. Especially I ask of you, since I have every hope of getting to the city soon, to let me see you there, so I can avail myself of your advice, influence, standing, and help in all matters. To return to my point: you must forgive my haste and the brevity of this message. You will learn everything else from Furnius.

### 14    March 20, 49 BC, Cicero's Reply to Caesar, Stating His Obligation to Pompeius (*Ad Atticum* 9.11A)

Cicero imperator to Caesar imperator, greetings. On reading your letter, handed to me by our friend Furnius, in which you ask me to come to the city, I was not so surprised at your wishing to "avail yourself of my advice and standing." But as to my "influence and assistance" I had to ask myself what you meant. Still, I was led by my hopes to the thought that, in accordance with your admirable and singular wisdom, you wanted to talk about peace, about reconciliation, about bringing all the people of Rome together. I thought myself well suited to the job by nature and character to come up with a good plan. [2] If that is what you want, and if you are at all anxious to maintain our friend Pompeius and win him back to yourself and the Republic, you will find no one more fit for that purpose than myself. I have always advocated for peace from the moment I could, both with Pompeius and in the Senate. When arms were taken up I had nothing to do with the war, and judged that it was you who were being wronged in that war, and that your enemies and jealous rivals were attempting to strip you of an honor granted by the favor of the Roman people.[98] Still, just as at that time I was not only a supporter of your position, but also encouraged others to help you, so now I am deeply concerned with the position of Pompeius. It is now a good number of years since I

---

97. This letter is included in the group of letters to Atticus because Cicero sent him a copy.

98. The right to run for consul *in absentia*, or else the consulship itself.

chose you and him as two men to cultivate above all others and to be my friends, and I remain so now.

[3] And so I ask you, or rather I beg and implore you with all my heart, to spare amid your grave preoccupations some time to consider how you might do me the kindness of allowing me to meet the claims of honor, gratitude, and loyalty, by showing myself mindful of the very great benefits he conferred upon me. Even if my request concerned only myself I would still hope to obtain it from you. But in my judgment it is relevant to your own reputation for good faith and to the Republic that I, a friend of peace and of each of you, be preserved as the most appropriate agent for restoring peace between yourself and Pompeius and between Romans in general.

I have thanked you concerning Lentulus, for saving the man who saved me.[99] Yet after reading a letter from him in which he speaks with the utmost gratitude of your generous treatment and kindness to him, I felt that the safety you gave him was given to me as well. If my gratitude to Lentulus is clear to you, then I beg you to let me show the same gratitude to Pompeius.

## 15     November 27, 48 BC, On His Post-War Position and the Death of Pompeius (Ad Atticum 11.6)

Cicero to Atticus, greetings. I see that you are anxious about your own and the common fortunes, but above all about me and my distress.[100] The fact that your distress is joined to mine hardly lessens my grief but in fact makes it worse. True, you sense with your usual perceptiveness the kind of comfort that can best relieve me: you approve of my course of action, and tell me that nothing else could have been done at such a time. And you add that my actions have earned the approval of all the rest—the ones who count, anyway—something that carries less weight with me than your opinion, but still does carry some weight. I would be in less distress if I thought it was all true. "Trust me," you will say. [2] I do trust you, but I know how much you want to lessen my distress. I have never regretted quitting the war. There was so much cruelty on our side, such association with barbarian races[101]—so much so that proscription lists were being drawn up, not just by name, but by whole classes of people. It had already been

---

99. Lentulus Spinther, who as consul in 57 BC helped obtain the recall of Cicero from exile. Caesar took him captive at Corfinium during the march on Rome, but rather than take revenge on his political opponents he released Spinther along with other senators—keeping with his policy of *clementia*, or forgiveness of political enemies.

100. After Caesar's victory in the civil war the economic outlook was unsettled. Tribunes such as Dolabella were agitating for an abolition of debts, which would have hurt Atticus financially. Cicero was ill in Dyrrachium while the battle of Pharsalus was fought in August 48 BC, and Pompeius was subsequently murdered in Egypt. Rather than fight on with the Pompeian remnant in North Africa, Cicero returned disconsolately to Brundisium, where he had to cool his heels for a year from November 48, awaiting Caesar's permission to return to Rome.

101. Pompeius in his desperation had enlisted peoples outside Roman sway, including, according to Cicero in another letter (Ad Att. 9.10.3, not in this volume), those as far away as the Getae and Colchians, located to the north of the Danube and to the far eastern coast of the Black Sea.

decided by universal consent that the possessions of all of you should be considered the plunder of the victors. When I say "you" I mean it literally: when it comes to you personally there were never any but the most ferocious intentions.

So while I will never regret my attitude, I do regret my course of action. I wish I had stayed quietly in some town or other until I was sent for. I would have been less exposed to gossip, suffered less distress. And I would not be faced with this anguishing choice. To be stuck in Brundisium is disagreeable in every way. But to come closer to Rome as you advise—how can I do that without the lictors that the people gave me, and which cannot be taken away so long as I retain my rights as a citizen?[102] I recently had to disperse them among the crowd with their sticks as I was approaching Brundisium, for fear of an attack by the soldiers. Since then I have stayed indoors.

[3] I have written all this to Balbus and Oppius,[103] and asked them to consider the matter, since they want me to come closer to Rome. I think they will advocate on my behalf. They vouch for the fact that Caesar is concerned not just to preserve my position but actually to augment it. They urge me to be of good courage, to hope for the highest distinctions.[104] They give promises and assurances, which I could rely on more if I had remained in Italy. But I'm dwelling on the past.

So please follow up. Sound them out, and if you think it's a good idea and they agree, have Trebonius, Pansa, anyone available called in, get them to write to Caesar that whatever I've done has been on their advice. Caesar will be more receptive to my actions if he sees them as coming from the advice of his friends.

[4] My dear Tullia's illness and weakness frightens me to death. I gather that you are taking great care of her, for which I am deeply grateful.

[5] As for Pompeius' death I never had any doubt.[105] All the rulers and peoples had become so convinced of the hopelessness of his cause that no matter where he went something like this was bound to happen. I cannot but grieve for his fate. I knew him to be a man of integrity, clean living, and serious principle.

[6] Should I offer you consolation about Fannius? He used very threatening language about your staying behind in Rome. As for L. Lentulus, he had promised himself Hortensius' house, Caesar's gardens, and the place at Baiae. Of course such confiscations are happening on the victorious side as well. But with them there was no limit to it. Everybody who stayed in Italy was considered the enemy, and fair game. But I'd like to talk more about this some day when I have less on my mind.

[7] I hear that my brother Quintus has set out for Asia to make his peace. About his son I have heard nothing. But ask Caesar's freedman Diochares, who brought the letter you mention from Alexandria. I have not seen him. He is said to have seen Quintus on his way—or perhaps in Asia itself. I am expecting a letter from you, as the occasion requires. Please have one brought to me here as soon as possible. Sent November 27.

---

102. Cicero had still not entered Rome itself since being governor in Cilicia, and so had not yet forfeited the power as a commander (*imperium*) that entailed having the lictors that so embarrassed him now.

103. Close confidants of Caesar.

104. A triumph is probably implied; see above, *Letters* 10.5.

105. Pompeius was killed in Egypt after he had fled there following his defeat at Caesar's hands at Pharsalus in August 48 BC.

**16**    **Mid-April 45 BC, On Tullia's death** (*Ad Familiares* 4.6)

Marcus Cicero to Servius Sulpicius, greetings.[106] Yes, I do so wish, my dear Servius, that you had been at my side in my time of most crushing loss, as you say.[107] Even reading your letters has calmed me somewhat, so I can easily imagine how much your presence could have helped, both with words of consolation and by sharing with me your nearly equal grief. You wrote the kind of things that can lessen grief, and in the process of helping me feel better you revealed your own not inconsiderable grief. Still, your son Servius has done for me all the kindnesses that one could ask at a time like this, which shows both his deep regard for me and also that he thought his attention to me would be pleasing to you as well. I have often felt more pleasure in his attention than I feel now (as you may imagine), but never more gratitude.

It is not just what you say, and your comradeship in grief, as it were, that consoles me, but also your authority. It would be a disgraceful thing not to bear my misfortune in the way a man of your wisdom would have me bear it. Yet sometimes I am over-whelmed, and can scarcely withstand my pain, because I lack the consolation that was available to all those other men who suffered similar misfortunes, and whom I look to as models of strength. You know how Fabius Maximus lost his son, who was an ex-consul, a distinguished man of great achievements; how Lucius Paullus lost two sons within seven days; how your kinsman Sulpicius Gallus and Marcus Cato lost sons of great talent and virtue. But their losses occurred at a time when some consolation for their bereavement could be offered by the prominence and standing the Republic had bestowed upon them.

[2] But I have lost all those public distinctions which you yourself mention, and which I gained through unceasing toil. I had only one consolation left, and that is what has been taken away. I couldn't take my mind off things by assisting my friends with their affairs, or by administering the state; I had no interest in pleading in the courts, and couldn't bear to even look at the Senate house. I merely reflected on the truth that I had completely lost all the rewards of my hard work and good fortune. But while I pondered these miseries (which I have in common with you and certain other men as well), and while I checked myself and forced myself to take it all in stride, I had a refuge, a person with whom I could be at peace, whose conversation and charm could relieve all my anxieties and pain.

But now, under the impact of this heavy blow, scars that seemed to have healed reopen. After all, I cannot now turn to the state to find peace in its successes when I am in mourning at home, just as before I used to come home to alleviate the grim sadness of politics. And so I am a stranger both in my house and in the Forum. The pain I receive from politics cannot be soothed in my house, nor can the pain from my house be eased with politics.

---

106. Ser. Sulpicius Rufus, held in high regard by Cicero, who once hoped to see him as a future husband for Tullia. The same Sulpicius was probably the father of the poet Sulpicia, who mentions him in her surviving elegies, translated in this volume.

107. In February 45 BC, Tullia, aged approximately thirty-three, died after giving birth to a son who also died soon after. Cicero, in deep mourning for his beloved daughter, so similar to him in character, planned a kind of sanctuary in her memory, which was never built, and wrote a *Consolation*, which has not survived.

[3] This is why I am looking forward to your arrival and long to see you as soon as possible. Nothing will bring me greater relief than being with you and talking with you. I hope you will arrive any day (for that is what I am told). There are many reasons that I badly want to set eyes on you as soon as possible, but especially so we can deliberate in advance how we are supposed to conduct ourselves in this day and age, when everything has to conform to the will of one man. He is both shrewd and generous and, as I think I can discern, not hostile to me and quite friendly to you. In these circumstances we nonetheless have to consider our strategy carefully—not to accomplish anything, but how we may best lay low by his permission and favor. Farewell.

## 17    December 45, On A Visit from Caesar (*Ad Atticum* 13.52)

Cicero to Atticus, greetings. Strange to have a guest be such a burden and not regret the visit. It really was quite pleasant. He had arrived at Philippus' villa on the second day of the Saturnalia[108] in the evening, and the place was so packed with soldiers that there was scarcely a free room where Caesar could take his dinner. Two thousand men, no less! So I was more than a little apprehensive about what lay in store for me the next day. But Cassius Barba came to my rescue and posted sentries. Camp was pitched in a field, and a guard placed on the house. He spent the third day of the Saturnalia at Philippus' house, until the seventh hour,[109] and admitted no visitors. He was looking at accounts with Balbus, I believe. After that he took a walk on the shore, then went into the bath after the eighth hour. That's when he heard about Mamurra.[110] His expression did not alter. After anointing he took his place at dinner. He is taking a course of emetics, so he ate and drank heartily and with obvious pleasure. It was really magnificent and sumptuous; not only that, but (as the poet Lucilius says) "well-cooked and seasoned with good talking, too—in fact a pleasant meal."

[2] What's more, his entourage was lavishly entertained in three other dining rooms. And his humbler freedmen and slaves lacked for nothing. The more elegant ones I entertained in style. In short, I showed I know how to live. But this is not the kind of guest to whom you say, "Come back whenever you're in the area." Once is enough. Our conversation included nothing about politics, but lots on literary topics. All in all he was pleased and enjoyed himself. He said he would spend one day at Puteoli, the next near Baiae.

There you have the story of a visit, or should I say a billeting, that was a lot of trouble, but as I said, not at all unpleasant. I will stay here for a while, then move on to Tusculum.

When Caesar passed Dolabella's villa (and nowhere else) his whole armed escort rode on the right and the left, and he in the saddle.[111] This detail comes from Nicias.

---

108. December 19.

109. Around 1:00 p.m.; see Appendix "Roman Time Reckoning."

110. A Roman equestrian and Caesar's head engineer in Gaul from 58 BC. In Rome his luxurious house caused a scandal, and Catullus (poem 29 in this volume) depicts him as a spendthrift war profiteer and a philanderer. Caesar's association with Mamurra was criticized, as is implied here. We do not know what Caesar heard about him on this occasion; perhaps it was his death.

111. Evidently a compliment (?).

**18**      **April 44 BC, On Caesar's Assassination and Its Aftermath** (*Ad Atticum* 14.10)

Cicero to Atticus, greetings. So is this it? Is this the upshot of the deed of Brutus, your friend and mine, that he spends his time skulking at Lanuvium? That Trebonius is forced to use back roads to reach his province? That all of Caesar's deeds, writings, words, promises, and plans are more effective now than when he was still alive? Do you remember how I cried out on the very first day of the occupation of the Capitoline[112] that the Senate should be summoned to the spot by the praetors? Immortal gods, think of the things we could have accomplished then, in the midst of the joy felt by all the honest men, even the moderately honest, and when all those bandits had been crushed! You put the blame on the Senate meeting on the Liberalia (March 17). But what could be done then? By that time it was all over—we were doomed. Do you remember when you shouted out that the cause was lost if Caesar was given a public funeral? Well, he was actually cremated in the Forum, and given that pathetic eulogy, while slaves and beggars were unleashed on our houses with lit torches. And the result? Now they dare to say, "Are *you* opposing Caesar's will?" This and similar things I cannot take, so I am planning to go traveling from land to land; but *your* land is sheltered from the storms.

[2] Have you fully recovered from that stomach trouble? It seems so, to judge from your letter. To return to the subject of men like Tebassus, Scaeva, and Fango: do you think that these men will ever feel secure in their gains as long as we are still standing? They thought we had more backbone than we actually showed. No doubt they are lovers of peace, and not the instigators of robbery.[113] But when I wrote to you about Curtilius and Sextilius' farm, I was talking about Censorinus, Messalla, Plancus, Postumus, the whole gang. It would have been better to die when Caesar was killed (though that never would have happened) than to live to see this.

[3] Octavian[114] arrived in Naples on April 18. Balbus met him there early on the following day, and Balbus was with me on the same day at my villa in Cumae. He says that Octavian will accept the inheritance. But as you say in your letter, that will mean quite a quarrel with Antonius. I am coping with your Buthrotum problem, as is right, and I will continue to do so. You ask whether the Cluvian property comes to 100,000 a year yet. It seems about to get there; but in the first year I have cleared 80,000.

[4] Quintus senior wrote to me in a serious tone about his son, the main complaint being that he is giving in to his mother's wishes, though previously when she was behaving well he was all against her. He sent me letters raging against him. As to Quintus the son, if you know what he is up to and you have not yet left Rome, please write to me about it, and about anything else, too, to be sure. I take great delight in your letters.

---

112. On the Ides (15th) of March 44 BC, when Caesar was assassinated, the assassins occupied the Capitoline Hill in the center of Rome.

113. Successors of Caesar were buying up the confiscated property of the politically disgraced at knock-down prices—a disreputable but very profitable activity.

114. C. Octavius, the future Augustus, adopted by Caesar in his will and named as his principle heir. He cultivated senators and Cicero in particular in a successful effort to gain official legitimacy.

**19      September 44 BC, Urging Cassius to Return and Fight Antonius**
(*Ad Familiares* 12.2)

Cicero to Cassius, greetings.[115] I am delighted that you approve of my motion in the Senate and my speech.[116] If it were possible to give speeches like that more often it would be no trouble to recover our freedom and restore the constitution. But that crazy desperado—much worse than the one whom you declared the worst man ever killed—is looking for an excuse to begin a bloodbath,[117] and accuses me of being the man behind Caesar's assassination, simply to incite the veterans against me. I'm not afraid of that, so long as he succeeds in connecting my reputation with the glory that you and your partners won with your deed.

As it is, none of us can enter the Senate in safety, not Piso, who was the first to criticize Antonius publicly, without anyone to support him; not I, who did the same a month later; not Publius Servilius, who did so shortly after me. That gladiator is just looking for a chance to use his sword, and thought that he was going to start with me on September 19. He came primed, after studying his speech for many days in Metellus' villa—but then again, how do you "study" when you're getting drunk in a make-shift brothel? The result seemed to everyone to be not public speaking, but his usual public puking.[118]

[2] You write you are sure that my influence and eloquence can do some good. As for that, you might say it's done a bit of good, considering the enormity of the evil. For the Roman people fully understand that there are three former consuls who, because they patriotically spoke their minds, cannot come in safety to the Senate.

That's all you can expect anyway, given that your relative is so thrilled with his new marriage connection.[119] He no longer cares about the games, and is bursting with envy at the applause your brother gets. That other family connection of yours has been placated by the new batch of Caesar's diaries.[120] One can put up with all that. But what is unendurable is that a certain man thinks that his son can be consul in the year projected for you and Brutus, and for that reason declares his loyal subservience to this bandit.[121]

[3] My close friend Lucius Cotta comes less often to the Senate, yielding to what he calls a "despair ordained by fate." Lucius Caesar, though an excellent and courageous

---

115. C. Cassius Longinus, one of Caesar's assassins. In April he had left Rome for Latium and Campania, and in late summer was assigned the province of Cyrenaica in N. Africa.

116. Attacking Antonius, the first *Philippic*.

117. The opportunity came in late 43 BC when Antonius and Octavian joined forces. Cicero was among the first victims of the widespread purge of anti-Caesarian senators.

118. Antonius' tendency to vomit in public is featured in Cicero's second *Philippic* and attested by Plutarch (*Life of Antony* 9).

119. Cassius' nephew L. Aemilius Lepidus (brother of the triumvir, consul in 50 BC) had been betrothed to Antonius' daughter.

120. Claudius Marcellus (consul in 50 BC) was the cousin of Cassius' wife.

121. Marcus Philippus (consul in 56 BC) advocated for his son (praetor in 44 BC), who was eligible for the consulship in the same year as Cassius, 41 BC.

citizen, is suffering from ill health. Servius Sulpicius, who wields immense influence and holds the most reasonable views, is not in town. As for the others, pardon me if I do not reckon them consular, with the exception of the consuls-designate. Those are all the men capable of making policy. They were few enough even in better days. So you can imagine what it's like in the present disastrous situation. You are our only hope. And if your reason for not coming to Rome is that you cannot do so safely, then there is no hope in you either. But if you are planning some master stroke worthy of your glorious reputation, I just pray I live to see it. But even if that cannot be, still at least the Republic will soon recover its legal rights, thanks to you. I am not failing to support your friends, and will continue to do so. Whether they turn to me or not, I will offer you proof of my good will and good faith.

## 20    October 44 BC, On the Tyranny of Antonius (*Ad Familiares* 12.3)

Cicero to Cassius, greetings. It grows daily, the insanity of your friend Antonius. To start with, he had this inscribed below the statue he had placed on the rostra: "To the Father, for his Outstanding Services." So you all are now condemned not only as murderers, but as parricides! But why do I say "you all"? Rather I should say "we" are condemned. That madman asserts that I was the ringleader of that most glorious deed of yours. If only I had been! *He* would not be troubling us now. But it is you and your comrades who are responsible for this, and since it is past and done with, I only wish I had some advice to give you. But the fact is, I cannot decide what I ought to do myself. For what can be done against force without having any force oneself?[122]

[2] Now the entire strategy of that faction is to punish the death of Caesar. So on October 2nd he was brought on stage at a public rally by Cannutius.[123] True, Antonius left the speaker's platform in utter humiliation, but he spoke about the saviors of the fatherland in terms only appropriate for traitors. He said without a trace of doubt that I was the inspiration for everything that you did and that Cannutius is now doing. You can judge how the rest of it went from the fact that they have deprived your legate of his travelling money. And what do you suppose is the plain implication they are making there? That the money is being sent to an enemy of the state.[124]

What an awful thing! We could not endure the master, and now we are in thrall to our fellow slave. Yet even now a glimmer of hope lies in your courage, though I am supportive rather than hopeful. But where are your troops? As for the rest, I would rather you deliberate with yourself than listen to words of mine.

---

122. This is the dilemma that induced Cicero to broker an alliance with Octavian, who had raised a private army of perhaps 10,000 strong, to assert his position as Caesar's heir. Cicero was instrumental in giving Octavian official legitimacy.

123. Ti. Cannutius, a tribune this year and a fierce critic of Antonius.

124. Cassius had been appointed governor of Cyrenaica, and Antonius was attempting to undermine him.

### 21    April 23, 43 BC, On the Defeat of Antonius at Forum Gallorum (*Ad Brutum* 1.3)

Cicero to Brutus, greetings.[125] Our side seems to be in a better position.[126] I'm sure that you have gotten letters describing the developments. The consuls have lived up to my descriptions of them in my previous letters to you. And the boy Caesar has proven to have a surprisingly bold character. Now he is riding high with honors and popularity. I just hope I can guide and restrain him as easily as I have so far. That will be quite a difficult trick, but still I'm optimistic. For the young man has been convinced, especially by me, that our salvation lies in his hands. At any rate, if he had not diverted Antonius from Rome, all would have been lost.

[2] A few days before this glorious victory every man from the city was streaming out with wife and children, in a panic, and headed for you. The same city was restored to life on the 20th of April and now, rather than set out to join you, would prefer that you come here. It was on that day that I reaped the richest of rewards for my great labors and my many sleepless nights—if there is any reward in true, genuine glory. As big a crowd as our city can contain came to my house, escorted me to the Capitoline, and put me on the speakers' platform amid thunderous cheers and applause. I have no vanity in me, nor should I. Yet I am thoroughly moved by the unison of all classes, their expressions of thanks and rejoicing. For to be popular in seeking after the people's welfare is a fine thing. [3] But these things I would rather you hear from others.

Please inform me of your own affairs and plans in detail. And do be careful that your generosity does not take on the appearance of weakness. The Senate and the Roman people take the view that no enemies have ever merited all forms of punishment as much as do the citizens who have taken up arms against their country in this war. In every speech I make in the Senate I call for vengeance upon them and attack them amidst the applause of all the honest men. What you think about this is up to you. But in my opinion all three brothers[127] stand on one and the same ground.

### 22    April 43 BC, On the Defeat of Antonius at Mutina (*Ad Brutum* 1.3A)

Cicero to Brutus, greetings. We have lost our two consuls—good men, or at any rate good consuls. Hirtius fell in the moment of victory, having also won a great battle only

---

125. M. Junius Brutus, one of Caesar's assassins. Brutus had left for Greece in August of 44. There, while posing as a student of philosophy, he recruited an army, which included the young Horace, and Cicero's son Marcus. Brutus' first objective was to control Macedonia and eject Marcus Antonius' brother Gaius, who was the legitimately appointed governor there. Gaius Antonius was now Brutus' captive, and in this letter Cicero advocates that he be executed.

126. The consuls of 43 BC, Hirtius and Pansa, with some help from Octavian (who had taken his adoptive father's cognomen "Caesar") had won a partial victory against Marcus Antonius at the battle of Forum Gallorum (April 15).

127. The Antonii. Lucius Antonius was serving with Marcus Antonius in northern Italy. Gaius Antonius, the Caesarian governor of Macedonia, was captured by Brutus at Apollonia around this time.

a few days before.[128] As for Pansa, he had retreated after receiving wounds, but he could not overcome them. Decimus Brutus and young Caesar are chasing the remnants of the enemy. All those who followed the faction of M. Antonius have been declared enemies of the state. And so, most people interpret the Senate's decree to apply to those under your guard as well, no matter whether they were captured or if they surrendered. When I proposed a decree mentioning Gaius Antonius by name I refrained from calling for any harsh punishment, since I had determined that the Senate ought to be informed by you of the merits of his case.[129] 27 April.

### 23    July 43, On the Voting in the Senate of Honors to Octavian and Penalties for Antonius (*Ad Brutum* 1.15)

Cicero to Brutus, greetings. Messalla[130] is with you now, and he can describe better than any detailed letter from me what is going on, and the political situation. He is extremely knowledgeable and can bring you all the news and explain it all very articulately. Brutus, you should never think—there is no need to tell you what you already know, but I can't pass over such outstanding and praiseworthy excellence—you should never think that Messalla here has any equal in honesty, firmness of purpose, attention to detail, and desire to help the state. In fact, eloquence (an art in which he is extraordinarily accomplished) barely seems an adequate tool with which to praise him. Yet his very eloquence is a real sign of his wisdom: with solid judgment and consummate skill he has chosen to train himself in the most restrained and classical style of rhetoric. He works so hard at the study of it and for such long hours that his natural talent (and he is exceptionally talented) seems the least of his assets.

[2] But my affection for him is getting me carried away. It wasn't my purpose in this letter to praise Messalla—especially to you, Brutus, who are no less familiar than I am with his excellence, and even more familiar with this eloquence that I am praising. I hated to see him go, but was consoled by one thing—that he was setting off to be with my second self, as it were, and that in so doing he was both fulfilling a duty and pursuing great glory. But enough of this.

[3] Now I come after quite a delay to a letter in which, amidst many compliments, you criticize me for being too enthusiastic, lavish even, in the granting of honors.[131] This is your criticism. Others would probably call me too harsh in punishments and

---

128. On April 21, just six days after their success at Forum Gallorum (see above, *Letters* 21), the republican forces decisively defeated Antonius at Mutina, and he was forced to retreat. Immediately after this, however, Antonius teamed up with Octavian and Lepidus to form the second triumvirate.

129. Cicero here withdraws the advice to execute him, given in the previous letter. Brutus would eventually execute him, in revenge for the murder of Cicero by the triumvirs, according to Plutarch (*Life of Antony* 22).

130. M. Valerius Messalla Corvinus, then aged twenty-one. He went on to great prominence as a soldier, statesman, orator, author, and patron of poets. He survived proscription in 42 BC and vicissitudes of the triumviral period to become consul with Octavian in 31 BC, and died aged seventy-two in AD 8. He brought this letter to Brutus.

131. To Octavian.

penalties—but perhaps you hold both views. And so I want to be very clear to you in expressing my thoughts on both matters. And I'm not relying here only on the dictum of Solon—one of the seven wise men and the only one to be a lawgiver—who said that the state is kept together by two things: reward and punishment. Of course there are limits to both, as to everything else, a kind of middle ground in each case. [4] My intention here is not to debate on such a big question. Yet I think it's not out of place to explain, in the case of this war, what I intended to achieve as I made motions in the Senate.

After the death of Caesar and your unforgettable Ides of March, Brutus, I spoke about what you and the others had left undone, and what a great storm was threatening the Republic—I'm sure you remember. Thanks to you, a great plague was averted, a great stain on the Roman people was eradicated, and for you the reward was a superhuman glory. But the tools of tyranny were handed over to Lepidus[132] and Antonius. The former is more fickle, the other more polluted, but each of them feared peace and loathed stability. They were burning with desire to throw the state into confusion, and we had no force with which to oppose them. The citizen body had risen as one, determined to hold on to liberty. [5] But at that point I was perhaps too eager for action, and you perhaps were wiser to leave the city which you had just liberated, and when Italy offered you her services you declined them. And so, when I saw that the city was occupied by criminals, that neither you nor Cassius could be safe there, and that Antonius was using armed force to oppress it, I decided to leave as well. The citizen body oppressed by wicked men, all means of resistance cut off—it was too revolting a spectacle. But my mind, always and consistently focused on love of the fatherland, did not allow me to walk away from those dangers. And so, in the middle of the journey to Greece, when even the winds had pushed me back to Italy, as if trying to argue me out of my decision, I saw you at Velia, and I was deeply distressed. For you were retreating, Brutus, retreating, even though our Stoics say the wise man never flees. [6] As soon as I arrived in Rome I threw myself into opposition to Antonius' criminal lunacy. Once I had provoked him against myself I began to form a quite Brutine plan (for this is what Brutuses do) of liberating the Republic.[133]

[7] The sequel is a long story I must pass over rather than blow my own horn. I'll just say that this boy Caesar (thanks to whom we are all still alive) flows from the fountainhead of my policies, if we want to admit the truth. To him I voted honors, yes, Brutus, but none beyond those he deserved, none but those that were necessary. For when we first began to recover our liberty, when not even the superhuman courage of Decimus Brutus had begun to stir so that we could be aware of the fact, and our entire protection lay in the hands of the boy who had removed Antonius from around our necks, what honor was too great for him? Yet all I proposed for him then was a complimen-

---

132. M. Aemilius Lepidus, prominent Caesarian and consul with Caesar in 46 BC. In 43, as governor of Gallia Narbonensis and Hispania Citerior, he led his troops to the side of Antonius after the defeats of Mutina and Forum Gallorum, a fatal blow to the republican side. He went on to become triumvir with Antonius and Octavian, approving with them the proscription and murder of Cicero among many others.

133. A reference to both his addressee and L. Junius Brutus (consul 509 BC), who was traditionally credited with the inauguration of Roman liberty and the end of the kingship. See Livy chs. 56–60 in this volume.

tary vote of thanks, and one expressed with moderation at that. I also proposed a decree conferring *imperium* on him, which, although it seemed too great a compliment for one of his age, was yet necessary for one commanding an army—for what is an army without a commander with *imperium*? Philippus proposed a statue. The privilege of running for office early was proposed by Servius, and later Servilius proposed he be allowed to run even earlier.[134] At that time no honor seemed too great for him.

[8] But somehow it's easier to find people generous in a state of alarm than those who are grateful in time of victory. For when Decimus Brutus was liberated[135] and that most joyful day dawned (a day which by chance was also Brutus' birthday), I proposed that the name of Brutus should be entered in the *fasti* under that date.[136] In this I followed the example of our ancestors, who paid such an honor to the woman Larentia, at whose altar in the Velabrum you pontiffs are accustomed to offer sacrifice.[137] In granting that honor to Brutus I wanted an everlasting notice of that most welcome victory to live on in the *fasti*. Yet on that very day I discovered that the spiteful in the Senate are rather more numerous than the grateful. During those very days I showered (if that's the way you want to put it) honors on dead men, Hirtius and Pansa, even Aquila. And who would criticize that, except those who forget the danger once the fear has past?

[9] In addition to the grateful memorializing of a service, there was a further motive, one that will benefit posterity: I wanted a permanent monument of our public loathing of vicious enemies of the state. I suspect you won't think much of what I'm about to add, since your friends did not approve—they are excellent citizens, though somewhat naive about politics—that I voted to let young Caesar enter the city in a minor triumph.[138] But it seems to me at least—perhaps I am wrong; it is not my way to be particularly pleased with my own performances—that in the course of this war I never took a more prudent step. Why this is so I must not say, else I would come off as more far-sighted than grateful. I have already said too much. So let us look at something else.

I voted honors to Decimus Brutus, and to L. Plancus. Men of outstanding talent are spurred on by the glory of public recognition. But the Senate is also wise to use all means, so long as they are honorable, to give *every* man an incentive to help the state. But, you say, I am blamed in regard to Lepidus, for having placed his statue on the Rostra, then voting for its removal. I was trying to use public honor to recall Lepidus from his madness. But the insanity of that extremely unstable man rendered my prudence futile. Yet on balance more good was done by demolishing the statue of Lepidus than harm by putting it up.

---

134. By law the minimum age for a consul was forty-two. Though exceptions had been made, Octavian at nineteen was by far the youngest to stand.

135. Antonius had been laying siege to him at Mutina. See above, *Letters* 21 and 22.

136. The *fasti* (calendar) included state holidays and festivals, and could include significant days of important individuals (such as the imperial family under Augustus: see "A Roman Calendar: April" in this volume).

137. This is Acca Larentia, the wet-nurse of Romulus and Remus (see Livy ch. 4 in this volume). The Larentalia, celebrated on December 23, took place in the Velabrum, the low-lying area between the Capitoline and Palatine Hill, near where the twins were exposed and saved.

138. The *ovatio*, granted to a general not qualified by the scale or completeness of his victory for a full triumph. See Glossary.

[10] Enough about honors—now a few words about penalties. I understand, based on frequent statements in your letters, that you would like to be praised for clemency toward those you have beaten in war. In my view, at any rate, you have acted wisely in every instance. But to forgo the punishment of crime (for that is what "pardoning" amounts to), even if it is tolerable in every other circumstance, is I think pernicious when it comes to this war. For in every Roman civil war I can remember, at the end, whatever side won, there would be some kind of organized state left standing. In this war, if we win I find it difficult to say what kind of Republic we're going to have left. If we lose it will be gone for good. This is why I proposed harsh penalties for Antonius, and why I proposed harsh penalties for Lepidus. It wasn't so much for the sake of revenge as to use fear to deter wicked citizens from attacking the fatherland right now, and to set an example to discourage anyone from imitating their lunacy in the future.

[11] Still, this opinion belonged to me no more than it belonged to everybody else. The thing that seemed cruel was that the penalty extended to the children, who did not deserve any. But this is an old and universal custom—even the children of Themistocles ended up in destitution. And if the same penalty apples to citizens legally condemned in court, why would we be more indulgent to public enemies? What actions of mine could be criticized? Clearly if Antonius had won he would have been even more vengeful toward me.

So there you have my reasons for proposing what I did, at least when it comes to honors and punishments. For I imagine you have already heard about my opinions and motions regarding other matters.

[12] But none of this is all that urgent. What really matters, Brutus, is that you come to Italy with an army as soon as possible. There is great anticipation of your arrival. Touch the shores of Italy and everyone will rush out to meet you. If it turns out we have won—and we would have won quite handsomely if Lepidus had not set his heart on ruining everything and perishing himself with all his friends—we will need your advice in establishing some form of constitution. And even if there is still some fighting left to do, our greatest hope is both in your personal influence and in the material strength of your army. But by the gods, hurry! You know the importance of seizing the right moment, and of speed.

I am tending carefully to the interests of your sister's children, as I trust you will learn from your mother's and sister's letters. My purpose in going to this effort is not mere consistency, as some people allege, so much as a desire to earn your good will, which is most precious to me. But my greatest wish of all is to be, and to seem to be, steadfast in my affection toward you.

# QUINTUS CICERO

(102–43 BC, wrote in Latin)

## Introduction

"Campaigning and the struggle for positions of honor is an altogether wretched practice," says Marcus Cicero in one of his philosophical works (*On Duties* 1.87). Though he possessed a burning desire to exercise leadership in the state, Cicero disliked the glad-handing and flattery that were (and still are) needed to win elections. In 64 BC he ran successfully for the consulate of 63. In this treatise (*Commentariolum Petitionis* in Latin), which is framed as a letter, Quintus Cicero, the orator's younger brother, urges him to get over his scruples, work as hard as possible to make friends, and win over every sector of the electorate.

This work was written in early 64 BC. Its authenticity has been doubted by some scholars, both because of the close similarities of certain sentences in it to passages in Cicero's speeches from the period (see Marcus Cicero, *Letters* 1 in this volume), and also because it seems strange that Quintus would presume to give political advice to his older, more politically experienced brother Marcus. These scholars see the work as a later pastiche by an unknown author based on Marcus' speeches. On the other hand, it can hardly be surprising if writings by the two brothers, who worked closely together on the campaign, share talking points. And Quintus himself suggests in the introduction and conclusion that the work is meant not just for Marcus but for anyone who wants an organized account of how to run a successful campaign. In fact, although Cicero's case and this election were exceptional in some ways, the treatise is more widely applicable, and gives a vivid impression of the culture of Roman politics, one that would probably have been familiar to most candidates, even in smaller towns (see Inscriptions no. 13). If it is by a forger, he was extremely well informed, and the treatise remains a key text for understanding the personal side of Roman politics.

To understand it one needs to know the basics of the idiosyncratic Roman electoral system of the late Republic. Every year Roman officials or magistrates were chosen by three different popular assemblies. Quaestors and aediles were chosen in the *comitia tributa*, tribunes of the people in the *concilia plebis*, and praetors and consuls in the *comitia centuriata*. The *comitia tributa* voted by blocks in thirty-five voting districts or "tribes" (*tribus*), into which the entire citizenry was enrolled. These did not, however, correspond to coherent geographical territories. The gradual expansion of citizenship over the history of the Republic to cover all of Italy meant that a candidate who wanted to reach all his fellow tribesmen had to travel far and wide. The four "urban tribes" did not participate in this expansion, so that by the late Republic, when the city was very large, there were a great number of citizens enrolled in the four urban tribes, while a smaller portion of the voters was enrolled in the thirty-one *tribus rusticae*. This number shrank even further when it came to actual voting, since only those with the money and leisure to travel came from far away to vote in the city (see Appian B, ch. 14).

Thus the votes of members of different tribes were by no means equally weighted, and this gave rise to considerable manipulation of the system and jockeying to gain membership in a more influential tribe, as the author of this treatise implies (ch. 18, "those who owe to you or hope to get from you their place in a tribe"). He also alludes to the importance of voters from the rest of Italy outside Rome, who are treated as especially worthy of the candidate's attention.

The Roman citizen body was also divided by the censors into census classes, based on wealth; these classes were further subdivided in various ways to form 193 centuries or voting units in the *comitia centuriata*, each of which would originally have been made up of a hundred men (*cent-* = 100). The upper classes, men of senatorial or equestrian rank, who had to have enough capital to live comfortably off of the proceeds (one million sesterces for senators, 400,000 sesterces for equestrians), occupied the top eighty-nine centuries, with everybody else distributed among the lower 104. Voting was done from the top down, and stopped as soon as a candidate attained a majority of centuries (that is, ninety-seven). So while every citizen could potentially vote, in practice the votes of the wealthy counted more heavily and could be decisive if the aristocracy was united. But as the following text shows, this might well not be the case.

Quintus proceeds methodically, dealing first with the advantages and disadvantages of Marcus' status as a "new man," that is, one with no famous ancestors; then he formally defines and divides campaigning into two parts and deals with each in turn. In this translation a few important political terms have been left in Latin for clarity's sake, and are defined either in a footnote or in the Glossary. The use of bullets and subject headings, while not in the original Latin, is likewise intended for ease of reading.

---

# Running for Office: A Handbook

Quintus sends greetings to his brother, Marcus.

You have every advantage one can have through natural talent, or acquire through experience or hard work. Still, given our affection, I didn't think it would be out of place to write up for you what I have been thinking about as I consider your campaign night and day—not to teach you anything new, but so that things that seem scattered and disorganized in real life might be organized and viewed in one coherent presentation.

## Running as a New Man

[2] Think about what city this is, think what you are seeking, and consider who you are. Most every day as you walk down to the Forum you must say to yourself: "I am a new man.[1] I am seeking the consulate. This is Rome." You will overcome your status

---

1. "New," because none of his ancestors had held public office at Rome. See Plutarch's discussion of this term in his *Life of Cato the Elder* ch. 1, in this volume.

as a new man above all by your fame as a speaker. That is something that has always contributed a great deal to one's prestige. A man who has been considered worthy to defend ex-consuls can hardly be thought unworthy of the consulate. Your reputation as an excellent speaker: that is where you begin. Whatever you are, you are because of that. So when you go to speak, prepare for each and every case as if your entire reputation is on the line. [3] Make sure you have ready and available all the tools you have set aside to help you in this task. And often recall what Demetrius wrote about the training and preparation of Demosthenes.[2]

Next, make sure to show off the number and variety of your friends. For not many new men have been as strong in that department as you are. You have all the *publicani*,[3] just about the entire equestrian order, many entire municipalities,[4] many men of every rank who have been defended by you, several of the trade associations (*collegia*), and what is more, a large number of young men drawn to you by their study of public speaking, and the daily attendance of your crowd of friends and supporters. [4] Take care that you hang on to these by reminding them and soliciting their support. Use every means to make them understand that those who are in your debt will never have another opportunity to pay you back, and those who have good will toward you will never have another opportunity to put you in their debt.

Another big potential advantage for a new man is the backing of the nobles,[5] and especially of the ex-consuls. It is beneficial to be thought worthy of attaining that rank by the very men whose numbers you wish to join. [5] All those men must be diligently canvassed, and intermediaries must be sent to them. They must be convinced that we have always agreed with the *optimates* in politics and are not at all of the popular faction.[6] If we ever seemed to say something in a more popular vein, remind them that we only did so to attach Cn. Pompeius[7] to our cause, so that he, with his very great power, would be an ally in our campaign, or at least not an adversary. [6] And work hard to get the aristocratic youth, or rather to hold on to those aristocratic protégés which you have. They bring a lot of status. You have a great many of them. Make sure that they

---

2. The famous Greek orator (384–322 BC), noted for the lengths to which he went to develop his speaking voice. Demetrius of Phaleron was an Athenian statesman and philosopher (350–280 BC).

3. Wealthy citizens who formed companies (*societates*) that acted as private contractors and performed various functions for the state, such as provisioning armies, building aqueducts, or collecting taxes. They allowed the state apparatus to remain relatively small. As a group they formed a politically influential subset of the class of *equites* or Roman knights, with whom they are often mentioned, as here.

4. Semi-autonomous townships (*municipia*, see Glossary) which possessed full Roman citizenship since the time of the Social Wars (91–89 BC).

5. *Nobiles* belonged to families at least one of whose members had reached the consulate.

6. The *optimates* favored the interests of the *optimi* or "best men" (their own flattering term), and upheld the authority of the Senate, resisting distributions of wealth and property. The "popular faction" refers to politicians who claimed to represent the interests of the people, as opposed to the Senate and the upper orders generally, stressing the sovereignty of the popular assemblies and the importance of the office of tribune of the people, and advocating economic and social reforms to help the poor (see Glossary).

7. Cn. Pompeius Magnus, "Pompey the Great" (106–48 BC), the brilliant and popular general.

know how important you consider them. It will help a great deal if you can persuade those who do not support you to do so.

## Cicero's Competition[8]

[7] Another fact that compensates greatly for your status as a new man is the character of your noble competitors. No one would dare say that their nobility should benefit them more than your merit benefits you. Some men (like, say, P. Galba or L. Cassius) are born into the highest nobility, yet it is unthinkable that they would ever run for the consulate. Men of the most distinguished families, you see, cannot match you because they have no backbone or energy. [8] But you will say that your adversaries Antonius and Catiline are hard men to beat.[9] On the contrary, for a person such as you—hard working, industrious, upright, learned, and influential among the people who sit on juries—these are just the kind of opponents you want. Both of them were killers from boyhood, both rakes, and both have squandered their patrimony. We've seen that one of them, Antonius, has had his entire property put up for public sale. And we heard him remark under oath that he could not get a fair trial in Rome in front of a "Greek" praetor.[10] We know that he was ejected from the Senate on the decision of excellent censors. When we were running against him for the praetorship he had as his supporters Sabidius and Panthera, since he had nobody else to vouch for him when officially registering.[11] And even after election to that magistracy he lived openly with a girlfriend whom he had bought from the slave auction block. And there's more: when it comes to his campaign for the consulate, he preferred to be abroad, fleecing all of the innkeepers during his disgraceful provincial appointment, rather than to be present in Rome to solicit the votes of the Roman people.

[9] But the other one—good gods, what is his distinction? First of all, is he of equal nobility? No. But he is of greater vigor. What makes you say that? Because Antonius is afraid of his own shadow, but Catiline doesn't even fear the laws? This man was born amid the poverty of his father, brought up amid his sister's debaucheries, grew to manhood amid the slaughter of his fellow citizens, and his initiation into public life was the murder of Roman knights! For it was Catiline that Sulla put in charge of those Gallic murderers, we all remember, when they were cutting off the heads of every Tom, Dick,

---

8. See Marcus Cicero, *Letters* 1 in this volume.

9. C. Antonius and L. Sergius Catilina (Catiline) were the other candidates for the two consular spots of 63 BC. After losing this election, Catiline became the ringleader of a conspiracy to violently overthrow the government. Apprehending and executing the Catilinarian conspirators was Cicero's proudest moment as consul. C. Antonius is not to be confused with M. Antonius ("Mark Antony"), Cicero's nemesis in 43 BC.

10. C. Antonius was prosecuted for provincial mismanagement in 76 BC by the Greeks he had robbed in an official capacity. The Greeks were represented successfully by a young Julius Caesar, and the praetor hearing the case was M. Lucullus, who seemed to Antonius to have shown favoritism toward the Greeks.

11. The names Sabidius and Panthera are evidently meant to designate thoroughly unimportant people, and to emphasize that Antonius did not, like Marcus, have respected citizen backers to vouch for him.

and Harry. Among the victims was that great man Q. Caecilius, a Roman *eques*—his own sister's husband!—a man of no political opinions, who was always a quiet man by natural inclination and also because of his age. Catiline killed him with his own hands. [10] But why should I even mention that you are running for the consulate against the killer of a man very dear to the Roman people, Marcus Marius? While the Roman people looked on, Catiline drove M. Marius all around the city, beating him with a wooden staff, and finally to his place of death, where he inflicted on him every kind of torture; then, while Marius was still just barely breathing, Catiline grabbed the hair on the top of Marius' head with his left hand, took his sword in his right, and chopped through his neck. He carried the head in his own hands while streams of blood flowed through his fingers. Later, Catiline lived with actors and gladiators, the former his accomplices in lust, the latter his accomplices in crime. He never entered a place so sacred and holy that he did not leave it with some suspicion of disgrace from his own wickedness—even if there was no fault to be found in the others present. He took as his closest friends from the Senate men like Curius and Anius, from the auctioneers' halls men like Sapala and Carvilius, and from the equestrian order men like Pompilius and Vettius. Catiline is so brazen, so depraved, and so skilled in the arts of lust that he has sexually violated freeborn young men practically in the laps of their parents.

Why should I write to you now about Africa,[12] or about what the witnesses said at his trial? These things are well known, and you should read over the transcripts often. Still, it seems to me that I ought not to pass over the fact that, first of all, he exited his acquittal just as poverty-stricken as some of the jurors were before the trial. Secondly, he is so hated that demands for a new trial are raised daily. His condition is such that, far from fearing him while he is keeping quiet, I would scorn him if he makes trouble.

[11] You are far, far luckier in your opponents than was that other new man recently, C. Coelius.[13] He was running against two individuals whose high nobility was the least of their assets. They had great talent, the highest ethical standards, a great many services to the state, great skill and energy in campaigning. Yet Coelius, though much inferior in birth, and superior in practically no respect, ended up beating one of them.

[12] And so, if you do what you are well capable of doing thanks both to your natural talent and the training you have always pursued, if you do what the circumstances require, what you can do, what you must do, it will not be a difficult contest with competitors who are much more notable in their vices than noble in their lineage. For what citizen is so irresponsible as to wish to unsheathe two daggers against the state in a single election?

## Cultivating Political Friendships

[13] Now that I have covered what you have or could have in the way of compensations for your status as a new man, it is time to speak about the importance of the campaign itself. It is the consulate you seek, an office of which no one would believe

---

12. Catiline had been put on trial for corruption following his stint as governor of the Roman province of Africa, which corresponds roughly to modern Tunisia.

13. C. Coelius Caldus, consul in 94 BC with L. Domitius Ahenobarbus.

you unworthy, but many would begrudge you out of ill will.[14] For you are a man of equestrian rank running for the very highest position in the state. Its glory is such that it confers more status on a man who is courageous, eloquent, and upright than it does on other men. You can be sure that the men who have held the office already see how much status you will acquire when you attain the same thing. In fact, I suspect that those who were born into consular families and have not obtained the office held by their ancestors envy you, unless they are personally quite fond of you. The new men as well who have risen to the praetorship, unless they are bound to you by some favor you have done for them, would prefer not to be surpassed by you in the ladder of offices.[15] [14] And I know that it will occur to you as well how many among the voting public already envy you, and how many are hostile these days to the election of new men. There are also necessarily some who are angry at you because of legal cases you have pleaded. And you should look around and consider whether you think that some are also unfriendly to you because you have so enthusiastically devoted yourself to enhancing the reputation of Pompeius. [15] Thus, since you are seeking the highest position in the state and you see what powerful interests are aligned against you, you must campaign with the utmost skill, care, energy, and diligence.

[16] Campaigning for office can be divided into two distinct efforts, one of which has to do with the support of friends, the other with public opinion. Support of friends should arise from a) favors and services you have performed for them, b) long standing relationships, and c) a winning personality and natural charisma. But when it comes to campaigning, this term "friend"[16] has a somewhat wider application than in normal life. *Anyone* who shows you any good will, who attends you, who keeps coming to your house, is to be considered a friend. Yet those who are your friends on the more compelling basis of family relationship, whether by blood or by marriage, companionship or some other connection, it is extremely helpful to stay on close and friendly terms with them. [17] In short, the closer to home and the more intimate a man is, the more he must love you and the more passionately he must want you to succeed—your fellow tribesmen, for example, or your neighbors, your freedmen, and lastly even your slaves. For practically all the word of mouth around the Forum emanates originally from sources within your household.

[18] You should seek out friends of every type:
- those distinguished by public office or family name (this is for show; even if they are not out hunting up votes, they still bring the candidate some prestige)
- the magistrates, especially the consuls, as well as the tribunes of the people (for asserting your legal rights)

---

14. On the ill will routinely directed at new men running for office, see Horace, *Satires* 1.6.19–45 in this volume.

15. The *cursus honorum*. See Glossary.

16. Latin *amicus*. "Friendship" (*amicitia*) included several kinds of relationships, including personal friendships, but also political alliances, the bond of patron and client, and alliances between states and rulers. An *amicus* might be a friend, a lover, a political supporter or associate, a king's courtier or counselor, or a philosopher's disciple. In politics, argues Quintus, the word applies even more broadly than usual.

- men of exceptional influence (for carrying the votes of centuries)
- those who have already gotten or hope to get from you their place in a tribe or a century, or some kind of favor.

You should strive especially hard to obtain and strengthen their support. These days, ambitious men work extremely hard with every resource at their disposal to get what they want from their fellow tribesmen. You should try by whatever means necessary to see that such men support you sincerely and with the greatest good will.

[19] If people showed the appropriate amount of gratitude, all these things should be taken care of, as I am sure they are. For in the last couple of years you have made indebted to you four clubs (*sodalitates*)[17] of men extremely influential for campaigning; those of C. Fundanius, Q. Gallius, C. Cornelius, and C. Orchivius.[18] Because I was involved, I know what their fellow members received and how they benefited from bringing their legal cases to you. And so, this is what you must do: extract from them now what they owe you by frequently reminding, soliciting support, encouraging, and by making sure that they understand that they will never have another opportunity for showing their gratitude. Men can be spurred to active interest both by your recent services to them and by the expectation of your services in the future. [20] And in general, since your campaign is especially bolstered by that type of friendship that derives from legal defense, make quite sure that every person bound to you in this way has his own particular duty defined and assigned. You have never bothered them in any way. Make sure they understand that you have waited for precisely this moment to call in all of their debts to you.

[21] People will be excited by and support a campaign by three main things: a) favors, b) expectation of favors, and c) like-minded thinking. Take note how to cultivate each type. Quite small favors induce people to think they have sufficient reason to support your campaign—to say nothing of the very many men who owe their salvation to you, and who should understand that if they do not come through for you in this your time of need, no one will ever think that they can be counted on again. Although this is true, still, they must be approached, and convinced that those who have been put under obligation to us can in turn put us under obligation to themselves.

[22] As for those who are held by expectation of a favor, this sort of person is actually far more diligent and eager. Make sure that they see that you are ready and willing to help, and moreover that they understand that you are watching closely their services to you. You should make it clear that you're taking note of how much comes from each person. [23] The third type of supporters are the volunteers. You should invigorate them by saying thank you, by tailoring your talk to the motivations for which each person seems to be in favor of you, by treating them with comparable good will yourself, and by suggesting that their friendship with you can turn into a close and personal relationship. And in all these types judge and weigh how much each person is capable of, so that you know in what way you can cultivate each person, and what you can demand and expect from each in return.

---

17. Neighborhood clubs whose influence and sometimes violent participation in politics is a notable feature of the late Republic.

18. All of these distinguished men were defended by Cicero in court between 66–65 BC against various charges of corruption and embezzlement.

[24] After all, there are certain men, influential in their own neighborhoods and towns, diligent and resourceful men who, even if in the past they have not been eager to exercise this influence, still, if given an opportunity, can easily mobilize support on behalf of someone they owe or like. Make sure that these types of men fully understand that you see what you are expecting from each person, that you realize what you are receiving, and that you remember what you have gotten. On the other hand, there are others who either count for nothing, or are even hated by their fellow tribesmen, some who don't have enough energy or skill to apply themselves as the occasion demands. Be sure to distinguish these. Don't place too much hope in someone who will deliver too little help.

[25] And although a campaign should rely on and be bolstered by already established friendships, still, you can develop very many and very useful friendships in the course of the campaign itself. Among the various annoyances of the campaign there is also this advantage: you can court the friendship of whomever you want without losing face, a thing that you cannot do in ordinary life. At other times it would look quite strange if you dealt with these people and urged them to make use of your services; but in a campaign if you don't do this widely and thoroughly you seem like a terrible campaigner. [26] But I promise you this: if you try, you can easily persuade anyone (unless he has personal ties to one of your competitors) to do you some favor so that you love him and owe him in return—provided that he understands that you think highly of him, that you are acting sincerely, that he is making a good investment, and that the friendship that arises will be not temporary and election-based, but solid and durable. [27] Believe me, no one who has any brains would pass up the opportunity of establishing friendship with you, especially since chance has brought it about that your competitors' friendship is considered either worthless or an actual liability. These men could not successfully follow the advice I am giving you here, or even begin to try.

[28] For how could Antonius even begin to solicit the friendship of men he cannot even call by name on his own?[19] To me at any rate nothing seems stupider than to count as a supporter a man whom you do not even recognize. It takes some kind of outstanding reputation or status or spectacular achievement to be elected to office by strangers, with no one campaigning on your behalf. But a lazy, good-for-nothing man, with no sense of duty, without talent, disgraced and friendless, cannot surpass one fortified by the good opinion of all and the support of a great many, at least not without sheer negligence being to blame.

[29] So make sure to use your many and varied friendships to solidify the allegiance of all the centuries. First of all, obviously, embrace the senators and Roman knights, and the energetic and influential men of all the other social classes. Many hardworking citizens of the city spend their time in the Forum, as do many influential and energetic freedmen. If possible, on your own or through mutual friends, take the greatest care that they become enamored of you, seek them out, send agents to them, show them that you feel they are doing you a great favor.

[30] Then take account of the whole city, its clubs, its hills, its neighborhoods, its districts; if you make friends with the leading men from these, you will easily carry the multitude through them. After that, keep a mental inventory of all of Italy, divided up

---

19. The implication is that he could do so only with the help of an accompanying slave (called a *nomenclator*) who reminded him of their names.

and categorized by tribe. Let there be no municipality, no colony, no rural district, in short no place in Italy where you do not have adequate support. [31] Investigate and track down men from every region, get to know them, solicit their support, strengthen their allegiance; take care that in their home districts they campaign on your behalf as if they were candidates themselves. They will want you as a friend if they see that their own friendship is valued by you; to make sure they understand this, use the kind of speech that is conducive to that end. Men from the outlying towns and the countryside think they are amongst our friends if we simply know their names. But if they also think that they are establishing some protection for themselves, they lose no opportunity for doing a service. Other candidates, and especially your competitors in this race, do not even know these men. You both know them and will easily recognize them, without which friendship is impossible. [32] Important as it is, however, recognition alone is not enough if no hope of personal benefit and friendship follows from it. If not, you appear to be not a good friend but just a good rememberer of names.

Win the support of those men in the centuries who, due to their own ambition, are most influential amongst their fellow tribesmen. Clinch the enthusiasm of the others who have some pull amongst some part of their tribe by reason of their home town, or neighborhood, or membership in a trade association (*collegium*). Then your hopes of victory should be high.

[33] It should be much easier to carry the centuries of *equites*, given care. First of all you should get to know the men in these centuries—not a problem, since they are few. Then you can solicit their support—also not a problem, since it is much easier to make friends with younger men such as these. And you can already count on the cream of the equestrian youth, all those most interested in humanistic study. Moreover, since the equestrian class as a whole is on your side, these centuries will follow the example of their order, as long as you take some pains to have the allegiance of those centuries not just through the general good will of the whole order, but also because of friendships with individual men. Support of the youth, whether they are voting for you, lobbying on your behalf, carrying messages, or forming part of your entourage, is incredibly important and brings honor to you.

## Maintaining an Entourage

[34] Speaking of your entourage, you should take care about this, too, that it is there every day and that it is composed of men of every type and rank and age. For people will be able to infer from its very size how much strength and resources you will have in the election itself. The entourage consists of three parts: a) those who attend the morning reception, b) those who escort you to the Forum, and c) those who follow you around.

[35] In the case of the men who attend your morning reception—I mean the common herd who visit with many patrons, as happens nowadays—make sure that even this tiny service of theirs seems extremely pleasing to you.[20] Signify to those who come to your house that you notice them (mention it to their friends who will report back to them, and if they are present frequently tell them this in person). It often happens

---

20. See Glossary, *salutatio*.

that people who go to the morning receptions of various competing candidates and see that one of them especially notices this service devote themselves to him and abandon the rest, and little by little emerge as staunch personal supporters instead of everybody's fair weather friends.

Now hold carefully to this: if you hear or perceive that someone who has committed himself to you is blowing smoke, as they say, pretend not to have heard or noticed it. If somebody wants to clear his name because he thinks he is under suspicion, affirm that you never doubted his loyalty, nor have any right to doubt it. The person who does not think he is in good standing with you cannot be a friend at all. Moreover, it is important to know each person's attitude, so you can establish the degree to which you can trust him.

[36] Now, as for the service of those who escort you to the Forum: this is a greater service than attending the morning reception, so make it clear that it is more pleasing to you. So far as possible, go down at the same time every day.[21] A large daily entourage while going down to the Forum carries a great deal of prestige and status.

[37] The third thing of this type is the supply of constant followers. Some are there voluntarily. Make sure they understand that you are forever in their debt for a very large favor. Others are there because they owe you a favor. Absolutely insist on this service. Have them stay with you in person if they can, given their age or their business. If they cannot follow you around themselves, have them designate associates for the job. I very much want you—and I consider this to be crucial—to be with a crowd of supporters at all times. [38] Furthermore it will bring you great glory and high status if you are attended by men who have been defended by you and who have been saved and liberated by you in the courts. Absolutely make sure to request this from them. After all, some of them obtained their property, some of them their civil status, others their entire salvation and fortunes through you, at no expense to themselves.[22] Tell them there will never be another time when they can show their gratitude, and that *this* is the moment for them to pay you back.

## Dealing with Enemies and False Friends

[39] And since this entire discussion has to do with the support of friends, it seems to me that I should not pass by one aspect that requires caution. Deceit and intrigue and double-crossing are everywhere. This is not the time to rehearse the extensive debates over how to tell a real friend from a pretended one; the important thing now is just to remind you: that outstanding talent of yours drives men simultaneously to pretend they are your friends and to feel envy for you. So keep in mind that old saying of Epicharmus,[23] that the heart of wisdom is "Never trust rashly."

[40] Once you have made sure of the support of your friends, learn also the varieties

---

21. At this time Marcus lived in the district of Carinae, on the rise between the Forum Romanum and the Oppian Hill.

22. Roman advocates did not accept formal fees for legal services.

23. A Greek comic playwright active under the Sicilian rulers Gelon and Hieron of Syracuse, 485–467 BC.

and motivations of your critics and enemies. Of these there are three types: a) those you have harmed, b) those that dislike you for no good reason, and c) those who are close friends with your opponents. Those you have harmed by speaking against them in court on behalf of a friend, by all means apologize to them; tell them there was no avoiding it, lead them to expect that you would show the same zeal and energy on their behalf if they joined in friendship with you. Those who dislike you for no good reason, endeavor to lead them away from their misguided opinion by doing them a favor, or by making them expect such, or by demonstrating your good will toward them. As for those who are disinclined to support you because of their friendship with your opponents, approach them in the same manner as the others, and, if you can do so convincingly, make it clear that you yourself are also well disposed toward your competitors.

## Securing Popular Support

[41] Enough about establishing friendships. It is time to speak about the part of campaigning which, as I mentioned, has to do with securing popular support. This requires

- the calling of people by name
- flattery
- persistence
- generosity
- good publicity
- good political visibility
- political promises

[42] First, show off the fact that you know people. Make it obvious; increase and improve this ability daily. Nothing is so popular or so pleasing to people. As for the second item, which is not in your nature, concentrate on faking it in such a way that it looks natural. For you have no lack of charm such as is worthy of a good and elegant man. But what you really need is to flatter people, which, even if it is a fault and disgrace in normal life, is nonetheless necessary in campaigning. Mindlessly agreeing with somebody is only a vice when it makes him a worse person; it is not so blameworthy when it makes him friendlier, and in fact it is essential for a candidate, whose face and expression and talk must be altered and accommodated to the opinions and beliefs of whomever he meets.

[43] As for persistence, there is no need for explanation; the word itself shows what it means. It is most useful never to leave town. But the most important aspect of persistence is not just being in Rome and in the Forum, but persistently campaigning, approaching the same men repeatedly, making sure that no one can say that he was not canvassed by you, and canvassed energetically and diligently. This you can do.

[44] As for generosity, this has wide application. Generosity within your own household does not directly touch the multitude. Still, if it is praised by your friends, it will please the multitude. You can do this with dinner parties, which you should put on personally and have put on by your friends, both for people in general and for members of the individual tribes. You can do this by performing services, which you should spread far and wide. Make sure you are accessible day and night, not only in

the foyer of your house, but also in your face and expression, which are the doorways to your mind. If these suggest that your will is hidden and secluded, it's no use having an open door.

## Making Promises

For people don't just want promises, especially from a candidate. They want promises in grand style and with a shower of compliments. [45] So this, at any rate, is an easy rule to follow: whatever you are going to do, make it clear that you are going to do it willingly and gladly. But here is something that is more difficult and will not come naturally to you, but which the situation demands: when you are going to say no, either do so pleasantly, or else don't say no at all. The former course is that of a good man, the latter of a good candidate. Suppose someone asks you a favor which you cannot promise honorably, or which damages yourself, such as when someone asks you to take some legal case against a friend. Decline elegantly. Explain your close relationship to your friend, and show how sorry you are you cannot help. Convince him you will make it all up to him in some other way.

[46] I have heard a certain man say, regarding some advocates to whom he had brought his case, that he was more pleased by the words of the one who turned him down than by the one who took the case. Such is the tendency of men, to be taken in by facial expression and speech rather than by the reality of the favor itself. That is a plausible enough piece of advice. Of the following, however, it will be very hard to persuade a philosophically inclined individual such as yourself, yet I shall keep your best interests in mind. When it comes to those you will refuse to help because of some prior obligation to a friend, even they can walk away feeling satisfied and well disposed. But when you turn people down and say it is because you are busy, or because of business with closer friends, or more important cases, or prior engagements, then they depart your enemies. Every one of them is in the mood that they would prefer you to lie rather than to say no.

[47] Gaius Cotta,[24] who was a master at campaigning, used to say that he promised his help to everybody, as long as he wasn't being asked to do something counter to his duty, but that he only followed through with those in whom he judged he was making the best investment. The reason he didn't say no to anyone, he said, was that it often happened that for some reason the person to whom he made the promise did not follow up on it. And he often discovered that he had more time than he thought. One would never get a full house, he reasoned, by receiving only those with whom it was actually possible to meet. Chance brings it about that something you never expected occurs, and that a matter you thought was well in hand for some reason does not come to pass. In fact, the possibility is remote that someone for whom you have failed to follow through will become angry with you. [48] If you make a promise, you don't know what will happen, and the matter is both postponed and known to relatively few. But if you say no, you will surely alienate people, and immediately, and many. Those who

---

24. C. Cotta (124–73 BC, consul in 75 BC), considered by Cicero to be one of the best speakers of his age.

request someone else's assistance are far more numerous than those who actually use it. Better to have some of the people angry at you in the Forum some of the time, than to have everyone angry at you in your house all of the time, especially since people get far angrier at those who say no than at someone who in their view is prevented for a reason from doing what he promised, although he wants to do it somehow if at all possible.

[49] Just so you don't think I have deviated from my outline, since I am supposed to be discussing the popular part of campaigning, my intent is for everything I am saying here to be relevant to popular opinion rather than to the support of friends. Although something from this latter category enters in—responding warmly, assisting friends carefully in their affairs and when they are under attack—still, here I am talking about how to capture the multitude, so as to fill your house with clients from the predawn hours, so that many men will hope for your protection and depart more friendly than they came, and so that as many ears as possible will be filled with excellent reports of you.

## Getting Good Publicity

[50] This brings me to publicity, to which you must pay extremely close attention. All the assets I have mentioned so far are also effective at creating good public opinion, that is:

- fame as a speaker
- the support of the *publicani* and the equestrian order
- the good will of the nobles
- accompanying crowds of younger men
- the attendance of those who have been defended by you
- the crowds from the towns who will visibly come out to support you
- that people say and believe that you know people well, address them courteously, seek their support carefully and diligently, and that you are kind and generous
- that your house is full of people well before dawn, and that crowds of people of all sorts are present
- that everyone is satisfied by your words, many by your deeds and assistance

Do what can be done, thoroughly, with energy, skill, and care—not so that good report will flow to the common people from these men, but so that the common people themselves will feel invested in supporting you.

## Appealing to the Masses

[51] Now when it comes to the multitude in the city, and the support of those who hold sway in the public rallies,[25] these you have already secured by glorifying Pompeius,

---

25. These could be rowdy; see *contio* in Glossary.

both when you took up the case of Manilius, and when you defended Cornelius.[26] We must mobilize a degree of support from that quarter that has been available to no one before, at least to no one who also has such backing among the more well-to-do. And you will have to make sure that everyone knows that Cn. Pompeius supports you fully, and that it is very much in his interest that you attain the office you seek. [52] Finally, make sure that your entire campaign is full of pomp, glamorous, eye-catching, and popular, that it has the maximum of visibility and prestige. Also, be sure if at all possible that your competitors acquire a bad reputation for vice, or lust, or bribery, depending on their character.[27] [53] Most of all, let it be clear in this election that the Republic respects you and has high hopes for your political future. Still, do not try to deal with political issues in the midst of the campaign, neither in the Senate nor at a rally. Rather, focus on the following goals:

- let the Senate believe on the basis of your past acts that you are a defender of its clout and influence
- let the Roman knights and the good and wealthy men believe, from the way you live your life, that you favor peace and stability
- let the multitude believe, based at any rate on what you have said in a popular vein during rallies and trials, that you will not be hostile to their interests.

## Concluding Advice

[54] It occurs to me regarding those two morning time mantras that I said you should meditate on every day as you walk down to the Forum—"I am a new man; I am running for the consulate"—there is a third: "This is Rome." Rome is a state formed out of the confluence of peoples. In it there are many plots, many deceptions, many vices in every type of person. One has to deal often with arrogance, often with truculence, often with malevolence, haughtiness, hostility, and otherwise annoying behavior. I see that in the midst of so many vices belonging to such a variety of men it takes amazing wisdom and skill to avoid giving offense, to avoid malicious talk, to avoid plots, to be one man, yet adaptable to deal with such a great variety of character, speech, and will.

[55] And so, always and ever, hold to that course of life that you have set for yourself. Excel at speaking. In Rome this is how men are kept loyal and attracted, and how they are dissuaded from attacking and getting in your way. Rome's biggest failing is that people forget all about merit and worth when bribery gets involved. When it comes to this, know yourself well, that is, understand that you are the kind of man who can strike the hearts of his competitors with the greatest fear of judicial prosecution. Make sure they know that you are on guard and watching them. Make sure they live in fear of your diligence, your influence, your oratorical power, and especially of

---

26. C. Manilius sponsored a bill as tribune in 66 BC that gave Pompeius a wide ranging military command in the East. Marcus spoke in favor of this law in the extant speech *On the Manilian Law*. Cornelius, a tribune of the people in 67 prosecuted for electoral corruption, was another Pompeian supporter whom Marcus defended. See above, ch. 19.

27. See above, ch. 10, where Quintus urges Marcus to read often the transcripts of Catiline's trial for provincial mismanagement.

your support among the equestrian order.[28] [56] And I want you to lay these things out before them, not so that you seem to be already contemplating filing suit, but so that thanks to their anxiety you can more easily accomplish what you are trying to do.

Above all, strain absolutely every nerve to attain what we seek. I see that no election is so polluted by bribery that some centuries do not support, free of charge, those with whom they feel a close connection. [57] And so, if we

- exercise a vigilance commensurate with the importance of the election
- motivate our supporters to the highest level of enthusiasm
- assign each of our supporters and influential men his own task
- lay before our competitors the prospect of prosecution
- instill fear in the middle men and stop the bribery agents however we can,

then it will be possible to ensure that there is no bribery, or else that it has no effect.

[58] I am under no illusion that I know this subject better than you do. But I thought that, given how busy you are now, I was in a better position to collect all this in one place and send it to you in writing. And even though it is written in such a way as to apply specifically to you and to this campaign of yours, rather than to everyone who is running for office, still, I want this handbook on running a campaign to be considered a thorough and rational treatment of the subject. So please let me know if anything seems in need of alteration, or complete omission, or if I have left anything out.

---

28. The Aurelian Law of 70 BC established that juries would be composed of members of the equestrian class, not senators as before.

# EPICTETUS

(ca. AD 50–120, wrote in Greek)

## Introduction

Epictetus was born a slave in Hierapolis (in modern day Turkey), and lived, at least for a time, as a slave of the powerful imperial freedman Epaphroditus, the secretary of petitions for the Emperors Nero (reigned AD 54–68) and Domitian (AD 81–96). While he was still a slave, he studied under the most prominent teacher of Stoic philosophy at the time, Musonius Rufus, and himself began teaching in Rome soon thereafter, probably as a freedman. Epictetus taught with great success there until 95, when Domitian expelled all philosophers not only from the city but from all of Italy.[1] Epictetus moved to Nicopolis, an affluent city in Greece, where his school continued to flourish, drawing young men from all stations of life looking for philosophical instruction. Like his own hero Socrates, Epictetus lived an ascetic life and never wrote for publication, but one of his students, the future consul Arrian (in AD 129 or 130), copied down his lectures and conversations, which survive today in four books under the title *Discourses*. Arrian also excerpted parts of the *Discourses* and organized them into the shorter work translated here, the *Handbook of Stoic Philosophy* (*Encheiridion*).

The *Handbook* is in essence a summary of Epictetus' teaching, reduced to a simplified form for easy consultation and memorization. In so far as it is a summary of his ideas, the *Handbook's* style is somewhat more abrupt than the more leisurely and varied *Discourses*. But its very straightforwardness and urgency is no doubt partly responsible for the *Handbook's* popularity from antiquity until the modern period. It was, for instance, probably not the *Discourses* but the *Handbook* that was read by the Emperor Marcus Aurelius (reigned AD 161–180), whose own *Meditations* are deeply influenced by Epictetus' teachings.

Epictetus describes philosophy as a way of training or preparing for what will happen to us (*Discourses* 3.10.6). Those who do not engage in philosophy are likely to be ill-equipped to face the inevitable difficulties of life. In order to deal with these challenges, he argues in Stoic fashion, we should not try to change the things that happen to us, but rather change our outlook concerning them (*Discourses* 1.12.17). Epictetus' writings on Stoic ethics, then, are an attempt to show us how to find peace

---

1. Expulsion of philosophers was not uncommon in the early principate. Stoic philosophers in particular gained a reputation for being aggressive and public critics of the more autocratic Roman emperors. Roman ambivalence toward Greek philosophy, however, goes back to the earliest encounters in the 2nd century BC; see Plutarch, *Life of Cato* 22–23 in this volume.

in a troubling world by directing our thoughts and actions to what we can affect and by accepting those things that we cannot.

---

## A Handbook of Stoic Philosophy

[1] Some things are up to us, some are not. What is up to us? Our beliefs, impulses, desires, aversions—in short, everything that is our doing. What is not up to us? Bodily health, wealth, reputation, public office—in short, everything that is not our doing.

What is up to you is by nature free, unhindered, and unobstructed. What is not up to you is weak, servile, subject to obstruction, and belongs to others. So remember: if you believe that things that are naturally servile are free, and that things that belong to others belong to you, you will be frustrated, pained, disturbed, and you will blame both gods and men. Yet if you believe that only what belongs to you is actually yours, and that what belongs to others does not belong to you (as is the case, in fact), then no one will ever compel or hinder you. You will not blame or accuse anyone, and you will never do a single thing against your will. No one will hurt you, and you will not have any enemies—for you will never be able to suffer any harm.

These are your lofty aims, so remember that you must not strive to reach them half-heartedly. Some things you will have to give up permanently, others for the time being. If you desire philosophical freedom *and* political office and wealth, you will probably not attain political office and wealth, because you are also pursuing philosophical freedom. But you will certainly fail to achieve philosophical freedom, which alone provides us with independence and well-being.[2]

So with every unpleasant mental impression[3] get in the habit of saying immediately, "You are only an impression and do not necessarily represent reality." Then scrutinize it and examine it with the tools you have at your disposal—first and foremost, by asking whether it is one of those things up to us or not. And if it involves things not up to us, be ready to recognize that it has nothing to do with you.

[2] Remember that the goal of desire is attaining what you desire, while the goal of aversion is to avoid encountering what you are trying to avoid. Now, the person who fails to achieve his desire is miserable. So too is the person who encounters what he is trying to avoid—he's bound to fail. Well now, if you focus only on avoiding those undesirable conditions that are up to us, you will never encounter what you're trying to avoid. But if you try to avoid disease, death, or poverty, you are doomed to fail. So stop trying to avoid all things that are not up to us and concentrate on avoiding those undesirable conditions that are. As for desire, for the time being you must do away

---

2. *Eudaimonia*: a stable, enduring flourishing, not just temporary pleasure or happiness. Deciding how to achieve this flourishing, and how to make it permanent, was a main task of ancient Greek and Roman ethics.

3. *Phantasia*: a physical alteration of the soul that represented the external object that caused it. Impressions had to be scrutinized by the governing mental faculty.

with it entirely. For if you desire something that is not up to us, you will inevitably be disappointed. And none of the things that are up to us, and which it would be proper to desire, is yet within your reach. Use only positive and negative impulses, but lightly and with reservation.[4]

[3] When it comes to something appealing or useful to you, or something you cherish, remember to tell yourself what sort of thing it is. Start with the smallest things and work your way up. For instance, let's say you cherish a pot. Say to yourself, "It is a pot that I cherish." That way, when it breaks, you won't be upset. When you kiss your child or wife, tell yourself, "It is a human being that I am kissing." That way, if one of them dies, you won't be upset.

[4] Whenever you are about to engage in some activity, remind yourself what kind of activity it is. If you are heading out to bathe, anticipate what happens in baths: people splash around, push and shove, hurl insults, and steal. You will engage in the activity more securely if you say at the outset, "I want to bathe *and* keep my volition[5] in accordance with nature" (and so likewise for each activity). This way, if something gets in the way of your bathing, you are ready to counter, "I wanted not only to bathe, but also to keep my volition in accordance with nature. I will not be able to do so if I am annoyed at what is going on."

[5] People are upset not by things, but by their judgments[6] about those things. Take death, for example. There is nothing awful about it, or else Socrates would have thought so. No, it is our judgment about death—that it *is* awful—that makes it awful. So whenever we feel frustrated, upset or pained, we should never blame anyone else but ourselves—by which I mean our own judgments. An untrained person accuses others when he himself acts incorrectly; someone who has begun philosophical training blames himself; a person fully trained in philosophy blames neither others nor himself.

[6] Do not be proud of any superiority that is not really your own. If your horse were to say proudly, "I'm a fine-looking horse," that would be acceptable. But if *you* proudly say, "I've got a fine-looking horse," know that you are priding yourself on a quality that belongs to the horse. What belongs to you? The use of impressions.[7] And so, when you are able to stay in accordance with nature in the use of mental impressions, then you can be proud, because you are priding yourself on your own good quality.

[7] Suppose you're on a voyage and the ship is at anchor. If you disembark to get water, you may wish to pick up a shell or some exotic plant as a secondary part of your mission. But you must always keep your attention directed toward the ship and constantly turn back in case the captain calls. And if he calls, you must drop all of those

---

4. Since the true Stoic "desire"—goodness of character—is not yet within the grasp of beginning students, they must for now rely on "impulses" regarding what it is reasonable to aim at in the external sphere, where the outcome is not "up to us."

5. Volition (*prohaeresis*) is a key term in Epictetus' philosophical outlook. Volition is what persons are in terms of their mental faculties, consciousness, character, judgment, goals, and desires. You and I are not our bodies; rather we, our essential selves, *are* our volitions. The sentence might be paraphrased, "I want to bathe *and* stay true to myself."

6. *Dogmata*, another key term: our opinions and assessments about life, goodness, badness, etc., which condition all our mental states, including all emotions.

7. See note 3 above.

things that you've collected, or else you may be tossed on board and tied up like the livestock.

It's the same in life. If instead of flowers and shells you are given wives and children, there is nothing stopping you from taking them. But if the captain calls, you must run to the ship, leaving all of those things behind, not even looking back. And if you are old, never stray too far from the ship, or you will be left behind when he calls.

[8] Do not expect events to happen as you wish, but wish for things to happen as they do, and you will pass through life untroubled.

[9] Illness is a hindrance to your body, but not to your volition, unless your volition itself gives its consent. Lameness is a hindrance to your leg, but not to your volition. Make this your response to everything that happens to you; you'll discover that every obstacle is a hindrance to something, but not to you.

[10] When something happens to you, remember to look inward to find some power to cope with it. If you see a beautiful man or woman, you will find self-control to deal with it. If you are faced with hard work, you will find stamina. If you are insulted, you will find patience. If you get into this habit, you will never be carried away by mental impressions.

[11] Never say of anything "I lost it," but rather "I have returned it." Did your son die? No, he's been returned. Did your wife? No, she's been returned. Was your land confiscated? This too was merely returned.

"But the one who took it from me is an evil man," you say? Why should you care who the giver sends to demand it back from you? So long as it is in your possession, take care of it, but remember it is not yours—just like guests at an inn.

[12] If you want to make progress, banish all thoughts such as these: "If I do not take care of my affairs, I will not have the means to live," or "If I do not chastise my slave, he will be a good-for-nothing." It is better to die of starvation without distress and fear than it is to live in the lap of luxury but always be worried. It is also better for your slave to be a good-for-nothing than for you to be unhappy. So begin with the little things. Suppose a little oil spills or some wine is stolen. Tell yourself, "This is the price of serenity, this, the price of tranquility. Nothing is gotten for nothing." Whenever you call your slave, keep in mind that he might not come, and even if he does, he might not do what you want him to. But he is not in so fine a position that it's in his power to spoil your tranquility.

[13] If you want to make progress, steel yourself to being considered foolish and naive when it comes to external possessions. You should not want to be considered knowledgeable. And if people think you're a somebody, don't believe it. Know that it is difficult to keep your volition in accordance with nature while watching over external possessions. Paying attention to the one necessarily results in the neglect of the other.

[14] If you want your children, wife, and friends to live forever, you are naive. For you want to control what you cannot control, and you want what belongs to another to belong to you. Likewise, if you want your slave not to make a mistake, you are a fool since you want what is worthless to be something else besides worthless. But if you want not to be disappointed in your desire, this is up to you. Just work at what you *can* control.

A person's master is the one with power over the things that he wants or wants to avoid, to either provide them or take them away. So anyone who wants to be free must not wish for anything or try to avoid anything that is in other people's power. Otherwise, he is necessarily a slave.

[15] Remember that you should act as if at a party. If someone brings some hors d'oeuvres to you, stretch out your hand politely and take some. If he passes by, don't grab and detain him. If he hasn't gotten around to you, don't fling your desire forward, but wait until he is near you. Act the same way in regard to your children, your wife, public offices, and wealth, and you will eventually be a banqueter worthy of the gods. But if you do not take any of the things set down before you, but despise them, then you will share not only in the banquets of the gods, but in their power as well. It was by acting like this that Diogenes, Heraclitus, and all those like them were rightfully divine and spoken of as such.[8]

[16] Whenever you see someone crying in grief, either because his son is abroad or he has lost his possessions, be careful that you are not carried away by the impression that this man is in bad shape because of external circumstances. Rather, be ready to say to yourself, "This fellow is not distressed by what happened—after all, it does not distress anyone else—but by his own judgment about these things." Still, do not refrain from comforting him as far as words go or lamenting outwardly with him if you feel it necessary. Yet be careful not to groan *inwardly*, too.

[17] Remember that you are the actor of a theatrical play of the director's choosing. It will be short if he wants it short, long if he wants it long. If he wants you to play a beggar, make sure you play it skillfully. Whether he wants a lame man, a public official, or a private citizen, this is your role and you must play the given part nobly. The selection of that part, however, belongs to another.

[18] Whenever a raven croaks inauspiciously, do not get carried away by the mental impression, but immediately make this distinction: "None of these signs predicts the future for me, but rather for my worthless body, some unimportant possession of mine or my reputation, my children, or my wife. All signs are auspicious for me, if I will it so. No matter what happens, it is up to me to find some benefit from it."

[19] You can be invincible if you refuse to enter any contest where victory is not under your control. Make sure that when you see someone who is greatly esteemed, has achieved great power, or is distinguished in some other way, do not pronounce him blessed because you've been carried away by your mental impression of him. If the essence of the good is to be found in those things that are up to us, there is no room for jealousy or envy. Your wish is not to be general, councilman, or emperor, but to be *free*. There is but a single path to this, contempt of those things not in our power.

[20] Remember that it is not the person abusing or beating you who is offending you, but the judgment that they are being offensive. Whenever someone is annoying you, know that it is your judgment that has caused you annoyance. Therefore you must above all strive not to be carried away by the mental impression. Once you find time and practice, you will more easily gain self-control.

[21] Put death, exile, and all the other seemingly awful things before your eyes on a daily basis, but most of all death. You will never have any lowly thoughts or desire anything excessively.

[22] If you have your heart set on philosophy, get ready at the outset to be ridiculed,

---

8. Diogenes the Cynic (412?–321 BC) and Heraclitus (lived around 500 BC) were early Greek philosophers whose ascetic ways of life were models for the Stoics.

because many will mock you and say, "Look, he's come back to us a *philosopher*!" and "Where did he get this look? Such haughtiness!" Don't have a haughty look about you, but do cling to those things that seem best to you, as you have been appointed by god to this post.[9] Remember that if you remain true to the same beliefs, those who once mocked you will later admire you. But if you yield to their insults, you will earn double the ridicule.

[23] If you ever turn outward[10] because you want to please someone, know that you have lost your way. So be content with being a philosopher in every aspect of life. If you also want to appear to be a philosopher, appear so to yourself and it will be enough.

[24] Don't let the following considerations bother you: "I'm going to live a life without distinction. I'll never be anybody!" Even if lack of distinction is bad (and it is), you cannot be in a bad state because of someone else, no more than you can be in a state of disgrace. Do you have any control over whether you land a public office or get invited to a banquet? Not at all! How, then, is this lack of distinction? How will you be a nobody? You should only be concerned with matters that are up to you. In these you can be of the highest importance!

"But I won't be able to help my friends." What do you mean, "won't be able to help"? Because they won't get some petty cash from you? Because you won't be able to make them Roman citizens? Who told you that these things are up to us and do not belong to others? I mean, who can give to another what he himself never had?

"Then go get rich so that we can have a little something, too!" If I can get rich while remaining judicious, loyal, and charitable, show me the way and I'll get rich. But if you're asking me to jettison good character so that you can acquire possessions that aren't really good, do you not realize that you're being entirely unfair and inconsiderate? Which do you want more, money or a loyal and modest friend? I thought so! So assist me in my quest and do not ask me to pursue wealth at the expense of those virtues.

"But my country won't be helped, at least not by me." Is this your objection? Again, what sort of help do you mean? You won't be able to furnish it with stoas and baths? So what? It doesn't get shoes from the blacksmith or weapons from a shoemaker, does it? It's enough if each person fulfills just his own job. If you furnished the city with another citizen who was loyal and judicious, wouldn't you be helping it in some way?

"Well, yes."

Then you would not be entirely useless to your city.

"So what role will I have in the city?" Whatever role you are able to do, so long as you maintain your loyal and judicious ways. But if you give up those good traits in your desire to help the city, what help can you be when you've rendered yourself shameless and untrustworthy?

[25] Suppose someone has been preferred over you at a dinner party, in a greeting, or in being asked for advice. If these are good things, then you should be happy that the other person got them. If bad, you should not be annoyed that you did not get them.

---

9. By "god" the Stoics, who were monotheists, referred to the pervasive divinity that coursed through and providentially guided the whole cosmos.

10. That is, to externals (things "not up to us"), like career, money, public office, or skills in public speaking. Epictetus' young, philosophically inclined audience would be under considerable pressure to enter lucrative and prestigious careers instead (see the next chapter).

But keep this in mind: if you don't pursue external distinction—something which is not up to us—with the same vigor as others, you won't be treated the same way.

Think of it this way: does a person who does not visit a patron's door, or escort him around, or fawn upon him[11] have the same relationship as the person who does all these things? Of course not. It's not possible. You are being unfair and greedy if you are unwilling to pay the price for preferential treatment and want it for free.

Think of it this way. How much does lettuce cost? Let's say an obol. If someone paid an obol and took the lettuce, and you did not, would you think that you had less than the one who got the lettuce? He has the lettuce. You have the obol you did not spend. It's the same with the topic we're discussing. You weren't invited to someone's dinner party. Why? Because you didn't pay the host the required fee for the dinner: flattery and paying court to him. Pay the balance if it is to your benefit. But if you are unwilling to pay the price but still want the invitation, you are being greedy and foolish. Are you troubled that you don't have anything in place of the dinner? Don't have your self-respect since you did not have to praise a man against your will or put up with his doormen?

[26] You can learn the will of nature from situations in which all of us react the same. For instance, when a slave-boy breaks someone else's drinking cup, we all immediately say, "Such things happen!" So you should know that, whenever it is one of *your* cups that is broken, you should act the same way as when it is someone else's. Now apply this message to more important matters. If someone else's son or wife dies, everyone is ready to say, "That's human nature." Yet when someone's own son or wife dies, right off the bat it's "Woe is me!" or "I'm so miserable!" We'd do much better if we bore in mind how we feel when we hear the same about others.

[27] Just as a target is not set up to be missed, so too the natural existence of evil does not occur in the universe.[12]

[28] If someone handed over your body to some passerby, you'd be quite upset. Well, what about the fact that you hand over your own judgment to all and sundry, such that your judgment becomes cloudy and confused if someone happens to insult you?[13] Aren't you ashamed of this?

[Chapter 29 is a near copy of *Discourses* 3.15, and seems to have been added to the *Handbook* at a later stage. It is omitted here.]

[30] The appropriateness of our actions is generally measured in terms of our relationships to other people. Take your father: you are obligated to take care of him, yield to him in all matters, and to put up with him even if he insults you or strikes you. "But

---

11. For these characteristic behaviors of Roman clients and patrons, see Martial, *Epigrams*, especially nos. 16, 17, 22, 34, 46 in this volume.

12. This cryptic statement seems to derive from the Stoic principle that the Stoic god was a beneficent entity, and that what is commonly considered "bad" in the universe was simply an aftereffect of the creation of the "good." No one would set up a target so that an archer would shoot away from it, and similarly the Stoic god would not create and sustain the world with the specific purpose that evil should exist in it.

13. The point here seems to be that one should not judge events according to someone else's values, but judge them for what they are. Insults, then, would not affect right-thinking Stoics.

he is a bad father!" Well, you aren't related by nature to a good father, but simply to a father.

Suppose your brother does you wrong. Even so, maintain your proper relationship toward him. Do not look at what he does, but what you have to do to keep your volition in accord with nature. No one else can harm you unless you consent. You will be harmed only when you believe that you are harmed. You will discover what you ought to expect from your fellow citizen, your neighbor, and your general if you get into the habit of considering their relationships to you.

[31] Let us turn to devotion to the gods. You should know that the most important aspect in this is having correct beliefs about the gods, that they exist and guide the whole universe properly and justly. You must also be disposed to obey them, yield to everything that happens, and willingly accept it in the belief that it is brought to pass by the best judgment.

If you think like this you will never blame the gods nor accuse them of not caring about you. And the only way this can happen is if you remove the good and the bad from matters that are not up to us and assign them to matters that are. Whenever you believe that there is some good and bad in externals, it is absolutely unavoidable that when you fail to achieve what you want, or fall into a situation you did not want, you'll blame and loathe those responsible. Why? Because every living creature by nature avoids and shuns what seems harmful and what causes it, but seeks out and admires what appears beneficial and what causes it. So it is impossible for a person who believes he is being harmed to be happy with the person who seems to be causing that harm, just as it is impossible for someone to be happy with the harm itself.

This kind of misguided thinking is why a son reviles his father whenever the son doesn't get from him the things the son *thinks* are good. This is what made Eteocles and Polynices enemies to each other—they thought that being a tyrant was good.[14] This is why the gods are reviled by farmers, sailors, merchants, and those who have lost their wives and children. Devotion to the gods is found wherever it is in our interest.[15] And so, all those who are concerned with directing their desires and aversions correctly are also, by this very act, concerned with devotion to the gods as well.

As for offering libations, blood sacrifices, and first fruits,[16] each nation should, in accordance with the customs of their countries, perform their rites in correct fashion and not perfunctorily, carelessly, stingily, or beyond their means.

[32] Whenever you have a need to use divination, remember that while you do not know what is going to happen—*that* is what you came to learn from the seer—you did come knowing full well what sort of matter it is, if you are a philosopher. What do I mean? Well, if it involves something not up to us, it is by definition neither good nor bad. So do not bring desire or aversion to the seer, and do not tremble when you

---

14. The sons of Oedipus, who fought and killed each other because neither had been given unambiguous control of Thebes by their father at his death. Because it was removed from reality, myth was frequently used to criticize imperial politics from a safe distance.

15. That is, people are generally devoted to the gods only when they think the gods are acting in their interest; but the gods are always acting in our (long term) interests, argues Epictetus, so we should always be devoted to them.

16. The portion of a harvest that is offered to the god(s) in thanks for providing a successful crop.

approach him. Rather, be resolved that whatever happens is indifferent (*adiaphoron*)[17] and means nothing to you. After all, you will be able to turn whatever happens into a positive, and no one will be able to prevent you from doing this.

So go confidently to the gods as your advisers, and from here on out, whenever you receive advice from them, remember what advisers you chose for yourself and whose advice you'll be ignoring if you disobey.

You should consult an oracle in cases where Socrates thought it was best to do so, when the entire inquiry looks to the outcome and when neither reason nor any other knowledge provides a starting point for understanding the problem. But whenever it is necessary to face danger alongside your friend or country, do not inquire of the oracle whether you should face the danger. No, for if the seer declares that the sacrifices have turned out adversely, it is clear that death, the loss of some bodily part, or exile is forecast for you. But reason directs us, even in these circumstances, to stand by our friend and to face danger alongside our country. Heed that greater seer, Pythian Apollo, who cast out of his temple the man who did not help his friend while he was being killed.[18]

[33] Establish for yourself a character and personality which you will maintain both when you are by yourself and when you are in a social setting. Keep silent for the most part. Speak only when necessary, and even then use as few words as possible. Occasionally, the situation will call for us to engage in conversation. On those occasions do not talk about common subjects, such as gladiator shows, horse racing, athletic contests, and eating and drinking—the trite topics everyone talks about. Most of all, do not discuss people. Do not criticize, praise, or compare anyone. If you are able, shift the conversation you and your friends are having to more suitable topics. But if you are stuck in the middle of complete strangers, keep silent.

Laughter: keep it to a minimum. Don't laugh over many things nor do so excessively.

Oaths: refuse to take them at all, if possible. Do so only when absolutely necessary.[19]

Dinner parties: avoid those offered by outsiders who are ignorant of philosophy. If the occasion does arise, you must take great care not to slip back into the habits of ordinary folk. Know that if one of your fellow guests is tainted, all those around him are bound to become tainted, too, no matter if they happen to be pure.

Bodily needs, such as food, drink, clothing, housing, and household slaves: take only the bare minimum. Reject everything meant for show or luxurious living. As for sex, one should keep oneself pure before marriage as much as possible; but if one is to

---

17. A technical Stoic term that describes those conditions that, whether positive or negative, have no bearing on our happiness and well-being (such as health or sickness, wealth or poverty). All that matters is training oneself to think correctly and accept the way the world works.

18. The story goes that three men were attacked by robbers while on their way to Apollo's oracle at Delphi. One of the men ran away, while another accidentally killed the third while trying to defend him. When the remaining two made it to the temple, Apollo absolved the man who had accidentally killed his friend but cast the coward out of his temple (Aelian, *Various History* 3.44).

19. The 6th-century philosopher Simplicius, who wrote a commentary on Epictetus' *Handbook*, gives two examples of when an oath might be necessary, "to save a friend from danger or to provide assurances on behalf of one's parents or country."

engage in it, then that person should engage only in customary and lawful acts.[20] Do not, however, be oppressive to or critical of those who enjoy a sexual lifestyle, and don't go around boasting to everyone that you are abstinent.

If someone informs you that a certain person is speaking ill of you, do not defend yourself against the criticisms, but reply, "I guess he does not know all of my other faults, since otherwise he would have included those as well!"

Public spectacles: generally you should not attend these. But if the occasion should present itself, show yourself to be a supporter of no one but yourself. What I mean is that you should not want anything else to happen than what actually happens, or anyone else to win than the person who actually wins. If you do this, you won't be frustrated. As for cheering for or jeering at someone, or getting all worked up, you should avoid this altogether. And after it's all over, do not have a long conversation about what happened since this contributes nothing to your improvement and only proves that you were awed by the spectacle.

Public readings:[21] you should not be eager to attend them or go to them randomly. If you do attend one, make sure you keep your propriety and stay calm, but take care at the same time not to give offense.

Now, whenever you are about to meet someone, especially someone remarkably important, prepare by imagining what Socrates or Zeno would do in that situation. If you do this, you will not be at a loss how to deal with any contingency appropriately. Whenever you go to visit some powerful man, think about the fact that you may not find him home, that you may be locked out, or have the door slammed in your face, or that he may not pay you any attention whatsoever. And if, even knowing all these possible outcomes, you judge it appropriate to go, you should endure whatever happens and never say to yourself, "That wasn't worth it!" That is the reaction of an ordinary person showing dissatisfaction with external matters.

When you are with company, refrain from constantly bringing up your own accomplishments and ventures. You might enjoy reminiscing about them, but others may not find so much pleasure in listening to your exploits.

You should also refrain from provoking laughter. This habit is liable to cause you to slip back into ordinary behavior, and people around you are likely to lose respect for you. Falling into obscenities is likewise dangerous. So whenever the conversation descends into this sort of talk, you should rebuke the person who crossed the line, if the moment is right. If not, make your displeasure with the conversation clear by keeping silent, blushing, and generally looking unhappy.

[34] When you receive a mental impression of some pleasure, you should, as in the other situations, guard against being carried away by it. Let the matter wait for you, and force yourself to delay a bit. Then reflect on both moments, first, when you enjoy the pleasure, and second, when you realize the error of your ways and reproach yourself

---

20. Probably a reference to avoiding adultery and other dangerous liaisons. See *Discourses* 2.18.15: "Today, when I saw a handsome boy or a beautiful woman, I did not say to myself, O that I could sleep with her! And, How happy is her husband! (For he who says this, says too, How happy is the adulterer!)." (Trans. R. Hard.)

21. Recitations of poetry (see Juvenal 1 in this volume) or of practice speeches, both popular types of entertainment in this period.

for it. Now balance against these feelings how much joy you will have and how much you will praise yourself when you abstain from the pleasure. But if it seems clear to you that it is an appropriate time to engage in the pleasurable act, be sure that you are not overcome by its seductive and enticing qualities—think, rather, of the other side of the ledger, how much better it will feel knowing that you have achieved this victory.

[35] Whenever you are doing something that you've determined must be done, do not shrink from doing it in full view of others, even if most people are bound to think that it's strange. If you are not acting correctly, it is the act itself you should avoid; if you are acting correctly, why fear those people who are incorrectly criticizing you?

[36] Here are two statements: 1) It is day. 2) It is night. To use these in a disjunctive proposition—that is, to say "it is day *or* it is night"—is logical. But to use them in a conjunctive proposition—that is, to say "it is day *and* it is night"—is illogical. Similarly, taking the greater amount of food at a dinner party may be logical in regard to your hunger, but it is illogical if you want to maintain a healthy social atmosphere. So whenever you are eating with others, remember not only to look at the value of the morsels set before you to your body, but also to maintain the proper respect toward your host.

[37] If you adopt a role[22] beyond your ability, you will disgrace yourself in the role you did choose, and you will have passed over a role that you might have filled successfully.

[38] When you go on a walk, aren't you careful not to step on a nail or twist your ankle? So be careful that you don't harm your governing faculty![23] If we safeguard this in each action, we will tackle each situation more securely.

[39] Each person's body should dictate the size of his possessions, just as his foot should dictate the size of his shoe. If you stop at bare needs for the body, you will be observing the proper measure; once you go beyond this, however, you will inevitably be carried away, as if falling over the edge of a cliff. It's the same with shoes: if you go beyond your foot's proper measure, first you'll get a gold sandal, then a purple one, then an embroidered one. Once you go beyond the proper measure, there is no stopping.

[40] The moment females turn fourteen, men start calling them "ladies." Since in their minds nothing else is available to them but to sleep with the men, they begin to beautify themselves and to put all of their hopes and dreams in their looks. So it is important for us to make sure that they understand that we value them only for their good behavior and decency.

[41] It's a sign of weakness to spend all one's time on one's body, for example, by exercising, eating, drinking, excreting, or copulating a lot. These things are to be done only secondarily to your main purpose, which is to pay complete attention to your judgment.

[42] Whenever someone treats you badly or speaks ill of you, keep in mind that

---

22. Greek *prosopon* (Latin *persona*, the origin of our word "person") originally meant "theatrical mask" but came to be an important term in Stoic philosophy. According to the fullest account, we have four *personae* ("roles") according to 1) our nature as human beings; 2) our individual natures; 3) the circumstances imposed on us by chance and time (e.g., into what city we were born); and 4) the choices we make based on the kind of life we want to lead.

23. *Hegemonikon*: the standard Stoic term for the human mind—the seat of rationality and the center of the person—largely synonymous with volition.

he is acting or speaking in the belief that it is appropriate for him to do so. He can only be guided by what appears right to *him*, not what appears right to *you*. Now, if what appears to him is mistaken, then he has been harmed inasmuch as he has been deceived. If someone assumes that a true proposition is false, it is not the proposition that is harmed, but the one that was fooled. If you take these principles as your starting point you will be more kindly disposed toward people who insult you. In each case say, "That's what he thinks is right."

[43] Every matter has two handles, so to speak: one that is bearable and one that is unbearable.[24] Suppose your brother does you wrong. Do not think, "He is doing me wrong." That is the "unbearable" handle. Instead, approach it by the other handle, the "bearable" one, and say, "He's my brother; he was raised with me."

[44] The following statements are logically unsound:

"I am richer than you, so I am superior to you."
"I am more literate than you, so I am superior to you."

These, however, are logically sound:

"I am richer than you, so my estate is superior to yours."
"I am more literate, so my diction is superior to yours."

But you, at least, are neither estate nor diction.

[45] Suppose someone bathes quickly. Do not say he is doing so "incorrectly," but rather "quickly." Someone drinks a lot of wine. Do not say he drinks "incorrectly," but rather "a lot." How, after all, can you tell they are doing it "incorrectly" before you determine what they were thinking? This way, you will only assent to impressions that are absolutely true and clear.

[46] Under no circumstances call yourself a philosopher, and do not, in the presence of ordinary folk, go on and on about your philosophical principles. Just put them into action. For instance, at a dinner party do not tell people how they should eat. No, just eat as one should. Remember that it was because Socrates had completely abstained from showing off that people came to him in the desire to have him put them under the guidance of *other* philosophers, and he would do so! This is how well he endured being underrated. If in the company of ordinary folk talk happens to turn to some philosophical principle, keep quiet for the most part. Why? There is the great danger that you will immediately spew out what you haven't yet digested.

When someone tells you that you don't know anything and that doesn't sting you, that's when you know that you've started to make progress. Do sheep show how much fodder they have eaten by bringing it to their shepherds? No, they digest the grasses on the inside and produce wool and milk on the outside. You should do the same. Do not reveal your philosophical ideas to ordinary folk but show them the results of their digestion by your actions.

[47] Once you've adapted your body to need little, don't go on boasting about it. Do not on every occasion that you drink water say, "Look, I'm drinking water!" And if you ever want to condition yourself to doing hard work, do it for yourself and not for

---

24. The Greek term translated here—"bearable"—also has the meaning of "by which one can carry the object," and "unbearable" the meaning "by which one cannot carry the object," playing on both the literal and metaphorical meanings of "handle."

an audience. Don't go embracing statues.[25] And if you are ever remarkably thirsty, take a drink of cold water, spit it out, and do not tell anyone.

[48a] This is the condition and character of an ordinary person: he never expects help or harm from himself but thinks it comes from the outside. This is the condition and character of a philosopher: he expects that all help and harm come from himself.

[48b] Here are the tell-tale signs of someone making philosophical progress: he does not criticize, praise, fault, or blame anyone, nor does he claim that he is somebody or knows something. Whenever he is frustrated or hindered in some way, he places the blame on himself. If someone praises him, he internally laughs at the person doing so. If someone criticizes him, he does not try to defend himself. He goes around like a sick person, careful not to disturb any part of him that is healing before it is perfectly fixed. He has driven from himself every kind of desire and has focused his aversion only on those undesirable things that are within our power. His impulse toward everything is calm. He does not care at all if he appears foolish or uneducated. Put simply, he watches himself closely, as if an enemy plotting against himself.

[49] Whenever someone gloats about being able to understand or explain the books of Chrysippus,[26] say to yourself, "If Chrysippus hadn't written so unclearly, this person wouldn't have any reason to gloat." What do I want? To understand nature and use it as my guide. So I look for someone to explain it to me, and when I hear that Chrysippus can, I go consult him. Well, I cannot understand what *he* wrote. So I look for someone to explain those to me. So far, there's nothing special about all this. But once I've found someone who can explain it, it's up to me to put into practice the precepts communicated to me. Now *that's* something special. But if I'm amazed at the interpretation itself, what else have I turned into but a literary scholar?[27] The only difference is that I'm interpreting Chrysippus instead of Homer. Whenever someone says to me, "Read me the works of Chrysippus," I end up blushing because I am not able to show that any actions of mine are consistent and consonant with his words.

[50] Whatever rules you have set for yourself, abide by them as if they were immutable laws, as if you would be committing an act against the gods if you were to transgress them. Do not concern yourself with what others will say about you. That is no longer up to you.

[51] How long will you put off demanding excellence from yourself? When will you stop ignoring correct thinking in every matter? You have learned the philosophical principles; you have made the necessary calculations. What sort of teacher are you waiting for now? One to whom you would hand over the responsibility of correcting yourself? You are no longer a boy, but a full-grown man. If you are not attentive now, if you do not feel a sense of urgency now, and if you keep putting things off, always

---

25. Diogenes the Cynic famously used to embrace statues in winter in order to toughen his constitution—an outward show of his philosophical principles (Diogenes Laertius, *Lives of the Philosophers* 6.23).

26. Chrysippus (ca. 280–207 BC) was the third head of the Stoic school in Athens and regarded as the "second founder of Stoicism." He wrote works on many topics, and because of his systematic exposition, his views became the standard Stoic position, even though his language and thoughts are sometimes obscure. None of his works survives except as excerpted by later writers.

27. The Greek word is *grammatikos*, the trained literature and language teacher, usually of teenage boys; see the introduction to Quintilian in this volume.

deciding that you will focus on yourself *tomorrow*, you will make no progress—and not even know it. You will continue to live—and die—an ordinary person. So on with it! Demand that you live like a grown-up, like someone eager to improve. If something seems best to you, you should treat it like an unbreakable law. No matter what you face, be it painful or pleasant, esteemed or despised, keep in mind that the contest is *now*, that the Olympic Games are here *now*, and they cannot be put off any longer. Remember that progress stands on a razor's edge, destroyed or preserved in one day, by a single action. How did Socrates become who he was? By never allowing himself to pay attention to anything but reason. Fine, you're not Socrates. But you should live your life as if you want to be Socrates.

[52] The first and most important matter in philosophy is the application of philosophical precepts, such as, "One should not tell lies." The second matter involves proofs, for instance, "Why should we not tell lies?" The third concerns confirming and explaining the proofs themselves, asking questions like, "How do we know this is a proof? What is a proof? What is a sequence of arguments, an inconsistency, truth, or falsity?"

This third topic is necessary because of the second, the second because of the first. But the first is the most important and the one on which we should focus. And yet we do the opposite; we waste time on the third topic, and we apply all of our energy toward it, having no concern for the first. And so we tell lies—this despite being ready to explain how we might construct a proof that we should not tell lies.

[53] At every moment you should have the following at hand:

> Lead me, Zeus! Lead me, Fate!
> Wherever you decide I should have my post,
> I will follow without hesitation. Even if I do not want
> to go in my wickedness, I will follow nonetheless.[28]

Or this:

> Whoever submits gracefully to Necessity
> is wise in our eyes and knows the ways of god.[29]

Or this:

> Well, dear Crito, if this is how the gods want it, let it be so.[30]

Or this:

> Anytus and Meletus can kill me, but harm me? Never.

---

28. A quotation from Cleanthes (331–232 BC), who was the second head of the Stoic school in Athens.

29. A quotation from an unknown tragedy of Euripides.

30. This is an adapted quotation from Plato's *Crito* (43d); the next paraphrases a dramatic statement by Socrates in Plato's *Apology* (30d). Both are from accounts of the trial and death of Socrates, whom Epictetus greatly admired and emulated.

# HORACE

(65–8 BC, wrote in Latin)

## General Introduction

Quintus Horatius Flaccus was from southern Italy (Venusia on the border between Lucania and Apulia). The son of a successful and wealthy freedman, Horace later achieved equestrian status. As a student in Athens he was caught up in the confusion of the civil wars; Junius Brutus, a leader of the murderers of Caesar, conferred on him a surprisingly high military rank—that of military tribune. After the defeat of the anti-Caesarians by Caesar's heirs Antonius and Octavian at Philippi, Horace lost his entire inheritance. But he subsequently obtained the coveted post of a *scriba quaestorius* (the *scribae* were trusted secretaries and accountants for short-serving Roman magistrates). Despite having been on the "wrong" side against Octavian, thanks to his literary talent and personal charm Horace became a friend of Octavian through the latter's close advisor Maecenas. Maecenas was patron to several of the great poets of the day, including Horace's dear friend Vergil. Later Octavian, now the Emperor Augustus, chose Horace to write a poem for an important public occasion: the secular games of 17 BC (the *Carmen Saeculare*) and even wanted to have him as private secretary. Horace's refusal to take the job of personal secretary to the emperor, according to an ancient biography of Horace by Suetonius, did not lead to any ill feeling. He died at the age of fifty-seven, naming Augustus as his heir.

---

## Introduction to *Satires*

Horace's *Satires* are among his early works, Book 1 being written mainly in the early 30s BC. The Latin title is *Sermones* ("chats"), and their gentle, conversational tone is somewhat at odds with the fiery malice one associates with the genre of satire (see, for instance, Juvenal's *Satires* in this volume). Yet the subject matter of satire—the social world—is still the focus, and all the expected characteristics of Latin verse satire are present: critique of vice, (gentle) ridicule of persons, wit and humor, some moral precepts and advice, a setting in the city with contrasting glances at the country, the mixture of high and low stylistic elements, and a well-developed persona of the speaker.

All three of the *Satires* included here deal indirectly with Horace's influential friend Maecenas, and present more or less realistic vignettes from Horace's own life. "A Journey to Brundisium" (*Satires* 1.5; the titles are editorial additions) shows Horace tagging along at Maecenas' invitation on what was in fact a very important diplomatic mission: an attempt to reconcile Octavian with Antonius in order to avoid another civil war. But instead of talking about politics Horace gives a vivid travelogue and makes

106

it clear that friendship is what he values most. "On Ambition and Noble Birth" (1.6) explains why Horace refuses to run for elected office as Maecenas suggests he should. He alludes to the prejudice he endures as a freedman among the Roman upper classes, the tough road walked by all "new men" who enter politics in the face of aristocratic disdain and hostility, and speaks movingly of his love for his freed slave father. In "The Pest" (1.9) Horace is waylaid in the street by an overly-talkative man who, it emerges, wants to use his very slight acquaintance with Horace to get access to Maecenas. The poem explores Horace's discomfort as he tries and fails to summon the courage to brush the man off. Horace's gentleness, charm, and lack of pretension will emerge from these anecdotal poems, which reflect on Roman society and values from a strikingly different perspective from that of Cicero, for example. Horace is a literary man who lacks Cicero's passion for public life, and certainly has no noticeable affection for the old republican form of government. Horace can be seen as an example of the kind of person who most benefited from Augustus' regime: Italian, but not from Rome; well-off, but not of one of the old senatorial families; educated, but not politically ambitious.

# Satires

## A Journey to Brundisium (*Satires* 1.5)

I left mighty Rome and came to a little inn at Aricia,
with Heliodorus the rhetorician, an unbelievably learned Greek.
From there it was on to Forum Appi, a place packed with ferrymen[1]
and surly, stingy inn-keepers. We took it slow, you see, and broke the trip
in two—more determined travelers can do it straight through, but
the Appian Way is easier if you take your time. The water there
was so vile I declared war on my stomach, and just waited,
in a grumpy mood, as my companions finished their dinner.
Now the night was preparing to spread her shadows upon the earth
and to unfurl the constellations in the sky. Our slaves began to heap        10
abuse on the ferrymen, and vice versa: "Here! Put in over here!
Moron, you're packing in way too many! Enough!" Between this,
the fare-collecting, and the yoking of the mule, we lost a full hour.
Sleep was out, with the damned mosquitoes, and frogs croaking away
in the marshes. Then the ferryman, quite drunk on cheap wine,
began singing to some absent girlfriend. Worse, a passenger
decided to give him some competition. Finally, the passenger gets
tired and drops off to sleep, and the lazy ferryman ties the halter for
the mule (let out to graze) to a stone, and snores, flat on his back.
It's nearly dawn when we realize the ferry is stopped dead.        20

---

1. The ferrymen and their mules dragged barges overnight down the sixteen-mile canal through the Pomptine marshes, south of Rome.

Some hot-headed passenger leaps out of the boat and starts hammering
at the head and sides of mule and ferryman both with a willow club.
We're lucky to get ashore, at last, by the fourth hour.[2]

                                     At the temple and
grove of Feronia we wash our faces and hands in the water of her spring.
Then, after lunch, we creep on three miles and make the climb to Anxur,
perched on gleaming, towering cliffs. Maecenas was to meet us here,
with the excellent Cocceius, both sent as ambassadors on a matter
of importance: reconciling friends who had become estranged—again.[3]
Here conjunctivitis obliged me to use some black ointment on my eyes.        30
In the meantime Maecenas arrived, and Cocceius, and along with them
Fonteius Capito, that superbly polished man—one of Antonius'
closest friends. We were glad to exit Fundi, where Aufidius Luscus
was the big cheese.[4] We laughed at the regalia of this crazy one-time clerk:
his magistrate's toga and wide-striped tunic, his pan of incense.
Then we arrived, exhausted, at Formiae, the city known as the
home of Mamurra;[5] there we stayed at Murena's villa, and
ate at Capito's.

                      The next day was by far the best of the journey,
for Plotius and Varius and Vergil[6] met us at Sinuessa—the purest        40
souls the earth ever produced, to whom no one is more devoted than I.
What happiness it gave me to embrace them there! Call me mad
if I ever prefer anything to a delightful friend. Next stop: a post house
for official travelers near the bridge at the edge of Campania;
it provided lodging, and the public officers gave us our allotment
of fuel and food. From there we arrived early in Capua, and as the mules
put down their loads Maecenas decided to get in a game of ball,
but Vergil and I had a siesta instead. Ball games are no good for those
with eye complaints (like me) or chronic indigestion (like him).
From here we moved on to Cocceius' sumptuous villa, which lies        50
above the town of Caudium and its inns.

                          I must pause now, and
invoke the Muse: O Muse, sing briefly, if you will, the epic battle
fought there between the buffoon[7] Sarmentus and the scrapper Messius.

---

2. Roughly 10:00 a.m. See Appendix "Roman Time Reckoning."

3. The friends at odds are Octavian (the future Augustus) and M. Antonius, who will try to
resolve their differences with the help of legates at a summit in Tarentum in 37 BC (which gives
a dramatic date for this poem).

4. Literally *praetor*, which Horace uses in jest.

5. The notoriously rich and spendthrift friend of Julius Caesar, his chief engineer or *praefectus
fabrum*. See Catullus 29 and Cicero, *Letters* 17 in this volume.

6. M. Plotius Tucca and L. Varius Rufus later acted as Vergil's literary executors and published
the *Aeneid* after his death—against his express wishes to burn it. The three probably joined
Horace from the Naples area, where Vergil was living.

7. *Scurra* (see Glossary).

Who bore these mighty competitors? The illustrious lineage
of Messius was Oscan, Sarmentus was slave-born (his mistress still lives).
Sprung from such noble families as these, they came to the combat.
"Messius," began Sarmentus, "to me you look a lot like a mean old
unicorn." We all laughed at this. "I resemble that remark," said Messius,
bucking his head in jest like a unicorn. "What must you have
been in the old days, Messius, if that's the way you menace the table now,
post horn-ectomy?" Messius, you see, had a scar amidst the bristly hair          60
on the left side of his forehead. Sarmentus kept it up, hurling continual
ridicule at his "Campanian disease"[8] and at his burly physique. He kept
begging Messius for an interpretative dance: the shepherd Cyclops in love.
"No mask, no costume required," he winked. Messius gave it back:
"Sarmentus, have you consecrated your chains to the household gods
like you vowed? I know you're a clerk now, and a free man and all,
but does your mistress still take her . . . services from you? Why did you
ever run, when you could easily have saved up to buy your freedom?
A puny bastard like you wouldn't need more than one-fifth of the usual
slave rations, I reckon." Banter like this enjoyably prolonged our dinner.          70
From there we headed straight for Beneventum, where an
over-enthusiastic innkeeper nearly burned the place down while trying
to roast some poultry. Some coals fell out of his dilapidated stove
and the flames rose and licked the roof beams. Imagine the scene
as panicked diners and terrified slaves snatch their suppers and
everyone tries to put out the fire.
                              After this we began to see
the mountains of Apulia that I know so well, mountains scorched
by the hot wind they call "Atabulus," and from which we never
would have emerged, had not a house near Trivicum taken us in.
There was smoke there, too, that brought tears to our eyes,          80
this time from some green and leafy logs put in the furnace.
Here, like the great fool I am, I waited until midnight for a girl
who never appeared. Meditating there in erotic anticipation,
I dropped off to sleep; and pornographic dreams caused me to soil
my nightclothes and my belly as well, as I lay there on my back.
From here our carriages whisk us along for twenty-four miles,
to stop in a little town whose name won't fit in verse, but which
is easily known by description: water, normally all but free,
is sold there for a hefty price; the bread, though, is fantastic.
Seasoned travelers know to buy extra to take along to the next stop—          90
Canusium. There the bread is hard as rock, and water just as scarce,
but they say it was founded once upon a time by the valiant Diomedes.
At Canusium we say a tearful goodbye to our dear friend Varius.
Next we arrive at Rubi, exhausted, since the road was long
and made rougher by the heavy rains. Next day the weather was better,

---

8. An unknown malady.

but the road was worse, all the way to Barium that abounds in fish.
Next stop, Gnatia, a town built despite the anger of the water nymphs.[9]
The place gave us a laugh, though, as the locals tried to persuade us
that when placed on the temple threshold, incense miraculously burns
by spontaneous combustion. The Jew Apella may believe this, but not I.[10]     100
For I have learned that the gods dwell in a state of tranquility, and that
if nature produces some wonder, it is not because the gods have sent
it from the high canopy of the heavens because they are unhappy.
Brundisium marks the end both of my long journey and of my poem.

## On Ambition and Noble Birth (*Satires* 1.6)

You don't turn up your nose, Maecenas, at those from unknown
families—or men like me, whose father was only a freedman—
as most people do. You don't, even though no one's more well-born
than you, nobler than any other Etruscan aristocrat with roots way
back in ancient Lydia—even though your ancestors on both sides
were the sort of men to be entrusted with the command of great armies.
You say it makes no difference what parentage one has, provided
he is himself free-born, and your perfectly valid reasoning's as follows:
even before the reign of that slave-born monarch Servius Tullius[11]
it happened all the time: men with no ancestors at all to boast of          10
showed excellent character, and were rewarded with high public office.
Laevinus, to take the opposite case, was descended from great Valerius,
who founded the Republic and ejected Tarquin, the last of the kings,
yet was judged utterly worthless at election time by the voting public—
that same public who, as you know, routinely puts dolts into office,
being foolish slaves to reputation and moronically dazzled by
ancestor masks and the pompous inscriptions that go with them.
Shouldn't we, then, in a different world than the batty crowd,
do the same?
          Well, fine with me if the people prefer to see a Laevinus
in office, rather than a new man like Decius. And Appius the censor[12]     20
would kick me out of the Senate, like anyone who turned out not to have
a free-born father. Rightly so, since I had not been content to live
in my own skin. Still, Ambition pulls us all, bound to her gilded car,
the low- and high-born alike. Just look at Tillius: what good was donning

---

9. That is, the water there was bad.

10. The Romans thought that Jews were particularly superstitious.

11. The sixth king of Rome; see Livy chs. 39–41 in this volume.

12. Decius Mus, consul of 340 BC, sacrificed himself in battle to preserve victory, famous and
noble despite not having noble parents. The Appius mentioned may be Appius Claudius Pulcher,
censor of 50 BC and notoriously strict. For "new man," see Glossary.

that wide-striped tunic again and entering the Senate as a tribune?[13]
He's surrounded by malice and envy—hardly a problem if he stayed
a private citizen. When you're mad enough to don those dark senatorial
boots, and let the broad purple stripe fall over your chest,
that's when the questions begin: "Who is this man? Whose son is he?"
It's as if one came down with a case of Barrus' disease, and strutted                30
around town, wanting to be thought handsome, and firing the girls
with curiosity wherever he goes, so they inquire after the details—
what does he look like, how are his legs, his feet, his teeth, his hair?
In the same way, a man who commits to being responsible for citizens
and their city, for the empire, for Italy, for the shrines of her gods,
such a man makes everyone curious and anxious to know who his
father is, or whether he's low born on his mother's side. "You," they ask
indignantly, "son of a slave like Syrian Dama or Dionysius, would *you*
dare toss a Roman citizen from Tarpeia's rock? Send him to the executioner?"
"But my colleague, Novius," you reply, "he's a rung below me on the ladder;      40
my father had the same status that he has now." So that makes you some
kind of Paullus or Messalla?[14] Yet he campaigns on regardless, shouting
in the Forum in a voice so loud it would drown the din of two hundred
wagons, plus three funerals; blaring horns and trumpets can't compete.
At least he's got our attention.
                            Now to my own case, the freedman's son.
That's what everyone keeps calling me with biting malice: the freedman's son.
The complaint now, Maecenas, is that I spend my time with you;
it used to be that I commanded a Roman legion as a military tribune.[15]
But the cases are quite unlike: I suppose a man might fairly grudge me
a tribune's rank. But no one can feel aggrieved that I am your friend,              50
especially since you are so careful to take on only those who deserve it
and have no part in corrupt ambition.[16] I can't call myself "fortunate"
in this respect, as though I somehow lucked into your friendship—
it was no mere chance that threw you in my way. Vergil, long ago,
that best of men, and Varius later on, told you what kind of man I was.
When I was introduced to you I stammered out a few words

13. Apparently Tillius was a freedman's son like Horace who was removed from the Senate but got back in by being elected tribune of the people. The tunic with wide purple stripes was worn by those with senatorial ambitions (see Ovid, *Tristia* 4.10.29–36 and Pliny, *Letters* 4 in this volume).

14. That is, a member of an illustrious aristocratic family.

15. After the assassination of Julius Caesar, Horace was living in Athens. Brutus the tyrannicide came to Athens to recruit supporters, and Horace, despite a lack of military experience, was given a junior commission as one of Brutus' military tribunes (see Glossary) in 43 or 42 BC. This kind of position was normally held by the sons of senators or equestrians who would go on to pursue military or official careers. The appointment gave Horace equestrian status, and exposed him to the sneers alluded to here.

16. A vague reference to common abuses of the patron-client system for disreputable ends.

(it was tongue-tied awe that kept me from talking at greater length):
I did not claim to be the son of a noble father; I didn't boast of riding
around some vast estate perched on a south Italian mare; rather,
I just told you what I was. You answered briefly, as is your custom.                    60
I went my way, and nine months later you called me back, and invited
me to count myself among your friends.
                                        It gives me great pride
to have found favor with you, who draw the line between a good man
and a bad one based not on his lineage, but on the conduct of his life
and the content of his character. But let's not get carried away:
if my nature is generally straight, if my vices are relatively small
and few, like moles you notice on an otherwise praiseworthy body,
if no one can truly charge me with greed, pettiness, or sensual self-
indulgence, if (to sing my own praises) I lead a pure and guiltless life
that makes me dear to my friends, then I owe all of this to my father—        70
my father, who was a relatively poor man with a small estate,
and yet refused to send me to the school of Flavius, where the burly
sons of burly centurions went to learn their letters, toddling off with
writing tablets and a case for school supplies slung over their shoulders,
and bringing eight *asses* on the Ides of every month for the teacher's fee.
No, he had the daring to transport me to Rome as a boy to learn
the same arts that any knight or senator would have his children taught.
He provided clothes and slave attendants of the kind boys have in
the big city, and if anybody saw me he would think these things
had been purchased from some massive ancestral fortune. And my              80
father was present in person as I made my rounds to all the teachers,
a guardian above reproach. To make a long story short, he protected
my chastity (for sexual purity is the first step in a virtuous life)
not only from actual violation, but from every scandalous rumor, too.[17]
He didn't worry that someday people would say it was all wasted
if I ended up a modestly paid auctioneer, or an auction-broker like him,
and I wouldn't have complained in the least: but now, the way things
are, the greater praise is due to him, the greater thanks from me.
It would be mad for me to feel regret over having had such a father,
or to get defensive, as many people do, protesting it's not their fault        90
if their parents didn't happen to be free-born or famous. This is not
what I say, and not how I think. What if Nature should suddenly give us
permission to rewind the years to a certain date,
and then choose new parents to suit our fancy and pride?
I'd stick with mine, and skip those ennobled by fasces
and by curule chairs[18]—a foolish choice in the view of the mob,
but wise, perhaps, in yours—because, truth be told,

---

17. The implication is that teachers often took sexual advantage of their students, to the moral
detriment of the latter. See Quintilian, section D in this volume. A (slave) *paedagogus*, or child-
minder, would normally have played the guardian role that Horace's father took upon himself.
18. The tokens of high office.

I wouldn't want the heavy and unaccustomed burden.
I would have to go out and acquire a much greater fortune, and quick;              100
I would have to start making and receiving morning visits; I'd have to
get friends for an escort so as not to travel alone to the country or abroad;
I'd have to keep a stable of horses and grooms, and travel with baggage
by the cart full. As it is, I'm free to go, just me and my mule, all the way
to Tarentum in the heel of Italy if I feel like it, with my single saddle
bag chafing the mule's rump, while I, the rider, wear down his front.
No one will accuse me of pathetic poverty, as they do you, Tillius,
when you travel the road to Tivoli as a magistrate with a sad retinue
of five slaves to attend you, lugging chamber pots and wine vessels.
In this and a thousand other ways I live more comfortably than you,              110
noble senator.
                    I walk—on my own—to wherever I feel like going.
I check on the current prices of vegetables and grain; I wander about
the Circus Maximus amid the hucksters; I take an evening stroll through
the Forum when the day's business is done; I watch the fortune tellers.
Then I head home for a bowl of leeks and chickpeas with hot cakes
on the side. Dinner is served by three slaves; a marble slab supports
a pair of drinking cups and a ladle. Close by there stands a salt-cellar,
an oil-flask, with its saucer, both simple Campanian earthenware.
After that I go to sleep, not worried that I have to get up early
the next day and face the statue of Marsyas in the Forum,                        120
the one who shields his face so he won't have to look at young Novius.
I lie in bed until the fourth hour, then maybe go for a walk or,
after reading or writing whatever I like to beguile my quiet hours,
I rub down with oil (not the sort which cheapskate Natta uses,
cheating the lamps) and play a game of ball. Then, when I'm tired,
and the sun gets too hot, it's time to leave the exercise ground and go
have a bath. After a light lunch, just enough so that I don't feel
I'm fasting all day, I stay at home and take my ease. This is the life
of those free from the worries and burdens of public ambition.
I console myself that in this way I will live a happier life                      130
than if my father, uncle, and grandfather had been senators.


## The Pest (*Satires* 1.9)

The other day I was walking along the Sacred Way and turning over
in my mind, as I often do, some poetic trifle. I'm totally absorbed,
when a man whose name I barely know comes up to me, grabs
my hand, and says, "How are you, my dearest friend?" "Just fine,
at the moment," I reply. "Have a nice day." He keeps following me;
so I stop and say first, "Is there something I can do for you?"
"You should get to know me," he urges. "I'm a literary man."
"Well, that's great," I said.
                    Painfully eager to get away,

I walked more quickly, then stopped at random and whispered
something to my slave, all the while beginning to sweat profusely.                    10
"O Bolanus," I thought to myself, "if only I had your surly temper!"
Meanwhile my pesky friend was nattering on about anything and everything,
saying how much he liked the city, its various neighborhoods.
When I made no reply he said, "You're very anxious to get away.
I realized that a while ago. But it's no use: I'm not letting you go.
Wherever you're off to, I'll just tag along." "No need," I say,
"to go out of your way. I want to visit a friend—no one
you know. He's, uh, sick, bedridden. It's a long way across the Tiber,
close to Caesar's gardens." "No problem," he said. "I've got time, and
I'm not lazy; let's go."

        I droop my ears, like an uncooperative ass                    20
taking too great a load. Then he launches into his monologue:
"Yes siree, you're going to like having me around, as much as Viscus
and Varius. I'm the fastest poet in town, and the most prolific.
And you can't find a better dancer. The songs I sing, why, even
Hermogenes would be jealous." I saw my chance to interrupt:
"So, do you have parents or friends who depend on you, need you healthy?"
"Not one, I'm sorry to say: I've laid them all to rest." Lucky bastards,
I'm thinking. And I'm the next victim. Finish me off, and fulfill
the grim prophecy that once upon a time an old country witch
delivered to me in my youth, with a shake of her divining urn:                    30
"This boy will be destroyed not by dreadful poison, nor enemy sword;
no lung infection, no hacking consumption, no crippling gout
will do him in. No, someday a chatterbox will be the death of him.
When he's grown up, let him be wise and avoid all such characters."
By now we had come to the temple of Vesta, and it was about
the fourth hour, the time, it happened, when he was supposed to be
in court: non-appearance would mean losing his suit. "Please," he begged,
"come along in support. It will be quick, I promise." "Totally impossible.
I'm too beat to stand, and I know nothing of civil procedure. Plus,
I've got a date, as you know." "I can't decide what to do," he frets.                    40
"Should I quit the case, or you?" "Me, me, please!" "I won't," he says,
and leads me forward. I follow, as it's hard for a beaten man to fight.
Now he starts in again:

        "So, you and Maecenas are pretty close, eh?
A gentleman of rare quality, he is, and of very sound judgment.
No one else uses his wealth for better purposes. If only you'd introduce
yours truly to him, I'd be a big help, you know—your wing-man,
so to speak. With me on your side, you'll beat all your rivals."
"Life there is not what you think," I assured him. "No circle is more
honest, none more free from back-stabbing. It's no hindrance to me                    50
if another is richer or more learned: each of us has his proper place."
"It's amazing what you say, scarcely believable," he gasped. "And yet
that's how it is," I replied. "You are firing me up with even more desire

to get close to him." "You have only to wish it. With merit like yours,
you will take him by storm: but mark, he knows he can be captured,
so he guards his outposts well." "Ok, ok. I won't let myself down.
I'll bribe his slaves. If I'm turned away today, I'll keep coming back.
I'll bide my time, make sure I 'accidentally' run into him on the street
and escort him to the Forum. As the saying goes, nothing good in life comes
without great toil."

       In the midst of this patter we saw Aristius Fuscus,      60
a good friend of mine, who knows exactly what this fellow is like.
"So, where have you been, and where are you off to?" he asks,
and answers the same questions. Meanwhile, I begin to pull at
his toga, and pinch his evidently insensible arms, nodding,
twisting my eyes in an effort to get him to save me. That evil
son of a bitch just smiled, pretending not to notice. "Aristius," I say,
boiling with fury, "weren't you just saying you needed to talk to me
about something, privately?" "Ah yes, I remember, but I'll tell you
at some better time. Today's, uh, thirtieth Sabbath. Wouldn't want
to fart in the faces of the snipped-off Jews, would we? "No, really,      70
I'm not orthodox." "But it's a problem for me. I'm a bit superstitious,
like most people, I suppose. You'll forgive me. I'll talk to you
some other time."

       Oh, what a black day! That rat scurries off and leaves
me under the sacrificial knife. At this point the opponent in the court
case shows up, yelling, "Hey! Where are you going, you scoundrel!"
then looks at me: "Will you be my witness?" I readily present
my ear.[19] He hurries him to court: there's shouting on both sides,
and a confused melee. And that's how, at last, Apollo rescued me.

---

## Introduction to *Odes*

In 23 BC Horace published three books of *Odes* (Latin title *Carmina*, "songs"), with a total of eighty-eight lyric poems; a fourth book with fifteen songs was published later, at the urging of Augustus, around 15 BC. The *Odes* would come to be seen as his crowning achievement, and indeed one of the glories of all European poetry. They draw on early Greek poetic models such as the lyric poems of Alcaeus and Sappho, adapting their metrical forms to Latin poetry with unparalleled elegance and economy.

Elsewhere (*Ars Poetica* 83–85), Horace defines the conventional themes of lyric poetry as follows: hymns and songs of praise to the gods and heroes, songs of praise for victors in athletic and other contests, erotic and sympotic ("banquet") poetry. In the *Odes* we find also songs of mourning, tributes to the ruler (Augustus) and his house, conversations with friends of different ranks, reflections and moral exhortations,

---

19. Touching one's ear was a traditional gesture used to remind someone about an obligation (see Seneca, *The Ascension of Claudius* ch. 9); hence it became the way to engage a witness.

thoughts on the transience of life and encouragement to enjoy it, and calls to moderation by pursuing the true "golden" mean. Private and political poems sit side by side in a way rather different from modern poetry books. On political themes the "Cleopatra Ode" (1.37) is notable, as are the so-called "Roman odes" (3.1–6), where the poet turns to his people and calls the young to the traditional values of the state, which he later summarizes as "good faith, peace, honor, modesty, and courage" (*Carmen Saeculare* 57–58).

## *Odes*

### To Maecenas[20] (*Odes* 1.1)

Maecenas, descendant of ancient kings,
my sweet glory and protector,
some men delight in Olympic dust
caked on their chariot as they round
the turning post on hissing wheels,
and in the palm of victory that lifts them up
among the gods who are masters of this earth.
Another rejoices if the fickle mob of voters
seeks to elevate him to triple honors.[21]
Another man smiles if his silo contains                                    10
the product of all Libya's threshing floors.
The one who loves to wield a hoe
on his ancestral plot of ground,
you'd never make a sailor—
not for the royal fortune of the Attalids—
and persuade him to cut the Myrtoan sea,
trembling in a Cypriot ship. The merchant,
his heart pounding as the south winds wrestle
the Icarian waves, praises the quiet life
in a country house; but soon enough
he rebuilds his battered ship, so unable
is he to endure an honest poverty.
Some favor goblets of old Massic wine
and are quite happy to shorten a solid                                     20
workday, lounging beneath a green
arbutus tree or at the gentle headwaters

---

20. A close associate of the Emperor Augustus, and Horace's friend, sponsor, and patron, who figures in all of the *Satires* above.

21. That is, the offices of aedile, praetor, and consul.

of a sacred spring. Many men love army life,
the battle-trumpet's clarion, and war,
hateful to mothers. Take the huntsman:
if a stag is seen by his trusty dogs, or if
a Marsian boar breaks through the nets,
he sleeps under Jupiter's cold stars,
thinking not of his tender wife at home.
Me? The ivy crown, prize for learned brows,                    30
exalts me to a spot among the gods.
The chorus of light-footed nymphs and satyrs
takes me away from the crowd, as long as
Euterpe lends me her pipes, and Polyhymnia
keeps loaning me the lyre that played on Lesbos.[22]
Maecenas, count me among the lyric
poets, and my head will touch the stars.

## To Augustus (*Odes* 1.2)

Enough. Father Jupiter has sent snows
and dreadful hail, and terrified the earth,
striking our sacred Capitoline with his
     lightning right hand.

He has terrified the people: they dread the
return of the Age of Pyrrha,[23] who bewailed
strange prodigies when Proteus drove his herd
     to high mountains,

when schools of fish got stuck, stranded in the
elm's lofty branches (before then the familiar                  10
seat of doves), when frightened does swam
     in overwhelming flood.

We have seen the sandy Tiber's waters turn
violent, overflowing the Etruscan bank, advancing
to demolish the monuments of Roman kings
     and Vesta's temple,

---

22. Euterpe ("Giver of Joy") was one of the nine Muses, whose specialty was flute-playing; Polyhymnia ("Of Many Songs") was a Muse of various responsibilities, here understood as one who immortalizes great matters with great songs. The Greek island of Lesbos was famous for its lyric poets, including Sappho (ca. 600 BC) and Alcaeus (born ca. 625 BC), two of Horace's models.

23. Pyrrha and her husband Deucalion were the sole human survivors of a massive flood sent by Jupiter in anger at human wickedness.

and now the River boasts of taking vengeance
for Ilia (who complains "it's too much"), and spills over
its left bank widely, though Jupiter disapproves,
    a river concerned for his wife.[24]                              20

Tomorrow's generations, thinned by the crimes
of their parents, will hear of these battles,[25] will hear
of swords, better used to slay formidable Parthians,
    sharpened against citizens.

To what god will people turn to restore
the fortunes of their crumbling empire?
What prayer will the holy Virgins offer to Vesta,
    now deaf to their litanies?

To whom will Jupiter give the solemn task
of expiating the crime? Prophetic Apollo!                            30
Come at last, we pray, your gleaming shoulders
    shrouded in mist.

Or you come, if you prefer, Venus, smiling lady
of Eryx, attended by flitting Mirth and Cupid.
Or perhaps Mars, author of our line, *you* care for
    your neglected progeny,

and are sated with our warrior games gone on,
alas, far too long—you who love war shouts,
smooth helmets, and the Marsic soldier's battle lust
    as he faces the bloody foe.                                      40

Or could it be that you, Mercury, winged son
of nourishing Maia, have transformed, and now
a young man, allow yourself to be called
    Caesar's Avenger?[26]

Delay your return to heaven, and be glad to dwell
a long time among the people of Quirinus.

---

24. There was flooding in Rome shortly after Julius Caesar's assassination. This was interpreted by some as supernatural punishment for that act, as well as a vendetta by Ilia (= Rhea Silvia), mother of Romulus and Remus (and by extension of all Romans). After the birth of her children Ilia was thrown into the Tiber as punishment for breaking her vows as a Vestal Virgin. Her "husband" Tiber now takes vengeance on her behalf by flooding the city.

25. The civil wars in the decade after Julius Caesar's assassination.

26. Horace imagines Mercury come to earth as a savior in the guise of Octavian/Augustus, avenging the murder of his adoptive father, Julius Caesar. Octavian rose to power as Caesar's heir and avenger.

Do not fly away breeze-quick in displeasure
     at our vices.

Rather stay and enjoy great triumphs, delight
at being called "father" and "first citizen";                                    50
Be our general, Caesar. Do not allow the Parthians
     to ride on with impunity.


## To Vergil (*Odes* 1.3)

Look here, ship, Vergil's been entrusted
     to you, and you owe me his return.[27] I ask you,
ferry this man—half my soul—
     safely on to Attica. Do so, and I will pray that the gods
guide you well: Venus, mighty
     goddess of Cyprus, and Helen's brothers
who guard over sailors and gleam
     at their masts, and Aeolus, father of winds.
May he restrain all his gusts,
     save only those of south Italian Iapyx.                                      10
That reckless man who first set
     flimsy raft on ferocious sea had a heart
made of oak and three-fold brass.
     He had no fear: not of the swooping
squalls of Africus that collide
     and wrestle with the northerly Aquilones;
not of the grim Hyades, harbingers
     of storm; nor of Notus, the Adriatic's most
formidable tyrant, who heaves
     or calms the waters according to his whim.[28]                              20
Indifferent to death's approach
     he was, gazing with tearless eyes at swimming
monsters, the roiling sea,
     and the notorious rocks of Acroceraunia.
Some god in his wisdom parted
     the lands with dividing ocean—but in vain,
if impious ships still skip across
     water that ought not to be touched.
The human race is bold enough
     for anything: it barges ahead to the forbidden,                             30
as Iapetus' son Prometheus brought

---

27. A "bon voyage" poem (*propempticon*) for Vergil, who is about to sail to Greece.

28. The references are to unpredictable winds that make navigation in the Adriatic Sea between Italy and Greece hazardous. The Hyades are a part of the constellation Taurus, which was thought to indicate rain at certain times of year.

fire to the peoples of earth with wicked deceit.
After the theft of fire from heaven,
   a new troop of fevers fell upon the land. Death's
Necessity, once remote, slow-moving,
   picked up her pace. Daedalus took to the empty
sky with wings not granted to man;
   Hercules broke into and escaped from hell.
No challenge is too steep for mortals.
   We seek to scale heaven itself in our foolishness,                    40
and our crimes do not permit
   Jupiter to put aside his thunderbolts of fury.


## To Sestius (*Odes* 1.4)

Now winter's bitter grip loosens, yielding to spring's warming Zephyrs.
   Now the ships' dry keels are winched down to shore.
Flocks no longer cling to their stables, nor the ploughman to his hearth.
   Fields no longer grow white with glistening frost.
Now Venus of Cythera leads her dances beneath the overhanging moon;
   the lovely Graces join hands with the nymphs,
exchange steps, feet slapping the earth, while fiery Vulcan tends
   the toilsome workshops of the Cyclopes.
Now is the time to place upon your glistening head green myrtle
   wreaths, or the flowers that the loosening earth now bears.            10
Now is the proper time to make sacrifice to Faunus—a lamb
   if he so demands, or a kid should he prefer.
Pale Death kicks at the door of the poor man's shack no less than
   the king's tower. O, dear fortunate Sestius,
the tiny span of our life rules out all long-term hopes. Soon night
   will overwhelm you; the fabled hoards of dead souls
await, and the meager house of Pluton. No casting knuckle-bones there
   to decide who presides over a drinking party,
no Lycidas to behold in wonder—he now fires the passions
   of all men, and soon will make the girls grow warm.                   20


## To Lydia (*Odes* 1.8)

   Lydia, enlighten me please,
and by all the gods be honest. Why must you rush to ruin Sybaris
   with your love? Why does he keep away
from the bright light of the Campus?[29] He used to quite like
   dust and sun. Why isn't he riding
with his age-mates in military array, or guiding Gallic horses

---

29. The Campus Martius ("Field of Mars") in Rome was a favorite spot for exercise and military training on horseback.

with a spikey bit? Why is he afraid
to touch Tiber's pale waters? Why does he avoid an oil
    rubdown as if it were snake's venom?
Why do his shoulders no longer show bruises from armor?                    10
    This in a man so often admired
for his surpassing discus and javelin throws. Why does he hide,
    like the sea-nymph Thetis' son did,
they say, in the face of the tear-stained killing fields of Troy,
    afraid that a man's clothing would get him
snatched off to face the armies of Lycia and the carnage of war?[30]


## To Thaliarchus (*Odes* 1.9)

You see Soracte there, how it stands, gleaming,
capped deep in snow?[31] How the forest trees bend
    beneath the weight, how rivers
        freeze in the needling cold?

Banish the chill, Thaliarchus. More wood
on the fire, load it on, and pour (be generous!)
    that four-year-old vintage,
        from its Sabine jar.

As to the world outside, leave it to the gods,
who can still the clashing winds on a roiling sea,                          10
    so not a single cypress
        or ancient ash tree stirs.

What will tomorrow bring? Do not even ask.
Every day that Fortune provides should be
    put down to profit. While you're young
        and green, before your head is grey

and dour, join the dance, don't turn down sweet love.
Now is the time for a date on the Campus
    or some city square, for soft whispers
        in the evening, for the lovely laugh                                20

that reveals the hiding spot of the girl you've
been chasing, for the bracelet or ring, a pledge
    of love, that you take from
        a quite un-stubborn finger.

---

30. Because Achilles was predestined to die at Troy, his mother Thetis disguised him as a girl at
the court of Lycomedes on the island of Scyros.

31. Monte Soratte, 2,400 feet high, about forty miles north of Rome.

## To Leuconoe (*Odes* 1.11)

Leuconoe, do not ask the stars to tell what end the gods
have allotted to you, or to me. This knowledge is forbidden.
Attempt no Babylonian calculations.[32] Better simply to endure
whatever will be. Whether Jupiter affords us many more winters,
or if the one now smashing the Etruscan sea on rocky shore is our last,
be wise: strain the lees and drink your wine, and prune your
long-range hopes back to a brief compass. Mean-spirited time
flees as we talk. Seize the day. Place no trust in tomorrow.

## The Fall of Cleopatra (*Odes* 1.37)

Now, friends, is the time to drink, now is the time
to dance with abandon, to set banquets worthy
    of the Salian priests before
        the festal couches of the gods.

Before this it was unthinkable to bring out
the Caecuban wine from ancient cellars
    while the demented queen was planning ruin
        for the Capitol, doom for the Empire—

she with her corrupt retinue of foul, perverted
eunuchs—wild with extravagant hope, drunk                    10
    on good fortune's sweetness.
        But her frenzy was checked

when she barely escaped the fires with a single ship.[33]
Caesar pursued from Italy under oars as she fled,
    and brought her mind, giddy
        on Egyptian wine,

into well-justified fear. He followed (as a hawk chases
soft doves, or as a swift hunter pursues the hare

---

32. Astrology, a field of knowledge derived ultimately from the Babylonians, was respected by many educated Romans, including some emperors, as a scientific, if fallible, method of predicting the future. It also had its critics. One of the most common reasons for consulting an astrologer was to ascertain the date of a person's death—one's own, a family member's, or a lover's. Augustus forbade the consultation of astrologers about death, but at the same time he published his own horoscope.

33. At the battle of Actium off northwestern Greece in 31 BC. Cleopatra and Marcus Antonius (the main opponent, despite being unmentioned here) escaped with about sixty ships and fled to Egypt. The battle marks the unofficial beginning of Octavian's reign as Rome's first emperor (named "Caesar" here).

in the fields of snowy Thessaly),
    trying to put chains upon                        20

that deadly monster. But she preferred a nobler death—
no womanish fear of the sword, no hurried flight
    to secret shores. She dared to look
        with serene composure

upon her royal city, lying in ruins, and steeled herself
to handle scaly serpents, to drink black venom in her flesh,
    still more defiant in the face of death.
        Doubtless she wished

to deprive the swift Roman galleys of the chance
to lead her back, stripped of rank, and to adorn          30
    the haughty triumphal procession[34]—
        no humble woman to the last.

## The Meaning of *Virtus* (*Odes* 3.2)

Boys should grow tough in harsh military service,
and learn to treat its strict privations like a friend.
    The cavalryman with his terrifying
        lance should harass the fierce Parthians,

and live a life of danger outdoors. When the warlike
tyrant's wife, and his grown daughter, too,
    gaze upon our soldier from enemy walls
        let them sigh, afraid that

her royal bridegroom, new to combat, will rashly
attack the young lion, whom it is perilous to touch,    10
    since raging bloodlust drives him
        through the midst of the slaughter.

Sweet and honorable it is to die for one's native land.
Death hunts down the man who runs away, too.
    Death does not spare the retreating back
        or hamstrings of a young coward.

Valor cares not about defeat at the polls, but shines
in untarnished honors. It does not pick up or put down
    the axes, emblems of office,
        at the whims of the popular breeze.    20

---

34. See "triumph" in the Glossary.

Valor opens heaven to those who deserve
not to die. It attempts to travel the impossible
    path, and with soaring wings spurns
        vulgar company and the dank earth.

Faithful silence, too, has its reward. A man who
divulges the secret rites of Ceres, I will not
    have him under my roof, nor will I
        let him sail in a fragile boat with me.[35]

Many a time Jupiter, when neglected, has included
the innocent with the guilty. The wicked man                    30
    advances, but Punishment, though lame of foot,
        has rarely let him escape.

## A Plea to the Romans (*Odes* 3.6)

Citizen of Rome, though innocent you will pay
for your ancestors' crimes, till you repair the temples,
    the crumbling shrines of the gods,
        cult images fouled with black smoke.

You rule because you hold yourselves inferior
to the gods. Make *this* the beginning and end
    of every enterprise. Neglected, the gods
        have given Italy many reasons to grieve.

Twice now Monaeses and the army of Pacorus
have crushed our attacks, made without proper                    10
    auspices, and they grin with joy to add
        plunder from us to their worthless

torques.[36] Preoccupied by civil strife, Rome
was nearly destroyed by the Dacian—superior
    thanks to his volleys of arrows—and the
        Ethiopian—formidable due to his fleet.[37]

---

35. Ceres (Greek Demeter) was worshipped along with her daughter at Eleusis. Participants had to be initiated into the rites and were sworn to secrecy about the rituals.

36. Stiff, honorary neckbands worn by Parthian (and Celtic) nobles and soldiers.

37. The Parthian general Pacorus attacked and defeated the Roman garrison in Syria under Antonius' general L. Decidius Saxa. Monaeses was probably in command of the Parthian forces that routed Antonius' invasion in 36 BC, during which Antonius lost two whole legions. Horace suggests it was due to Antonius not being duly constituted as augur and thus improperly campaigning without consulting the gods by taking the auspices (see Valerius Maximus, section B in this volume). The Dacians, tribesmen from what is now Romania, fought on Antonius' side

Generations prolific in sin first polluted their
marriages, lineage, and homes. From this
   fountainhead the disaster flowed out across
      the country and its people.                     20

The grown girl delights to learn sensual Greek
dances. Her wiles are learned early on,
   and with deep relish she plans
      out her obscene love affairs.

Later she seeks younger lovers at her husband's
drinking parties. She doesn't pick a man to give
   quick and forbidden pleasures in secret,
      when the lamps are extinguished—

no, asked quite openly she gets up before
her fully complicit husband, if perchance some         30
   peddler or Spanish sea captain
      pays enough to buy her shame.

These were not the parents who bore the men
who dyed the sea with Punic blood, and cut down
   Pyrrhus, mighty Antiochus,
      and the dreaded Hannibal.[38]

It was a manly breed of country soldiers,
taught to turn the earth with Sabine mattocks,
   to cut and carry wood at their
      stern mother's command                  40

when the sun was lengthening the mountain
shadows and taking the yokes off tired oxen,
   receding on its chariot, bringing
      the longed-for hour of rest.

What has injurious time failed to degrade?
Our parents' generation, worse than their own parents',
   brought forth us, even more worthless,
      and our children will be baser still.

---

in the Roman civil wars, as did the Egyptians (under Cleopatra), here called "Ethopians" for
derogatory rhetorical effect.

38. Allusions to great victories of the mid-Republic that secured Rome's Mediterranean-wide
empire: that over Pyrrhus, king of Epirus in northwest Greece in 275 BC; over Antiochus the
Great, king of the Seleucid empire centered in Babylonia, who was defeated by the Romans in
191 BC after he invaded Greece; and over Hannibal, the great Carthaginian (Punic) general
whose defeat at Zama in 202 BC resulted in the capitulation of Carthage.

## Poetic Immortality (*Odes* 3.30)

I've finished it, a monument more lasting than
bronze, higher than the royal seat of the pyramids,
one that cannot be eroded by biting rain,
by the winds' wild rage, nor by the passing
of countless years in time's headlong flight.
I will not entirely die, and a great part of me will
escape Libitina.[39] I will grow, always fresh with
posthumous glory, as long as the Great Priest scales
the Capitoline in the company of the silent Vestal.
I will be spoken of where the rushing river                    10
Aufidus clamors, and where Daunus, poor in water,
rules over his country people.[40] They will say that,
rising high from humble origins, I was the first
to spin Aeolian poetry into Italian rhythms.
Melpomene, enjoy a pride won by my merits,
and willingly wreathe my head in Delphic laurel.[41]

---

39. Goddess of death.

40. References to a remote rural region in the south of Italy, Horace's homeland. The Aufidus (modern Ofanto) is a river near Venusia and the farm where he grew up. Daunus, a Greek from Illyria, was the legendary founder of Daunia, the northern part of Apulia.

41. Melpomene ("She Who Sings") was one of the nine Muses, and for Horace the most exalted, the inspirer of lyric poetry. Victors in the athletic and artistic competitions at Delphi received a wreath of laurel.

# JUVENAL

(1st–2nd centuries AD, wrote in Latin)

## Introduction

Decimus Iunius Iuvenalis came from Aquinum in Campania, and was active as a satirist primarily in the reigns of Trajan (AD 98–117) and Hadrian (AD 117–138). Like his friend Martial, Juvenal lived in Rome as a literary associate to wealthy friends and patrons, a frequently demeaning social situation that provides much of the grist for his mill. His sixteen surviving satires are characterized by a sometimes white-hot indignation at various perceived social ills and at the hypocrisy of contemporary Roman society, especially among the upper class. Below we offer translations of two of his most famous poems (*Satires* 1 and 3).

Juvenal's favorite targets include bad mythological poetry (which, along with the vice that surrounded him everywhere, drove him to write), sexual immorality, the flamboyant display of newly acquired or ill-gotten wealth, the selfishness of patrons and their humiliation of clients, vicious informers, the wasting of inherited wealth, greed, and conspicuous consumption. *Satire* 3 is a famous indictment of life in the city of Rome, put in the mouth of a friend, the disgusted Umbricius, who is about to leave Rome and move to a small town. Juvenal contrasts the morally healthy life of the country with the corruption of the city, and the decadence of contemporary morals with the sturdy uprightness of the Romans of old times (those discussed, for instance, in Plutarch's *Life of Cato* in this volume).

Juvenal's persona as a ranting client is not dissimilar to that of Martial, but angrier and more hyperbolic. For his free-wheeling freedom of speech he cites as a precedent Lucilius, a writer of the 2nd century BC, and the founder of the Roman genre of satire (*satura*). But times had changed a great deal since the days of Lucilius, and Juvenal justifiably felt, as he explains in *Satire* 1, that to attack prominent living persons as Lucilius had done would be hazardous to his life. Instead he satirized social types and figures from relatively recent history (in particular the hated Emperor Domitian), and probably relied on contemporaries to fill in the corresponding names from their own times.

## Satires

### Why I Write (*Satires* 1)

Forever trapped in the audience? Shall I never fight back?
The torment, having to listen to Codrus recite himself hoarse
on his *Epic of Theseus*! I need payback for so-and-so's
toga plays,[1] and the other guy's elegies, for the days that I
squandered on what's-his-name's endless *Telephus* play, and *Orestes*—
the script jammed every square inch of papyrus, spilled over the back,
and still wasn't done. No man knows his own house as I know
the grove of Mars, and Vulcan's cave near the craggy island of Aeolus.[2]
What are the winds up to? Which poor bastards is Aeacus torturing
in hell? Where did some other guy steal his fleece of gold?                    10
Just how big were the ash-trees hurled by Monychus the centaur?
The boom of continuous high-volume recitation on such topics
rattles Fronto's plane-trees, topples his statues, and brings his columns
crashing down. It's the same from all poets, the great and the small.
Well, I too went to school and had my hand whacked. I too composed
"Advice to Sulla," urging him to lay down power and sleep in peace.[3]
When a poet lurks on every corner, it's misguided mercy
to spare paper that's destined for destruction in any case.
But why choose this particular field of play, this track once driven
by Aurunca's favorite poetic son?[4] If you've the time and inclination        20
to hear the thoughts of a reasonable man, I shall explain.
A soft eunuch takes a wife. Mevia impales a Tuscan boar and,
breasts exposed, grasps the hunting-spears.[5] A single man,
a former *barber* who cut my youthful beard, now challenges
the whole class of patricians in wealth. Crispinus! That member of
the Nile's rabble, that native born slave of Egyptian Canopus,
now sports Tyrian purple cloaks and fans the summer heat
with a gold ring[6] on his sweaty fingers, its gem nearly
more than he can lift. With all this, it's hard *not* to write satire.

---

1. Comedies in Roman dress (as opposed to those adapted from the Greek); none have survived.

2. (Overly) elaborate descriptions had become a literary commonplace by the early empire.

3. An example of the kind of (highly artificial) model speech assigned by rhetoric teachers (see Quintilian H in this volume). Juvenal claims this education as qualification to become a poet. Sulla, in fact, did retire to Campania after taking Rome by force and reshaping the constitution (see Appian A ch. 3 in this volume).

4. Lucilius, founder of Roman satire.

5. Evidently a woman of good family who participated in beast hunts in the arena. A number of emperors and senatorial decrees tried (mostly in vain) to prevent members of the equestrian and senatorial orders from demeaning themselves by appearing for pay as gladiators and beast hunters.

6. A sign of equestrian status.

Who is so tolerant of this outrageous city, so steeled to injustice,                30
that he can contain his bile when the new litter of Matho
the lawyer glides by, his girth spilling over the sides,
followed by the one who informed on his own prominent patron,
and plans now to gobble up what's left of the old nobility.[7]
Even Massa fears *him*, and Carus placates *him* with gifts;
Thymele approaches *him* on behalf of terrified Latinus.[8]
Men elbow you out of the way who earn their massive fortunes
by night, men exalted to the sky by what is now the best way
to make it big: sex with some rich old lady. Proculeius got a twelfth
of her estate, but Gillo got eleven-twelfths—each inherited                40
in proportion to his crotch's endowment. Fine! I suppose they earned
the reward for their . . . um . . . exertions, going pale as a man
who has stepped on a snake, or stepped up to speak at the altar of Lyons.[9]
Why even mention the fiery rage that parches my liver
when I see a man who took the property of his prostituted ward[10]
strutting down the street with his massive entourage of clients;
and this other man, condemned on a trumped-up charge.
Legal disgrace? Who cares, if you get to keep the ill-gotten cash?
Marius?[11] The man starts drinking in exile at 2:00 each day
in the face of the angry gods, while you, his victorious province,                50
are left to weep. Aren't these events worthy of Horace's satiric verse?
Shouldn't I assail these outrages? Or should I write about . . . oh . . .
Hercules instead, or Diomedes, or things that go moo in the labyrinth,
or the flying carpenter, how his boy struck the sea?[12]
But here's the husband-pimp, a skilled ceiling-gazer, good at
"passing out" next to a wine cup with a wakeful snore,
and raking in the goods of his wife's lovers (if she can't legally
take them herself).[13] Look at that boy charioteer as he flies down
the Flaminian way in his swift rig. His ancestors were rich,
but he's spent it all on the stables. And now he thinks he has the right                60

---

7. Informers were common in the 1st century AD under certain emperors. They stood to receive one-quarter of the property of anyone condemned on their information.

8. Latinus was a famous actor and may have been part of the Emperor Domitian's private council. Thymele was his leading lady.

9. A reference to the whippings, water torture, and other punishments suffered by the losers in Caligula's oratory contests held at Lyons (Lugdunum).

10. The motif of the crooked guardian was common in Roman satire. The ward is forced into prostitution by poverty.

11. Marius Priscus, the corrupt governor of Africa. For an account of his trial see Pliny, *Letters* 2.11 in this volume.

12. Daedalus, who built the labyrinth on Crete to house the Minotaur (half-man, half-bull), also built wings for himself and his son to escape imprisonment. His son flew too close to the sun and fell to his death.

13. The woman's husband is encouraging his wife to have affairs with rich men and stands to benefit (why the wife is unable to receive their property is unclear).

to hope for a post in charge of a cohort? Please. He was holding
the reins himself, posing to impress his girlfriend in her fashionably
mannish cloak. Don't you just want to stand in the crossroads
and write it all down in spacious wax tablets, when you see
that forger carried around on the necks of six litter-bearers (six!),
flaunting himself on that womanish armchair, both sides open,
like some languid Maecenas.[14] He's made himself sleek and rich
with short documents sealed with a kiss on his damp seal ring.
And here comes the grand matron who mixes mellow wine
with toad's poison and hands it to her thirsty husband.                    70
This new and improved Locusta[15] instructs her naive neighbors
on the art of carrying their husbands out feet first, black with poison,
never mind what people say. Want to be somebody? Commit a crime
worthy of prison, or exile to tiny Gyara island. Honesty? She's praised,
but left in the cold. Crime's what got them their gardens, palaces,
costly tables, antique silver dishes, goblets with goats in relief.
Who can sleep, thinking of the man who seduced his own
daughter-in-law, a girl greedy for gold, or the wicked brides,
or the teenaged adulterer? If my talent fails, my verse—such as it is,
or such as Cluvienus would write—will come from sheer indignation.     80
I begin from the beginning of time, when Deucalion braved the flood to climb
a mountain in a ship and consulted the oracle there, when the stones
gradually grew warm and soft with life, and Pyrrha showed naked girls
to men:[16] my book will be a mishmash of whatever men do, their hopes,
fears, anger, pleasure, joys, their scurryings back and forth.
And when has the world ever offered us a richer store of vice?
When has the pocket of greed gaped wider? When has gambling
ever been such the rage? People approach the hazards of the gaming-table,
not with their wallets, not anymore: now they bring their entire
fortunes in a strong-box. Oh, what battles transpire there, each man     90
with a bodyguard—his treasurer! Is it not plain lunacy
to squander a hundred thousand sesterces in this way, and yet
deny a tunic to a shivering slave? Who among our honest ancestors
erected so many villas as we see today? Which among them dined on
seven courses, all alone? Nowadays the crowd of toga-wearing clients
must furtively snatch the little dole that sits on the threshold
of the patron's house,[17] as he uneasily examines your face, afraid you
might be coming to ask for a handout under false pretenses.

---

14. Famous patron of the arts and friend of the Emperor Augustus. He was criticized for his effeminacy.

15. A famous poisoner from the mid-1st century AD.

16. Deucalion (the Greek equivalent of Noah) survived the primeval flood with his wife Pyrrha. They landed on Mt. Parnassus, home of the Delphic oracle, which instructed them to create a new race of people by throwing over their shoulders rocks that became endowed with life.

17. See Glossary, *sportula*.

You only get it when your identity has been verified. He orders clients
to be announced by a herald, first the very blue-blooded men                          100
of Trojan descent—for even they besiege the threshold along with us.
"Serve the praetor first, then the tribune!" But a freedman stands
in front of you: "I got here first," he says. "Why should I be afraid,
or hesitate to defend my place in line, just because I was born
on the Euphrates (even if I don't admit it—see the tell-tale effeminate
earring holes)? But I own five shops, and they provide four hundred
thousand sesterces.[18] Who needs the *latus clavus*? Corvinus
watches over rented sheep in the lands around Laurentum, but I
have more wealth than Pallas or Licinus!"[19] So let the tribunes wait,
let riches rule, let a man who only recently entered this city                          110
with chalk on his feet[20] take precedence over this sacred official.
The fact is, among us the most sacred and revered power of all
has long been that of Cash—even if destructive Money does not yet
have her own temple, and we have yet to erect altars to Coin,
as we worship Faith, Victory, Virtue, and Concord, the one
whose shrine twitters when the nest of her sacred birds is saluted.
It makes no difference at the end of the year in the account books
of a consul, whether he receives the dole or not. But what of
the clients, who must use it to buy a toga, shoes, daily bread,
and cooking fuel at home? A dense crowd of litters comes in search                      120
of a measly hundred *quadrantes*,[21] including sick or pregnant wives
brought along for sympathy. Or sometimes a man cleverly seeks extra
for a missing wife by pointing to a closed and empty sedan chair
that ostensibly holds her within—a well-known trick.
"That's my Galla," he says. "Quick, hand it over. What's the problem?
Galla, stick out your head, dear! Oh, don't trouble her; she's resting."
These are the days of our lives, and what a lovely routine:
first the dole, then the Forum, and Apollo the legal expert,[22]
then off to the place of triumphal statues, where
some Egyptian magnate has dared to insert his inscriptions.                             130
Pissing on his statue would be a good start.[23] Finally the clients, old

---

18. A hefty sum, equivalent to the property qualification for equestrian status.

19. The *latus clavus* (see Glossary) was a sign of senatorial status; Corvinus is a noble who is so
down on his luck that he has no land of his own, but manages a flock of rented sheep; Pallas and
Licinus were famously wealthy freedmen of the Emperors Claudius and Augustus respectively.

20. Foreign slaves were put up for sale with chalk on their feet, to distinguish them from locally
born slaves.

21. A modest sum; a *quadrans* was the smallest copper coin, worth one-quarter of an *as*. The
actual sum of the hand-out by patrons no doubt varied, but Juvenal makes it sound pathetically
small.

22. The Forum of Augustus, where court cases were judged, featured a statue of Apollo.

23. Probably a reference to Tiberius Julius Alexander, a Jew who became Prefect of Egypt in AD
66–70.

and weary, abandon the thresholds and their desires, though mankind's
longest-lasting hope is for a dinner invitation. The poor guys
must buy their own cabbage and fire. Meanwhile, King Patron
will devour the choicest products of sea and forest, reclining
in splendid isolation, alone on his couch. These men consume whole
family fortunes at a single table, chosen from their extensive
collections of lovely antiques. Soon the parasite will disappear.[24]
Who can endure such tight-fisted extravagance? How big is the gullet
that serves an entire boar to itself, an animal designed for banquets?          140
But retribution is at hand. You'll strip down and enter the bath
with undigested peacock in your bloated paunch. Then, wham!
Your unforeseen demise, an old man without a valid will; the story
will fly through all the dinner parties, and no one will shed a tear.
Your pissed-off clients will greet your funeral cortege with applause.
Men of the future will have nothing to add to our rotten ways.
Our descendants will crave and act exactly the same;
all vice has reached its acme. So . . . I'll spread my sails
and full speed ahead! Yet perhaps at this point someone might
object, "Where will you find the talent to match your theme?          150
And where will you find the . . . the . . . guts to write, as your
predecessors did, whatever your blazing mind desires?"
I'm not afraid of naming names. Who cares if Mucius
forgives my words, or not?[25] "Go ahead! Attack Tigellinus:[26]
You'll light up the night, a living torch where men stand and burn
and smoke with throats fixed on a stake; your remains will trace
a nice wide furrow across the arena." But look, what am I to do when
*that* man rides by, the one who poisoned three uncles, gazing
down upon us from the eminence of his cushioned litter?
"When he comes near, put your finger to your lips and keep mum.          160
Just say 'that's him!' and it'll be as if you'd accused him in court.
You'll have no worries if you stick to portraying the battles
of Aeneas and his fierce Rutulian foe; no one minds the death of
Achilles, or the search for Hylas who fell in after his water jug.[27]
True, whenever Lucilius roared in anger, as if with a drawn sword,
guilty listeners blushed at their own crimes, their hearts sweating

---

24. *Parasitus* is a derogatory term, an extreme version of a client who makes a profession of living off others, and was familiar as a stock figure of Roman comedy.

25. Mucius Scaevola was the target of the venom of the 2nd-century BC satirist Lucilius.

26. C. Ofonius Tigellinus was Nero's praetorian prefect in AD 62 and was an example of the kind of powerful man one should not cross. He was responsible for punishing the Christians, after they were blamed for setting the great fire of 64, by covering them with pitch, putting them on crosses, and setting them alight "as nocturnal illumination," according to Tacitus (*Annals* 15.44).

27. Examples of epic subject matter. Aeneas' Rutulian foe is Turnus. Hylas was a member of the crew of the *Argo* and the lover of Hercules, who went missing while gathering water when he was drawn into a pool by a group of water nymphs.

with silent remorse. Hence rage and tears. So think it over,
friend, long and hard, before the war trumpet sounds.
Once helmeted up, it's too late to regret going to battle."
Ok, I'll try and see what's permitted to say against those                    170
whose ashes are covered by the Flaminian and the Latin roads.[28]


## Umbricius Leaves Rome in Disgust (*Satires* 3)

My old friend is leaving. I'm upset, but good for him!
I understand why he'd decide to settle down in that ghost-town
Cumae, and give to the Sibyl there at least one fellow-citizen.
It's the gateway to Baiae, after all, a pleasant
seaside retreat. Hell, I'd even take barren Prochyta
over the Subura.[29] What land is so grim and deserted
that you'd rather be *here*, living in fear of fire,
of buildings incessantly collapsing, of the thousand perils
of the savage city, and—good lord!—poets reciting in August?
Umbricius had his entire estate loaded in one wagon.                    10
We met when he stopped at the old damp arch of the Capena gate,
where King Numa used to meet his girlfriend at night.[30]
Now, of course, the sacred spring's grove and shrine are rented
to Jews with their boxes and hay. Every tree's a place
for the people to make a profit. The forest goes begging.
The Muses? Evicted. Anyway, we headed down
to Egeria's hollow. The caves seemed so unnatural.
The sacred spring's divinity would be much more authentic
with just a border of grass, not these marble pavements
that insult the native-born tufa beneath. In this setting,                    20
Umbricius began: "A good, respectable man, I'm afraid,
can find no place for his skills in this city. No pay
for his efforts. I've got less net worth today than yesterday,
and tomorrow more will be whittled away from that small sum.
So I've decided to go away, to the place where Daedalus
doffed his weary wings.[31] I'm going while my hair
is still recently grey, while my old age is young and not yet
hunched over, while Lachesis still has something to spin,[32]

---

28. That is, the dead. Burial within the city was forbidden (see *The Twelve Tables* 10.1 in this volume); major roads were lined with the tombs of people with the means to afford them.

29. Subura was one of the busiest neighborhoods in Rome, known for shops and brothels; Prochyta was a rugged island near Cumae.

30. Numa, second king of Rome, claimed his religious institutions were inspired by meetings with the nymph Egeria. See Livy ch. 19 in this volume.

31. According to Vergil, Daedalus ended up in Cumae in southern Italy. For Daedalus, see note 12 above.

32. One of the three Fates who spun the thread of a person's life, as if spinning wool.

while I walk on my feet, and no cane supports my hand.
It's time to leave my homeland. Artorius can have it,
and Catulus—men who know how to turn black into white.          30
Easy for them to turn contractor, fixing up temples,
cleaning rivers, harbors, dredging out muck, hauling
corpses to the pyre, putting themselves up for sale.
Men who once played trumpet at municipal shows—
doing the rounds of Italian towns, puffing their cheeks—
now sponsor the shows themselves! When the mob turns
a thumb, these big shots kill for the people's amusement.[33]
Then they go back to leasing latrines. And why not?
Whenever Fortune feels like a good joke, she raises
these nobodies from insignificance to the pinnacle of success.          40
What's for me at Rome? Lying is not my strong suit.
If a book is bad, I can't say it's good and ask for a copy.
Heavenly motions are beyond my ken, so I cannot employ
astrology to forecast a father's death—nor would I want to.[34]
Divination by frog guts? Not for me. And as for carrying
adulterers' love notes to a young bride, that's someone
else's job. I won't aid a corrupt magistrate, so no one asks
me to be on his staff—it's like I'm maimed, one-handed,
physically useless. The only people valued are fellow conspirators,
accomplices whose minds seethe with awful, permanent secrets.          50
Has someone confided in you, told you an *innocent* secret?
He won't think he owes you a thing. No hush money from him.
But Verres—he'll take care of the people who could put him away
on a whim.[35] It's not worth all the gold the dark Tagus River
spews into the sea: the sleepless nights, the bribes you'll
have to give back, and being your patron's worst nightmare.
But what people are the true darlings of our Roman rich,
the same group that makes me run the other way? I'll tell you.
Greeks! There's no shame in saying it. One thing I cannot abide,
dear citizens, is a Greek Rome. But then, what percentage          60
of the bilge are authentic Achaeans? For a long time now
the Syrian Orontes River has spilled directly into the Tiber,
bringing its language and customs, its weird music
and native drums, its girls who sell themselves around
the Circus—fine for those who want a barbarous whore
tricked out in a multi-colored headscarf. Romulus,

---

33. The wealthy sponsors of gladiatorial games consulted the crowd as to whether gladiators who lost but fought well should be spared. See Martial, *Spectacles* 31 (no. 8 in this volume).

34. Compare the huckster Regulus in Pliny, *Letters* 6 in this volume, who pretends to know astrology to gain a legacy.

35. Verres was the famously corrupt governor of Sicily, prosecuted successfully by Cicero in 70 BC; here the name is used generically for any corrupt provincial governor.

your stout Roman farmers have exchanged their boots
for dainty Greek slippers. We compete, naked, for prizes
on the Greek wrestling ground. Meanwhile every Greek town—
high Sicyon, Amydon, Andros, Samos, Tralles, Alabanda—                    70
has sent its sons to the Esquiline and Viminal Hills.
And why? To gut the great houses and become our masters.
The Greek is a quick thinker, desperately bold, with a torrent
of words on his tongue. Go ahead, think of a role.
He can be whatever you want: grammarian, rhetor, geometer,
painter, seer, masseur, tightrope walker, doctor, mystic priest.
If a little Greekling is hungry for a dinner, he knows it all.
Tell him to take to the air and he'll find a way to fly.
Tell me, who was it who took to wing? A North African tribesman?
A Sarmatian nomad? No, it was a man from downtown Athens.[36]          80
Get their purple gowns away from me. Will *he* sign a document
before me, or dine in a more honored place? He was shipped
to Rome on the same wind that brings our plums and figs!
Does it count for nothing, then, that I breathed the air
of the Aventine from infancy and grew up on Sabine olives?
These Greeks, you see, are masters of flattery, brilliant
at praising the elegant speech of some illiterate patron,
the beauty of an ugly one. Are you a skinny-necked weakling?
He'll say you're like Hercules lifting Antaeus. "Bravo!"
he will say as his patron sings in a voice like a rooster
in the act of screwing his hen. We praise such things, too,                   90
but the Greeks are more believable. What actor is more
convincing as he impersonates a woman—Thais the courtesan,
or a matron, or the slave girl Doris who's removed her cloak
and gotten to work? None! When a Greek plays the part you'd think
he's no actor, that a genuine woman was speaking.
You'd swear below his waist was smooth as can be,
penis-free, just a little crack. Over in Greece,
the leading lights of the Roman stage—Antiochus, Stratocles,
Demetrius, or supple Haemus—would be nothing special.
It's a nation of actors. You laugh. He guffaws. He spots                        100
a tear on a patron's eye and weeps, without grief.
Call for a bit of fire to warm up in wintertime, and he
reaches for a heated blanket. Say you're hot, and he starts to sweat.
We can't compete. The Greek is simply *better*. He can take
his expression from another's, any time, day or night.
He's ready to throw out his hands and shout in praise
if his patron gives a good burp, manages to pee straight,
or releases a particularly golden fart. And another thing:
nothing is sacred or safe from his cock, not the matron

---

36. Daedalus.

of the house, not the virgin daughter, not even her fiancé                    110
still beardless, or even the son, hitherto unfamiliar with sex.
If none of these candidates is ready and available
he'll bed down his patron's *grandmother*. And since
I have gotten started on Greeks, forget about
what goes on at the gymnasia, and listen to a crime
of a whole different order: A Stoic killed Barea, turning
informer on his patron, a teacher victimizing his pupil.[37]
And where was this teacher reared? Tarsus, that shore where
fell the feather of the Gorgon's horse.[38] There is no place
here for any Romans at all. Some Protogenes rules, some          120
Diphilus, or Hermarchus—the sort who by a fault of the race
never shares a patron, but keeps him all to himself.
Once he has dripped in his patron's gullible ear a few drops
of the national poison, I am shooed away from the threshold,
my long servitude wasted. One fewer client—who cares?
But I go too easy on us Romans. What service, what favor
can a poor man perform here when he puts on his toga
and rushes out pre-dawn, only to see a praetor there first,
telling his lictors to hurry, since Albina and Modia,
the childless widows, are already awake. He mustn't
let his praetorian colleague pay his respects first!                         130
Look, it's a rich man's slave, escorted by the son
of freeborn parents. And there's a slave who gives
Calvina or Catiena what a legionary tribune earns,
so he can pant over her once or twice. But if *you* see a
pleasing prostitute, you pause, concerned at the expense.
Can you afford to call Chione from her lofty chair?
Choose anyone in Rome to be a witness. He may be honest,
honest as the host of Cybele,[39] and as upright as old Numa himself
or the man who saved hot Minerva from the flames.[40]
The last thing inquired of a witness is his character.                       140
The first is the size of his fortune. "How many slaves
does he feed? How much land has he got? How big is his dinner?
How many courses?" One's bank account is the measure of trust.

---

37. The Stoic professor P. Egnatius Celer in AD 66 gave evidence against his patron and pupil Barea Soranus, who had been indicted under the Emperor Nero (Tacitus, *Annals* 16.21–33). As often, Juvenal attacks vicious behavior by using a real example of a prominent person, but from well before his own time.

38. Tarsus ("feather" in Greek), a wealthy and prosperous Greek city, was located in southeast Asia Minor (modern Turkey).

39. In 204 BC, P. Cornelius Scipio Nasica was chosen, as being the most virtuous man, to escort the image of the goddess Cybele from Phrygia to Rome.

40. L. Caecilius Metellus, as *Pontifex Maximus* in 241 BC, lost his sight rescuing the image of Minerva (the Palladium) from the burning temple of Vesta.

Swear by all the gods in Samothrace, and by our own as well.
If you're poor, people will think you're completely godless,
but even the gods don't care. What's worse,
the poor man here is the butt of everyone's jokes,
if his cloak is dirty or torn, if his toga has a few stains,
if one shoe has an open rip in the leather, or its often-sewn                    150
wounds show a scar, thick thread, and recent mending.
Poverty makes you a laughing stock, and that's the hardest part.
"Get out! Have you no shame? Leave the equestrian seats,
if your property falls short of the law!⁴¹ The pimp's boys
need to sit here, and whatever else was born in a brothel.
The dandy son of an auctioneer will applaud the show
right here, alongside the cultivated sons of the gladiator,
and his trainer."⁴² So it pleased that fool Otho, who divided
the classes in the theater. What potential father-in-law
will choose a poorer man, one with less luggage                                 160
than his daughter? What poor man gets named in a will?
When do the aediles call him into their councils?
The poorer citizens should have formed a line and left
town long ago. It's never easy to get ahead when your merits
go unnoticed since you've got no cash. But it's harder in Rome.
It's big money to rent your lousy flat, big money to feed
your slaves, and big money for your measly dinner. You feel
ashamed of earthenware dishes that'd be perfectly fine
were you suddenly transported to a country table
among the Marsi or the Sabines. A rough cloak is all                            170
you'd need to wear. The truth? In most of Italy no one
puts on a toga except when dead. The festival days themselves
are spent on the grass—quite majestic!—as people return
to the theater to see that well-known rustic play
revived once more. The country-bred infant cowers in his
mother's lap in fear of the pallid mask's gaping mouth.
In that theater you'll see everyone—orchestra seats
and common people—wearing the same kinds of clothes.
Even the garb of noted office-holders is simple: just a white tunic
for the highest aediles. In Rome, we don't have enough
to achieve the glamor that's required. At times we borrow                       180
to finance some superfluous fashion. We're all guilty of the same vice:
we live here in ambitious poverty. In short, everything
comes at a price in Rome. What do you spend just to call

---

41. The first fourteen rows of seats behind the orchestra, where the senators sat, were reserved
for the *equites* in accordance with the *lex Roscia theatralis* passed by L. Roscius Otho in 67 BC.
See Cicero, *Letters* 5 section 3 in this volume.

42. Typically low-prestige professions, but these have supplanted the old (and now impoverished) equestrian class.

on Cossus in the morning, or so Veiiento can give you a cold,
closed-lip glance? Meanwhile they're throwing parties
for their favorite slaves, dedicating first beard- or hair-clippings
to the gods. The house is full of cakes, but you'll have to pay.
"Here, take your coin and keep your blasted cakes." We clients
pay tribute, and enlarge the pocket money of fancy slaves.
If you lived in chilly Praeneste, or Volsinii nestled on a wooded ridge,                190
or in simple Gabii or Tibur with its sloping citadel, would you
ever worry about a building collapsing? But *we* live in a city
of skyscrapers, perched on slender props. Building managers
stand in front of their unsteady structures, covering
old gaping cracks, and say "sleep well!" as catastrophe looms.
Better to go where there are no fires, where no one lives
in fear at night. Ucalegon cries out "Water!" and gathers
up his meager possessions. Now smoke pours out of
the third story window. But *you* have no idea. The alarm
may be raised at the bottom floor, but the last to burn                                      200
is the man whom only the roof tiles shelter from the rain,
up where gentle doves lay their eggs. What did Cordus[43]
possess? A bed too small even for that waif Procula, six little
jugs to put on his sideboard, a small clay wine cup,
a recumbent centaur made out of the same "marble,"
and a book box, now old, that contained some Greek tomes,
glorious poetry being steadily gnawed by barbarian mice.
Cordus had nothing—who could deny it? And yet in the fire
he lost all his nothing, poor man. The crowning misery?
When he was naked and begging for scraps, not a soul                                    210
helped him out with food or with shelter. Meanwhile,
if the great house of Asturicus[44] falls, notable matrons
go around in mourning, the city fathers wear black, and the praetor
suspends legal business. *Then* we bemoan the disasters of the city,
*then* fire makes us angry. Donors appear while the place
is still blazing to replace his marble statues, take care of expenses.
One man supplies gleaming marble nudes, another some
bronze masterpiece by Euphranor or Polyclitus, the ancient
ornaments of Asia's sanctuaries. Another man donates books
and bookshelves, and a Minerva for the library. Yet another,
a bushel of silver. Persicus, richest of the childless widowers,                            220
ends up with more and better than he had in the first place—

---

43. Apparently a generic figure, resident of a housing block, a man of modest means. The name Cordus, however, is an old Roman name—the implication being that no one cares for a poor blue-blooded Roman.

44. Not a known person, probably a generic figure whose name is invented from the name of a people of Spain. The implication is that wealthy people, no matter their origin, are fawned upon in Rome. The same goes for Persicus ("The Persian") below.

people suspect he set the fire himself, and for good reason!
If you can tear yourself from the Circus, an excellent home
can be had at Sora, Fabrateria, or Frusino for what it costs
to rent a shadowy flat in Rome for a year. There you'll have
a small garden, a shallow well—no need for a rope when
drawing water to pour on your tender vegetables.
Live as a lover of the hoe, the overseer of a well-tended garden
that will supply a banquet for a hundred Pythagoreans.[45]
It's something, wherever you are, in whatever backwater,                    230
to be master of one little spot of ground. Here in Rome,
scads of people grow sick and die of sleep deprivation.
The cause? Indigestion, the food that sticks in a burning gut.
What kind of lodgings can you get that actually allow you to sleep?
It costs a fortune in the city to get a good night's rest.
The origin of this affliction? Noisy wagons passing through our winding
streets, the din of herds stuck at a standstill. It's enough to keep
Emperor Claudius awake, or a herd of seals![46]
Does duty to a patron call? On the streets the rich man is carried
right through as the crowd makes way. He glides along
over our heads in a great ship-like litter, and reads along the way,       240
or writes within, or catches a nap—the closed windows
on the litter make him sleepy—and he still gets there before me.
We may hurry, but a wave of humanity stands in the way,
and a human wedge presses on from behind. One man strikes me
with his elbow, another with the hard pole of a litter, or knocks
my head with a beam or a jar. My legs are thick with mud, my feet
trampled by massive boots everywhere, as the military hobnail
sticks in my toe. Now the gift baskets are being distributed.[47]
Can you believe the smoke? A hundred diners, each with
his own cook and kitchen. The mighty Corbulo could                         250
scarcely support all the pots and pans, so much stuff
put on the head of a poor little slave, fanning the fire as he runs.
Your tunic gets ripped again—it was just mended! Watch out!
Long timbers jostle and shake as a truck passes by,
and a pine tree carried by a wagon looms threateningly
over the people. If the vehicle carting that Ligurian marble
should break, and pour its mountainous load upon the crowd,
what would be left of their bodies? Who would find their
mangled limbs or collect their bones? Every crushed corpse
would vanish utterly, gone like their souls. Meanwhile, at home          260

---

45. The followers of the Greek philosopher Pythagoras were strict vegetarians.

46. On the alleged stupidity and somnolence of Claudius, see Seneca, *The Ascension of the Pumpkinhead Claudius into Heaven* in this volume. Seals were thought to be exceptionally deep sleepers.

47. See Glossary, *sportula*.

their servants wash plates for dinner, carefree, and fire up the oven.
The baths are alive with the sounds of a good massage.
As the slaves go about their various tasks, their master already sits
on the shores of Hades, a newcomer, terrified
of the foul ferryman of Styx, and with no actual hope of
catching a ride, since the poor man lacks a coin in his mouth,
no fare with which to cross the dismal swamp of the dead.
Consider all the other perils that infest the night:
the sheer height of the buildings from which a piece of crockery
might strike your head, as some cracked or broken jar is tossed                270
out a window. You can judge the force of the blow by all the pits
in the pavement. People will think you a thoughtless, lazy man,
unprepared for the worst, if you head to dinner without a will in place.
At night, a potential killer awaits in each open window you pass.
Your best hope—and bring this wretched hope along—
is that they merely dump out their chamber pots on you.
Some impudent, drunken hooligan is in anguish because
it happens that he has yet to beat anyone up tonight.
He tosses and turns in his bed, like Achilles mourning
lost Patroclus.[48] Only a brawl can get him some rest.                        280
Though unruly in youth and hot with wine, he's cautious
to avoid the man with a rich scarlet cloak, a long train
of companions, and a throng of blazing bronze lamps.
Me? I travel the streets by moonlight, or else the light
of a small candle, whose wick I'm careful not to waste.
So I'm an easy target. Here's how it goes
at the beginning of the brawl—if you define "brawl"
as a fight where he does the beating and I take the blows.
He stands opposite and orders me to halt. Nothing to do
but obey. What *can* you do when a madman gives an order,                       290
and he's stronger? "Where've you been?" he demands. "Whose
cheap wine and crappy beans have filled your belly with wind?
What miserable cobbler has been gobbling up giant chives
and boiled sheep's head with you? What, no answer?
Talk, or feel my boot! Tell me where you're holed up. What Jew's
prayer hall can I find you in?" Whether you try to say something,
or withdraw in silence, it's all the same. He'll beat you either way,
then sue you for assault. This is the poor man's freedom:
having taken his brutal beating, he's free to beg and plead
to be allowed to go home with a few teeth left.                                300
Your fears aren't over, though. On your way home there are
others to rob you, now that the houses are shuttered,
the shops closed, chained, and silent all around. Sometimes
a mugger will suddenly appear and do his dastardly work

---

48. The restlessness of Achilles (Homer, *Iliad* 24.10–11) was proverbial.

armed with a sword—that is, when the Pomptine Marsh
and the Gallianaria Forest are well and safely policed.[49]
Then all the bandits converge on Rome, as if to a well-stocked
fish pond. Surely every forge, every anvil is used for the making
of heavy chains, right? Most iron that comes out of the mines
goes to shackles. It's a wonder any's left for ploughshares,                310
hoes, and rakes. Blessed were our ancestor's ancestors, blessed,
you would say, was that age of the early kings and tribunes
that looked upon Rome when she was content with a single jail.
I could go on, add other reasons to head out, but the sun
is sinking, and the draught animals call. It's time to go.
The mule driver's been nodding at me and waving his whip
for some time. And so, goodbye. Be well, and remember me.
And whenever Rome lets you go for a quick refreshing visit
to your place in Aquinum, call me up from Cumae to see the
Helvian temple of Ceres, and the Diana you all worship.                320
I'd like to hear your satires in your cool and pleasant lands—
as long as they don't mind a listener in big country boots.

---

49. The Pomptine marshes covered a large area on the coast south of Rome, along the *Via Appia*.
See Horace, *Satires* 1.5 (lines 3–23) in this volume. Like the Gallinaria Forest in Campania, their
inaccessible reaches harbored pirates and bandits.

# Livy

(59 BC–AD 17, wrote in Latin)

## Introduction

Titus Livius was born and buried in Padua in northern Italy, though he spent much of his adult life, and probably received his higher education, in Rome. Growing up in the turbulent and violent period of the Roman civil wars, he did not pursue a political career, but devoted himself to writing a history of Rome that covered the period from its foundation in 753 BC up to 9 BC. It was a monumental work, over forty years in the making. Only thirty-five of the original 142 books survive complete, although we do have summaries for most of the lost books. Below, we offer a selection from Book 1, which covers the legendary period of the kings. (We omit chapters 22–33, Livy's account of two kings, Tullus Hostilius and Ancus Martius, but add brief summaries of their reigns written by Eutropius in the 4th century AD.)

Since most if not all of the evidence for this early period had disappeared by Livy's day, he relied on historians from the 3rd and 2nd centuries BC, who were probably themselves piecing together a narrative from disparate scraps of evidence. Livy himself admits in his preface that the events of the early period are "embellished with poetic tales rather than based on uncorrupted records of historical events." But Livy, a talented storyteller, was able to catch the essence of these stories in a compelling narrative, and make them revealing of enduring Roman values and ideas. He also related this distant material obliquely to the problems and developments of his own day, especially the civil wars and the rise of autocratic rulers such as Julius Caesar and Augustus.

Livy, in fact, had a personal friendship with Augustus. Yet he did not write primarily to praise the *princeps*, and he retained a certain independence of thought in the tradition of the Republic. As the Roman historian Tacitus tells us, "Titus Livius, in the top rank of historians for both eloquence and reliability, praised Gnaeus Pompeius so enthusiastically that Augustus used to call him 'Pompeianus,' yet it did not affect their friendship" (*Annals* 4.34).

Livy's aims are primarily exemplary, that is, his history is set as a series of episodes that provide examples of conduct to emulate and avoid. He refers to his history as a *monumentum*, literally "reminder, memorial," a word that was also used for roadside tombs and other sculptural monuments.[1] While the Greek term *historia* connotes research or enquiry, *monumentum* as a word for historical writing presents a much more Roman conception of the craft: not just the recording of information for its own sake (as if the mere collection of facts were sufficient), but the public memorialization of important deeds as a call to virtue, achievement, and reflection. This sort of "moti-

---

1. The same word is also used by Livy's contemporary, the poet Horace, to describe his three-book collection of *Odes*; see *Odes* 3.30 in this volume.

vational history" seems embedded in Roman culture; we see, for instance, the same sort of public recollection of great deeds in Polybius' description of Roman funerals in this volume (chs. 53–54). For the places mentioned in the selection below, see map of Latium in the Period of the Kings (p. xxvi).

---

## The History of Rome from Its Foundation (1.1–21, 34–60)

### A    Preface

Whether I am going to receive any return for the effort if I record the history of the Roman people from the foundation of the city, I do not really know. Nor, if I did know, would I dare to say so. Indeed, I see that the subject is both old and generally known, because new writers always believe either that they are going to bring some greater authenticity to the subject matter or that they will surpass the unpolished attempts of antiquity in literary style.

However that will be, it nevertheless will be a pleasure to have celebrated, to the best of my ability, the memory of the past achievements of the greatest people on earth. If my own reputation should remain obscure amid such a crowd of writers, I would console myself with the renown and greatness of those who stand in the way of my fame. The subject, moreover, is an immense undertaking, since it goes back more than 700 years and, having started from small beginnings, has so increased that it is now laboring under its own size. I have no doubt that the earliest origins and the immediately succeeding period will give less delight to the majority of readers who are hurrying to these recent times in which the might of a most powerful people has long been destroying itself.[2]

But, on the contrary, I shall seek this additional reward for my labor so that I may turn away from the contemplation of the evils that our age has seen for so many years and, for the short time that I am absorbed in retracing those early days, be wholly free from the concern, which, even though it could not divert the writer's mind from the truth, might nonetheless cause anxiety.

The intent is neither to affirm nor refute the traditions that belong to the period before the foundation of the city or the anticipation of its foundation, for these are embellished with poetic tales rather than based on uncorrupted records of historical events. To antiquity is granted the indulgence of making the beginnings of cities more impressive by mingling human affairs with the divine. And if any people should be allowed to sanctify their origins and reckon their founders as gods, surely the military glory of the Roman people is such that, when they claim that their father and the father of their founder was none other than Mars, the nations of the world tolerate this claim with the same equanimity with which they tolerate our dominion. But these and

---

2. Livy refers to the period of civil strife (133–31 BC) that preceded the emergence of Augustus, the first emperor of Rome.

similar things, however they will be regarded and judged, I shall not for my own part regard as of great importance.

The following are questions to which I would have every reader direct close attention: the kind of lives men lived; what their moral principles were; by what individuals and by what skills, both at home and in the field, our dominion was born and grew. Then let him follow how at first, as discipline gradually collapsed, there was, as it were, a disintegration of morals; then note how more and more they slipped and finally began to fall headlong until we have reached the present times in which we can tolerate neither our own vices nor their remedies.

This is the particularly healthy and productive element of history: to behold object lessons of every kind of model as though they were displayed on a conspicuous monument. From this, you should choose for yourself and for your state what to imitate and what to avoid as abominable in its origin or as abominable in its outcome.

But either the love of the task I have undertaken deceives me, or there has never been a state that is greater, or more righteous, or richer in good examples. Nor has there been one where greed and luxury migrated so late into the citizenry, nor where there has been such great respect for small means and thrift. The less men had, the less was their greed. Recently riches have brought in avarice, and excessive pleasures have led to a desire to ruin ourselves and destroy everything through excess and self-indulgence.

But complaints are bound to be disagreeable, even when they will perhaps be necessary; so at least let them be absent from the beginning of this great enterprise. Rather we would begin with good omens and, if we had the same custom as the poets, with prayers and entreaties to the gods and goddesses to grant us the blessing of success as we start this great undertaking.

## B    From Aeneas to the Foundation of Rome (1.1–7)

### 1    The Arrival of the Trojans Antenor and Aeneas in Italy

Now, first of all, there is sufficient agreement that when Troy was captured, vengeance was visited upon the other Trojans. In the case of Aeneas and Antenor, however, the Greeks observed the ancient right of hospitality and did not impose the right of conquest on these two men, since they had always advocated peace and the return of Helen. Each of them had different adventures. Antenor is said to have come to the uppermost gulf of the Adriatic sea, together with a group of Eneti who had been driven from Paphlagonia by revolution. They had lost their king, Pylaemenes, at Troy and were seeking a home and a leader. Driving out the Euganei who lived between the sea and the Alps, the Trojans and Eneti took possession of this territory. The place they first landed is named Troy, and so the district is called Trojan. The entire people are known as Veneti.

Aeneas was an exile from his home because of a similar disaster; but the fates guided him to initiate greater achievements. First he came to Macedonia, then he sailed to Sicily as he sought a place to settle, and from Sicily he held course for the territory of Laurentum. This place is also called Troy. There the Trojans disembarked. Having nothing except their arms and ships after their almost endless wanderings, they began to plunder the fields. King Latinus and the Aborigines, the occupants of the region at that time, armed themselves and rushed from the city and fields to repel the violence of the invaders.

At this point, there are two versions of what happened next. Some sources say that Latinus was conquered in battle, made peace with Aeneas, and contracted a marriage alliance. Others report that when the battle lines were drawn up, Latinus came forward among his chieftains before the signal could be given and summoned the foreigners' leader to discuss the situation. He asked what kind of men they were, where they had come from, what misfortune had caused them to leave their home, and what they wanted in Laurentine territory. He was told that they were Trojans; their leader was Aeneas, son of Anchises and Venus; their fatherland had been burned; they were exiles from their home and were looking for a place to settle and a site on which to found a city. Latinus marveled at the noble renown of the race and the man, and at his spirit, prepared alike for war or peace. So, he offered his right hand as a pledge of their future friendship. A treaty was made between the leaders, the armies saluted each other, and Aeneas became a guest in the house of Latinus. There, before his household gods, Latinus added a domestic treaty to the public one by giving his daughter in marriage to Aeneas.

This event strengthened the Trojans in the hope that their wanderings were at last ended and that they were settled in a permanent abode. They established a town that Aeneas called Lavinium after the name of his wife, Lavinia. Soon a child was born of the recent marriage, a boy whom his parents named Ascanius.

## 2    War against Local Italians and Aeneas' Death

War was soon made on the Aborigines and Trojans alike. Turnus, the king of the Rutulians, had been engaged to Lavinia before Aeneas' arrival. Angry that a foreigner had been preferred to him, he attacked both Aeneas and Latinus. The outcome of the conflict did not bring joy to either side. The Rutulians were conquered; the Aborigines and Trojans, though victorious, lost their leader Latinus. Discouraged by the situation, Turnus and the Rutulians turned for help to the realm of the Etruscans and their king, Mezentius, who ruled over Caere, a wealthy town at that time. From the beginning, Mezentius had been by no means pleased with the birth of the new city, thinking that the Trojan state was growing far too much for the safety of its neighbors. So, he readily joined forces with the Rutulians.

Confronted with such a formidable war and the need to win over the minds of the Aborigines, Aeneas called both peoples Latins so that everyone would not only be under the same law, but also the same name. From that time on, the Aborigines' dedication and loyalty to King Aeneas was no less than those of the Trojans. Aeneas relied on the spirit of these two peoples, who daily became more united. But Etruria was so powerful that not only the lands, but also the sea along the extent of Italy from the Alps to the straits of Sicily were filled with the glory of her name. Although he had the power to drive an enemy from the city walls, Aeneas nonetheless led his troops into the field to fight. The Latins were successful in battle, but it was the last of Aeneas' mortal labors. Whatever it is lawful and right that he be called, be it god or man, he is buried by the river Numicus. Men call him Jupiter Indiges.

## 3    The Descendants of Aeneas

Aeneas' son Ascanius was not yet old enough to rule. Nonetheless his realm remained intact until he reached manhood, thanks to Lavinia. She was such a strong character that the Latin state and kingdom of Ascanius' grandfather and father stood firm in the meantime, under a woman's guardianship. I shall not dispute this matter—for who could confirm as a certainty something that is so ancient?—whether it was this Ascanius or an elder brother whom Creusa bore while Troy still was intact, the one who was his father's companion in his flight and whom the Julian family claims as the founder of its name.[3] This Ascanius, wherever he was born and whoever his mother was—it is certainly agreed that his father was Aeneas—left Lavinium to his mother (or stepmother), since it was already a comparatively flourishing and wealthy city with an excess of people. He founded another new town at the foot of the Alban Mount, which was called Alba Longa because it stretched along a ridge. Between the foundation of Lavinium and the establishing of the colony of Alba Longa, there was a period of thirty years. Their resources had increased so greatly, especially after the defeat of the Etruscans, that neither Mezentius nor the Etruscans nor any other neighbors dared stir up war; not even after Aeneas' death, nor later during the woman's guardianship and the young man's first attempts at ruling. Under a peace treaty, the river Albula, which men now call the Tiber, became the boundary between the Etruscans and Latins.

Silvius, the son of Ascanius, was the next to reign; he happened to have been born in the woods (*silvae*). He was the father of Aeneas Silvius. Next came Latinus Silvius. He planted several colonies that were called the Ancient Latins. All those who ruled at Alba had the name Silvius. From Latinus came Alba; from Alba, Atys; from Atys, Capys; from Capys, Capetus; from Capetus, Tiberinus. This last king was drowned while crossing the river Albula, thus giving to posterity the river's famous name. Then came Agrippa, the son of Tiberinus. Romulus Silvius ruled after Agrippa, receiving the kingship from his father. He was struck by a thunderbolt and was succeeded by Aventinus, who is buried on that hill which is now part of the city of Rome, thus giving his name to the hill. Proca, the father of Numitor and Amulius, was the next ruler. He bequeathed the ancient kingdom of the Silvian family to Numitor, his eldest son. But violence was more powerful than the father's wishes or respect for age. Amulius drove his brother out and became king. Adding crime to crime, he killed his brother's male children and, under the pretext of honoring his brother's daughter Rhea Silvia, selected her to be a priestess of Vesta.[4] By condemning her to perpetual virginity, he deprived her of the hope of bearing children.

## 4    The Miraculous Survival of Romulus and Remus

To the fates, as I suppose, was owed the origin of this great city and the beginning of the mightiest empire that is second only to that of the gods. The Vestal was raped

---

3. Ascanius was also called "Iulus," from whom the Julian family (e.g., Julius Caesar) claimed descent—a common type of prestige-enhancing invention among the Roman nobility.

4. That is, one of the Vestal Virgins, who in historical times were required to remain chaste and (among much else) maintain the sacred fire in the Temple of Vesta. See Glossary.

and produced twins. She claimed that Mars was the father of her doubtful offspring, either because she believed this or because it was more honorable to put the blame on a god. But neither gods nor men protected her or her children from the king's cruelty. The priestess was put in chains and imprisoned, and the king ordered the baby boys to be thrown into the current of the river. By some heaven-sent chance, the Tiber had overflowed its banks, forming stagnant pools that made it impossible to approach the actual river. The men who brought the children hoped they might be drowned despite the sluggish water. Making a pretense of discharging the king's orders, they exposed the children on the edge of the floodwater where the Ruminalis fig tree now stands. Formerly, they say, it was called the Romularis.[5]

The area at that time was a vast deserted region. The story persists that the floating basket in which the children had been exposed was left high and dry by the receding water. Coming down from the surrounding mountains, a thirsty she-wolf heard the infants' cries and turned in their direction. She gave the infants her teats so gently that the master of the royal flock found her licking them with her tongue. This man's name was Faustulus, as the story goes. He took the children to his hut to be reared by his wife Larentia. There are some who think that this miraculous story originated because Larentia was called "she-wolf" among the shepherd community, since she had been a prostitute.[6] This, then, was the birth and rearing of the boys. As soon as they were grown to manhood, they began to hunt in the forests, while also working on the farm and with the flocks. In this way they achieved strength of body and mind. They not only confronted wild beasts but attacked robbers who were laden with plunder. What they took they divided among the shepherds, joining them in work and play as their group daily grew larger.

## 5    Romulus and Remus Avenge their Grandfather

Tradition has it that the merry festival of the Lupercalia was already established on the Palatine.[7] This hill was named Pallantium after Pallanteum, a city in Arcadia; it later became Palatium. Evander, an Arcadian who inhabited the area many years before, is said to have established the annual rite, importing it from Arcadia. At this festival young men run about naked, sporting and frolicking as they honor Lycaean Pan, whom the Romans afterward called Inuus. The day of the ritual was generally known. So when Romulus and Remus were engrossed in this celebration, they were ambushed by some robbers who were angry at the loss of their plunder. Romulus forcibly defended himself, but Remus was captured and handed over as a prisoner to King Amulius. Accusations were freely made, the main charge being that the youths had attacked Numitor's fields and plundered them with an organized gang of youths, just like an enemy. And so, Remus was handed over to Numitor for punishment.

Now right from the start Faustulus had hoped that the children he was rearing were of royal birth. He knew that children had been exposed on the king's order and that the time matched the very time that he rescued them. He had, however, been

5. This was in Rome, near the southwest slope of Palatine Hill.

6. A play on the Latin word *lupa*, which can either mean "she-wolf" or "prostitute."

7. The Lupercalia, a ritual celebrated in Rome on February 15. See Glossary.

unwilling to reveal the matter prematurely until either opportunity or necessity intervened. Necessity came first. Forced by fear, he revealed the facts to Romulus. By chance Numitor was also reminded of his grandsons. For he had heard of the twin brothers while Remus was in his custody. Then he had thought about their age and temperament, which was not at all slavelike. And so, after making further enquiries, he had all but acknowledged Remus. From all sides, a net of guile was being woven against King Amulius. Romulus made his attack on the king, though not with his band of youths—he was not yet strong enough to use open violence. He ordered his men to come by different routes to the king's palace at an appointed time. Remus collected another group and came to their assistance from Numitor's house. And so he killed the king.

## 6    Romulus and Remus Depart to Found a New City

At the beginning of the disturbance, Numitor kept insisting that an enemy had invaded the city and attacked the palace. He drew off the Alban fighting men to defend and garrison the citadel. After the killing of Amulius, he saw the young men approaching to congratulate him. He immediately summoned a council and revealed his brother's crimes against him, his grandsons' parentage—how they had been born, reared, and recognized—and lastly the killing of the tyrant, for which he was responsible. Romulus and Remus marched with their men through the midst of the assembly and saluted their grandfather as king. From the entire crowd there arose a unanimous shout of assent, thus ratifying the king's name and his power.

After entrusting the government of Alba to Numitor, Romulus and Remus were seized by a desire to establish a city in the places where they had been exposed and raised. The number of Albans and Latins was more than enough; in addition to this group, there were also the shepherds. All of these men easily created the hope that Alba and Lavinium would be small in comparison with the city that they were founding. But these thoughts were interrupted by the ancestral evil that had beset Numitor and Amulius—desire for kingship. From quite a harmless beginning, an abominable conflict arose. Since Romulus and Remus were twins and distinction could not be made by respect for age, they decided to ask the protecting gods of the area to declare by augury who should give his name to the new city and who should rule over it after its foundation. Romulus took the Palatine and Remus the Aventine, as the respective areas from which to take the auspices.[8]

## 7    The Death of Remus; the Story of Hercules and Cacus

Remus is said to have received the first augury, six vultures. This augury had already been announced when twice the number appeared to Romulus. Each man was hailed as king by his own followers. Remus' men based their claim to the throne on priority; Romulus' followers on the number of birds. Arguments broke out, and the angry conflict resulted in bloodshed. Amid the throng, Remus was struck dead. The more

---

8. For augury and taking the auspices, see Valerius Maximus section E and Glossary in this volume.

common story is that Remus leaped over the new walls, jeering at his brother. He was killed by the enraged Romulus, who added the threat, "So perish whoever else shall leap over my walls."[9] Thus Romulus became the sole ruler and the city, so founded, was given its founder's name.

Romulus' first act was to fortify the Palatine where he himself had been raised.[10] He offered sacrifice to the other gods according to the Alban ritual, and to Hercules according to the Greek ritual instituted by Evander.[11] There is a tradition that, after killing Geryon, Hercules drove his cattle into this area.[12] He swam across the Tiber river, driving his exceptionally fine cattle in front of him. Weary from his journey, he lay down near the river in a grassy spot where he could let the cattle rest and refresh themselves with the abundant pasture. Heavy with food and wine, he fell into a deep sleep. A ferociously strong shepherd called Cacus, an inhabitant of the area, was taken with the beauty of the cattle and wanted to steal them. But he realized that if he drove them directly into his cave, the tracks would lead their master there when he began to look for them; and so he dragged the finest animals backward by the tail into the cave. At dawn Hercules awoke, looked over the herd and realized that some were missing. He went to the nearest cave to see whether by chance the tracks led in that direction. But all the tracks faced in the opposite direction and did not lead anywhere. Confused and puzzled, he began to lead the herd out of the strange place. While they were being driven away, some of the cows lowed because, as often happens, they missed the bulls that were left behind. The responding low of those that were shut in the cave caused Hercules to turn around. As he advanced to the cave, Cacus forcibly tried to keep him off. Calling in vain for the shepherds to help him, he was struck by Hercules' club and fell dead.

At that time, Evander, an exile from the Peloponnese, controlled the area more by personal authority than sovereign power. He was revered for his wonderful skill with the alphabet, a novelty among men who were untutored in such arts. He was even more revered on account of his mother, Carmenta, who was believed to be divine and was admired as a prophetess before the Sibyl's arrival in Italy.[13] Evander was aroused by the throng of shepherds who were excitedly mobbing the foreigner and accusing him of blatant murder. Seeing that the man's bearing and stature were greater and more impressive than those of a human, Evander listened to what had happened and the reason for the deed. Then Evander asked which hero he was. On hearing his name, father, and country of origin, he said, "Hail Hercules, son of Jupiter! My mother, a truthful interpreter of the gods, declared that you would increase the number of the gods and

---

9. See a similar account in Ovid, *Fasti* in this volume.

10. Excavations in the late 1980s uncovered evidence of a wall on the northern slope of the Palatine Hill that can be dated to the mid-700s BC, consistent with the legendary date of the founding of Rome in 753. There are also remains of huts on the Palatine that date to roughly the same period.

11. That is, with head covered and uncovered, respectively. Evander was a Greek from Arcadia in the central Peloponnesus.

12. Geryon was a triple-bodied monster located in Spain by the Atlantic Ocean. The area where Hercules stopped in Rome was called the "Forum Boarium" ("The Cattle Forum"). See map of The City of Rome and the Forum.

13. The Sibyl was a prophetic priestess of Apollo residing in Cumae on the Bay of Naples.

that here an altar would be dedicated to you, which the race that was destined one day to be the most powerful on earth would call the Greatest Altar, tending it with rites in your honor."

Hercules offered his right hand, saying that he accepted the omen and would fulfill the prophecy by establishing and dedicating an altar. A fine cow was taken from the herd, and the first sacrifice was made to Hercules. Officiating at the feast were the Potitii and Pinarii, families who at that time were especially prominent in the area. By chance it happened that the Potitii arrived on time and were offered the victim's entrails. The Pinarii, however, came after the entrails had been eaten but in time for the rest of the feast. Thus, as long as the family of the Pinarii endured, the practice remained that they did not eat entrails at this festival. Trained by Evander, the Potitii officiated at this sacrifice for many generations until the whole family died out when this solemn family function was handed over to public slaves. This was the only foreign rite undertaken by Romulus. Even then Romulus was already honoring the immortality that is won by valor, an honor to which his own destiny was leading him.

## C    The Reign of Romulus (1.8–17)

## 8    Romulus Establishes Symbols of Power and the Senate

After duly performing the religious observances, Romulus summoned his men to an assembly and gave them laws, since there was no way other than by law that they could become a unified community. He thought the rustic population more likely to be bound by these laws if he made himself venerable by adopting symbols of office. Not only did he make himself more impressive in his way of dressing, but he also assumed a retinue of twelve lictors.[14] Some sources think that this number derived from the number of birds that had augured and portended his rule. But I have no problem with the opinion of those who consider that the attendants and their number derive from the neighboring Etruscans, who also are the source of the magistrates' curule chair and the *toga praetexta*. The Etruscans had this number because each of their twelve communities contributed one lictor after they united to elect a king.

Meanwhile the city was growing as the Romans included one area after another within the city's defenses. They were building more in expectation of a future population than for the number of men they currently had. Then, so that this large city was not empty, Romulus resorted to a plan for adding to the population that had long been used by founders of cities, who gather a host of shady, low-born people and put out the story that children had been born to them from the earth. In this way, Romulus opened a place of asylum in the area that is now enclosed between the two groves as you come down the Capitoline. The entire rabble from the neighboring peoples fled there for refuge. They came without distinction, slaves and freemen alike, eager for a fresh start. This was the first move toward beginning the increase of Rome's might.

Now that he was satisfied with Rome's strength, Romulus prepared to add delibera-

---

14. Official attendants of Roman magistrates (see Glossary). Livy honors this and other Republican institutions (the *fasces*, the curule chair, toga praetexta, and Senate, mentioned below) by attributing their establishment to the first king of Rome.

tion to strength. He appointed a hundred senators, either because that number was sufficient or because there were only a hundred men who could be made senators. They were called "fathers" (*patres*) because of their rank, and their descendants were called "patricians."

## 9    The Romans Abduct the Sabine Women

Already Rome was so strong that she was the equal of any of the neighboring states in war. But the lack of women meant that Rome's greatness would only last for the current generation, since the Romans neither had the hope of offspring at home nor intermarriage with their neighbors. On the advice of the senators, Romulus sent ambassadors around the neighboring tribes to seek alliance and intermarriage for the new people. The envoys argued that cities too, like everything else, start from the most humble beginnings; that great wealth and a great name are achieved by those cities that are helped by their own valor and the gods. It was enough to know that the gods had attended Rome's birth and that its people's valor would not fail. The Romans were men like themselves, and so, as neighbors, they should not be reluctant to mingle their blood and stock with them.

Nowhere did the embassy get a kindly reception. The neighboring peoples rejected them, at the same time fearing, for both themselves and their descendants, the great power that was growing in their midst. Dismissing the envoys, many asked whether the Romans had also opened a refuge for women, since that at least would be a way to get wives who were their equals. The young Romans resented this attitude, and things were undoubtedly beginning to look violent. In order to arrange an appropriate time and place for his plan, Romulus hid his resentment and carefully prepared a solemn festival in honor of Neptune as patron of horses, which he called the Consualia.[15] Then he ordered that the spectacle be announced to the neighboring peoples. With all the pageantry within the knowledge and resources of those times, the Romans prepared to celebrate this festival, publicizing it to create expectation.

Many people came in their eagerness to see the new city, particularly the nearby inhabitants of Caenina, Crustumerium, and Antemnae. All the Sabines came too, together with their children and wives. They were hospitably entertained in every home, and, after seeing the layout of the city with its walls and numerous buildings, they marveled at the rapidity of Rome's growth. The time for the show arrived, and, while everyone's eyes and thoughts were intent upon it, the prearranged violence broke out. At a given signal, the Roman youths rushed in every direction to seize the unmarried women. In most cases the maidens were seized by the men in whose path they happened to be. But some exceptionally beautiful girls had been marked out by the leading men of the senate and were carried off by plebeians who had been given that task. One girl who far outshone the rest in appearance and beauty was seized, as the story goes, by the gang of a certain Thalassius. When asked to whom they were taking her, they kept shouting "To Thalassius" to prevent anyone else from violating her. This is the origin of the wedding cry (*Thalassio!*).

---

15. The Consualia, dedicated to Consus, the god who protected stored grain, was celebrated on August 21 with horse races.

The games broke up in fear and confusion. The maidens' parents fled, charging the Romans with the crime of violating hospitality. They invoked the god to whose solemn rite they had come only to be deceived in violation of religion and good faith. The abducted maidens were no more hopeful of their plight, nor less enraged. But Romulus himself went around, telling them that this had happened because of their parents' arrogance in refusing intermarriage with neighbors. Nevertheless, he said, women would have the full rights of marriage, having a share in their possessions, Roman citizenship, and the dearest possession that the human race has—children. They should calm their anger and give their hearts to those to whom chance had given their bodies. For, he said, often affection has eventually come from a sense of injustice. They would find their husbands kinder because each would try not only to fulfill his obligation, but also to make up for the longing for their parents and homeland. The men spoke sweet words to them, trying to excuse their action on the grounds of passionate love, a plea that is particularly effective where a woman's heart is concerned.

## 10    Romulus Wins his First Battle

The resentment of the abducted women had already been greatly mollified, but their bereft parents, wearing squalid garments, were arousing their states to action with tears and lamentations. Nor did they confine their expressions of anger to their hometowns, but converged from all directions on the house of Titus Tatius, king of the Sabines. Embassies also came there because of the greatness of Tatius' name in the area. The people of Caenina, Crustumerium, and Antemnae who were most affected by this injustice thought that Tatius and the Sabines were slow in taking action. So, these three peoples prepared a joint campaign. Yet not even the peoples of Crustumerium and Antemnae moved quickly enough to satisfy the burning anger of the people of Caenina, who invaded Roman territory on their own. But Romulus encountered them with his army as they were scattered and engaged in plundering. In a quick fight he taught them the futility of anger without strength. He routed their army, put them to flight, and pursued them in their disarray. In the fighting, he killed the king and stripped the armor from the corpse. Once the enemy leader was dead, Romulus took the city at the first attack.

Romulus then led back the victorious army. Magnificent in action, he was no less eager to publicize his achievements. So, he hung the spoils of the slain enemy commander on a frame made to fit the purpose and went up to the Capitol, carrying it himself. He set it down by an oak tree sacred to the shepherds and, at the same time as he made his offering, marked out the boundary of a temple to Jupiter and gave the god an additional title, declaring: "To you, Jupiter Feretrius, I, Romulus, victor and king, bring (*ferre*) spoils taken from a king. On this site that I have just marked out in my mind, I dedicate a precinct to be a place for the spoils of honor[16] that men of the future, following my example, will bring to this place when they have slain kings and enemy commanders." This was the origin of the first temple that was consecrated in Rome.

In the ensuing years, it has been the will of the gods that the words of the temple's

---

16. The spoils of honor (*spolia opima*) were given to generals who killed an enemy commander in hand-to-hand combat. It happened only three times in Roman history.

founder were not in vain when he declared that posterity would bring spoils to this place; nor has the honor of the gift been cheapened by many sharing it. Twice since then, over so many years and so many wars, have the spoils of honor been won: so rare is the good fortune of winning that distinction.

## 11    More Wars against Neighboring Peoples and the Treachery of Tarpeia

While the Romans were busy in Rome, the army of the Antemnates took the opportunity of their absence to raid Roman territory. But a Roman legion was quickly led against them; scattered in the fields, the Antemnates were overwhelmed. At the first shout and attack, the enemy was routed and their town taken. As Romulus was exulting in his double victory, his wife Hersilia, wearied by the entreaties of the abducted women, begged him to grant amnesty to their parents and grant them citizenship, saying that by this means the state would grow in strength and harmony. Her request was easily granted. Romulus then set out against the people of Crustumerium who were marching on Rome. In this case, there was even less of a struggle, because their spirit had collapsed as a result of the defeat of the others. Colonists were sent to both places, although more people were found to enroll their names for Crustumerium because of the fertility of its soil. On the other hand, a number left and migrated to Rome, particularly parents and relatives of the abducted women.

The last war was with the Sabines, and it was by far the greatest. These people were not acting through anger or greed. Nor did they show any hint of war before the actual attack. Deception was also added to their strategy. Spurius Tarpeius was in command of the Roman citadel. With gold Tatius bribed this man's maiden daughter to let armed men into the citadel. By chance the girl had gone outside the walls to get water for a sacrifice. Once inside, they overpowered her with their weapons and killed her, either to make it appear that the citadel had been taken by force or to set an example that no one should anywhere keep faith with a traitor. There is also a tale that, because the Sabines generally wore heavy gold bands on their left arms and magnificently studded rings, she made a deal for what they had on their left hands. But instead of gifts of gold, they piled their shields on her. There are those who say that, in keeping with the agreement to hand over what they had in their left hands, she asked outright for their weapons, and, when it was apparent that she was tricking them, she perished by the reward she had demanded.[17]

## 12    The War against the Sabines Continues

Whatever the case, the Sabines got control of the citadel. The next day, when the Roman army was drawn up, covering the ground between the Palatine and the Capitoline hill, the Sabines did not come down to level ground until the Romans were coming up the

---

17. The figure of Tarpeia may have been invented to explain the name of the Tarpeian Rock, a cliff on the Capitoline Hill from which convicted traitors were thrown to their deaths. She also serves as a face-saving explanation of a crucial Roman failure to guard their central citadel.

hill on the attack, their minds goaded by anger and eagerness to recover the citadel. On either side the commanders led the fighting: Mettius Curtius leading the Sabines, and Hostius Hostilius the Romans. In the front line, though on unequal ground, Hostius upheld the Roman cause with courage and daring. When he fell, the Roman line immediately collapsed and was routed. Even Romulus himself was driven by the mob of fugitives to the old gate of the Palatine. Raising his weapons to the sky, he said, "Jupiter, it was at the bidding of your augural birds that I laid the city's first foundations here on the Palatine. The citadel has been bought by a crime and is in the hands of the Sabines. They have conquered the valley between the two hills and are now upon us, sword in hand. But, father of gods and men, keep them back, at least from here. Rid the Romans of their terror and stay their shameful flight! I hereby vow a temple to you as Jupiter the Stayer, to be a memorial for posterity that the city was saved by your presence and help." With this prayer, as if he realized that his words had been heard, he cried, "It is here, Romans, that Jupiter the Best and Greatest bids us stand and renew the fight!" As if bidden by a voice from the sky, the Romans made a stand, and Romulus himself rushed into the front line of battle.

On the Sabine side, Mettius Curtius had led the charge from the citadel, driving the Romans in disarray over the whole area of the forum. Now he was not far from the Palatine gate, shouting, "We have beaten our faithless hosts, a cowardly enemy. Now they know that it is one thing to steal maidens, another to fight with men." As he was uttering these boasts, Romulus attacked him with a band of the most ferocious Roman youths. Mettius happened at the time to be fighting on horseback. For that reason, he was more easily driven back. The Romans pursued him in his flight. Fired by their king's audacity, the rest of the Roman battle line put the Sabines to flight. Mettius' horse was terrified by the din of pursuit and plunged him into a swamp. The danger to their great hero caused the Sabines to wheel around. Mettius, his spirit encouraged by the support of the throng as his men gestured and shouted to him, made his escape. Romans and Sabines renewed the fighting in the valley that lies between the two hills. But the Romans had the upper hand.

## 13    The Sabine Women Bring the Romans and Sabines together

At that point the Sabine women, whose abduction had given rise to the war, dared to advance amid the flying weapons, their womanish fear overcome by the terrible situation. With loosened hair and torn garments, they rushed in from the side, parting the battle lines and checking the battle rage. Appealing on the one side to their fathers, on the other to their husbands, they begged fathers-in-law and sons-in-law not to defile themselves with impious bloodshed, nor stain with parricide the offspring of their blood—grandfathers their grandchildren, fathers their children. "If you cannot bear the relationship between you," they cried, "If you cannot bear the marriage bond, turn your anger upon us. We are the cause of war; we are the cause of wounds and death to our husbands and our fathers. Better that we die than live as widows or orphans, without either of you." Their appeal moved both leaders and the rank and file. There was silence and a sudden hush.

Then the leaders came forward to make a treaty. They made not only peace, but also one state from two. They shared the kingship, transferring all power to Rome. In this way the city was doubled, and, so that the Sabines should be given something, the citizens were called Quirites, a name deriving from Cures.[18] As a memorial of the battle, they gave the name of Curtian Lake to the place where Curtius' horse first emerged from the deep swamp and set him in the shallows. The sudden joyful peace after such a grievous war made the Sabine women dearer to their husbands and parents, and above all to Romulus himself. And so, when he divided the people into thirty wards, he named the wards after the women. Although the number of women was undoubtedly considerably more than thirty, the tradition does not say whether those who gave their names to the wards were chosen by lot, age, or according to their own rank or that of their husbands. At the same time, three centuries of knights were formed.[19] The Ramnenses were named for Romulus, the Titienses for Tatius; the reason for the name and origin of the Luceres, however, is unknown. From this time the two kings ruled not only jointly, but also harmoniously.

## 14    The Death of Titus Tatius and War with Fidenae

Several years later, relatives of King Tatius assaulted envoys of the Laurentians who protested under the law of nations. Tatius, however, was more influenced by partiality for his relatives and their pleas. As a result of this, he got what should have been their punishment. A mob gathered and killed him when he had gone to Lavinium for the annual sacrifice. The story is that Romulus took this less badly than was proper, whether because of the disloyalty that is inherent in shared rule or because he thought that Tatius' murder was not unjustified. Consequently Romulus refrained from war but renewed the pact between Rome and Lavinium in order to expiate the insults to the envoys and the murder of the king.

Against all expectation, there was peace with the Laurentians. But another war broke out much nearer, indeed almost at the very gates of the city. The men of Fidenae, perceiving the increasing strength of such a close neighbor, decided to make war before Rome achieved the might that she clearly would. They sent out an armed band of young men who plundered the territory lying between Rome and Fidenae. Then, because the Tiber prevented them on the right, they turned left, causing devastation and great fear among the farmers. The sudden stampede from the fields into the city served as the announcement of war. Romulus immediately reacted—war with a neighbor made delay impossible. He led out the army and pitched camp a mile from Fidenae. Then, leaving a small guard, he marched on with all his forces, ordering some of the soldiers to lie in ambush in concealed positions amid the dense undergrowth. He himself set out with the greater number of the troops and all the cavalry.

By making a disorderly and menacing assault in which the cavalry rode almost to the very gates, he achieved his aim of drawing out the enemy. The same cavalry engagement provided a less surprising reason for their retreat, which had to be feigned. The

---

18. A Sabine town; the etymology is implausible.

19. A century is literally "one hundred men;" the word "knight" translates *eques*, "cavalryman." See *equites* in the Glossary.

cavalry were apparently undecided whether to fight or flee, and the infantry also began to retreat. At this point the enemy suddenly thronged the gates, pouring forth as the Roman battle line gave way. And so, in their eagerness to press on and pursue, the Fidenates were drawn into the place of ambush. There the Romans suddenly sprang out and attacked the enemy's flanks. To add to the panic, the standards of those who had been left on guard were advancing from the camp. Almost before Romulus and his men could rein in their horses and wheel around, the men of Fidenae turned tail and ran, stricken with terror from every direction. They made for the city in much greater disarray than that of the pretended fugitives whom they had previously pursued, though this time the flight was real. But they did not escape the enemy. The Romans followed close behind them, and, before the gates could be closed, both pursuers and pursued burst into the city, as if in a single line.

## 15     War with Veii[20]

The people of Veii were aroused by the war fever that spread from Fidenae, and by their kinship with the people of Fidenae, for they too were Etruscans. A further stimulus was the very proximity of Rome, should Roman arms be directed against all their neighbors. The Veientines invaded Roman territory more like marauders than men on a regular campaign. They did not pitch camp or wait for the enemy's army but returned to Veii with the booty they had seized from the fields. The Romans, when they did not find the enemy in the fields, crossed the Tiber, prepared and eager for a decisive fight. On hearing that the Romans were pitching camp and would be making an attack on the city, the people of Veii went out to meet them, preferring to fight a regular battle rather than to be besieged and forced to fight for their homes and city. By sheer force and without employing any strategy, the Roman king prevailed simply by the might of his seasoned army. He routed the enemy and pursued them up to the walls. But he refrained from attacking the city itself, since it was strongly fortified by both its walls and natural position. On his return he plundered the fields, more from a desire for revenge than for booty. The people of Veii, impelled by this disaster no less than by their defeat in battle, sent envoys to Rome to sue for peace. They were deprived of part of their land and given a truce for one hundred years.

These were the main achievements of Romulus' reign, at home and in the field. None of them is incompatible with the belief in his divine origin and the divinity that is attributed to him after his death—neither his spirit in recovering his grandfather's kingdom, nor his wisdom in founding the city and strengthening it by both war and peace. Indeed, the strength that he gave to Rome enabled her to have untroubled peace for the next forty years. He was more popular with the people than with the senators. Far above all, however, he was dearest to the hearts of the soldiers. Not only in war, but also in peace, he had 300 armed men as a bodyguard, whom he called the Swift Ones.

---

20. Located thirteen miles north of Rome, this Etruscan city rivaled Rome for quite some time until it was finally captured in 396 BC.

# 16   The Mysterious End of Romulus

After accomplishing these mortal deeds, Romulus was one day holding an assembly of the people on the Campus Martius near the Goat Swamp to review the army. Suddenly a storm arose with loud claps of thunder, enveloping him in a cloud so dense that it hid him from the view of the people. From then on Romulus was no longer on earth. The Roman people finally recovered from their panic when the turbulence was succeeded by a bright and sunny day. Seeing the king's throne empty, they readily believed the assertion of the senators who had been standing nearby that he had been snatched up on high by the storm. Nevertheless, they remained sorrowful and silent for some time, stricken with fear as if they had been orphaned. Then, on the initiative of a few, they all decided that Romulus should be hailed as a god, son of a god, king, and father of the city of Rome. With prayers they begged his favor, beseeching him to be willing and propitious toward the Roman people and to protect their descendants forever.

I suppose that there were some, even then, who privately claimed that the king had been torn into pieces by the hands of the senators. This rumor also spread, though in enigmatic terms. But men's admiration for the hero and the panic felt at the time have given greater currency to the other version, which is said to have gained additional credence thanks to the plan of a single man. The citizens, however, were troubled by their longing for the king and were hostile toward the senate. So, Proculus Julius, a man of authority, as the tradition goes—he was, after all, vouching for an extraordinary event—summoned a public assembly. "My fellow citizens," he declared, "Today at dawn, Romulus, the father of this city, suddenly descended from the sky and appeared before me. Overcome with fear and awe, I stood there, beseeching him with prayers that it might be permissible for me to gaze on him. But he said, 'Depart, and proclaim to the Romans that it is the gods' will that my Rome be the capital of the world. So let them cultivate the art of war; let them know and teach their descendants that no human strength has the power to resist the arms of Rome.' With this pronouncement," concluded Proculus, "Romulus departed on high." It is astonishing what credence was given to this man's story, and how the longing for Romulus felt by the people and army was alleviated by belief in his immortality.

# 17   The Interregnum (Period between Kings)

Meanwhile an ambitious struggle for the kingship engaged the minds of the senators. It had not yet come to a question of individuals, since no one in the new populace was particularly preeminent. There was a struggle between factions from two groups. Those of Sabine origin wanted the king to be chosen from their own body, because they had had no king from their side since the death of Tatius and so they did not want to lose control of government, despite their equal status. The original Romans, on the other hand, rejected the idea of a foreign king. Nevertheless, despite their different inclinations, all wanted to be ruled by a king, for they had not yet experienced the sweetness of liberty. Then, since many neighboring states were disaffected, the senators became alarmed that a state without government and an army without a commander would be assailed by violence from outside. It was decided that there should be some head of state, but nobody could make up his mind to yield to another. And so the hundred senators shared the power among themselves, setting up groups of ten and appointing one man for each group to preside over the government. Ten men exercised authority, but only one had the insignia of command and the lictors; the command was limited to a period of five days and passed to all in rotation. For a year the kingship (*regnum*) lapsed. This interval was called an *interregnum*, a name that it still has today.

The people were grumbling that their servitude had been multiplied: they now had a hundred masters instead of one. It was apparent that they would allow nothing except a king, one chosen by them. When the senators realized that these ideas were stirring, they thought that they should spontaneously offer what they were about to lose. So, they won the people's favor by granting them supreme power on such terms that they gave away no more of their privilege than they retained. They decreed that, when the people had chosen a king, their choice should be valid only if it was ratified by the senators. Today also, the same right is exercised in voting for laws and magistrates, though it is robbed of its force because the senators ratify the outcome of an election in advance, before the people can vote. Then the *interrex* summoned the assembly and said, "Citizens, may what you are about to do be propitious, favorable, and fortunate. Choose your king! This is the will of the senate. Then, if you choose one who is worthy to succeed Romulus, the senate will ratify your choice." This so pleased the people that they did not want to give the appearance of being outdone in goodwill, and so they merely resolved that the senate should decide who should be king in Rome.

# D    The Reign of Numa (1.18–21)

## 18    The Sabine Numa Pompilius becomes King

In those days, Numa Pompilius was famed for his justice and his sense of obligation to the gods. He lived in the Sabine town of Cures and was most learned—inasmuch as anyone of that time could be—in all law, both divine and human. In default of another name, people claim that Pythagoras of Samos was his teacher. But it is established that Pythagoras lived in the reign of Servius Tullius, which was more than a hundred years later, and that he gathered bands of devoted disciples on the distant shores of Italy around Metapontum, Heraclea, and Croton. So, even if he had belonged to that time, how could his fame have reached from that area to the Sabines? What common language would he have used to excite anyone with a desire to learn? How could a solitary man have safely made his way through peoples so different in speech and customs? Therefore, I think that Numa's mind and moral principles derived from his own native disposition. He was trained not by foreign learning, but by the strict and severe teaching of the Sabines, the most incorrupt of ancient peoples.

When Numa's name was proposed, the Roman senators thought that the power would shift to the Sabines if the king were chosen from them. Nevertheless nobody dared to propose himself, anyone of his own faction, or indeed any other of the senators or citizens in preference to this great man. So they unanimously decided that the kingship be offered to Numa Pompilius. When summoned, Numa ordered that, just as Romulus had assumed the kingship by augury at the foundation of the city, so too the gods should be consulted in his case. Then he was led to the citadel by an augur[21] who thereafter, as a mark of honor, held a sacred office that became a permanent function of the state. Numa sat on a stone, facing south. On his left sat the augur, his head covered, holding in his right hand a crooked staff without knots, which is called a *lituus*. There, looking out over the city and countryside, he prayed to the gods and marked the regions from east to west, designating those to the south as "right," and those to the north as "left." He fixed in his mind a sign opposite him, as far as the eye can reach. Then, transferring his staff to his left hand and placing his right hand on Numa's head, he uttered the following prayer: "Father Jupiter, if it is the will of the gods that this man, Numa Pompilius, whose head I am touching, be king in Rome, then reveal to us sure signs within the boundaries that I have set." Then he specified the auspices that he wished to be sent. Sent they were, and so Numa was declared king and came down from the sacred area of augury.

## 19    Numa Establishes the Foundation of Roman Religion

Having received the kingship in this way, Numa prepared to give the new city that had been founded by force of arms a new foundation in justice, law, and proper observances. But he realized that it was not possible in the midst of wars to accustom men whose minds were brutalized by military service to such changes: the warlike spirit of his people must be softened by their giving up the use of arms. He therefore built a temple of Janus at the foot of the Argiletum, as an indicator of peace and war so that, when open, it signified that the state was at war; when closed, that all the surrounding people were pacified. Twice since the reign of Numa, it has been closed: once during the consulship of Titus Manlius after the First Punic War, and the second time, which the gods granted our generation to see, after the war at Actium, when the commanding general Caesar Augustus achieved peace on land and sea.[22]

Numa closed the temple after he had first won over the minds of all the neighboring peoples with alliances and treaties. But he was afraid that relief from foreign dangers might cause the spirit that had been held in check by military discipline and fear of the enemy to become soft from idleness. The first thing to do, he thought, was to instill in them a fear of the gods, on the assumption that it would be most effective with a populace that was unskilled and, for those days, primitive. Since he could not get through to their minds without inventing some miraculous story, he pretended that he had nocturnal meetings with the goddess Egeria. On her advice, he said, he was establishing rites that had the highest approval of the gods and he was appointing priests for each of the gods.

First of all, he divided the year into twelve months, according to the revolutions of the moon. The moon, however, does not supply thirty days for each individual month, and so the lunar year is eleven days short of the full year that is marked by the sun's revolution. Accordingly, he inserted intercalary months in such a way that in the twentieth year, the solar and lunar calendars would again coincide, the days coming round

---

21. See Glossary.

22. In 235 BC and 29 BC respectively. The First Punic War ended in 241 BC; the battle of Actium took place in 31 BC.

to the same position of the sun from which they had started.[23] He also appointed days on which state business could or could not be done, since it would be desirable to have times when nothing could be brought before the people.[24]

## 20    Numa Establishes New Priesthoods

Numa then turned his attention to the appointment of priests, but he himself performed most rites, especially those that now belong to the *flamen Dialis*.[25] He realized, however, that in a warlike nation there would be more kings like Romulus than like himself, and that they would go off to war. So, he appointed the *flamen Dialis* as a permanent priest, distinguishing him with special dress and a regal curule chair. To him he added two *flamens*, one for Mars and the other for Quirinus.[26] He chose virgins for the service of Vesta, a priesthood that originated in Alba and was thus associated with the race of Rome's founder. For them, so that they might be perpetual attendants of her temple, he decreed a stipend from the public treasury, marking their revered and inviolable status by their chastity and other signal honors. Likewise he chose twelve Salii for Mars Gradivus, granting them the distinction of wearing an embroidered tunic and, over the tunic, a bronze breastplate. He ordered them to carry the shields from heaven called *ancilia* and to go through the city, singing hymns and dancing their triple-beat war dance.[27]

Next from the senators he chose Numa Marcius, son of Marcius, as pontiff, entrusting to him all the written and authenticated sacred rites that specified with what victims, on what days, and in which temple sacrifices should be made, and from what sources they should be funded. All other public and private rituals he made subject to the decrees of the pontiff, so that there should be somebody to whom the people could come for advice to prevent any disturbance of the gods' rights as a result of the neglect of the ancestral rituals and the adoption of foreign ones. The same pontiff was to teach not only the ceremonies of the gods above, but the proper funeral rites and appeasement of the spirits of the dead, and also what prodigies sent by lightning or other visible signs were to be recognized as significant and requiring attention.[28] To elicit this information from the minds of the gods, Numa dedicated an altar on the Aventine to Jupiter Elicius (The "Eliciter" or "Enticer") and consulted the god by augury to find out what portents were to be recognized.

---

23. An intercalary month of twenty-two days was inserted, on the command of the *Pontifex Maximus*, after February 23.

24. See introduction to "A Roman Calendar: April" in this volume.

25. A priest (*flamen*) devoted to the cult of Jupiter.

26. Quirinus was identified as the deified Romulus, whose father was Mars.

27. The Salii were the "leaping" (*salire*) priests of Mars, who on March 1 (the traditional opening of the season for campaign) "set the arms in motion," bringing them forth from the temple into the public eye.

28. For prodigies, see Valerius Maximus section G in this volume.

## 21    The Success of Numa's Institutions

Consideration and attention to these matters turned the thoughts of the entire people away from violence and arms. They had something to occupy their minds, and, since the heavenly powers seemed to have an interest in human affairs, the people's constant preoccupation with the gods had imbued the hearts of all with such devotion that the state was governed by regard for good faith and oaths, rather than by fear of punishment under the law. And since Numa's subjects were modeling themselves on the character of the king as their unique example, so too the neighboring peoples—who had previously felt that a military camp, not a city, had been put in their midst to disturb the general peace—came to feel such a respect for the Romans that they considered it sacrilege to do violence to a nation that had so entirely turned to the worship of the gods.

There was a grove watered by a never-failing spring that flowed through its midst from a dark cave. Here Numa frequently went, without witnesses, as if to meet the goddess. He dedicated this grove to the Camenae, because, he said, they gave advice to his wife Egeria.[29] He also established an annual cult of Faith. He ordered that the *flamens* should drive to this shrine in a two-horse, covered carriage, and should make sacrifice with their hands wrapped as far as the fingers, thus signifying that faith must be kept and that, when men clasp hands, there too is the sacred temple of Faith. He established many other rites, as well as the places for sacrifice that the pontiffs call the Argei.[30]

But the greatest of all his works is that, throughout his entire reign, he safeguarded peace no less than he did his kingdom. Thus two successive kings, each in a different way, promoted the state: the one by war, the other by peace. Romulus ruled thirty-seven years, Numa forty-three. The state was not only strong but moderated by the arts of both war and peace.

[We omit Livy's account of two kings, Tullus Hostilius and Ancus Martius. The following brief summaries of their reigns were written by Eutropius in the 4th century AD:

Tullus Hostilius succeeded Numa. He renewed the previous wars and conquered the Albans (who were 12 miles from Rome) and the peoples of Veii and Fidenae (the latter were 6 miles from Rome, the former 18). He added the Caelian hill to Rome. In the 32nd year of his reign he was struck by lightning and burned along with his house.

After him Ancus Martius, the grandson of Numa on his mother's side, took power. He fought against the Latins. He also added the Aventine and Janiculum hills to the city and established a city on the sea 16 miles from Rome at the mouth of the Tiber river.[31] He died from disease in the 24th year of his reign.

We rejoin Livy with the fifth king, Tarquinius Priscus.]

---

29. Originally goddesses of natural springs and fountains, these deities were later associated with the Greek Muses.

30. On May 14 the Vestal Virgins visited twenty-seven stations around Rome to collect a series of straw dolls (called *Argei*), then threw them ritually into the Tiber River from the Wooden Bridge.

31. This is Ostia ("Mouth"), the port of Rome.

**E    The Reign of Tarquinius Priscus** (1.34–40)

## 34    Tarquinius Moves from Tarquinii to Rome

During the reign of Ancus, Lucumo, an energetic and wealthy man, took up residence at Rome, mainly because of his desire and expectation of achieving the high position that he had not been able to get in Tarquinii.[32] Though he came from there, he was of foreign origin, being the son of Demaratus of Corinth who had been exiled from his home by political faction. Demaratus had settled in Tarquinii, married, and produced two sons whose names were Lucumo and Arruns. Lucumo survived his father, inheriting all his property. Arruns died before his father, leaving a pregnant wife. The father did not long survive the son, but, being unaware of his daughter-in-law's pregnancy, died without providing for his grandson in his will. The son was born after his grandfather's death without any share in his property and so was called Egerius ("The Needy One") because of his poverty.

On the other hand, Lucumo was the heir to the whole estate. His wealth was already giving him self-confidence, but his fortunes were increased by his marriage to Tanaquil, a woman of upper-class birth who would not easily tolerate a situation as a wife that was inferior to that into which she had been born. The Etruscans despised Lucumo as the son of a foreign exile, and Tanaquil was unable to bear this indignity. Prepared to disregard her natural love for her fatherland provided that she could see her husband in a position of honor, she got the idea of leaving Tarquinii. Rome seemed to be the most promising place for her purpose. Among a new people, where nobility was quickly acquired and based on merit, there would, she reckoned, be room for a brave and energetic man. The Sabine Tatius had held the kingship; Numa had been summoned to rule from Cures; Ancus was born of a Sabine mother and had only one noble ancestor, Numa. Tanaquil had no trouble in persuading a man who was yearning for high office and whose claim to Tarquinii as his native city was only on his mother's side.

And so they took their possessions and moved to Rome. They happened to have reached the Janiculum when an eagle came gently down, poised on its wings and, as Lucumo was sitting in the wagon with his wife, removed his cap. Then, after flying over the wagon with loud screeches, it deftly replaced the cap on his head, sent, as it were, by the gods for this purpose. This augury, it is said, was joyfully accepted by Tanaquil, a woman skilled in interpreting prodigies from the sky, as Etruscans generally are. Embracing her husband, she told him to expect a high and exalted position. The type of bird was significant; likewise the area of the sky from which it had come and the god whose messenger it was. It had performed the auspice around the highest part of a man; it had removed the adornment placed on a mortal's head, only to put it back with divine approval.

Such were their hopes and reflections as they rode into the city. They bought a house and announced his name as Lucius Tarquinius Priscus. His newness and wealth made him conspicuous among the Romans. He himself advanced his good fortune, winning support wherever possible by his friendliness, courteous hospitality, and generosity until his fame reached the king's palace. His acquaintance with the king soon developed into the privileges of a family friend because of his generous and efficient

---

32. This is an important Etruscan town (modern Tarquinia) fifty-five miles north of Rome.

service. He was involved equally in state and private decisions, in both war and domestic affairs. Finally, after being tested in every way, he was named in the king's will as guardian of his children.

## 35    Tarquinius Becomes the Fifth King of Rome

Ancus reigned for twenty-four years, a king who was the equal of his predecessors in the arts of war and peace and in the glory he achieved. Since Ancus' sons were now almost adults, Tarquin was becoming all the more insistent that an assembly to choose a king be summoned as soon as possible. The meeting was proclaimed and, as the time drew near, he sent the sons off on a hunting expedition. Tarquin is said to have been the first to canvass votes for the kingship and make a speech that was designed to win over the hearts of the people. He pointed out that he was not seeking anything unusual: he was not the first—a move that might have occasioned indignation and surprise—but the third foreigner in Rome to aspire to the kingship. Tatius had become king after being not only a foreigner, but also an enemy; Numa was a stranger to the city and, without seeking the kingship, had been invited to come and take it. He himself, when he had become his own master, had moved to Rome with his wife and all his property. For the larger part of life in which men serve their city, he had lived in Rome, rather than in the city of his birth. Both in domestic and military matters, he had had no mean teacher, King Ancus himself; and so he had learned Roman laws and Roman rites. He had emulated everybody in obedience and deference to the king, rivaling the king himself in his goodwill to others.

As he recounted these claims that were by no means false, the Roman people chose him as king, with a huge consensus. This man, so outstanding in other ways, continued even when king the same kind of politicking that he had employed in seeking the kingship. Thinking as much of strengthening his own position as enlarging the state, he added a hundred members to the senate who were called senators of the "lesser families." They belonged, of course, to the faction of the king to whose favor they owed their admission to the senate.

Tarquin's first war was with the Latins, and he took the city of Apiolae by storm. Returning with more booty than reports of the war had led him to expect, he gave games that were more lavish and elaborate than those of the earlier kings. It was then, for the first time, that the area was marked out for a circus, the one that is now called the Circus Maximus. Places were set apart for senators and knights, where they could each have viewing stands for themselves. They were called *fori*, "seating sections." They watched the spectacles from seats raised on props, twelve feet from the ground. Horses and boxers, mostly imported from Etruria, provided the entertainment. From then on, the games were held at regular annual intervals, being variously called the Roman and Great Games. The same king also apportioned to private citizens building sites around the forum; colonnades and shops were also erected.

## 36    The Miracle of the Augur Attus Navius

Tarquin was also preparing to surround the city with a stone wall when war with the Sabines interrupted the undertaking. The invasion was so sudden that the enemy were crossing the Anio before the Roman army could march out and stop them. In Rome there was panic. The first encounter was indecisive, with great slaughter on either side. The enemy forces withdrew into their camp, giving the Romans time to prepare anew for war. Tarquinius thought that his cavalry was especially lacking in strength. To the Ramnes, Titienses, and Luceres that Romulus had enrolled, he decided to add others and to distinguish them by giving them his own name. But because Romulus had done this only after taking the auspices, Attus Navius, a famous augur of that time, said there could be no change or innovation unless the birds gave their consent. This angered the king, who mocked his skill, as the story goes, with the words, "Come, inspired seer, determine by augury whether what I am now thinking can actually be done." Attus took the auspices and replied that it would surely come to pass. Then the king said, "What I have in mind is that you will cut a grindstone in two with a razor. Here, take these things, and do the thing that your birds foretell can be done." Then, they say, the augur split the grindstone in two without hesitation. There was a statue of Attus, his head covered, in the *Comitium*, on the very steps at the left of the senate house, on the spot where the event took place. Tradition has it that the stone also was placed in the same spot to be a memorial of that miracle for posterity. Whatever the case, such great honor accrued to augury and the office of augur that thereafter nothing was done, either at home or in the field, unless auspices had been taken, whether it be assemblies of the people, mustering of armies, or the most vital affairs—all were postponed if the birds did not give their consent.

Tarquin made no change in the organization of the centuries of knights but doubled their numerical strength so that there were now 1,200 knights in three centuries. The centuries kept the same names, but those that were added were called the Later Ones. Now, however, the centuries are known as the six centuries because their number was doubled.

## 37    The Romans Rout the Sabines

After the expansion of the cavalry there was a second conflict with the Sabines. But in addition to their increased strength, the Roman army was also helped by a covert stratagem. Men were sent to ignite a great quantity of firewood lying on the bank of the Anio and throw it into the river. With the help of the wind, the wood blazed up and the greater part, packed on rafts, lodged against the piles of the bridge, setting it on fire. This also alarmed the Sabines during the battle, hindering their flight once they were routed. Many escaped the enemy only to perish in the river. Their arms were recognized as they floated down the Tiber toward the city, making the Roman victory apparent even before the official news could arrive. In this battle the cavalry especially distinguished themselves. The story is that they were placed on either flank and rushed in from both sides when the center line of their infantry was driven back. They not only checked the Sabines who were pressing fiercely on the heels of the Roman infantry as they gave ground, but suddenly routed them. Scattered in disarray, the Sabines were running toward the hills and a few of them made it. But the majority, as was mentioned earlier, were driven into the river by the cavalry.

Tarquin thought that he ought to go after the enemy while they were in a state of panic. So, he sent the booty and captives to Rome and made a huge pile of the enemies' arms, setting it on fire in fulfillment of a vow to Vulcan. Then he proceeded to lead his army into Sabine territory. Although things had gone badly for the Sabines and they could not hope to do any better, they nevertheless took the field with a hastily levied army, since circumstances did not give time for deliberation. They were then routed a second time and, in an almost desperate situation, sued for peace.

## 38    The Town of Collatia Surrenders; Tarquin Builds in Rome

Collatia and whatever land the Sabines held on the side of the town nearer to Rome were taken from them. Egerius, the son of the king's brother, was left in Collatia with a garrison. I find that the people of Collatia capitulated according to the following formula for surrender. The king asked: "Are you the envoys and spokesmen who have been sent by the people of Collatia to surrender yourselves and the people of Collatia?" "We are." "Are the people of Collatia free to make their own decisions?" "They are." "Do you surrender yourselves, the people of Collatia, your city, territory, water, boundary markers, shrines, movables, and all things belonging to gods and men into my control and that of the Roman people?" "We do." "And I receive the surrender." At the conclusion of the Sabine war, Tarquinius returned to Rome and triumphed.[33] Then he made war on the Ancient Latins. In this campaign there was no general battle to decide the whole issue, but the king subdued the entire Latin race by leading his troops against each town individually: Corniculum, Old Ficulea, Cameria, Crustumerium, Ameriola, Medullia, Nomentum. These were the towns that were captured from the Ancient Latins or from people who had gone over to the Latins. Peace was then made.

   Thereafter, Tarquin undertook the tasks of peace with a greater enthusiasm than he had expended in war, with the result that the people had no more rest at home than on campaign. He prepared to surround the unfortified parts of the city with a stone wall, the beginning of which had been interrupted by the Sabine war. He drained the lowest parts of the city around the forum and the other valleys between the hills. There was no easy runoff for the waters from the flat areas, and so he constructed sewers that sloped down toward the Tiber. On the Capitol, in a spirit that foresaw the future grandeur of the site, he laid the foundations for a temple to Jupiter that he had vowed in the Sabine war.[34]

## 39    A Miraculous Flame Appears around the Head of a Future King

A prodigy occurred in the palace at this time, miraculous in both its manifestation and outcome. The story is that the head of a child named Servius Tullius burst into flames as he was lying asleep, a sight that many people saw. The king and queen were aroused by the great uproar caused by this amazing miracle. One of the household slaves was bringing water to put out the flame, but the queen restrained him. Calming the uproar, she ordered that the boy not be moved until he awoke of his own accord. Soon, as sleep

---

33. See "triumph" in the Glossary.

34. This will become the Temple to Jupiter Optimus Maximus, the largest temple in Rome, completed by his son Tarquinius Superbus (see ch. 55 below).

left him, so too did the flame. Then Tanaquil took her husband aside and said, "You see this boy that we are raising in such humble circumstances? We should realize that he will be a beacon for us when we are in jeopardy and a safeguard for our royal house when it is stricken. Henceforth let us rear him with every indulgence that we can, since he will be a source of great distinction to the state and our family." From then on, Servius was looked on as their son and trained in those skills by which men are roused to aspire to great fortune. It worked out easily because it was the will of the gods.

The youth turned out to be truly of a regal disposition. When Tarquinius was looking for a son-in-law, none of the Roman youth could be compared to Servius in any skill, and so the king betrothed his daughter to him. For whatever reason such a great honor was conferred upon him, it is difficult to believe that he was the son of a slave woman and was himself a slave in his childhood. I am more of the opinion of those who say that, after the capture of Corniculum, the pregnant wife of Servius Tullius, the slain leader of that city, was recognized among the other captives; then, because of her outstanding nobility, she was rescued from slavery by the Roman queen.[35] And so the woman gave birth in Rome in the house of Priscus Tarquinius. Because of this act of generosity, a friendship developed between the two women and the child was held in affection and esteem, since he was raised in the palace from infancy. The belief that he was born of a slave woman is the result of his mother's misfortune to have fallen into the hands of the enemy upon the capture of her native city.

## 40    Tarquin is Murdered

Some thirty-eight years after the beginning of Tarquin's reign, Servius Tullius was held in the greatest esteem, not only by the king, but also by the senators and the people. The two sons of Ancus had always been outraged that they had been driven from their father's throne by their tutor's deceit and that Rome was ruled by a stranger who was not of neighboring stock, still less Italian. Their sense of outrage was vastly increased at the prospect that the kingdom would not return to them even after Tarquin's death but would fall headlong into the possession of slaves. In the same state where, a hundred or so years earlier, Romulus, son of a god and himself a god, had reigned as long as he was on earth, the royal power would be held by a slave, the son of a slave woman. It would be a disgrace shared not only by the Roman name, but particularly by their family if, while Ancus' sons still lived, the Roman kingship should be open not just to foreigners, but also to slaves. They decided to prevent the insult by murder. But resentment at their injustice spurred them on against Tarquin more than Servius. For if the king survived an assassination attempt, he would be a more formidable avenger than a private citizen. But if Servius was killed, Tarquinius was likely to choose another son-in-law and make him his heir. For these reasons, the plot was aimed at the king himself.

Two of the most ferocious shepherds were chosen to do the deed. Armed with their usual rustic implements, they feigned a brawl in the forecourt of the palace, and by making as much of a disturbance as possible, they attracted the attention of all the

---

35. The origin of Servius was much debated in antiquity; see Inscriptions no. 59 (column 1) in this volume.

king's attendants. As they called out the king's name, their shouts reached the innermost part of the palace. So, they were summoned into the king's presence. At first both raised their voices, each one trying to shout the other down. They were restrained by a lictor who ordered them to speak in turn. When finally they stopped railing at each other, one of them began his speech as arranged. While he had the king's full attention, the other raised an axe and brought it down on the king's head. Leaving the weapon in the wound, both of them dashed for the doors.

## F    The Reign of Servius Tullius (1.41–48)

### 41    Tanaquil Secures the Succession of Servius.

As those around him took the dying Tarquin in their arms, lictors seized the fugitives. There was an uproar as people rushed in, wondering what was going on. In the midst of the commotion, Tanaquil ordered the palace to be closed and threw out all the witnesses. At the same time, as if hope still remained, she busily got together what was needed for healing a wound, while also preparing other safeguards in case her hopes should fail. Quickly she sent for Servius and showed him her husband's almost lifeless body. She took his right hand, begging him not to allow the death of his father-in-law to go unavenged nor his mother-in-law to become the laughingstock of her enemies. "The kingship is yours, Servius, if you are a man," she cried. "It does not belong to those who used the hands of others to commit this terrible crime. Arouse yourself and follow the leadership of the gods who long ago surrounded your head with divine fire, portending your future fame. May that flame from heaven now stir you! Now be truly awakened! We too were foreigners and yet we reigned. Consider who you are, not your birth. If your mind is too numb to make plans in this sudden crisis, at least follow mine."

Since the shouting and pushing of the crowd could scarcely be withstood, Tanaquil addressed the people from the upper story of the house through the windows that faced onto New Street (the king lived near the temple of Jupiter Stator). She bade them be optimistic, saying that the king had been rendered unconscious by a sudden blow, but the weapon had not gone deep into his body. He had already regained consciousness; the blood had been wiped away and the wound examined. All the signs were healthy. She was confident that they would see him in a day or so. Meanwhile she ordered the people to obey Servius Tullius: he would dispense justice and perform the king's other duties. Servius appeared in the royal robe, attended by lictors. Sitting in the royal seat, he made some decisions and pretended that he would consult the king about others. And so, for several days after Tarquin had already breathed his last, his death was concealed, as Servius strengthened his position by pretending to act on another's behalf. Then at last, when the ritual lament was raised in the palace, it became clear what had happened. Servius surrounded himself with a strong guard and was the first to assume the kingship without being chosen by the people. He did, however, have the consent of the senators. Ancus' sons had already gone into exile in Suessa Pometia, when the hired killers had been caught and the announcement made that the king still lived and Servius was in control.

## 42     Servius Strengthens his Position and Organizes Rome

Servius now proceeded to secure his position by private as well as public measures. Fearing that Tarquin's sons might show the same animosity toward him that Ancus' sons had exhibited to Tarquin, he married his two daughters to the king's sons, Lucius and Arruns Tarquinius. But his human wisdom did not break the force of destiny. Even among his own family, jealousy for the kingship created an atmosphere of distrust and hostility. Most opportunely for the peaceful maintenance of the prevailing situation, a war was undertaken against the Veientines (the truce had now expired) and other Etruscans. In that war, the bravery and good fortune of Servius Tullius shone forth. He routed a huge enemy army and returned to Rome, having proved himself the undisputed king in the minds of both senators and people.

Then Servius embarked on what was by far his most important peacetime work. Just as Numa had been the author of divine law, so posterity would regard Servius as the one who established all the distinctions among the citizen body and the ranks whereby there is a clear differentiation between the various grades of wealth and prestige. He instituted the census, a most useful thing for a state that was to achieve such great dominion.[36] A man's duties in war and in peace would be determined, not indiscriminately on an individual basis as before, but in proportion to a man's wealth. It was at this time that Servius distributed the people into classes and centuries in accordance with the census, an arrangement that was suitable for either peace or war.[37]

## 43     The Constitutional Reforms Attributed to Servius Tullius

For those who possessed 100,000 *asses* or more, Servius created eighty centuries, forty each of seniors and juniors.[38] These were all known as the first class; seniors were to be prepared to guard the city, juniors to wage war in the field. These men were required to supply a helmet, a round shield, greaves, and breastplate, all of bronze, to act as protection for their bodies; their offensive weapons were a spear and sword. To this class were added two centuries of craftsmen who were to serve without arms. Their task was to attend to the siege equipment in war. The second class came from those whose rating was between 100,000 and 75,000 *asses*; from these, twenty centuries were enrolled for seniors and juniors. They were required to supply an oblong shield rather than a round one, and everything else except for a breastplate. Servius set the rating of the third class at 50,000 *asses*; it had the same number of centuries as the second and the same age distinctions. Nor was there any change in the arms, except for the omission of greaves. In the fourth class, the rating was 25,000 *asses*; they formed the same number of centuries, but there was a change in the arms: they were given nothing except a spear and

---

36. Livy's assertion that the census (see Glossary) was established during the period of the kings is probably not accurate.

37. A "century" was originally a military unit of one hundred men, but here they represent the classes of the so-called *Comitia Centuriata*, the main voting assembly. See the introduction to Quintus Cicero, *Running for Office: A Handbook* in this volume.

38. The junior centuries included men between seventeen and forty-five years old, the senior from forty-six to sixty in age.

a javelin. The fifth class was made larger, forming thirty centuries. They carried slings and stones for missiles. Added to these were the trumpeters and horn-blowers, distributed over three centuries. The rating of this class was 11,000 *asses*. Those whose rating was less than this formed the rest of the population; they were put in one century and were exempt from military service.

When he had organized the distribution and equipment of the infantry, Servius enrolled twelve centuries of knights from the leading men of the state. He likewise formed six other centuries, three of which had been instituted by Romulus, keeping the same names that they had received by augury. For the purchase of horses, they were given 10,000 *asses* each from the state treasury. Unmarried women were assessed for the maintenance of these horses, and they had each to pay 2,000 *asses* per year.

All these burdens were shifted from the poor to the rich. The latter were then granted a special privilege. Under the tradition handed down by Romulus and preserved by the other kings, the vote of each individual implied an equality of rights and power. But now suffrage was no longer given indiscriminately to all. Gradations were made in such a way that no one seemed to be excluded from voting, but all power was in the hands of the leading men of the state. For the knights were called upon to vote first, and then the eighty centuries of the first class.[39] At that point, if there was any disagreement—which rarely happened—the order was given to call on the second class. Almost never did they descend as far as the lowest citizens.

Nor should we be surprised that the present organization is not consistent with the total number of centuries instituted by Servius Tullius, for the former came into existence after the number of tribes had increased to thirty-five and their number had been doubled in the centuries of the juniors and seniors. When Servius divided the city into four parts according to the areas and hills that were inhabited, he called them "tribes," a word that, I think, derives from "tribute." He also planned a method of collecting tribute equitably, on the basis of the census. But these four tribes were not connected with the distribution or number of the centuries.

## 44    Servius Extends the Pomerium[40]

Servius expedited the completion of the census by passing a law that threatened those who failed to register with death or imprisonment. He then proclaimed that all Roman citizens, both cavalry and infantry, were to assemble at dawn on the Campus Martius, each in his own century. When the whole army was drawn up there, he purified it with the sacrifice of a pig, sheep, and bull (*suovetaurilia*). This was called the "closing of the *lustrum*" because it marked the end of the census. Eighty thousand citizens are said to have been registered at this census. Fabius Pictor, our oldest written authority, adds that this was the number of people capable of bearing arms. Given this large number, it was apparent that the city also needed to be expanded. Servius added two hills, the Quirinal and Viminal, and then developed the Esquiline, living there himself in order to enhance its prestige. He surrounded the city with a mound, ditch, and wall, and

---

39. On voting procedures, see Quintus Cicero, *Running for Office: A Handbook*, with introduction, in this volume.

40. The sacred boundary of the city; see Glossary.

so extended the *pomerium*. Those who look only at the meaning of the word derive it from *postmoerium*, "the part behind the wall;" but rather it is *circamoerium*, "the area on both sides of the wall"—the space that the Etruscans, whenever they founded a city and selected a site for a wall, used to consecrate after taking auspices at fixed points along the boundary. They did this so that, on the inner side, the buildings should not touch the walls (the general practice today is to join them) and, on the outside, there should be some space that was kept clear and free from human use. The space where divine law forbade habitation or cultivation is called the *pomerium*, as much because the wall was behind it as because it was behind the wall. Whenever the constant growth of the city created a need to advance the walls, the consecrated boundary stones were also moved forward.

## 45    The Temple to Diana is Built on the Aventine

The king had promoted the state by enlarging the city and arranging domestic affairs to meet the needs of both war and peace. Then, to avoid always being dependent on force of arms for asserting Roman interests, he tried to increase his dominion by means of diplomacy, at the same time adding splendor to the city. Already at that time, the temple of Diana at Ephesus was famous, reputedly built as a joint enterprise by the cities of Asia. Servius lavishly praised this cooperation and community of worship to the Latin leaders, with whom he had assiduously cultivated ties of hospitality and friendship in both a private and official capacity. By reiterating the same points, he convinced the Latin peoples to join with the Roman people in building a temple to Diana at Rome.

This was an admission that Rome was the capital city[41]—an issue that had so often caused armed conflict. Although this had apparently now ceased to be a concern to the Latins after their many unsuccessful efforts, there was one of the Sabines who imagined that he had a chance of recovering their dominion by a plan of his own. It is said that a heifer of wondrous size and beauty was born in Sabine territory, on the property of a certain head of a family. For many generations, its horns have been fastened up in the vestibule of the temple of Diana to commemorate this marvel. This heifer was considered to be a prodigy, as indeed it was. Soothsayers prophesied that dominion would belong to the state whose citizen should sacrifice the animal to Diana. The priest of Diana's temple had heard of this prophecy. On the first suitable day for sacrifice, the Sabine led the heifer to the temple of Diana in Rome and set it before the altar. The priest was impressed by the famed size of the victim but, mindful of the prophecy, asked him, "Stranger, what do you think you are doing? Surely you aren't going to make a sacrifice to Diana without first purifying yourself? Why don't you first bathe in running water? The Tiber is flowing down there in the valley." The stranger, touched by a sense of religious obligation, immediately went down to the Tiber because he wanted to do everything with the proper ritual so that the outcome would match the

---

41. Livy's point here is that there was already a Temple to Diana in Nemi, located south of Rome in the heart of Latium. The establishment of the same cult in Rome was meant to negate the importance of the Latin cult center, although in reality the cult of Diana at Nemi continued to prosper.

prediction. Meanwhile the Roman sacrificed the heifer to Diana, an act that was wonderfully gratifying to both the king and the citizens.

## 46    Servius' Daughter and the Younger Tarquin Conspire against Him

Servius was now undoubtedly king *de facto*, but he kept hearing that the young Tarquin was from time to time making remarks that the king was ruling without the consent of the people. So, first he won over the goodwill of the people by dividing the territory captured from the enemy among all the citizens; then he ventured to ask the people whether they were willing to vote for him as their king. Servius was declared king with a unanimity as great as that accorded to any previous king. But this event did not diminish Tarquin's hopes of obtaining the kingship. Indeed, he had realized that Servius' action of giving land to the people was contrary to the wishes of the senators, and so he thought that he had been given an opportunity to censure the king in the senate and increase his own power in that body. He himself was a young man of fiery spirit, and he had a wife, Tullia, who goaded the restlessness of that spirit.[42] For even the royal house of Rome produced an example of a crime worthy of Greek tragedy, in order that hatred of kings might hasten the coming of liberty and the last kingship be one that was obtained by a criminal act.

This Lucius Tarquinius—it is not at all clear whether he was the son or grandson of King Tarquinius Priscus, though I follow the majority of sources, and so would declare that he was the son—had a brother, Arruns Tarquinius, a young man of a gentle nature. These two young men, as noted above, were married to the king's two daughters, who were very different in their characters. By chance it happened that the two violent characters were not married to each other—thanks, I suppose, to the good fortune of the Roman people—so that Servius' reign would be prolonged and the state's traditions become established. It was distressing to the fierce Tullia that her husband did not have the stuff of ambition and boldness. So, she turned completely from him to his brother; he was the one she admired, calling him a man and one of true royal blood. She despised her sister, because, as she said, now that the other woman had a real man as a husband, she had lost the boldness that a woman should have. Similarity quickly brought the two together, as usually happens, since evil is most drawn to evil.

But it was the woman who began all the trouble. She got into the habit of conversing secretly with another woman's husband and spared no insults when speaking about her husband to his brother, nor about her sister to her husband. She said that it would have been better for her to be unmarried and for him to be without a wife than for them to be married to their inferiors. In the present situation, however, they had to remain inactive because of others' cowardice. If the gods had given her the husband she deserved, she would soon have seen in her own house the royal power that she now saw in her father's. Quickly she filled the young man's mind with her own recklessness.

---

42. Tullia is the daughter of the king; daughters typically took the feminine form of their father's surname, in this case *Tullius* (see Appendix "Roman Naming Conventions"). In fact, both of Servius' daughters took the name Tullia, adding to the confusion of the account here.

Deaths followed in quick succession, ensuring vacancies in their homes for new spouses. And so Lucius Tarquinius and the younger Tullia were married. Servius did not prevent the marriage but hardly gave his approval.

## 47    The Younger Tarquin Assumes the Throne

From that time on, Tullius' old age was increasingly a source of danger, and his rule became more endangered day by day. Already the woman was looking from one crime to another, and she did not allow her husband any peace either by night or day, urging him not to let the murders they had committed prove ineffective. She had not wanted a husband simply to be called his wife and endure slavery with him in silence. What she had lacked was a man who thought himself worthy to be a king, who remembered that he was the son of Tarquinius Priscus, and who preferred to have the throne rather than to hope for it. "If you are the man that I think I married," she said, "I salute you both as husband and king. But if not, then the situation has changed for the worse, for crime is compounded by cowardice. Why don't you rouse yourself to action? You don't come from Corinth or Tarquinii. Unlike your father, you don't have to take over a foreign kingdom. Your household gods, the gods of your ancestors, your father's image,[43] the royal palace and the royal throne in your home, and the name of Tarquin declare and summon you to be king. Or, if you have so little nerve for this, why do you disappoint the citizens? Why do you allow yourself to be seen as a prince? Get out of here and go to Tarquinii or Corinth; take yourself back to your roots! You are more like your brother than your father."

With these and other taunts, she goaded the young man. She herself could not bear the thought that Tanaquil, a foreign woman, had had the nerve to be kingmaker twice in succession, once for her husband and then for her son-in-law; whereas she, a king's daughter, was unable to have any influence in making and unmaking a king. Tarquin, spurred on by his wife's frenzy, went round soliciting the senators, especially the heads of the lesser families. He reminded them of his father's kindness to them, seeking their favor in return. The young men he attracted by gifts, increasing his influence everywhere not only by extravagant promises but also by slandering the king. Finally, when it seemed the time for action, he surrounded himself with a band of armed men and rushed into the forum.

Then, amid the general consternation and panic, he seated himself on the royal throne in front of the senate house and ordered a herald to summon the senators to come before King Tarquin at the senate house. They came immediately, some by prearrangement, others fearing that their nonappearance might prove harmful to them. Astonished at this strange miracle, they thought that Servius was finished. Then Tarquin began by maligning the king, going back to his family origins. Servius, the son of a slave woman, was a slave himself who, after the undeserved death of Tarquin's own father, had seized the kingdom, thanks to a gift given by a woman. There had been no *interregnum* as on previous occasions; no elections had been held; there had been no

---

43. These are the *imaginēs* or wax masks of one's ancestors. See Glossary, and Polybius, *History* chs. 53–54 in this volume.

vote of the people or ratification by the senators. Such was Servius' birth; this was how he came to be king. He had promoted the lowest types of society, to which he himself belonged. His hatred of others' noble birth had caused him to take land from the leaders of the state and divide it among the rabble. All the burdens that had formerly been shared, he had transferred to the city's foremost men. He had initiated the census to make the fortunes of the rich a conspicuous mark for envy and a source for extravagant gifts that he could give to the most needy whenever he wished.

## 48    Servius is Murdered, his Corpse Defiled

Servius, alerted by this alarming news, interrupted this harangue, calling out in a loud voice from the vestibule of the senate house, "What's all this about, Tarquin? How dare you have the audacity to summon the senators and take my seat while I yet live?" Tarquin ferociously replied that he was occupying his own father's seat; a king's son was a much better heir to the throne than a slave. Too long had Tullius had the license to mock and insult his masters. Shouts arose from the partisans of each man. People rushed to the senate house. It was clear that the victor would become king. Then Tarquin was forced by sheer necessity to dare the ultimate. Being far stronger because of both his age and vigor, he seized Servius around the waist, carried him out of the senate house, and flung him to the bottom of the steps. Then he returned to the senate house to control the senators. The king's companions and attendants fled. Servius himself, faint from loss of blood and half dead, was making his way back home without his royal retinue when the men that Tarquin had sent in pursuit caught up with him, and he was killed.

There is a belief that Tullia suggested this deed, which is not inconsistent with the rest of her wickedness. In any case, it is generally agreed that she drove in a carriage into the forum and, unafraid of the men who had gathered there, summoned her husband from the senate house and was the first to hail him as king. He ordered her to get out of the fray. On her way back home, she came to the top of Cyprius Street, where the shrine of Diana recently stood. As she sought to turn to the right toward the Urbian slope to reach the Esquiline hill, her driver recoiled in terror and, pulling in the reins, pointed out to his mistress the murdered king lying there. Abominable and inhuman is the crime that is said to have ensued. The place itself is a reminder, for they call it the Street of Wickedness. Crazed by the avenging spirits of her sister and husband, Tullia is said to have driven her carriage over her father's body. Spattered and defiled by the blood of her murdered father, she brought some of it on her vehicle to the gods of her own household and those of her husband's. These deities, in their anger, saw to it that the evil beginning of this reign was soon followed by a similar end.

Servius Tullius ruled for forty-four years. His reign was such that even a good and moderate successor would have found it difficult to match him. But this renown has been enhanced by the fact that just and legitimate kingship perished along with him. Mild and moderate as his rule was, some sources say that he intended to resign because it was rule by a single individual. This he would have done had not wickedness within his own family interrupted his plans to give freedom to his country.

**G    The Reign of Tarquinius Superbus** (1.49–60)

**49    The Despotic Reign of the Younger Tarquin Begins**

Such was the beginning of the reign of Lucius Tarquinius, who, because of his actions, was given the name of Superbus ("Arrogant"). He forbade the burial of his own father-in-law, asserting that Romulus had also not received burial after his death. Then he killed those leading senators whom he believed had been Servius' supporters. Aware that the precedent he had set of seeking the kingship by criminal means might be used against him, he surrounded himself with a bodyguard; for he had no judicial right to the kingship, since he ruled without the bidding of the people or consent of the senators. In addition, his rule had to be protected by fear, since he had no hope of the citizens' affection. To instill this fear into the majority, he alone, without advisers, carried out the investigation of capital charges. For this reason, he was able to execute, exile, or fine not only those whom he suspected or disliked, but also those from whom he had nothing to gain but plunder. It was mainly senators whose numbers were depleted in this way. Tarquin, moreover, was determined not to replace them, so that the fewness of their number would bring more contempt on the senate, which, in turn, would be less able to express anger at its lack of participation in state business.

Tarquin was the first of the kings to break with the custom of consulting the senate on all matters, a custom handed down by his predecessors. He governed the state by consulting only members of his own family. On his own initiative, without the consent of the people or the senate, he made and unmade war, peace, treaties, and alliances, dealing with whomever he wanted. He concentrated on winning over the Latin peoples, in order that assistance from abroad might give him greater safety among the citizens at home. He created not only ties of hospitality with their leading men, but also marriage ties. He gave his daughter in marriage to Octavius Mamilius of Tusculum, who was by far the most important of the Latin peoples, being descended, if we believe the report, from Ulysses and Circe.[44] Through this marriage he gained ties with Mamilius' many relatives and friends.

**50    A Leader of the Latins Criticizes Tarquin**

Tarquin's influence among the Latin leaders was already considerable when he proclaimed a day for them to assemble at the grove of Ferentina, saying that there were matters of common interest that he wanted to discuss. They gathered in large numbers at dawn. Tarquin himself did indeed keep the appointment but only arrived shortly before sunset. Throughout the day there had been much discussion in the council on various topics. Turnus Herdonius from Aricia made a vehement attack on the absent Tarquin, saying that it was no wonder that he had been given the name Superbus in Rome—for already that name was current, though whispered behind his back. Could anything be more arrogant than to make a mockery of the entire Latin race as he was doing? Their leaders had been brought from their distant homes, whereas the very

---

44. The promontory of Circeii in Latium was traditionally identified as the location of the home of Circe from Homer's *Odyssey*. A great many places in Italy became connected with the travels of Odysseus. Latinus was said to be the son of Odysseus' son Telemachus by Circe.

man who had proclaimed the council was not present. Clearly his aim was to try their patience. If they submitted to the yoke, he would press them into servitude. Who couldn't see that he was aiming at sovereignty over the Latins? If his own citizens had done well in entrusting power to him, or if it had been entrusted and not stolen by parricide, then the Latins also should entrust it to him. But no, not even in that case, because he was of foreign birth. But if his own people were discontented with him—indeed, one after another they were being butchered, exiled, and deprived of their property—what better prospect was portended for the Latins? If they would listen to him, each man would go back to his own home, thereby keeping his appointment at this meeting no better than did the man who had called it.

These and other pertinent remarks were being uttered by Turnus, a rebel and trouble-maker who had won influence in his hometown by employing these very skills, when Tarquin arrived. This put an end to the speech. All turned to greet Tarquin. Silence was imposed and Tarquin, warned by those near him that he should apologize for the time of his arrival, said that he had been arbitrating a dispute between a father and his son and had been delayed by his concern to reconcile them. Because the matter had taken up that day, he would deal with his agenda the following day. Turnus is said not to have let even this pass without comment, remarking that there was no shorter legal investigation than that between father and son. It could be dealt with in a few words: if a son did not obey his father, it would be the worse for him.

## 51    Tarquin Gets His Revenge

With this gibe against the king of Rome, the man from Aricia left the council. Tarquin was considerably more angry than he seemed. Immediately he began to plot Turnus' death, so that he might inspire in the Latins the same fear that he had used to oppress the spirit of the citizens back home. Because his power at Rome did not enable him to kill Turnus openly in this place, he trumped up a false charge and so destroyed an inno-cent man. Through some of the opposing faction in Aricia, he bribed one of Turnus' slaves with gold to permit a large quantity of swords to be brought secretly into the place where Turnus was staying. This was accomplished in one night.

Then, shortly before dawn, Tarquin summoned the Latin leaders, pretending to have received some alarming news. He said that by some divine providence, his late arrival had proved to be both his and their salvation; for he had been told that Turnus was plotting to kill both him and the peoples' leaders in order to gain sole control over the Latins. He would have made his attack in the council on the previous day, but the attempt had been put off because his main target, the man who had sum-moned the council, was not there. This was the reason for Turnus' invective against him in his absence, because his delay had frustrated the Arician's hopes. There was no doubt, if this information was true, that Turnus would come at dawn when the meeting assembled, armed and attended by a band of conspirators. A large number of swords were said to have been brought to his lodging. Whether or not this was an empty rumor could be immediately discovered. So, he asked them to accompany him to Turnus' quarters.

Turnus' fierce disposition, his speech the previous day, and Tarquin's delay made the accusation plausible, because it seemed likely that the massacre might have been postponed on that account. So, they went with the king, inclined to believe his story but prepared to think the rest of the charges false if they did not find the swords. On their arrival, they awoke Turnus, surrounded him with guards, and seized the slaves who, out of concern for their master, were preparing to use force. Then the swords that were hidden in every part of the lodging were produced. Everything seemed clear. Turnus was put in chains, and, amid a great commotion, the council of the Latins was immediately summoned. The sight of the swords placed in their midst aroused such fierce hostility that, without being given a hearing, Turnus was condemned to a novel kind of execution: he was plunged into the source of the Ferentine Water and drowned beneath a wicker crate heaped up with stones.

## 52    Tarquin Renews a Treaty in the Romans' Favor

Tarquin then summoned the Latins back to the council and praised them for giving the rebellious Turnus the punishment that a murder plot deserved. He went on to say that he was empowered to act in accordance with an ancient right, the treaty made by King Tullus Hostilius, whereby the entire state of Alba, together with its colonies, had come under Rome's control. Since all Latins originated from Alba Longa, they were bound by that treaty. But he thought that the interests of all would be better served if the treaty were renewed. In this way, the Latin people would share in the good fortune of the Roman people, rather than continually expecting or suffering the destruction of their cities and devastation of their land that they had endured first under Ancus, and then in his own father's reign.

The Latins were easily persuaded, though Roman interest was uppermost in that treaty. But they saw that the Latin chiefs stood with the king and were in agreement with him. For everyone there was the recent lesson of the danger of opposing Tarquin. So, the treaty was renewed and the Latin men of military age were ordered to assemble on a fixed day at the grove of Ferentina, armed and in full force, in accordance with the treaty. Recruits from all the peoples assembled in response to the king's command. But Tarquin did want them to have their own leaders, or a separate command, or their own standards. He therefore divided the existing fighting units into two, forming new ones with one half taken from the Latins, the other from the Romans. Centurions were put in command of the recombined units.

## 53    Tarquin Makes War against the Volscians and Gabii

Unjust as the king was in peacetime, he was not a bad general in war. Indeed he would have equaled his predecessors in military skill if his glory in this sphere too had not been offset by his degeneracy in other matters. He was the first to make war on the Volsci, a struggle that would last for 200 years after his time.[45] He took Suessa Pometia by storm and raised forty talents of silver by selling off the booty. He envisioned a

---

45. The Volscians were a people who inhabited the area of southern Latium, and were distantly related to the Latins.

temple to Jupiter whose magnificence would be worthy of the king of gods and men, of the Roman empire, and of the majesty of the site itself. To build this temple, he set aside the money from the captured city.

Then Tarquin became engaged in a war that took longer than he expected. After attempting in vain to storm the neighboring city of Gabii,[46] hope of a siege was also lost when he was driven back from the walls. Finally he resorted to guile and trickery, a thoroughly un-Roman stratagem. Pretending to have given up the war and to be concentrating on laying the foundations of the temple and other urban projects, Tarquin arranged for Sextus, the youngest of his three sons, to go as a deserter to Gabii and complain of his father's unbearable cruelty to him. His father's arrogance toward strangers, Sextus said, was now directed against his own family. The king was also annoyed by the large number of his children and wanted to create the same solitude in his own house as he had in the senate, so as to leave no descendant and no heir to the kingship. Indeed he himself had escaped from the midst of his father's weapons and swords, believing that his only safety lay with Tarquin's enemies. They should make no mistake: the war still remained. It was a pretense that it had been abandoned. Tarquin would seize an opportunity to invade when they were off their guard. But if they had no place for suppliants, he would wander all over Latium and then seek out the Volsci, Aequi, and Hernici until he reached men who knew how to protect children from the cruel and impious tortures inflicted by a father. Perhaps he would even find some enthusiasm for war against a most arrogant king and his most ferocious people.

When it appeared that he was going to depart in anger if they disregarded him, the people of Gabii gave him a generous welcome. They told him not to be surprised that in the end the king had treated his children as he had treated his citizens and allies. If all else failed him, he would finally vent his cruelty upon himself. Indeed, they were glad that Sextus had come and believed that, with his assistance, the war would soon be shifted from the gates of Gabii to the walls of Rome.

## 54    Sextus Tarquinius Becomes Master of Gabii

Then Sextus was invited to their councils of state, in which he said that he deferred to the long-established residents of Gabii on matters about which they were better informed. Over and over again, however, he advocated war. He assumed a special knowledge in this sphere because he was acquainted with the strength of both peoples and knew that the king's arrogance was hateful to his citizens, since even his children had not been able to put up with it. In this way, little by little, he was prodding the leaders of Gabii to reopen the war. He himself went out to plunder and reconnoiter, together with the boldest Gabinian youths. All his words and deeds were designed to deceive, increasing their misplaced trust. Finally he was chosen as their war leader. The people had no idea of what was going on, but when skirmishes broke out between the Romans and the people of Gabii, in which the latter generally gained the upper hand, then all the citizens of Gabii, both high and low, enthusiastically believed that Sextus Tarquinius had been sent as a gift from the gods to be their leader. By sharing

---

46. Gabii was a thriving city twelve miles east of Rome.

in their dangers and hardships and by liberally distributing the booty, he so won the affection of the soldiers that the son became as powerful in Gabii as his father Tarquin was in Rome.

When Sextus saw that he had amassed enough strength for any enterprise, he sent one of his followers to Rome to ask his father what he wanted him to do, since the gods had granted that he was the only one who controlled public affairs at Gabii. King Tarquin said nothing in reply, because, I suppose, the messenger seemed of questionable loyalty. He went into the garden as if to ponder, followed by his son's messenger. There, as he walked up and down without speaking, he is said to have struck off the heads of the tallest poppies with his stick. Tired of asking and waiting for a reply, the messenger returned to Gabii, his mission apparently unfulfilled. He reported what he himself had said and what he had seen. Whether from anger, he said, or hatred, or his innate arrogance, the king had not uttered a word. When Sextus realized what his father wanted and what he was telling him by his unspoken enigmas, he killed the city's leaders, accusing some before the people and taking advantage of the unpopularity of others. Many were executed openly; others, in whose case an accusation was less plausible, were murdered in secret. Exile was open to those who chose it, or else they were forced into it. The property of exiles and murdered alike was made available for distribution. Largesse and booty ensued, and the sweetness of personal gain eliminated the sense that the state was being wronged. In the end, deprived of anyone to advise or help, Gabii was handed over to the king of Rome without a fight.

## 55    Tarquin Builds the Temple to Jupiter Optimus Maximus on the Capitoline Hill

Once he had possession of Gabii, Tarquin made peace with the Aequi and renewed the treaty with the Etruscans. Then he turned his attention to affairs in the city. His first concern was to leave a temple to Jupiter on the Tarpeian Mount as a memorial of his reign and of his family, indicating that of the two Tarquins, both of them kings, the father made the vow and the son fulfilled it. But because he wanted the site on which he was building the temple of Jupiter to be free from all other religious associations, he decided to deconsecrate the several sanctuaries and shrines that had been first vowed by King Tatius in the crisis of his battle against Romulus, and later consecrated and inaugurated. There is a tradition that, when the foundations were first being laid, the gods exerted their will to show the greatness of this mighty empire. Although the birds permitted the deconsecration of all other shrines, they refused their consent in the case of the sanctuary of Terminus.[47] This was interpreted as an omen and augury: the fact that the seat of Terminus was not moved and that he alone of all the gods was not summoned from his consecrated boundaries portended that everything would be stable and secure. After this auspice of permanence had been received, another prodigy portending the greatness of empire ensued. It is said that a human head, its features intact, was found by the men who were digging the foundations of the temple. This phenomenon undoubtedly foretold that this was to be the citadel of empire and the

---

47. Terminus was the god of boundaries.

head or capital of the world. This was the interpretation of soothsayers, both those in the city and those who were summoned from Etruria to advise on the matter.

The king's enthusiasm to spend money on the project increased. The spoils from Pometia that had been intended to complete the building right up to the roof scarcely sufficed for the foundations. I am inclined to believe the figure of a mere 40 talents[48] given by Fabius (apart from the fact that he is the earlier source), rather than that of Piso, who writes that 40,000 pounds of silver were set aside for this project. The latter is a sum of money that could not be expected from the booty of a single town of that time, and one that would exceed the cost of the foundations of any building, even in modern times.

## 56    The Cleverness of Brutus

Intent on completing the temple, Tarquin called in workmen from everywhere in Etruria, using not only public funds but also laborers conscripted from the people. The work was considerable and was in addition to their military service. The people, however, were less annoyed that they were building temples of the gods with their own hands than they were later, when they were transferred to other, less spectacular projects that were considerably more laborious. These were the erection of seats in the Circus and the construction of the Cloaca Maxima, which served as the drain for the whole city. The new splendor of modern times has scarcely been able to match the greatness of these two original structures. After making the people labor on these projects, Tarquin felt that their large numbers were a burden on the city when there was no work for them. Wishing to extend the limits of Roman power by sending out colonies, he sent colonists to Signia and Circeii to protect the city by land and by sea.

While he was busy with this, a terrible portent was seen: a snake glided out from a wooden column, causing people to flee in terror into the palace. The king himself was not so much stricken with sudden panic; rather, his heart was filled with anxious foreboding. Only Etruscan seers were summoned to deal with state prodigies, but Tarquin was so alarmed by this apparition, which he regarded as affecting his own household, that he decided to consult Delphi, the most famous oracle in the world. Not daring to entrust the oracle's reply to anyone else, he sent two sons to Greece, through lands unknown at that time and over seas yet more unknown. Titus and Arruns set out. Lucius Junius Brutus, the son of the king's sister Tarquinia, also went with them as their companion, a young man of a far different character from what he pretended to be. After hearing that the leading men of the state, including his own brother, had been executed by his uncle, Brutus had determined to leave nothing either in his own conduct for Tarquin to fear, or in his possessions for Tarquin to desire. He would secure his safety by being despised in a situation where justice offered little protection. And so he deliberately put on an act of being stupid, allowing himself and his property to become the spoil of the king. Nor did he refuse the name Brutus ("Simpleton"), so that under its cover, the great spirit that was to free the Roman people might lie low and bide its time. This was the man who was taken to Delphi by the Tarquins, more as a

---

48. A talent was an enormous sum of money, equivalent to eighty Roman pounds of silver, about sixty modern pounds.

buffoon than as a companion. He is said to have brought as a gift to Apollo a golden staff enclosed within one of cornel wood that was hollowed out to fit it, an enigmatic representation of his own character.

When they arrived and had carried out their father's instructions, the two Tarquins were possessed by a desire to ask which of them would succeed to the kingship. From the depths of the cave, so the story goes, came the reply: "Whoever of you shall be the first to kiss his mother will hold the highest power in Rome." The Tarquins ordered the matter to be kept absolutely secret, so that Sextus, who had been left in Rome, should be unaware of the response and thus excluded from power. They themselves decided by lot which of them should be the first to kiss their mother on their return. But Brutus thought that the Pythia's words had a different meaning. Pretending to slip, he fell and touched the earth with his lips, evidently regarding her as the mother of all mortals. Then they returned to Rome, where preparations for war with the Rutulians were vigorously underway.

## 57    Sextus Tarquinius Becomes Infatuated with Lucretia

Ardea was held by the Rutulians, a race that, for both that time and place, was extremely wealthy. Their wealth was the cause of the war, since the Roman king, impoverished by his magnificent public works, wanted to enrich himself while also mollifying the feelings of the people with booty. For they were hostile to his rule, not only because of his general arrogance, but also because they were angry that the king had kept them employed for so long, like workmen doing the job of slaves. The Romans tried to capture Ardea at the first assault. When that did not succeed, they began to blockade the city with siegeworks. Here in their permanent camp, as usually happens in a war that is protracted rather than intense, furloughs were rather freely granted; more freely, however, to the leaders than the soldiers. The young men of the royal house were whiling away their free time in feasting and drinking among themselves. They were drinking in Sextus Tarquinius' quarters, where Tarquinius Collatinus, the son of Egerius, was also dining, when the subject of wives happened to come up. Each man praised his own wife in extravagant terms. Then, as the rivalry became inflamed, Collatinus said that there was no need for words: in a few hours they could discover how his Lucretia far excelled the rest. "Come!" he cried. "If we have the vigor of youth, why don't we mount our horses and see for ourselves what kind of women our wives are? Let us each regard as decisive what meets his eyes when the woman's husband shows up unexpectedly." They were heated with wine. "Right! Let's go," they all cried. At full gallop, they flew off to Rome.

Arriving there at early dusk, they went on to Collatia. There they found Lucretia occupying herself differently from the king's daughters-in-law. These they had seen whiling away their time at a luxurious banquet with their young friends. In contrast, though it was late at night, they came upon Lucretia sitting in the middle of the house busily spinning, surrounded by her maidservants who were working by lamplight. The prize of honor in this contest about wives fell to Lucretia. As her husband and the Tarquins approached, they were graciously received. The victorious husband courteously invited the young royals to be his guests. It was there that Sextus Tarquinius was seized by an evil desire to debauch Lucretia by force. Not only her beauty but also her proven chastity spurred him on. Meanwhile they returned to the camp after their youthful nocturnal prank.

## 58    Raped by Sextus Tarquinius, Lucretia Commits Suicide

After the lapse of a few days, Sextus Tarquinius went to Collatia with just one companion. He was graciously received by a household unaware of his purpose. After supper he was led to the guest bedroom. Burning with passion, once he saw that it was safe all around and everyone was asleep, he drew his sword and went to the sleeping Lucretia. Pressing his left hand on her breast, he said, "Keep quiet, Lucretia! I am Sextus Tarquinius. My sword is in my hand. You will die if you utter a sound!" Terrified out of her sleep, Lucretia saw no help at hand, only imminent death. Then Sextus confessed his love and pleaded with her, mingling threats with prayers and trying in every way to play on her feelings as a woman. When he saw that she was resolute and unmoved even by fear of death, he added the threat of disgrace to her fear: after killing her, he would murder a slave and place him naked by her side, as evidence that she had been killed because of adultery of the lowest kind. With this terrifying threat, his lust prevailed as the victor over her resolute chastity. Sextus Tarquinius departed, exulting in his conquest of a woman's honor. Lucretia, grief-stricken at this terrible disaster, sent the same message to her father in Rome and her husband in Ardea, bidding each to come with a trustworthy friend. This they must do and do quickly; a terrible thing had happened. Spurius Lucretius came with Publius Valerius, the son of Volesus; Collatinus with Lucius Junius Brutus, with whom he happened to be returning to Rome when he encountered his wife's messenger.

They found Lucretia sitting in her bedchamber, grieving. At the arrival of her own family, tears welled in her eyes. In response to her husband's question, "Is everything all right?", she replied, "Not at all. What can be well when a woman has lost her honor? The marks of another man are in your bed. But only my body has been violated; my mind is not guilty. Death will be my witness. But give me your right hands and your word that the adulterer will not go unpunished. Sextus Tarquinius is the man. Last night he repaid hospitality with hostility when he came, armed, and forcibly took his pleasure of me, an act that has destroyed me—and him too, if you are men." All duly gave her their pledge. They tried to console her distress by shifting the guilt from the woman who had been forced to the man who had done the wrong, saying that it is the mind that errs, not the body. For where there has been no intent, there is no blame. "You shall determine," she replied, "what is his due. Though I absolve myself of wrongdoing, I do not exempt myself from punishment. Nor henceforth shall any unchaste woman continue to live by citing the precedent of Lucretia." She took a knife that she had hidden in her garments and plunged it in her heart. Falling forward onto the wound, she died as she fell. Her husband and father raised the ritual cry for the dead.

## 59    Brutus and Lucretia's Family Vow to Rid Rome of Kings

While the rest were absorbed in grief, Brutus took the knife from Lucretia's wound and held it up, dripping with blood, as he proclaimed, "By this blood, most chaste until it was defiled by a prince, I swear and take you, O gods, to witness that I will pursue Lucius Tarquinius Superbus, together with his wicked wife and all his children, with sword, fire, and indeed with whatever violence I can. Nor will I allow them or anyone else to be king at Rome." Then he handed the knife to Collatinus, and from him to Lucretius and Valerius. They were stunned at the miracle, wondering what was the source of the new spirit in Brutus' heart. They swore as bidden. Switching from grief to anger, they all followed Brutus' lead as he summoned them to overthrow the monarchy. They carried Lucretia's body out of the house and took it down to the forum, attracting crowds in amazement and indignation at this strange event, as generally happens. Everybody made his own complaint about the criminal rape committed by the prince. They were moved not only by the father's grief but also by Brutus, who reprimanded them for their tears and idle complaints, urging them, as befit men and Romans, to take up arms against those who had dared such acts of hostility. All the boldest young men seized their weapons, offering their service, and the rest also followed. Then, leaving a garrison at Collatia and posting guards to prevent anyone taking news of the uprising to the royal family, the rest of the armed force set out for Rome under Brutus' command.

Arriving there, the armed populace caused panic and confusion wherever it advanced. But when the Romans saw the leading men of the state marching at the head of the forces, they realized that, whatever it was, this was no random business. The dreadful event created no less an emotional uproar in Rome than it had in Collatia. People rushed from every part of the city into the forum. As soon as they were assembled there, a herald summoned the people before the tribune of the Swift Ones, an office that Brutus happened to hold at that time.

There he gave a speech that was quite inconsistent with the spirit and disposition that he had feigned up to that day. He spoke of Sextus Tarquinius' violent lust, his unspeakable rape of Lucretia, her pitiful death, and the loss sustained by her father Tricipitinus, for whom the reason for his daughter's death was more outrageous and pitiful than her death itself. In addition, he spoke of the arrogance of the king himself and the wretched forced labor of the people who were plunged into ditches and sewers and forced to clean them out. The Romans, conquerors of all the surrounding peoples, had been changed from fighting men into workmen and stonecutters. Invoking the gods who avenge parents, he recalled the shameful murder of Servius Tullius and how his daughter had driven over her father's body with her accursed carriage. With these and, I suppose, recollections of other more savage deeds, the sort suggested by an immediate feeling of outrage that is by no means easy for historians to relate, he inflamed the people, driving them to revoke the king's power and order the exile of Lucius Tarquinius, together with his wife and children.

Brutus himself enrolled a band of young men who voluntarily offered their names. Arming them, he set out for the camp at Ardea to stir up that army against the king. He left Lucretius in control of Rome as prefect of the city, a position he had been given by the king some time before. In the midst of this revolt, Tullia fled from her house, cursed wherever she went, as men and women called down upon her the furies that avenge the wrongs done to parents.

## 60     The Tarquins are Banished and Two Consuls are Chosen

When news of these events reached the camp, the king, terrified by this unexpected crisis, set out for Rome to suppress the revolt. Brutus had anticipated the king's arrival and so changed his route to avoid encountering him. At almost the same time, though by different routes, Brutus arrived at Ardea and Tarquin at Rome. Tarquin found the city gates closed and his exile pronounced. But the camp received the city's liberator joyfully and the king's sons were driven out. Two followed their father and went into exile at Caere in Etruria. Sextus Tarquinius set out for Gabii, as if returning to his own kingdom, and was killed there by men avenging old feuds that he himself had stirred up by murder and pillage.

Lucius Tarquinius reigned for twenty-five years. The rule of kings at Rome, from the foundation of the city to its liberation, lasted 244 years. Two consuls were then chosen in the *Comitia Centuriata* under the presidency of the prefect of the city, in accordance with the precepts laid down in the commentaries of Servius Tullius. Lucius Junius Brutus and Lucius Tarquinius Collatinus were chosen.

# LUCRETIUS

(early 1st century BC, wrote in Latin)

## Introduction

T. Lucretius Carus wrote *On the Nature of Things* (*De Rerum Natura*) in six books as a way of putting the philosophy of Epicurus (341–270 BC) into Latin poetry, and of winning over his Roman contemporaries to Epicurus' ideas. Nothing certain is known about his life, except that he was a friend or client of C. Memmius, to whom he dedicates the poem, and who was praetor in 58 BC. We also know from one of Marcus Cicero's letters that both he and his brother Quintus had read the work by 54 BC.

Just as Epicurus' philosophy, written in prose, challenged his Greek contemporaries, *On the Nature of Things* challenged conventional Roman ideas about the world, the gods, and what was important in life. In a sometimes lyrical, sometimes argumentative style, Lucretius argues that all matter is composed of atoms, and describes their movements (Books 1 and 2). He says that the soul itself is made of atoms, and is therefore mortal, and that we should not fear death (Book 3). He discusses the theory of sense perception and emotion (Book 4), cosmology and the origin of culture, and argues that the world is not divinely made and governed, and that the gods are not to be feared (Books 5 and 6). Throughout, Lucretius' goals are both scientific and therapeutic. He intends to remove the fear of death and other misconceptions about the nature of the world, arguing that they threaten the mental equilibrium (*ataraxia*, "freedom from disturbance") that is the most important goal of Epicurean philosophy.

We include four excerpts from Lucretius' poem: (A) 1.1–264: Lucretius' famous invocation of Venus; science as an antidote to superstition; a critique of poets' tales of punishment after death, and ghosts; the principle that nothing can come from nothing, and that atoms are indestructible. (B) 2.1–124: freedom from pain and worry is the goal, which is only achieved through philosophy; further comment on atoms and the "swerve." (C) 2.570–660: the cycle of destruction and birth; the Earth, which contains countless substances, is immensely fertile, but is not divine; Epicurean gods are aloof and tranquil. (D) 3.784–1094: mind and body are inseparable and terminate together, so death is nothing to us. The traditional torments of the underworld are actually seen here on earth.

# On the Nature of Things

## A    Epicureanism and the Concept of Atoms (1.1–264)

Mother of Aeneas' people, delight of human beings and the gods, Venus,[1] power of life, it is you who beneath the sky's sliding stars inspirit the ship-bearing sea, inspirit the productive land. To you every kind of living creature owes its conception and first glimpse of the sun's light. You, goddess, at your coming hush the winds and scatter the clouds; for you the creative earth thrusts up fragrant flowers; for you the smooth stretches of the ocean smile, and the sky, tranquil now, is flooded with effulgent light.

Once the door to spring is flung open and Favonius'[2] fertilizing breeze, released from imprisonment, is active, first, goddess, the birds of the air, pierced to the heart with your powerful shafts, signal your entry. Next wild creatures and cattle bound over rich pastures and swim rushing rivers: so surely are they all captivated by your charm and eagerly follow your lead. Then you inject seductive love into the heart of every creature that lives in the seas and mountains and river torrents and bird-haunted thickets and verdant plains, implanting in it the passionate urge to reproduce its kind.

Since you and you alone stand at the helm of nature's ship, and since without your sanction nothing springs up into the shining shores of light, nothing blossoms into mature loveliness, it is you whom I desire to be my associate in writing this poem *On the Nature of Things*, which I am attempting to compose for my friend Memmius.[3] Through your will, goddess, he is always endowed outstandingly with all fine qualities. So with all the more justification, Venus, give my words charm that will ensure their immortality.

Meanwhile, cause the barbarous business of warfare to be lulled to sleep over every land and sea. For you alone have the influence to obtain for mortals the blessing of tranquil peace, since barbarous war is the province of Mars mighty in arms who often stretches himself back upon your lap, vanquished by the never-healing wound of love; throwing back his handsome neck and gazing up at you, in open-mouthed wonderment he feasts his greedy eyes with love; and, as he reclines, his breath hangs upon your lips. As he rests upon your holy body, bend, goddess, to enfold him in your arms; and from your lips, worshipful lady, let a stream of sweet, coaxing words flow in an appeal on behalf of the Romans for placid peace. For at this tempestuous time in my country's history, I cannot tackle my task with tranquil mind, and the gravity of the situation is such that the noble descendant of the Memmii cannot fail the cause of public security.[4]

As for what follows, Memmius, lend open ears and an alert mind, released from cares, to true philosophy. My gifts have been arranged for you with steadfast zeal; be

---

1. Goddess of love and fertility who bore Aeneas, the legendary ancestor of the Romans.

2. The west wind.

3. C. Memmius, a wealthy, politically unscrupulous bon vivant and connoisseur of literature. He served as praetor in 58 BC. As governor of Bithynia in the following year he took along the poet Catullus as part of his staff (see Catullus 10 in this volume).

4. A reference to the political turmoil of the 50s BC, and to Memmius' political career.

sure that you do not contemptuously discard them without having understood them. For I will proceed to explain to you the working of the heaven above and the nature of the gods, and will unfold the primary elements of things[5] from which nature creates, increases, and sustains all things, and into which she again resolves them when they perish. In expounding our philosophy I often call these elements "matter" or "generative particles of things" or "seeds of things;" and, since they are the ultimate constituents of all things, another term I often use is "ultimate particles."

When all could see that human life lay groveling ignominiously in the dust, crushed beneath the grinding weight of superstition, which from the celestial regions displayed its face, lowering over mortals with hideous scowl, the first who dared to lift mortal eyes to challenge it, the first who ventured to confront it boldly, was a Greek.[6] This man neither the reputation of the gods nor thunderbolts nor heaven's menacing rumbles could daunt; rather all the more they roused the ardor of his courage and made him long to be the first to burst the bolts and bars of nature's gates. And so his mind's might and vigor prevailed, and on he marched far beyond the blazing battlements of the world, in thought and understanding journeying all through the measureless universe; and from this expedition he returns to us in triumph with his spoils—knowledge of what can arise and what cannot, and again by what law each thing has its scope restricted and its deeply implanted boundary stone. So now the situation is reversed: superstition is flung down and trampled underfoot; we are raised to heaven by victory.

In this connection, I fear that you may perhaps imagine that you are starting on the principles of an irreligious philosophy and setting out on a path of wickedness. But in fact more often it is that very superstition that has perpetrated wicked and irreligious deeds. Consider how at Aulis the elite of Greece's chieftains, the flower of its manhood, foully polluted the altar of the Virgin Goddess of the Crossroads with the blood of Iphianassa.[7] As soon as the ribbon[8] had been fastened about her virgin locks so that it flowed down either cheek in equal lengths, and as soon as she had noticed her father standing sorrowfully before the altars, and near him attendants trying to keep the knife concealed, and the people moved at the sight of her to streaming tears, struck dumb with dread and sinking on her knees, she groped for the ground. Poor girl! Little could it help her at such a time that she had been the first to give the king the name of father. For uplifted by masculine hands, she was led, trembling with terror, to the altars. Instead of being escorted by the wedding hymn's cheerful ring, when the solemn service of sacrifice had been performed, she was to be immolated by her father and fall a sorrowful and sinless victim of a sinful crime, cheated of the marriage for which she was just ready. And all to what purpose? To enable a fleet to receive the blessing of a prosperous and propitious departure. Such heinous acts could superstition prompt.

---

5. This is the concept of the atom, which in Greek means "indivisible particle."

6. Epicurus.

7. Agamemnon, commander-in-chief of the Greek expedition to Troy, sacrificed his own daughter Iphianassa (or Iphigenia) to Diana, in order to appease the goddess, who was delaying his fleet with contrary winds at the port of Aulis. Iphigenia had been told that she was being brought to Aulis to marry Achilles.

8. The mark of a sacrificial victim.

The time may come when you yourself, terrorized by the fearsome pronounce-ments of the fable-mongers,[9] will attempt to defect from us. Consider how numerous are the fantasies they can invent, capable of confounding your calculated plan of life and clouding all your fortunes with fear. And with reason; for if people realized that there was a limit set to their tribulations, they would somehow find strength to defy irrational beliefs and the threats of the fable-mongers. As it is, they have no way, no ability, to offer resistance, because they fear that death brings punishment without end. They are ignorant of the nature of the soul: they do not know whether it is born with the body, or whether on the contrary it insinuates itself into us at the moment of birth; and they are uncertain whether it is dissipated by death and so perishes when we perish, or whether it visits the gloom and yawning wastes of Orcus,[10] or whether it miraculously steals its way into other creatures as described by our own poet Ennius, who first brought down from lovely Helicon a garland of perennial leafage, to send his fame flashing through all the peoples of Italy.[11] And yet in his immortal verses Ennius also declares that there are precincts of Acheron,[12] where neither soul nor body sur-vives, but only a kind of wraith weirdly wan and pale. From these parts, so he relates, the apparition of Homer, of never fading genius, rose and appeared to him and began to shed briny tears and disclose nature's secrets.

So it is imperative that I give a correct account of celestial phenomena, explaining what principle governs the courses of the sun and moon, and also what force is respon-sible for all that happens on earth; above all, my penetrative reasoning must reveal the nature of the mind and spirit, and disclose what it is that visits us when we are buried in sleep or lie awake in the grip of sickness and gives us the terrifying illusion of hear-ing and seeing face to face people who are dead, and whose bones are embosomed in the earth.

I am wide awake to the difficulty of the task of illuminating the obscure discoveries of the Greeks in Latin verse. The main obstacles are the inadequacy of our language and the novelty of my subject—factors that entail the coinage of many new terms. But your fine qualities, Memmius, and the hope of gaining the pleasure of your delightful friendship spur me to make a success of my task, however laborious, and induce me to forego sleep and spend the still calm of the night in quest of words and verses that will enable me to light the way brightly for your mind and thus help you to see right to the heart of hidden things.

This terrifying darkness that enshrouds the mind must be dispelled not by the sun's rays and the dazzling darts of day, but by study of the superficial aspect and underlying principle of nature.

The first stage of this study will have this rule as its basis: nothing ever springs

---

9. "Fable-mongers" translates the derogatory *vates*, which refers to those who, whether poets or priests, are professional promoters of traditional religion and mythology.

10. The underworld.

11. Ennius was a famous early Latin poet, greatly admired by Lucretius. In his works he claimed to have been reincarnated, alluding to the doctrine of "exchange of souls" or metampsychosis held by Pythagorean philosophers, among others. Helicon is a mountain in Greece, sacred to the Muses.

12. A river in the underworld; hence the underworld itself.

miraculously out of nothing. The fact is that all mortals are in the grip of fear, because they observe many things happening on earth and in the sky and, being at a complete loss for an explanation of their cause, suppose that a supernatural power is responsible for them. Therefore, as soon as we have seen that nothing can be created out of nothing, we shall have a clearer view of the object of our search, namely the explanation of the source of all created things and of the way in which all things happen independently of the gods.

If things could be created out of nothing, any kind of thing could be produced from any source; nothing would need a seed. In the first place, human beings could spring from the sea, squamous fish from the ground, and birds could be hatched from the sky; cattle and other farm animals and every kind of wild beast would bear young of unpredictable species, and would make their home in cultivated and barren parts without discrimination. Moreover, the same fruits would not invariably grow on the same trees, but would change: any tree could bear any fruit. Seeing that there would be no elements with the capacity to generate each kind of thing, how could creatures constantly have a fixed mother? But as it is, because all are formed from fixed seeds, each is born and issues out into the shores of light only from a source where the right matter and the right ultimate particles exist. And this explains why all things cannot be produced from all things: any given thing possesses a distinct creative capacity.

A second point: why do we see the rose bursting out in spring, the corn in scorching summer, the vine at autumn's coaxing, if it is not because, only when the fixed seeds of things have streamed together at their appropriate time, is any created thing uncovered, while the attendant seasons assist the prolific earth to deliver the frail objects into the shores of light in safety? But if they were produced from nothing, they would suddenly spring up at unpredictable intervals and at unfavorable times of the year, for there would be no ultimate particles that could be debarred by the unpropitious season from entering into creative union. Moreover, so far as growth is concerned, the lapse of time required for the confluence of seed would be unnecessary, if things could arise out of nothing. Children, too young to talk, in an instant would become young adults, and trees would suddenly bound up out of the ground. But it is evident that none of these things happens, since in every case growth is a gradual process, as one would expect, from a fixed seed and, as things grow, they preserve their specific character; so you may be sure that each thing increases its bulk and derives its sustenance from its own special substance.

There is the further point that, if there were no rain at regular times of the year, the earth would be unable to thrust up her luxuriant produce; and if deprived of food, animals naturally could not propagate their kind and keep alive. Therefore the supposition that, as there are many letters common to many words, so there are many elements common to many things, is preferable to the view that anything can come into being without ultimate particles.

Furthermore, why has nature not succeeded in producing human beings so huge that they could wade across the open sea, making it seem shallow, and who could dismember mighty mountains with their hands and outlive many generations? Surely the reason is that things are created from a definite, appointed substance, and it is firmly laid down what this substance can produce. Therefore we are bound to admit that nothing can come into being from nothing, because a seed is essential as the source from which each thing can be produced and committed to the care of the air's soft breezes.

Finally, since we see that cultivated ground is superior to uncultivated and rewards the labor of our hands with improved yield, it is evident that the earth contains elements of things which we rouse from dormancy when we turn up the fertile clods with the plowshare and trench the soil. If this were not so, our labor would be unnecessary, because you would see things everywhere improve considerably of their own accord.

The complement of the foregoing doctrine is the principle that, although nature resolves everything into its constituent particles, she never annihilates anything. For if anything were subject to destruction in all its parts, anything might be whisked out of sight in a flash and cease to exist: no force would be needed to effect the dispersion of its parts by unraveling its interlaced fabric. But as it is, because all things are composed of imperishable seeds, nature does not allow us to witness the destruction of anything until it has encountered a force that dashes it to pieces or works its way inside through the interstices and so breaks it up.

Moreover, if time wholly destroys the things it wastes and sweeps away, and engulfs all their substance, whence does Venus escort each kind of creature back into the light of life? Or, when this is done, from what store does the creative earth furnish the food to sustain and strengthen each? From what source is the sea provided with an unfailing supply of water by its native springs and by the rivers that rise far beyond its bounds? Where does the ether find fuel to feed the stars? For everything of perishable substance must inevitably have been swallowed up by the sweep of infinite time and days that are no more. But if through that space of ages past the elements that compose and reshape the universe have survived, it is certain that they are endowed with an immortal nature. Therefore it is impossible for anything to return to nothing.

Furthermore, the same force would cause the destruction of all things without exception, if there were no imperishable substance, more or less closely interwoven, to give them stability. The fact is that a mere touch would be enough to cause their death, since there would be no imperishable elements to form a web that in each case could be unwoven only by a real force. But as it is, because the elements are interwoven in various ways, and their matter is imperishable, things survive intact until they encounter a force sharp enough to unweave their particular fabric. Nothing, therefore, returns to nothing, but everything dissolves and returns to the elements of matter.

Lastly, the rains disappear, when father sky has sent them spurting down into the lap of mother earth; but crops spring up and show a sheen, branches clothe themselves with green leaves, and trees grow and become heavy with fruit. This is what provides the human race and beasts with nourishment; this is what gives us the happy sight of cities blooming with children, and leafy woodlands full of the song of newhatched birds; this is what causes cattle and sheep, exhausted by their very plumpness, to lie down in luxuriant pastures, and white moist milk to ooze from distended udders; this is what enables newborn creatures to frisk and play on unsteady legs in the tender grass, their young minds intoxicated with neat milk.

And so no visible object ever suffers total destruction, since nature renews one thing from another, and does not sanction the birth of anything unless she receives the compensation of another's death.

**B**      **Freedom from Pain and Worry** (2.1–124), **The Swerve and Free Will** (216–93)

It is comforting, when winds are whipping up the waters of the vast sea, to watch from land the severe trials of another person: not that anyone's distress is a cause of agreeable pleasure; but it is comforting to see from what troubles you yourself are exempt. It is comforting also to witness mighty clashes of warriors embattled on the plains, when you have no share in the danger. But nothing is more blissful than to occupy the heights effectively fortified by the teaching of the wise, tranquil sanctuaries from which you can look down upon others and see them wandering everywhere in their random search for the way of life, competing for intellectual eminence, disputing about rank, and striving night and day with prodigious effort to scale the summit of wealth and to secure power. O minds of mortals, blighted by your blindness! Amid what deep darkness and daunting dangers life's little day is passed! To think that you should fail to see that nature importunately demands only that the body may be rid of pain, and that the mind, divorced from anxiety and fear, may enjoy a feeling of contentment!

And so we see that the nature of the body is such that it needs few things, namely those that banish pain and, in so doing, succeed in bestowing pleasures in plenty. Even if the halls contain no golden figures of youths, clasping flaring torches in their right hands to supply light for banquets after dark, even if the house lacks the luster of silver and the glitter of gold, even if no gold-fretted ceiling rings to the sound of the lyre, those who follow their true nature never feel cheated of enjoyment when they lie in friendly company on velvety turf near a running brook beneath the branches of a tall tree and provide their bodies with simple but agreeable refreshment, especially when the weather smiles and the season of the year spangles the green grass with flowers. Fiery fevers quit your body no quicker, if you toss in embroidered attire of blushing crimson, than if you must lie sick in a common garment.

Therefore, since neither riches nor rank nor the pomp of power have any beneficial effect upon our bodies, we must assume that they are equally useless to our minds. Or when you watch your legions swarming over the spacious Plain[13] in vigorous imitation of war, reinforced with numerous reserves and powerful cavalry, uniform in their armor, uniform in their spirit, can it be that these experiences strike terror into your irrational notions, causing them to flee in panic from your mind? Can it be that the fears of death leave your breast disburdened and eased of care? But if we recognize that these suppositions are absurd and ridiculous, because in reality people's fears and the cares at their back dread neither the din of arms nor cruel darts, and strut boldly among kings and potentates, respecting neither the glitter of gold nor the brilliant luster of purple raiment, how can you doubt that philosophy alone possesses the power to resist them? All the more so, because life is one long struggle in the gloom. For, just as children tremble and fear everything in blinding darkness, so we even in daylight sometimes dread things that are no more terrible than the imaginary dangers that cause children to quake in the dark. This terrifying darkness that enshrouds the mind must be dispelled not by the sun's rays and the dazzling darts of day, but by study of the superficial aspect and underlying principle of nature.

Now then, by what motion do the generative particles of matter produce different

---

13. The Campus Martius. See Glossary.

things and then disintegrate them? By what force are they compelled to do this? What speed of movement through the vast void has been granted to them? I will explain; as for you, be sure to lend attentive ears to my words.

Certainly matter does not cohere in a solid mass, since we observe that everything loses substance, and we perceive that all things ebb, as it were, through length of days, as age steals them from our sight. Nevertheless the aggregate of things palpably remains intact, because, although the particles that withdraw from each object diminish it by their departure, they join another object and favor it with increase. They cause some things to decline, others to mature, but never stay with them. So the aggregate of things is constantly refreshed, and mortal creatures live by mutual exchange. Some species grow, others dwindle; at short intervals the generations of living things are replaced and, like runners, pass on the torch of life from hand to hand.

If you suppose that the primary elements of things can stay still, and by staying still can produce new motions in compound bodies, you are straying far from the path of sound judgment. Since they are wandering through the void,[14] the primary elements of things must all be propelled either by their own weight or by a chance blow from another atom. For the consequence of the frequent meetings and collisions that occur as they move is that they rebound instantly in different directions—not surprisingly, since their solid weight makes them absolutely firm and there is no obstruction behind them.

To grasp more firmly the restless movement of all the particles of matter, remember that the whole universe has no bottom and thus no place where the ultimate particles could settle; space is infinite and measureless, being of boundless extent in every direction on every side, as I proved by sound argument in the course of a lengthy demonstration.[15] Since this is an established fact, it is certain that the ultimate particles are allowed no rest anywhere in the unfathomable void; rather they are harried by incessant and various movement, some rebounding to considerable distances after they have clashed, others leaving short interspaces when they have been jerked back from collision. And all those that are concentrated in closer union and rebound only a very short distance apart, entangled by the interlacement of their own shapes, form the basis of tough rock, the bulk of stern steel, and other such substances. Of the rest that pursue their roving course through the vast void, a few spring far apart and rebound to considerable distances, thus furnishing us with unsubstantial air and radiant sunlight; but there are many other atoms roaming the vast void whose inability to adapt their movements to those of any compound bodies has debarred them from gaining admittance.

It occurs to me that this activity is mirrored and reflected in a phenomenon of our everyday experience. Watch carefully whenever shafts of streaming sunlight are allowed to penetrate a darkened room. You will observe many minute particles mingling in many ways in every part of the space illuminated by the rays and, as though engaged in ceaseless combat, warring and fighting by squadrons with never a pause, agitated by frequent unions and disunions. You can obtain from this spectacle a conception of the perpetual restless movement of the primary elements in the vast void, insofar as a trivial thing can exemplify important matters and put us on the track of knowledge.

---

14. One of Epicureanism's boldest claims was the existence of void, through which the atoms moved. Most thought that the world was one long interconnected chain of matter.

15. 1.958–1007, not translated in this volume.

## The Swerve and Free Will

[Lucretius explains the speed and linear downward direction of the atoms' movement. We pick up again with his most controversial concept, "the swerve," which Lucretius argues allows for the concept of free will.]

In this connection, I am anxious that you should grasp a further point: when the atoms are being drawn downward through the void by their property of weight, at absolutely unpredictable times and places they deflect slightly from their straight course, to a degree that could be described as no more than a shift of movement. If they were not apt to swerve, all would fall downward through the unfathomable void like drops of rain; no collisions between primary elements would occur, and no blows would be effected, with the result that nature would never have created anything.

Anyone who happens to believe that heavier atoms are carried straight through the void more swiftly than lighter ones, fall on them from above, and so cause the blows capable of producing the movements necessary for creation, is diverging far from the path of sound judgment. Everything that drops through water and unsubstantial air falls with a velocity proportional to its weight, because the body of water and air with its fine nature are unable to retard all bodies equally, but yield more quickly to the superior power of heavier objects. On the other hand, empty void cannot offer any resistance to any object in any part at any time: it must give way at once in conformity to its own nature. Thus all the atoms, despite their unequal weights, must move with equal velocity as they shoot through the unresisting void. The heavier will therefore never be able to fall on the lighter from above, or of themselves cause the blows determining the varied movements that are the instruments of nature's work.

So I insist that the atoms must swerve slightly, but only to an infinitesimal degree, or we shall give the impression that we are imagining oblique movements—a hypothesis that would be contradicted by the facts. For it is a plain and manifest matter of observation that objects with weight, left to themselves, cannot travel an oblique course when they plunge from above—at least not perceptibly; but who could possibly perceive that they do not swerve at all from their vertical path?

Moreover, if all movements are invariably interlinked, if new movement arises from the old in unalterable succession, if there is no atomic swerve to initiate movement that can annul the decrees of destiny and prevent the existence of an endless chain of causation, what is the source of this free will possessed by living creatures all over the earth? What, I ask, is the course of this power of will wrested from destiny, which enables each of us to advance where pleasure leads us, and to alter our movements not at a fixed time or place, but at the direction of our own minds? For undoubtedly in each case it is the individual will that gives the initial impulse to such actions and channels the movements though the limbs.

Have you not observed too that, at the very moment when the starting gates are opened, the horses, despite their strength and impatience, cannot burst forward as suddenly as their minds desire? The reason is that the whole mass of matter throughout the whole body must be actuated: only when the whole frame has been actuated can it respond with energy to the eagerness of the mind. So you can see that the initial movement is produced by the mind: it originates from the act of mental will, and is then diffused through every part of the body.

But it is a quite different matter when we are thrust forward by a blow delivered with formidable force and powerful pressure by another person; for in that event it is transparently clear that the whole bulk of our body moves and is swept along involuntarily until the will has reined back all our limbs. So do you now see that, even though an external force pushes a crowd of us, often compelling us to move forward against our will and sweeping us along precipitately, there is in our breasts something with the ability to oppose and resist it? At its bidding the mass of matter through every member and limb at times is compelled to change direction or, when thrown forward, is reined back and brought back to rest.

Thus you are obliged to acknowledge that the seeds have the same ability, and that, besides blows and weight, they have another cause of motion form which this innate power of ours is derived, since we see that nothing can come into being from nothing. Weight ensures that all movements are not caused by blows, that is to say by external force. But the factor that saves the mind itself from being governed in all its actions by an internal necessity, and from being constrained to submit passively to its domination, is the minute swerve of the atoms at unpredictable places and times.


**C      The Gods Are Far Removed from Our World** (2.570–660)

And so the destructive motions cannot hold sway eternally and bury existence forever; nor again can the motions that cause life and growth preserve created things eternally. Thus, in this war that has been waged from time everlasting, the contest between the elements is an equal one: now here, now there, the vital forces conquer and, in turn, are conquered; with the funeral dirge mingles the wail that babies raise when they reach the shores of light; no night has followed day, and no dawn has followed night, which has not heard mingled with those woeful wails the lamentations that accompany death and the black funeral.

In connection with this topic, it is advisable to keep this further truth under seal and retain it in the depository of your memory: no object whose substance is plainly visible consists only of one class of atoms; each is composed of a mixture of different seeds. The extent of the properties and powers that an object possesses indicates the multiformity of its constituent atoms.

First and foremost, the earth contains the ultimate particles that enable bubbling springs of cool water to replenish the boundless sea. She contains too the atoms that generate fire: for in many places her crust blazes up in flames, while from her bowels bursts the fury of Etna. She also contains seeds that enable her to raise up lustrous crops and exuberant trees for the races of humanity and to supply the mountain-prowling tribe of wild beasts with rivers, foliage, and luxuriant pastures. Consequently she has at the same time been titled Great Mother of the gods,[16] mother of wild beasts, and parent of human beings.

She it is whom the erudite poets of ancient Greece represented as enthroned in a chariot drawn by a pair of lions, thereby teaching that the world, for all its vastness, is suspended in airy space, because earth cannot rest on earth. They gave her a team

---

16. The cult of the Phrygian goddess Cybele, the Great Mother, was brought to Rome from Pessinus (central Turkey) in 205–204 BC.

of wild beasts to show that every offspring, no matter how savage, is bound to be softened and tamed by parental kindness. They encircled the top of her head with a turreted crown, because earth in prominent places is fortified, and so protects cities. Even today this diadem adorns the image of the divine Mother, as she is processioned through great countries, striking awe into the people. She it is whom many different nations, in accordance with the ritual usage of ancient times, call Mother of Ida; and they provide her with an escort of Phrygians, because they declare that the production of cereals originated in Phrygia and spread from there to every region of the earth. They assign her eunuch-priests, because they wish to indicate that those who have profaned the divinity of the Mother, and have been found wanting in gratitude to their parents, must be judged unworthy to bring forth offspring into the shores of light and life. All around the statue rolls the thunderous percussion of taut timbrels; concave cymbals clash, raucous-voiced trumpets snarl, and the Phrygian rhythm of the hollow pipe goads on the devotees, who brandish before them weapons that symbolize their violent frenzy, to terrorize the ungrateful minds and irreverent hearts of the populace with the power of the goddess. And so, as soon as her silent figure is processioned into great cities to bless mortals with mute benediction, the people strew her path all through the streets with bronze and silver, enriching her with liberal offerings, and shade the Mother and her escort with showers of snowy rose-blossoms. From time to time during the ceremony an armed company, whom the Greeks call Curetes,[17] caper among the Phrygian retinue, leaping rhythmically in ecstasy at the shedding of blood and shaking their terrifying plumes with the nodding of their heads. Their antics recall the Curetes of Dicte in Crete, who, according to the legend, once upon a time drowned that famous wailing of Jupiter; it was the occasion when around the baby boy those boys clad in armor danced swiftly, rhythmically clashing bronze on bronze, to prevent Saturn from finding his son and devouring him in his jaws, thus inflicting a never-healing wound in the Mother's heart. This may explain why armed men accompany the Great Mother; alternatively, the significance of their presence is that the goddess demands that men should be determined to defend their native land with valiant feats of arms and should prepare to be both a shield and an honor to their parents.

But although these ideas are conceived and expressed in a fine and impressive manner, they are far divorced from the true explanation. For it is inherent in the very nature of the gods that they should enjoy immortal life in perfect peace, far removed and separated from our world; free from all distress, free from peril, fully self-sufficient, independent of us, they are not influenced by worthy conduct nor touched by anger. The fact is that the earth is at all times destitute of sensation, and the reason why it brings forth many things in many ways into the light of the sun is that it is possessed of the primary elements of many substances.

In this connection, if people choose to call the sea Neptune and corn Ceres, and prefer to misapply the name of Bacchus rather than use the proper term for liquor of grapes, let us concede that they may designate the earth as Mother of the Gods, on

---

17. The Curetes, who lived in Crete, were said to have protected the infant Jupiter by drowning out his cries in a cave on Mount Dicte, where his mother hid him to protect him from his father, Saturn. The cult of Rhea came to be confused with that of Cybele, and Lucretius here conflates the Curetes with Cybele's attendants, the Corybantes.

condition that they really and truly refrain from tainting their minds with the stain of superstition.

### D    Mind and Body Are Inseparable; Death Is Not to Be Feared
(3.784–1094)

Again, a tree cannot exist in the sky, or clouds in the depths of the sea; fish cannot live in fields; blood is not found in timber, or sap in stones. The place where each thing may grow and exist is fixed and determined. Thus the substance of the mind cannot come to birth alone without the body or exist separated from sinews and blood. But even if this were possible, the mind could far more easily reside in the head or the shoulders or the base of the heels, or be born in any other part of the body, and so at least remain within the same person, within the same vessel. However, since even within our body it is evident that a special place is firmly fixed and reserved for the existence and growth of the spirit and mind, it is all the more necessary for us to deny that they could survive or come to birth wholly outside the body. Therefore, when the body has died, you must acknowledge that the soul too has perished, torn to pieces all through the body.

Moreover, to yoke together the mortal and the everlasting, and to imagine that they can share one another's feelings and experiences, is fatuous. What notion can be more preposterous, incongruous, and inharmonious than that of a mortal thing being united with something immortal and imperishable, and of the two together weathering pitiless storms?

Furthermore, all things that subsist eternally must either be composed of solid substance, so that they repel blows and are impenetrable to anything that might destroy the close cohesion of their parts from within—like the elements of matter, whose nature I have already demonstrated; or their ability to survive throughout all time must be due to their immunity from blows—as is the case with void, which is always intangible and never experiences any impact; or else the cause of their indestructibility must be the absence of any surrounding space into which their substance might disperse and dissolve—as is the case with the totality of the universe: for outside the universe there is no space into which its substance can escape, and no matter capable of striking it and shattering it with a powerful blow.[18]

If by chance the preferred supposition is that the soul is to be considered immortal because it is fortified and protected by the forces of life, or because things fatal to its existence never approach it, or because those that do approach it are repulsed by some means before they can inflict any injury upon us, <it must be said that this supposition is at variance with the facts>.[19] Besides sharing the diseases of the body, the soul is often visited by feelings that torment it about the future, fret it with fear, and vex it with anxious cares, while consciousness of past misdeeds afflicts it with remorse. Remember also madness and loss of memory—afflictions peculiar to the mind; remember the black waves of coma into which it sinks.

---

18. The soul's failure to satisfy any of the three conditions of immortality shows that it must be mortal.

19. Editorial supplement for a lost line.

Death, then, is nothing to us and does not affect us in the least, now that the nature of the mind is understood to be mortal. And as in time past we felt no distress when the advancing Punic hosts were threatening Rome on every side, when the whole earth, rocked by the terrifying tumult of war, shudderingly quaked beneath the coasts of high heaven, while the entire human race was doubtful into whose possession the sovereignty of the land and the sea was destined to fall;[20] so, when we are no more, when body and soul, upon whose union our being depends, are divorced, you may be sure that nothing at all will have the power to affect us or awaken sensation in us, who shall not then exist—not even if the earth be confounded with the sea, and the sea with the sky.

And even supposing that the mind and the spirit retain their power of sensation after they have been wrenched from our body, it is nothing to us, whose being is dependent upon the conjunction and marriage of body and soul. Furthermore, if in course of time all our component atoms should be reassembled after our death and restored again to their present positions, so that the light of life was given to us a second time, even that eventuality would not affect us in the least, once there had been a break in the chain of consciousness. Similarly at the present time we are not affected at all by any earlier existence we had, and we are not tortured with any anguish concerning it. When you survey the whole sweep of measureless time past and consider the multifariousness of the movements of matter, you can easily convince yourself that the same seeds that compose us now have often before been arranged in the same order that they occupy now. And yet we have no recollection of our earlier existence; for between that life and this lies an unbridged gap—an interval during which all the motions of our atoms strayed and scattered in all directions, far away from sensation.

If it happens that people are to suffer unhappiness and pain in the future, they themselves must exist at that future time for harm to be able to befall them; and since death takes away this possibility by preventing the existence of those who might have been visited by troubles, you may be sure that there is nothing to fear in death, that those who no longer exist cannot become miserable, and that it makes not one speck of difference whether or not they have ever been born once their mortal life has been snatched away by deathless death.

So, when you see people indignant at the thought that after death they will either rot in the grave or be devoured by flames or the jaws of wild beasts, you may be sure that, however emphatically they themselves deny belief that they will retain any feeling in death, their words do not ring true, and that deep in their hearts they are pricked by some secret fear. In my judgment, they grant neither the conclusion they profess to grant, nor the premise[21] from which it is derived; they do not completely uproot and detach themselves from life, but unconsciously suppose that something of themselves survives. Whenever people in life imagine that in death their body will be torn to pieces by birds and beasts of prey, they feel sorry for themselves. This is because they do not separate themselves from the body or dissociate themselves sufficiently from the outcast corpse; they identify themselves with it and, as they stand by, impregnate

---

20. The reference is to the Punic Wars, especially the second (218–201 BC), when Hannibal invaded Italy and defeated the Romans in several battles.

21. The premise is that the soul does not survive after death; the conclusion is that there is no feeling after death.

it with their own feelings. Hence their indignation at having been created mortal; hence their failure to see that in real death there will be no second self alive to lament their own end, and to stand by and grieve at the sight of them lying there, being torn to pieces or burned. I mention being burned, because, if in death it is disastrous to be mauled by the devouring jaws of wild beasts, I cannot see why it is not calamitous to be laid upon a funeral pyre and consumed by scorching flames, or to be embalmed in stifling honey, or to grow stiff with cold, reclining on the smooth surface of an icy slab of stone, or to be pulverized by a crushing weight of earth above one.

"Never again," mourners say, "will your household receive you with joy; never again will the best of wives welcome you home; never again will your dear children race for the prize of your first kisses and touch your heart with pleasure too profound for words. Never again can you enjoy prosperous circumstances or be a bulwark to your dependants. Wretched man," they cry, "one wretched, damnable day has dispossessed you of every one of life's many precious gifts." They omit to add: "No craving for these things remains with you any longer." If only they fully grasped this fact and expressed their feelings accordingly, they would relieve their minds of great anguish and fear.

I imagine another saying: "You, for your part, are wrapped in the sleep of death and will remain so for the rest of time, exempt from all painful sufferings. But we, as we stood near the dreadful pyre upon which you were reduced to ashes, wept and wept for you insatiably; our sorrow is undying: the day will never dawn that will banish it from our hearts." The person who takes this attitude should be asked how a happening that involves a return to sleep and repose can be so bitter that anyone should pine away in undying grief.

It often happens too that people reclining at a banquet, drinking-cup in hand and garlands shadowing their brows, earnestly declare: "All too short-lived is the enjoyment of these things for us puny humans; soon it will be gone, and we will never be able to recall it." As if the most miserable misfortune awaiting them in death was to be consumed and parched by a burning thirst or indeed to be afflicted with any other craving! In fact, people never feel the want of themselves or their life, when mind and body alike are sunk in sound sleep: as far as we are concerned, this sleep might continue for ever without any craving for ourselves affecting us. And yet, at the moment when people jerk themselves out of sleep and gather themselves together, the primary elements of the spirit scattered throughout their limbs cannot be straying far from the motions that produce sensation. It follows that death should be considered to be of much less concern to us than sleep—that is, if anything can be less than what we perceive to be nothing. For at death a greater disturbance and dispersion of matter takes place, and no one wakes and rises once overtaken by life's cold stoppage.

Furthermore, suppose that nature suddenly burst into speech, and personally addressed the following rebuke to one of us: "What distresses you so deeply, mortal creature, that you abandon yourself to these puling lamentations? Why do you bemoan and beweep death? If your past life has been a boon, and if not all your blessings have flowed straight through you and run to waste like water poured into a riddled vessel, why, you fool, do you not retire from the feast of life like a satisfied guest and with equanimity resign yourself to undisturbed rest? If, however, all your enjoyments have been poured away and lost, and if life is a thorn, why do you seek to prolong your existence, when the future, just as surely as the past, would be ruined and utterly wasted? Why not rather put an end to life and trouble? There is nothing further that I can devise and discover for your pleasure: all things are always the same. Though your body is not yet shrunk with age, and your limbs are not exhausted and enfeebled, all things remain the same—yes, even if in length of life you should outlast all generations, or indeed even if you should be destined never to die." What can we say in reply, save that nature's complaint is just, and that in her plea she sets out a true case?

And if someone older and more advanced in years should sorrowfully bewail and bemoan the approach of death to an immoderate degree, would she not be justified in rating that person still more roughly and delivering an even sharper rebuke: "Stop sniveling, you dolt! Away with your whinings! You had full use of all the precious things of life before you reached this senile state. But because you continually crave what is not present and scorn what is, your life has slipped away from you incomplete and unenjoyed, until suddenly you have found death standing at your head before you are able to depart from the feast of life filled to repletion. Quick then, discard all behavior unsuited to your age and with equanimity yield to your years; for yield you must." In my opinion, she would be justified in making this plea, justified in delivering this rebuke and reproof. The old is ever ousted and superseded by the new, and one thing must be repaired from others. No one is consigned to the black abyss of Tartarus: everyone's component matter is needed to enable succeeding generations to grow—generations which, when they have completed their term of life, are all destined to follow you. The fate in store for you has already befallen past generations and will befall future generations no less surely. Thus one thing will never cease to rise out of another: life is granted to no one for permanent ownership, to all on lease. Look back now and consider how the bygone ages of eternity that elapsed before our birth were nothing to us. Here, then, is a mirror in which nature shows us the time to come after our death. Do you see anything fearful in it? Do you perceive anything grim? Does it not appear more peaceful than the deepest sleep?

Next let me assure you that all the punishments that tradition locates in the abysm of Acheron actually exist in our life.

No tormented Tantalus, as in the story, fears the huge rock suspended over him in the air, paralyzed with vain terror; but in life mortals are oppressed by groundless fear of the gods and dread the fall of the blow that chance may deal to any of them.

No Tityos[22] lying in Acheron has his insides devoured by winged creatures. It is certain that they could not find anything for their beaks to explore throughout eternity even in the depths of that huge breast: even if the sprawling extent of his body were so enormous that his splayed-out limbs covered not merely nine acres, but the whole orb of the earth, he would not be able to endure eternal pain or furnish an inexhaustible supply of food from his own body. However, Tityos does exist among us on earth: he is the person lying in bonds of love, who is torn by winged creatures[23] and consumed by agonizing anxiety or rent by the anguish of some other passion.

Sisyphus too exists in this life before our eyes: he is the man who thirstily solicits from the people the rods and grim axes[24] of high office and always comes away disap-

---

22. A giant who attempted to rape Latona, the mother of Apollo and Diana.

23. Cupids, the gods of erotic love.

24. The *fasces* (see Glossary).

pointed and despondent. For to seek power that is illusory and never granted, and to suffer continual hardship in pursuit of it, is the same as to push up a mountain with might and main a rock that, after all this effort, rolls back from the summit and in impetuous haste races down to the level plain.

Then again, to keep feeding an ungrateful mind with good things, without ever being able to fill it and satisfy its appetite—as is the case with the seasons of the year, when they come around with their fruits and manifold delights and yet never satisfy our appetite for the fruits of life—this, in my opinion, is what is meant by the story of those maidens[25] in the flower of their age pouring water into a riddled vessel that cannot possibly be filled.

But what of Cerberus[26] and the Furies[27] and the realm destitute of light? What of Tartarus vomiting waves of fearful fumes from its jaws? These terrors do not exist and cannot exist anywhere at all. But in life people are tortured by a fear of punishment as cruel as their crimes, and by the atonement for their offenses—the dungeon, the terrible precipitation from the Rock,[28] stripes, executioners, the execution cell, pitch, redhot plates, torches. Even though these horrors are absent, the mind, conscious of its guilt and fearfully anticipating the consequences, pricks itself with goads and sears itself with scourges. It fails to see how there can be an end to its afflictions, or a limit to its punishment; indeed it is afraid that its sufferings may increase in death. In short, fools make a veritable hell of their lives on earth.

Now and again you might well address yourself in the following terms: "Shame on you! Even good Ancus closed his eyes and left the light of life,[29] and he was a far, far better person than you. Since then, many other kings and potentates, rulers of mighty nations, have passed away. Even that famous monarch[30] who once constructed a road-way over the great sea and opened a path for his legions across the deep, teaching his infantry to march over the briny gulfs while his cavalry pranced upon the ocean in defiance of its roars—yes, even he was deprived of the light of life and gasped out his soul from his dying body. Scipio,[31] that thunderbolt of war, the dread of Carthage, surrendered his bones to the earth as though he were the meanest of menial slaves. Remember too the inventors of sciences and arts; remember the companions of the Heliconian maidens,[32] among whom unique Homer bore the scepter and yet is wrapped in the same sound sleep as the others. Democritus, warned by ripe old age that the motions of his mind's memory were failing, voluntarily went to meet death and offered him his

---

25. Forty-nine of the fifty daughters of Danaus (called the Danaids) killed their husbands on their wedding night. They are punished with futilely trying to fill a pot full of holes in the Underworld.

26. The monstrous three-headed dog that guarded the entrance to the lower world.

27. Chthonic goddesses of vengeance.

28. The Tarpeian Rock from which criminals were thrown to their deaths (see Glossary).

29. A quotation from Ennius. Ancus Marcius was the fourth king of Rome (642–617 BC).

30. The Persian king Xerxes, who invaded Greece in 480 BC, constructed a pontoon bridge to enable his troops to cross the Hellespont.

31. P. Cornelius Scipio Africanus the Elder, who in 202 BC defeated Hannibal at Zama.

32. The maidens are the Muses, who inspire poets ("the companions").

life.[33] Epicurus himself died, when the light of his life had accomplished its course—he who outshone the human race in genius and obscured the luster of all as the rising of the ethereal sun extinguishes the stars. Will *you*, then, be hesitant and indignant, when death calls? You, even while you still have life and light, are as good as dead: you squander the greater part of your time in sleep; you snore when awake; you never stop daydreaming; you are burdened with a mind disturbed by groundless fear; and often you cannot discover what is wrong with you, when, like some drunken wretch, you are buffeted with countless cares on every side and drift along aimlessly in utter bewilderment of mind."

People evidently are aware that their minds are carrying a heavy load, which wearies them with its weight; and if only they could also understand what causes it, and why such a mass of misery occupies their breasts, they would not live in the manner in which we generally see them living, ignorant of what they want for themselves, and continually impatient to move somewhere else as if the change could relieve them of their burden. Often a man leaves his spacious mansion, because he is utterly bored with being at home, and then suddenly returns on finding that he is no better off when he is out. He races out to his country villa, driving his Gallic ponies hell-for-leather. You would think he was dashing to save a house on fire. But the moment he has set foot on the threshold, he gives a yawn or falls heavily asleep in search of oblivion or even dashes back to the city. In this way people endeavor to run away from themselves; but since they are of course unable to make good their escape, they remain firmly attached to themselves against their will, and hate themselves because they are sick and do not understand the cause of their malady. If only they perceived it distinctly, they would at once give up everything else and devote themselves first to studying the nature of things; for the issue at stake is their state not merely for one hour, but for eternity—the state in which mortals must pass all the time that remains after their death.

Finally, what is this perverse passion for life that condemns us to such a feverish existence amid doubt and danger? The fact is that a sure end of life is fixed for mortals: we cannot avoid our appointment with death. Moreover, our environment is always the same, and no new pleasure is procured by the prolongation of life. The trouble is that, so long as the object of our desire is wanting, it seems more important than anything else; but later, when it is ours, we covet some other thing; and so an insatiable thirst for life keeps us always openmouthed. Then again, we cannot tell what fortune the future will bring us, or what chance will send us, or what end is in store for us. By prolonging life we do not deduct a single moment from the time of our death, nor can we diminish its duration by subtracting anything from it. Therefore, however many generations your life may span, the same eternal death will still await you; and one who ended life with today's light will remain dead no less long than one who perished many months and years ago.

---

33. Democritus (ca. 460–370 BC), a philosopher and the inventor of atomism, is said to have starved himself to death.

# MARTIAL

(ca. AD 40–104, wrote in Latin)

## Introduction

M. Valerius Martialis was from the Roman colony Augusta Bilbilis (modern Calatayud, Spain). He came to Rome in his twenties, and gained fame as a writer of satirical epigrams (short poems on various topics with some kind of punch-line, ironic observation, or mocking insult at the end). He celebrated the inauguration of the Flavian Amphitheater (the Colosseum) in AD 80 with a book of epigrams, *On the Spectacles*, which is preserved only in excerpts. This book is in some ways atypical of the main body of his work, the *Epigrams*. These took shape gradually in the years 86 to around 102, and contain a varied mix of observations on daily life, the battle of the sexes, and the always fraught relationship between the rich and the not rich, between patrons and clients.

Martial adopts the persona of the hard-up *scurra*—a type of social hanger-on who earned his dinner by entertaining the guests with his sarcasm and mockery. This was, perhaps, close to his real position at the beginning of his career, but he later achieved equestrian rank on the basis of a titular tribunate awarded to him. He owned an estate northeast of Rome near Nomentum, and later also a house in Rome. He also received certain legal privileges from the Emperors Titus (reigned AD 79–81) and Domitian (reigned AD 81–96)—the latter of whom Martial frequently mentions and praises.

In tone Martial's epigrams range widely, from gentle humor to hair-raising obscenity, from rapturous praise to cruel mockery. He can also turn philosophical, and occasionally shows tender feeling, as when he commemorates the death of a six-year-old slave (*Epigrams* no. 33, below). He says clearly that he refrained from attacking actual people—a sensible precaution at this period, when writers who offended the powerful for whatever reason might well be exiled, killed, and their works burned. Unlike his favorite model Catullus, Martial avoided controversial political topics. The selections below begin with some of the poems from *On the Spectacles*, whose purpose was mainly to celebrate the games put on at the opening of the Colosseum, then continue with selections from throughout the *Epigrams* themselves.

# On the Spectacles

### 1    The Colosseum Outshines All the Wonders of the World
(*Spectacles* 1)

Uncivilized Memphis can shush about the miracle of the pyramids.
  Babylon's walls? Stop bragging, Assyrians, about your toil.
Let Diana's temple bring no more glory to the soft Ionians.
  Delos can keep mum about its altar of many horns,
and please, stop the Carians from lifting the towering Mausoleum
  to the stars with their immoderate praise.[1]
Every wonder must now yield to the Emperor's Amphitheater.[2]
Posterity will forgo the rest and speak only of this.

### 2    A Spectacular Execution (*Spectacles* 9)

Think of Prometheus, tied to his Scythian crag, feeding the tireless
  bird of prey with his ever-growing chest.
Just so "Laureolus," hanging on no mock theatrical cross,
  gave his naked guts to a Scottish bear.[3]
His mangled limbs lived on, dripping with gore, until his body
  became no body at all. So, what heinous crime
merited such retribution? Perhaps the condemned man had
  slit his master's throat with a sword,
or in his madness robbed a temple of its hidden gold, or else
  he put a savage torch to you, dear Rome.                          10
This criminal's deeds outdid those of yore, but in his case
  what was fiction became a punishment quite real.

---

1. The Seven Wonders of the World were traditionally given as the temple of Diana at Ephesus; the Mausoleum or tomb of Mausolus, ruler of Caria 377–353 BC, built in Halicarnassus by Artemisia his widow; the Colossus of Rhodes, a huge bronze statue of the Sun god; the statue of Jupiter at Olympia by Pheidias; the palace of Cyrus at Ecbatana; the walls of Babylon; and the Pyramids of Egypt. Other lists included, in place of Cyrus' palace, the lighthouse of Alexandria, or the altar on Delos made by the four-year-old Apollo from the horns of animals slain by Diana.

2. The work of the Emperors Vespasian and Titus of the Flavian dynasty, it was often called the "Flavian" amphitheater. The name "Colosseum" was first used in the Middle Ages.

3. Sometimes a slave criminal, consigned to be executed in the arena by the beasts, was dressed up as a figure from the theater and executed in a way that recalled a well-known mime (see Glossary). In this case the mime was a historical one, describing the capture and execution of a notorious bandit called Laureolus. The condemned convict "plays the part" of Laureolus at his execution in the Colosseum while being tied up and exposed to a (real) bear.

**3      A Beast-Fighter** (*Spectacles* 17)

Meleager, what's your crowning achievement? A slaughtered boar?[4]
    That's but a tiny fraction of the glory of Carpophorus.
*He* plunged his spear into a charging bear as well, a bear like the one
    in the northern heavens,[5] and *he* dispatched a lion
of unheard-of size, a sight to behold, worthy of the hands
    of Hercules; and *he* sent a speedy panther
sprawling with a wound inflicted at long range.
    [*two lines missing*]
    since one bore off glory as his reward, the other a dish.


**4      A Trained Elephant** (*Spectacles* 20)

The elephant bows in devotion and worships you, Caesar—
    the same one who was just now so formidable
to the bull. It's not that he was ordered, or taught by his trainer:
    believe me, he, too, feels the presence of our god.


**5      A Tame Tigress Made Savage** (*Spectacles* 21)

She used to lick the hand of her trainer, who felt no fear,
    that tigress, the rare glory of the Hyrcanian hills.
Now she has savagely mauled a wild lion with her ravenous teeth.
    Strange sight, never witnessed before.
She was never so savage when living in the high mountain forests.
    Now that she's spent time with us, she's found new ferocity.


**6      A Sea-Battle in the Colosseum** (*Spectacles* 27)

Spectator! In case you're from distant shores and have shown up late,
    and this is your first day at the sacred games,
what you see here was recently land. Don't let the ships and naval battle
    fool you, or the water that looks like the sea.
You doubt me? Keep watching as the water exhausts the fighters.
    Soon you'll say, "Just now there was a sea here!"


**7      Synchronized Swimming** (*Spectacles* 30)

They played over the whole surface, a well-trained chorus
    of sea-nymphs, dotting the yielding waters

---

4. Meleager was a mythological hero famous for hunting the Calydonian boar.

5. Some sort of comparison with Ursa Major is meant, but the exact text and meaning are unclear.

with various patterns: a threatening trident, then a curved anchor.
    Then we believed we saw an oar, then a boat,
then the shining constellation welcome to sailors—the Dioscuri!—
    and broad sails billowing in distinctive folds.
Who invented such aquatic wizardry? Thetis herself must have taught
    these displays, or else learned them from you.[6]


**8    Gladiators Fight to a Draw** (*Spectacles* 31)

Priscus and Verus were each dragging out the contest,
    and for a long time the struggle stood equal.
The crowd shouted again and again, demanding discharge
    for the men.[7] But Caesar obeyed his own rule—
once the palm had been set up the fight had to go on until
    a finger was raised.[8] What Caesar could do,
he did: he often doled out dishes and presents. Finally, an end
    to the deadlock was found: equal they fought,
equal they yielded. Caesar sent a rod and a palm to each.[9]
    Such was the reward for their valor and skill.                    10
This has happened under no other emperor but you,
    Caesar: two men fought, and both won.


# Epigrams


**9    To My Readers** (Book 1, preface)

I have exercised enough restraint in my writings, I hope, that no one with any self-respect can complain about them, in as much as they make fun without infringing on the dignity of actual people, even those of the lowest status. This is a trait that

---

6. Thetis was a goddess of the sea in Greek mythology.

7. Discharge (*missio*) allowed a gladiator to return to his barracks and train for further engagements; it did not mean discharge from service as a gladiator. A gladiator who had technically surrendered to his opponent might be awarded a reprieve, if the spectators could convince the sponsor of the games that his performance merited it; alternatively, two gladiators who fought to a draw could both be judged worthy of a reprieve, as here. See Inscriptions, no. 79.

8. A sign of surrender; many images from Roman art show a defeated gladiator, his shield lying on the ground beside him, holding up his left arm with the index finger raised.

9. The palm signified victory. The *rudis* was the rod carried by the owner of the gladiatorial school (*lanista*) as a symbol of authority. Its awarding to a gladiator signified not just *missio* (see note 7 above), but *liberatio*, total release from service. The *rudis* was not, as is often stated, a wooden sword, but a kind of wand.

was completely lacking in the satirists of old: they not only abused real people, but prominent ones, too. Fame to me is not worth so much, and the last thing I want is a reputation for cleverness.[10] Malicious critics should steer clear of my straightforward humor, and refrain from writing my epigrams for me: it's a wicked thing to exercise one's own ingenuity on another's book. I would apologize for using frank, indecent language—that is, the language of epigram—if I had been the first to do so. This is the way Catullus wrote, and Marsus, Pedo, Gaetulicus—all the authors whose books people actually finish. But if there is anyone so hell bent on being morose that no actual Latin may be spoken on any page he reads, he can be content with this prefatory letter—or rather just the title. Epigrams are written for those who like to attend the Games of Flora. Let Cato not enter my theater or, if he enters, let him watch.[11] I think I'll be within my rights to close this letter with some verse:

> You knew about the merry rites of Flora's games,
> the playful festivities, the uninhibited crowds.
> So why, stern Cato, enter the theater in the first place?
> Or is it that you went in just so you could leave?

## 10    The Book Addresses Its Reader (*Epigrams* 1.1)

> Hello, it's me. The one you're reading,
> the one you long for: the famous Martial,
> known the world over for his shrewd little
> books of epigrams. You, devoted reader,
> have granted him glory while he's still alive
> and here to enjoy it, such as very
> few poets attain in their graves.

## 11    A Sexual Exhibitionist (1.34)

> Your door's always open and unguarded when you have sex,
>     Lesbia. You don't conceal your forbidden trysts.
> You get more pleasure from being watched by another
>     than from the adulterer himself. You can't
> enjoy it if it's hidden. A prostitute, by contrast, drives away
>     all witnesses with a curtain or door-bolt,
> and rarely does a crack appear in the brothel's wall.
>     Learn some modesty from Chione and Ias!

---

10. That is, a reputation for cleverly attacking real, living people under fictitious names.

11. The games for the Italian goddess Flora were celebrated in late April and early May—a boisterous affair that included racy theatrical performances, including the dancing of unrobed prostitutes (Martial, *Epigrams* 1.35). Valerius Maximus (2.10.8) tells the story that the stern moralist Cato the Younger attended in 55 BC, but became embarrassed when the crowd started urging the mime actresses to strip. He left the theater on finding that his presence was inhibiting the show, to the loud applause of the crowd.

Even a filthy whore hides behind some grave monument.
    Do these strictures seem too harsh?                                    10
Lesbia, I'm not asking you not to get fucked,
    I only want you not to get caught.


## 12    A Doctor (1.47)

Diaulus was a doctor until recently; now he's an undertaker.
    His daily routine hasn't changed, not a bit.


## 13    A Neighbor Never Seen (1.86)

Novius is my neighbor, and we can reach
out through our windows to shake hands.
Who wouldn't envy me, call me happy
as the day is long, to be able to enjoy
a dear friend's company at such close quarters?
In fact, though, Novius is as distant from me
as Terentianus, the current governor
of Syene on the Nile. I can't dine with him,
I can't even see him, or hear him.
No one in this whole city is so close, and yet
so far. That's it. I'm moving out, or *he* has to.
You should only be a neighbor or suitemate
of Novius if you never want to see him.


## 14    Hard on the Outside, Soft on the Inside (1.96)

If it's not a bother and you don't mind, my
limping verse,[12] please speak a few words
to my friend Maternus—whisper so only he hears.
"You know that lover of stern and manly cloaks,
who dresses in drab grey Spanish wool?
He thinks that wearers of scarlet are not real
men at all, and calls lilac-colored cloaks
'women's clothes,' and praises pure un-dyed
fabrics. *Well*, even if he wears somber colors
every day, his character is neon green."                                   10
Maternus will no doubt ask what leads me
to suspect that this man is soft and effeminate.
We go to the same baths, he and I,

---

12. The "limping" meter is scazon, so called because it unexpectedly reverses the stress at line-end.

and he never looks up. He gazes at the athletes
with devouring eyes, and licks his lips as
he stares at their cocks. You ask who it is?
Oops, the name has just slipped my mind.

## 15    Desperate for a Dinner Invitation (2.11)

Rufus, do you see Selius there, how his brow
is clouded, how he walks around, wearing out
the portico floor in the late afternoon? See how
his glum face leaves some sorrow unvoiced,
stooping, his ugly nose nearly touching the ground?
See how he beats his chest, pulls at his hair?
He's not mourning the death of a friend or a brother.
Both his children live (I pray they continue to).
His wife is doing fine, and so are his possessions,
and his slaves. Nor have his tenant farmers and
overseers squandered his cash, not at all. So what
could be the cause of his grief? He's dining at home.

## 16    A Client's Client (2.18)

Maximus, I'm trying to catch an invitation to dinner at your house.
    It shames me to say it, but that's what I'm after.
Then again, *you're* trying to catch an invitation to someone
    else's dinner, so we're equal. In the morning
I show up to pay you my respects. But they say you've already
    gone to call on someone else, so we're equal.
I escort you, walking in front of my pompous patron.
    But you escort somebody else, so we're equal.
It's enough to be a slave. I won't be a slave's slave any longer.
    A patron, Maximus, should not have a patron.

## 17    An Eager Supporter (2.27)

Giving a recitation? Pleading in court? Bring along the praise-giving
    Selius when he's spreading his net for a dinner.
"Way to go!" "A hit!" "Bang!" "Cunning!" "Nice!" "Well done!"
    "Perfect, Selius. You earned your meal. Now shut up."

## 18    The Outside Doesn't Match the Inside (2.36)

Please don't curl your hair, but don't let it run riot, either.
    Skin should not glisten, nor yet be filthy,

beard like neither the hair-net crowd, nor shaggy defendants.[13]
    Pannychus, don't be too much a man, nor too little.
As it is, you've got hair on your legs, and your chest is quite shaggy.
    What's depilated, Pannychus, is your mind.


## 19     A Cruel Master (2.82)

Why do you cut out your slave's tongue before crucifying him?
    Ponticus, the people are saying what he no longer can.


## 20     Dinner Replaces Handouts (3.7)

Goodbye, you miserable few bucks,[14]
hand-out for a tired entourage, once shared
by us with the boiled bath-keeper, goodbye.
The dole given out by the proud patron is no more.
What do you say, you starving clients?
"No tricks. We deserve a salary!"


## 21     A Corpse at Dinner (3.12)

You gave out a fine perfume yesterday
at dinner, I admit. But you carved nothing.
That's pretty funny, to smell good and be hungry.
A man who is anointed but does not eat,
Fabullus, seems to me truly dead.[15]


## 22     Hopes and Dreams of a Life in Rome (3.38)

Tell me, Sextus, why come to Rome, what prospect attracts you?
    What are you after, what are your dreams? Tell me!
"I'll argue cases, and be more eloquent than Cicero himself.
    No man in the three Forums will be my equal!"[16]

---

13. Defendants in court stopped bathing and let their beards grow to elicit sympathy. The *mitra* was a kind of cap or hairnet with a pointy top and ties under the chin, worn by women and allegedly effeminate men.

14. Literally "100 *quadrantes*" = twenty-five *asses*, a small amount of money. Martial complains because a "dinner" is now given in place of the money *sportula* (see Glossary).

15. Hosts gave guests unguents to anoint their hair at dinner parties, but corpses were also anointed. See Catullus 13 in this volume, likewise addressed to one Fabullus, a poem which Martial is parodying.

16. There were two types of "lawyers" in the Roman world. A *iuris consultus* would give advice on the substance of the law, while a *rhetor* would offer his skill in speaking, usually for a fee. The

Atestinus and Civis argued cases—you knew them both—
    but neither managed to pay the bills.
"Well, if that doesn't pay off, I'll write poetry. When you hear it,
    you'll swear it's the work of Vergil himself."
You're crazy. You see those men there, shivering in frosty cloaks?
    They're all would-be Ovids and Vergils.
"I'll schmooze with the wealthy in their *atria*!" That racket feeds    10
    three, maybe four. The rest? Pale with hunger.
"So give me some advice, then. I am determined to live in Rome."
    If you're an honest man, Sextus, you can live at random.[17]

## 23    A Man to Be Avoided (3.44)

Do you want to know why it is, Ligurinus,
that no one is glad to run into you,
that wherever you go people vanish,
leaving a vast solitude all around you?
Why? Because you are too much of a poet.
This is a fault quite dangerous, more feared
than the swift tiger deprived of her pups,
than the viper scorched by the midday sun,
than the ruthless scorpion. For I ask you,
who would endure such ordeals? You read to me    10
as I stand and you read as I sit.
You read as I run and you read as I shit.
I try to escape to the baths:
you boom in my ear. I head for the pool:
I can't even swim. I hurry off to dinner:
you stalk me as I go. I head into dinner:
you drive me away as I eat. Worn out, I sleep:
you wake me up when I'm down. You want to see
how much damage you do? You are a fine,
upright, innocent man. And yet you are feared.    20

## 24    Perfume (3.55)

Wherever you go, we think that Cosmus has moved shop
    and is waving about an open vial of cinnamon oil.
I wish you didn't like this foreign junk, Gellia. You know
    it could make my dog smell just as good.

---

distinction is analogous to that of the English legal system, where solicitors do the paperwork and barristers (often called "advocates") argue in court. Trials took place in the basilicas surrounding the various forums.

17. That is, from hand to mouth. Satirists liked to say that only rogues could make a regular living at Rome. See Juvenal, *Satires* 3 in this volume.

### 25    An Unequal Dinner Party (3.60)

Since I now come to dinner as a guest, and not at a price as before,[18]
 how come you don't serve me the same dinner as you?
You enjoy oysters that grew fat in the Lucrine lake,
 I cut my mouth sucking on a mussel.
You have mushrooms. I get pig fungi. You dine on
 a fine turbot. I'm stuck with bream.
A golden turtle dove fills you up with its oversized rump.
 I am served a magpie that died in its cage.
Ponticus, why do I dine without you when we dine together?
 The dole's gone, so how about it: let's eat the same thing.

### 26    An Elegant Man (3.63)

Cotilus, you're an elegant man. So everybody says, Cotilus.
 I hear it. Tell me, what exactly *is* an elegant man?
"An elegant man keeps his hair curled and carefully placed.
 He always smells of balsam, always of cinnamon.
He hums the tunes from Egypt and Spain, he moves his
 smooth arms in time with the music.
He sits all day among the ladies' chairs, and is constantly
 whispering in somebody's ear.
He reads and writes notes on tablets sent hither and yon.
 He avoids brushing the cloak on a neighbor's elbow.
He knows who's in love with whom, flits among dinner parties,
 and knows Hirpinus'[19] ancestry by heart."
What? That's it? This is an elegant man, Cotilus? An elegant man,
 Cotilus, is a whole lot of trifling bullshit.

### 27    A Boy Lover Grows Up (4.7)

Hyllus, my boy, why deny me today what you granted yesterday,
 so suddenly cruel when just now you were kind?
Beard, body hair, your age: these are the excuses now. What a
 long, long night to have made you so old!
Why do you mock me? Yesterday you were a boy, Hyllus.
 Tell me, how can you be a man today?

---

18. The dole ("handout") is now an invitation to dinner, not money as before (see no. 20 above, with note).

19. A racehorse. See Novatian, *On Spectacles* ch. 5 in this volume.

**28    A Day in Imperial Rome** (4.8)

The first and second hours[20] tire out clients making their rounds.
  The third makes the lawyers go hoarse.
Rome extends its various labors into the fifth. The sixth means
  rest for the weary,[21] which ends at the seventh.
The eighth to the ninth suffice for oily wrestling bouts,
  the ninth bids us lie down on our couches.[22]
The hour for my books, Euphemus,[23] is the tenth, when
  you dutifully attend to the ambrosial feast,
and good Caesar relaxes with heavenly nectar, holding
  a modest goblet in his massive hand.                                    10
That's the right time for humor. My Muse walks like a tart,
  and dares not approach Jupiter in the morning.


**29    A Rich Atheist** (4.21)

Segius claims there are no gods, that the sky
is empty. And he proves it: in the midst of
these denials he sees that he's become rich.


**30    An Urban Villa** (4.64)

Julius Martialis' few acres,
lovelier than the Hesperides' gardens,
lie on the long ridge of the Janiculum.[24]
The lofty villa can be seen above the hills.
Its level or slightly rising peak enjoys
a calmer air. When clouds cover the winding
valleys, it gleams alone in private sunlight.
The elegant peaks of the lofty villa's
roof gently approach the unclouded stars.
From here one can see the seven hills that rule                          10
the world, take the measure of all Rome,
the hills of Alba and Tusculum, too,
and every chilly retreat in the region,

---

20. Just after daybreak. See Appendix "Roman Time-Reckoning."

21. Siesta, a word that derives from the Latin *sexta hora* ("sixth hour").

22. For dinner.

23. A Greek freedman who served as chief steward (*tricliniarches*) of the Emperor Domitian. He seems to have remained on duty during dinner, and is imagined here as arranging for a reader to recite Martial's poems to the emperor as after-dinner entertainment.

24. A ridge of hills on the western side of the Tiber.

old Fidenae, and tiny Rubrae as well,
and the fruitful grove of Anna Perenna
that rejoices in the shedding of maiden's blood.[25]
Over there, you can clearly see a traveler
on the Flaminian or Salarian road,
yet his wagon is completely silent, as if
to keep noisy wheels from disturbing your nap.                    20
And no boatswain's holler will shatter your rest,
nor any barge puller's shout, even though
the Mulvian bridge lies so close, and the boats
glide speedily along the sacred Tiber.
This estate—or should it be called a palace?—
gains charm from its owner. You will think the place
your own, so unfailingly gracious it is,
so open in warm hospitality.
It's like being at the home of Alcinous
or of Molorchus with his newfound wealth.                         30
You who think nothing is ever big enough,
go ahead, farm cool Tibur or Praeneste
with a hundred mattocks, assign Setia
and its slopes to a single inhabitant.
Just know that, for me, they take second place
to Julius Martialis' few acres.

**31    A Mystery in the Country (4.66)**

Your life, Linus, has always been the municipal kind,[26]
     positively the least expensive life there is.
You shook out your toga only on rare occasions.
     A single dining suit[27] lasted ten summers.
The glens supplied boar meat, the fields rabbits, unbought;
     you beat the forest: out came the thrushes.
Your fish arrived, snatched from the river's swirl;
     a ruddy cask poured cheap local wine.
The servants were no exquisite Greek boys: a rustic crowd
     stood round an unsophisticated hearth.
When your organ grew warm, inflamed by wine, you bedded
     the overseer's wife, or a rugged tenant-farmer's.[28]

---

25. There was a popular and raucous festival of the Italian goddess Anna Perenna on the Ides of March in an open area near the Tiber (Ovid, *Fasti* 3.523–542). But the allusion here to "maiden's blood" is obscure.

26. *Municipia* were Italian towns outside of Rome. See Glossary.

27. *Synthesis*, a set of loose garments worn at dinner parties.

28. Rather than expensive urban prostitutes.

Your buildings suffered no fires, your crops no drought,
    no ship sank at sea—in fact, you never had one!
You never felt the draw of dice, and stuck to knucklebones.
    Your only gambling stakes? Inexpensive nuts.
So now where's that million your money-mad mother left you?
    Nowhere? Linus, now *that's* quite a feat.

## 32    Roman Girls Never Say No (4.71)

I've long been searching the whole city, Safronius Rufus,
    for a girl who says no. No girl says no.
It's as if it's not right to say no, as if it's a disgrace,
    not permitted. No girl says no.
So none are chaste? There are a thousand. What does a chaste girl do?
    She doesn't put out, but she doesn't say no.

## 33    Epitaph for a Slave Girl (5.34)

Father Fronto and mother Flacilla,[29] to you I commend
    this girl, my sweet darling and delight.
Make sure little Erotion isn't frightened of the shadowy blackness
    of Hades, the dread jaws of Tartarus' hound.
She was about to see the end of her sixth winter,
    had she not lived that many days too few.
Let her sport and play among her old patrons, and let her
    speak my name with a childish stammer.
May the turf lie not rough on her soft bones, and Earth,
    be not a burden for her—she never was for you.

## 34    Escaping the *Salutatio* (7.39)

Caelius said he could no longer take it:
the morning routine of rushing around,
of visiting place after place to receive
the greetings of powerful, arrogant men.
And so he pretended to suffer from gout.[30]
To make it look good he started to treat,

---

29. Martial's parents. The child, evidently a favorite in Martial's house, died and was presumably buried on his land. He commends her to his parents, already dead and awaiting her in the underworld.

30. A type of acute inflammatory arthritis typically affecting the big toe and making it difficult to walk.

plaster, and bandage his quite healthy feet,
to walk with slow, labored gait, until—wham!
See what's been done by this artist of pain:
Caelius now has gout, and no need to feign.


## 35    Troubling Dreams (7.54)

Every morning you tell your weird dreams involving me,
and they disturb and distress my mind.
A fortune-teller has been trying to exorcize your nightmares for me—
She's drained all of last year's wine, and this year's is next.
I've used up all my salt sacrificial cakes, and piles of incense.
My dwindling flocks have lost lamb after lamb.
No hogs, no poultry, no eggs are left. Nasidienus, please,
either stay awake, or dream about yourself.


## 36    An Effeminate Husband (7.58)

So you've married a *cinaedus*,[31] Galla? Is he number six, or seven?
You do love a neat beard and long hair.
But what about the sex, the penis like a wet leather strap, one
that no hard-working hand can compel to arise?
So you leave the pacifist bed of your effeminate man,
but soon find yourself back in the same kind of bed.
Find yourself a man who constantly talks of the Curii and Fabii:
tough, hairy, harsh, and rustic.
You'll find him. But beware, this grim tribe also has its *cinaedi*.
It's a hard thing, Galla, to marry a real man.


## 37    Clearing the Streets (7.61)

Reckless retail had gobbled the city,
no shop entrance was kept within bounds.
Germanicus,[32] you ordered the strangled streets to grow;
what was a narrow track has reemerged as road.
No column hangs with chained wine jugs; the praetor is not
compelled to track through muck.
The razor is not drawn blindly in a thick crowd,
the grimy pubs don't monopolize the streets.

---

31. See Glossary and Pliny, *Letters* 24 in this volume.

32. In AD 92, the Emperor Domitian (given the name Germanicus for his victories in Germany) issued an edict prohibiting stalls and shops from spilling into the streets.

Barber, taverner, cook, and butcher, all keep within bounds.
  It's Rome again, which was lately one giant shop.


## 38      Rich Wives in Charge (8.12)

I won't marry rich, Priscus. Would you like to know why?
  I prefer not to be the bride of my wife.
A woman should be under her man's social status.
  It's the only way to an equal match.


## 39      Punishing a Cook (8.23)

Rusticus, do I seem cruel, a too-obsessive gastronome,
  because I beat my cook on account of a dinner?
If that seems to you a trivial cause, then tell me
  just when *should* a cook be beaten?


## 40      Diminishing Gifts for Saturnalia (8.71)

Ten years ago, Postumianus, you sent four pounds of silver
  at the time of the winter solstice ritual.
I was hoping for more next time—gifts should either stay
  the same or increase—but two came, more or less.
The third and fourth years brought quite a bit less; the fifth
  was only a pound, and Septician silver[33] at that.
The sixth year we went down to one eight-ounce dish,
  then a bare half-pound in the shape of a cup.[34]
The eighth sent a spoon weighing in at less than two ounces.
  The ninth year brought a snail pick, light as a needle.
Now the tenth year has nothing left to send to me.
  Postumianus, let's go back to four pounds.


## 41      A Way to Stay Young (8.79)

All your friends, Fabulla, are old biddies,
or ugly and still more repulsive than that.
You lead them around as companions,
and drag them along to dinner. With them
you stroll the porticoes, attend the theater.
That's how you stay pretty, Fabulla, and young.

---

33. That is, inferior.

34. The Roman pound (*libra*) contained twelve ounces (*unciae*); eight ounces would therefore
be two-thirds of a pound.

**42    A Loud Schoolmaster** (9.68)

Schoolmaster, you wretch, bane of girls and of boys,
    why on earth do you plague us? The rooster has yet
to break the silence of the night, yet there you are
    thundering, grumbling, thwacking away.
When hammer pounds on anvil, as a sculptor mounts
    a lawyer's mug on some equestrian statue,
when a gladiator wins and the Colosseum goes mad,
    the sounds are far less grating than this.
Your neighbors ask only for sleep—and not the whole night.
    A brief interruption, that's fine. But insomnia
is hard. Send your students away. Here's a deal, how about
    you take as much to be quiet as you get to shout?

**43    Gold-Digging** (10.8)

Paula wants to marry me, but I would rather not. She's old.
    I might be willing if she were older.

**44    An Ungenerous Friend** (10.15)

You say you are second to none of my friends, Crispus.
    But tell me, how do you back up the claim?
I asked for a loan of five thousand. You said no. Yet your groaning
    cash box cannot hold all your wealth.
I don't recall a single bushel of beans or grain, despite your
    plantations tilled by Egyptian tenants.
When have you sent a short toga in chilly winter time?
    When has a half pound of silver come my way?
I see no evidence of your friendship, Crispus, except for the fact
    that you habitually fart in my presence.

**45    The Good Life** (10.47)

Here are the makings of a happy life,
my dear Martialis:[35] money not worked for,
but inherited; a farm that's productive;
a hearth fire always roaring; law suits never;
the toga rarely worn; a calm mind;
a gentleman's vigor and healthy body;
circumspect candor, friends who are your equals;
relaxed dinner parties, a simple table,

---

35. L. Julius Martialis, the poet's closest friend.

nights not drunken, but free from cares;
a bed not prudish, yet modest;
plenty of sleep to make the dark hours short.
Wish to be what you are, and prefer nothing more.
Don't fear your last day, or hope for it, either.

## 46    A Poet Must Eat (11.24)

I escort you around town and back home,
and I lend, Labullus, an ear to your chat.
I praise the things you say and do.
In the time it took to do all that,
just *think* what verse I could have produced.
Does it not seem a waste that what Rome likes to read,
what visitors demand, what *equites*
enjoy and senators learn by heart
what lawyers praise and poets criticize,
thanks to you, Labullus, it *dies*.
For real, Labullus? Who could stand it?
To up the size of your toga'd entourage,
you lessen the number of my little books?
In a month I've scarcely finished a page.
So it goes when a poet will not dine at home.

## 47    A *Paedagogus* (11.39)

Charidemus, you rocked my cradle. And when I was a boy
    you were my constant protector and companion.
But now the barber's towel grows black with my beard, and my
    girl complains of red marks left by my lips.
To you, though, I've not grown at all. My farm's overseer
    shudders at your approach. The house-manager—
the very house itself—lives in fear of you. You won't let me
    have fun, or a love affair. If you have your way,
I'm not allowed any freedom, and you have total control.
    You scold, spy, complain, heave deep sighs,
and when angry you scarcely spare the rod. When I put on
    purple and anoint my hair, you exclaim,
"That's something your father never did!" You count
    my drinks and frown as if the wine
came from your private cellar. Stop. I cannot endure a freedman
    Cato.[36] I'm a man now—just ask my girlfriend.

---

36. A byword for a rigid overseer of morals.

**48    An Impoverished Philosopher** (11.56)

Hey Chaeremon! You, the Stoic! You're all too fond of praising death,
    and for that I'm supposed to admire your courage?
What's the source of your "valor?" A jug with broken handle,
    a grim hearth never warmed by a fire,
a rush mat and bedbugs, a bare couch with no cushions,
    and the same short toga worn night and day.
Oh, what a hero you are, to be able to do without the dregs
    of red vinegar and straw and black bread!
But come now, if your pillows were stuffed with fine Gallic wool,
    if your cushions were draped with silky purple,
if you went to bed with a boy who lately tormented the guests
    with his rosy face as he mixed the fine Caecuban wine,
how eager you'd be to live the lifespan of Nestor three times,
    how you'd wish not to lose an instant of any day!
It's no trick to despise life in straightened circumstances:
    the brave are those with something to lose.


**49    A German War-Captive** (11.96)

Hey, German! It's water from the Marcian aqueduct
    that leaps up here, not from the Rhine!
Why are you in the way, keeping a boy from the rain
    of this rich basin? Barbarian, it's not right
for you to elbow a citizen aside and quench your servant's thirst
    on these waters meant for your conquerors.[37]


**50    A Prudish Wife and Her Adventurous Husband** (11.104)

Wife, conform to my ways or get out of the house.
    I am no Curius or Numa or Tatius.
I like to prolong the evening with a pleasant drink or three;
    you drink water and hurry grimly from the table.
In bed, you like it dark; I like to play with a lamp for witness,
    let in some light when I'm bursting my loins.
You cover up with a breast band, tunic, and obscuring cloak;
    for me no girl can be naked enough.
I like kisses that imitate the flattering doves; you give pecks
    like your grandmother gets in the morning.

---

37. Both are slaves, but the native born one is facetiously called a citizen, by contrast to the German war captive. The Aqua Marcia, erected 144–140 BC, brought the purest and coolest water of all Roman city aqueducts.

You're too good to assist with your voice or your fingers.
    It's as if you were preparing incense and wine.[38]
Whenever Hector's wife hopped on and rode her man, the Trojan
    servants would masturbate in the hall,
and although the Ithacan was snoring beside his chaste Penelope,
    she always used to keep her hand *there*.[39]
You won't let me sodomize. But Cornelia used to do this
    for Gracchus, Julia for Pompey, and Porcia
for you, Brutus.[40] Before the Dardianian cupbearer mixed wine
    for Jupiter, Juno was his Ganymede.
If *gravitas* is what you want, go ahead, be Lucretia all day.
    But at night, what I want is Laïs.[41]

---

38. For ritual purposes.

39. Andromache and Penelope were famous and exemplary wives from the epics of Homer;
Martial is inventing his mythology with tongue in cheek.

40. These are all famous and famously upright Roman women, married to powerful men. It is
doubtful that Martial had any information about their habits in bed.

41. Lucretia was the legendary paragon of chastity (see Livy chs. 57–60 in this volume). Laïs was
a famously beautiful, quick-witted, and expensive courtesan from Corinth (400s BC).

# NOVATIAN

(3rd century AD, wrote in Latin)

## Introduction

Novatian was a prominent Christian theologian in the city of Rome at the time of the Decian persecution in AD 250 (see Inscriptions nos. 98–100 in this volume). He became famous after the persecution for his unbending position that no one who had lapsed by making the required sacrifice during that time, or who had cooperated with the Roman authorities in any way, should ever be readmitted to the church, no matter how penitent. In AD 251 he accused the newly elected bishop of Rome, Cornelius, of having purchased a bogus certificate of sacrifice in 250, and promptly set himself up as a rival bishop or "anti-Pope," an act that secured Novatian's subsequent designation as a heretic and schismatic in the Roman church. The relationship in time between these events and the following attack on the Roman games is unclear, but the treatise certainly reflects Novatian's hardline attitudes. Like the earlier, longer work of the same name by the north African bishop Tertullian, this letter forcefully articulates the Christian clergy's objections to the various types of Roman spectacles, games, and theatrical shows, and indirectly suggests how popular they remained with some members of Christian congregations. The same sorts of appeals were being made from the pulpit by St. Augustine in Carthage after AD 400, a full hundred and fifty years after the writing of this letter. Beyond his fiery denunciations, what Novatian reveals is the immense variety of shows and spectacles, theater, athletic, and musical events enjoyed in his time. Novatian deals with the various types of shows in turn: public executions, chariot races, comedy and mime (see Glossary), pantomime (see Glossary), boxing, wrestling, athletics, and more. He strangely has little to say about gladiators. He emphasizes the (pagan) religious aspects of the games, though the extent to which the spectacles were felt to be religious in this period is debated.

---

## On the Spectacles

Novatian to the flock who are steadfast in the Gospel, greetings.[1] It saddens me and greatly distresses my mind when no opportunity to write to you presents itself. Not to communicate with you is my loss. By the same token nothing brings me as much joy and happiness as having another opportunity to do so. For when I speak with you

---

1. The identity of the addressees is unclear.

through the medium of a letter, I feel that I am there with you. And so, although I know that you are sure that what I have just said is true, that you have no doubt about my affection, actions speak louder than words, and the fact that I'm writing shows how much I mean it. For love is proven when absolutely no occasion for writing is passed over.

I am certain that you are no less serious in the conduct of your lives than you are steadfast in the sacrament of faith. Still, there are some clergy who, by being seductive advocates and indulgent patrons of vice, lend authority to it. Even worse, they twist the sound judgment of the holy scriptures into support of sinful activity, arguing that the purpose of the spectacles is mere innocent and blameless pleasure, mere mental relaxation. Priestly discipline, once vigorously steadfast, has so far weakened and declined due to all sorts of laxity and wickedness that vice is no longer merely excused but actually recommended! Because of this I have decided to say a few words now, not to instruct you but simply to remind you of what you already know, in the hopes of preventing those spiritual wounds, which were not sutured properly and are only apparently healed, from breaking open through the scar tissue once more. No vice is harder to stamp out than that which can easily return because it is championed by the whole common crowd and enabled by the church's toleration.

[2] Is it not shameful, I say, shameful that men of faith, men who claim for themselves the title of the Christian name, use heavenly scripture to defend the vain superstitions of the pagans that are part of the spectacles, and lend divine sanction to idolatry?[2] For when faithful Christians attend a ritual that is being performed in honor of some idol by the pagans at a spectacle, pagan idolatry is strengthened. The true and divine religion of God is insulted and trod under foot. I am ashamed to repeat the sophistries and special pleading that those men employ in this cause. "Where," they ask, "are those things written, where are they prohibited? What's more, Elijah rode in a chariot, and David himself danced before the arc of the covenant. In the Bible we read of harps, lyres, tambourines, citharas, and dances. And the Apostle Paul as well, in his spiritual struggles, urges us to fight against the spirits of evil with boxing and wrestling. Again, when he takes his examples from the stadium, he also imagines our reward as an athlete's wreath of victory. Why would it not be permitted for a faithful Christian to watch the kinds of things that could lawfully be written about in the sacred book?"

In this connection I might justifiably say that it would have been far better for those men to be illiterate than to read the Bible in this way. For the words and examples that were set down to preach gospel virtue are being twisted to plead the cause of vice. Those things were not written to encourage spectacle-going, but so that greater enthusiasm might be excited in our minds for profitable pursuits, since there is such great enthusiasm among the pagans for unprofitable pursuits. [3] The intent is to encourage virtue, not to grant permission or freedom to gaze at pagan waywardness. Through this metaphor the mind is to be more fired up to the pursuit of gospel virtue that leads to divine rewards, just as athletes strive through all sorts of sufferings and painful adversity to arrive at mere earthly gains.

The fact that Elijah rode a chariot in Israel is not an argument for looking at circus races; for he did not race in a circus. And the fact that David led dances in the presence

---

2. Literally the worship of idols, though by this period "idolatry" had taken on a very wide meaning, including all types of sins (see Tertullian, *On Idolatry*).

of God is no defense for faithful Christians sitting in the theater; for never did he distort his limbs with obscene motions and dance a salacious Greek myth. The harps, lyres, tambourines, and citharas were played for God, not for an idol. Thus there is no scriptural warrant for gazing at forbidden spectacles.

Thanks to the work of the devil these things, once sacred, have become forbidden. So if those men are incapable of being guided by holy writings, let them at least be guided by a sense of decency. For certain things scripture prohibited more by not taking account of them. Guided by a sense of modesty, it has forbidden much simply by not talking about it, afraid that it would have held the faithful in too little esteem if it lowered itself so far. In general, when giving out precepts some things are better left unsaid. After all, prohibition often amounts to encouragement. Even if there is no explicit mention of these things in sacred scripture, moral strictness speaks in place of rules, and reason teaches what the Bible passes over in silence. Each man must deliberate with himself and speak with his own faith as interlocutor: he will never do anything unworthy. Conscience will have more weight if it trusts itself above all else.

[4] What is it that scripture has forbidden? It has forbidden us to look at that which it prohibits doing. It has condemned, I say, all those types of spectacles, because it has banished idolatry, which is the mother of all the games, the source of these abominations of vanity and frivolity. For what spectacle is there without an idol, what game without a sacrifice, what contest that is not consecrated to a dead man? What business has a faithful Christian among such things, if he shuns idolatry? What pleasure can he derive from these scandalous displays if he is already blessed? Why does he approve of ungodly superstitions, for which he shows his love by watching? But he should know that all these things are the inventions of demons, not of God. Shameless! He goes to church and exorcises the very same demons whose pleasures he praises at the spectacles. And although everything is forgiven when he renounces the devil in baptism, once he goes to the spectacle of the devil after knowing Christ, he renounces Christ just as he does the devil.

Idolatry, as I have already said, is the mother of all the games. In order to get faithful Christians to come to her she flatters them through the pleasures of the eyes and the ears. Romulus first consecrated circus games to Consus, a kind of god of strategy, for the purpose of seizing the Sabine women.[3] And the rest are consecrated to various other gods. When a famine had gripped the city, theatrical games were acquired as a consolation for the people, and later they were dedicated to Ceres and Liber and to the other idols, and to the dead. Those Greek contests, too, have various demons as their presidents, be they contests in vocal performance, or in string instruments, or in oratory, or in strength. And whatever else there is that moves the eyes or charms the ears of the spectators, if one considers its origin and founding, it carries the banner of idols or demons or of the dead. So clever an artificer is the devil. He knew that idolatry by itself, undisguised, would cause revulsion, so he mixed it with spectacles to make it be loved through pleasure.

[5] What need is there to elaborate on this, or to describe the hideous varieties of sacrifices that take place at the games? Sometimes even a human being becomes a victim of the sacrifice, thanks to the criminality of a priest. They savagely toast their

---

3. See Livy ch. 9 and Ovid, *The Art of Love* 1.101–34 in this volume.

god with blood taken hot from the throat into a foaming bowl, drunk down while still warm and tossed into the face of the idol as though it were thirsty.[4] To the delight of the crowd they spend a few lives all in the interest of teaching cruelty through a bloody spectacle—as if private savagery isn't enough and one must learn more in public! A fierce beast is reared as a pet, to be a punishment for men. To make it rage more cruelly before the eyes of the spectators, the beast is trained by a master of savagery, and would perhaps have been more gentle if its master, more cruel than the beast itself, had not taught it to thirst for blood.

To say nothing of the various other enthusiasms of idolatry, how pointless are those contests, the arguments over the chariot teams, the disagreements over charioteers, partisanship over their prizes, the joy when one's horse is rather swift, the grief when it is too slow, the calculations of the beast's age, the precise knowledge of its year of birth, the learning of its stages of life, the tracing of the pedigree, the recitation of horse's grandfathers and even more distant ancestors. How utterly useless is the whole business! How foul and disgraceful! Just ask any man who can calculate the entire stock of some equine clan with total recall and flawlessly recite this knowledge with the greatest of speed, who the parents of Christ are, and I'll bet he has no idea—or if he does know he is even more of a disaster. Again, if you ask this man by what road he came to that spectacle, he will confess that it was through the brothel, through the naked bodies of prostitutes, through sleazy lust, through public disgrace, through vulgar sensuality, through the reproaches of all right thinking men. But I should not charge him with what he has perhaps not actually done. Still, he saw what should not have been done, and led his eyes to the spectacle of idolatry through lust.[5] Such a man would have dared, if he had been able, to lead the Holy Spirit into the brothel. Such a man hurries to get to the show having just gotten out of Sunday services, and still bears the Eucharist within him, as is his custom. The infidel carried around the holy body of Christ amidst the obscene bodies of whores. He deserves damnation less from the pleasure of the spectacle than from the route he took to get there!

[6] But to pass now to the shameless witticisms of the theater: I am ashamed to describe what is said, ashamed also to indict what goes on there, the tiresome plot devices, the lies of adulterers, the lewd women, the filthy humor, the despicable parasites;[6] even the very *patresfamilias* in their togas are depicted sometimes as stupid, sometimes as rakes, and all the time as fools and utterly lacking in decency. No type of man or profession is spared such treatment at the hands of those reprobates. Yet everyone goes to see the shows. No doubt the immoral mob delights in reviewing its own vices—or in learning new ones. They run to that whorehouse of public shame, to that school of obscenity, so they can perform in private all the acts that are learned

---

4. The situation imagined is a grim parody of an ancient drinking custom, whereby a person proposing a toast tastes the wine in his cup and then hands it over to be drunk by the person honored.

5. Probably a reference to the congregation of prostitutes around Circus. See Juvenal, *Satires* 3.64–65 in this volume.

6.The "parasite" was a stock figure of Greek and Roman comedy, like the cunning slave, the pimp, the prostitute, or the braggart soldier. The braggart soldier was often portrayed in the company of a ridiculously flattering parasite, who was typically looking for a free dinner. The name derives from the Greek for "dining companion." See Juvenal, *Satires* 3.138 in this volume.

in public. Amidst the pomp of the laws they are taught the very things that the laws forbid.

What is a faithful Christian, who is not permitted even to contemplate sinning, doing amidst these things? Why is he finding delight in the images of lust? So that there he can shed his sense of decency and work up the courage to sin? As he gets used to watching sin, he also learns how to do it. At least those women who, because of their own misfortune have been forced into slave prostitution, serving the public's lusts, do it in a private place and take some consolation for their dishonor in concealment.[7] Even those prostitutes who work for money blush to be seen in public. But that public monstrosity is performed in plain view of everybody, surpassing even the obscenity of the prostitutes. When people commit adultery, at least they try to do it away from the eyes of men!

We may add to this disgrace a worthy follow-up, a wretched human being, effeminate and soft in every limb, a man melted to a state beyond the softness of a woman, whose skill consists in issuing words with his hands. And because of this one individual—man or woman, who knows?—the entire city gets worked up that the lusts of ancient mythology will be performed through dance.[8] So strong is love of the forbidden that memory brings back before our eyes sins that the passage of time had long since buried. [7] Lust is not satisfied with using its own present depravities, but adopts as its own from a stage play the sins of an earlier age. It is forbidden, I say, for faithful Christians to attend.

It is also completely forbidden for them to attend performances by those musicians whom Greece has sent all over the world, having instructed them in her vain arts intended to delight the ears. One man simulates the blaring noise of war on the trumpet; another produces a lugubrious sound by blowing into tibias.[9] A third man vies with choirs and the human singing voice by modulating the openings of the tibias. He employs his breath, which he draws with great effort from the depths of his guts into the upper regions of his body, now keeping it shut up and locked within, now releasing it and pouring it out into the air through the passageways of his instrument. In this way he manages to speak with his fingers by breaking the sound into fragments, showing ingratitude to his maker who endowed him with a tongue. Why should I speak of the pointless efforts of comedy, or that massive bombast of tragic recitations? Why should I mention stringed instruments and their clamorous harmonies? Even if such things are not consecrated to idols, still, faithful Christians ought not to attend and watch them. If they are not sinful, they yet have in them a vanity which is both very great and ill-befitting the faithful.

[8] Now, that other madness that the rest pursue is clearly an activity for indolent, shiftless men: they do themselves harm by stuffing their bellies to bulk up, the better to take and receive blows. The first victory for these "athletes" is to be able to eat beyond human endurance. In the name of this prize for gluttony we see a disgraceful trade:

---

7. See Martial, *Epigrams* 11 in this volume.

8. Pantomime (see Glossary).

9. The *tibia* was an instrument consisting of a tube with holes for stops, fitted with a reed mouthpiece. They were often used in pairs.

wretched men rent out their faces for blows, so that they can all the more wretchedly stuff their bellies. And furthermore, how disgraceful are the fights themselves: a man lying under a man is tied up in ignoble embraces and holds. In a contest like that, no matter who wins, decency loses. Look now, one man does the long jump in the nude, another hurls in the air a bronze disc with all his strength. This is the glory of the insane. Take away the spectators, and you expose its emptiness. As I have said repeatedly, faithful Christians must avoid such vain, pernicious, and sacrilegious spectacles. Our eyes and ears must be protected from them. We quickly become accustomed to what we hear, and even more quickly to what we see. The human mind on its own tends toward vice. What will happen if it has examples to encourage it? The flesh is by nature on slippery ground, and falls of its own inclination. What will happen if it is given a push? The mind must be called back from such things.

[9] The Christian has his own, better spectacles, if he wishes. He has his own pleasures that are true and beneficial, if he comes to his senses. To say nothing of those wonders that we cannot yet contemplate, the Christian has the loveliness of the world to see and marvel at. Let him gaze at the rising sun, then its setting, which in their exchange call back the day and the night. Let him gaze at the orb of the moon that marks the passage of time with its waxing and waning. Let him gaze at the dance of the flashing constellations as they move perpetually on high, the seasons of the year in their subdivided cycle, and the days themselves with the nights, divided into the procession of hours, and the balanced mass of the earth with its mountains, and the rushing rivers with their sources, the sprawling seas with their waves and shores, and meanwhile the air, ever unchanging and uniform, balanced in perfect concord and binding harmony, spread out wide and invigorating all things in its delicacy. Now it gathers together the clouds and pours forth rain, now it thins out and regains its serene clarity.[10] And each of those elements has its own special inhabitants, the birds in the air, the fish in the waters, and man on earth. These, I say, these and other such divine works are the spectacles for faithful Christians. How can any theater built by human hands compare with those works? So what if it is built from huge piles of stone? Mountain peaks are higher. Do the ceiling coffers glint with gold? The gleam of the stars is superior. The man who has recognized himself as a son of God will never admire human works. The man who can admire anything apart from God has hurled himself down from the peak of his human nobility.

[10] Let the faithful Christian pay attention to holy scripture. There he will find spectacles worthy of faith. He will see God creating the earth, man, all the other animals— the whole amazing fabric of the world—and making it all better. He will see the earth in its sinfulness. He will see well-deserved shipwrecks, the rewards of the just and the punishment of the wicked, the sea made dry for His people, and the sea rising again from the rocks to save the same people. He will see crops falling from heaven, not from a threshing floor or planted with a plow. He will see rivers providing dry crossings, with the troops of their waters restrained. He will see in certain passages faith struggling with fire, and beasts made tame, overcome by religion. And he will see souls called back from the point of death, and he will also witness the bodies of the very dead

---

10. Novatian here echoes the Stoic idea that the perfection and harmony of nature proves that the world is governed by a benevolent deity.

themselves amazingly restored to life from their tombs. And in all these things he will see the greatest spectacle of all, the devil, who had triumphed over the whole material world, lying beneath the feet of Christ. What a glorious spectacle, my brothers, how pleasant, how necessary, to gaze always at one's own hope, and to open one's eyes to one's own salvation! This is a spectacle that can be seen even by the eyes of the blind. This spectacle is not put on by the praetor or the consul, but by Him who is alone and before all things and over all things, nay, rather the source of all things, the father of our Lord Jesus Christ, to whom honor and glory be forever and ever. I hope, brothers, that you are well.

# OVID

(43 BC–AD 17 or 18, wrote in Latin)

## General Introduction

P. Ovidius Naso was from the Italian town of Sulmo. He spent most of his celebrated career as a love poet in Rome, where he had been educated to pursue, but ultimately rejected, the practice of law. Early in his career he wrote a series of medium-length love elegies (*Amores*) addressed to a woman he called Corinna, as well as a series of letters in the voices of famous heroines of mythology, the *Heroides*. Around the year 1 BC he produced a kind of quasi-technical manual, *The Art of Love* (*Ars Amatoria*). It was originally conceived in two books addressed to men, about where and how to meet women, begin a love affair, and make it last. Ovid added, by popular request, he says, a third book for women, and a fourth, addressed to both sexes, *Cures for Love*. He later wrote two large, ambitious works simultaneously, the *Metamorphoses*, an encyclopedic epic poem on myths of transformation, and the *Fasti*, a poetic elaboration of the festivals of the Roman calendar, month by month.

In AD 8 Ovid was sentenced by the Emperor Augustus to *relegatio*, a form of exile to a particular place, which allowed nonetheless the preservation of property and citizen status. Writing in misery from his wild and barbaric place of banishment (Tomis, in what is now Romania), Ovid assigned at least some of the blame for his disgrace to the Emperor Augustus' displeasure at *The Art of Love*. He also admits he made a serious "mistake," though what exactly it was he never specifies. His works from exile defending himself and pleading (unsuccessfully) for reinstatement are collected in two sets of medium-length elegies, *Sorrows* (*Tristia*), and *Letters from Pontus* (*Epistulae ex Ponto*). We translate here the first Book of the *Art of Love*, a section of the *Fasti* that deals with the Parilia festival, and *Tristia*, 4.10, which gives the poet's autobiography.

---

### Introduction to *The Art of Love*, Book 1

Young upper-class men in Augustan Rome would be accustomed to having a variety of romantic and sexual possibilities, from prostitutes, to their own slave women, other people's slave women, free women of lower status, and married women. The most taboo and riskiest by far were married women and unmarried women of high status. This kind of affair risked, besides the scandal, serious and lasting legal consequences for both parties. Much of the excitement of the *Art of Love* lies in its studious ambiguity about the exact marital and social status of the women being talked about, and in Ovid's playful exploration of the tensions surrounding potentially illicit affairs.

It is often assumed that women in the ancient world were cloistered and confined to the home. But if there is any truth to Ovid's humorous seduction manual, in his day at least Roman women were out and about in public, ready to be approached by an ambitious lover. His suggestion that women like to be forced (1.673–676) will rightly shock modern readers, and was probably meant to shock Roman ones as well. It should be balanced against the overwhelming emphasis in the book on flirtation, persuasion, flattery, and playfulness. Much of the *Art of Love* is meant to raise eyebrows, such as his contention that sincerity is not really a requirement, or that the highest goal is to enter into an affair without having to give presents first. Likewise playful is Ovid's approach to Greek and Roman mythology, which is a pervasive source of examples. The speaker cheerfully twists the traditional meanings of all sorts of myths to suit his less-than-honorable purposes.

The title itself is somewhat outrageous, implying that love is a kind of learned skill, like rhetoric, carpentry, or medicine, and can be the subject of a didactic ("teaching") poem written by a self-proclaimed expert. There was a tradition of such poems and treatises with the first word *Ars*, intended to organize and convey a field of knowledge and skill. Thus the title (and perhaps the poem as a whole) is a paradox, seemingly a bit of an insult both to love and to the pretensions of didactic poetry. But Ovid plunges in with characteristic verve and confidence, and the result is one of the most arresting and witty of Latin poems.

# *The Art of Love,* Book I

People of Rome! Are any here unfamiliar with the Art of Love?
    If so, read on, and learn to love expertly.
Skill with oar and sail keeps ships afloat and on the move.
    Skill moves the chariot. Love, too, requires skill.
Achilles had Automedon to handle the supple reins of his chariot,
    and Jason's ship had Tiphys to pilot the Argonauts.
Me? I'm the specialist that Venus put in charge of tender Love.
    Call me the Tiphys, the Automedon of Love.
Love, though, is a wild boy and will buck against my sage advice.
    Yet a boy he is, soft and ready to be governed.          10
When Achilles was a boy, Chiron taught him to play the lyre
    and tamed his savage mind with civilizing art.
The mighty hero who often terrified both enemies and allies
    was cowed, they say, by one old man.
The hands that would crush great Hector tamely submitted
    to a thwack when his master demanded.
As Chiron was to Achilles, I am Love's learned authority;
    each boy wild, each from a goddess born.
No matter: a feisty bull will bear the plough upon his neck,
    a proud stallion takes the bit between its teeth.          20

Yes, Love will yield to me, no matter how many arrows he plants
    in my chest or fiery torches he hurls my way.
The more he skewers my soul, the more he serves my heart flambé,
    the more effectively will I avenge those wounds.
Lord Apollo! I will not lie and call you the source of my skill.
    No prophetic bird song instructed me.
I never saw the Muses—Clio and her dancing sisters—
    while shepherding, Hesiod-like, on Mt. Helicon.[1]
No, this work comes from personal experience. Listen to the expert;
    my song's the truth. Aid my work, Venus, mother of Love.    30
But you there, stand back, you ladies who wear the thin fillets
    and long dress, signs of respectable modesty.
I will sing of love that's safe, pleasures to be lawfully stolen.
    There will be nothing criminal in my poem.
Task number one for you green recruits in Love's army:
    try to find a suitable object for love.
Next, you've got to win over the girl you want.
    Third, ensure your love will last a long time.
This is the plan, this the track my chariot will take,
    this the turning post my breakneck wheels will hug.    40
You're still unattached, a horse with no one yet holding the reins,
    so choose a girl to whom you can say, "You're
the only one for me." But don't expect her to fall from heaven.
    Use your eyes. Go looking for a suitable girl.
The hunter knows where to place his nets to catch the doe;
    he knows in what vales the snorting boar resides.
The bird catcher knows his shrubbery; the baiter of hooks
    knows where the waters teem with fish.
You, too, are hunting—for a lasting love affair—and so you must
    learn in advance where girls congregate.    50
No need to set sail over open seas in your search,
    no need to travel far and wide by land.
Perseus went to dark India to pick up Andromeda. So what?
    So what if Trojan Paris had to go to Greece to snatch Helen?
Rome will supply such a raft of dazzling beauties, you'll say,
    "Everything in the world is now in this city."
Gargara has its countless wheat fields, Methymna its loads of grapes.
    The sea has its fish, trees have their birds,
and the sky has stars. Rome? She has beautiful girls. Venus has
    come home to stay in her son's own city.[2]    60

---

1. The Greek poet Hesiod (around 700 BC) begins his *Theogony* by saying that he met the Muses while tending his sheep on Mt. Helicon, and that they inspired his poem.

2. The Romans traced their ancestry back to Venus through her son, Trojan Aeneas, who founded the city of Lavinium on the shores of Italy and whose descendants would found the city of Rome. See Lucretius, *On the Nature of Things* Section A in this volume.

If young girls still growing are to your taste, a real babe
   will appear right before your eyes.
If you're looking for a young lass, a thousand will please you
   and make you wonder which to choose.
Or perhaps a mature and wiser age appeals. Believe me,
   there will be plenty of those as well.


## Where to Find Women

Just take a leisured stroll beneath the shade of Pompey's portico,[3]
   when the sun nears the back of Hercules' lion,[4]
or visit Octavia's Colonnade (by the theater of Octavia's son),[5]
   with its rich and splendid imported marbles.                    70
Or pay a visit to the Colonnade called Livia's after its builder,
   the one packed with ancient paintings;
or the one where the Danaids are plotting to murder their husbands,
   and savage father Danaus stands with sword drawn.[6]
Don't miss the festival of Adonis, over whom Venus wept,
   or the sacred Sabbath observed by Syrian Jews.
Drop in at the temple of Isis, that linen-wearing bovine[7]
   (she makes many girls what she was for Jupiter).
Even the Forum itself is suited to passion, believe it or not,
   and one often finds love amongst the lawyers.                   80
You know where the Appian fountain jets into the air,
   just below the marble temple of Venus?[8]
Here many an attorney is ensnared by love, and one who looks
   after others' interests fails to look after his own.
There many an eloquent man finds himself at a loss for words,
   and defends a case without precedent—his own.
Venus laughs at the sight from her temple nearby: he who was

---

3. A rectangular courtyard with covered colonnades built next to Pompeius' Theater (55 BC), which at once became a resort for elegant women. For this and other buildings in Rome, see "Map of the City of Rome and the Forum."

4. The sun enters the constellation Leo (said to be the lion killed by Hercules) in July, the beginning of the hottest part of summer. Porticoes were built to protect the population from the elements.

5. The Theater of Marcellus, Octavia's son.

6. The portico mentioned here surrounded the Temple to Apollo on the Palatine Hill, which was filled with statues depicting the daughters of Danaus.

7. The priests of the Egyptian goddess Isis wore linen garments as a sign of ritual purity. She had a temple in the Campus Martius. Greek and Roman myth identified her with Io, whom Jupiter loved and later turned into a cow to hide her from Juno's wrath.

8. In the Forum of Julius Caesar there was the fountain of the Appiades, and behind it the temple of Venus Genetrix ("Mother" of the Roman people).

recently a patron wishes he were a client.
Above all, go hunting in the curving theaters; this is terrain whose
    bounty will exceed your wildest dreams.          90
There you will find a girl to love, a girl you might deceive,
    a girl for a one-night stand, a girl you'd like to keep.
Picture the ants that come and go in a long, dense line,
    the usual grains of food in their mouths.
Think of the bees reaching their groves and fragrant pastures,
    flying about amidst the blooming thyme.
So all the most elegant women flock to the crowded festivals—
    so many, it has been at times hard to choose.
They come to watch—and to be watched as well.
    The theater can harm a good woman's chastity.          100

## The Abduction of the Sabines

Romulus, you were the first to trouble the games, back when
    the wifeless Romans stole Sabine brides.[9]
No marble theaters were hung with awnings in those days,
    no saffron perfume reddened the stage;
the backdrop was simple, artless: whatever foliage
    the leafy Palatine happened to provide.
They sat in rows on the hillside turf, the only shade
    for their bristly heads came from overhead trees.
Each Roman man marked out a Sabine girl with his eyes,
    restless in silent anticipation.          110
At last the dancer stomped the earthen stage three times
    as the rough Etruscan flute played a tune;
next, applause—not artful or organized, as now.
    Then the king gave the long awaited signal.
The men leapt up, betraying with a shout their intentions,
    and eagerly seized the Sabine girls.
Picture meek doves fleeing eagles, or tender lambs
    taking flight at the sight of a wolf.
As the men rushed around, such was the girls' panic;
    each one's face lost its color.          120
All felt the same fear, but they showed it variously:
    some tore at their hair, others sat in shock;
some kept grim silence, others shouted "mother!" (in vain).
    Complain or stare, stay or run, it's the same:
the plundered girls were led off as spoils for the marriage bed;

9. The seizing of the Sabine women, supposedly motivated by the early Romans' pariah status
and their lack of women, was enshrined in Roman legend (see Livy chs. 9–13 in this volume).
Ovid's retelling is a good example of his humorous and often subversive approach to mythology.

and in a way, fear became them.[10]
If a girl fought too much and refused to go along
    the man would lustfully lift her up, saying,
"Now, now, why spoil your lovely eyes with tears? As your father
    was to your mother, so I will be to you."                              130
Ah, Romulus, you knew how to give a soldier a bonus;
    with that kind of perk, even I would enlist.
That's the story. Ever since then the theaters have been,
    and still are, a trap for beautiful girls.


## At the Circus

Then there is the capacious Circus with its contests
    of noble thoroughbreds—go there, too!
No need there to speak to a girl using hand signals
    or cryptic nods of the head.[11]
Sit down right next to her, if no one's in the way, and get up close,
    touch her side with yours.                                             140
Thanks to the seat-marking lines, proximity is required,
    and house rules dictate touching the girl.[12]
At this point, find a way to start up a friendly conversation:
    let small talk provide your opening line.
Make sure to inquire warmly whose horses are parading by.
    Whatever team she cheers, you should cheer, too.
When the thronging parade of ivory images of gods goes by,
    give your heartfelt applause to Lady Venus.
Some sand or dust may fall, as often happens, in her lap.
    Be sure to flick it off with your fingers.                            150
No dust, no sand? Flick it off anyway. No excuse
    is too small to do her a service.
Perhaps her cloak hangs too low and drags upon the filthy ground:
    gather it and hold it up with care.
The immediate reward for this service, if she allows,
    will be a clear look at her legs.
Make sure whoever sits behind her does not poke
    his knee into her tender back.
Small things do captivate a fickle mind. Just arranging a cushion
    has done the trick for many men.                                       160
So has cooling her down with a thin fan, or placing

---

10. Ovid seems to have some pictorial representation of the scene in mind, perhaps the frieze of the Basilica Aemilia in the Roman Forum, which represented the abduction of the Sabine women.

11. As was necessary at the theater (see next note) and dinner parties (see lines 569 ff. below).

12. Co-ed seating was a feature of the Circus Maximus; in the theater seating was segregated by sex.

a hollow stool beneath a tender foot.
Opportunities exist in the Circus, and also at gladiatorial games
    when the anxious Forum is grimly strewn with sand.
Cupid often does battle on that sand, and the spectator of wounds
    has often felt a wound himself:
one minute he's chatting, shaking hands, asking for the program,
    guessing who will win, and placing bets,
then—ouch!—he feels Cupid's flying arrow and groans at its sting;
    the spectator has become the spectacle.                          170
Another case: just recently[13] Caesar staged a mock naval battle
    of Persian and Athenian fleets.
Young men and girls arrived from the corners of the earth, as if
    the whole world had converged on Rome.
Who did not find something to love in *that* crowd?
    How many felt the flame of exotic desire!


## Gaius Caesar's Campaign in the East (or Girls at a Triumph)

As for our empire—behold!—here's Caesar now to add the final piece:
    Orient, you will at last be ours.[14]
Parthian, vengeance is coming. Crassus, you and your son, rejoice.
    Rejoice, you standards defiled by barbarian hands.[15]          180
Your Avenger is coming: the boy general is coming
    to handle a war not meant for a boy.
But then the Caesars have always had courage beyond their years.
    No need to count the birthdays of the gods.
Precociously divine, the courage of Gaius is on the rise
    and chafes at sluggish delay.
Hercules was but a babe when he throttled the snakes,
    worthy of father Jupiter while still in his crib.
Bacchus—still a boy today—was quite a boy when India, vanquished,
    bowed its head to his thyrsus staff.                            190
You, boy, will do battle under the mature auspices of your father,
    and under them you shall conquer.
Such should be your first military campaign, befitting your great name,
    now Prince of the Youth, one day Prince of the Elders.[16]
You yourself have brothers; avenge brothers who have been harmed;

---

13. August, 2 BC (see *The Accomplishments of the Deified Augustus* 23).

14. In the year 1 BC Augustus was planning a military expedition against Parthia (in what is now Iran), to be led by his biological grandson (and adopted heir) Gaius.

15. In 53 BC the Parthians inflicted a humiliating defeat on a Roman expedition near the Mesopotamian town of Carrhae, killing its general Crassus and his son and capturing the legionary standards.

16. In 5 BC Gaius was proclaimed *princeps iuventutis*, "Leader of the Youth," by the *equites*, an honor granted to the best and brightest young men of the state before they entered the Senate.

as a son, vindicate a father's rights.[17]
Your father is the nation's father; he entrusts its arms to you;
    the enemy took his father's throne by force.
You will bear the arms of Loyalty, he the arrows of Treachery;
    Justice and Devotion will serve at your side.        200
The Parthians would lose in court; let them lose in battle now.
    May our leader add their Eastern riches to Latium!
Father Mars—a god—and father Caesar—a god-to-be—
    assist young Gaius with your divinity.
A prediction, and a vow: you will conquer, and I will write a poem
    to proclaim your deeds in epic style.
In it you will inspire the troops with words of my invention
    (may they do justice to your courage!);
I will describe Parthians retreating and Romans advancing,
    the enemy's mounted archers firing behind.        210
Parthian cowards! Since you flee to win, what will you do in defeat?
    Your tactics already do not bode well.
So it's assured, most handsome boy: your day will come to triumph,
    clad in gold, drawn by four snow-white horses.
The enemy commanders will precede you, their necks heavy with chains,
    no longer capable of fleeing to safety.
At your triumph a mixed crowd of young men and girls will watch
    in joy and relaxation on that day.[18]
If one of the girls should ask you the name of a king, or of lands,
    mountains, or rivers on the placards,        220
provide all the answers—and not only if she happens to ask.
    What you don't happen to know, invent:
"Right here's the Euphrates—see the reed on his forehead?
    The blue-haired one, he's the Tigris.
Armenian prisoners are here, those are Persians, Danaë's descendents,
    and yonder's the city in Achaemenid lands."
Go ahead, give names to this or that general, accurate if you can;
    if not, at least make them sound plausible.

## Hunting Girls at Dinner Parties

Dinner parties also give you an in. The tables have been set out;
    there is something more than wine to be enjoyed.        230
Here Love and Wine get to wrestling—the rosy boy gets Bacchus
    in his tender hammer lock.

---

17. An allusion to the fact that one of the motivations for Gaius' expedition was, in part, to install Artavasdes in Armenia, whose father, Phraates IV, a pro-Roman sympathizer, had been murdered.

18. The triumph never materialized. Gaius died in the East in AD 4 after settling the Armenian question by diplomacy.

Then Love gets stuck himself (as his wings absorb the wine),
    and weighs down a young man's captured heart.
But Love shakes it off and flies away, leaving Wine still tinged with Love
    and the man's heart still feels the sting.
Ah, wine, you give us courage and ready us for love!
    Worries flee, diluted by undiluted wine.
Then we laugh, then the poor man finds his courage, then it's
    goodbye to cares and furrowed brows.             240
We speak our minds with a candor now all too rare,
    all pretense banished by the wine god.
At such times girls have often stolen the hearts of men;
    Venus in the wine is fire within fire.
Beware, though, the tricks of the lamp. Both nighttime and wine
    make it hard to be a judge of beauty.
Full daylight it was when Paris judged the goddesses, saying,
    "Venus, you beat the other two."              250
Flaws lurk beneath the darkness, every blemish forgiven:
    Every woman is a beauty in the dead of night.
Daylight is required to judge a gem, or a piece of purple-dyed fabric;
    the same should go for a body or a face.
The places where women congregate, ready for hunting—why list
    them all? There are fewer grains of sand.
Why mention Baiae and Baiae's notorious beaches,
    its bubbling hot springs?[19]
Many a heart-wounded man has left here muttering, "These waters
    are not as therapeutic as they say."
Or consider the grove and temple of Diana, where the priesthood
    changes hands by death-dealing swordplay.[20]      260
The goddess is a virgin and hates Cupid's arrows, but delights in
    wounds inflicted on the people time and again.

## How to Win the Lady's Affections

The unequal wheels of my Muses' car[21] have so far been spinning
    on where to cast your nets and find your love.
Now for a somewhat more specialized topic: the skills you need
    to capture the girl you have chosen.
Be quiet, men, whoever you are, and pay close attention;
    I promise it will be worth your while.

---

19. A fashionable resort town on the bay of Naples south of Rome, Baiae was well known for its beaches, its hot springs, and its relaxed sexual mores. See Seneca, *Letters* 5.

20. The sanctuary of Diana of Nemi, about ten miles south of Rome, was a popular place of pilgrimage. For reasons that are not clear, the priest there was called "King of the Grove," a position won only by killing the incumbent priest in single combat.

21. A reference to the unequal lengths of the two lines of Ovid's verse (elegiac couplet).

First you must believe that every woman can be caught.
    You will catch her; just lay out your snares.                    270
Sooner will the birds fall silent in spring, or crickets in summer,
    sooner will the hound run from the hare,
than will a girl say no when approached in a pleasing manner—
    even ones you would never expect to be game.
Furtive love is just as pleasing to a girl as to a man. Men just hide it
    poorly—she desires more discreetly.
If men agreed never to make the first approach, women would soon admit
    defeat and play the part of the asker.
Out in the gently rolling fields the cow lows for her bull,
    the mare always whinnies for her stallion.                       280


## Women Desire Sex More Than Men

Fact: sexual desire is more moderate and less frenzied in the male;
    masculine passion has proper limits.
Example? Take Byblis: full of forbidden lust for her brother,
    she bravely paid for her crime by hanging herself.
Or Myrrha. She loved her father as no daughter should, and now,
    post-metamorphosis, lies imprisoned in bark—
her tears are fragrant myrrh we use to anoint ourselves,
    in its drops the poor lady's name lives on.
In the shady foothills of Mt. Ida there was once a bull, all white,
    the glistening pride of the herd.                                290
A small black spot stood between its horns, but apart from
    that flaw, he was entirely white as milk.
All the cows from Cnossus and Cydonia on Crete
    wanted to have him on their backs.
But Queen Pasiphae yearned to be the bull's adulterous lover,
    and in jealousy hated all those pretty cows.
The story is well known. All the liars who live in the hundred
    cities of Crete cannot deny it.
Pasiphae clipped the freshest, softest grass for the bull
    with her own inexperienced hand.                                 300
Without a thought for her husband, she accompanied the herd.
    King Minos was jilted for a bull.
Pasiphae, why put on such precious clothes? Your adulterer
    is quite unable to appreciate them.
Why the mirror, if your goal is rustic cattle? Foolish woman,
    why do you fuss with your hair?
Trust the mirror—see, it proves you're no heifer. O how you would
    wish that horns were sprouting on your forehead!
If you love Minos, then do not cheat. If you must cheat on him,
    at least do it with a man.                                       310

Out she goes, into the woods, leaving her bedroom behind,
    like some Bacchant possessed by the Theban god.
Ah! How often did she cast a hostile look at a cow and say,
    "What does my master[22] see in *her*?
Look at her prancing in front of him in the soft grass! No doubt
    the fool thinks she's attractive."
So saying, she would order some innocent heifer removed from the herd
    and forced beneath the curving yoke,
or compel the poor beast to fall before the altar in some invented rites,
    and smiled as she held her rival's entrails.          320
Placating the gods with the blood of her foe, she'd hold the liver and say,
    "Ha! Let's see how you please him now!"
And now she longs to be Europa, or Io: the one became a cow,
    the other was carried by a bull.
Hidden in a wooden cow, Pasiphae was filled with the alpha bull's seed;
    the baby Minotaur had his father's looks.
Aerope of Crete. If only she had refrained from loving Thyestes!
    Was it so hard to be without this one man?
The sun would not have reversed in mid-course and turned
    its chariot back toward the dawn.[23]          330
Take Scylla, daughter of Nisus, who stole her father's purple lock of hair;[24]
    her private parts are ringed with ravenous dogs.
Agamemnon survived the perils of Mars by land and Neptune by sea,
    but fell victim to Clytemnestra's sexual jealousy.
Medea! Every poet laments her crimes, the flaming death of Creusa,
    the blood of children red on their mother's hands.
Phoenix wept through hollow eye sockets; frightened horses
    ripped Hippolytus limb from limb.
Phineus, why are you gouging out the eyes of your innocent sons?
    That punishment will just rebound on you.[25]          340
All these events were set in motion by female lust, which is clearly
    keener than ours, more full of frenzy.
Have no doubt: all girls desire. Pick a few random dozens,
    scarcely one will be found to turn you down.
True, some women accept, others decline, but they *all* enjoy being asked,
    so the rare rebuff carries no unpleasantness.

---

22. *Dominus*, a word commonly used for a lover in Roman love poetry, as is the feminine equivalent *domina*, "mistress."

23. Aerope's husband Atreus got revenge on his brother Thyestes by cooking the latter's sons and feeding them to him, causing the sun to recoil in horror.

24. Scylla treacherously cut her father's lock of hair out of love for Minos, who was besieging Nisus' city, Megara.

25. Phineus blinded his sons after they were falsely accused by their stepmother of some wrongdoing. Later, Phineus suffered blindness in return and was beset by the Harpies, "The Snatchers," who stole and fouled his food when he tried to eat.

But why feel rejected, when variety is the spice of life,
>    as they say, and the grass is always greener?
The crop is always richer in someone else's field, his cow's udders
>    seem a bit more swollen with milk.                                    350


## Get to Know the Girl's Maid

First, get to know the maidservant of the girl you wish to catch.
>    She'll smooth the way for your approach.
See to it that she is very close to her mistress' counsels,
>    the trusted confidant of her secret jokes.
Entice her with promises, entice her with pleas; if she is willing
>    you'll get what you want, with ease.
Let *her* pick the moment (as doctors pick times for treatment),
>    when her mistress' mind is receptive,
when she is happy as can be, like a rich crop standing
>    ready for harvest in the fertile earth,                               360
when her heart is not shut tight by grief, but lies open in joy—
>    that's when the wiles of Venus have a chance to get in.
Troy was well defended when the mood was grim; in gladness
>    she took in the horse pregnant with soldiers.
Or try when she is angry at being cheated on herself; then your task
>    will be to see that she gets her revenge.
Get her hairdresser to rile her up and add fuel to the fire
>    as she combs her hair in the morning.
First have her say to herself with a sigh, "Ah, I don't suppose you would
>    pay him back in his own coin?"                                        370
Then have her talk about you; lay it on thick, and swear
>    you are dying of mad love for her.
But hurry. Anger, like a breeze in sails, or a thin layer of ice,
>    vanishes quickly if you delay.
Does it help, you ask, to sleep with the maid herself? Such a gambit
>    carries with it a large throw of the dice.
A maid might become more diligent after sex, or she might slow down;
>    one gives you to her mistress, another to herself.
Things might fall out either way. You can indulge in such
>    rakishness, but my advice is to refrain.                             380
I don't risk walking on the razor's edge or a sheer mountain cliff;
>    follow my lead and avoid a fall.
Still, if, as she passes your notes, you like not only
>    her work, but her body as well,
just make sure to win the mistress first, then follow up with her;
>    your love affair should not *begin* with the maid.
One warning, if you trust my expertise, if my
>    words are not gone with the wind:
either finish the job, or don't even try. Once the maid is your accomplice,

a dangerous informer has been removed.                                    390
Do we let the bird fly away once its wings are smeared with lime,
    or let the boar escape once caught in the net?
When the fish tastes the hook, make sure it sticks fast. Same with the maid:
    stay on her and don't let go till you win.
But secrecy is key. If your spy is well hidden, your girlfriend-to-be
    can be constantly under surveillance.[26]


## Time Your Moves Carefully

It's wrong to suppose that only those who farm or sail
    need to pay attention to the seasons.                           400
We don't plant Ceres' seeds at any old time of year, nor does
    the hollow ship set sail whenever you please.
Likewise, it's not always safe to hunt for tender girls. Frequently
    holding back will yield a better result.
If her birthday is coming, put things off; also on the first of the month
    that joyously connects Venus and Mars,[27]
or if the Circus is hosting a market, not of old-fashioned
    statuettes, but of baubles fit for kings.[28]
During the stormy season, when the Pleiades are threatening,
    when the Kid is submerged in the watery sea,                      410
it's better to back off. The man who sails then ends up wrecked,
    clutching a plank from his mangled ship.
A better day is the sad anniversary of Allia, the place that ran
    with blood from the wounded men of Latium.[29]
Or pick the seventh day held holy by the Jews from Palestine,
    a day less suitable for buying and selling.
Her birthday is a day of dread. Whenever presents are required,
    that day should be considered Black.[30]
Still, even if you avoid these carefully, she will rob you blind.
    A woman finds a way to fleece an eager lover.                     420
The loose-robed peddler will arrive to serve your shopping-mad lady;
    out comes his merchandise as you sit nearby.

---

26. Lines 395–96, which do not occur in the main manuscripts, have been omitted here.

27. Presumably the first of April (Venus' month), which follows the last day of March (Mars' month) and is a day when Venus is worshipped (see also April 1st in "A Roman Calendar: April").

28. A reference to the day during Saturnalia festival in December—called the Sigillaria (*sigilla* = "statuette")—when *objets d'art* were sold, to be given as presents.

29. July 18, the date of the catastrophic defeat by the Gauls in 390 BC. The shops would be closed to mark the anniversary, so the lover would not have to buy presents for the girl, as he would during the other days mentioned above.

30. Days were marked black on anniversaries of disastrous events, such as the day on which the Battle of Allia took place (see previous note).

She will ask you to look, as though you were a connoisseur.
    Then with a kiss she asks you to buy.
"This will keep me content for years to come," she'll swear,
    "I *really* need it. What a bargain!"
Plead no cash on hand, and you'll be asked for an IOU—enough
    to make you wish you'd never learned to write.
What about the "birthday" cakes and consequent demands for a gift?
    How many times per year can she be born?          430
Or crocodile tears over some nonexistent gem that—allegedly—
    slipped somehow out of her pierced ear?
They borrow all sorts of things, then never give them back.
    The losses are yours, but none of the thanks.
If I had ten mouths and ten tongues they would be insufficient
    to describe all the wicked tricks of *meretrices*.[31]

## First, Send a Note

First, test the waters with a message on a wax tablet.
    Let this be the emissary of your thoughts.
Focus on flattery, imitate a lover's words, and, no matter what
    your station in life, don't forget to beg.          440
Achilles, won over by pleas, gave Hector's body back to Priam.
    Even an angry god is moved by a pleading voice.
Make promises—where's the harm in that? Any man at all
    can be rich when it comes to promises.
Hope is a deceptive goddess, yet useful. Once believed,
    she holds on for a long, long time.
If you do give a gift, the girl has every good reason for walking away:
    benefit received, nothing spent.
But if you withhold, you seem always about to come through.
    Just so, the sterile field deceives its owner.          450
This is why losing gamblers keep losing—so they won't lose more;
    the dice call out, "Again, again!"
Love without gifts—this is the task, this the struggle.[32] So as not to give
    without reward, she will continue to give.
So send her a letter in beguiling words. Sound her out,
    take the first tentative steps.
It was a letter sent on an apple that deceived Cydippe, and the girl
    was unwittingly caught as she read it aloud.[33]

---

31. A *meretrix* (literally, a "woman who earns") was a prostitute of a relatively dignified kind, who did not necessarily charge a fee but expected to be kept in style by their lover's gifts.

32. A humorous allusion to a line in Vergil's *Aeneid*, where the Sibyl instructs the hero Aeneas how to get to the underworld. The descent is easy, she tells him, but to return to the upper world, "This is the task, this the struggle" (6.129).

33. The apple was inscribed with the words, "I swear by Artemis to marry Acontius."

Young men of Rome, get a good education! And not just for success
    aiding nervous clients in the courts.                                    460
It is eloquence that wins over the people, the serious judge,
    the elite Senate—but also your girl.
Still, do not flaunt your verbal abilities. Conceal your skills,
    and avoid pretentious words.
Only a madman would turn a love letter into a speech.
    That's sure to get you snubbed!
Your language should be believable, the words familiar
    but pleasing, as if delivered in person.
Perhaps she sends back your note unread. Don't give up.
    There is reason to hope she will read it yet.                          470
Time brings troublesome oxen under the plough; time teaches
    horses to submit to unyielding reins.
A ring made of iron is worn down by continuous use,
    and the plough is slowly eroded by the earth.
What's harder than rock, what could be softer than water?
    Yet hard rocks are pitted by soft water.
Given time you will win Penelope herself. Only be persistent.
    Capturing Troy took a while, yet captured it was.
Say she's read your letter but won't write back. Don't push.
    Just keep on sending the flattering notes.                            480
What she's been willing to read she'll be willing to answer.
    Have patience. All things in good time.
Perhaps you'll receive a sour reply at first, one that
    asks you to please not bother her.
What she asks for, she fears; she wants what she does *not* ask.
    Pursue, and you'll get what you want.
Meanwhile, if she moves through the streets on a litter,
    approach nonchalantly and have a small chat.
Or, to avoid hostile ears, stealthily slip her a note, if you can,
    that masks your intent in ambiguous phrases.                          490
Perhaps she takes a leisurely stroll through a spacious portico.
    Spend some sociable hours there yourself.
Be sure to walk sometimes ahead, sometimes behind,
    and adjust your pace accordingly.
Don't be too bashful to move up through a few intervening columns,
    or to brush your side against hers.
Be there as well when she sits in the curved theater, a lovely sight:
    her arms will provide quite a show.
Here you can look back at her and marvel. Communicate extensively
    by eyebrow movements and secret signs.                                500
Applaud the mime playing the girl, show your support
    for the actor who plays her lover.[34]

---

34. Mime was a type of comic dramatic performance (see Glossary).

When she gets up, you get up. While she is sitting, you sit.
    Waste your time at the lady's whim.


## Personal Appearance

No curling iron should twist your hair, no abrasive pumice
    should scour the fuzz off your legs.
That is for men who sing and chant for the mother goddess Cybele,
    wailing in a frenzy to a Phrygian tune.[35]
The rugged look befits a man. Theseus swept Ariadne off her feet
    without the services of a comb.                                                510
Phaedra loved Hippolytus, who never dressed up. Adonis was fit for
    forest living, yet was the beloved of a goddess.
Be well-groomed, be tan from exercise on the Campus Martius.
    The toga should fit well, and be clean.
Your shoes should not be too stiff, nor their fastenings rusty;
    your foot should not swim in leather too loose.
Don't let a bad haircut ruin your mane and make it bristly. Mop and beard
    should be trimmed by a qualified hand.
Fingernails should neither be dirty nor protruding; no wild hairs
    should protrude out your nose.                                                520
No rank breath should issue from a malodorous mouth,
    nor a billy goat's stink offend surrounding nostrils.
Other refinements? Leave them to the playful girls, and unmanly men
    who seek another man for a partner.


## Bacchus and Ariadne

I hear Bacchus calling. I am his poet, and he, too, helps lovers;
    indeed, he felt the flame of love himself.
Once Ariadne was wandering, out of her mind, on an unknown
    shore, the small Aegean island of Dia.
There she was in disarray, just awoken, her tunic unbelted,
    barefoot, her saffron hair unbound.                                                530
She cursed cruel Theseus to the unhearing waves, as tears,
    undeserved, wet her tender cheeks.
She shouted and wept by turns—both became her,
    and tears did nothing to spoil her beauty.
Again and again she pounded her delicate breast as she cried,
    "That liar has gone. What will become of me?
What will become of me?" But then cymbals clanged
    along the shore, and drums beaten by frenzied hands.

---

35. The effeminate, castrated priests of the Phrygian goddess Cybele (see "Galli" in Glossary).

Ariadne fainted with fear in mid-utterance. No blood
    flowed through her lifeless body.                      540
But look: Bacchants with their hair flowing loose down their backs.
    Look: nimble satyrs—the god's entourage.
Look: Silenus, drunk old Silenus, on his snub-nosed donkey,
    scarcely staying aboard by clutching its mane,
chasing the Bacchants, who flee and return, while he spurs on
    his four-footed beast—quite a poor equestrian!
Down Silenus falls off his long-eared donkey and onto his head.
    The satyrs shout: "Up, Father, get up!"
Now the god himself arrives, carriage topped with grape clusters,
    driving his team of tigers with golden reins.           550
The girl lost color, voice, and all thought of Theseus.
    Three times she thought to flee, but was held back by fear.
She shuddered like the fields of wheat caressed by wind,
    like the reeds in a watery marsh.
Then said the god, "Ariadne, here I am, a more faithful love.
    Fear not, you shall be the bride of Bacchus.
Your bridal gift? A place in the heavens. Your star shall be seen in the sky,
    your crown shall often guide the doubtful sailor."
He dismounted from his chariot (so the tigers would not frighten her),
    and the sand yielded to his steps.                560
He picked her up (for she had no strength to resist) and then
    carried her off: all things are easy for the gods.
Some raised the marriage hymn, others cried "Euhion euhoe!"[36]
    God joined with girl on a divine wedding couch.
The moral? When you find yourself on a dining couch with a woman,
    and the gifts of Bacchus are laid out before you,
say a prayer to father Bacchus and his nighttime rituals
    that the wine will not dull your wits.
You'll be able to say quite a bit discreetly, coded messages
    that she will perceive to be meant for her.          570
Use liquid wine to write out flirtatious words: she can read
    on the table that you are smitten with her.
Give her a look that confesses your passion.
    A silent glance speaks volumes.
Be the first to grab the cup that she has touched with her lips;
    drink from the same place on the rim.
She has sampled a dish with her fingers: reach for it yourself,
    and while reaching make sure your hands touch.
You should also hope that the girl's husband likes you;
    it is useful if he becomes your friend.            580
If the lot falls to you in a drinking game, have him drink first;
    give him the garland that falls from your head.

---

36. A ritual cry associated with the cult of Bacchus/Dionysus.

If he is your social equal or inferior, gallantly defer to him;
    chime in supportively when he speaks.

    [ *four lines that are doubtlessly a later addition are omitted here*]

As for drinking, here is a clear limit: never imbibe so much
    that mind and feet can no longer function.                590
Above all, avoid the quarrels that can be started by wine,
    when the fists become all too ready for war.
Eurytion the centaur died after foolish indulgence in alcohol.
    At wine and dinner, stick to good jokes.
If you have a decent voice, then sing. If you can move, then dance.
    What pleasing gift you have, use it to please.
Just as real drunkenness hinders, feigned drunkenness can help.
    Let your crafty tongue stammer and lisp.
That way, any future indecent remarks or acts can easily
    be put down to too much wine.                  600
Give a toast to the lady, and the man with whom she sleeps;
    but think a silent curse upon that man.
When the tables are removed and the diners rise to leave,
    the crowd itself will give you opportunities.
Wade into the crush and gently sidle up as she is leaving;
    give her a pinch and touch her foot with yours.
Now is the time to talk. Rustic Modesty, be gone, far away!
    Venus, like Fortune, favors the bold.
Your eloquence need not submit to any guidelines of mine.
    Merely desire, and eloquence will come.           610
You must play the lover and mimic the wounds of passion.
    Strive for believability, however you can.
It's not hard to be believed: every girl thinks she's a catch
    and good-looking, unlovely as she may be.
Frequently, though, the insincere lover begins to love for real,
    becoming what at first he only pretends to be.
So, girls, be indulgent and kind to play-acting lovers.
    The love that was recently false will soon be true.
Now subtly undermine her resistance with flattery,
    as the stream undermines the river bank.          620
Don't hold back: lavish praise upon her face or her hair,
    her slender fingers, her tiny feet.
Advertisement of their beauty delights even the chaste;
    virgins, too, care about their looks.
Why else would it still chafe Juno and Minerva to have lost
    that beauty contest in the Phrygian woods?
Juno's peacock displays its brilliant feathers when praised;
    gaze in silence and it hides the treasure of its tail.
Fleet-footed stallions between vigorous races like
    their manes combed and their necks patted.         630

When making promises, don't be shy, for promises draw girls on.
    Invoke whatever gods you like.
Jupiter smiles from on high at the perjured oaths of lovers
    and has them voided by Aeolus' winds.
Jupiter used to make Juno false promises by the Styx;
    now he favors those who follow his example.
The existence of the gods is a helpful thing; so let us believe in them.
    Let us offer wine and incense on ancient altars.
The gods do not live in a state of quiet repose, like sleep.[37]
    Divine power is all around us: live a moral life!                    640
Return property held in trust, live up to agreements, be honest;
    keep your hands free from bloodshed.
If you're smart, you'll stick to deceiving girls—that goes unpunished.
    In this one area, take truth in moderation.
Deceive the deceivers; they're a largely unprincipled lot
    and deserve to be caught in traps like their own.
Egypt, they say, was stricken with drought—nine long years
    without rain to nourish the fields—
till one Thrasius arrived and told Busiris, the king, that Jupiter
    required the blood of a foreigner.                                   650
"Right," replied Busiris, "you shall be Jupiter's first victim;
    you, visitor, will give Egypt water."
Savage Perillus was first to be roasted alive in the bull of Phalaris;[38]
    the inventor stained his own invention with blood.
Both kings had right on their side. There's no law more fair:
    inventors of destruction should perish by their own inventions.
And so it's only right to use a little perjury on the perjurers;
    a woman should feel the sting of her own favored weapon.
Tears are useful as well; tears can melt a heart of stone.
    If you can, wet your cheeks with tears.                             660
Tears don't always show up on cue, so when they fail,
    merely touch your eyes with a little oil.
It's also wise to mix kisses with your seductive banter;
    if she demurs, snatch them anyway.
At first she may resist and say, "Stop it, you brute!" Still,
    such resistance wants to be overcome.
Just make sure those stolen kisses do not hurt her tender lips,
    and she cannot complain that they are rough.
If you take kisses and fail to take the rest, then you deserve
    to lose also what she's already given.                             670
How much distance between those kisses and your true desires?
    Stopping short isn't decency—it's unsophistication!

---

37. A reference to the view of the Greek philosopher Epicurus, who believed that the gods were entirely unconcerned with human conduct.

38. A 6th-century tyrant of Agrigentum in Sicily.

I suppose you can call it "force," but such force is welcome to girls.
　　Many who don't comply wish they had.
The woman violated by the sudden seizing of pleasure is glad,
　　and this "wickedness" is seen as a kind of gift.
She who could have been forced but leaves untouched
　　might smile on the outside, but frowns within.
Phoebe was raped, and so was her sister, but each was later quite fond
　　of her assailant. It's a well-worn tale,                                                    680
but here goes: Deidameia, they say, did it with Achilles—
　　the girl from Scyros with the man from Thessaly.
This was after Paris had praised Venus' looks and won his baleful
　　reward in the foothills of Mt. Ida,
and after Priam's daughter-in-law had arrived from overseas,
　　to be a Greek wife in a Trojan city.
Everyone swore loyalty to her spurned husband, for one man's
　　pain became a national rallying cry.
Achilles had disguised his sex under a long dress—a disgrace,
　　but due, he said, to his mother's entreaties.[39]                                        690
What are you doing, Achilles? Working a loom's not your job!
　　You excel at Minerva's other craft.
Why does the hand by which mighty Hector would fall
　　hold a wool basket instead of a shield?
Put down those spindles covered with laborious thread
　　and pick up your Pelian spear.
The king's daughter happened to be in the same bedroom;
　　she learned he was a man when she was raped.
She was overcome by his strength (so the most plausible version),
　　yet she desired nonetheless to be overcome.                                             700
She often said "wait" when Achilles was hurrying to leave—
　　for now he was his soldierly self.
So where is that "force" now, Deidameia? Why do you cling
　　to the author of your deflowering?
No doubt: they feel shame at being the first to begin an affair,
　　but are pleased to receive when the other leads.
The man who waits to be approached by the woman
　　relies too much on his own good looks.
The man should make the first approach; it's his job to woo;
　　the girl's, to humor his flattering pleas.                                               710
Ask, so you may succeed. She just wants to be asked.
　　If you want the job you have to apply.
Even Jupiter came to heroines of old on bended knee—
　　no girl ever hit on great Jupiter!
But if you perceive that your entreaties are being met

---

39. Achilles' mother Thetis attempted to keep him from the Trojan War by disguising him as a
girl amidst the daughters of Lycomedes, king of Scyros. Deidameia was one of these daughters.

with haughty disdain, lay off, retreat.
Many girls want that which flees, and hate what insists.
    Relieve her of your annoyance, chase less energetically.
Nor should the seducer always reveal that he hopes for sex;
    let love enter disguised as friendship.                                    720
This friendly approach has softened many a puritan heart;
    the devoted attendant can become a lover.
Pale skin on a sailor is a disgrace; he ought rather to be
    blackened by sun's rays and sea swells.
Likewise the farmer, who tills his fields under open sky
    with curved plough and heavy rake.
The athlete who seeks Olympic crowns would be ridiculous
    if his body were ivory and wan.
But every lover should be white as a sheet. This is the lover's hue,
    both fitting and also quite useful.                                        730
Orion was pale as he haunted the forests in love with Side;
    Daphnis went pale over the reluctant Nais.
Let your wasting body declare your mental state. Why not conceal
    your well-groomed hair with the invalid's hood?
Sleepless, anxious nights, and the grief of intense longing
    emaciate the bodies of young lovers.
If you want to achieve your desire, be pathetic; they'll see
    at a glance and say, "He's in love."
Morality is scarce these days. Shall I lament, or just give my advice?
    Friendship, Trust: mere names without substance.                          740
Praise your love to a friend, and the moment he believes you,
    alas, he tries to take your place.
"But," you may reply, "Achilles' man Patroclus never violated his bed.[40]
    As far as Pirithous goes, Phaedra was quite chaste.
Pylades loved Hermione like a sister, as Apollo loved
    Minerva, or as Castor loved Helen."
Fool, you're too naive. You probably hope to get fruit from a tamarisk,
    or honey in the midst of a river.
These days only wickedness delights, and it's every man for his own
    pleasure, sweetest from another man's pain.                               750
Oh, the criminality! Fear not your enemy, but those you think
    trustworthy; avoid them and be safe.
Watch out for your cousins, your brother, your dear companion;
    that crowd should give you real anxiety.
I'm ending, but one more point: the hearts of girls are quite diverse;
    you need many tricks for many tempers.
It's like land. One region is suited to grapes, another to olives,
    a third is green with fields of spelt.
There are as many types of characters as there are of faces.

---

40. That is, by sleeping with his concubine Briseis.

The wise man adapts to countless bents.                                    760
Like Proteus, he will melt into insubstantial water, and become
   now lion, now tree, now bristling boar.
There are fish one catches by casting-net, others need hook and line,
   still others require a bulging drag net.
Nor can one method be applied to every age. The aged
   hind will see the trap from afar.
Come off learned to an uneducated girl, or forward to one who's shy,
   and she will soon lose confidence in herself.
This is why girls too meek to go with a man of high status
   often embrace their social inferiors.                              770
Part of my work is done, but part still remains. Let my ship
   cast anchor and pause at this point.


## Introduction to *Fasti*, April 21

Ovid's *Fasti* ("Calendar") is an ambitious poetic treatment of Roman cult and ancient religion. In it, Ovid describes Rome's various religious customs and then provides the mythological or legendary stories behind them, all keyed to the festival calendar. Of a projected twelve books, one per month, Ovid finished the first six before he was exiled (AD 8) and broke off the project. A poetic complement to a scholarly work like Verrius Flaccus' publicly displayed calendar (see "A Roman Calendar: April" in this volume), Ovid's *Fasti* are a fascinating compendium of lore about Roman religion and a key source for anyone trying to understand its often curious rituals. We give here the entry for April 21, which describes the Parilia, the festival honoring the ancient Italian goddess of shepherds (Pales), which happened to fall on the same day as the traditional foundation of Rome in 753 BC.

Ovid describes some characteristic elements of the Parilia, which he says he himself participated in many times: the fetching of incense from the Vestal Virgins, as well as the ashes of calves burned at another festival called the Fordicidia, bean stalks, and blood from the festival of the "October Horse." Participants in the Parilia ran three times through a straw fire while water was flicked at them with laurel twigs. We hear from other sources that young people in particular celebrated the Parilia boisterously under the greening trees and put up improvised tents, tables, and couches made of turf for a picnic. In the country, the shepherds cleaned the sheepfolds and then adorned them.

Ovid's account begins with an invocation of the goddess (721–30). He then describes the central elements of the festival: the obtaining of the incense (731–34), the purification of the sheep (735–42), the eating of special millet cakes with milk (743–46), the shepherd's prayer (747–78), the drinking of wine mixed with milk, and the jumping over the fires (779–82). This is followed by some possible explanations, some current, some contrived, of the combined use of water and fire in the ritual (781–806), and finally the story of Rome's walls, including the murder of Remus, with a stirring finale on the greatness of the city (807–62).

# *Fasti*, April 21 (4.721–862)

## Festival of Pales

Night fades as Aurora rises. The Festival of Pales calls.
   I will be up to the task, if nourishing Pales smiles on me.
Nourishing Pales, smile on me as I sing of shepherds' rites—
   if I do your festival justice with my song.
I myself have often carried the ash, the charred remains
   of the calf, and the beanstalks in my hands.
I have often leapt three times over the fires placed in a row
   and been sprinkled by a wet laurel branch.
The goddess stirs! She smiles on my endeavor! My ship has left
   the docks and sets sail on the deep.      730
People, go to the virgin's altar; ask for the stuff of purification.
   Vesta will give it. You will be pure through Vesta's gifts.
Two will be the blood of a horse and the ash from a calf,[41]
   a third the empty stalks of hard beans.
Shepherd, purify your fattened sheep at dawn's first light;
   sprinkle water first, then sweep the ground with brooms.
Festoon the pens with wreaths and leafy branches,
   hang long garlands over the doors.
Light the sulphur, fill the pens with dusky incense,
   and let the sheep bleat, stung by the smoke.      740
Burn rosemary, pinewood, juniper, and let laurel
   crackle as it burns on the hearth.
Bring millet cakes, then a small basket of millet—
   this food brings the rustic goddess great joy.
Bring the feast and milk-pail fit for her; divide the feast,
   pour warm milk, pray to Pales the forest-dweller.
Say: "Look after the flock and flock's shepherds alike;
   keep my stables free from harmful sickness.
If I pastured my flock on sacred land, or sat beneath a sacred tree,
   if my sheep nibbled on tomb-offerings without my knowing,      750
if I entered a forbidden grove and sent the sacred nymphs
   and the half-goat god[42] scattering from my sight,
if my pruning hook robbed a sacred wood of a dark branch
   to make a leafy basket for an ailing sheep,
forgive me! And may you pardon me if I sheltered my flock
   in a woodland shrine till a hail storm spent its fury.

---

41. The blood comes from the sacrifice of the "October Horse" after a race held on October 15.
The ash of the calf is that created during the sacrifice at the Fordicidia, held April 15.
42. Pan (Faunus).

Forgive me, nymphs, if a moving hoof muddied your waters;
    may disturbing a placid pool bring me no harm.
Pales, placate for us the springs and the gods of springs;
    pacify the gods scattered throughout the woods.    760
May we not espy Dryad nymphs or Diana's Baths,
    or Faunus when he sleeps in the fields at noon.[43]
Drive disease far away! May flocks and men flourish,
    may my alert pack of watchdogs flourish, too.
May I bring home as many sheep as I took to pasture, never sob
    as I bring back a bloody fleece, a wolf's victim.
Keep awful hunger away; let grasses and leaves grow in abundance;
    give us water to wash our limbs and slake our thirst.
May I squeeze full udders, may cheese bring me profit,
    and may the wicker sieve yield liquid whey.[44]    770
May the ram be lusty, ready to mount, may his mate be fertile,
    and may there be many a lamb about my pens.
May the wool my sheep produce not harm girls' fingers,
    and may it be soft, fit for the most tender of hands.
May my prayers come to pass, and each year let us offer
    abundant cakes to Pales, goddess of shepherds."
Appease the goddess with this prayer. Say it four times,
    facing east. Wash your hands with fresh water.
Then let a wooden bowl serve as your mixer,
    and quaff snow-white milk and mulled red wine.    780
Only then can you run and make a strenuous leap
    over the burning heaps of crackling hay.
I've explained the customs. What's left is the origin of the rites.
    So many explanations—I'm foiled by uncertainty.
Gnawing fire cleanses all, and strips out impurities from metals.
    Is this it? Does fire purify the flocks and their master?
Or is it that all things come from two opposing elements,
    fire and water, discordant gods?
Did our forefathers join these elements, and think it fit
    to graze the body with fire and sprinkled water?    790
Or is it that these two are the causes of life—which is why we deny
    them to exiles and give them to brides?[45]
I have serious doubts. Some think they symbolize Phaethon's
    fire and the floodwaters of Deucalion.
Another group tell the tale that when shepherds were striking
    rock on rock, a spark suddenly shot out;

---

43. It was dangerous to disturb Pan (Faunus) at midday, or to see satyrs and nymphs at play. Ovid also alludes to the story of Actaeon, who saw Diana bathing and paid for it with his life.

44. The byproduct of cheese-making, whey is high in protein and has many uses.

45. The legal formula for exile was to "deny someone fire and water," and these two elements were also presented to the Roman bride as she entered her new home.

the first was lost, but the second was caught in hay—
    does this explain the Parilian fire?
Or does this custom go back to that family-man, Aeneas,
    to whom the fires of Troy gave safe passage?        800
Or could it be that when Rome was founded, the Lares[46]
    were ordered to move to new homes,
and as they exchanged country shacks for city-dwellings
    they set fire to the woodland huts and pens?
Perhaps the livestock leapt trough these, and the shepherds, too,
    as happens today on the birthday of Rome.
This coincidence allows your poet to speak of Rome's foundation.
    Great Quirinus,[47] help me sing of your deeds.

## Foundation of Rome

Now that Numitor's brother[48] had paid the price,
    and the twins ruled the shepherd host,        810
each decided it time to urbanize the farmers
    and build walls. But who'd have that honor?
"No need to fight," said Romulus, "since birds are dependable.
    Let us put our faith in birds."
The other agreed. At daybreak one went to the crags
    of leafy Palatine, the other to Aventine's peak.
Six birds Remus saw. Romulus saw twice six in order.
    Case closed—Romulus rules the city.
He chose a proper day to mark the city walls with a furrow.
    The rites of Pales were at hand, this, the mighty beginning.    820
He digs a pit in the solid ground. Grain is pitched in.
    So, too, earth from neighboring places.
The trench is filled with soil, an altar built on top:
    the new hearth enjoys burning fire.
Then he presses down the plow, marks the walls with a furrow;
    a white heifer and snowy bull bear the yoke.
This was the king's prayer: "Jupiter, Father Mars, Mother Vesta,
    look with favor as I found this city,
and all you gods that I ought to invoke, smile upon me.
    Let this city soar beneath your auspices.    830
Let it be long lasting, powerful, master of the earth.
    Let the sun rise and set over its lands."
He prayed, and Jupiter sent a happy omen: thunder
    and lightning crashed and flashed on his left.
Overjoyed by the sign, they set to building, citizens now,

---

46. Household gods; see Glossary.

47. The deified Romulus.

48. Amulius, killed by the twins Romulus and Remus (see Livy chs. 3–7 in this volume).

and the new wall soon started to grow.
The man Romulus dubbed "Speedy" was urging them on;
    "Celer," said Romulus, "this is your task:
Let no one pass over this wall or the plow-made ditch.
    Should someone dare, deliver him to death."                              840
Remus, unaware, scoffed at those paltry walls and said,
    "*These* will keep our people safe? Ha!"
At once he leapt across. Before he landed Celer impaled him
    with a spade; Remus, bloody, lay heavy on hard earth.
When the king heard, sadness welled up inside, but this
    he swallowed and kept the deep wound hid.
No public tears—he had to set a tough example and said,
    "May every enemy who crosses my wall perish so."
Despite this, he gave a lavish funeral, no longer holding back tears.
    A brother's love, once concealed, now lay open.                         850
He gave a final kiss to his brother upon the bier, and said,
    "Brother, you were torn from me unwilling! Fare thee well!"
The limbs that were to burn he anointed, joined in the task
    by Faustulus and Acca, her hair let down in mourning.
His people (not yet called Quirites) cried for the young man:
    "Remus" was heard as the final flame was lit.
The city rose—who then would have believed it?—destined
    to place its victorious foot upon the earth.
May you rule all things, may great Caesar be your lord forever,
    and may you have many men of that name.                                  860
City of Rome, as your head towers above a conquered world,
    may everything else rise to below your shoulders!

## Introduction to *Tristia* 4.10

A rare example of autobiography by an ancient author, this poem focuses on Ovid's
family, his literary career, and his banishment to the shore of the Black Sea by the
Emperor Augustus. It comes from a collection of Ovid's writings from exile entitled
*Tristia* or "Sorrows." As a first-person sketch of his life and works, it bears comparison
with some of the epitaphs printed in this volume (e.g., Inscriptions nos. 40, 41, and 43).

## *Tristia* 4.10

Learn here, posterity, of that "I" whose works you peruse,
    the playful poet of tender love affairs.
Sulmo is my fatherland, rich in fields and chilly streams,

some ninety miles from the capital.
That's where I was born. What year, you ask? The year
  when both consuls met similar deaths in office.[49]
For what it's worth, I inherited my equestrian status
  from my ancestors; my fortune is not newly
acquired. I was not a first child, but had an older brother,
  born twelve months before.                    10
The same morning star shone on our births; we had one day
  to celebrate, and two birthday cakes.
It was one of the five feast days of warlike Minerva—the one
  that is first to be stained with blood in battle.[50]
Our education began early, and our father's loving care
  sent us to distinguished teachers in the big city.
My brother was early on headed for eloquence, born to wield
  the potent weapons of the talkative Forum.
But even then I was drawn to the heavenly rites of the Muse,
  who was stealthily pulling me into her service.       20
"Why are you wasting your time?" my father used to complain,
  "Your precious Homer died without a cent."
Swayed by his words, I left Mt. Helicon and abandoned verse
  completely. I tried to write prose.
But the words emerged in metrical form of their own accord;
  whatever I tried to say came out versified.
The years glided quietly by, and it was time for my brother
  and me to take up the free man's toga:
on our shoulders went the tunic with a broad purple stripe.[51]
  But our former interests remained.            30
My brother was only twenty when he died; and from that day
  I began to live without half of myself.
I won the young man's first official position, and served
  as a member of the Board of Three.
The Senate beckoned; but the weight was more than I could carry.
  I began to wear the narrower stripe.
My body was not tough, my brain unsuited to the grind;
  I'd no heart for the stress of campaigning.
The Muses kept luring me toward safety and leisure—
  always my own inclination.               40
In those days I saw in every poet the presence of
  the divine. I sought out and courted them all.

---

49. 43 BC, the consulship of Hirtius and Pansa, both of whom died during a civil war. See Cicero, *Letters* 22 in this volume.

50. March 20, the first of three days for gladiatorial spectacles during the five-day Quinquatrus festival.

51. The *latus clavus*, signifying an intent to pursue a senatorial career (see Glossary). Later Ovid renounced such ambition and wore the narrower stripe of an *eques* (see below, line 36).

Old Macer used to read to me from his works on birds,
    and on poisonous snakes and healing herbs.
Propertius would often recite to me his fiery love elegy
    honoring the friendship we shared.
Ponticus the epic poet and Bassus the master of iambics
    were beloved members of my inner circle.
I listened, mesmerized, to Horace as that metrical magician
    sang his polished *Odes* to the Italian lyre.        50
Vergil I only saw; as for Tibullus, greedy death robbed me
    of the chance for friendship with him.
Gallus' heir in love elegy was Tibullus. Propertius came after him.
    I myself was the fourth in the series.
Young poets cultivated me as I had sought out my elders;
    my works quickly became known.
I had only shaved my beard once or twice when first I debuted
    my early works in public performance.
The woman I decided to call Corinna inspired my poetry,
    which was recited all over the city.       60
I wrote a lot, it is true, but what I thought faulty I consigned
    to the flames for revision. Then, too,
when I was exiled I burnt some poems destined to please,
    enraged at my profession and my verse.
My soft heart was always impulsive, love-prone, an easy
    mark for Cupid's piercing weapons,
Yet despite my nature, though the smallest spark would ignite me,
    no scandal ever attached to my name.
I was married, briefly, still practically a boy, to a wife
    who was both worthless and useless.       70
My second wife, though blameless, was nevertheless not
    destined to be my permanent partner.
The last, who remained with me to old age, has remained
    the steadfast wife of an exiled man.
My daughter made me a grandfather twice (though not from the
    same man) while she was still quite young.
By then, my father had died, having lived for ninety years;
    and when he died I wept just as he would,
had I been taken first. Not long after that I endured
    to see my mother laid to rest.       80
How lucky they both were to be dead and buried before
    the day of my punishment and doom.
I am lucky, too, that they're not here to see my wretchedness,
    and felt no pain on my account.
But what if something beyond our name survives,
    if slender shades escape the funeral pyre?
If news has reached you, parents, and my case is being tried
    in some ghostly Stygian court of law,

please know my exile came about not of crime, but from a
   foolish mistake. Parents, I cannot lie to you.        90
Enough for the souls of the dead. I now return to you, curious
   readers, who want to know the story of my life.
The grey had now come and disarranged my hair;
   my best years were gone. Ten times
since my birth had victorious Olympic charioteers won
   their olive crown prizes.[52] The anger
of the emperor's offended majesty forced me to travel to Tomis,[53]
   on the western shore of the Black Sea.
I must not discuss the cause of my ruin, or inform against myself—
   it's all too well-known, in any case.        100
Why describe the crime of my friends, and the deceit of my slaves?
   Much of that was worse than exile itself.
My mind refused to submit to adversity; relying on its inner
   resources it rendered itself unbeaten.
I abandoned my life of leisure and steeled myself for necessity,
   ready for battle, which I'd never known.
My journey by land and sea held misfortunes, as many as
   the stars of the night sky. At last, after long
wanderings I arrived at this coastal outpost among Sarmatian
   Getae, a tribe of deadly archers.        110
Here, surrounded as I am on all sides by the clash of weapons,
   I nonetheless lighten my dreadful lot,
as best I can, with poetry. There is no one here to listen;[54]
   still, it helps me to pass the days.
So the fact that I live and confront my grievous sufferings,
   and have not grown tired of the light,
I owe to you, Muse; for you are my consolation, my respite
   from anxiety, a kind of medicine;
my leader and companion, you snatch me from the Danube
   and place me in the middle of Mt. Helicon.        120
Thanks to you, I have that rare possession: writerly fame while
   alive, something usually got, if at all,
postmortem. Nor has Envy, that hostile critic of contemporary
   authors, gnawed away at my work.

---

52. That is, he was fifty years old. Ovid reckons time using the old method of counting by Olympiads. The Olympic games were held every four years, which were sometimes thought of as five by inclusive counting. Ovid here makes an Olympiad five years, the same as the Roman *lustrum* (see Glossary). He was relegated in the autumn of AD 8, and had turned fifty in March of that year.

53. Tomis (or Tomi) was just south of the Danube delta, in the still unsettled province of Moesia. It is now Constanta, Romania.

54. Few if any natives of Tomi spoke Latin or cared about poetry. Inscriptions in the 1st century AD, however, show that Latin and Ovid's poetry eventually caught on there.

Our age has produced many great poets; yet the reading public
  has not been at all hostile to my talent.
I am thought no worse than many whom I consider my betters,
  and I am much read around the world.
And so, a forecast (if the prophecies of poets have value):
  when I die, Earth, I will not be yours.                          130
Whether my fame rests on real poetry, or mere popular fashion,
  I owe a debt of thanks, honest reader, to you.

# PERPETUA

(ca. AD 180–203, wrote in Latin)

## Introduction

Before Christianity received official sanction under Constantine (reigned AD 306–337), Christians were sometimes jailed and put to death as criminals, on the grounds that they were atheists who refused to worship the traditional gods, and thus endangered the whole community by provoking divine anger. Official persecutions of Christians were sporadic, local, relatively small in scale, and ineffective. Even the "great" persecutions of AD 303–313 varied in intensity across the empire. In this there is a marked contrast with the later suppression of non-Christian practices by Christian bishops once in power, which were systematic and effective. But punishment of unrepentant Christians occurred in every reign of any length from that of Nero (AD 54–68) on. Records of individual cases were kept by local Christian groups, and the reading of these accounts became a regular part of the church calendar on the anniversaries of the deaths of famous martyrs. Dozens of these "martyr acts" survive. They include transcripts of interrogations, vividly portray the anger of the non-Christian mobs and the frustration of Roman magistrates at Christian refusals to cooperate and save themselves, and record the words, bearing, and exact manner of the torture and death of the martyrs.

The following is an early and extraordinary example of the genre, because it contains not just an eyewitness report, but a first-person recounting of the ordeals leading up to exposure to the beasts in the amphitheater and subsequent execution. It is also an extremely rare instance of a memoir-like text authored by a Roman woman, by all accounts a remarkable one.

On March 7, AD 203, a small group of young women and men were led from prison to the arena of the amphitheater at Carthage in the province of Africa, destined for spectacular execution as part of the celebrations of the birthday anniversary of Geta, the reigning emperor's younger son. The group consisted of a young woman called Vibia Perpetua, whose words form part of this account, and her companion from prison, a young female slave named Felicitas. There were also three men: Revocatus, Saturninus, and Saturus. Perpetua, about twenty-two at the time of her execution, was of a well-to-do Roman citizen family from the town of Thuburbo Minus, near the great urban center of Carthage. She was well educated, as is shown by her accomplished Latin style. She had recently married, and was still, as she points out, breast-feeding her first child. The central account describes her imprisonment and public trial, and her anguished arguments with her non-Christian father (her husband, for reasons that are unclear, is not mentioned). It describes her anxiety over her infant son, and also the prophetic dream-visions she had while in prison.

Exposure to the beasts was not fatal; all five were put to the sword afterwards by gladiators, at the insistence of the crowd.

The text begins with an introduction (sections 1–2) and ends with a description of the ordeal of the arena itself (sections 15–21), both written by one of Perpetua's Christian associates. These chapters frame the central section, written by Perpetua (sections 3–10; sections 11–14, containing the dream-vision of Saturus, are omitted here). Identifiable scriptural quotations are signaled by italics, followed by a footnote giving the source.

---

## The Passion of Perpetua and Felicitas

[1] The reason for recording instances of outstanding faith from long ago, acts that testify to the grace of God and bring about the spiritual betterment of men, is to honor God and comfort men by the recollection of the past in the written word. Should not recent outstanding examples also be recorded that serve both purposes just as well? One day these things, too, will be ancient, and essential reading for future generations, even if right now the unchallenged veneration of antiquity grants them less prestige in their own time. But I leave that to people who rate manifestations of the single power of the single Holy Spirit according to the age in which they happen to occur. In fact, more recent events should be considered all the more significant for their very lateness, in accordance with the abundance of grace decreed for the end times. For *in the last days, says God, I will pour out my spirit on all mankind, and their sons and daughters will prophesy; and on my manservants and maidservants I will pour out my spirit; young men will see visions, and old men will dream dreams.*[1]

We honor and recognize as valid both the prophecies and the new visions, given according to the promise. As for the other miraculous works of the Holy Spirit, we count those among the aids of the church. For the same Spirit has been sent to distribute all his gifts to all, as the Lord apportions to each. Thus we regard it as imperative to write these events down and make them known for the greater glory of God, so that those weak and despairing of faith might not think that divine grace operated only among people of olden times, whether in the granting of martyrs or of revelations. God is always working to fulfill his promises, both as a testimony for non-believers, and as a blessing for believers.

And so, *what we have heard and touched with our hands* we proclaim to you as well, brethren and little children, *so that you*, too, who were involved will recall the glory of the Lord, and so those who now hear it through report *might share fellowship* with the holy martyrs, and through them *with our Lord Christ Jesus*,[2] to whom belong glory and honor forever and ever. Amen.

[2] Some young catechumens were arrested: Revocatus, his fellow slave Felicitas, Saturninus, and Saturus. In this group was Vibia Perpetua, a recently married woman of good family and upbringing. Her father and mother were still alive, and one of her two brothers was a catechumen like herself. She was about twenty-two, and was still

---

1. Acts 2:17.
2. I John 1:1–3.

nursing an infant son at the breast. What follows is the whole story of her martyrdom as she herself related it, just as she left it behind, written in her own hand and her own thoughts.

[3] When we were still with the guards,[3] my father, out of love for me, was eager to dissuade me and kept trying to undermine my resolution.

"Father," I said, "do you see that vase lying on the ground, for example, or this beaker or whatever?"

"Yes, I do," he said.

"Could it be called by any other name than what it is?" I asked.

"No," he said.

"In the same way, I cannot say I am anything other than what I am, a Christian."

Then my father, enraged by the word "Christian," came at me as if to tear my eyes out; but he merely shook me and went his way, defeated along with his diabolical arguments. Then my father stayed away for a few days, for which I gave thanks to God. I was comforted by his absence. During those few days, I was baptized, and I was inspired by the Holy Spirit to pray after baptism for nothing but courage to withstand bodily torture.[4]

After a few days we were taken to the prison, and I was terrified, having never experienced such darkness. What a terrible period! With the crowd, the heat was stifling; then there were the bribes demanded by the soldiers, and worst of all I was tortured with anxiety about my baby there. Then Tertius and Pomponius, those blessed deacons who were trying to help us, managed to get us some relief by bribing the soldiers to transfer us to a more comfortable part of the prison for a few hours. Then we left the prison, and were all free from constraint. For my part I tried to nurse my baby back to health. He was nearly dead from hunger. Worried about him, I spoke to my mother, tried to encourage my brother, and entrusted my son to their care. I was consumed with grief to see them grieving over me. These are the anxieties I endured over many days. Then I got permission to keep my baby with me in prison,[5] and immediately I recovered my strength and was relieved from suffering and worry about my infant. Suddenly, prison became to me a palace; there was nowhere else I wanted to be.

[4] Then my brother said to me: "Dear sister, you are greatly privileged; surely you are worthy to ask for a vision to show you whether martyrdom or freedom lies in store for you."

And I confidently promised that I would ask, since I knew I could speak with the Lord and had received great blessings from him. "I will tell you tomorrow," I said. Then I made my request, and this is the vision I had:

> I saw a bronze ladder of tremendous size, stretching all the way up to the heavens, but so narrow that only one person could climb at a time. All sorts of iron implements were attached to the rails—swords, needles, hooks, daggers, spikes—so that if anyone climbed inattentively or without looking up, his flesh would stick to the iron implements and he would be mangled. And underneath the ladder itself lay a serpent of

---

3. House arrest, including monitoring by guards (*prosecutores*), preceded their confinement in the military prison (see just below).

4. The first prayer after baptism was regarded as having a special power.

5. Presumably in better conditions than initially.

amazing size, ready to attack, intimidating those who try to climb. Saturus, however, went up first—he who turned himself in because of me afterwards, since he had given me religious instruction but had not been present when I was arrested. And he arrived at the top of the ladder and turned around and said to me: "Perpetua, I'm waiting for you. But take care; do not let the serpent bite you." And I said, "In the name of Jesus Christ, it will not harm me." And from under the ladder it slowly stuck out its head, as if it were afraid of me. And, as though stepping on the first rung of the ladder, I stepped on its head and climbed up. And I saw a vast garden, and seated in the middle a white-haired man in the dress of a shepherd—tall he was, and milking sheep. And around him stood people dressed in white, many thousands. And he lifted his head and looked at me and spoke: "Welcome, my child," he called out, and gave me some of the curds he was collecting, just a mouthful. I took it in my cupped hands and ate it, and all those standing around said, "Amen."

And at the sound of a voice I awoke, the taste of something sweet still in my mouth. Right away I told my brother, and we understood that I was to suffer martyrdom, and that from now on I would no longer have any hope in this life on earth.

[5] A few days later there was a rumor that we were to be given a hearing. My father suddenly arrived from the city, worn out with worry, and he came up to try to persuade me.

"Daughter," he said, "pity my grey head. Pity your father, if I am fit to be called that name by you. With these hands I raised you to the prime of life. I favored you above all your brothers. Do not bring on me such disgrace and infamy. Think of your brothers, think of your mother and her sister, think of your son, who will not survive without you. Give up your pride! You will destroy us all! For none of us will hold up our heads again if something happens to you."

This was how he spoke, like a father out of a father's love, but he was kissing my hands and throwing himself at my feet and crying, and he called me not "daughter" but "lady." I was sorry for my father's sake, because he alone of all of my family would not rejoice in my suffering martyrdom.

And I comforted him, saying, "What happens on that platform will happen as God wills it. For you may be sure that we are not set in our own power but in that of God." And he left me in great sorrow.

[6] One day, while we were eating breakfast, we were suddenly hurried off for a hearing. We arrived at the forum, and rumor spread quickly through the neighborhoods around the forum. A huge crowd gathered. We climbed up onto the platform. When questioned, the others acknowledged that they were Christians. When it was my turn, my father appeared carrying my son, and he dragged me from the step.

"Perform the sacrifice! Have pity on your baby!" he said.

And Hilarianus the governor, who had taken over judicial authority after the death of the proconsul Minucius Timinianus, said:

"Have pity on your father's grey head; have pity on your infant son. Perform a sacrifice for the welfare of the emperors."[6]

---

6. Professed Christians were required to renounce their faith by sacrificing to the state gods and the emperor (see Inscriptions nos. 98–100 in this volume). At this time there were two emperors, Septimius Severus (reigned AD 193–211) and his elder son Caracalla, whom he had appointed consul and colleague to himself in the previous year (AD 202).

And I responded: "I will not."

"Are you a Christian?" asked Hilarianus.

"I am a Christian," I responded.

And since my father was determined to remove me from the platform, Hilarianus gave the order to have him thrown down and beaten with a rod. And the suffering of my father grieved me as if I had been struck myself. Such was my grief for his wretched old age. Then Hilarianus pronounced the sentence on all of us: we were condemned to the beasts.[7] We returned to prison in high spirits. My baby was accustomed to breast feed and stay with me in prison, so I immediately sent Pomponius the deacon to my father to ask for the baby. But my father was unwilling to give him over. But as God willed, the boy no longer required the breast after that, and I did not suffer any swelling, and so I was relieved of any anxiety about the infant, and of any discomfort in my breasts.

[7] A few days later while we were all praying, suddenly in the midst of prayer a voice came forth from me and I uttered the name Dinocrates. I was surprised, since I had not thought about him for a while, and it pained me to be reminded of his misfortune. Immediately I realized that I was in a privileged state to ask for a vision about him, and I began to pray about him intensely and cried out to the Lord. That very night I had the following vision:

I saw Dinocrates coming out of a dark hole, where there were many other people also. He was very hot and thirsty, filthy and pale. On his face was the lesion he had when he died. This Dinocrates had been my brother according to the flesh. At age seven he had died an awful death due to a cancerous tumor on his face, and his death was a source of loathing to everyone. And so I had prayed on his behalf.

There was a great abyss between us, so that neither of us could approach the other. Where Dinocrates stood there was a basin full of water, with a rim higher than the height of the boy. And Dinocrates was stretching as if trying to get a drink. I was pained that the basin was full of water and yet he was not going to get a drink because of the height of the rim.[8]

I woke up and realized that my brother was suffering. But I was confident that I could help him in his trouble. And I prayed for him every day, until we were transferred into the military prison. (We were to fight at the military games, on the occasion of the Caesar Geta's birthday.)[9] I prayed for him day and night, moaning and crying in hope that I might be granted a vision.

[8] On the day we spent in chains, the following vision was shown to me:

---

7. Execution by exposure to beasts in the arena was an extreme, humiliating, and public form of death penalty, available to Roman judges as they saw fit. Most recorded instances, in which the type of offense is known, relate to heinous criminals such as brigands, political revolutionaries, and runaway slaves. Since there was a special element of public expiation in execution before a crowd in the arena, it was also applied in crimes of sacrilege.

8. The implication is that Dinocrates died before baptism.

9. P. Septimius Geta, born March 7, AD 189, was the younger son of the Emperor Septimius Severus. He and his brother Caracalla were styled "Caesars," that is, heirs to imperial power.

I saw the same place I had seen before, but Dinocrates was all clean and well-dressed and relaxed. I saw a scar where the lesion had been, and the basin I had seen before now had its rim lowered all the way to the waist of the child, and Dinocrates kept drinking water from it. On the edge of it was a golden cup full of water, and Dinocrates came up and started to drink from it, and the cup was never empty. When he had had enough he started to play around with the water, laughing, as children do.

I awoke, and realized that he had been delivered from his punishment.

[9] A few days later Pudens, a junior officer in charge of the prison,[10] began to think very highly of us, understanding that we possessed some great power within us. He began to allow many visitors to come and see us, for our mutual comfort. But when the day of the games was at hand, my father came in, completely worn out with grief, and began to rip out chunks of his beard and throw them on the ground, and he threw himself face down on the ground, cursed his old age, and said such words as would move any living being. And I grieved for the unhappiness of his old age.

[10] On the day before we were scheduled to fight with the beasts, I saw the following vision:

Pomponius the deacon had come to the door of the prison and was banging hard on it. And I came out and opened it for him. He was dressed in an unbelted white tunic, and wearing embroidered slippers. And he said to me, "Come, Perpetua, we are waiting for you." And he took me by the hand, and we started to walk on a rough and winding path. After much difficulty we finally arrived, gasping for breath, at the amphitheater. He led me into the middle of the arena, and said: "Do not be afraid. I am here struggling with you." And he left. I looked at the enormous crowd watching expectantly. I knew I had been condemned to the beasts, so I was surprised that the beasts had not yet been let loose on me. And there came out against me an Egyptian, hideous to look at, ready to fight, accompanied by his seconds. Handsome young men came to me as well, my supporters and seconds. My clothing was stripped off, and suddenly I became a man. My seconds began to rub me down with oil, as they do at athletic contests. I saw that the Egyptian on the other side was rolling in the wrestling sand.[11] There emerged a man of amazing size who stood taller than the amphitheater itself. He wore an unbelted tunic with purple stripes going down over his chest on either side, and embroidered slippers made of gold and silver. He carried a staff like a trainer of gladiators, and a green bough, upon which were golden apples. He called for silence and said: "If this Egyptian wins, he will slay that woman with his sword. If she conquers him, she will receive this bough." And with that he left. We approached each other and began to throw punches. He tried to grab my feet, but I kicked him in the face with my heels. I was lifted up in the air and began to pummel him as if not treading on the ground. But when I noticed there was a lull, I joined my hands so that my fingers were interlaced, and grabbed his head. He fell on his face and I trod his head under my foot.[12] The crowd began to shout,

---

10. Pudens was an *optio*, or an assistant to the officers of his legion, tasked in this case with guarding the prison. He is distinct from the jailers (*cataractarii*) and their servants, who are mentioned in ch. 15, and from the *tribunus*, a senior officer of the legion, who is mentioned as supervising the prison in ch. 16.

11. *Haphe*, the yellow sand with which wrestlers were sprinkled after being anointed, so as to be able to get a better grip on their opponents.

12. A sign of victory. See Joshua 10:24.

and my supporters began to sing. I came up to the gladiator trainer and took the bough. And he kissed me and said to me: "Daughter, peace be with you." And I began to go with glory to the Sanavivaria gate.[13]

Then I woke up, and I understood that I was going to fight not against the beasts but against the Devil. But I knew that I would win.

This is what I did leading up to the eve of the spectacle; as for the events of the spectacle itself, someone else who wants to can write about that."[14]

[15] As for Felicitas, she too enjoyed the Lord's favor, in the following way. She had been pregnant when arrested, and was now in her eighth month. The day of the spectacle was approaching, and she was very distressed at the thought that her execution would be postponed due to her being pregnant (since it was not allowed for pregnant women to suffer capital punishment), and she might have to shed her holy and innocent blood later, among common criminals. And her fellow martyrs were also very saddened at the prospect of abandoning such a good ally and fellow traveler, as it were, to go alone on the path of their shared hope. And so, two days before the spectacle, they poured forth prayer to the Lord in one torrent of common grief. Immediately after the prayer she went into labor. As she was experiencing the agonies to be expected in a birth of the eighth month, one of the servants of the jailers said to her: "You think you are in pain now. What are you going to do when they expose you to the beasts? You weren't thinking about *that* when you refused to sacrifice, were you?" And she responded: "What I am suffering right now I suffer by myself. But in the arena there will be another in me who will suffer on my behalf, because I, too, will suffer for him." She had a baby girl, whom one of the sisters took and raised as her own daughter.

[16] The Holy Spirit has permitted the writing down of what happened at the spectacle itself, and in so permitting has willed it. Even if I am unworthy of the task of finishing such a glorious narrative, still, I will follow the last wishes and the testament, so to speak, of Perpetua,[15] and add also one further example of her determination and greatness of soul: The tribune in charge of the prison was treating them with extreme harshness because he believed, based on the warnings of certain very foolish men, that they would be spirited away from prison by some sort of magic spell. Perpetua spoke right to his face:

"Why on earth are you not allowing us to refresh ourselves? We are the veritable elite of death row—Caesar's own, and destined to fight on his birthday. Isn't it all the more glory for you if we are led out there looking fat and healthy?"

The tribune became disturbed and grew red. And he ordered them to be treated more humanely, letting their brethren and others visit and dine with the prisoners. And by now the military guard himself was a believer.[16]

[17] On the day before the games came the prisoner's last meal, called "the free

---

13. The "Gate of Life," through which victorious or pardoned gladiators exited the amphitheater at Carthage. This contrasted with the *Libitinensis* gate ("Gate of Death"), through which the dead bodies of gladiators were carried.

14. This ends the direct account of Perpetua, and the narrator again takes center stage. Sections 11–14, which consist of the dream-vision of Saturus, are omitted here.

15. Evidently a reference to Perpetua's words at the end of ch. 10.

16. This is Pudens, the *optio* mentioned in ch. 9 as being sympathetic.

banquet."[17] They turned it into a Christian feast,[18] to the extent they could, and while doing so they continued to throw out remarks at the people with the same determination, warning them about the coming judgment of God, insisting on how lucky they were to be suffering martyrdom, and ridiculing the voyeurism of the those who rushed up to observe.

Saturus said, "Isn't tomorrow enough for you? Why do you enjoy looking at what you hate? Are we your friends today, but tomorrow your enemies? [19] Ok, look at our faces carefully, so you can recognize us on the judgment day." And so they all left there in confusion, and many of them became believers.

[18] The day of their victory dawned, and they emerged from prison into the amphitheater joyfully, as if they were walking into heaven, with faces composed, trembling, if at all, with joy rather than fear. Perpetua followed, her face radiant, her gait calm, as a beloved of God, as a wife of Christ, deflecting the stares of all onlookers with the intensity of her gaze. Felicitas was the same: glad that she had safely given birth so that now she could fight the beasts, going from one bloodbath to another, from the midwife to the gladiator, ready to wash after childbirth in a second baptism. After they were led into the gateway, they were forced to put on costumes—the men were to be dressed as priests of Saturn, the women as priestesses of Ceres.[20]

But Perpetua resisted with noble determination to the end. "This is why we have come here voluntarily," she said, "so that our liberty will not be crushed. This is why we are giving our lives, so that we will not have to do anything of this sort. That was our deal."

Even injustice itself recognized justice: the tribune yielded, and they were simply brought in as they were. Perpetua was singing a victory song about trampling on the head of the Egyptian.[21] Revocatus and Saturus were issuing dire threats at the gawking crowd. Then, when they came in front of Hilarianus,[22] they began to gesture and nod as if to say, "You are punishing us, but God will punish you." At this the people ran out of patience and demanded that they be beaten with whips through a line of beast-fighters.[23] And doubtless they rejoiced at obtaining something of the sufferings of the Lord.

---

17. Criminals condemned to the beasts were given a lavish dinner in public the day before the games.

18. One of the features of early Christian ritual was the communal meal (called *agape*, or "love") held the evening after a morning of worship. See Pliny, *Letters* 33 in this volume.

19. Reminiscent of the contemporary remark of Tertullian regarding the social ostracism of gladiators (*On the Spectacles* 22): "and for the same reason for which the spectators glorify them, they also degrade and belittle them. . . . What perversity. They love whom they punish. They depreciate whom they value."

20. It was not unusual for criminals facing spectacular execution to be dressed in a costume somehow relevant to their crime (see Martial, no. 2 in this volume). Saturn and Ceres were the most important divinities of Roman North Africa (= Baal and Tanit).

21. See above, ch. 10.

22. The governor of the province of Africa; see above, ch. 6.

23. Beast-fighters (*venatores*) fought with beasts for pay, and were armed. They also carried long cowhide hunting-whips, and it was not unusual to force criminals to run the gauntlet before them.

[19] But he who said, *Ask and you shall receive*, answered their prayers and granted the sort of death that each desired. For whenever they talked among themselves about how they wished to be martyred, Saturninus, for his part, declared that he wanted to be exposed to all sorts of beasts, no doubt so his victory crown would be all the more glorious. And so at the beginning of the spectacle he and Revocatus endured a leopard, and also were attacked by a bear while on the platform. Saturus, by contrast, dreaded bears most of all, and anticipated being finished off by one bite of a leopard. And so when he was being tied to a boar, it was rather the beast fighter tying him to the boar who himself got gored by that very beast, and died the very next day. Saturus was merely dragged along. And when he had been tied to a bear on the platform, the bear declined to emerge from its cage. Thus Saturus left the arena unscathed a second time.

[20] For the young women, however, the Devil contrived an enormously fierce heifer. It was an unusual animal, chosen to match the sex of the beast to theirs. They were stripped naked and led out covered by nets. The crowd was horrified by this, looking now on a delicate young girl, now on one who had just given birth, her breasts still dripping milk. So they were sent out and brought back in dressed in loose, unbelted tunics. The heifer threw Perpetua first, and she landed on her back, exposing her genitals. As she sat up she adjusted her tunic, now ripped at the side, to cover her thigh, more conscious of her modesty than of her physical pain. Then she asked for a pin to fix her disarranged hair, for it was not proper that she suffer martyrdom with her hair unkempt; otherwise she would seem to be in mourning in the midst of her triumph. Thus she got up, and when she saw that Felicitas had been knocked down, she went and gave her a hand and lifted her up, and they both stood there, side by side. Then the hard hearts of the mob softened, and the women were spared and dismissed through the Sanavivaria gate. There Perpetua was received by a certain Rusticus, at that time a catechumen who stayed close to Perpetua.

As if waking from a dream (so thoroughly had she been in a trance, possessed by the Spirit), she began to look around, and to everyone's amazement she said, "When am I to be led in to face that heifer, or whatever it is?"

When she was told what had happened, she did not believe it until she recognized certain signs of the trauma on her own body and clothing. Then she asked for her brother, and that catechumen, and said to them: "*Stand fast in the faith*,[24] love one another, and do not let my martyrdom shake your belief."

[21] Meanwhile, at another gate, Saturus was giving encouragement in a similar fashion to Pudens the soldier, saying: "In short, it happened just as I anticipated and predicted: so far I have not felt the bite of a single beast. Now you should believe with all your heart. Look, I'm going in there and I'm going to be killed by one bite of the leopard."

And immediately thereafter, at the end of the spectacle, he was exposed to the leopard, and after one bite he was drenched with such a quantity of blood that, as he was leaving the amphitheater, the crowd shouted out, "Well-bathed! Well-bathed!"—a testimony to his second baptism, for certainly he who has bathed in this way is quite well saved.[25]

---

24. I Corinthians 13:16.

25. The crowd tauntingly uses a formula of good wishes from the public baths, *salvum lotum*, literally "well-bathed." The writer reinterprets the words in the Christian sense, *salvum* as "saved" and *lotum* as "washed (in baptism)."

Then to Pudens the guard he said, "Goodbye. Remember your faith, and me. What happened here should not disturb you, but should strengthen your faith."

As he said this he asked Pudens for the ring from his finger, dipped it in his wound, and returned it, leaving it to him as a kind of legacy, a pledge and reminder of his bloodshed. Shortly thereafter, now unconscious, he was laid out with the others to have his throat cut in the usual place.[26]

But the crowd demanded that the victims be brought back out into the middle of the arena, so their very eyes could join in, as murderous accomplices to the sword as it penetrated their bodies. The martyrs got up of their own free will and went where the crowd wanted, but not before exchanging kisses, so as to consummate their martyrdom with the sign of peace. The others took the sword in silence and standing still, especially Saturus, who had ascended the staircase first, and was the first to die. For once again he was waiting for Perpetua.[27] Perpetua, however, so she could savor the taste of pain, gave out a wail as she was stabbed to the bone. Then she took the faltering hand of the gladiator—he was a young trainee—and guided it to her throat. Perhaps a woman as great as she, an object of fear even to an unclean spirit, could not be killed unless she herself actively desired it.

Ah, most valiant and blessed martyrs! Truly are you called and chosen for the glory of our Lord Christ Jesus. Anyone who exalts, honors, and adores that glory should read these new deeds of heroism, which are no less beneficial for the edification of the church than older ones. These new examples of courage will bear witness that one and the same Spirit, God the omnipotent father, and his son Jesus Christ our Lord, to whom is the glory and immeasurable power forever, still operates even today. Amen.

---

26. Presumably the *spoliarium*, where armor (*spolia*) was stripped from dead gladiators.

27. A reference to Perpetua's vision (ch. 4), where she saw Saturus at the top of the ladder, "waiting for her."

# PETRONIUS

(1st century AD, wrote in Latin)

## Introduction

P. Petronius Niger was a member of the court of the Emperor Nero (reigned AD 54–68). He is described by the historian Tacitus (*Annals* 16.18–19) as a voluptuary, a Roman who abandoned himself to idleness and luxurious living. Despite this, Petronius served as consul in AD 62 and later as governor of the important province of Bithynia. He gained influence with the emperor as an "authority in matters of elegant living" (*elegantiae arbiter*), according to Tacitus. Amid the turmoil of the Pisonian Conspiracy, a rival succeeded in turning Nero against him. Petronius opted for suicide, which he carried out with theatrical panache (AD 66).

Petronius' now fragmentary novel *Satyricon* is the earliest surviving example of a novel in Latin. The novel was not seen as a prestigious form, like epic, but as a kind of light entertainment. The typical ancient novel, as known from Greek examples, features the separation of two young lovers and their successful reunion after much wandering and many trials. The *Satyricon*, by contrast, is less romantic and more satirical. The title seems to mean "Book of Satyr Stories," which suggests racy, sexual content. But an allusion to the genre of *satura*, Latin satire, is also probably intended. The plot of the *Satyricon* is difficult to reconstruct in full, since most of the work is lost. But it is clear that it follows the episodic misadventures of the narrator, Encolpius, and his comrade Ascyltos, as they travel around Italy. Both Encolpius and Ascyltos are impoverished, vagrant young scholars. They are joined in the excerpt given here by Giton, a pretty, adolescent boy (Encolpius' darling), and by Agamemnon, a professor of rhetoric. Agamemnon has been invited to dinner by Trimalchio. Trimalchio, once a slave, is now a rich and ridiculously tasteless freedman who shocks his guests with bizarrely pretentious and vulgar displays of his wealth, as well as showing a lack of basic education that was a mark of the true Roman aristocracy. "Trimalchio's Dinner Party" begins with a preliminary visit to the baths, followed by hors d'oeuvres. Then there is some conversation among the other freedmen around the table; a joke that Trimalchio plays on his guests; two ghost stories; and finally Trimalchio's description of his rise from slavery to riches and his rehearsal of his funeral.

Besides being a comic and satirical tour de force, the dinner party of Trimalchio is valuable for its (inevitably distorted and exaggerated) depiction of Roman social life in a wealthy freedman's house around the time of the destruction of Pompeii. (The story seems to be set in Puteoli, modern Pozzuoli, not far from Pompeii.) Some aspects of the life described in it can be paralleled in Roman inscriptions and other texts, and these can be followed up via the footnotes. Ellipses (". . .") indicate places in the text that have been lost, not purposeful excerpting on the part of the editors.

## Trimalchio's Dinner Party

[26] It was the third day now, and we were expecting our farewell dinner, but we were dug through with so many holes that we preferred to flee rather than wait and see. While we were glumly and nervously debating which tack would get us out of the looming storm, a slave of Agamemnon's broke in. He said, "Say, you don't know where it's happening today? Trimalchio, who is one high-living individual . . . keeps a water clock in his dining room, and a trumpeter in a sort of uniform, so that the master can always tell how much of his life he's wasted." We forgot all about our troubles and got dressed in our best. Giton was happy to play our slave for the occasion, and we told him to come along to the baths[1] to help us get ready. . . .

[27] Then we wandered around, still in our clothes, making jokes and mingling with the circles of ballplayers. But suddenly we saw a bald old man, dressed in a dark red tunic, tossing a ball among long-haired boys. These boys were worth looking at, but they weren't what drew us to the performance. It was the head of the household in his slippers, working out with a chartreuse ball. He didn't even retrieve the balls that fell to the ground—an attendant slave had a full bag of them with which to keep supplying the players. Another innovative feature of the scene was the two eunuchs on the side of the circle facing the master. One was holding a silver chamber pot, and the other was counting the balls—not the number whizzing in the air, but those that fell to the ground. While I was gaping at these fripperies, Menelaus[2] ran up to me and said, "This is where you're propping up your head tonight. What you're seeing now is the way a dinner party starts for him." Menelaus was still talking when Trimalchio snapped his fingers and the one eunuch held the chamber pot for him. He emptied his bladder, asked for water, sprinkled his fingers lightly and dried them on a slave's hair. . . .

[28] We didn't have time to take everything in. We went in to bathe, took a sauna, and leapt into the cold water. Trimalchio, soaked in scented oil, was already being patted down, not with the usual linen towels, but with cloths of the finest wool. In the meantime, three masseurs were guzzling Falernian wine in front of him. They even squabbled and spilled a lot of it. Trimalchio laughed and said they were making a funeral libation for him.[3] Then they wrapped him up in a scarlet bathrobe, put him on a litter, and carried him down the street. There were four attendants ahead of him, dressed in uniforms with badges, and a little cart carried his pet slave,[4] a wizened little boy with cruddy eyes, uglier than Trimalchio himself. The whole of the old man's way home, a musician walked along beside him and played tiny pipes right in his ear, as if he were telling a secret.

---

1. These would be public baths, which filled most of the functions of a modern gym or health club. A daily trip to the baths was usual for Romans, especially before a dinner party. See *A Roman Schoolbook* chs. 10–11 in this volume.

2. An assistant to Agamemnon. In Greek myth, Menelaus is Agamemnon's younger brother.

3. Wine was poured onto the ground to appease the spirits of the underworld. See Catullus, poem 101 in this volume.

4. On the pampered "pet" slaves sometimes kept by the Roman wealthy, see Juvenal, *Satire* 3.185–89 in this volume.

We were already sated with wonder. But we followed, along with Agamemnon, and came to a door with this notice nailed to the frame: ANY SLAVE WHO GOES OUT WITHOUT THE MASTER'S PERMISSION WILL RECEIVE A HUNDRED LASHES. Inside the entrance there was a doorkeeper dressed in a chartreuse tunic and a cherry-colored belt, shelling peas on a silver tray. A gold cage hung over the threshold, and the spotted magpie inside greeted us.

[29] While I was casting my eyes about in amazement, I saw something that nearly made me fall on my back and break my legs. To the left as you came in, near the door-keeper's cubicle, was a wall painting of an enormous chained dog, above an inscription: BEWARE OF DOG. My partners in this dining venture thought my reaction was hilarious, but I ignored them. Catching my breath, I looked along the whole wall. There was a slave market, with the slaves all carrying signs describing themselves, and Trimalchio as a long-haired boy was entering the city. Minerva led him, and he held a herald's wand like the one Mercury carries.[5] Then you saw him learning how to keep accounts, then becoming manager—the conscientious painter had shown it all and put captions everywhere. At the end of the portico Mercury took Trimalchio by the chin and lifted him up to the magistrates' platform.[6] The goddess Fortune was present at the scene, holding a horn of plenty, and the three Fates were spinning golden threads.[7] There was more to see in the portico: a group of runners was exercising with their trainer, and a large cabinet stood in a corner, with a miniature shrine containing silver Lares, a marble statue of Venus, and a gold box of no petty size. Somebody told me that the hairs from the first shave of Himself were stored there. . . .[8]

I ventured to ask the steward what the other paintings on display depicted. "The *Iliad* and the *Odyssey*," he said, "and those gladiator games Laenas sponsored." [30] I didn't have time to look at everything in detail. . . .

Now we came to the dining room, in front of which a bookkeeper was checking accounts. What looked really strange to me was a bundle of rods and axes on the door post, with a sort of ship's beak coming out of the bottom of the bundle. On this was inscribed, "For Gaius Pompeius Trimalchio, a sevir of Augustus, from Cinnamus his manager."[9] There was also a two-branched lamp with the same inscription, hanging from the ceiling. A plaque hung on each side of the door. One said, "On December 30

---

5. Minerva here represents astuteness and the skilled trades. Mercury (Hermes in Greece) was the patron god of businessmen.

6. The painting depicts the crowning moment of Trimalchio's career, his elevation to service as a public official on the Board of Six (*seviri Augustales*), one of the colleges of priests for the cult of divinized Roman emperors that existed in many towns in Italy and the provinces. It was the highest public distinction to which a freedman might aspire. For a real life example of a freedman who obtained this rank, see Inscriptions no. 47 in this volume; and see just below, where Trimalchio is called "sevir of Augustus."

7. The threads the Fates spun governed the length and quality of a mortal life.

8. The Lares (small statues of household gods), the statue of a patron deity, and the souvenir of the ceremonial first shave would all be normal objects in a domestic shrine—but for an aristocratic Roman, not for a freedman like Trimalchio.

9. A strange hybrid image of the *fasces*, reserved for high magistrates, and ships beaks, which were symbols of a victory in a sea-battle.

and 31, our Gaius[10] is dining out"; the other had the phases of the moon and the movements of the sun and the six planets painted on it, and the lucky and unlucky days had markers of different colors.

We were simply stuffed full of delights. When we tried to go into the dining room, a slave yelled, "Right feet first!" Evidently, that was his job. Of course, we were alarmed at the thought of breaking the rule. But as we lifted our right feet in tandem, a stripped slave collapsed before us and launched into a plea for us to deliver him from a whipping. He hadn't sinned greatly, he claimed, or not in proportion to the punishment threatened. He had been left to watch the manager's clothes in the public baths—scarcely ten thousand sesterces' worth of clothes[11]—and someone had stolen them. We drew back our feet and went to find the manager. Locating him in a little office counting gold coins, we delivered our entreaties on the slave's behalf. Haughtily, he lifted his face to us and said, "It isn't the material loss that troubles me, as much as the carelessness of that worthless chattel. He lost my evening clothes, which a client of mine gave me for my birthday—Tyrian-dyed fabric and all, you know—but they'd already been washed once. Oh well. I'll let him off as a favor to you."

[31] We felt ourselves bound by such a substantial service. Now we went back to the dining room. There, our beneficiary ran up and nailed a dense series of kisses on us before we could think of resisting. He was full of praise for our kindness and remarked, "You're going to find out soon that I'm a person who knows how to return a favor. It's the master's wine, but that doesn't matter as long as the waiter's your friend."

We lay down, and slave boys from Alexandria poured water cooled with snow over our hands. Others came along and gave us pedicures with a good deal of skill. They weren't silent even in such a disgusting task—they sang the whole time. I wanted to find out if the whole household sang, so I asked for a drink. The waiter answered me most readily with a shrill musical comedy number. Anyone who was asked for anything responded in the same way, so that it sounded like a stage chorus, not the staff of a respectable dining room.

In any case, they brought us really swell hors d'oeuvres. (Everybody had taken his place but Trimalchio; the place of honor was saved for him, a practice I had never seen before.)[12] On the relish platter was a donkey made of Corinthian bronze, and he was wearing little dishes in the form of saddlebags containing black olives on the one side, white on the other. Two other platters (with Trimalchio's name and the weight of the silver inscribed on the rim) flanked the donkey. On one were welded little bridges, receptacles for cooked dormice that were dipped in honey and sprinkled with sesame seed. On the opposite platter was a toy silver grill, sausages on top and Syrian plums and pomegranate seeds underneath standing for hot coals.

[32] We were deep in this luxury when they carried in Trimalchio—to musical

---

10. When he was a slave Trimalchio would have had a single name; as a freedman he assumed the full three names of a male Roman citizen. Freedmen typically reveled in their first name (*praenomen*), which they received when they were freed. See Appendix "Roman Naming Conventions."

11. An absurdly large sum for clothing.

12. In a traditional Roman dining room, the couches formed three sides of a square, with tables inside, in front of the couches. There was a clear hierarchy to the placement of guests; a host was not supposed to occupy the place of honor, which was reserved for a guest.

accompaniment—and placed him among a lot of minuscule pillows. Those of us who hadn't known what to expect burst out laughing. The host had on a tightly clasped scarlet cloak that squished his closely shaven head out the top and weighed on his neck in massive folds. He had a napkin, with a senatorial stripe and tassels on it, shoved in there too. On the little finger of his left hand he wore a big gilded ring. The ring on the knuckle of the next finger looked like solid gold—except for the iron star shapes welded onto it.[13] As a further display, he bared his right arm, on which he wore a gold bracelet and a circlet of ivory fastened with a glittering metal plate.

[33] He picked his teeth with a silver toothpick and said, "Friends, it didn't suit me to come in yet, but to keep from holding you up I gave up all my own pleasure. But I hope you'll let me finish my game here." A slave came up to him with a board made of rare terebinth wood, and crystal tiles, and then I saw the daintiest thing of all: instead of black and white counters, he was using gold and silver Greek coins. As he played, he munched on a lot of crude language—the sort of thing blacksmiths and weavers say over their work.

While we were still busy with the hors d'oeuvres, they brought in a stand that had on it a wooden hen holding her wings out in a circle, as if she were brooding. Two slaves came up quickly. At a blast from the musicians, they rooted in the straw for peacock eggs and distributed them to the guests. Trimalchio turned his face to this tableau and said, "Friends, I ordered them to put peacock eggs under the chicken, and, by Hercules, I think they may be already turning into chicks. But let's check and see if they're still suckable." We got egg spoons that weighed at least half a pound each, so we could pierce the shortbread outer layer. I almost threw away my egg, because it looked as if the chick was already formed. But then I heard a veteran guest of Trimalchio's say, "This ought to be something good." I broke the shell with my hand and found a fat fig-pecker bird cooked in a peppered yolk.

[34] Trimalchio interrupted his game to demand a helping of everything for himself, and was yelling that if anybody wanted a mulled drink, he gave permission for one. Then suddenly the band gave a blast, and a trilling chorus took away all of the hors d'oeuvres at once. In the uproar, a dish happened to fall. A slave picked it up. Trimalchio noticed, and ordered an ear-boxing for the boy and a re-dropping of the dish. The slave in charge of furnishings came in and proceeded to sweep the pieces of silver to the side along with the other rubbish.

Then two long-haired Ethiopian slaves came in with tiny bottles (like the ones used for sprinkling the sand in amphitheaters to keep the dust down), from which they poured wine onto our hands. Nobody offered water.

Praised for these elegant touches, the master said, "Mars likes a fair fight—everything equal. That's why I had everybody assigned his own table. It also means that these stinking slaves won't crowd around and get us in a sweat."

Right then, they brought wine bottles tightly sealed with gypsum. Labels were stuck on the necks saying, "Falernian Wine Bottled in the Consulship of Opimius. One Hundred Years Old." While we were reading this, Trimalchio clapped his hands and said, "Too bad! Wine lives longer than we do—it's pitiful. So down the hatch with this,

---

13. Again, Trimalchio appropriates symbols of the aristocracy for himself. The purple senatorial stripe (on a toga) represented high officials, and gold rings could be worn only by equestrians and senators.

huh? Drink some wine, life is fine. This is real Opimian I'm giving you. I served worse stuff yesterday, and the guests were much more substantial people." We guzzled, and rendered some carefully calibrated praise of the host's taste.

A slave brought a silver skeleton, put together in such a way that the joints and the backbone could be bent in any direction. He tossed it onto the table and moved the limbs in order to form different sexual positions. Trimalchio provided the commentary:

> "Woe is us!
> This is what happens, for all our fuss.
> When Orcus[14] comes to get us, this is what we'll all become.
> So while we're still alive, let's have some fun!"

[35] Following our praises, there came a dish more modest in size than the previous one had led us to expect. But its novelty drew everyone's attention. It was a round platter with the twelve signs of the zodiac on it, above each of which the architect of the thing had placed an appropriate food. Above the Ram there were "ram's head" chickpeas, above the Bull a piece of beef, above the Twins a pair of testicles and a pair of kidneys, above the Crab a crown, above the Lion an African fig, above the Virgin the uterus of a barren sow, above the Scales a set of scales with a different kind of cake in each tray, above the Scorpion . . . a stinging fish, above the Archer a crow, above the Goat a lobster, above the Water Carrier a goose, and above the Fish two mullets. In the middle was a chunk of sod with a honeycomb sitting on the grass. An Egyptian slave carried around bread in a silver basket . . . while the master mutilated a song from the mime called "The Silphium Gatherer."[15] As we glumly approached this crude repast, Trimalchio said, "C'mon, let's dine. It's fine to dine."

[36] No sooner was this said than there was a honk of music and four Mars dancers[16] rushed out and snatched away the top layer of the platter. This revealed fattened fowls and sows' udders and a hare that had been fitted with wings to make it look like a tiny, furry Pegasus. There were also four Marsyas figures, and out of little wineskins they were pouring a peppery garum sauce.[17] It flowed down into a sort of channel, where there were cooked fish arranged as if they were swimming. The slaves started the applause, and we took it up before we approached in mirth these most select substances.

Trimalchio's delight at the device was no less than ours. "Carver!" he said. A carver strode forward and, moving to music, sliced the food in such a way that he looked like a gladiator fighting from a chariot to the rhythm of a water organ. Softly, Trimalchio kept piling on the word "carver." Suspecting that so much repetition had to mean another piece of wit, I did not hesitate to ask my neighbor in the place above mine about this very matter. He had often witnessed things of this kind, and he said to me, "See the guy who's carving? He's called Carver. Whenever you say his name, you're giving him an order too. 'Carver, carve 'er.' Get it?"

---

14. A god of the dead.

15. Silphium was an aromatic plant from North Africa. For the theatrical form "mime," see Glossary.

16. The Salii ("Leaping Dancers"), whose dance was swift and rhythmic.

17. The delicacy "garum" was a sauce made from fermented fish.

[37] I couldn't swallow any more of the first course, so I turned in my naïveté to my previous informant and tried to get the whole story. I asked him who the woman was running back and forth. "She's Trimalchio's wife," he said, "called Fortunata,[18] don't count her money, measures it in bushel baskets. And what was she a little bit ago? Your guardian spirit is gonna have to forgive me for saying this: you wouldn't of wanted to take bread from her hand. Now she's on top of the world, somehow or other—she's Trimalchio's all or nothing. Anyway, if it was high noon and she told him it was midnight, he'd believe her.

"Himself doesn't know what he's got: he's that loaded. But that whore takes care of everything, she's everywhere—you wouldn't believe it. She's dry sober, knows exactly what she's talking about. You can see where all this gold comes from. But she's got a nasty mouth on her, like a pet magpie sitting on your bed and squawking at you. She likes you—great. She doesn't like you—ouch.

"Himself has got property as far as hawks can fly, plus cash on top of cash. He's got more silver lying in his doorkeeper's office than anybody else ever inherited. His slaves—hell's bells—I don't think a tenth of 'em know their master by sight. He could toss any of these rich bastards into a pan and braise 'em. [38] Don't you think he buys stuff. Everything's homegrown: wool, cedar resin, pepper. Looking for chicken's milk? You'll find it. Anyway, he wasn't happy with the wool from his estates, so he brought rams from Tarentum and had them ball his herd. He wanted his own Attic honey, so he had bees imported from Athens. Some are gonna breed into his stock and make his own little boys a little better. Just a couple days ago he ordered mushroom spoor from India. Hasn't got a single mule that a wild ass didn't sire. All these pillows here: they got purple or scarlet stuffing. This is a guy who's found true inner peace.

"But don't put down them other freedmen. They're loaded. The one in the lowest place on the lowest couch—eight hundred thousand at the moment. Grew from nothing. Not long ago used to carry wood on his back. They say—I don't know a thing about it, I've just heard—he stole a gnome's hat and found a treasure. But he's kind of a blowhard, wants to show how good he's doing. Just lately, when he had to advertise for a tenant, he put up a sign that said, 'Gaius Pompeius Diogenes is letting his apartment from the first of July. He's buying a house for himself.' The one in the 'freedman's place'[19] had it great. I got nothing against him. He saw a million sesterces in his day, but then it all started to sway. I bet he's mortgaged his own hair. Not his fault, of course. There's no better man than him, but some asshole freedmen took over everything. Listen: even water don't boil worth a damn if the cooks are a committee, and when your business starts to slip, there go your friends. Look at him. He had such a respectable profession too: undertaker. He used to dine like a king: boars in blankets, cakes like works of art, birds, . . . cooks, bakers. More wine got spilled under his table than other people have in their cellars altogether. He wasn't a man, just a piece of theater. When his business started to slide, and he was afraid his creditors would find out he was about to go belly-up, he advertised an auction with a sign like this: 'Proculus is holding an auction of his spare possessions.'"

[39] Trimalchio interrupted these winning tales. The dish had been removed, by the

---

18. "Lucky," or "Rich."
19. The middle place on the lowest couch.

way, and the lighthearted guests were investing all their efforts in wine and gossip. So Trimalchio propped himself and said,

"This wine—it's all I got, but I hope you enjoy it. Fish gotta swim. Hey, did you think I'd be happy with the food on the top of the dish? 'Is this the Ulysses you know?'[20] How come I did it? Well, you've gotta know a little literature, even if it's only for the dinner table. God bless my master—rest his bones!—who wanted me to be as good as the next man. There's nothing that's new to me—as you can see from that dish. The sky here, where the twelve gods live, turns itself into twelve pictures: same number, hey? First you get the Ram. Whoever's born under that sign has lots of herds and lots of wool. But he's got a hard head and a face that shoves in where it's not wanted, and a sharp horn. A lot of mutton-headed schoolteachers were born under this sign."

We praised his astrological sophistication, and he continued: "Then the whole sky becomes a Bull-y boy, where you get people who kick out at you, and plowmen, and people grazing in green pastures. In the Twins are yokes of horses and yokes of oxen and people with big balls and people who play both sides of the fence. I was born in the Crab. I've got a lot of things propping me up, and I own a lot of stuff both on land and sea—a crab fits in both places. So I don't never put anything over the Crab, 'cause I don't wanna crowd my sign. In the Lion, you get gluttons and bosses; in the Virgin, skirt chasers and runaway slaves and slaves in chains. In the Scales, there are butchers and perfume dealers and anybody else who weighs anything; in the Scorpion, poisoners and assassins; in the Archer, wall-eyed people—in the marketplace you see them looking at the vegetables and picking up the lard; in the Goat, those poor bastards who grow horns on their heads from worrying so much. In the Water Carrier, you get innkeepers who water the wine, and people with water on the brain; in the Fish, caterers and fish-faced rhetoricians. The world turns like a grindstone, and there's always something iffy going on, people getting born, people dying, you name it. Okay, the sod in the middle and the honeycomb on the sod? I don't do nothing for no reason. Mother Earth is the sod, round like a big egg, and she's got everything good in her like a honeycomb."

[40] "Brilliant!" we all yelled, lifting our hands up toward the ceiling, and we swore that, compared to Trimalchio, Hipparchus and Aratus[21] were practically subhuman. Then servants came in and hung valances on the couches—backdrops that showed nets, and hunters lying in wait with spears, and everything else you would associate with hunting. We didn't know yet where our suspicions should be headed, but soon an immense racket came from outside the dining room, and now there were Spartan hounds running around the tables. A platter followed, with a gigantic boar on it—a freedman's cap on its head, no less. From its teeth hung little baskets woven from palm leaves, the one full of Syrian dates, the other of Egyptian ones. Set up to look as if they were pressed to the udders were little piglets made of biscuit dough; obviously, it was a mother sow. These piglets turned out to be party favors. Carpus, who had hacked up the fat fowls, was not the one to carve the boar; instead, it was an immense man with a beard and leggings and a multicolored short cape. He drew a hunting knife and slashed the side of the boar passionately, and thrushes flew out of the gash. As these

---

20. A quotation from Vergil, *Aeneid* 2.44. Ulysses (Odysseus) was known for his cleverness.
21. Famous Greek astronomers.

fluttered around the dining room, bird catchers with limed reeds caught them in no time. Trimalchio had one bird brought to each of us, and added, "You see what juicy acorns that oinker was eating in the forest."

As soon as they heard this, slaves ran up to the baskets hanging from the tusks and divided the different figs among the guests by careful count. [41] Meanwhile, in the privacy of my mind, I was pulled apart by various speculations concerning why the boar had come in with a freedman's cap on. After I had internally used up all of my stupid guesses, I steeled myself to ask my informant about this matter that was torturing me. He said, "Even your slave could tell you this: it's not a riddle, just common sense. This boar was supposed to be the high point of the dinner yesterday, but the guests *let it go*. That's why it comes back to our party today as a freedman." I cursed my thick-headedness and didn't ask any more questions, afraid that it would look as if I had no experience of decent society.

During this interchange, a comely boy came in, crowned with vines and ivy leaves. He called himself Bromius, then Lyaeus, then Euhius.[22] He carried bunches of grapes around in a little basket and travestied his master's poems in a squealing voice. Trimalchio faced this sound head-on and said, "Dionysus, have your Liber-ty!" The boy took the cap of freedom off the boar and placed it on his own head. Then Trimalchio added, "You're not gonna be able to say I don't have Father Liber, which means 'a free father,' ya know!"[23] We praised this pun, and when the boy came around for congratulations, we kissed him thoroughly.

After this course, Trimalchio got up to go to the toilet. Seizing our own liberty in the absence of our tyrant, we tried to get the other guests to talk some more. . . . Dama, after asking for a bigger wine cup, sighed, "A day's nothing. Turn around, and it's night. There's nothing better than goin' straight from bed to the dining room. It's a helluva cold day we've had here too. The baff—*bath*—barely warmed me up. But a hot drink's a clothes dealer who sells you a good thick cloak. I've poured whole jars down me, and I'm really pissed. The vine—*wine*—went straight to my head."

[42] Seleucus took up the tale in turn. "I don't take a bath every day. In the bath, you're like a cloth at the laundry—the water's got teeth in it. Your heart melts a little every day. But when I drink a pot of mulled wine, I tell the cold to go screw itself. But today I couldn't wash nohow. Had to go to a funeral.[24] That fine man, decent man, Chrysanthus, gave up the ghost and is no more. Just a few days ago he was there in the street, said hi to me. It's like he's still here now. It's just too damn bad: we're walking around, but there's nothing more inside us than if we was them blown-up bladders. We're worth the same as flies—no, flies've got something to them. We're like bubbles. If he just hadn't gone on that diet. For five days he didn't put a drop of water in his mouth, and not a crumb of bread neither. Well, he's gone off where most people have gone already. The doctors did him in—no, it was bad fates or somethin', 'cause a doctor's good for nothin' but to make you think you're gonna feel better.[25] But he had

---

22. Cult names of Bacchus, or Liber, the wine god.

23. The pun is on the Latin words *Liber Pater*, the Romans name for Bacchus. A slave was defined legally as "having no father."

24. It was a Semitic, not a Roman, custom to avoid bathing during periods of mourning.

25. Compare Martial *Epigram* 12 in this volume.

good rites, proper couch, nice blankets on it. Got a fine show of breast-beating from the guests, too—bunch of them were former slaves he set free—though his wife barely bothered to cry. Okay, so he didn't treat her as good as he might of. But women—you know women—they're like a flock of vultures. It don't help to do no good to nobody. It's like throwing it down a well. But love's a festering sore under your skin."

[43] He was being a pain, and Phileros shouted him down. "Let's talk about the living, huh? He got what was owing to him. Decent life, decent death. What has he got to complain about? He had it made, started from nothing, and he would have taken a penny out of a manure pile with his teeth. Everything he touched grew like a honeycomb. By Hercules, I think he left a good hundred thousand, all in cash. But I'll tell you the truth, and I wouldn't lie to you any more than a dog would: he was a mean bastard, had a real mouth on him—he was a walking fight. His brother was a straightforward kind of guy, treated his friends right, what was his was theirs, knew how to throw a party. But when Chrysanthus was getting started the bluebird of happiness crapped on him; still, he wiped himself off, and with his first vintage he was walking tall: he could sell as much wine as he had. And what really gave him a lift was that he got an inheritance that gave him a chance to swipe more than he got left. But he got mad at his brother and willed his money away out of the family, to somebody with no more background than a weed growing out of the dirt. It's a long trip when you leave your own people behind. But he had these slaves he listened to as if they had a direct link to the gods, and they did him down. If you believe what people tell you, you'll never get it right, at least if you're a businessman. But he had a good time, long as he lived. No justice in this world. He was Lady Luck's fair-haired boy, lead turned to gold in his hand. It's easy, when all your blocks of stone roll along like wheels. And how old do you think he was when he went? More than seventy. But he was hard as horn, aged well, hair black as a crow. I knew the man from way back, and he was as randy as ever. I don't think he left the dog alone. He was mostly one for the boys, but a jack of all trades, I guess. I've got nothing against it. That's the only thing you take with you."

[44] Thus spake Phileros. Ganymedes answered him thus: "What you're talking about has got nothing to do with anything. Nobody seems to care how the cost of bread gets you. Today I couldn't find a mouthful I could afford. And the way this drought is keeping up—for a whole year now it's pure starvation. I hope the aediles[26] get what they deserve for playing the bakers' game. 'You scratch my back, I'll scratch yours.' That's why the little people are having such a hard time, and the bigwigs have Saturnalia[27] all year round. If we just had those lions I found here when I first came from Asia. That was living. If the high-grade flour from Sicily went downhill, the magistrates used to pound them sellers on the heads like the wrath of the gods. I remember Safinius; when I was a boy he used to live by the old arch. He was a peppercorn, not a man. He used to sear the ground when he walked. But he was upright, reliable, a loyal friend if you treated him right. You could have played guess-how-many-fingers in the dark with him. When he was in the Senate house blasting away at people one by one, he didn't do any of those rhetorical dances, just talked straight. When he was arguing

---

26. Officials responsible for the regulation of marketplaces.

27. The Saturnalia was a festival in December that featured great merrymaking. See Glossary.

a case in court, his voice blared like a horn. And he never sweated or spat. I think the gods blessed him with a real solid-like constitution. And he was so civil in answering your greeting, remembered everybody's name, just like one of us. Back then, bread was dirt cheap. The loaf you could buy for a penny, you couldn't gobble up with a friend's help. I've seen bull's-eyes bigger than what you get now. Damn it, it's worse every day. The town's growing backwards like a calf's tail. How come? Well, we've got this two-bit aedile who'd sell us all for a penny. He's sittin' all cozy at home, makes more money in a day than anybody else has got in the family. And now I know where he got that thousand gold denarii, though I'm not sayin'. If we had any balls, we'd wipe that grin off his face. But the people are lions at home and foxes in public. As for me, I've sold every rag I owned just to feed myself, and if prices don't go down I'm going to have to let that little shack of mine go. What's going to happen if nobody, god or man, takes pity on this town? I'll bet anything that this is all a judgment on us. Nobody thinks the gods are real, nobody observes the fast,[28] nobody gives a damn about Jupiter. They pretend to be praying, but while their eyes are closed they're figuring out how rich they are right now. Before, the matrons in their long dresses went up the hill, barefoot, hair loose, pure in their thoughts, and asked Jupiter to send rain. And right away it started pouring by the pitcher like it was never gonna get another chance. And they all went back looking like drowned rats. But we're not observant anymore, so the gods have turned their backs on us. The fields are lying—"

[45] "Hey!" said Echion the rag dealer. "Watch what you're saying! The gods can hear it. 'Some black, some white, some shades of gray,' like the farmer described his lost spotted hog. Wait till tomorrow if you're not happy with today. That's how life lumbers along. By Hercules, we'd have a perfect town if it weren't full of these pesky human beings. These are hard times, but there're hard times everywhere. We shouldn't be picky: we all stand under the same sky. If you were somewhere else, you'd say that here the pigs walk around already roasted.

"Anyway, we're gonna have a great show in three days, on the holiday. It's not some pack of slaves from a gladiator school, but mostly freedmen. Titus's got big ideas, and he really goes for it. One thing or another, there'll always be something. I'm in and out of that house all the time, and, believe me, he don't do things by halves. It's gonna be pure steel, no mercy, a butcher's shop in that amphitheater, plenty for the crowd to see. He's got the wherewithal. He got left thirty million sesterces when his father died. Too bad! If he spends four hundred thousand his inheritance isn't gonna feel it, and people will be talking about him forever. He's got some dwarves, and a woman who fights from a chariot, and Glyco's steward, who got caught entertaining his mistress. You're gonna see the people slugging it out in the stands over this guy, the jealous husbands against the lover-poos. But Glyco's a two-bit character for giving his steward to the wild animals. He's just making a fool of himself. The poor slave only did as she ordered him. That piss pot of a woman is the one the bulls ought to be tossing. But if you can't beat the donkey, you beat the saddle. How did Glyco think Hermogenes' brat would turn out, anyway? That guy could have trimmed the nails of a hawk flyin' past him, and she's the same. A cobra don't sire a rope. Glyco—I mean it—Glyco's had it. As long as

---

28. Traditional Roman religion did not include fasts. Ironically, a speech in favor of old Roman ways reveals Eastern influences.

he lives, he'll have the mark of what he's done, and nothing but Hades will take it off. But everybody's got their own sins to worry about.

"At any rate, I'm getting a whiff of the banquet Mammea's gonna give us soon, with a gift of two denarii each for me and mine.[29] If that's what he does, he's gonna get all of the votes and beat Norbanus. Full speed ahead, he's gonna win. I mean, what did Norbanus ever do for us? Twobit, broken-down gladiators—blow on them and they fall over. I've seen people thrown to the animals who did better. He killed us a bunch of toy horsemen, who put up the same kind of fight chickens would. The one was thin as a stick, the one *he* fought was bandy-legged, and the challenger of the winner was a hamstrung wreck as dead as the loser. The Thracian[30] was the only one with any spirit, and he just fought by the rules, and that's no fun. They all got whipped in the end, there was so many people yelling, 'Give it to them!' It was like a rout. 'Well,' he said, 'I gave you a show.' Good for you. Add it up, and I give you more than I got. One hand washes the other.

[46] "I know what you're thinking, Agamemnon: 'What's that boob blabbing about now?' Well, you could conversicate, but you don't. You're not our sort, so you look down on the talk of people with a lower so-so economic status. We know you're off your head from reading—but what are we gonna do? Am I gonna talk you into coming out to the farm someday to see my little house? We'll find something to get our teeth into, a chicken, eggs, whatever. It'll be nice, even if the weather this year has shot everything to hell: we'll find something to fill up on.

"That little squirt of mine's growing up. He'll be a student for you soon. He can already recite his times table up to four. If he lives, you'll have a little servant at your side. Any time he's free, he's got his head bent over his writing tablet. He's bright, he's good stuff, but he's crazy about birds. I killed three of his finches and said that a weasel ate them. He's found other hobbies, though, and mostly he likes to paint. He's done with the Greeks now, and he's coming at Latin literature,[31] not doing so bad neither, even if his teacher thinks the world of himself and never sticks to the point. There's another one, though, who doesn't know much but takes some trouble, and he teaches more than he knows himself. He spends holidays at the farm, and he's happy with any tip you give him.

"Now I've bought the boy a bunch of them law books, 'cause I want him to learn a little law to use in the family business. That kind of thing buys groceries. He's already had more literature than's good for him. If he doesn't cooperate, I've decided to get him trained in a trade: barber or herald or at least advocate. Nothing but death can take your trade away. Every day, I yell at him, 'Primigenius, believe me, whatever you learn, you're learning it for yourself. You've heard of Philero the advocate? If he hadn't learned a trade, he'd be hungry every day. He used to carry peddler's goods around on his back. Now he's squaring up against Norbanus. Books is a treasure, and a trade don't die.'"

---

29. Cash gifts by potential, sitting, or former town councilors on special occasions were not uncommon. See Inscriptions no. 76 in this volume. Such people also financed gladiatorial games. See Inscriptions no. 73.

30. "Thracians" were a category of light-armed gladiators.

31. Compare the remarks on elementary education by Quintilian, *The Instruction of an Orator* selections B and G in this volume.

[47] These were the sort of monologues fluttering around when Trimalchio came back in. He wiped his forehead, washed his hands with perfume, and after a brief pause said, "Friends, forgive me. For days now my stomach hasn't answered the summons. The doctors don't know what to do. I got some help from pomegranate rind and pine resin in vinegar, though, and I hope my tum's gonna behave again. But for right now it's roaring like a bull. So if any of you wants to take some pressure off yourself, I understand. There's no reason to be ashamed. We're not born solid inside. I don't know of any torture that's so bad as holding it in. Even Jupiter can't hold it in. What are you laughing at, Fortunata? You're the one who keeps me up at night with your noises. In my dining room, I never kept nobody from doing what they needed to, and the doctors tell you not to keep it in. If you get the urge to do a bit more, everything's ready outside: water, pots, all the other odds and ends. Believe me, you can have the noxious vapors going to your brain and spreading through your whole body. I've known lots of people to die that way, not wanting to say what was going on, even to themselves."

We thanked him for his kindness and generosity and hurried to repress our laughter with uninterrupted gulps of wine. But we didn't know yet that we had toiled only halfway up the slope, as they say. After the tables were cleared—more music for this—three white pigs, with harnesses and bells on, were brought into the room. The announcer said that the one was two years old, the second three, and the third six. I thought it was going to be an acrobat show, that the pigs were going to do tricks, as in street performances. But Trimalchio banished this expectation. "Which one do you want to have for dinner right away? Yokels serve chicken, casseroles, all that nonsense. My cooks know how to boil calves whole in a pot." Right away he called a cook, and without waiting for our choice, ordered the oldest pig cooked. "Wait!" he shouted. "What division are you in?"

"The fortieth."

"Were you bought or born in the household?"

"Neither. Pansa left me to you in his will."

"Do a good job, then, or I'll have you put in the messengers' squad." The cook, admonished of his master's power, trailed the victual into the kitchen. [48] Trimalchio turned to us with a gentle mien. "If you don't like the wine, I'll change it. It's crap, I know, but that don't matter if you're enjoying yourself generally. By the favor of the gods, I don't buy it, or anything else. Everything to make your mouth water grows on my country estate, which I've never seen myself. They say it borders on Tarracina on one side and Tarentum on the other.[32] I want to add Sicily to my property now, so that when I feel like going to Africa, I can go through my own territory.

"But Agamemnon: what controversia did you do in declamation today?[33] I don't argue cases, but I've learned to read and write for business. I'm not one to put down book learning: I've got two bookcases, one Greek, one Latin. So go on and give me a précis (hey!) of your declamation."

"A rich man and a poor man had a dispute—"

---

32. Ridiculous. These Italian towns are a good 250 miles apart.

33. A reference to the practice debates on hypothetical legal cases employed in Roman rhetorical education. Agamemnon is a teacher of rhetoric. See Quintilian, *The Instruction of an Orator* selection H in this volume.

"What's a poor man?"

"Very witty," said Agamemnon, and outlined some controversia or other. Immediately, Trimalchio said, "If that actually happened, there's nothing *controversial* about it. If it didn't happen, then why bring it up at all?"

We followed up all of this with drooling eulogies, and he continued. "Agamemnon, I'm crazy about you. Tell me if you remember the twelve labors of Hercules? Or that story about Ulysses and how the Cyclops tore his thumb out with a pair of pliers? I used to read that in Homer when I was a boy.[34] I saw the Sibyl at Cumae with my own eyes. She was hanging in a bottle, and when the guys asked her, 'What do you want, Sibyl?' she said, 'I want to die.'"[35]

[49] Before all of the intellectual world had succumbed to the disease of his conversation, a platter with an immense pig on it took over the table. We were struck by the speed of the cooking, and we swore that even a chicken couldn't be done in so short a time. We were even more suspicious in that the pig looked bigger than before. Trimalchio inspected it more and more closely, and burst out, "What the—? This pig isn't gutted! By Hercules, it really isn't!"

The cook stood in front of the table and cringed and said he'd forgotten to gut the pig. "What?! You forgot?! He says it like he just forgot to put in pepper and cumin. Strip him."

In a moment, the cook was stripped and standing between two of the punishment crew. We started to beg him off. "It happens. Please, let him go. If he does it again, none of us will say a word for him." But I, as usual, was feeling intolerant and punitive. I couldn't hold myself back from leaning over to whisper in Agamemnon's ear, "I've never seen such a worthless slave in my life. How could somebody forget to gut a pig? By Hercules, I wouldn't pardon him if it had been a fish he'd forgotten to gut." But Trimalchio's face relaxed into a grin.

"Okay. Since you can't remember nothin', gut it in front of us."

The cook got his tunic back on, snatched a knife, and jabbed cautiously at the pig's stomach here and there. In no time, the weight of the flesh widened the cuts, and sausages and black puddings began to pour out.

[50] The slaves applauded this trick and shouted, "Long live Gaius!" The cook got a drink and a silver crown as a reward, and the cup came to him on a tray of Corinthian bronze.[36] When Agamemnon moved up for a closer look at this, Trimalchio said, "I'm the only one in the world who's got real Corinthian ware." I thought that, in line with his other bragging, he would say that he imported tableware directly from Corinth, but he outdid himself.

"Maybe you want to know why I'm the only one who's got real Corinthian ware. The dealer I buy from's called Corinthus, that's why. It's Corinthian because it comes

---

34. An outrageous error on the part of Trimalchio. Homer (*Odyssey* 9) has Odysseus blind the Cyclops with a stake. Trimalchio, though rich, lacks the education of a typical elite Roman.

35. The Sibyl at Cumae (near Naples) was a legendary prophetess. Apollo offered to grant her any favor she chose: she asked to live as many years as the number of grains of sand she held in her hand, but neglected to ask for eternal youth. Therefore, she aged continually, and was finally reduced to a sort of tiny mummy.

36. In the 1st century AD there was a craze for implements made of expensive "Corinthian" bronze, an alloy of bronze, silver, and gold.

from Corinthus—see? But I don't want you to think I'm a diddle-head. I know exactly where Corinthian bronze first came from. When Ilium was captured, Hannibal, that sly bastard, piled up all of the bronze and gold and silver statues in one pile and lit a fire under them.[37] They turned into a sort of mixed bronze; out of this glob the crafts-men took chunks and made plates and dishes and figurines. That's where Corinthian comes from—it's everything together, not one thing or another, but one big glob. If you'll pardon my saying so, I like glass better—doesn't smell, anyway. If it didn't break, it would be better than gold, but like it is, it's not worth havin'.

[51] "But did you know that there was a smith who made a glass bottle that didn't break? They let him in to see Caesar with his gift. . . . He made like he was gonna take it back from Caesar, but instead he threw it on the tiles. Caesar just about shit. But the smith picked up the bottle from the floor. It had a dent in it, like a bronze vase. Then he pulled a little hammer out of his pocket and took his sweet time mending the vase. When he was done, he thought he had Jupiter by the balls—he sure thought that after the emperor asked, 'Nobody else knows about this glass-making technique, right?' And get this: when the smith said no, the emperor had his head cut off, 'cause if word got out, gold would be the price of mud. I admit I'm a fan of silver. [52] I got three-gallon goblets . . . that show how Cassandra kills her sons, and the kids are lying there so real you'd think they were alive. I got a bowl King Minos left my old master, where Daedalus is shutting Niobe up in the Trojan horse.[38] Plus I've got all of the fights of Hermeros and Petraites[39] on cups, they weigh a ton. I wouldn't sell my taste for no money."

While Trimalchio was lecturing to us, a slave dropped a cup. The master gave him a look. "Go kill yourself, you useless piece of trash."

The slave pouted and begged for mercy.

"Why're you asking me? I'm not the one who's a pain in the ass. Go tell yourself not to be so useless."

We extracted a pardon for the slave, who then began to run around the table in his relief. . . .

Trimalchio was yelling, "Water out, wine in!" That was so hilariously clever that we had to show our appreciation—especially Agamemnon, who knew how to qualify for a repeat invitation. Encouraged by our praises, Trimalchio soused cheerfully. When he was close to flat-out drunk, he said, "Nobody's asked Fortunata to dance. Believe me, nobody beats her at the cordax."[40] Then he himself raised his hands above his head and imitated the actor Syrus. The slaves all sang along with a fake incantation from some play. He would have gone to the center of the room to dance where we could see him better, but Fortunata came up to whisper in his ear, probably saying that such trifling

---

37. Trimalchio, as usual, gets his facts mixed up. Ilium is the mythical city Troy, while Hannibal was the historical general from Carthage who invaded Italy in the late 3rd century BC. It was commonly thought by the Romans that Corinthian bronze, an alloy of bronze, silver, and gold, was first made by accident when Corinth was burned by the Roman army in 146 BC.

38. Again, Trimalchio is confused. It is Medea, not Cassandra, who kills her children, and the rest of the sentence is a garble of other mythological stories, all wrong.

39. These gladiators were mentioned elsewhere during the 1st century AD, which encourages scholars to date the *Satyricon* to this period.

40. An erotic dance.

behavior did not befit his position. I never saw anyone so unpredictable. Sometimes—now, for example—he listened to Fortunata, and sometimes he went his own way.

[53] In any case, he was distracted from his lust for dancing by an accountant, who read what sounded like the daily news at Rome. "July 26: On the estate at Cumae thirty boys and forty girls were born. Forty thousand bushels of grain were transferred from the threshing floor into storage. Five hundred oxen were broken to the yoke. The slave Mithridates was crucified for cursing the guardian spirit of our Gaius. On the same day, ten million sesterces were returned to the treasury, for lack of investment opportunities. Also, there was a fire in the Gardens of Pompey; it broke out in the mansion of the overseer Nasta."

"What?" said Trimalchio. "When did I buy the gardens of Pompey?"

"Last year," said the accountant. "This is the first time they've figured in the accounts."

Trimalchio was furious. "If I buy a piece of land and I don't hear about it within six months, then I don't want it in the accounts at all."

Now the aediles[41] read their reports. A couple of foresters' wills gratefully acknowledged that Trimalchio had declined to be one of the heirs.[42] Then came the reports of bailiffs, and an account of a comptroller's separation from his freedwoman partner, who had been caught with a bath attendant. Finally, we learned that a steward had been banished to Baiae, a manager had been indicted, and a dispute between two valets had gone to court.

At last that was all over, and acrobats came onto the scene. Some big lunk held up a ladder so that a boy could climb it and dance to music on the top rung. There was jumping through flaming hoops and lifting of a six-gallon jug with teeth, and that sort of thing. Trimalchio was the only one impressed. He said that this art form was sadly unappreciated. Acrobats and trumpet players—that's what he liked. Other entertainments were pure crap. "I bought some slaves who knew Greek comedy, but I had them do Atellan farce.[43] And I made my Greek flute player play pop tunes."

[54] He hadn't finished this critical summary when the boy . . . fell on top of him. The slaves made an uproar—we guests did too, but not because of the low-life acrobat. He could break his neck for all we cared. We just didn't want the dinner party to end with us going into mourning for someone we didn't give a damn about.

Trimalchio sobbed and groaned and nursed his arm, which really didn't look badly injured to me. Doctors came running from all directions, and Fortunata was in the first wave of them, tearing her hair and bringing a basin. Woe was her, what had she done to deserve this? she exclaimed. The acrobat who had fallen wasted no time in making the rounds, throwing himself at all of the guests' feet and asking us to intervene on his behalf. I had an irritable suspicion that these pleas were the prelude to some new trick. I still had in mind the cook who had "forgotten" to gut the pig. I peered around the

---

41. Trimalchio's own private officers, not the public officers in charge of weights and measures.

42. The practice of making one's friends and family "co-heirs" with the emperor arose during the more abusive imperial regimes. The emperor was in effect bribed with a large portion of an estate, in the hope that he would allow the other heirs to keep the remainder. Trimalchio has graciously declined the perk of a tyrant.

43. A coarse form of slapstick comedy, native to Italy. On slaves kept for domestic entertainment as readers of comic plays, see Pliny, *Letters* 14 and 24 in this volume.

dining room, half expecting some stage machinery to burst out of the walls. I was even more on my guard when somebody began to beat a slave for wrapping the master's arm in a bandage that was plain white rather than purple. I wasn't far wrong about what was to come: Trimalchio ordered the acrobat who had fallen on him to be set free rather than punished. That way, no one could ever say that so great a man had been injured by a slave.

[55] We voiced our approval of this decision, and began to natter about the propensity of good fortune to take a tumble. "Right," said Trimalchio. "And I wanna commemorate this downfall with a couple of lines." He asked for a writing tablet and, without racking his brains too long, recited:

"The unexpected always hits you from behind.
And Fortune has her own agenda in mind. Waiter,
    bring us more Falernian wine!"

This epigram opened up the subject of poets. Mopsus the Thracian seemed to be held in the highest favor generally. But Trimalchio said to Agamemnon, "You're a teacher: how does Cicero stack up against Publilius?[44] Cicero's more sort of 'eloquent,' but I think Publilius has got solider values. Ever hear anything finer than this?

"The citadel of Mars is pining away,
Caught in the massive maw of luxury.
The peacock, clad in Babylonian tapestry
Of plumage, fattens in captivity
To sate your appetite. Numidian hens
And eunuch capons serve you. Even the stork,
Sweet, welcome foreign guest with slender legs
And castanet bill—so gentle with its young—
Avian avatar of spring, exile from frost,
Has nested in your cooking pot of greed!
What use the costly pearl, white berry grown
In India? Should matrons wearing these
Insignia of the seas lie on strange beds
And spread their legs with overwhelming lust?
What good are emeralds, prized virid glass,
Or carbuncles, those stones of crimson fire?
Does virtue shine more brightly clad in gems?
Should brides put on a fabric made of wind,
And naked walk the streets in linen clouds?

[56] "Okay, being a scholar is the hardest, but what's the second hardest? I think it's being a doctor or a money changer. A doctor's gotta be able to guess what's going on in people's guts. He's gotta predict when a fever's gonna start. But I hate doctors. They put me on a diet of nothing but duck meat. Your money changer's got it hard because he has to see through the silver coating to the worthless copper. If we're talking about

---

44. Again, Trimalchio mixes up genres, comparing the orator Cicero to Publilius the writer of mimes (see Glossary). The following lines are probably a parody of Publilius rather than a quotation from his work.

animals, then the hardest working ones are oxes and sheep. The oxes feed us all by pulling them plows, and we owe it to the sheep that we can strut around in good clothes. I think it's outrageous that some people wear clothes and eat lamb at the same time. In my opinion, bees are magic animals, barfing up honey that way—even though they're supposed to be getting it from Jove. They sting, but where there's something sweet there's gotta be something that hurts too."

On he went, putting the philosophers out of work, but he was interrupted by a slave coming around with a jar full of cards and reciting the names of party favors as the cards were drawn.

> "Hamstrung:" the prize was a ham tied up with string.
> "Headrest:" a joint of neck meat
> "Too soon old and too late smart:" some wilted parsley and musty stinging nettles
> "Contumely:" a sow's vulva and some ground meal
> "Fig-pecker and fly-catcher:" a fig tied to a dildo and some Attic honey
> "All dressed up for dinner or the forum:" a piece of meat and a writing tablet
> "Dog treat and a house for feet:" a hare and a shoe
> "Parrot fish:" a dead parrot and fish tied together
> "The letter Beta:" a beet

[57] Ascyltos[45] never did bother to hold back. He threw his hands up in sarcastic wonder and laughed himself to tears. This angered one of Trimalchio's fellow freedmen—the one next to me, in fact—who demanded, "What are you laughing at, you dumb ox? Ain't the gentleman our host elegant enough for you? Sure, you've got more money than he's got. Your parties are lots better. The gods of this place help me: if I were lying next to that guy I'd shut his bleating mouth up. Nice job, laughing at other people, when you're nothing but a runaway, not worth your own piss! If I let that dumb-ass have it, he wouldn't know which way to turn. By Hercules, it takes me a while to get worked up, but he's asking for it. Like they say, if the meat's rotten the worms are gonna breed. He's laughing. What's he got to laugh at? Yeah, I bet his father vowed heaps of money to the gods, to get a son as fine as him. You're a Roman knight?[46] Sure, and I'm a king's son. So why was I a slave? I volunteered. I thought it was better to become a Roman citizen someday than stay a provincial just payin' the taxes. And I hope I live a life that don't make me nobody's joke. I'm a man good as any other, walk with my head high and don't hide from nobody. I don't owe a red cent. Nobody hauls me into court, nobody stops me in the forum and says, 'Pay up!' I've bought a bit of land and some precious metals. I feed ten stomachs and the dog as well. I bought my partner out of slavery, to keep her master's dirty hands off her. I paid a thousand denarii for my own freedom. I was voted onto the board in charge of the emperor's worship,[47] and they waived the usual fee. When I'm dead, I won't blush about the life I led. You're busy passing judgment on other people? Why don't you watch your own ass? You see a louse on someone else, but there's a tick on you. You're

---

45. Friend and comrade of the narrator, Encolpius.

46. "Knight" here refers to a member of the equestrian class. See Glossary, *equites*.

47. The Board of Six. See Glossary, *Augustalis*.

the only person here who thinks we're funny. Look at your teacher, he likes us—and you oughta take your cue from somebody like him, who's been around. You're still nursing, haven't said your first words. I could break you like a clay jar, rip you like a piece of leather that's rotted in the water. So you've got more money than we do? You can have two lunches and two dinners every day, for all I care. My good name is worth more to me than piles of money. Here's the bottom line: I pay when the bill comes. I was a slave for forty years, but nobody knew whether I was a slave or free. I was a little boy with long hair when I came here. The town hall wasn't even built yet. But I took care to live up to my master's expectations. He was the finest man that ever was—his little pinkie was worth more than all of you is. There were people in that house who tried to trip me up—the usual stuff—but my master's guardian spirit looked out for me, and I came out smelling like a rose. That was a real workout, because, I'm telling you, being born free is as easy as ordering lunch. What are you staring at? You look like a goat that's stuffed hisself on vetch and's just standing there waiting to fart."

[58] At this trenchant observation, Giton[48] (who was standing in attendance) let out his long-suppressed laughter in loud snort—rather unseemly. Ascyltos' adversary turned to the boy, redirecting his harangue. "You too? *You're* laughing, you curly-haired little prick? Happy Saturnalia, hey? It's December already? When'd you pay your freedom tax? . . .[49] You're not good for nothing but to get nailed on a cross and feed the crows with your body while it rots. I'm so mad you're gonna think it's Jove himself coming down on you—and on that guy too, who don't bother to control you. I swear by the bread that fills my belly, I'd make short work of you right now if it wasn't for the gentleman our host, who's a freedman like me.

"We were all having a nice time, but then you worthless—like master, like slave. I can barely keep my hands off you—not that I'm mean by nature, but once I get started I wouldn't give two cents for my own mother. I'm gonna meet you afterwards, out in public, you little piece of shit. I'm gonna put your master in a damn tight place, and I won't forget about you either, by Hercules. You can scream to Jupiter on Olympus if you want, but it's not gonna do you no good. If I don't keep my word, then I'm not alive and sitting here in front of you. Lot of help that two-bit wig and your two-bit master's gonna be then. Just let me get my teeth into you. Either I don't know myself or you're not gonna be laughing for long, even if you put on a gold beard like a god's statue. I'm gonna bring Athena down on you like a ton of bricks—you and that guy, bet he's in your pants. I never studied geometry, or critical theory, or any of that crap, but I can read block letters, and I know my times table, which is good for small change or weights and measures or big cash amounts, doesn't matter. Let's settle this with a bet. Come on, put down a wager. I'll show you your daddy wasted his money, even if you do know rhetoric.

"What part of the body comes from all over? Or this one: What darts around but never changes place? What part keeps growing but keeps getting shorter?[50] I've got you now, I can see. You're stumped, you're scurrying around for a way out, like a mouse in a piss pot. So you can shut up now and leave your betters alone. They don't even know

---

48. A pretty, adolescent boy, Encolpius' darling.

49. A tax of five percent was levied on the market value of freed slaves.

50. Possible answers: the foot, the eye, hair.

you exist. Unless you think I'm impressed by that fake gold ring[51]—I can see it's made out of boxwood. Did you steal it from your girlfriend? I swear, by the god of getting ahead—let's go to the forum and do some business. You'll find out what my iron ring can do.[52] You'd look about as good as a fox soaked in the rain. I'm your executioner; I'm gonna chase you down. If I don't, the gods can make it so I don't make money and die like a gentleman, and nobody in town says, "Gods, I wanna die like that." The guy who taught you to behave like you do isn't a teacher, he's a turd. When we were young, we learned what we had to know. Our teacher said, 'Have you got your things together? Go straight home. No looking around. No back talk to your elders.' Now it's pure crap. Nobody grows up worth a damn. If I'm the man that's sitting in front of you, I owe it to my training."

[59] Ascyltos was poised to respond to this abuse. However, Trimalchio thought that the choice eloquence of his fellow freedman had charmed us long enough. "Come on, no more squabbling," he said. "Let's all calm down. Hermeros, let the boy alone. He's young and hotblooded. You should set an example for him. There's one way to win a fight like this: you back down. When you were a kid—hell, you didn't have no brains either. Let's start over and enjoy ourselves. Look, it's my Homer reciters."

A gaggle of them came in, slamming their shields and spears together. Trimalchio took a seat next to them on a big pillow and read aloud in Latin, with a singsong voice, while the reciters went through their usual pretentious exchanges of Greek verse. Well, it did end after a while.

Then Trimalchio said, "Ya know what myth they're doing? Diomede and Ganymede were two brothers. Helen was their sister. Agamemnon kidnapped her and left a doe so Diana wouldn't know the difference. So Homer tells us how the Trojans and the Tarentines had this big war. Agamemnon won, of course, and had Achilles marry his daughter. So Ajax went crazy—but he'll tell you about it himself."[53]

The Homer reciters started yelling, the slaves rushed out of the way, and, on a tray that must have weighed two hundred pounds, an entire boiled calf was brought in. It had a helmet on its head. Ajax came in next, with a drawn sword to signify that he was indeed insane. He hacked up the calf and with forehand and backhand motions gathered up the pieces and shared them out among the startled guests.

[60] But we didn't have long to gape at this tasteful turn of events. The ceiling panels began to groan, and the whole dining room shook. Alarmed, I got up—for all I knew, an acrobat was about to climb down through the roof. No less stunned than I was, the other guests looked up to see what divine portent was on its way. But the ceiling tiles merely swung aside, and a giant hoop was lowered down into the room. All around it hung gold garlands and alabaster bottles of unguent.[54] These, we were told, were our party favors to take home. Looking at the table. . . .

---

51. The accusation is of false display of social status.

52. Signet rings were used to sign contracts (an imprint was made in the document's wax seal). An iron ring indicated a status below equestrians.

53. As usual, Trimalchio completely garbles the myth of the Trojan War and the events leading up to it, except for the fact that the greater Ajax did go crazy and hacked up livestock in the belief that they were the Greek chieftains who had dishonored him.

54. For the use of scented oils at dinner parties, see Catullus, *Poems* 13 in this volume.

Now there was a tray covered with cakes. In the middle stood a pastry Priapus,[55] and from his ample appendage hung a sling full of different fruits, in the usual way it's pictured. We laid our greedy hands on this new display and found—imagine!—that it was another joke. At the slightest touch, every single cake and piece of fruit spewed out saffron—damp, messy stuff all over our faces, quite disgusting. We thought that a dish perfumed with this ritual substance was probably part of some important rite, so we jumped up and yelled, "Hail, Augustus, father of our country!" But we noticed that other people were grabbing fruit during our display of reverence; so we went ahead and got as much as we could tie up in our handkerchiefs—and I was particularly efficient at loading Giton's pockets: I thought that nothing was too much or too good for the boy.

Meanwhile, in came three boys with gleaming white tunics hiked way up. Two of the boys placed on the table a collection of household gods with amulets hanging around their necks. The third carried a dish of wine around, shouting, "May the gods be gracious to us!". . .

He said that the three were called Handy, Lucky, and Moneymaker. An image of Trimalchio himself—ugh, a good likeness too—appeared as well. The others kissed it, so we more or less had to.

[61] After all of the usual prayers for health and steadiness of mind, Trimalchio turned to Niceros and said, "You used to be more fun at a party. Don't know why, but I don't hear a mumble out of you now. Come on—if you care about me at all, you'll tell about that thing that happened to you."

Niceros was thrilled at the kind words. "May I never make no money no more if I'm not bustin' to pieces with happiness, 'cause I see you're doin' so well. So I'll tell you a real funny story—even if I'm scared of them scholars laughin' at me. Well, I'll just go ahead, and they can think what they want. They can laugh too—it won't hurt me none. It's better to get laughed at than to have somebody spit in your face or somethin'." Thus he spoke, and began the following tale.

"When I was still a slave, we lived in this narrow alley. It's Gavilla's house now. It must of been the will of the gods, 'cause when I was there I fell in love with the wife of Terentius who had the inn.[56] You guys all knew Melissa from Tarentum, what kind of gorgeous little dumplin' she was. But Hercules is my witness, I didn't love her because of her body. It wasn't no physical thing at all, but because she was such a decent woman. Anything I asked for, she gave me, never said no. . . . If she made a penny, that meant I had half a penny. I dumped everything I made into her lap, and she never done me wrong.

"Well, wouldn't you know, her partner out there in the country died. So I was frantic, tried to rig things every which way so I could go out and be with her. When you're in a tight spot, you find out who your friends are, so I wasn't gonna let her down. [62] It just so happened that the master was out at his estate at Capua to check up on some dumb thing or other. I grabbed the chance and persuaded a guest of ours to go

---

55. God of fertility whose phallus was extraordinarily large.

56. The inns of ancient Italy were as well known for prostitution as for rest and food. But this is a case of true love between the slave Niceros and the inn-keeper's wife—or perhaps the inn-keeper's informal companion, since he is referred to below as her "partner" (*contubernalis*), the word for a spouse in a quasi-marriage among slaves.

with me as far as the fifth milestone. He was a soldier, strong as hell. We get our butts moving when the cocks are starting to crow, but the moon was shining bright as noon. We came to a graveyard, and this pal of mine went off to the tombstones to take a piss while I say a spell or two to keep off evil and count how many stones there are. But when I turned back to him, he'd taken off all his clothes and put 'em in a pile beside the road. That sure knocked the wind outta me. I stood there like I was dead. He pissed around his clothes, and all of a sudden he turned into a wolf. I'm not joking. I wouldn't lie for all the money in the world. But like I was saying, once he was a wolf he started howling and ran off to the woods.

"First I was so scared I didn't even know where I was. Then I went up to get his clothes, but they'd turned to stone. I was just about ready to fall over dead. But I drew my sword and jumped on every little shadow, and I finally got to my girlfriend's place. By that time I looked like a ghost myself, I was practically takin' my last breath, sweat runnin' down through my crotch, blank eyes. The people there had some hard work bringin' me around.

"But my Melissa was amazed that I was out so late. She said, 'If you'd come a little earlier, you could of helped us out. There was this wolf that got into the stock. . . . It looked like a butcher'd been here. Well, he got away, but at least he don't have nothin' to laugh about. Our slave stuck his neck through with a spear.'

"When I heard that, I wasn't gonna sleep that night, that's for damn sure. But when the sun was up I ran home fast as an innkeeper runs after the guy that's gone without paying the bill. When I got back to the place where the clothes turned into rocks, I didn't find nothing but blood. Then when I got home the soldier was lying in bed helpless like a sick ox, and a doctor was looking at his neck. I knew then that he was a werewolf, and I wouldn't of sat down at the table with him if you'd killed me. You can have any opinion you want about what I've said. If I'm lying, your guardian spirits can get me for it."

[63] We were all struck with wonder and admiration. Trimalchio said, "I don't mean to say nothin' against your story—but believe me, my hair was standin' straight up, 'cause I know Niceros don't talk nonsense. No, you can count on him, he don't jabber for its own sake. But I can tell you a scary story too, amazing thing, like a donkey getting up on a roof.

"When I was a long-haired little boy—'cause I lived a pampered life the whole time—our master's favorite slave boy died. By Hercules, he was a pearl of a kid, sexy little number, nothing wrong with *him*. Well, his poor little mother was beating her breast, and a bunch of us were in mourning too, when all of a sudden the witches began to howl. It sounded like a dog running down a hare. We had this guy from Cappadocia[57] in the household—tall, not afraid of anything, and strong like you wouldn't believe! He could of gone against a bull that was in a bad mood. Doesn't hesitate, draws his sword and runs out the door. But first he's careful to wrap up his left hand. He sticks one of the women clear through, right here in the middle—may the gods protect what I'm touching now. We heard a groan, and then all the women disappeared. Weird, huh? But if I was lying, you could tell. Then that big lug of ours came back in and threw hisself down on the bed. He was bruised all over like he'd been

---

57. Producing a reputedly bold and hardy race.

whipped—it had to be 'cause them witches touched him. We closed the door and went back to keep mourning the little boy. But when his mother picked up the body to give it a hug, it was just a dummy full of straw. Didn't have no heart, no guts, nothing. The witches had taken the corpse and left this stuffed decoy.

"Listen, you better believe that there are these sorceress women. They go around at night turning everything upside down. The big guy, though—he never did look normal again. He went crazy, and a couple of days later he died."

[64] We were as amazed as we were credulous. We kissed the table and prayed to the creatures of the night to keep to themselves when we went home from the party. . . .

By this time, I was gazing at a single lamp and seeing several. The whole dining room looked different. Trimalchio said, "Hey, Plocamos, no stories? Nothing to enter-tain us? You used to be more fun, with the great stuff from plays you used to recite and sing and all. Too bad, all gone, like figs from last year."

"I've got the gout now," he said. "I'm a wreck. But when I was young I used to sing till I practically got TB from the strain—and that's sayin' nothin' of the way I used to dance and recite scenes, and do imitations of the talk in a barbershop. Apelles[58] was the only one who was ever half as good as me." He put his hand to his mouth and whistled out some garbage, which afterward he said was Greek.

Trimalchio himself was imitating the sound of a trumpet, but then he looked at his pet slave, who was called Croesus.[59] This was a cruddy-eyed little boy with teeth covered in scum. He had a black puppy, obscenely fat, that he was wrapping in a char-treuse scarf. He also put a half-eaten hunk of bread on the couch in front of the animal and forced the poor thing to eat, making it gag and heave.

[65] This scene of thoughtful husbandry reminded Trimalchio to have Scylax,[60] "the protector of hearth and home," brought into the room. In no time, the door-keeper fetched an immense dog on a chain and kicked it into a sitting position beside the table. Trimalchio took some of the white bread and tossed it to the beast, remark-ing, "Nobody in this house loves me more."

The boy was upset at such lavish praise directed toward the brute. He placed the puppy on the floor and urged it to fight. As a dog will do, Scylax filled the dining room with ear-splitting barking and lunged forward, nearly dismembering Croesus' little Pearlie. The tumult spread beyond the dogfight when a lamp on the table was tipped over, breaking all the crystal dishes and spattering some of the guests with hot oil.

Trimalchio, however, was chiefly concerned with appearing indifferent to the destruction of his treasures. He kissed the boy and offered him a piggyback ride. The little slave did not hesitate to mount his master and slap him again and again on the shoulder blades, laughing and shrieking the whole time, "Come on, horsy, how many fingers am I holding up?" This quieted Trimalchio down for a while, but then he ordered punch mixed in a giant bowl and divided among all of the slaves who sat at our feet. He stipulated one thing, though: "If there's anybody who won't take it, pour it over his head. The day's for work. Let's have some fun now."

---

58. The name of a tragic actor associated with the court of Caligula, in the late 30s AD.

59. Croesus, the name of a fabulously rich Lydian tyrant, is a ridiculously overblown designation for the child, but in a certain way appropriate for a representative of Trimalchio's household.

60. Greek for "Puppy Dog."

After this gracious gesture came a plate of snacks. Even the memory of them annoys me. Fattened chickens were passed around instead of the traditional thrushes. There were also garnished goose eggs. Trimalchio ordered us to eat up, adding the joke that the eggs were "boneless hens." During this course a lictor came banging on the double doors. In came a reveler, who was dressed in white and had an immense number of attendants. I was terrified at this display of authority and thought I must be facing the local praetor. I started to rise and set my bare feet on the floor, but Agamemnon laughed at my trepidation. "Calm down. You must be the dumbest man on earth. That's Habinnas, a sevir.[61] Also a stone mason. Makes nice tombs, I've heard."

Relieved, I put my elbow back on the couch, and, greatly impressed, observed Habinnas' entrance. He was already drunk, and dragged himself along by his wife's shoulders. A number of garlands weighed him down, and unguent dripped from his forehead into his eyes. He lowered himself into the place customarily reserved for the praetor and called for wine and hot water.

Trimalchio was charmed by this witty performance, called for a bigger cup himself, and asked how the previous party had turned out.

"We had everything but you," his friend answered. "My heart was here. By Hercules, though, it was nice. Scissa was having a memorial service for that poor slave of hers, the one she set free after he was dead. But now I guess she's having a big fight with the collectors of the five percent tax. They valued him at fifty thousand, just as a corpse. It was swell, though, even if we had to pour half our drinks over his bones."

[66] "But what'd you have at dinner?" Trimalchio asked.

"Let me see if I can tell you. Great memory I've got nowadays—forget my own name sometimes. The first course was a roast pig with a sausage garnish, plus blood pudding and chicken gizzards cooked just right, and—I know: beets and whole-wheat bread, which I think is better than white; it's nutritious, and I don't moan and groan when I do my business. The next course was a cold cheesecake, and warm honey with this great Spanish wine. I had a big gob of the cake, and honey up to my neck. On the side we got chickpeas and lupines, as many hazelnuts as we wanted, and an apple apiece. I sneaked two, though. Got 'em here in my handkerchief, 'cause if I don't bring a present to that little tyke of mine, I'll have trouble. Oh, my dearest here reminds me: we had a hunk of bear meat on the menu. Scintilla was stupid enough to try some, and she almost heaved her guts up. But I ate more than a pound. Tasted like boar. If bears eat up us poor people, then I don't know why people shouldn't eat bears. To finish off, we had soft cheese in wine sauce, and one snail each, and a piece of tripe, and chopped liver in little portions, and garnished eggs and turnips and mustard and a dish in that sauce that looks like poop—the recipe's called 'That's Plenty, Palamedes.'[62] Also we got served pickled olives in a big trough. Some of those bastards took three handfuls. We sent the ham back. [67] But tell me, Trimalchio: why doesn't Fortunata come lie down?"

"Oh, you know what she's like. She's gotta know where all the silver is, divide up the scraps among the slaves. She won't even have a drop of water till that's done."

---

61. Member of the Board of Six. See Glossary, *Augustalis*.

62. Palamedes was an important leader in the Greek campaign against Troy, but the meaning here is obscure.

"If she doesn't take her place on the couch right now, then my ass is out of here." He started to get up and was stopped only by all the slaves calling four or five times, on Trimalchio's cue, "Fortunata!" She arrived with her clothes hiked up by a bright yellow belt, so that underneath you could see her cherry-colored tunic, her anklets in a twisted shape, and her gilded slippers. She was wiping her hands on a towel that hung around her neck. She arranged herself on the couch on which Habinnas' wife Scintilla was lying. "Is it really you, honey?" Fortunata asked, bestowing a kiss, while Scintilla clapped her hands in glee.

It quickly got excessive. Fortunata pulled the bracelets off her hideously fat upper arms to give her admiring friend a better look. She finally unsnapped her anklets and took from her hair a net that she boasted was made of refined gold. Trimalchio noticed, and ordered all of this brought to him. "You see the shackles our women wear," he announced. "This is what we lunkheads get stripped bare for. This stuff must weigh six and a half pounds. But I've got an armband that weighs ten pounds, myself. It's made out of Mercury's thousandth share of my profits."[63] He didn't want us to think that he was lying, so he had a set of scales fetched and taken around to each of us, so that we could check the weight for ourselves.

Scintilla did not rise above these proceedings. She took from her neck a little gold locket—she even had a name for it: "Lucky." From this, she extracted dangly earrings and presented them for Fortunata's examination. "My man is so good to me," she said. "No woman's got a better pair than this."

"What are you talking about?" Habinnas interrupted. "You cleaned me out for a couple of glass beads. If I had a daughter, I'd just cut her ears off. Everything would be dirt cheap if it weren't for you women. You use up everything good: ice for your drinks, but plain hot piss comin' out of you."

But the women were already the worse for the wine and occupied with private laughter and sloppy kisses. The one was braggingly complaining about how much work it took to run a household; the other was loudly sharing her opinion about her husband's neglect of her and his preference for his pet slave. While they were clinging together, Habinnas sneaked off his couch and over to theirs. Seizing Fortunata's feet, he tossed her upside down. She shrieked, and we could see her dress go up over her knees. After putting herself back together, she huddled with Scintilla and hid her blazing blushes in a napkin.

[68] After a while, Trimalchio ordered the second course.[64] The slaves took away all of the tables and brought new ones, and scattered sawdust tinged with saffron and vermilion—also powdered mica, which I had never seen used this way. Trimalchio was not slow in commenting. "You think I'd be happy with an ordinary second course? Of *course* not. Get it? Of *course* not. Okay, if you've got anything good, boy, let us have it."

The Alexandrian slave boy in charge of the hot water started an imitation of nightingales, but Trimalchio snarled, "Not that!" The slave who sat at Habinnas' feet—suddenly, under orders from his master, it appeared—struck up a chant:

---

63. Trimalchio has apparently used for jewelry an offering owed to a god.

64. "Second course" here translates *secunda mensa*, literally "second table," which was the dessert course.

"'Meanwhile, Aeneas, with his fleet on the high seas. . . .'"[65]

It was the shrillest, sourest sound that had ever struck my ears; the voice veered up and down in a barbaric version of meter—and there were lines from Atellan farce mixed in! For the first time in my life, Vergil was painful to me. Finally, the boy grew tired and stopped, and Habinnas remarked, "He does that naturally—never went to school. But I educated him by having him follow the hawkers around. Nobody's as good as him at imitating them hawkers, plus mule drivers too. Incredibly talented kid: he's a tailor, a cook, a pastry chef at the same time. Sometimes the Muses just smile on a slave, you know? He'd be perfect if he didn't have two faults: he's circumcised and he snores. Okay, he's got a squint, but I don't care: so does the goddess Venus. He's always lookin' around, and he never keeps quiet. I paid just three hundred denarii for him."

[69] Scintilla interrupted. "You don't know all of that shit's tricks. I'm going to have him branded one of these days, the little pimp."

"I know what your husband's like," Trimalchio laughed. "He's a Cappadocean, damn sure to do right by himself. But I like that. You sure can't get it after you're dead. But don't be jealous, Scintilla. Believe me, we know what you get up to. So help me, I used to bang my own mistress. The master actually suspected, so he sent me off to run one of his farms. But there goes my mouth again. I'll give it some bread and make it shut up."

The slave was really abominably spoiled: he thought what he'd heard was to his credit. He took a clay lamp out of his pocket and spent more than half an hour imitating the sound of a trumpet on it. Habinnas hummed along, pressing down his lower lip. The slave even stepped to the center and mimed a flute player by brandishing a couple of reeds around. Then he wrapped himself up in a cloak, took a whip, and enacted the adventures of a mule driver. Habinnas called him over, kissed him, gave him a drink, and said, "You get better all the time, Massa. I'll give you a pair of boots for this."

There would have been no relief from all of this if another dessert hadn't been brought, pastry doves stuffed with raisins and nuts. Quinces followed; they were stuck full of spines, to look like sea urchins. We could have put up with this, but there was a dish that was simply horrific, and we would have died of hunger rather than touch it. When it was set before us, it looked like a fattened goose, with fish and all kinds of smaller birds around it. But Trimalchio said, "My friends, everything you see here is made out of just one thing."

I thought I was pretty smart, as right away I had a guess as to what the stuff was. Turning to Agamemnon, I said, "I wouldn't be surprised if the whole thing were made out of wax or clay. I've seen artificial meals like this during the Saturnalia at Rome, and—"

[70] Trimalchio cut me off. "I swear—and if I'm lying, then let my belly get bigger, instead of my investments, ha, ha!—my cook made all of that outta pork. He's the most valuable slave I have. If you want, he'll make a fish from a sow's belly, a pigeon from lard, a dove from ham, a chicken from pork knuckles, you name it. I had this amazing inspiration and called him Daedalus.[66] He's never put his foot wrong, neither,

---

65. Vergil, *Aeneid* 5.1.

66. This mythical character constructed, among other things, wings that allowed a human being to fly.

so I ordered him steel knives from Rome. They were made at Noricum."[67] He had these brought so that he could inspect and admire them. He also gave us permission to test the points against our cheeks for sharpness.

Two slaves came in, looking as if they had just had a fight at a well. They had the requisite jars balanced on their shoulders, at any rate. Trimalchio passed his judgment, but neither of them liked his decision, and there was a mutual bashing of jars with walking sticks. We were horrified at this drunken misbehavior, but as we gaped at their brawling we saw oysters and clams falling out of the jars. A slave gathered them onto a tray and handed them around. But the genius of a cook offered some competition for this elegant show. He served snails on a silver grill and sang in a hideous, trembling voice the whole time.

I almost hesitate to say what happened next. It was so tasteless and unheard of. Long-haired boys brought unguent in a silver dish and smeared our feet as we lay there. That was after they wrapped garlands around our legs and ankles. Some of this same unguent was dumped into the wine bowl and the lamp.

Now Fortunata showed signs of wanting to dance, and Scintilla was applauding more often than she spoke. Trimalchio spoke up: "Philargyrus, you can come join us, even if you're a damn Green and everybody knows it.[68] Tell your partner Menophila that she can take a flop here too."

To be brief, we were almost thrown off our couches by all the slaves who came crowding into the dining room like some sort of victorious army. Right beside me— toward the more prestigious end of the couch, in fact—was the cook who had made goose out of pork. He stank of brine and spicy sauces. He wasn't happy just to lie down: right away, he started imitating the tragic actor Ephesus and offered to bet his master that the Greens would win first place at the next races.

[71] Trimalchio enjoyed this sparring. "Friends," he said, turning to us, "slaves are people too. They drank mother's milk the same way we all did. It's just that an evil fate got 'em down.[69] But if I've got anything to do with it, they're gonna feel how different a cup of water tastes if you're free. What I mean is, I'm settin' 'em all free in my will. I'm also gonna leave Philargyrus a farm and his partner, and Cario's gettin' an apartment block and his five percent tax and a bed with pillows and blankets. You see, I'm makin' Fortunata my heir so she'll take care of all my friends. I'm saying this now so that everybody loves me as much as if I'm dead."

They all started to thank the master for his kindness. Wanting to do nothing by halves, he ordered a copy of his will brought, and read it aloud from beginning to end while the entire household groaned in chorus.

Trimalchio turned to Habinnas. "You're my best buddy, you know? So are you building my tomb the way I ordered? At the base of my statue you've gotta paint a puppy and garlands and bottles of perfume and all the fights of Petraites.[70] It'll feel like I'm still alive, and I'll owe it all to you. Make the building a hundred feet across the front and two hundred feet back. Lots of fruit trees all over and plenty of grapevines,

---

67. An area in the Alps famous for the manufacture of steel weapons.

68. The "Greens" were one of the chariot racing teams.

69. For a similar "philosophical" view of slaves, see Seneca, *Letters* 4 in this volume.

70. A favorite gladiator, mentioned also in ch. 52, above.

okay? It's a pile of crap to have gorgeous houses when we're alive and not worry about where we're gonna stay a lot longer. So first of all put up a sign: 'This property shall not pass to the heir.' And I'm gonna make sure in my will that nobody does me dirty after I'm dead. One of my freedmen's gonna be on guard duty, or the whole town'll be running to crap on my tomb. Do a ship sailing with the sails full of wind, and do me sitting up on a dais in a senator's robe. Give me *five* gold rings, and have me pouring money out of a bag to give away. You know the banquet I gave, with a handout of two denarii a head. Do some dining rooms, too, with the whole town having a great time. Put Fortunata on my right, and have her holding a dove. And give her a little dog tied to her belt. Don't forget that kid who's my favorite. And big jars, and seal 'em with gypsum so the wine won't run out. One of them should be broken, with a boy standing above it and bawling.[71] In the middle put a sundial, so that anybody who wants to know the time has to look at my name. And see what you think of this inscription: 'Here lies Gaius Pompeius Trimalchio, Freedman of Maecenas.[72] He was elected sevir, though he was not even here to campaign. He could have been in all of the guilds at Rome, but he said no. He had old-fashioned values, he was brave, faithful, and he started small and made it big. He left a fortune of thirty million sesterces. He never in his life paid any attention to a philosopher. Farewell to him. And to you, stranger.'"[73]

[72] As Trimalchio finished, he burst out richly in tears. Fortunata was crying too, and Habinnas—then the whole household, like a pack of funeral guests, filled the dining room with lamentation. Actually, even I was crying at this point.

"Okay," said Trimalchio, "since we know that we've gotta die, why don't we do some living? I just wanna make you all happy: let's jump in for a bath. Count on it, you won't be sorry. It's as hot as a furnace."

"Sure," said Habinnas. "I don't like nothin' more than makin' two days outta one." He got up barefoot and followed the gleefully exiting Trimalchio.

I looked at Ascyltos. "What do you think?" I asked. "As for me, if I take one look at a bath, I'll die on the spot."[74]

"Let's pretend to go along with it," he said. "While the rest are headed there, we can get out under cover of the crowd."

Accordingly, we set out, and Giton led us along the portico to the door. But the dog chained up there greeted us with so much noise that Ascyltos fell into a fish pool. And I, who was just as drunk, and who had been afraid of a painted dog—as I went to the aid of the poor overboard sailor, I was dragged into the same abyss. The steward saved us, intervening to quiet the dog and pull us onto dry land. But Giton had ransomed himself from the dog from the start: everything we had given to him from dinner, he scattered before the baying beast, whose rage was eased by the distraction. Then, wet and shivering, we asked the steward to let us out the door, but he refused.

---

71. A typical funerary symbol of the fragility of life.

72. Maecenas, an associate of the first emperor, Augustus, was notorious for his effeminate luxury. It seems appropriate that Trimalchio's master also had this name.

73. For actual epitaphs of wealthy and successful freedmen, see Inscriptions nos. 47–49 in this volume.

74. A hot bath after a rich meal was considered dangerous. See Juvenal, *Satires* 3.141–45 in this volume.

"You're mistaken if you think you can go out the way you came in. No guest is ever dismissed through the same door. One is an entrance, another an exit."

[73] We were the most wretched of mortals. What were we going to do now, shut up as we were in a new version of the labyrinth?[75] Actually, we *were* wanting to bathe now. We came right out and asked to be taken to the baths. Once there, we threw off our clothes, which Giton undertook to dry for us in the entranceway, and we approached the pool, a narrow one like a cold water tank.

Trimalchio was standing in the water, and even under these circumstances it was impossible to get away from his disgusting boasting. He claimed that nothing was better than to bathe without a crowd around, and that there had been a bakery on this very spot. In a while he sat down, tired. Under the lure of the room's acoustics, he leaned back, opened his drunken mouth to the vaulted ceiling, and proceeded to dismember some songs of Menecrates[76]—or that's what they were according to those who could understand Trimalchio's utterances.

Other guests ran around the rim of the pool, hand in hand, and through the room came an enormous echo of their giggling. Some were trying the stunt of lifting a ring from the floor while their hands were tied behind their backs; or, from a kneeling position, bending back to touch the tips of their toes. We shunned these games and went down into the pool, which had been heated to Trimalchio's specifications.

When our drunkenness evaporated we were led into another dining room, where Fortunata had laid out a collection of amenities. . . . We took note of lamps with bronze fishermen decorating them, solid silver tables set with gilded earthenware cups—and wine being strained through a cloth right out in the open.

Trimalchio said, "Friends, today a slave of mine had his first shave—damn good guy, doesn't waste a crumb. So let's throw a few back and keep the party going till dawn."

[74] While he was still speaking, a cock crowed. Trimalchio was upset and ordered libations poured under the table and unmixed wine sprinkled on a lamp. He even moved a ring to his left hand. "There's some reason for that," he said. "It's like the trumpet before a battle. There's gonna be a fire, or somebody in the neighborhood is gonna croak. The gods spare us! Anybody who brings me that bad-omened little bastard gets a tip."[77]

Before he could finish, the cock was brought, and Trimalchio ordered it stewed in wine. Daedalus, that same expert cook who had made fish and birds out of pork a little while ago, hacked up the cock and tossed the pieces into a pot. While he drained off the boiling broth, Fortunata ground pepper in a little boxwood mill.

When we had consumed this tasty dish, Trimalchio took a look at the contingent of slaves around us. "Huh? You still haven't eaten? Get out, and let the others do their shift." Another squadron accordingly came as a replacement, shouting, "Greetings, Gaius!," whereas from those on the way out it was "Farewell, Gaius!"

At this point came the first real disruption of our good times. Among the new

---

75. The original "labyrinth" was a maze built to house the monstrous Minotaur.

76. A harpist at the court of Nero (reigned AD 54–68).

77. Trimalchio superstitiously attempts to avert a fire or some other disaster announced by what he sees as the bad omen of the cock crow.

batch of waiters was a boy particularly easy on the eyes. Trimalchio descended on him and kissed him rather persistently. Fortunata, in a forthright and principled assertion of her rights, began to take Trimalchio apart, calling him a piece of filth and a disgrace, with no control over his libido. At last she used the word "dog." Trimalchio, offended, launched a drinking cup into Fortunata's face. She screamed as if she had lost an eye, and moved her shaking hands to her cheek. Scintilla was upset and sheltered her trembling friend in her bosom. An officious slave also applied to her cheek a chilled jug. She leaned against it, weeping and moaning.

"Terrific," said Trimalchio. "The slut's forgotten everything. I took her off the auction block and made a human being out of her. But now she's all puffed up like a frog, thinks her luck's endless. She's got no more sense than a block of wood. Maybe somebody born in a hut shouldn't dream about a mansion. So help me, I'm gonna put her in her place—she's nothin' but a bitch in army boots. Back when I was worth two bits, I could of married a dowry of ten million. You know I'm not lying. And Agatho the perfume dealer took me aside just the other day and said, 'C'mon, don't let your family end with you.' But I'm trying to be a good guy, don't wanna seem like a jerk, so I ram an axe in my own leg. You wanna scratch me in the face? I'll give you a reason. I'm not gonna make you wait to find out how much damage you've done yourself: Habinnas, don't put her statue in my tomb. I at least want some peace after I'm dead. And wait a second, I can give as good as I get: she's not allowed to kiss my corpse."

[75] This thunderbolt roused Habinnas to plead for an end to Trimalchio's anger. "There's none of us who's never done nothing wrong. We're just people, not gods." Scintilla wept and appealed to Trimalchio's guardian spirit, called the man by his first name, Gaius, and begged him to relent. Trimalchio himself no longer held back his tears. "Habinnas, c'mon, be an honest judge, and the gods will let you enjoy your savings. If I did anything wrong, you can spit in my face. That boy is the decentest slave I've got, and I didn't kiss him because he's pretty, but because he's so decent. He can say his times-ten table, he reads straight off just by looking at the words, bought himself a gladiator suit out of his allowance, plus an armchair and two wine dippers. I think a lot of him, yeah, but he's earned it. But Fortunata says no way. So I get this decided for me by you, a bitch who's spent her life with her legs in the air? You damn buzzard, you better think about what's good for you. And don't make me show my teeth, sweetie. You don't wanna be in the way when I'm really angry. You know what I'm like: once I decide something, it's nailed in with a three-inch nail.

"But let's not let this spoil our good time. Life's short. Go on, you people, enjoy yourselves. I was like you once, but I got to where I am because of my character. Guts is what makes a man what he is. Everything else is crap. Buy low, sell high, is what I say, but maybe that's just me. But I'm doing so well that I'm gonna explode or something. Hey, are you still sniveling and crying? I'll give you something to cry about.

"But as I was saying, my character got me where I am today. When I first come out of Asia, I was as tall as that lamp stand. Used to measure myself by it every day. And so as to get a beard on my beak here quicker, I'd rub the lamp oil all around my mouth. Still, I was the master's favorite for fourteen years. It's not wrong if the master makes you do it. Anyway, I managed to do okay by the mistress as well. You know what I'm talking about. But I won't talk about it, 'cause I don't like to brag.

[76] "At any rate, the gods must of been okay with it, 'cause I got in charge of the

whole place, and the master was crazy about me. To make a long story short, he made me his heir (along with the emperor, of course), and I got a senator's fortune. But nobody's ever got enough of nothing. I had this itch to go into business. I don't want to bore you with the story, but I built five ships and got a cargo of wine—like solid gold at the time—and I sent them off to Rome. You would of thought I gave *orders* for the ships to get wrecked, 'cause every one got wrecked. It's the truth I'm telling you; I didn't make this up. Neptune ate up thirty million sesterces in one day. You think I gave up? I'll be damned if I did: I didn't give a shit, it was like I didn't lose a thing. I built more ships, that was bigger and better and luckier. You know, a big ship's not afraid of nothin'. I loaded up more wine, plus lard, and beans, and ointment, and slaves. Nobody was gonna say that I didn't have any balls. And Fortunata did a real loyal thing: she sold all her jewelry and all her clothes and put a hundred gold coins in my hand. That was the yeast that started my fortune rising.

"Well, what the gods want to happen happens fast. On that one trip I piled up ten million sesterces. Then I got out of hock all the property that'd belonged to my master. I built a house, bought myself some slaves, some stock. Everything I touched grew like a honeycomb. As soon as I owned more than the whole town put together, I got out, stopped trading, and started loaning money with freedmen as agents. When I was thinking about getting out, this astrologer comes to town, Greek guy called Serapa, who was so good he could of given the gods advice, and he told me what to do. Shit, he told me stuff that I'd forgot myself. From the ground up, he said everything that was goin' on with me, even in my guts—everything but what I ate the day before. You'd think he'd lived with me my whole life.

[77] "You were there, Habinnas, right? Didn't he say, 'We all know how you got your lady. You've been unlucky in your friends. Nobody is grateful enough toward you. You have large estates. You're sheltering a viper under your wing'? I probably shouldn't tell you this, but I've still got thirty years, four months, and two days to live. And I'm going to get an inheritance real soon. That's what's in store for me, according to the soothsayer. But if I get my property to go as far as Apulia,[78] then I'll have done enough with this life of mine. But while Mercury was watching over my business, I built this house. It was a shack, and now it's a temple. It's got four rooms for eating, twenty bedrooms, two marble porticoes, a bunch of rooms upstairs, the room where I sleep, a sitting room for this viper here, a real good doorkeeper's lodge, and a guest house for a hundred. Just to show you: when Scaurus came here, this was the place he wanted to stay, and his family always stayed at their place by the sea. There's a lot of other stuff, too, that I'll show you just now. Believe me, if a penny's all you've got, it's all you're worth. You have something, you'll get respect. Yours truly here was a frog, but now he's a king. Stichus, bring out the grave clothes I wanna wear at my funeral. And bring me a gob of that unguent, and some of the wine from the jar I ordered set aside for cleaning my remains."

[78] Stichus didn't hesitate, but brought into the dining room a white winding sheet and a toga with a senatorial stripe on it. . . .[79]

---

78. In southeast Italy.

79. See Glossary, *latus clavus*.

Trimalchio ordered us to feel them to check the quality of the wool. Smirking, he added, "Stichus, see that the mice and the moths don't get at them, or I'll burn you alive. I wanna look snazzy at my funeral, so that the whole town heaps blessings on me."

Then he opened a jar of spikenard, smeared a little on each of us, and said, "I hope that when I'm dead I enjoy this just as much as when I'm alive." He had wine dumped into a bowl and said, "Okay, pretend that you're my guests at the remembrance day for the dead."

Things were reaching a sickening climax. Trimalchio was weighed down with a loathsome drunkenness. He summoned a new kind of entertainment, trumpeters, into the dining room, and stretched himself out on numerous pillows over his couch. "Pretend I'm dead," he said. "Play something pretty." The trumpeters gave the traditional funerary blast all together. The loudest was the slave of the undertaker, who was the most respectable man there; that noise woke the neighborhood. The sentinels keeping watch in the area must have thought that Trimalchio's house was on fire, as they broke down the door and created pandemonium with axes and water in their usual way. This was a perfect opportunity for us to give Agamemnon the slip, and we rushed out with no more hesitation than if there *had* been a fire.

# PLINY THE YOUNGER

(ca. AD 61–113, wrote in Latin)

## Introduction

C. Plinius Caecilius Secundus was born in Como in northern Italy, and probably died in the Roman province of Bithynia on the Black Sea, where he was serving as governor. He took the name of his uncle C. Plinius Secundus (Pliny the Elder, author of the *Natural History*) after being adopted by him. He is generally called Pliny the Younger to distinguish him from his uncle. Pliny came from a wealthy family and received a sophisticated education at Como and Rome, where he studied rhetoric with Quintilian. He went on to a brilliant political career under the Emperors Domitian, Nerva, and especially Trajan, holding in succession the offices of quaestor, praetor, consul and augur, suffect consul, and finally governor of Bithynia. At the same time, Pliny was active as an orator and advocate in court, founded educational institutions, and wrote and performed poetry as well. He serves for modern readers, and to some extent presents himself, as a model of a Roman senator in the early empire.

Pliny wrote his letters to a variety of friends, family members, and colleagues. Although they are addressed to real people and were based on actual circumstances, they are probably not real correspondence as such. Their style is artful—not artificial, but careful enough to suggest substantial revision. Pedestrian details of the kind one finds in Cicero's letters are omitted. That and the fact that each letter restricts itself to a single theme suggest that Pliny probably selected parts of his actual letters and published them in edited form as literary works. The naming of the addressee thus functions as a kind of dedication of a mini-essay. We have added a title to each letter to indicate the contents.

Despite their literary character, the letters are often drawn on today by scholars as a primary source for Roman social and intellectual life and political events. They give important insights into matters such as Roman politics, provincial administration, literature, marriage, education, entertainment, patronage, slavery, religion, and many other topics. Pliny's correspondence with Trajan includes the so-called "Christian letters" (nos. 33 and 34 below), in which Pliny asks how he should deal with people accused of being Christians. The letters about the eruption of Mt. Vesuvius in AD 79 are vivid eye-witness accounts of the eruption itself and the resulting chaos (nos. 15 and 16 below). Several letters illuminate the lives of the women of his circle (see nos. 6, 12, 13, 18, and 20), and those about his unfortunate tenant farmers (nos. 10 and 25) give a rare glimpse into the plight of free Italian peasants.

Pliny avoided chronological ordering and did not give specific dates or places of composition for the letters. But it seems that most of them were written from AD 97 on. The correspondence with Trajan (Book 10) dates to around AD 110, and was probably published posthumously.

## *Letters*

### 1    **False Activity and Authentic Leisure** (1.9, to Minucius Fundanus)

When in Rome it's amazing how you can give a full and correct accounting of each day's activities—or seem to—but when you put a number of days together, things just don't add up. If you were to ask someone, "What did you do today?" he would reply, "Well, I attended the ceremony of a young man's coming of age, a betrothal, a wedding. One man invited me to the signing of his will, another to appear at a trial on his behalf, another to a legal consultation." It all seems quite important at the time, but when you look back and realize you've been at them day after day, they seem pointless—all the more so when you have gotten out of Rome. That's when it dawns on you how many days you've wasted, and on what dreary stuff.

That's how I feel as soon as I reach my villa at Laurentum,[1] and read something or do some writing, or take the time to exercise—these are the props that support the mind. I don't hear anything there I would regret having heard, or say anything I would regret having said. No one feeds me malicious gossip about a third party, and I don't criticize anyone either, except maybe myself for not writing very well. No hopes, no fears to disturb me, no rumors to distract me. I speak only with myself and my books. This is really living. This is leisure that is sweet and honorable, and more satisfying than almost any type of business. The seashore, that true and secret haunt of the Muses, sparks my imagination and gets me writing. You too, my friend, should do likewise the first chance you get. Turn your back on all that bustle, the idle back and forth, the utterly inane drudgery, and abandon yourself to study, or just to rest. It is better (as our friend Atilius says, with equal wisdom and wit) to have nothing to do than to be doing nothing.

### 2    **Long and Short Speeches** (1.20, to Cornelius Tacitus[2])

I often argue with a certain man of learning and experience who says that when it comes to pleading a case in court there is nothing as effective as brevity. A good rule to follow, I admit, if the case allows it. But sometimes it is a dereliction of duty to pass over things that ought to be said, a dereliction to touch only briefly and cursorily on points that should be emphasized, repeated, hammered home. For most topics a longer treatment lends a sort of force and weight. A speech is to the mind what a sword is to the body: the effect is achieved not so much by the blow as by the sustaining of it.

At this point my friend starts citing authoritative examples. Of the Greeks, he points out the works of Lysias, and of the Romans, those of the Gracchi and Cato, most of whose speeches certainly are terse and crisp. Against his Lysias I cite Demosthenes,

---

1. On the sea-coast between Ostia and Lavinium, about sixteen miles from Rome.

2. The famous historian and author of the *Annals* and *Histories*. He was a friend and colleague of Pliny's, and the addressee of eleven of the extant letters, including the ones on the eruption of Mount Vesuvius, nos. 15 and 16 below, and co-counsel in the trial of Marius Priscus (see *Letters* 5).

Aeschines, Hyperides, and many others; against the Gracchi and Cato I offer up Pollio, Caesar, Caelius, and especially Marcus Tullius Cicero, whose longest speech is generally considered his best. Like other good things, a good book is in fact better for being longer. Think about statues, pictures, and paintings. Think about the shapes of men, and of many animals—of trees, even. So long as they are beautiful, bigger is better. The same is true of speeches. Even the scrolls themselves gain some authority and beauty from their very bulk.

I like to make these and many similar points in support of my argument, but my friend, being a slippery debater and hard to pin down, escapes. These very orators which I cite spoke more concisely in their live speeches, he says, than they wrote in the published versions of them. I am of the opposite opinion. My evidence? In a number of orations by a number of orators (for example, those of Cicero for Murena and for Varenus), certain charges are listed in a short and bare formal notification, in outline form only. Clearly the published speech leaves out a great deal that Cicero must have said in court. The same Cicero tells us that when speaking on behalf of Cluentius he argued the whole case himself from beginning to end, without assistance, as they did in the old days; and that his speech for Gaius Cornelius lasted four days. Obviously he later pruned the long speech he gave over several days (how could he not?), and condensed it into a single book—a big one, but still only one.

But a good live speech and a good published oration are just different things, right? I know this is the popular view. I could be wrong, but I believe that though some poor written speeches can be improved in delivery, a good written speech always yields a good live one. The written version is the model or archetype of a live speech.[3] That's why in all the best written speeches we find a thousand apparently improvised turns of phrase, even in those which we know to have been only published. For instance, in one of Cicero's speeches against Verres: "But the artist, what was his name? That's right, thank you. They said it was Polyclitus."[4] It follows that the most perfect live delivery is that which is most closely molded in the likeness of the script—provided, of course, that it is given the just and appropriate amount of time. If that is denied, then the judge is very much to blame, the speaker not at all.

I am backed up in this opinion by the laws themselves, which lavish oceans of time on speakers, and urge them on not to brevity but to abundance (by this I mean diligence), which brevity cannot supply, except in cases of the narrowest scope.

Just to add what I've learned from the best of teachers, experience: having often pleaded in court, served as judge, and sat as an assessor, I've seen that different people are moved by different factors, and frequently it's the little things that decide great issues. People have all kinds of different opinions and predispositions. Those who have listened to the same speech at the same time often come to opposite conclusions, and occasionally to the same conclusion from opposite routes. Besides, everyone is fond of his own ingenuity. We embrace most readily what another person says when we have previously thought it ourselves. So give them all something they can take in and recognize as their own.

Regulus said to me once, when we were on the same case, "You think you have to

---

3. On this analogy the live speech would be like a copy made from an original sculpture.

4. *Against Verres* II.4.3.

follow up on every last point in the case. I look for the throat of the matter immediately and grab *that*." True, he grabs what he chooses, but he often chooses mistakenly. "What you think is the throat," I replied, "might well be a knee or an ankle. I can't see the throat, so I poke around everywhere, try everything. In short, I leave no stone unturned." It's just like farming. I take care to cultivate not just vineyards but also orchards, not just orchards but also fields. In these fields I sow not just spelt or wheat but also barley, beans, and other crops. Just so, in a speech I scatter many seeds far and wide so I can harvest whatever happens to sprout. And believe me, the minds of jurors and judges are just as impenetrable, uncertain, and deceptive as weather and soil. I keep in mind how the great orator Pericles was praised by the comic playwright Eupolis:

> He not only had speed,
> but a kind of Persuasiveness rested on his lips.
> He cast a spell, and was the only orator
> who left behind his sting on the audience's ears.

But even Pericles could not, without the richest gifts of expression, have gotten this "persuasiveness," this "spell" by mere brevity or rapidity—or both (for they are different things). To delight and persuade an audience requires a profusion of words and time to speak them. You can only "implant a sting" in the minds of the audience if you don't just prick, but drive it in. Consider also what another comic playwright says of the same Pericles—

> He lightened, he thundered, and threw Greece into a stir.[5]

No truncated and stunted oration, but only one that is broad, majestic, and elevated can thunder, lighten, and, in short, throw everything into confusion and tumult.

Still, moderation in all things, they say. Who would disagree? But too little is just as immoderate as too much. Speaking too briefly is just as immoderate as speaking at too great a length. One often hears the criticism, "Undisciplined and repetitive!" but also this one, "Pathetic and weak!" One man has overshot his subject matter, the other underplayed it. Both go wrong, one in feebleness, the other through energy—which is characteristic of a great talent, if not of a polished style. I'm not saying I approve of what Homer called the "man of unlimited words," but rather the man whose "words are like the wintery snows." And it's not that I don't admire very much one who says "a few words, but very clearly."[6] Given the choice, I would prefer the winter snow type of oratory, that is, falling thick, constant, plentiful, as if coming from the gods and the heavens. "But to many people short speeches are more agreeable." So they are, to careless listeners. It would be ridiculous to treat their self-indulgent laziness as if it were some kind of critical judgment. If you want to take their advice, best not merely to speak briefly, but not to speak at all.

That's how I see things so far, but if you disagree I am willing to change my view. I only ask that you explain clearly why you disagree. I should bow to your authority and example, though I would rather be won over not by authority but by logical argument

---

5. Aristophanes, *Acharnians* 531.

6. Thersites, Odysseus, and Menelaus, respectively (Homer, *Iliad* 2.212, 3.222, 3.214).

in a matter of such importance. And so, if you think I'm correct, write and say that in as short a letter as you please. But still write, since you will be confirming my judgment. If I'm wrong, compose an extremely long letter. But wait—maybe it's bribery to ask for a short letter if you agree, but a long one if you don't? Farewell.

### 3    Status-Grading at Dinner Parties (2.6, to Avitus)

It's a long story to tell you exactly how I got there, and it doesn't really matter how, so I'll just jump in mid-tale: I found myself at dinner at the house of a certain man—I don't know him very well—a man who unites, in his own view, elegance and economy, but in my view, miserliness and extravagance. For himself and a few others he served the best of everything. But to the rest of the guests he served cheap food and tiny portions.[7] Even the wine he had divided into three grades, in little cups, not so that people could have the ability to choose, but so they would have no ability to refuse. One grade was for himself and us, another for his friends of lower status (he puts his friends into categories), another for his and our freedmen. The man reclining next to me noticed this, and asked me if I approved. "No," I said. "So, what's your system?" he asked. "I serve the same thing to everybody. It's a dinner party, not a census review.[8] When I treat people as equals by inviting them to share the same couches and tables, I treat them as equals in all respects." "What, your freedmen, too?" "Certainly. In that setting I see them as my guests, not freedmen." "It must cost you a pretty penny," he said. "Not at all," I replied. "How can that be?" "Because my freedmen don't drink the same wine that I do; I drink the same wine as my freedmen."

It's no great burden to share what you have with many others if you can only restrain your gluttony. Check that, keep that in line, so to speak, if you want to moderate your expenses. And it is preferable to do so by curbing yourself rather than by insulting other people.

So why am I telling you all this? So you won't be fooled, excellent young man that you are, by a show of frugality at certain people's tables that is in fact mere self-indulgence. It is consistent with my affection toward you that, whenever a case of this kind occurs, I send you an example of What Not To Do. Remember, then, that there is nothing more to be avoided than this weird combination of extravagance and miserliness—vices which are foul enough on their own, and still more foul when combined.

### 4    A Solicitation of Electoral Support (2.9, to Apollinaris)

The candidacy of my friend Sextus Erucius has me worried and tense. I'm feeling anxiety as though for another self, the kind of stress I didn't even feel over my own campaigns. As a matter of fact, my honor, my reputation, my status are all at stake. It

---

7. The custom of grading clients and dinner guests by status and serving cheaper food to the lower-status ones is recorded as early as the time of Cato the Elder, and impressed the 2nd-century AD Greek writer Lucian as a characteristic of Roman senatorial society (*Salaried Posts in Great Houses* 26). See also Martial, *Epigrams* 25 in this volume.

8. The Latin is elegant here (*ad cenam, non ad notam*), with *nota* being the mark placed by one's name in the censor's rolls that assigned citizens to particular classes.

was I who obtained the broad stripe for Sextus from our Caesar,[9] I who procured the quaestorship for him. It was on my recommendation that he obtained the right to run for the tribunate, and if he does not get the office from the Senate, I am afraid it will look like I misled Caesar. So I must do everything I can to make sure that everyone else judges him to be the sort of man the emperor, on my recommendation, believed him to be. But even if I did not have this reason for getting behind his candidacy I would still want to campaign for a young man of great virtue, principle, and attainments, one, in short, worthy of all praise. The same is true of his whole family as well. His father is Erucius Clarus, an upright man of old-fashioned character, a fine speaker, and an experienced attorney who conducts his cases with equally high conscientiousness, determination, and modesty. His maternal uncle is C. Septicius, who is the most genuinely reliable, frank, and trustworthy man I know. They all compete in showing their loyal affection to me, and do so equally; now I can repay the kindness of all of them by coming through for one. And so I am lobbying my friends, beseeching, canvassing, making the rounds of homes and public meeting places, and spending all the political capital that I possess in impassioned support for him. And here I am, begging *you* to think it worth your while to shoulder some of my burden. I will return the favor if you ask, in fact, even if you don't. People love you; they court you and come to your house. All you have to do is say what it is that you want, and there are people for whom your wish will be their passionate desire.

### 5    A Dramatic Trial in the Senate (2.11, to Arrianus)

I know you love it when something happens in the Senate that is worthy of that body. True, your love of the quiet life has led you to withdraw to the country. Yet there remains lodged in your mind a regard for the dignity of the commonwealth. So listen to an account of a trial held over the last few days, a notorious one thanks to the high social standing of the accused, a healthy one thanks to the severity of the example set, and an immortal one owing to the sheer magnitude of the affair.

Marius Priscus stood accused by the people of the province of Africa, whom he had governed as proconsul.[10] He offered no defense, but asked that the matter be referred directly to the board of judges.[11] Cornelius Tacitus and I, appointed counsel for the

---

9. The emperor in question is probably Nerva, which would date this letter to late AD 97. The "broad stripe" is the *latus clavus*, stitched on the tunic, betokening senatorial ambitions (see Glossary).

10. Marius Priscus was accused by certain prominent men of Lepcis Magna of taking bribes to deliver corrupt judicial verdicts. He pleaded guilty and tried to get a lighter sentence by appealing for a quick penalty phase administered by a board of judges. Pliny prevented this and was the lead attorney in the successful prosecution in the full Senate, which also entailed the conviction of other members of Priscus' circle.

11. The board of judges would have consisted of five senators selected according to strict requirements. Priscus' maneuver was aimed at bypassing a full trial in the Senate and thus preventing further crimes not named in the original indictment from being added later; he was unsuccessful, as becomes clear.

provincials, considered it a part of our duty to inform the Senate that Priscus' crimes were so monstrous and vicious that they went beyond the proper scope of the board of judges, in so far as he had taken money for the condemnation and even the execution of innocent persons.[12]

Fronto Catius, in reply, claimed that no inquiry could be made into anything that was not covered by the law against bribery and extortion. Fronto is a past master at making an audience weep, and he filled the sails of his entire speech with a wind of pathos and pity. There was a big dispute, with much shouting on both sides. One group said the jurisdiction of the Senate was restricted by the law, the others that it was free and unfettered, and that the accused must be punished in proportion to his crimes. In the end the consul-elect, Julius Ferox, an honest and upright man, moved that Marius should be given a panel of judges in the interim, but at the same time the individuals should be produced to whom he was said to have sold the conviction and punishment of innocent men. Not only did this opinion win out, but, after all that rancor, it was in fact the only one widely supported—proof positive that bias and pity toward a defendant, though overpowering on first impact, will dissipate little by little when neutralized by reason and good sense. This is why an opinion that many will support in the midst of a confused clamor, no one will dare articulate when the rest are silent. Separated from the crowd, you get a clear view of many things which the crowd serves to conceal.

The men summoned to attend made their appearance: Vitellius Honoratus and Flavius Marcianus. Honoratus was charged with having purchased, for 300,000 sesterces, the exile of a Roman knight and the execution of seven of his friends. Marcianus was charged with having purchased, for 700,000, a combination of penalties inflicted on a single Roman knight, who had been beaten with cudgels, condemned to work in the mines, and finally strangled in prison. Honoratus, however, was spared the Senate's investigation by a timely death.[13] Marcianus was brought before the court while Priscus was not present. At that point an ex-consul, Tuccius Cerialis, made a special request to the presiding consul that Priscus should be informed, thinking either that Priscus would arouse greater compassion if present, or perhaps greater indignation, or else (as I am strongly inclined to believe) because the fairest thing in a shared charge is for both men to defend themselves, and for both to take the punishment if they cannot be cleared.

The matter was postponed until the next Senate meeting, which was an extremely impressive sight. The emperor presided (he was consul). Add to this that it was the month of January, which brings great crowds to Rome, both senators and ordinary people. Furthermore, throngs of people had come from all over, drawn by the importance of the case, the rumors, and the anticipation, which had only grown because of the delay, and by the innate human fascination with what is big and unusual. Imagine

12. Such doings went beyond the mere extortion of money (*repetundae*), and were classed as *saevitia*, intolerable brutality, too serious for consideration merely by the board of judges. Roman provincial governors, who were generally unsupervised, had many opportunities to solicit or accept bribes, especially in their capacity as judges in their provinces, hence the expedited procedure.

13. Doubtless by suicide.

my anxiety, my fear at the prospect of speaking on such an important case before such a crowd, in the presence of the emperor! True, this wasn't the first time I'd spoken before the Senate; in fact, that is where I usually find my audience most receptive. But at that moment everything seemed strangely new, and filled me with unaccustomed fear. Besides the factors I mentioned, the difficulties of the case were clear: there stood a man only recently of consular rank, only recently a member of a board of priests; now, neither. It was an extremely disagreeable task to accuse a man already condemned.[14] Although he had the viciousness of the charges going against him, he was still protected by the sort of pity reserved for a man whose conviction is essentially a done deal. Still, once I collected my mind and my thoughts, I began to speak and felt approval from the audience comparable to the anxiety in myself. I spoke for nearly five hours. My normal allotment of twelve water-clocks was allowed to run slowly, and I was given four extra.[15]

It turned out that the very factors that seemed difficult and problematic when I was preparing to speak worked in my favor when I was actually speaking. Caesar, at any rate, showed such favor toward me, such care for me even (perhaps solicitude would be too strong a word), that he frequently suggested to my freedman, who was standing behind me, that I spare my voice and my strength, whenever he thought I was straining myself with greater vehemence than my delicate frame could bear. Claudius Marcellinus, representing Marcianus, delivered the reply to my speech. The Senate adjourned, to be recalled on the following day, for by this time a fresh speech could not have been started without being cut short by nightfall.

Next day Marius was defended by Salvius Liberalis. As a speaker he is precise, well-organized, incisive, and eloquent, and in this case he showed all his considerable skills. Cornelius Tacitus answered him with great eloquence, and with the majesty that is the outstanding feature of his style. Fronto Catius replied on behalf of Marius, in an excellent speech, and—as the situation now demanded—spent more of his time asking for mercy than defending his client. The fall of evening brought Fronto's speech to a close, though not in a way that seemed premature. Thus the presentation of evidence lasted into a third day. This in itself was a fine and good old-fashioned thing: that the Senate session was ended at nightfall, and called together for a third consecutive day. The consul-elect Cornutus Tertullus, a man of great distinction and rock-solid integrity, moved that the 700,000 sesterces which Marius had received should be paid into the state treasury, and that Marius himself should be barred from Rome and from Italy;[16] Marcianus from Rome, Italy, and also from Africa. At the end of his motion he added that since Tacitus and I had discharged the office of advocate imposed on

---

14. He had already been found guilty of simple extortion, and had already lost his place in the Senate along with membership in the *septemviri epulonum*, a prestigious board of priests responsible for organizing banquets in honor of the gods.

15. Normally four cycles of the water-clock took an hour, but here they were made to run more slowly, so that sixteen made nearly five hours. Elsewhere Pliny mentions speaking continuously for seven hours (*Letters* 4.16.3, not included in this volume).

16. As mentioned below, this was ultimately the final punishment for Marius Priscus, who had to give the money to the treasury and suffered relegation (a form of exile; see Glossary, *relegatio*). He ended up settling comfortably in Massilia (modern Marseille, France). See Juvenal, *Satires*

us with diligence and courage, the Senate commended us for acting in a way worthy of the functions assigned. The consuls-elect assented to Cornutus' motion, and all the ex-consuls, until we got to Pompeius Collega. *He* moved that the 700,000 should be paid into the treasury, that Marcianus should suffer relegation for five years, but that, in the case of Marius, his punishment should be restricted to that for extortion which he had already suffered. There were many supporters for each view, perhaps a greater number for the latter, more easy-going and lenient one. Some, too, who had seemed to agree with Cornutus now changed and followed Collega's lead, even though he had spoken after themselves. But when there was a division, those who stood by the consuls' chairs began to go over to the side of Cornutus.[17] At this point, those who still clustered around Collega crossed to the opposite side of the House, and Collega was left with scarcely anyone. He later complained a good deal about the people who had encouraged him, and especially about Regulus, who told him what to say and then abandoned him. So it goes with the fickle mind of Regulus, prone to audacious moves that he later regrets.

Such was the end of this spectacular inquiry. There still remains, however, a public matter of some importance—the affair of Hostilius Firminus, a staff-officer[18] of Marius Priscus. He was implicated in the case, and got very roughly handled. For according to both Marcianus' account books, and also a speech which Firminus made to the senators of Lepcis, it was clear that Firminus had leant his services to Priscus in a particularly disgraceful way.[19] He had also bargained with Marcianus to receive 200,000 sesterces, and he himself had taken 10,000 sesterces under a disgraceful false pretext of being a "perfume dealer"—actually not far off for a man whose hair was always done up and whose skin was always silky smooth from pumice-applications. It was resolved, on the motion of Cornutus, that his case should be put before the Senate at its next meeting. As it turns out, Firminus happened to be absent, either by accident or because of a guilty conscience.

So now you have the news of the town. Write me in return that of the country. How are your shrubs doing, and your vineyards, your crops, and those prize sheep of yours? In a word, send me back a letter as long as my own, or else expect only the shortest of notes from me.

## 6    **Legacy Hunting** (2.20, to Calvisius Rufus)

Give me your spare change, since I've got a golden little story for you—stories in fact, for this new one has reminded me of some older ones, and it doesn't matter which I tell first. Verania, the wife of Piso—I mean the Piso whom Galba adopted[20]—lay seriously

---

1.49–50 in this volume: "Marius starts drinking at the eighth hour in exile and lives it up in the face of the angry gods, while you, his victorious province, you weep."

17. The Senate voted by gathering in groups on the floor of the House. They were then counted, if necessary.

18. *Legatus*; see Glossary.

19. Firminus had aided Priscus in his extortions from the leading citizens of Lepcis.

20. AD 69.

ill. Regulus[21] paid her a visit. The impudence of calling on a sick woman, when he had been the greatest enemy to her husband, and was extremely hateful to herself, is one thing. No problem, though, if he just paid her a visit. But he also sat down on her bed and interrogated her on the day and hour of her birth! Hearing the answer, he composes his face, focuses his eyes, moves his lips, fiddles with his fingers, and does some calculations.[22] Not a word. He keeps the poor woman dangling in suspense for a long time, then says, "You are in a critical period! However, you will escape. To reassure you of this, I will consult a *haruspex*[23] whom I have frequently employed." Immediately he goes and offers a sacrifice, and declares that the entrails agree with the indications of the stars. With the usual gullibility of those in danger, she calls for her will and writes down a legacy for Regulus. Before long she grows worse. With her dying breath she cries out against him, calling him a worthless traitor, and worse than a perjurer, since he had sworn falsely to her on the life of his own son. This behavior of Regulus is as frequent as it is wicked, since he is bringing down the anger of the gods (which he always manages to escape himself) on the head of his unfortunate boy.[24]

Here's my second story. Velleius Blaesus, the well-known and well-heeled ex-consul, was struggling with the late stages of a terminal disease. He felt the need to alter his will. Regulus had lately taken to courting him, and hoped for something from a new disposition of his property, so he began to plead with the doctors to prolong the old man's life however they could. As soon as the will was executed, he changed his role, reversed his tone, and said to the same doctors, "How long will you torture the poor man? Why begrudge a good death when you cannot give him life?" Blaesus died, and, as though he had heard everything, left not a thing to Regulus.

Are two stories enough, or will you demand a third, as the rhetoric teachers do? Well, I've got material. An elegant lady named Aurelia was about to execute her will, and had put on very beautiful clothing. Regulus, having come to witness her signature, said, "Won't you please let me have those clothes?" Aurelia thought he was joking. But he insisted. Long story short, he compelled the lady to open her will and to bequeath to him the clothes she had on. He watched her writing, and then inspected the document to make sure she had written it. Aurelia, to be sure, is still alive, though he compelled her to do this just as if she had been at the point of death. And so he gets inheritances here, and legacies there, as if he deserved it all.

But why am I getting so worked up? In our city wickedness and dishonesty have long paid as well as—no, better than—honor and virtue. Look at Regulus. From poor and obscure beginnings he has advanced to such great wealth, thanks to his misdeeds, that (as he told me himself) he consulted the omens as to how soon he would get up to 60 million sesterces. He found double entrails, which portended that he would get 120 million. And he will, if he goes on like this, making people craft their wills to serve someone other than themselves—the most immoral kind of fraud.

---

21. The same unscrupulous Regulus from the previous letter; he also was responsible for the condemnation of Piso's brother under the Emperor Nero—and reportedly mutilated his head after death.

22. Regulus is pretending knowledge of astrology.

23. A type of diviner; see Glossary.

24. The boy died some five years later, as Pliny describes in *Letters* 4.2 (not in this volume).

**7      Choosing a Teacher** (3.3, to Corellia Hispulla)

Your father was a very serious and upright man. I'm not sure if I loved or respected him more. And I am especially fond of you, too, both in his honor and on your own account. This is why I desire and will work as hard as I can to see that your son turns out to be like his grandfather. I'd prefer him to be like his maternal grandfather, although his paternal grandfather was also a distinguished senator and respected man. And his father, too, and his paternal uncle were men of note and of excellent reputation. He will grow up to be like all of them if he gets a good education in the liberal arts. And it makes a huge difference from whom in particular he receives this education. So far, boyhood has kept him within your family circle; he has had tutors at home, where there is little to no opportunity for going astray. Now, however, his studies must be carried on outside your doors. Now it is time to look about for a Latin rhetoric teacher, and we have to be assured of his academic strictness, good character, and especially his sexual self-control. For our young friend, in addition to all the other gifts of nature and fortune, possesses remarkable physical beauty. At his critical age he needs not just a teacher but a guardian and guide as well.[25]

This is why I think I can point out to you Julius Genitor.[26] I have a great affection for him; yet this affection does not prejudice my judgment, since my high opinion of him is why I love him so. He is a person of spotless integrity and quite serious, perhaps even a bit too austere and blunt for the permissiveness of our age. As for his eloquence, there are many whose word you may take on that point. The ability to speak is evident on the surface and immediately perceptible. But a man's character is concealed in deep recesses and secret nooks, and on *this* point I will vouch for him. Your son will hear nothing from him that will not be beneficial; he will learn nothing which it would be better not to know. Genitor will remind him, as frequently as you or I would, of the ancestral images with which he is weighted,[27] of the names—the great names—that he has to uphold. So, with the favor of the gods, entrust him to a teacher from whom he will learn character first and then eloquence. After all, eloquence without character never comes to a good end.

**8      The Writings and Amazing Energy of Pliny the Elder** (3.5, to
        Baebius Macer)

I am very pleased that you are such an avid reader of my uncle's books that you want to own them all, and ask for the names of them all. I'll act like a catalog for you, and I'll even give you the order of composition (since this kind of information, too, is not unwelcome to a scholarly person like yourself):

---

25. The problem of teachers who took advantage of their pupils, and the bad effects of this on the morals of the student, are frequently mentioned in Roman discussions of education. See Horace, *Satires* 1.6.80–84 in this volume.

26. The addressee of *Letters* 9 and 24 below.

27. *Imaginēs*; see Glossary.

- *Throwing the Javelin from Horseback*. One volume.[28] Written while he was a junior officer in command of a unit of allied cavalry, it shows both literary talent and careful crafting.
- *The Life of Pomponius Secundus*.[29] Two volumes. A funeral gift, as it were, to the memory of his friend, by whom he was much loved.
- *The German Wars*. Twenty volumes. Collects all the wars we have ever fought with the Germans. He began this work while on campaign in Germany, in response to a dream. The image of Drusus Nero[30] stood over him as he slept (he who, after triumphing far and wide over the Germans, died in their country), commending his memory to my uncle, and begging to be rescued from unmerited historical oblivion.
- *The Student*. Three volumes, divided into six on account of their length. On the education of an orator, from infancy right up through advanced work.
- *Observations on Usage*. Eight volumes. Written in the last years of Nero's reign, when the slavery of the times made more independent and lofty kinds of literary pursuit dangerous.
- *A Continuation of Aufidius Bassus*. Thirty-one volumes.[31]
- *Natural History*. Thirty-seven volumes. A wide-ranging and learned work, no less varied than nature herself.[32]

Are you surprised that a busy man completed so many volumes, many of them on such intricate subjects? You will be even more surprised to learn that for some time he was a practicing attorney, that he died in his fifty-sixth year, and that in between he was much distracted and hindered, partly by important official posts, and partly by his role as advisor to the emperors.[33] But he had a keen mind, an incredible work ethic, and an extraordinary ability to do without sleep. Starting at the festival of Vulcan he would begin getting up in the middle of the night, not to take the auspices, but to study by lamp light.[34] In winter he was up by the seventh or the eighth hour at the latest, often the sixth.[35] To be sure sleep came to him very easily, even overtaking

---

28. That is, one roll of papyrus. This would correspond to perhaps forty pages or so of a modern book.

29. Legate of the armies of Upper Germany in the reign of Claudius, also a distinguished poet and tragedian.

30. Nero Claudius Drusus, brother of the Emperor Tiberius, died in Germany in 9 BC.

31. Bassus' history, now lost, covered the period from Julius Caesar's death to the accession of Caligula in AD 37. Pliny's continuation went into the 60s AD.

32. His sole surviving work, it well justifies the description.

33. The emperors kept an informal cabinet of advisors that consisted of men from various walks of life, including senators, administrators from the equestrian class, and even sometimes freedmen.

34. Consuls and augurs would regularly wake up before dawn to take the auspices. The festival of Vulcan began August 23.

35. The night was divided into twelve equal hours, whose exact length varied depending on the season. Most Romans went to bed after dark and rose at dawn. The wakeful Pliny the Elder rose four or five hours before dawn, but went to bed early.

him at times, or leaving him, in the midst of his studies. Before daybreak he would visit Emperor Vespasian (another night-owl), and after that tend to his official duties. Back home, he devoted the rest of his time to study. He ate a light and simple meal during the day in the old-fashioned style. Afterwards, in summer, he would often sunbathe, if he had any spare time. Meanwhile, a book was read to him, while he made notes and took extracts. Indeed, he read nothing without copying out extracts; he used to say that there was no book so bad that it did not contain something of value. After sunbathing he commonly took a cold bath, then had a snack and took a nap. Later, as though beginning a fresh day, he studied until dinnertime.[36] At this meal a book was read out and notes were made, just in passing. I remember a friend of his once, when the reader mispronounced some words, stopped the reader and made him repeat. At this my uncle said, "You understood him, didn't you?" His friend said, "Yes." "So why did you stop him? We lost more than ten verses by this interruption of yours." So economical was he with his time. In summer he went to bed while it was still light out; in winter within the first hour after nightfall, as though in obedience to some legal restriction.

This was his life when he was at work, amidst the hubbub of the city. While on vacation in the country, only his time at the baths was exempted from study. When I say the baths, I am speaking of the actual bath inside, for while he was being scraped[37] and dried off he was read to or dictated. When traveling, as though freed from every other care, he devoted himself exclusively to study. At his side, with a scroll and writing tablets, was a secretary, whose hands were protected in winter by gloves, so that not even harsh weather would rob my uncle of time for study. In Rome he used to be carried in a chair for the same reason. I remember once he scolded me for walking. "You could have avoided wasting those hours," he said, for in his view a moment not spent on study was a moment wasted. So intense was his focus that produced all those volumes. He also left me one hundred sixty books of "excerpts," written on both sides of the parchment and in an extremely small hand, so the number is really much larger. He used to say that when he was procurator in Spain, Larcius Licinus offered to buy these books for 400,000 sesterces—and at that time there was only a fraction of what he left me.

When you consider how much he read and how much he wrote, it seems impossible that he could have engaged in any public offices or served on the emperor's advisory council. On the other hand, when you hear how much he accomplished in his career, you can't imagine he had enough time to read or write. A career like his could get in the way of anything, but drive like his could get anything done. So you can see why when people call *me* studious it makes me laugh. Compared to him I am as lazy as can be. But I'm distracted, partly by public duties, partly by obligations to my friends. What about those who devote their whole lives to literary study? When compared with him, would they, too, not feel the shame of a habitual slacker?

---

36. For a more usual city routine for the upper class, see Martial no. 28 in this volume. See also in this volume Horace, *Satires* 1.6.119–128 (lawyers up early, but he sleeps in to the fourth hour).

37. During the bathing process the bathers would oil themselves down and often work up a great sweat; after the bathing process this grime would be scraped off by a curved instrument called the strigil, "scraper." See *A Roman Schoolbook* ch. 10.

I have gone on, though I intended to write only what you asked, the names of the books he left behind. Yet I am sure that all this additional information will prove as welcome to you as the books themselves, since it may inspire you with the spirit of emulation, not just to read them, but to work up something of the same kind yourself.

## 9     The Character of a Philosopher (3.11, to Julius Genitor)

Our dear Artemidorus has such an extremely kind nature that he exaggerates the services of his friends. That's why he goes around proclaiming my services to him in terms partly true and partly beyond what I deserve. True, after the banishment of the philosophers from Rome, I went to see him at his house outside the city, and what made the thing more talked about—in other words, more dangerous—was the fact that I was praetor at the time.[38] He needed a fair amount of money to pay off debts contracted by him under the most honorable circumstances. While some great and wealthy friends of ours were hemming and hawing over it, I borrowed the money myself and gave it to him interest free. I did this despite the fact that seven of my friends had been either put to death or relegated[39]—Senecio, Rusticus, and Helvidius had been put to death; Mauricus, Gratilla, Arria, and Fannia had been relegated. Scorched, so to speak, by so many thunderbolts falling around me, I divined from certain sure signs that the same destruction was looming over myself. Yet I do not believe that this makes me some kind of hero, as he claims, merely that I avoided disgracing myself.

You'll see why I had to when you consider our history. When I was a military tribune in Syria I had come to love and respect Artemidorus' father-in-law, C. Musonius,[40] so far as the difference in ages permitted, and had become close friends with Artemidorus himself. In fact, the first sign that I had any intelligence at all was that I realized that I could recognize a man who was either a sage or as close as you could come to one. Of all those who call themselves philosophers these days, you will hardly find one or two so thoroughly honest and genuine. I say nothing of the physical toughness with which he bears winter and summer alike; or of how he will undertake any labor and takes no account whatever of pleasure when it comes to food and drink; or of the self-control he displays both in his gaze and his emotions. Great qualities these, in any other man. In *his* case they are nothing compared with his other virtues, which got him chosen by C. Musonius as his son-in-law, in preference to various suitors of various ranks. When I recall these things, it is certainly gratifying to me that he heaps such praises on me in your presence and that of others. Yet I am afraid he goes beyond the proper limit, something he often exceeds in his kindness (I return, you see, to my starting-point). Though in other respects a most sagacious man, there is just one mistake that he falls

---

38. In the early 90s AD, partly due to the anti-monarchical agitation of some Stoic and Cynic philosophers, "many people were killed on a charge of philosophy" by the Emperor Domitian, and "all the rest" of the philosophers were expelled from Rome (Cassius Dio, *Roman History* 67.13.3). Pliny was probably praetor in 93.

39. A form of exile; see Glossary, *relegatio*.

40. C. Musonius Rufus, the leading Stoic thinker of the 60s and 70s AD, and teacher of Epictetus. Exiled by Nero in 65, he returned to Rome after Nero's death in 68 and was a respected and influential figure in the highest classes of Roman society.

into—an honorable one, but still a mistake: he values his friends more highly than they deserve.

## 10    A Farm Estate and Its Tenant-Farmers (3.19, to Calvisius Rufus)

Once again I need your financial advice. Some properties adjacent to my own lands, and even falling partly inside them, are for sale. There are many factors that tempt me to buy, and some equally important ones that warn me off. First, it would be a fine thing in itself to join the two properties. Second, it would be pleasant and convenient to be able to visit both at the same time and at the expense of one journey. They would be under the same estate manager, virtually the same staff.[41] I could stay in and furnish one villa, and merely maintain the other one. One also has to calculate the cost of equipment, the expense for head servants, gardeners, workmen, and hunting gear as well. It makes a big difference whether these are centralized or dispersed. On the other hand, I am afraid it will be a bad move to expose such a large amount of property to the same climate and the same risks. It seems safer to guard against the vagaries of fortune through diversification. Besides, it's quite pleasant, the change of scene and climate, the traveling around from one property to another.

But the chief point of consideration is this: the lands are fertile, rich, and well-watered, with meadows, vineyards, and woods that furnish timber. The revenue from this, though not huge, is steady. But the fertility of the soil is more than offset by the weakness of the tenant-farmers. The former owner often used to sell their security deposits,[42] and while this diminished their arrears, it drained their resources for the future. These losses, in turn, caused their debt to mount again. So I would have to supply them with slaves, and I'll have to pay extra to get honest ones—the more honest, the more costly. I don't use chained slave gangs, nor does anyone else in this area.[43]

There is one last thing to tell you—the likely price: three million sesterces. Once upon a time it was worth five. But owing to the miserable state of the tenant-farmers and the generally unfavorable times, the income from the land has gone down, and the price with it. You will ask whether I can readily raise three million. True, nearly all my property is in farmland, but I have some money out at interest, and it won't be difficult for me to borrow. My mother-in-law will accommodate me; her cash-box is at my disposal.[44] So don't let this influence you if the other factors are not in the way, all of which I want you to give careful consideration. For in real estate as in all other things, you are rich in experience and in judgment.

---

41. The bulk of the land was let out in small parcels to tenant-farmers, under the general control of a manager called a *procurator*. But some acreage around the owner's main villa was retained under the management of a slave overseer and slave workers. An absentee landlord like Pliny would visit his various estates occasionally to check up on things.

42. Collateral offered against non-payment of rent, including slaves, animals, and tools. When the tenant farmers fell behind on rent, the former owner took possession of these items and sold them.

43. Pliny the Elder also discourages this practice (*Natural History* 18.6.36).

44. Pompeia Celerina, the mother of Pliny's ex-wife, owned considerable properties herself, which Pliny helped manage.

**11    Hiring a Teacher for Comum** (4.13, to Tacitus)

It's good to hear you made it safely into Rome. I am always glad when you have arrived, but especially now. I'm going to stay a few more days here in Tusculum to finish a collection of poems that I've been working on. I'm afraid if I slack off at the last minute it will be hard to pick it up again. Meanwhile, since this is a matter of some urgency, I will now ask you the favor that I was going to ask of you when we meet, using this letter as a kind of advance courier. But first let me tell you the reasons for my request.

Recently when I was visiting my native region,[45] a boy still wearing the *toga praetexta*, the son of one of my fellow-townsmen, visited me on his morning rounds. "Are you studying?" I asked. "Certainly," he answered. "Where?" "At Milan." "Why not here?" His father—he had brought the boy to me—interjected, "Because we have no teachers here."[46] "No teachers?" I replied. "Surely it's in the best interest of you fathers"—and very opportunely there were several fathers within earshot—"that your children should be instructed here rather than somewhere else. Where better for them to spend their time than in their native land? What better moral supervision than the eyes of their parents? Where can they be educated at smaller cost than at home? It would cost you next to nothing if you pooled your money and hired some teachers here. After all, you can put toward their salaries everything you spend now on lodgings, travel expenses, and all the things which have to be purchased away from home (and everything has to be purchased when away from home). And I, though I have no children myself, am prepared on behalf of the commonwealth of Comum, as though she were a daughter or mother, to contribute a third part of whatever sum you decide to collect. I would even promise the whole amount, but I worry that such a gift might one day be squandered through favoritism. I see this happen in many places where teachers are hired at public expense. The only way to tackle this abuse is to make sure that the hiring is done by the parents alone, and that the requirement of making their own contributions adds an incentive to choose carefully. Those who might be careless with other people's property will certainly be careful with their own. They will see to it that only a deserving person receives my money, if he is to receive theirs as well. So get together and reach a consensus, and take encouragement from me, since I want the sum I contribute to be as large as possible. You can give no gift more noble to your children, or more rewarding to our commonwealth. Let those who are born here be educated here, and right from infancy let them grow accustomed to love and to inhabit their native soil. And I hope that you find such distinguished teachers that people from neighboring towns will seek their schooling here, just as your children now flock to other places."

I thought you should hear all this at length and from the source, as it were, so you will better understand how delighted I will be if you agree to undertake what I ask. I ask, or in view of the importance of the matter, I entreat that you look around for a teacher among the group of scholars that gather around you out of admiration for

---

45. Comum (modern Como) in northern Italy.

46. Teachers of rhetoric, that is. Students began the basic study in language and literature either at home or in local public or private schools, then a smaller number went on to study public speaking. See Quintilian, *The Instruction of an Orator* in this volume.

your talent.[47] Find me some that I might approach, but make sure they realize I will not make them a formal offer. I reserve complete freedom for the parents; *they* must judge, *they* must choose. All I want is to make the arrangements and pay my share. So if you can find anyone who has confidence in his own talents, let him go there with this understanding, that that confidence is the only guarantee he takes with him.

## 12     On His New Wife (4.19, to Calpurnia Hispulla, his wife's aunt)[48]

You are a model of devotion to family: that excellent brother of yours adored you as you did him, and you love his daughter as if she were your own. To her you are not just an aunt but a living embodiment of the father she lost. This is why I know it will be a great pleasure for you to learn that she is turning out to be worthy of her father, worthy of you, and worthy of her grandfather. She is gifted with remarkable savvy and remarkable frugality, and her love for me is a visible sign of her fidelity. Add to this her interest in literature, which she took up out of affection for me. She has my books, studies them, and even learns them by heart. How she worries when I'm preparing to speak in court, and how glad she is when it's all over! She arranges for messengers to report to her how much approving applause I get, and the result of the trial. It's the same when I give a reading: she sits nearby, separated from us only by a curtain, and enjoys listening to all the appreciative comments. She even sings poems I have written, and sets them to her cithara, with no teacher but love, which is the best of instructors.

All this makes me very confident that our marital concord will last and grow day by day. It's not my age and physique she loves—those are in their slow decline. Rather it is my good reputation. How appropriate for a girl raised by you personally, who has been molded by your precepts, and who witnessed in your house nothing but what was pure and honorable, who, finally, grew accustomed to love me through your commendations of me. You revered my mother as if she were your own. And so, from my very boyhood, you used to shape me, praise me, and predict that I would be the kind of man I now appear to my wife to be. She and I, then, compete in thanking you: I for giving her to me, she for giving me to her, as though you had chosen us for each other.

## 13     The Death of Fundanus' Daughter (5.16, to Aefulanus Marcellinus)

I write this to you in great sorrow. The younger daughter of our friend Fundanus is dead. I never saw a livelier or a more lovable young lady, or one more worthy not only

---

47. Like Pliny himself (*Letters* 6.11.23), Tacitus had a circle of students, evidently including people who would welcome a job opportunity in Comum. Prominent orators such as Tacitus, like legal experts, did not give regular instruction, but trained their followers by informal discussion, advice, and example.

48. Pliny was married three times. Nothing is known of his first wife. The second died in AD 97, and Pliny remained on friendly terms with her mother, Pompeia Celerina (see *Letters* 10 and note 44). His third wife, praised here, was Calpurnia, the orphaned granddaughter of Calpurnius Fabatus of Comum. Her miscarriage is described below in *Letters* 20.

of a longer life, but almost of one to last forever. She had not yet completed her four-teenth year,[49] and already she had an old woman's wisdom, a married woman's dignity, and yet a girl's sweetness, too, along with a maiden's modesty. It was wonderful, how she used to hang on her father's neck; how lovingly and with what affection and modesty she used to embrace us, her father's friends; how she cherished her nurses, minders, and tutors, each according to their own roles. How carefully she used to read aloud, and with what comprehension; how sparing and well-behaved she was in play; what self-restraint, what patience, indeed what courage she showed during her last illness!

She obeyed the doctors, kept telling her sister and her father not to worry, and sus-tained herself, after her bodily strength had failed, by sheer force of will. Her will to live lasted right up to the end, and was not shaken either by the length of her illness or by the fear of death, and her fortitude added even more weight to our stricken grief. What a terribly bitter, tragic death. Even more cruel than the fact of death was the time of life at which we lost her. She was already betrothed to an admirable young man. The wedding day had already been chosen, and we had already received our invitations. But now our great joy has become inconsolable grief. And grief ever finds ways to turn the knife. I cannot express how excruciating it was to hear Fundanus ordering that the money he had intended to spend on dresses and pearls and jewelry be spent on incense and unguents and perfumes.

Fundanus of course is a man of learning and wisdom, devoted from his earliest years to profound studies and sciences. Now he despises every philosophical principle he ever heard or spoke. Other virtues have gone by the wayside, all lost in love for his daughter. This is pardonable, even praiseworthy, considering what he has lost. He has lost a daughter who was like him in character no less than in face and expression, who bore a remarkably faithful resemblance to her father in all respects. So if you write to him about his all too well-justified grieving, be sure not to console him in a chiding or overly blunt way, but be gentle and friendly. The passage of intervening time will do much to help him receive this more readily. It's just like a wound. When it is still raw, it shrinks from healing hands, yet afterwards submits willingly and invites them. It's the same with a mental wound. When fresh, it rejects and runs away from consolations. Yet soon it yearns for them, and is calmed by them, provided that they are gentle.

## 14    A Freedman Comic Actor (5.19, to Valerius Paulinus)

I have seen how mildly you treat your slaves and freedmen, so I'm more ready to admit the indulgence with which I treat my own. I always keep in mind that Homeric expres-sion, "He was gentle as a father,"[50] and our own Latin term, "father of the household" (*paterfamilias*). Even if I were harsher and more callous by nature I would be deeply moved by the ill health of my freedman Zosimus. I feel all the more obliged to show him kindness now that he needs it so much. He is an honest and dutiful man, and a

---

49. Her epitaph, which survives on a stone found in Rome on the Vatican Hill, says she was almost thirteen (see *Inscriptions* no. 7 in this volume). Her father C. Minucius Fundanus was suffect consul in AD 107, and governor of the province of Asia under the Emperor Hadrian.
50. *Odyssey* 2.47.

literate one. His skill—his label, so to speak—is comic actor, and he excels in it. His delivery is sharp, witty, apt, even graceful. And he's a fine cithara player as well, better than a comic actor needs to be. What's more, he reads aloud orations and histories and poetry so skillfully you'd think he was trained to do nothing else.

Now, I'm giving you all this detail so you can better understand how many pleasant services this one man provides to me. Add to this my longstanding affection for him, which his dangerous illness has only increased. For it seems to be a law of nature that nothing excites and intensifies affection as much as the fear of bereavement, a fear I am suffering on his account, and not for the first time. A few years ago, while he was performing with intensity and vehemence, he began to spit blood. So I sent him to Egypt, and after a long stay there he recently returned in better health. Then he put too much strain on his voice for several days in a row; after a coughing fit that brought to mind his old illness, he spit up blood again. So I have decided to send him to the estate that you own at Forum Iulii.[51] I've often heard you say that the climate there is healthy and also that there is milk there particularly helpful for this kind of case.[52] I would ask you therefore to write to your people, so they open the villa and the house to him, and contribute to his living expenses, if he needs anything. But his requirements are modest. He is so frugal and restrained in his habits that he cuts back not just on luxuries but even in things necessary for his health. I will give him at his departure traveling money sufficient to get him to your place.

## 15     The Eruption of Mount Vesuvius and the Death of Pliny the Elder (6.16, to Tacitus)

You asked for an account of my uncle's death, so you can write about it more accurately for posterity. Thank you. I predict that his death will be forever renowned if you honor it in your histories. True, the manner of his dying, amidst the destruction of a supremely lovely region, in the unforgettable catastrophe of peoples and cities, guarantees him a sort of immortality. True, he himself wrote very many enduring monuments of scholarship.[53] Still, the immortal quality of your works will add much to keeping his memory alive. Blessed are those, it seems to me, whom the gods allow either to do what is worth writing about, or to write something worth reading. Blessed above all are those who attain both. This is the group to which my uncle will belong, thanks to his own books, and yours. So I am happy to comply, and even insist upon doing what you ask.

He was at Misenum, in command of the imperial fleet.[54] On the ninth day before

---

51. Fréjus, France.

52. Ancient medical writers, such as Celsus (Latin) and Galen (Greek), customarily treated tuberculosis with a diet of fresh air and milk, which was also regarded as treatment for headaches and fevers.

53. See above, *Letters* 8.

54. Misenum, on the northern arm of the Bay of Naples, was headquarters of the western fleet, whose command was a largely bureaucratic post, assigned to the Elder Pliny by the Emperor Vespasian.

the Kalends of September, at about the seventh hour,[55] my mother indicated to him that a cloud of unusual size and shape had appeared. He had already sunbathed, taken a cold bath, and eaten a snack (which he took reclining), and was engaged in study. He called for his sandals and ascended to a spot from which this astonishing sight could best be seen. A cloud was rising, but it wasn't clear from a distance what mountain was producing it (afterwards it was known to be Vesuvius). Its appearance and form could best be likened to a pine: a kind of trunk towered up to a great height and then spread out as if into branches. I believe the cloud was lifted up by an initial burst of air, then lost support as this grew weaker, yielded to its own weight, and thinned out sideways. It was sometimes white, sometimes dingy and spotted, depending on whether it carried earth or ash.[56] To a man of my uncle's scientific interests it seemed a remarkable phenomenon, and one to be observed from a nearer point of view. He ordered a Liburnian ship[57] to be made ready. He told me I could come along if I wanted. I said I would rather go on with my studies. It so happened that he had himself given me some writing to do. As he was leaving the house, a note arrived from Rectina, the wife of Tascius. She was terrified at the danger he was in, for his villa lay under the mountain, and there was no way out except by ship. She begged my uncle to rescue her from so desperate a situation. My uncle changed his plan, and what had begun as a learned enquiry ended as a heroic rescue mission. He launched quadriremes[58] and embarked in person to help not only Rectina but many others, since that lovely stretch of coast was thickly inhabited. He sped off in the direction from which everyone else was fleeing. He plotted a direct course and kept his helm set straight for the peril, so free from fear that he dictated notes as he observed all the shifting shapes of the evil phenomenon.

Ash was already falling on the ships, hotter and thicker the nearer they approached, then chunks of pumice and other stones, blackened, scorched, and cracked by the fire. Then suddenly the waters off the coast became shallow as the debris from the mountain made the shore unapproachable. He hesitated for a moment whether to turn back, then called out to the helmsman (who was urging him to do so), "Fortune

---

55. August 24, AD 79, around midday. Recent research strongly suggests that the eruption actually took place in November. The prevailing northerly winds as described in Pliny are typical of the winter season (late October to March); studies of storage vessels in and around Pompeii suggest the harvest of late fall produce; and a coin found there refers to an event that took place after August of 79.

56. An accurate description of the first phase of the eruption, called by modern volcanologists the "Plinian" phase in honor of our author, during which ash and various sizes of rocks and pumice stones were ejected along with hot gasses and water vapor. High altitude winds pushed the column south and southeast, until it spread over hundreds of square miles. Pliny aptly compares the sight to the Italian stone pine, also called the umbrella pine.

57. A fully equipped but light and fast oared vessel, mainstay of the Roman imperial fleets.

58. Large but fast and maneuverable warships with two levels of oarsmen, part of the imperial fleet at Misenum. Their relatively shallow draught made them suitable for coastal operations, and their capacity for carrying about seventy-five marines would have made them ideal for evacuating the coast beneath Vesuvius.

favors the bold! Head for Pomponianus."[59] He lived at Stabiae, across the bay (for the sea is embraced by a gently curving shoreline). When the danger was not yet imminent but was clearly going to come very close as it grew, Pomponianus had put his effects on shipboard, ready to sail the minute the unfavorable wind died down. My uncle was brought to shore by this same wind at his back. He embraced his trembling friend, consoling and encouraging him. He let his own cool-headedness reassure his friend, and ordered the slaves to carry them to the bath. After bathing, he reclined at dinner in a cheerful mood, or feigning good cheer, which is just as impressive.

Meanwhile vast sheets of flame and tall columns of fire were blazing from many points on Mount Vesuvius, their flashing brightness heightened by the darkness of night. "These are just fires left behind by panicked peasants," my uncle kept saying in an attempt to soothe their fears, "and deserted villas burning in the countryside." Then he went to bed and slept a perfectly sound sleep. His snoring (which due to his bulk was heavy and loud) was heard by those in attendance at his doorway. But the courtyard that gave access to the rooms was now so full of ash mixed with pumice that if he stayed much longer in his bedroom he would not be able to get out. Woken up, he emerged and rejoined Pomponianus and the others, who had stayed awake. They consulted together whether to remain under cover or roam about in the open; for the walls were swaying under the repeated and tremendous shocks and seemed to be moving back and forth as though detached from their foundations. Outside, on the other hand, there was fear of falling pumice, however light and hollow. Comparison of the hazards made them opt for this latter option. For his part, my uncle was making a rational calculation of the risks. With the others, one fear was simply stronger than the other. To protect themselves against the falling debris they covered their heads with pillows tied on with strips of cloth.

By this time it was day elsewhere, but there it was night, the blackest and thickest of nights, though many torches and lights of various kinds relieved it. They decided to go out to the shore to see at close hand if it was now possible for anything to sail. But the sea was still turbulent and hostile. At that point he lay down on a blanket, asked a couple times for water, and drank. Then there were flames and the smell of sulfur, the harbinger of more flames. This made others run away, but merely prompted him to get up. With the help of two slave boys he rose from the ground, and immediately fell back down. I infer that the dense air obstructed his breath and stopped up his windpipe, which was weak and narrow and frequently subject to wheezing. When day returned (two days after we last saw him) his body was found covered up, but whole and uninjured in the clothes he wore, looking more asleep than dead.

Meanwhile at Misenum, my mother and I—but this has nothing to do with history. You only wanted to know about his death, so I will leave it there. I will just add one last remark: everything I have described I either witnessed myself or heard about right away, when information is most reliable. But you should select the most important details. It is one thing to write a letter to a friend, quite another to write history for all to read.

---

59. Apparently the same person as Tascius mentioned earlier, the husband whom Rectina had asked him to rescue.

**16    The Eruption of Mount Vesuvius as Seen from Misenum** (6.20, to Tacitus)

You say that the letter I wrote for you about my uncle's death made you want to know about my own fearful ordeal at Misenum (this was where I broke off). "Although I shudder to remember, I shall begin."[60]

After my uncle left, I spent the rest of the afternoon studying (since that was why I had stayed behind). Then a bath, dinner, and sleep, though troubled and brief. There had been earthquakes for many days—a common occurrence in Campania and no cause for panic. But that night the quakes grew much stronger. Things seemed to be not just shaking but about to come crashing down. My mother burst into my room. I was in the midst of getting up myself and going to wake her if she was sleeping. We sat down in the small yard that lay between the house and the sea. I sent for a volume of Livy. I read and even took notes from where I had left off, as if it were a moment of free time—I don't know whether to call it bravery, or foolhardiness (I was seventeen at the time). Up comes a friend of my uncle's, visiting from Spain. When he saw my mother and me sitting there, and me even reading a book, he criticized her for being complacent, and me for being oblivious. But I kept on with my book.

It was now the first hour of the day, though the dawn was still doubtful, as if it were drowsy. Now the surrounding buildings began to shake violently. We were in an open area, but only a narrow one, so we were greatly afraid, in fact, certain of the impending building collapse. Finally, we decided to leave town. A stupefied crowd followed us, preferring our plan to their own (this is what passes for wisdom in a panic). The crush of the multitude pushed us on and swept us forward. Once we got out of the built-up area, we stopped. There we saw many amazing sights and had many frightening experiences. The carts we had ordered brought were moving in opposite directions, though the ground was perfectly flat. They wouldn't stay in place even with stone wheel blocks. In addition, we saw the sea had been sucked backwards, as if pushed back by the earthquakes. At any rate the shoreline had moved outwards, and many sea creatures were left stranded on dry sand. Behind us was a terrifying pitch-black cloud, broken by the frenetic twisting of fiery gusts, as it opened to reveal long flame-like shapes, similar to lightning, but bigger.[61] At that point the Spanish friend urged us strongly: "If your brother, and your uncle, is alive,[62] he wants you to be safe. If he is dead, he wanted you to survive him. What are you waiting for? Get out." We responded that we would not look to our own safety as long as we were uncertain about his. With no further delay he dashed off at a breakneck pace and got out of danger. Shortly thereafter a cloud descended upon the land and covered the sea. It surrounded Capri and made it vanish,

---

60. Vergil, *Aeneid* 2.12. The line is uttered by Aeneas as he begins to tell the story of Troy's destruction.

61. This evidently refers to the second phase of the eruption, in which the ash column, having collapsed onto the volcano, generated a very hot, dust-laden cloud of gas and incandescent rocks, called *nuées ardents* or "burning clouds" by volcanologists. Six of these surges swept down the steep sides of the mountain in the night and early morning hours, at speeds of perhaps sixty miles per hour, burying places such as Pompeii and Herculaneum; they did not reach north to Misenum or further south to Stabiae, which were merely covered in ash.

62. Addressing first Pliny's mother, then Pliny himself, referring in both cases to Pliny the Elder.

and hid Cape Misenum. Then my mother begged, urged, ordered me to flee however I could, saying that a young man could make it, but that she, weighed down in years and body, would die happy if she avoided being the cause of my death. I replied that I wouldn't save myself without her, and then I took her hand and made her walk a little faster. She obeyed reluctantly, and blamed herself for slowing me down.

Now came the ash, but only a dusting. I looked back: a dense cloud was looming behind us, following like a flood poured across the land. "Let's get off the road," I said, "I don't want to fall in the street and get crushed by the crowd in the dark." We had scarcely sat down when the darkness came—not like a moonless or cloudy night, but like a dark room when the lamp is out. Sounds: women shrieking, children wailing, men shouting. People kept calling out to their parents, children, spouses. They could only be recognized by their voices. Some bemoaned their own lot, others that of their near and dear. There were some so afraid of death that they prayed for death. Many raised their hands to the gods, and even more believed that there were no gods anymore and that this was one last unending night for the world. Some magnified real dangers with invented terrors, announcing that one or another part of Misenum had collapsed or burned. Lies, but they found believers. It got a bit lighter, but to us it seemed not like day but a sign of approaching fire. The fire itself actually stopped some distance away, but darkness and ash came again, a great amount of it. We got up to shake it off again and again, otherwise we would have been covered with it and crushed by the weight. I would tell you with pride that no groan or unmanly sound escaped my mouth in the midst of such terror, if not for the fact that I thought that I was perishing with the world, and the world with me, which was a great consolation for death.

At last the cloud thinned out into a kind of smoky fog. Soon there was real daylight. The sun was even shining, though with a lurid glow, like in an eclipse. The sight that met our still adjusting eyes was a changed world, buried in ash like snow. We returned to Misenum and cleaned ourselves up as best we could. We spent the night alternating between hope and dread. Dread had the upper hand, for the earth was still quaking, and a number of people who had gone mad were mocking others' misfortunes and their own with terrifying prophecies. Although we had been through many dangers and expected more, we still refused to go until we heard news of my uncle.

As you read this you will have no intention of writing about it, as the material is not at all suitable for history. But since you asked for it, you have only yourself to blame if it seems not even proper stuff for a letter.

## 17    A Mysterious Disappearance (6.25, to Baebius Hispanus)

You write that Robustus, a distinguished Roman knight, was traveling with my friend Atilius Scaurus, and got as far as Ocriculum, at which point their paths diverged and nothing further was heard of Robustus.[63] You've asked Scaurus to come and, if he can,

---

63. Robustus disappeared along with his slave retinue somewhere beyond Ocriculum on the Via Flaminia, about sixty miles north of Rome. The son of Robustus has visited Ocriculum and reported to Hispanus, Pliny's correspondent. Hispanus wants Pliny to put pressure on Pliny's friend, Atilius Scaurus, to return to Rome and help with the investigation. Atilius had been Robustus' traveling companion until their paths diverged at Ocriculum. This letter illustrates the hazards of travel outside cities even in central Italy, and the necessity of self-help.

to get us started in the search for clues. He will come, though I am afraid it will do no good. I suspect that what happened to Robustus is something similar to what once happened to a fellow-townsman of mine, Metilius Crispus. I had obtained an appointment for him as centurion, and had further presented him at his departure with forty thousand sesterces for his outfit and equipment.[64] After this, I never got any letters from him or any news with regard to his end. Whether he was killed by his slaves, or along with them, is a matter of doubt. Certainly neither he nor any of his slaves subsequently appeared, as is the case with Robustus. Nevertheless, we must try. We must send for Scaurus. We owe it both to your pleas and to the highly commendable pleas of his son, that excellent young man, who is searching for his father with such remarkable devotion and intelligence. May the gods favor him, so that he finds the object of his search, just as he already found his father's traveling companion, Scaurus.

## 18    A Roman Lady and Her Pantomime Troupe (7.24, to Rosianus Geminus)

Ummidia Quadratilla is dead, at almost eighty years of age, but she was vigorous right up to her final bout with illness, and with a body more compact and strong than you would expect in a matron.[65] She died leaving a will that did her great credit. She left two-thirds of her estate to her grandson, the remaining third to her granddaughter. The granddaughter I know only slightly, but the grandson I have the highest regard for. He's an outstanding young man, the kind even those outside the immediate family are bound to love like one of their own. First of all, though he is conspicuously handsome, he has remained untouched by malicious gossip, both in boyhood and youth. Married at twenty-three, he would be a father today if the gods had allowed it. In the house of a grandmother addicted to pleasure he lived a life of great self-discipline, and yet complied with every one of her wishes.

She kept a troupe of pantomime actors and spoiled them more than was fitting for a woman of her high rank.[66] Quadratus did not watch their performances, either at home or in the theater, and she did not ask him to. "I am a woman," I heard her say when she was entrusting her grandson's training to my care, "and we women have little to do. So I relax by playing backgammon,[67] and watch my pantomimists. But before I do either I instruct my grandson to go away and study."

You will be surprised at this, as was I: At the last games that were put on by the colleges of priests there was a contest of pantomimists, and as Quadratus and I were leaving the theater together, he said to me, "You know, today is the first time I ever saw one

---

64. Centurions could be created by promotion from within the ranks, or appointed by the emperor on the recommendation of influential persons. Centurions had to outfit themselves with equipment and expensive items such as a gold ring and a special white parade uniform.

65. She was the daughter of Ummidius Quadratus, suffect consul in AD 40 and governor of Syria.

66. The pantomime was a kind of drama performed by masked, sinuously moving dancers. See Glossary.

67. *Lusus calculorum*, some sort of board game.

of my grandmother's freedmen dancing." This is what her grandson said. But people who had no real connection with Quadratilla, by way of doing her honor—I hate to call it honor, rather they were doing their job as toadies—were running around the theater, jumping and clapping their hands, and admiring and imitating every gesture for the benefit of their patroness, all the while singing the music. And now these people will receive the tiniest of legacies, as a tip for their hard work at the theater,[68] from an heir who was never a spectator of these performances.

I have told you all this because when something new happens you generally don't mind hearing about it; also because it's a pleasure for me to renew my joy by writing about it. And I do rejoice both in the deceased's devotion to her son and in this young man's outstanding behavior. I am delighted, too, that the house which formerly belonged to C. Cassius (the man who was the chief and founder of the Cassian school)[69] should be headed by a man in no way his inferior. For my friend Quadratus will worthily fill it and do it credit, and once more restore to it its ancient dignity, fame, and glory, since he will emerge from it as great an orator as Cassius was a jurist.

## 19    Worship of an Italian River God (8.8, to Voconius Romanus)

Have you ever seen the source of the River Clitumnus? If you haven't—and I don't think you have, or else you would have told me—go see it. I recently did, and I regret waiting so long. There's a hill of moderate size, shaded by a grove of ancient cypresses. At its base the spring emerges, forced out through many channels of various sizes. It fights its way through a swirling pool of its own making, then opens into a broad pond, so clear and transparent you can count the small coins people throw in, and the glistening pebbles. From there the water is forced on not by the slope of the ground but by its own very abundance, as it were. No sooner does it leave its source than it becomes a real river, actually capable of bearing boats. Even when boats meet heading in opposite directions it allows them to pass and carries them on their way. The current is so strong and swift that, though the ground is level, you have no need of oars when going along with it, but against it you can just barely make progress with oars or poles. For those who are afloat for fun and recreation it is an enjoyable change of pace to work hard one minute and then turn around and ride the current. The banks are clothed with an abundance of ash and poplar trees, which the transparent river reflects one after another in countless green images, as though they were submerged in it. Its coldness rivals snow, and its color is just as pure.

Nearby is an ancient temple invested with religious awe: Clitumnus stands there in person, clothed and adorned with a *toga praetexta*.[70] The lots show that the god is

---

68. It was possible to be hired to applaud for a particular performer or orator (see Pliny, *Letters* 2.14.4–13, not in this volume), but these were volunteers, hoping for a spot in Ummidia's will.

69. C. Cassius Longinus, a prominent jurist and leader of a loosely defined "Cassian school" of legal thought in the mid-1st century AD.

70. The statue wore a real toga, like the ancient statue of Fortuna at Rome (see Pliny the Elder, *Natural History* 8.179). The toga was the scarlet bordered type (*praetexta*) which was the formal dress of magistrates and priests.

both powerful and prophetic.[71] A large number of shrines are scattered about, each with its own god, each with its own cult and name, and some even with their own springs. Besides the main parent spring there are other separate, smaller ones. But these flow into the river as well, which is itself spanned by a bridge. The bridge marks the boundary between what is sacred and what is profane: upstream from it only boats are permitted; below, one may swim as well.[72] A bath is provided at public expense by the people of Hispellum, to whom the late Emperor Augustus assigned this place. They also offer lodging. There is no lack of villas, either, which crowd around the outskirts, owing to the attractions of the river. In short, nothing there will fail to delight. You will even be able to study: you'll read inscriptions which hymn the waters and the god, written by people of all walks of life on every column and every wall. Many of these are not bad compositions, though others will make you laugh. On second thought, you, with your usual kindness, won't laugh at any of them.

## 20    On His Wife's Miscarriage (8.10, to Fabatus, his wife's grandfather)

Your eagerness to see us provide you with great-grandchildren will make you all the sadder to hear that your granddaughter has suffered a miscarriage. Young and naive, she did not know that she was with child, and because of this she neglected some precautions pregnant women should take, and did some things they should not do. For this mistake she has paid a great price, at serious risk to her life. And so, while I know you must take it hard that you have been deprived of descendants in your later years even though they seemed to be forthcoming, still, you should thank the gods. They refuse you great-grandchildren for the present, but preserve the life of your granddaughter, whose very fertility, even if proven in these unfortunate circumstances, gives us surer hope of those to come.[73] These same words I say to you I say to myself for encouragement, admonition, and strength. For my own desire for children is no less intense than yours for great-grandchildren. It seems to me that their inheritance, both from my side and from yours, will be a favorable path to public office, widely recognized family names, and *imaginēs* of no recent vintage.[74] May they only be born, and turn this sorrow of ours into joy.

## 21    Grief over Dying Slaves (8.16, to Plinius Paternus)

I am crushed by sorrow at the sicknesses of my slaves. Some are dying, too, and some of those quite young. Two thoughts bring me some consolation, and although not at all on a par with the depth of my grief, they do bring some comfort. One is my readiness to set them free. I will not feel like I've lost them quite so prematurely, it seems, if I lose

---

71. Oracular responses were sometimes written on slips of wood or metal called *sortes* or lots and shaken together in an urn until one emerged or was picked out.

72. It was thought that the human body could defile sacred waters.

73. In fact she did not conceive again.

74. See Glossary, *imaginēs*.

them as free individuals. The other is the fact that I permit them, even though they are slaves, to make a sort of last will and testament. I observe these just as if they were legal documents. They may instruct and request whatever they want, and I obey as if under orders. They may distribute, give, and bequeath their property—at least, within the limits of the household. For to slaves the household is a kind of republic, and stands in the place of a citizen community.[75]

Such consolations help, and yet I am weakened and broken by the very humanity of disposition that prompted me to allow these things in the first place. I would not for this reason like to become a harsher master. Other men, I know, call misfortunes of this sort a financial loss and nothing more, and hence seem to themselves great and wise men.[76] Whether they are great and wise, I cannot tell, but men they are not. For it is the part of a human being to be affected by grief, to have feelings, yet at the same time to struggle against them and to acknowledge consolations—in fact, to *need* consolation. About all this I have probably said more than I should, though less than I wished. There is a certain pleasure even in grief, particularly if you weep on the shoulder of a friend who is prepared to grant your tears either his approval or his indulgence.

## 22    Advice to a Provincial Governor (9.5, to Caelestrius Tiro)

You are doing an excellent job (I have my sources) in administering your justice to the provincials in a very civilized way.[77] Keep it up. The most important thing is to embrace and favor all the most honorable and decent people, and to win the affection of the lesser citizens in such a way as to keep the regard of the leading men. Many governors, afraid of seeming to cater too much to the powerful, earn a reputation for being rude, or even hostile. Of this fault you have kept yourself well clear, I know. But I can't help giving you praise that sounds a bit like advice, for you plot a middle course so as to preserve the distinctions of rank and dignities. If these are upset, disordered, and mixed up, nothing can be more unequal than the resulting "equality."

## 23    On Not Going to the Races (9.6, to Calvisius)

Sweet peace. I have been spending all my time lately among my writing tablets and my books. "In Rome?" you ask. "How is this possible?" Because the circus games are on, a type of entertainment in which I have not the slightest interest. There's no novelty, no variation, nothing one needs to see more than once. This makes me all the more astonished that so many thousands of people should have such a childish desire to see, over and over again, horses running, and men standing in chariots. If they were drawn by the speed of the horses or the skill of the drivers, maybe I could understand.

---

75. Compare Seneca, *Letters* 4 in this volume.

76. Like Cato the Elder. Compare Plutarch's discussion of this issue in his *Life of Cato the Elder*, ch. 5.

77. Pliny writes to the governor of the province of Baetica, in southwestern Spain.

No, they're fans of a jersey; it's the jersey they admire.[78] If the cars swapped colors in midstream during a race, the passion of the fans would change, too, and they would immediately abandon the very horses and drivers they recognize from afar, and whose names they repeatedly shout. Such is the authoritative prestige of a single cheap jersey, not merely among the mob, which I can forgive (after all, the mob is cheaper than the jersey itself), but even among some serious and important people. When I recall that such men can settle down so insatiably to this pointless, tedious, unending pursuit, I take some pleasure in the fact that I am not taken in by this pleasure. So during that whole time I spend my idle hours in literature, while others are wasting theirs in the idlest of occupations.

## 24    Entertainments at Dinner (9.17, to Julius Genitor)

I got your letter in which you complain that you were annoyed by an otherwise extremely elegant dinner party because jesters (*scurrae*), catamites (*cinaedi*), and fools were wandering among the tables.[79] Come on, shouldn't you stop frowning for a bit? True, I keep nothing of the kind, yet I put up with those who do. Why don't I keep them? Because I find nothing enjoyably shocking or humorous in some effeminate remark from a catamite, something rude from a jester, or something stupid from a fool. This is personal preference, not reasoned opinion. But then how many do you suppose there are who are alienated by entertainments that attract and enthrall you and me, and consider them either silly or positively annoying? How many are there who, when a reader, or a performer on the lyre, or a comic actor is introduced, head for the door,[80] or remain reclining with no less annoyance than that with which you sat through these monstrosities, as you call them. So let us be tolerant of other people's amusements, so they will be indulgent of our own.

## 25    Hopeless Debt among Tenant-Farmers (9.37, to Paulinus)

You are not the sort to demand the conventional formalities from your personal friends if you know they will be inconvenienced, and I am too steadfast a friend to think that you might take it the wrong way if I am not present to see you made consul on the first of this coming month.[81] I am prevented by the necessity of fixing leases on my farms for many years ahead, and for this I must come up with new ideas. During the last five-year term, despite considerable abatements in payments, arrears have only grown. Most tenants have stopped even trying to diminish debts which they despair of ever being able to pay in full. They even hoard and consume the produce, on the grounds that they have nothing to gain by keeping their hands off it. So I have to tackle this growing problem and try to fix it. The only solution seems to be to lease the farms, not

---

78. Color-coded jockeys drove chariots drawn normally by four horses each. The four factions were the Greens, Blues, Reds, and Whites.

79. For *scurrae* and *cinaedi*, see Glossary.

80. Literally, "call for their shoes"—which were removed before the *cena*.

81. Paulinus was suffect consul (see Glossary) from September to December 107.

for money, but for part of the produce, and appoint members of my household to collect and safeguard the harvest. There is no fairer type of income than the very products of the soil, the climate, and the seasons; but this plan requires a great amount of trust, sharp eyes, and numerous hands. Still, I will have to give it a try and see if, as with a disease of long standing, a change of approach may help. So you see it is no frivolous self-indulgence that prevents me from attending on the first day of your consulship, which I shall nevertheless celebrate here, just as I would if I were there, with prayers and joy and congratulations.

## 26    Rebuilding a Rural Temple (9.39, to Mustius)

The soothsayers[82] advise that I should rebuild the temple of Ceres on my estate into something bigger and better. It is quite old and small, though on festival days it is thronged with people. On September 13 a large crowd gathers from the whole district, much business is transacted, many vows are undertaken, and many paid. But there is no refuge nearby against rain or sun. So I think it will be an act of generosity and piety alike to construct as fine a shrine as possible, and add to it a colonnade—the temple for the goddess, the covered colonnade for the people. So please buy four marble columns of whatever sort you see fit, as well as marble for the improvement of the floor and the walls. We shall have to have a statue of the goddess made as well, because the old one is wooden and broken with age in some spots. As for the colonnade, at the moment nothing comes to mind that I need from you, unless you could draw up a plan suitable to the site. It cannot surround the temple, because the ground on which the temple stands is bounded on one side by a river with very steep banks, and on the other by a road. Across the road there is a large field where it might fit comfortably enough, facing the temple itself—unless you can think of some better solution, based on your long experience and skill with difficult sites.

[In 109 or 110 AD Pliny was appointed by the Emperor Trajan to govern the wealthy Greek-speaking province of Bithynia in northwest Turkey. Trajan states the reason for choosing Pliny: "I chose you for your good sense, so that you could guide that province in changing their ways and establish institutions that would lead to permanent peace there." (Pliny, *Letters* 10.117). The tenth book of his letters preserves exchanges in which Pliny consulted the emperor about various problems, and the emperor's brief responses. The eight letters translated below shed interesting light on life in a populous and urbanized Roman province, as well as the scope and workings of Roman provincial administration at this time.]

## 27    Financing a New Public Bath Building (10.23, Pliny to the Emperor Trajan)

The citizens of Prusa,[83] my lord, have public baths that are filthy and out of date, and so are very keen to build a new one. In my view you can assent to their request. There

---

82. *Haruspices*; see Glossary.
83. Bursa, Turkey.

will be money for the job, first from the amount I have already begun to call in and claim from private individuals. Second, they are now prepared to contribute toward the building of the baths the money that they have been spending on distributions of oil. Moreover, this is a work which is worthy of the importance of the city and of the splendor of your reign.

## 28    Reply (Trajan to Pliny, 10.24)

If the construction of a new bath building will not overburden the resources of Prusa, we can assent to their request, provided no new tax is imposed for this purpose, and it does not impair their ability to provide for necessary expenses in the future.

## 29    On the Treatment of Convicts (10.31, Pliny to Trajan)

I hope it will not be inconsistent with your eminence to help me with issues I confront, since you have given me permission, sir, to consult you in cases of doubt. In many cities, in particular Nicomedia and Nicaea, certain persons who had been condemned to the mines, or the arena, and similar kinds of punishment, are doing the jobs of public slaves, and receiving an annual stipend for their work as such. Since I learned about this I have long been debating what to do. I thought it would be too harsh to hand them over to punishment after so much time had passed. Most of them are old men, and by all accounts living quiet and honest lives. But to retain convicts in public employments does not seem proper. On the other hand, while there is nothing to be gained by supporting at public expense men who do no work, in my opinion to not support them could be dangerous. I thus felt compelled to leave the whole matter up in the air until I could consult with you. You may wonder how it came about that they escaped their appointed punishments. I asked that as well, but came away with no solid information to pass on. Records of their sentences were produced, but no documents proving their release. There were some, however, who said they had appealed and been released by former governors or their deputies, which makes sense, since no one else would dare to do this without proper authorization.

## 30    Reply (10.32, Trajan to Pliny)

You will recall that you were sent to the province you now govern precisely because there were many abuses that clearly needed correcting. Here is a prime example, that those who have been condemned to punishments have not only been released from them, as you write, without authorization, but have even been drawn into the category of respectable civil servants. Therefore, those who were condemned within the last ten years and released by no competent authority, must be returned to their punishment. If you find some old-timers, aged persons who were condemned more than ten years ago, let us assign them to jobs that are not far from being penal: it is normal to assign such persons to the baths, to cleaning out the sewers, or working on the roads and streets.

**31        On the Status of Exposed Children Raised in Slavery** (10.65,
           Pliny to Trajan)

An important question, my lord, and one affecting the whole province, is that of the status and costs of maintenance of those who are called "foundlings."[84] I have heard read the decisions of previous emperors on this subject and found nothing general or specifically applicable to Bithynia. So I thought I ought to consult with you for guidance, and did not think I could be content to rest on precedent in a matter requiring your authoritative judgment. An edict was cited to me, which was said to derive from the Emperor Augustus, relating to Andania; they also read out letters of the Emperor Vespasian to the Spartans, of the Emperor Titus to both the Spartans and the Achaeans, and of Domitian to the proconsuls Avidius Nigrinus and Armenius Brocchus, and also to the Spartans. I have not sent these to you, since they seemed to me to be inaccurate and in some cases of doubtful authenticity, and I felt sure that you had accurate and genuine versions in your files.

**32        Reply** (10.66, Trajan to Pliny)

This question—relating to those who were free born but exposed, then taken up by certain parties and raised in slavery—has often been discussed. Yet there is nothing to be found in the records of the emperors who have preceded me, in the shape of an established, universal rule for all the provinces. True, there are the letters of Domitian to Avidius Nigrinus and Armenius Brocchus, which, perhaps, ought to guide us. But Bithynia is not among the provinces which are the subjects of his rescript. I think, therefore, that the right of asserting free status should not be denied to those who wish to claim emancipation on this ground. Nor should their freedom be contingent upon their payment of maintenance costs.

**33        How to Conduct Trials of Christians** (10.96, Pliny to Trajan)

It is my custom, my lord, to consult you on all difficult questions, for no one is better able to resolve my doubts and inform my ignorance. I have never been involved in hearings concerning Christians before, so I do not know how or to what extent they are normally punished, or their cases prosecuted. And I was quite unsure whether to make an age distinction, or if there should be no difference between adults and children, no matter how young; whether a pardon should be granted to those who renounce their beliefs, or if once a person has been a Christian it brings him no benefit to cease; whether the title Christian itself is punishable, even if there is no criminal conduct, or rather the crimes associated with the name.

In the meantime, I have dealt with those turned over to me as Christians in the

---

84. Despite the difficulties many couples had in conceiving and raising healthy children, the practice of exposing unwanted offspring seems to have been common in the Greco-Roman world, perhaps especially among urban, unmarried women. Such exposed children often died, but some were rescued and treated as slaves, or else passed off as legitimate children.

following way.[85] I ask them directly whether they are Christian. Those who admit it I ask a second and third time, threatening them with punishment. If they persist, I order them led away for execution. For there is no doubt that, whatever it was they admitted or professed, their obstinacy and unyielding inflexibility should be sufficient reason for punishment. Some others possessed by a similar lunacy were Roman citizens, so I signed the order that they be sent to Rome for trial.

The very process of dealing with this has subsequently led, as so often happens, to the charge becoming more widespread and various. An anonymous pamphlet has been circulated which contains the names of a great many accused persons. I decided to dismiss charges against any who stated that they were not now, nor had ever been Christians, if they repeated after me a prayer of invocation to the gods, made an offering of wine and incense to your statue (which I had brought in to the court along with the statues of the gods for this purpose), and furthermore denounced Christ—things which I understand true Christians will never do.

A second group, whose names were supplied by an informer, admitted that they were Christians but then denied it. They said they had been, but stopped—some of these a few years ago, others even further back, and a few as many as twenty years previously. All of these also reverenced your statue and those of the gods, and denounced Christ. They stated, however, that the sum total of their error or misjudgment had been coming to a meeting on a given day before dawn, and singing responsively a hymn to Christ as to a god, swearing with a holy oath not to commit any crime, not to steal or commit robbery, not to commit adultery, not to break a promise or refuse to return a sum left in trust. When all this was finished, it was their custom to go their separate ways, and later re-assemble to take food, but only an ordinary and harmless kind.[86] But they said they had stopped doing even this after my edict forbidding secret brotherhoods, which followed on your instructions. So I deemed it necessary to determine the truth by interrogating under torture two slave women who were called the deaconesses of the group. I found nothing but an extreme and misguided superstition.

I have therefore postponed further examinations and made haste to consult with you. The matter seems to me worthy of your consideration, especially because of the number of people in jeopardy. A great many persons of every age, of every social class, men and women alike, are being brought in to trial, and this seems likely to continue. It is not only the towns, but also the villages and even the rural districts which are being infected by contact with this wretched cult.

Yet it seems capable of being stopped and corrected. At any rate, all reports indicate that the temples of the gods that were practically abandoned are now beginning to be filled again, sacred rites long in abeyance are being performed again, and flesh of sacri-

---

85. Note that there was no governmental policy of prosecuting Christians unless a private citizen brought a suit against them. Known examples of sporadic persecution from the 2nd century were led by private individuals. This would only change under the Emperor Decius (reigned AD 249–251), who instituted the first empire-wide persecution of Christians (see Inscriptions nos. 98–100 in this volume).

86. Christians were often charged with cannibalism because of the sacrament of the Holy Eucharist, when they would "eat the body of Christ," just as they were charged with incest for calling their spouses by the common (and just as harmless) Christian appellation "brother" and "sister."

ficial victims is now commonly sold, although until recently nobody would buy it. So it seems reasonable to think that a great many people could be persuaded to reform, if they were given some opportunity to repent.

## 34    Reply (10.97, Trajan to Pliny)

You have done the right thing, my dear Pliny, in handling the cases of those who were brought to you under the charge of being Christians. For it is impossible to lay down a single universally applicable rule, like a formula. These people must not be hunted out. If they are brought before your court and the case against them is proved, they must be punished. But in the case of anyone who declares that he is not a Christian and makes it perfectly clear that he is not, by offering prayers to our gods, he should obtain mercy on the basis of his expression of remorse, no matter how suspect his conduct in the past. But anonymous lists must not have any place in the court proceedings. That would set a terrible precedent, and one not at all in keeping with our times.

# PLUTARCH

(ca. AD 40–ca. 120, wrote in Greek)

## Introduction

A native Greek from the small town of Chaeroneia near Delphi, Plutarch is best known as the author of a collection of twenty-three pairs of biographies in which a famous Roman is matched with a Greek counterpart, the so-called *Parallel Lives*. The child of well-to-do parents, Plutarch was able to travel extensively (in Greece and abroad) and obtained the best education. When still young, he was sent to Athens, where he studied under Ammonius, who introduced him to Platonic philosophy. This would come to permeate his thought. A prolific author, he wrote many other works in addition to the *Lives*, including philosophical dialogues, literary essays, and therapeutic "self-help" books, all of which are generally grouped together under the modern title *Moral Essays*. But even his biographies could rightly be called moral essays because of their deep interest in philosophy and ethics. He is not interested, as he himself tells us elsewhere (*Nicias*, 1), in providing a mere storehouse of facts, but in creating a narrative thread that will reveal the character and personality of his subjects and establish them as models for virtuous behavior. As he says at the start of his life of Alexander the Great, "I'm writing biographies, not history." Plutarch, then, is offering his readers a series of examples to contemplate as they themselves consider their progress toward an ethical life.

We provide a translation for the entire *Life of Cato*, as well as a substantial passage from the *Life of Aemilius Paullus*. Cato (called "the Elder" to distinguish him from his great-grandson Cato "the Younger," the implacable opponent of Julius Caesar) is the epitome of an old-fashioned senator of the Republic. Tough and frugal, he worked the land himself, served in the army with distinction, and as censor sought to curb luxury. Although he was more versed in Greek language and culture than perhaps he would admit, in public he expressed strong disapproval of the obsession over things Greek displayed by some of his contemporaries—especially his political rival Scipio the Elder, the famed conqueror of Rome's most dangerous enemy, Hannibal. Old Roman values were being subverted, Cato thought, not only by the huge influx of wealth into the city following the Romans' defeat of Carthage and Greece, but also in the adoption of Greek ways of life. Plutarch himself takes a quite different view (ch. 22–23). He also takes Cato to task for his inhumane treatment of worn-out slaves (ch. 5), a passage in which Plutarch's humane philosophical outlook comes through clearly.

The excerpt of the *Life of Aemilius Paullus* is included because it lends insight into the practical and political issues surrounding the Roman triumph, one of the many public cultural practices that inspired young Romans (like Cato) to accomplish glorious deeds.

# The Life of Cato the Elder

Our sources tell us that Marcus Cato's family originally came from Tusculum, but prior to his military and political service Cato lived and worked on his father's land in the Sabine country.[1] His forefathers seem to have been complete unknowns, but Cato himself praises his father Marcus as a fine man and a good soldier. He also says that his great-grandfather Cato was often awarded military honors and that in recognition of his bravery he was repaid from the public treasury the price of the five war horses he lost in battle. The Romans traditionally dub those who make a name for themselves through their own accomplishments, rather than inheriting status from their family, "new men." They called Cato this, but he himself used to say that while he was "new" in terms of political office and fame, when one considered his ancestors' exploits and excellence in war, he was very "old" indeed. Originally his third name was not Cato, but Priscus. It was only later that he got the *cognomen* Cato because of his abilities— the Romans call a man who is shrewd *catus*.

As for his appearance, he had reddish hair and grey eyes, as we are informed by the author of this satirical epigram:

> Hair of red, wild grey eyes, with bite like an ornery snake;
>    when Porcius dies Persephone will say, "Him I refuse to take!"

Since from the very start he got into the habit of doing his own physical labor, followed a restrained way of life, and served in the army, he had a very fit body, ready for anything. His constitution was both strong and healthy.

He also took public speaking seriously and worked hard at it; it was, after all, a sort of second body, a necessary tool for a man aiming at glory and fame instead of a lowly and indolent life. He could often be found in the courts of the neighboring villages and towns, where he took up a case whenever someone needed an advocate. By doing so he acquired a reputation, first as a zealous defender, but soon enough as a capable orator as well. From this point on, people who dealt with him increasingly saw a certain gravity and resolution in his character that marked him out for great achievements and political leadership. Not only did he keep himself clean, refusing to accept a fee for his counsel at trials and hearings, but, what is more remarkable, he appears not to have cared much for the reputation garnered from his success in such cases. He much preferred the esteem that came from military action and battles with the enemy. In fact, when he was still a rather young man, the front of his body was already covered with wounds. Cato himself says that he went on his first campaign at the age of seventeen, when Hannibal was setting Italy ablaze with the flames of his success.[2]

In war he delivered a fierce blow with his hand, was steady and sure of foot, and had a ferocious look in his eyes. He unleashed threats and harsh war cries against the enemy; he rightly believed, and tried to convince others, that such yelling often terrifies the enemy more than the sword. On marches, he went on foot and carried his own arms, while a single servant followed with his provisions. They say that Cato never got

---

1. Just to the northeast of Rome; Tusculum is south of Rome.
2. 217–216 BC.

upset at this man or scolded him when he made his breakfast or supper; on the contrary, he often helped him prepare the meals if he had no military duties. On campaign he drank water. When he had a raging thirst he would call for some vinegar-water,[3] and when his strength was flagging he would add a little wine to his water.

[2] Near his fields was the villa that once belonged to Manius Curius, who had celebrated three triumphs.[4] He would frequently take a walk to this place, survey the small plot of land and the simple house, and reflect upon the man. Here he was, the greatest Roman of his time, who had subdued the most belligerent tribes, and driven Pyrrhus out of Italy. Yet he tilled this tiny plot of land himself and lived in this simple cottage—even after his three triumphs! It was here that a delegation of Samnites found Curius cooking turnips at his hearth and tried to bribe him with a great deal of money. He sent them packing, saying that a man who was content with such a simple dinner did not need gold, and adding that he found it more glorious to conquer people who had gold than to possess it. With these inspirational thoughts in mind Cato would return and would see his own home, fields, servants, and way of life in a new light. He redoubled his commitment to doing his own physical labor and pruning back extravagant living.

When Cato was still quite a young man, he happened to be serving under Fabius Maximus, when the latter took the city of Tarentum.[5] While there, Cato lodged at the house of a certain Nearchus, who was a follower of the Pythagoreans. Eager to get a taste of their philosophy, he listened as Nearchus discussed ideas that had been central to Plato as well: he called pleasure the greatest enticement to wrongdoing, and regarded the body as the greatest impediment to the soul, which can be freed and cleansed only by the exercise of the rational faculties that separate and remove it from bodily experiences. When he heard these precepts, he embraced the simple life and self-control all the more. Beyond this introduction into Greek philosophy, however, we are told that Cato came to Greek studies late in life and that it was only in extreme old age that he started reading Greek books. He learned a few things about rhetoric from Thucydides, but much more from Demosthenes. A fair number of Greek sayings and stories, however, are sprinkled throughout his writings, and among his collection of maxims and proverbs one will find that many are literal translations from the Greek.

[3] There was a man in Rome, as influential and well-born as any in the city, who had the unique ability to recognize excellence in its early stages and the goodwill to nourish it and turn it into true distinction. His name was Valerius Flaccus. His estate bordered on Cato's, and he learned from his servants about Cato's commitment to working the land himself and his restrained way of life. He was full of admiration when they described his routine, how early in the morning he would walk to the local forum and advocate for those in need, then return home, where he would work alongside his

---

3. Mixed with water, cider, or wine, vinegar was a thirst-quenching drink for simple people, and was the typical drink for soldiers in the field.

4. M'. Curius Dentatus, consul four times. He celebrated two triumphs in 290 BC for his twin victories over the Sabines and Samnites, and another in 275 after his victory over Pyrrhus at Beneventum.

5. Q. Fabius Maximus, "the Delayer," retook the wealthy south Italian city Tarentum in 209 BC, five years after it was delivered into the hands of Hannibal by a sympathizer.

slaves, wearing only a laborer's tunic in the winter or stripped down in the summer, and how he would recline beside his slaves at meals, eating the same bread and drinking the same wine. When Valerius heard these and other examples of Cato's mildness and moderation, as well as certain proverbs Cato was wont to say, he decided to invite him to dinner. He came to like him, and saw that his humane and refined character was like a plant that needed room to flourish and grow. So with encouraging words he persuaded Cato to take up a public career in Rome. Cato immediately headed to the city, where his efforts in the courts won him admirers and friends, apart from the considerable distinction and influence he got through his association with Valerius. He was elected first as a military tribune, and later to the office of quaestor. Now that Cato was well known and highly visible, he attained the top public offices right alongside Valerius, first as his consular colleague and later as co-censor.[6]

Among the elder Romans Cato devoted himself to Fabius Maximus, not just because he was a man of the highest repute and clout, but more importantly because he considered his conduct and way of life to be an excellent model for his own life. Because of his devotion to Fabius, Cato was ready and willing to oppose Scipio the Great,[7] who, although still young, had squared off against the powerful Fabius, and was generally thought to be resented by him. In fact, when Cato was sent as Scipio's quaestor in the African war and saw that the man was not only living extravagantly, as had become a habit for him, but also lavishing vast sums of money on his army, Cato did not hesitate to confront him face to face.[8] The most important thing, he said, was not the expense, but the fact that Scipio was corrupting the customary thrift of the soldiers, who were now turning to pleasures and luxuries because they had more than they needed. "I do not require," responded Scipio, "an overly scrupulous quaestor when I am heading into war under full sail. After all, I only owe the city an account of my performance, not my expenditures."

At this Cato left Sicily and returned to Rome and the Senate, where he, alongside Fabius, denounced Scipio's squandering of untold sums and frittering away of days, like a boy, in the wrestling grounds and theaters, as if he were not leading a war, but attending a festival. These protests convinced the Senate to send tribunes who, if the accusations appeared to have merit, were to haul Scipio back to Rome. Well, Scipio merely pointed out that victory in war depended upon the quality of the preparations, and that while he clearly enjoyed the company of friends in his times of relaxation, he never allowed his social life to make him careless in matters of the utmost importance and seriousness. Then he sailed off for war.

[4] Cato's clout increased a great deal because of his eloquence, and many Romans called him "Demosthenes." But it was his way of life that made him famous and

---

6. Cato was military tribune in 214 BC, quaestor in 204, consul in 195, and censor in 184.

7. P. Cornelius Scipio Africanus urged the Senate, against Fabius' opposition, to take the war to Africa, which in fact happened and led to Hannibal's retreat from Italy and his eventual defeat at Zama in North Africa in 202 BC.

8. The quaestor often served on campaign with a consul or praetor (see Polybius' description of the quaestor's tent in the Roman army camp in this volume) and was to keep the accounts of the general's expenditures. They could not legally deny their superior access to any funds voted to him by the Senate.

acclaimed. After all, every young man in Rome competed in the arena of public speaking, which was regarded as a universally desired prize. But a man who deigned to work with his hands like his ancestors had done, one who was content with a simple dinner, a cold breakfast, plain clothes, and an ordinary home, one who was less impressed by the possession of luxury than he was by the ability to do without it—now *this* was a rare bird. By this time Rome had grown too large to preserve its earlier integrity. Mastery over many lands and people meant the mixture of all kinds of customs, and exposure to a wide variety of lifestyles. So it is no surprise that the Romans, when they saw that all the other men were broken by hard work and were being made soft by pleasures, admired Cato all the more since he was overcome by neither. He was this way not only while he was still an ambitious young man, but even in extreme old age, with a consulship and triumph behind him. Just like a victorious athlete, he continued to follow his regimen of training and remained consistent until the day he died.[9]

He says, for example, that he never wore clothes that cost more than 100 drachmas, that he drank the same wine as the rowers, even when praetor and consul, and that he would buy in the marketplace a little extra meat or fish (thirty *asses'* worth) to supplement his rations of bread and wine—and he did this only for the sake of the city, so that he could keep his body strong while on campaign. He also says that once, when he inherited an ornate Babylonian carpet, he sold it immediately; that not a single one of his country houses[10] was plastered in stucco; and that he never bought a slave for more than 1,500 drachmas, because he did not need delicate young things, but hardy men to work the fields, such as stable hands and cattle drivers. And when these get old and useless, he thought, one should sell them off rather than pay to feed them. In general, he thought that nothing excessive was inexpensive—an unnecessary purchase is expensive even if it only cost a few cents. He purchased real estate not for watering and manicuring, but for farming and pasturing.

[5] Some people ascribed such practices to the fact that he was a cheapskate, but others more charitably felt that his belt-tightening was an attempt to correct and curb the excesses of others. I for my part, however, see it differently. His abuse of slaves, treating them like beasts of burden until they grow old and then driving them to market and selling them, is a symptom of an extremely stubborn insensitivity that recognizes no connection between human beings beyond that of utility. And yet clearly, compassionate behavior extends over a larger sphere than justice. We naturally apply the standards of law and justice only to human beings, but kindness and compassion, flowing from a good nature like water from an abundant spring, sometimes reach even mute animals.

For instance, a kind man will take care of his horses even after they are worn out with age, and his dogs, too, not only when they are young pups, but also when they

---

9. In fact his views and habits seem to have changed a good deal over his long life, as Plutarch himself acknowledges below (e.g., ch. 21).

10. It may seem incongruous to hear the possessor of several country houses praised for frugality, but being wealthy (measured in land holdings in antiquity) is not the same thing as putting one's luxurious lifestyle on display. For the Romans of the early Republic (so we're told), the only proper profit could come from productive farming of one's land. For Cato's attitude toward land-owning and his aggressive engagement in other forms of investment, see below, ch. 21. Plutarch's point here is that Cato refrained from the *ostentatious* display of his wealth.

are old hounds. When the Athenian people were building the Hecatompedon,[11] they set free all of the mules that they saw had been particularly hard working and allowed them to pasture unfettered and free. They say that one of them, however, returned of its own accord to the construction area, joined the pack animals that were pulling the carts up to the Acropolis, and took the lead as if to encourage and push them to the top. The Athenians passed a resolution that this mule be fed and stabled at public expense until it passed away. There is also the example of Cimon's horses, who gave him three victories in the Olympic games. Their graves lie next to his tomb. Like many men who have had dogs as close companions, Xanthippus, who lived long ago, gave a funeral to his dog, which swam next to his trireme all the way to Salamis when the Athenians abandoned their city.[12] The grave is located on a promontory of Salamis, which is still called Hound's Tomb.

We should not treat living beings like shoes or tools, discarding them after they've been beaten up and worn out from their years of service—if for no other reason than to practice our compassion. We have to train ourselves in these opportunities to be mild and gentle. Personally, I wouldn't sell an old ox that had worked for me, much less an elderly human being, forcing him, like some exile, to leave the place he grew up and the life he knows, all for a few measly coins. Isn't he going to be just as useless to the buyer as he was to the seller? But Cato, as if thriftiness were some badge of honor, says that he even left behind in Spain the horse that he rode all throughout his campaigns while consul. Why? So that he could save the city the cost of transporting it back home. Whether we should chalk up such behavior to unselfishness or to stinginess, well, one could argue convincingly either way.

[6] In other ways, however, his self-control made him a truly remarkable man. When serving as a military commander, for example, he used to take for himself and his staff no more than three Attic *medimnoi* of wheat per month and no more than 1 1/2 *medimnoi* of barley each day for his pack animals.[13] When he was assigned Sardinia as a province,[14] he was much more frugal than his predecessors. They were in the habit of charging their housing, couches, and clothes to the state treasury, and strained the finances of the provincials, who had to support the large entourages of their slaves and friends and pay for large, elaborate welcome dinners. Cato's frugality, by contrast, was a welcome change. He never made demands on the treasury for additional funds for any reason, and he used to visit the cities in the province on foot, attended by a single state-supplied servant who carried his religious garb and a vessel for sacrifices. The provincials under his jurisdiction found him an undemanding and unpretentious governor. On the other hand, he restored authority and seriousness to the position by his uncompromising administration of justice, and by the direct and no-nonsense way in which he carried out official edicts. For the islanders,

---

11. A building on the Athenian Acropolis, probably the original temple to Athena that predates the existing Parthenon.

12. During the Persian invasion of 480 BC, the Athenians abandoned Athens for the island of Salamis.

13. A *medimnos* was a dry measure of about fifty liters or 11.5 gallons. Compare the figures from Polybius ch. 39, and see Appendix "Roman Currency, Weights, and Measures."

14. In 198 BC, when Cato was praetor.

Roman rule was simultaneously more intimidating, and more welcome, than it had ever been before.

[7] His manner of public speaking reflected more or less the same dichotomies in the man. It was at once polished and imposing, pleasant and terrifying, playful and severe, sententious and contentious. It's just like what Plato said about Socrates: people who knew only his exterior thought him to be uncouth, rude, and insolent, but on the inside he was full of seriousness and profound ideas that could move his listeners' hearts and bring them to tears. In view of this I cannot understand the thinking of those who say that Cato's speeches resemble most closely those of Lysias.[15] Still, I will leave this matter to those in a better position than I am to judge Roman oratory. I will merely set down here a few of his sayings, since I maintain, contrary to what some people believe, that character is better revealed by what people say than how they look.

[8] The first comes from the time when the Roman people were determined to force a distribution of grain at a bad time and Cato was trying to dissuade them. He began with this: "It is difficult indeed, my fellow citizens, to talk to a belly, since it has no ears." When he was denouncing the excesses of his time, he said that it was difficult to rescue a city in which a fish sells for more than an ox.[16] Once he likened the Romans to sheep: "When you get sheep individually they go their own way, but in a group they blindly follow their shepherds. You're no different," he continued, "since whenever you come together you let yourselves be led by people whose advice you would never be willing to follow in private." When delivering a speech on the power of women, he said "All men rule their wives. We rule all men, but our wives rule us." The last, however, was adapted from a saying of Themistocles, who, when he found himself being ordered around by his son through his wife, said, "Wife, the Athenians rule the Greeks. I rule the Athenians. You rule me. Our son rules you. Our boy, hare-brained as he is, has the greatest power in Greece—make sure he treads carefully with it."

Cato said that the Roman people regulated the value not only of dyes, but also of people's behavior: "Just as dyers choose the colors that they see their customers like, so the young study and pursue the behavior which earns your praise." He used to urge the people, "If it was virtue and self-control that made the Romans great, then don't change a thing. If it was greed and wickedness, then make a change for the better—those former qualities have gotten you far enough already."

Then there's his jab at men who were always seeking public office, saying that they must be lost, since they always seemed to need lictors to show them the right road. He also rebuked the Romans for voting the same men into office over and over again. "You will give the impression," he said, "either that you don't think public office is worth much, or that you don't think many people are worthy of public office." Concerning a certain political enemy of his who everyone knew was living in a disgraceful and shameful way, he said, "Mothers often pray for their sons to outlive them, but *his* mother calls upon the gods to prevent that." Then there is the case of the man who had sold his ancestral land, which sat along the sea. Cato pointed to him, and, pretending

---

15. An Athenian speechwriter known for his artful simplicity—a trait that seems to match Cato's style. See Pliny, *Letters* 2 in this volume.

16. The consumption of extremely expensive fish by rich Roman gourmets attracted the ire of moralists.

to admire him as more powerful than the sea, said, "These vast lands, of which the sea hardly had a taste, this man swallowed with ease."[17]

When King Eumenes visited Rome, the Senate welcomed him with excessive ceremony, and the leading men of the state fell over each other in an effort to fawn upon him, but Cato did not conceal the fact that he did not trust him and kept his distance.[18] When someone remarked, "But he's a good man and an ardent supporter of Rome," Cato replied, "Fine, but keep this in mind: this creature you call king is by nature a carnivore." He went on to say that none of the kings that people called blessed in his time could hold a candle to Epaminondas, Pericles, Themistocles, Manius Curius, or Hamilcar Barca.[19] He used to say that his political enemies were bitterly disposed toward him because he would rise every day before dawn and, ignoring his domestic life, devote the whole day to state business. He also said that he would prefer to act nobly and receive no thanks for the good deed than to act disgracefully and escape criticism. And at another time he remarked that he pardoned everyone else's mistakes except his own.

[9] One time, the Romans elected three men to serve as ambassadors to Bithynia: one who had a case of gout, another who underwent an operation in which part of his skull was removed with a trepan, and a third who everyone thought was an idiot. Cato scoffed, saying that the Romans were dispatching an embassy that had no feet, head, or heart.[20] On another occasion Scipio (on Polybius' request) asked him for support on behalf of the Achaean exiles.[21] The speeches ran long in the Senate—some urging that they be sent home, others opposing the measure—until finally Cato stood up and said, "Here we are, sitting around as if we have nothing better to do, whiling away the whole day debating whether some old Greek men will be carried to their graves by Roman or Achaean undertakers!" The Senate voted in favor of their return to Achaea. A few days later, however, Polybius and his supporters wanted another hearing before the Senate, this time to request that the exiles be restored to the honors that they had formerly had in Achaea, and they asked Cato what he thought about it. He smiled and said to Polybius, "So you have escaped the Cyclops' cave, Odysseus, and now you want to go back in and get the hat and belt you left behind?"[22] He was accustomed to say that intelligent people benefited more from fools than the other way around, since the former were always trying not to repeat the latter's mistakes, while fools never try to imitate the successes of the wise. He remarked that it pleased him more when young men blushed than when they went pale, and that he had no use for a soldier who moved his hands while marching, or his feet while fighting, or one whose snoring was louder

---

17. The man had apparently sold this estate to pay for his extravagant tastes in food and wine.

18. King Eumenes of Pergamum, an ally of Rome who benefited greatly from their support, visited Rome in 172 BC to warn them of the looming threat posed by the Macedonian king Perseus.

19. Successful generals and leaders who were not monarchs.

20. In Cato's day the heart was considered the organ of intelligence.

21. After the Romans defeated Perseus at Pydna in 168 BC, the Romans deported 1,000 prominent members of the Acheaean league, including the historian Polybius, and detained them until Scipio Aemilianus secured their return in 150 or 149 BC.

22. In other words, don't be greedy, and get out of Rome while the getting is good.

than his battle cry. When he saw an exceedingly obese man, he asked reproachfully, "How could such a body as yours be of service to the city? Everything from your throat to your groin is a gut!" Once, a certain *bon vivant* invited Cato to join the circle of his acquaintances, but Cato said he could not spend time with someone whose palate was more discerning than his mind. One of his sayings was that the lover's soul resided in another person's body. He said he had only three regrets: that he once entrusted his wife with a secret; that he once went by boat when he could have walked on foot; and that he once spent a whole day without a last will and testament. To an old man who was acting dishonorably he said, "Poor fool, old age already has enough indignities of its own. Don't add to them the disgrace of wrongdoing." When a tribune, who had earlier been falsely accused of poisoning someone, was vehemently trying to pass a worthless law, he said, "My young fellow, I do not know which is worse, to quaff the drink you mix or to pass the law you author!" When a man who had lived a wanton and worthless life maligned him, Cato responded, "Unfair, this fight between you and me! You dish out insults at the drop of a hat and are unfazed when they are directed at you. I, on the other hand, find it distasteful to dish them out and am unused to hearing them." Such is the tenor of Cato's sayings.

[10] When he was elected consul [195 BC] with his friend and confidant Valerius Flaccus, he received as his province the area the Romans call "Nearer Spain." He was in the process of subjugating some tribes and winning over others through diplomacy when a large band of natives descended upon him and threatened to drive the Romans from the area in disgrace. He therefore appealed to the Celtiberians, who lived nearby, asking for aid in the war. In return for assistance they demanded a price of 200 talents. Everyone else thought it unendurable that the Romans pay barbarians for assistance. Cato, however, said it was not so terrible. If the Romans proved victorious, they could pay them with the spoils of the enemy, not out of their own funds, and if they were defeated, there would be no one either to demand or to make payment. Cato won this battle decisively, and carried out the rest of his duties in Spain with success and distinction. In fact, Polybius reports that on his orders the walls of every city this side of the River Baetis were demolished in a single day. (There were a great many of these and they were full of great warriors.) For his part Cato said that the number of cities he captured was greater than the number of days he spent in Spain—no idle boast, if indeed there were 400 of them.

His soldiers were greatly enriched by the campaign, but Cato distributed an additional pound of silver to each man. He said that it was better that many Romans return home with silver than a few with gold. As for himself, he says that the only spoils he accepted were what he drank and ate, adding, "I do not blame men for wanting to enrich themselves from war, but my goal is to compete with the best men in virtue, not with the wealthiest in cash or the greediest in avarice." He tried to keep both himself and those around him completely unsullied from the taint of profiteering. He had five servants with him on campaign, and one of these, Paccius by name, bought three young children from among the prisoners. When Cato got wind of this, Paccius hanged himself rather than face his master. Cato sold the children and returned the monies to the state treasury.

[11] While he was still busy in Spain, Scipio the Great, his political enemy, in a desire to block Cato's successes and steal command of the Spanish campaign from him, managed to get himself appointed as Cato's successor in that province. He headed

there as quickly as he could and put an end to his rival's command. Cato, however, took as an escort home five units of infantry and 500 cavalry, and on his way home he subjugated the Lacetani and put to death the 600 deserters he recovered from them. Scipio was absolutely furious over this, but Cato teased him, saying that Rome would be great if and only if men of high repute never allowed commoners to outdo them in excellence, and if commoners like himself strove to equal the excellence of men of higher birth and reputation. Despite Scipio's intentions, the Senate voted not to alter or reverse any measures Cato had made, and so Scipio's command passed idly, marked by inactivity and downtime, to the effect that it diminished Scipio's reputation more than it did Cato's.

Meanwhile, Cato celebrated a triumph, and did so in the right spirit. The majority of men strive not for excellence, but for reputation, and once they arrive at the highest honors—the consulship and triumphs—they leave public service to live out the remainder of their lives amidst pleasures and relaxation. But Cato never relaxed or lost his commitment to excellence. No, just like those entering public life for the first time, with their great thirst for esteem and renown, he leapt back into the fray, going out of his way to make himself available to his friends and fellow citizens, refusing no request, whether to plead in the courts or to serve in the field.

[12] For example, he assisted Tiberius Sempronius when he held consular command over the lands in Thrace and along the Danube, acting as his legate.[23] He also served as military tribune for Manius Acilius on a campaign in Greece against Antiochus the Great, who struck more fear in the Romans than any other enemy since Hannibal.[24] Antiochus had recently recovered nearly all the lands that Seleucus Nicator[25] once possessed in Asia and had subjugated a great number of warlike barbarian tribes. Inflated by his successes, he was ready to clash with the Romans, who were, in his view, the only worthy opponents left. He offered up a specious motive for going to war—to liberate the Greeks—and crossed over into Greece. (The Greeks hardly needed liberation since they had just been freed from Macedonian control under Philip and been given full autonomy by the goodwill of the Romans.)[26] Instantly Greece was thrown into a state of turmoil and uncertainty—she had lost her bearings at the hands of political agitators promising rewards from the king. So Manius dispatched ambassadors to the cities that were on the verge of an uprising. The majority of these Titus Flamininus restrained and calmed without any trouble, as you can read in the book about his life. But Cato delivered Corinth, Patrae, and finally Aegium.

Cato spent a great deal of time in Athens. It is said that he delivered a speech in Greek to the people there and that it still circulates. In it, he is supposed to have said that he was a great admirer of the virtue of the Athenians of old and was excited to

23. T. Sempronius Longus, consul in 194 BC.

24. M'. Acilius Glabrio, consul in 191 BC, led the successful Roman campaign against an invasion of Greece by Antiochus III, king of the Seleucid kingdom (roughly modern Iraq and Syria), as is described in the next chapters.

25. Seleucus I, surnamed Nicator ("the Conqueror"), was the successor of Alexander the Great and great-great-grandfather of Antiochus III. Seleucus' kingdom had become fragmented in the intervening period.

26. T. Quinctius Flamininus defeated Philip V, king of the Macedonians, at Cynocephalae in 197 BC, then proclaimed the Greek cities free and autonomous the following year.

be a visitor of a city of such size and beauty. But this is simply not true. He addressed the Athenians through an interpreter. True, he could have spoken directly to them, but he was deeply committed to the Roman way of doing things and had nothing but scorn for those who were enamored of things Greek. I'll give you an example. When Postumius Albinus composed a history, he begged his readers' pardon for having written it in Greek. Cato mocked him by saying that he would deserve pardon only if he had been compelled to undertake the task by a decree of the Amphictyonic Council.[27] He also informs us that the Athenians were impressed with the brevity and concision of his speech; although his statements were brief, it took the interpreter a long time and many words to relay the message. This is his general opinion on the matter: the Greeks speak from their lips, the Romans from their hearts.

[13] When Antiochus had blockaded the narrow pass at Thermopylae with his army, constructing walls and other fortifications to reinforce the natural defenses of the place, he slacked his efforts in the belief that he had completely locked out the war by barring the gates of Greece. The Romans completely gave up on any hopes of forcing their way through that narrow opening, but Cato recalled that famous move by the Persians, how they swung around and bypassed the narrows.[28] He selected a sizeable force and set out at night. But once they had progressed up the hill, the prisoner who was guiding them lost his way. As he wandered over the steep crags and impassable places, an eerie feeling of despair mixed with fear washed over the soldiers. When Cato saw how dangerous the situation was, he ordered the whole company to stay quietly where they were. Meanwhile, he took Lucius Manlius, a skilled mountaineer, and set out over the treacherous terrain under the profound darkness of a moonless night. It was quite the ordeal, made worse by the fact that their sight was severely blocked and obscured by wild olive trees and outcroppings of rock. Finally they stumbled upon a path, which led down to the enemy camp, or so they thought. They set up markers on some conspicuous ledges that rose over Callidromus, then went back to pick up the rest of the contingent.

They proceeded toward the markers, found the trail, and started their journey down the slope. They had not gone far when the trail disappeared and they were facing a giant ravine. Helplessness and fear set in again—little did they know, and they could not see, that they were right on the enemy's doorstep. But as soon as dawn began to break, someone thought he heard voices, and soon they thought they could make out a Greek outpost and guards at the foot of the cliff. Cato stopped his contingent on the spot and ordered the men of Firmum, whose loyalty and readiness he could count on, to meet with him apart from the others. When they had rushed to his side and stood all about him Cato addressed them: "Ok, men, I need to take an enemy soldier alive and question him to find out who these guards are, how many there are, how the rest of the Greeks are positioned or deployed, and what preparations they have made for our advance. The success of this mission requires you to act with the speed and boldness of lions who, though unarmed, attack those of their prey who lack spirit."

27. The Amphictyonic Council was a confederation of Greek states that regulated the cult at Delphi and represented interests of Greece as a whole.

28. In 480 BC a contingent of 300 Spartans famously held the Persian army at bay at Thermopylae, until a Greek informant showed them another path over the mountain (see Herodotus, *Histories* book 7).

At the end of Cato's speech the Firmians sped away and, just as they were, started running down the mountain toward the guards. They descended upon them unexpectedly and threw the whole outpost into confusion, routing them. They seized one of them, complete with his arms, and turned him over to Cato. From this man Cato learned that the Greeks' main force was stationed in the Thermopylae pass and was led by the king himself, but those guarding the mountain trails were 600 hand-picked Arcadians. Unimpressed with their small numbers and their carelessness, Cato immediately advanced upon them with blares of trumpets and battle-cries, and was himself the first to draw his sword. When the enemy saw the Romans rushing at them from the cliffs, they fled to the main camp, where they threw the whole army into terror and confusion.

[14] While Cato was attacking from above, Manius was assaulting the fortifications from below, storming the pass with his entire force. Antiochus was struck in the face by a stone, which knocked out his teeth. In extreme pain, he turned his horse and fled. After that, no part of the army held their ground against the Romans. Instead, despite the fact that they faced treacherous terrain where one could easily go astray—deep swamps and sheer crags meant slips and falls—the Greeks fled in those directions through the narrow passes, pushing each other in a crush of men. As they fearfully tried to avoid the enemy's sword stroke, they propelled themselves to their doom.

Now, Cato was apparently never one to refrain from singing his own praises, or from making a great boast when it followed upon a great achievement. But over no other deed did he ever gloat as much as over what he had done at Thermopylae. He says that those people who saw him pursuing and cutting down the enemy realized that the debt Cato owed to Rome was nothing compared to what Rome owed to Cato. He went on to say that the consul Manius, when the victory was still fresh for both of them, gave Cato a long embrace, hailing him and crying out in joy that neither he himself nor the whole Roman state could possibly repay Cato for his courageous deeds. Immediately after the battle he was sent back to Rome to announce his own victory. His voyage to Brundisium passed smoothly; from there it took him only a day to cross over to Tarentum, and then after four more days on the road he arrived in Rome on the fifth day after he touched Italian soil. He was the first to announce the victory. He filled the city with happiness and sacrifices, and the people with the conviction that they could be master over every land and every sea.

[15] In terms of Cato's wartime activities, what we have just described are more or less the most noteworthy. As for his political life, he thought that his most important role, and one deserving most of his energy, was denouncing and exposing wrongdoers. He prosecuted a great number himself, assisted other prosecutors, and convinced still others to prosecute, such as in the case of the Petilii vs. Scipio.[29] Scipio, however, on the merits of his great family name and genuine strength of will, crushed the trumped-up charges beneath his foot. Cato, realizing he could not secure a death sentence, abandoned that case and joined those prosecuting Scipio's brother, Lucius,[30] winning a

---

29. Two tribunes of this name prosecuted Scipio Africanus in the Senate in 187 BC, according to Livy, who also states that Cato was behind it (*Roman History*, 38.54.2).

30. L. Cornelius Scipio Asiagenes, consul in 190 BC, was accused of taking bribes from Antiochus in 187 BC.

conviction that carried with it an enormous fine to be paid to the state. Lucius did not have the resources to pay the fine, and was on the verge of being imprisoned, but just barely managed to escape imprisonment on appeal to the tribunes.

There is also the story of the young man who convicted a personal enemy of his dead father, depriving him of his civic rights. As the youth walked through the Forum after the trial, Cato ran up to him, shook his hand warmly, and said, "These are the sacrificial victims we should bring to honor our dead parents, not lambs and kids, but the tears and convictions of their enemies." Now, Cato himself did not survive unscathed in the political arena; whenever he exposed himself to his enemies—and this happened frequently—he found himself under prosecution and at risk of sanction. We are told, in fact, that he was prosecuted just under fifty times, the last time when he was eighty-six years old. In that case he uttered the memorable line, "It's rather difficult, when you've lived in one generation, to have to defend yourself in front of the next." This was not the last time he was involved in a trial, however. Four years later, when he was ninety, he brought charges against Servius Galba.[31] One could even argue that he, like Nestor, lived an active life into the third generation. As we mentioned above, he faced off against Scipio the Great many times in the political arena and lived down into the time of Scipio the Younger, who was the elder's grandson by adoption (he was the biological son of Paullus, the conqueror of Perseus and the Macedonians).[32]

[16] Ten years after his consulship, Cato ran for censor. This office is summit, so to speak, of all magistracies, and one may fairly say that it is the crowning achievement of a political career. The position has a great deal of power over many things, but most importantly it carries with it the responsibility of examining the characters and lifestyles of Roman citizens. Marriages, procreation, lifestyle, social life—all of these, the Romans thought, should be subjected to examination and scrutiny to uncover people's impulses and proclivities. You see, they thought that the character of a man was better seen through his private life than in his public or political career, and so they elected two men—one patrician, one plebeian—as guardians, correctors, and punishers to ensure that no one went astray because of pleasures or deviated from the customary ways of his ancestors. They called these officers "censors," and they had the power to take away a man's horse[33] or to banish him from the Senate if he led an undisciplined and wayward life. These men also conducted assessments of people's property and maintained the census lists in which they divided the citizen body into tribes and political classes. These are just a few of the great powers this office possessed.

It is for this reason that nearly all of the distinguished and powerful senators gathered together to oppose Cato in his candidacy for the censorship. The patricians were indignant, convinced that noble pedigree would be trampled in the mud if men from humble origins rose to the highest peak of honor and power. Crooked senators who were living a very un-Roman way of life (and knew it), meanwhile, feared the severity of the man, who would be inexorable and ruthless if he were in power. Therefore,

---

31. In 149 BC. Plutarch's details are faulty—Cato died in 149 at the age of eighty-five.

32. P. Cornelius Scipio Aemilianus Africanus (ca. 185/4–129 BC); see the excerpt of Plutarch's *Life of Aemilius Paullus* in this volume.

33. That is, to demote one from the equestrian class by taking away his state-sponsored horse.

they conspired and worked together to put up seven candidates to oppose Cato in the election.

These candidates wooed the multitude with marvelous promises, assuming that the people wanted their leaders to be soft and pampering. Cato did the opposite; he made no such concession to the people, but took to the speaker's platform, threatening wrongdoers in no uncertain terms and shouting that the city was in need of a thorough cleansing. He told them that, if they were smart, they would choose not the most pleasant doctor, but the one who was most aggressive. He was just that doctor, and so was Valerius Flaccus of the patrician class. Cato thought that only with Flaccus' help could he make any progress toward cropping and cauterizing the Hydra-like tentacles of softness and luxury. As for the other candidates, they were, in his view, forcing their way into an office and destined to govern it poorly because they feared those who would govern it well. And as it happened, the Roman people proved to be truly great and worthy of great leaders. Unafraid of Cato's inflexibility and imperiousness, they rejected those indulgent candidates whose every action seemed calculated to please them, and along with Cato they elected Flaccus, obeying his recommendations as though he were already in office, not just a candidate for it.

[17] And so Cato named as chair of the Senate his colleague and friend Lucius Valerius Flaccus,[34] then proceeded to expel a large number of men from its ranks, the most notable of whom was Lucius Quinctius. This man had been consul seven years earlier, but was even more well known for being the brother of Titus Flamininus, the conqueror of Philip. He expelled him for the following reason. Lucius had taken up with a boy who was known to make a living off of his youthful good looks, and kept him constantly at his side. He would even bring him on campaigns, giving him more honor and power than anyone else, even his closest friends and kin. At a certain drinking party during Lucius' campaign in his consular province, this young man was lying on the couch next to him as usual. Lucius was very susceptible to flattery when he had been drinking, and the young man started to lay it on in various ways. He said that he loved Lucius so much that "even though there was a gladiatorial contest going on in my home town, I rushed to your side—despite the fact that I'd never seen one and I very much wanted to see a man slaughtered." In an attempt to requite his lover's devotion, Lucius responded, "Well, I would not have you lying there pained by your loss. I will cure your pain." Then he ordered a prisoner already condemned to death be brought to the party and had a lictor stand beside him with an axe. He asked his beloved if he still wanted to see a man killed. When he said he did, Lucius ordered the man to be beheaded. This is the account that most narrate, and it is the one that Cicero puts into Cato's mouth in his dialogue *On Old Age*. But Livy claims that the man executed was a Gallic deserter and that Lucius did not have the man killed by a lictor, but did the deed with his own hands. He gives as his source one of Cato's speeches.

However that may be, when Lucius was expelled from the Senate by Cato, his brother took it hard. He made an appeal to the people and demanded that Cato give an account of his reasons for the expulsion. When Cato explained and recounted Lucius' actions at the drinking party, Lucius at first tried to deny the charges, but when Cato

---

34. Usually the longest serving senator of censorial or consular rank, the *princeps senatus* was the first to give his opinion on any matter before the Senate.

challenged him to repeat his denial in a trial where money was on the line, he backed down.[35] At the time the people thought that Lucius got just what he deserved. During a theatrical performance some time later, however, when Lucius passed by the seats reserved for those of consular rank and sat in a section far away from them, the people felt pity and protested. They insisted that he change his seat—thus correcting and alleviating, as far as was possible, his embarrassment for what had happened to him.

Cato also expelled a man who seemed destined for the consulship, Manilius, for showing his wife too much affection in broad daylight while his daughter looked on. Cato said that he never embraced his own wife except when it thundered loudly, adding, playfully, that he was a happy man when Jupiter decided to thunder.

[18] Cato received some intense criticism over his treatment of Lucius, the brother of Scipio. Here was a man who had celebrated a triumph, and Cato as censor stripped him of his horse. The move seemed motivated by a desire to get one last jab at Scipio Africanus, who was now dead. But the vast majority of people were annoyed most of all by his restrictions on luxury. There was no way that he could eradicate it completely, since by then most people had been infected and stricken by its contagion. So he took another route. Any item—be it clothes, vehicles, women's jewelry or other household accessories—that had a value exceeding 1,500 drachmas he assessed, for purposes of taxation, at ten times its worth. The idea was to make those people pay higher taxes through higher assessments. Then he added a luxury tax of three *asses* per 1,000 [.3 percent], so that extravagant spenders, burdened by the tax and seeing that their modest, frugal-minded peers were paying less into the state coffers, would be deterred from such displays of wealth. As it happened, he angered both groups, those who accepted the costs of the luxury tax, as well as those who gave up their luxurious lifestyle because of it. Most men, after all, think that being prevented from showing off their wealth is equivalent to being robbed of it, and one cannot show off ordinary items, but need something extraordinary.

They say that the philosopher Ariston was particularly surprised by this kind of thinking, namely, the notion that people who possess luxuries are considered better off than those who have been provided with all the necessary and useful things needed in life. And then there's Scopas the Thessalian. One of his friends once asked to have an item that Scopas didn't particularly need, explicitly noting that he wasn't asking for anything essential or useful to him. "And yet," Scopas replied, "my wealth and prosperity are judged precisely by how many unnecessary and excessive things I own." Well, there you have it, proof that our passion for wealth is not a natural-born impulse, but the by-product of a common, misguided belief imposed on us from the outside.

[19] In spite of everything, Cato gave not the slightest consideration to his accusers, and in fact redoubled his efforts. He cut off the water pipes that private homeowners were illegally using to divert the public water supply into their houses and gardens. He knocked down and demolished all structures that encroached on public spaces. He reduced the cost of contracts for public works through wage reduction, and set at the highest possible level the cost of winning tax-farming contracts. All these measures earned him the ardent hatred of a lot of people. Eventually Titus Flamininus and his supporters made a concerted effort to resist him. They managed to get the Senate to

---

35. Latin *sponsio*, where one party agrees to pay a fine if a claim is proved to be false.

rescind all the expenditures and outlay of money that Cato had earmarked for contracts on temples and public works, on the grounds that they did not benefit the state. Then they goaded the boldest of the tribunes into calling Cato before an assembly of the people to account for his actions, and imposing a fine on him of two talents. They also took many steps to oppose the construction of the basilica that he built with state monies along the Forum just below the Senate House, the one called the Basilica Porcia.[36]

The people, on the other hand, were clearly impressed with the job Cato did as censor. They put up a statue of him in the Temple of Health with a dedicatory inscription that did not celebrate Cato's military campaigns or his triumph, but said, as one may translate the Latin, "When Rome was in a state of decline and decay, he became censor and put it on the right path again with sound leadership, sober conduct, and instruction." And yet, Cato once used to scoff at people who prized such honors, saying that, although they would never admit it, what they were really taking pride in was the expertise of sculptors and painters, whereas the finest images of himself were the ones the people of Rome carried around in their hearts. When people expressed surprise that there were no statues of him, even though many insignificant characters had them, he said, "I would prefer people to ask why people had not erected a statue of me than why they had." One of his general principles was that no worthwhile citizen should let himself be praised, unless for the good of the commonwealth.

And yet he was prepared to sing his own praises more than anyone else. He himself tells us that when people were caught in some misdemeanor, they used to reply, "You shouldn't blame us. We can't all be Catos." He goes on to say that people who tried unsuccessfully to emulate some of his practices were called "left-handed Catos." One last bit of self-praise: he informs us that, in times of greatest danger, the Senate looked to him as seafarers look to the captain of the ship, and that frequently, if he was not present, they would postpone deliberation on the most important issues. All of these claims are indeed corroborated by others—for Cato had acquired great clout in the city because of his way of life, his eloquence, and his age.

[20] He was also a good father, a kind husband, and a highly capable manager of his estate. He gave the latter his full attention and did not treat it as some unimportant matter or afterthought. I think it is worthwhile to give a few examples of his success in this area. He married a woman who came from a family that was more noble than it was wealthy.[37] He was convinced that while both nobility and wealth could equally well endow a woman with dignity and good sense, women who could only claim high birth were more apt to be guided by their husbands to pursue what is honorable, since they detest disgrace.[38] He used to say that those who beat their wives and children were desecrating the most sacred objects in the world, and that he thought that being a good husband deserved more praise than being a great senator. Nothing impressed

---

36. Buildings and public works in Rome were often named after the *gens* of the person who commissioned the building, in this case after Porcius, Cato's *nomen gentilicum*.

37. Licinia, his first wife, whom he married around the year 192 BC.

38. Though it was obviously desirable to marry a wealthy woman, Roman men sometimes worried about being dominated by wives who were wealthier than themselves. See Martial, no. 38 in this volume.

him about Socrates from bygone times more than the fact that he always treated his nasty wife and numbskull kids with toleration and politeness.

When his son was born, nothing was so important—with the exception of affairs of state—as to prevent him from being next to his wife when she washed and swaddled the newborn. She nursed the child herself, and she also let the slaves' children suckle at her breast in order to foster feelings of goodwill toward her son through this common nurturing. As soon as his son could understand, Cato himself took charge of his learning, teaching him how to read—this despite the fact that he had a slave named Chilon who was an accomplished schoolteacher and had educated many children before. He did not think it was right, as he informs us himself, that his son be scolded or have his ears pulled by a slave if he did not pick up on things quickly enough. He also certainly did not want his son to be indebted to a slave for such an important area of learning.

Cato acted as his son's language teacher, instructor in the law, and physical trainer. Regarding the latter, his instruction did not just include javelin-throwing, armed combat, and horseback riding, but he also taught him how to box, to endure extreme heat and cold, and to swim forcefully through the rough, choppy currents of the Tiber. He wrote his *Histories*, he himself informs us, in his own hand and in large print so that his son might, in his own home, gain knowledge about ancient history and the age-old traditions of Rome. He avoided foul language around his son as if he were in the presence of the sacred virgins, the ones they call the Vestals. He never went to the baths with his son. This seems to be a custom once shared by all Romans; in fact, fathers-in-law made sure they did not bathe with their sons-in-law because they were shy about revealing their bodies. Later the Romans adopted the Greek practice of going naked, and even returned the favor, re-infecting the Greeks with the practice of going naked even in front of women.

Cato's attempt to mold and fashion his son into a model of excellence went well—no one could fault his son's eagerness, and his mind, naturally well-disposed, responded well to Cato's instructions. But since his body was clearly too fragile for hard labor, Cato let up on the excessively strict and punishing physical regimen he had set for his son. Despite his frailty he proved to be a brave soldier on campaign, fighting brilliantly for general Paullus in the battle against Perseus.[39] During the engagement, however, Cato's son lost his sword, which either had been knocked out of his hand or slipped out because the hilt was wet with perspiration. He was terribly upset about this and turned to his comrades for help. Supporting him, they made a second charge against the enemy. The struggle was great and violent, but he was finally able to clear the area and, after a long and tiring search, he found his sword amidst the many heaps of arms and indiscriminate piles of dead bodies, Roman and enemy alike. Even Paullus, his commander, marveled at the young man's bravery in recovering his sword.[40] In addition, a letter of Cato to his son still survives, in which he praises in glowing terms his son's love of honor and the pains he took to get the sword back. Later, the young man married Paullus' daughter Tertia (Scipio's sister), and it was due to his own merits as much as those of his father that he secured an alliance with such an important family—a worthy culmination of Cato's great investment in his son's upbringing.

---

39. At Pydna in 168 BC.

40. For the importance of recovering a lost weapon in battle, see Polybius ch. 37 in this volume.

[21] Cato owned a lot of slaves. When purchasing prisoners of war he sought out younger ones that were still capable of being nurtured and trained, like pups or foals. No slave entered another person's house unless Cato or his wife explicitly sent him to do so. And whenever a slave was asked what Cato was up to, the only answer he would ever give was "I don't know." A slave was expected to be doing one of two things, either performing some necessary task in the house, or sleeping. He did not mind at all if they slept, because he believed that it made them more docile than if they stayed awake, and that, if rested, they were apt to perform their chores better than those that were sleep-deprived. He was convinced that the thing that led most slaves astray was sex, so he laid down this rule: male slaves could sleep with the females at a set price, but none was to have sex with any other woman.[41]

Early in his career, when he was still poor and serving in the military, he never got upset with any of the meals his slaves prepared. He made it clear that he thought it was the height of disgrace to quarrel with one's slave on account of one's stomach. Later, however, as Cato's fortunes improved, whenever he put on a dinner party for his friends and fellow magistrates, he would immediately afterwards whip any slave whose preparation or service was at all subpar. He always contrived to create some dissent among the slaves, keeping them against each other—he distrusted and feared a united body of slaves. If any slave was thought to have committed some crime that deserved a death sentence, Cato thought it made sense to have them tried and, if convicted, be put to death in front of an assembly of all the slaves.

Once he put more effort into making money, he regarded farming as more of a hobby than a source of income, and he put his capital into safe and secure investments, buying up fisheries, hot springs, land for fulleries, estates with natural pastures and timber, investments that brought him great income but were not, as he puts it, subject to Jupiter's whim. He also used to engage in the most disreputable kind of moneylending, that on shipping. Here is what he did. He required prospective borrowers to form a consortium, and when there were fifty total, with just as many ships, he would take on one share. His agent was Quintio, his freedman, who would sail along with his clients and serve as a business advisor. Thus he did not assume the entire risk, only a small portion of it, but with a high likelihood of making a large profit.[42] He would also lend his slaves money if they asked for it. They would purchase their own slaves with it, train and teach them for a year (at Cato's expense), and then put them up for sale. Many of these Cato would keep for himself, crediting the account of the slave who owned him the price offered by the highest bidder. When he was urging his son to take making money seriously, he said that a real man would never allow his assets to diminish—that was what widows did. Now, the next remark of Cato is a bit excessive. He went so far as to say that the man who added more to his estate than he had inherited was a man of "wonderful and godlike glory."

---

41. This seems to have been an attempt to ensure monogamy, with a fixed payment to establish a relationship with a single woman. It is highly unlikely that he would have treated his entire cadre of female slaves as prostitutes.

42. The innovation seems to be the chopping up of the individual investments into fifty units each, so that the loss of one ship would not be catastrophic to one investor. Cato had to use his freedman as an intermediary because Roman senators were prohibited by law from owning large cargo vessels, and could not directly profit from shipping trade.

[22] He was already old when Carneades the Academic and Diogenes the Stoic came as ambassadors from Athens to Rome.[43] Their mission was to request that the Romans overturn a verdict against the Athenian people that carried a fine of 500 talents. (The Athenians had declined to defend themselves when the Oropians brought a suit against them, and the Sicyonians judged against them in their absence.) Well, the most scholarly young people in Rome immediately flocked to these philosophers and spent time with them, listening to their lectures, captivated with the men themselves. Carneades in particular was very charismatic—he had a powerful magnetism, and his reputation was hardly less of a draw—and so his lectures found large and receptive audiences. Talk of his greatness swept through the city like a rushing wind. A buzz filled the city: here was a Greek man who had a supernatural power to mesmerize his listeners. By beguiling and charming everyone he met, Carneades instilled in Rome's young people a fierce passion—one might call it obsession—for philosophy, one that caused them to abandon their customary pursuits and pastimes.

To many this phenomenon was welcome, and they looked on with pleasure as their youth got a taste of Greek culture and associated with such awe-inspiring men. Not Cato. From the very beginning he was bothered by the enthusiasm for words and dialectic that was pouring into the city. He was afraid that the young people of Rome would turn their ambitions to this and seek out the glory that comes from speaking, more than that which comes from military service and mighty deeds. When the philosophers' reputation kept spreading throughout the city, and no less a figure than Gaius Acilius volunteered to act as translator for their opening speeches before the Senate, Cato decided that it was time to act. He resolved to engineer the departure of all the philosophers from the city, but in such a way that they could save face. He came before the Senate and censured its leaders: "Why allow this delegation, whose ambassadors can easily win any argument they want, to sit idly around the city for such a long time? We should make our decision, with all due haste, and vote on their petition, so that they may return to their schools and lecture to Greek boys, and our Roman youth can get back to listening to the laws and their magistrates."

[23] This was not an act of personal spite against Carneades, as some people believe. The fact of the matter is that he was opposed to philosophy on principle and publicly tried to smear every kind of Greek cultural or educational practice. I mean, he goes so far as to say that Socrates was a babbler and a bully who tried, in every way possible, to take over his city as tyrant, doing away with age-old customs and brainwashing its citizens into thinking in ways contrary to the laws. He also ridiculed the school of Isocrates, saying that his students continued to study under him into old age so that they could employ their skillful rhetorical tricks when pleading their cases before Minos in Hades. When he was trying to dissuade his son from pursuing things Greek, he made a remark that is rather brash for an old man. He predicted, like a seer or prophet, that Rome would lose its supremacy when it became infected with Greek learning. But now we can see that this slander of his is hollow, since the city rose to the pinnacle of preeminence as it took on all of Greek learning and culture as its own. But Cato was not just bothered by Greek philosophers. He was also suspicious of Greeks practicing medicine in Rome. He must have heard, it seems, Hippocrates' response

---

43. 155 BC, a landmark moment for the introduction of Greek learning in Rome. The Academics were descendants of Plato's school.

when the great king of Persia invited him to his court to act as his physician for a sum of many talents: "I would never offer my services to foreigners if they are enemies of the Greeks." Cato used to say that all Greek doctors took this same oath, and instructed his son to keep a close eye on the whole bunch of them. He also informs us that he composed a little medical handbook himself, and he used it to care for and treat sick members of his household. He never prescribed fasting; instead he gave them a diet of garden vegetables or bits of duck, pigeon, or rabbit. He thought that such a diet was light and agreeable to people in a weakened state, the only drawback being that it often caused dreams. Using treatments and dieting like these, he said, he kept himself in good health and kept his household healthy as well.

[24] Well, in this case, it seems, his self-confidence did not go unpunished, since he lost both his wife and his son. As for Cato himself, since he had a strong body and healthy constitution, he held out against the onslaughts of old age for a long time—so much so that even as an old man he remained quite sexually active, and remarried when he was well past the marrying age. Here is the story. After the death of his first wife he arranged for his son to marry one of Paullus' daughters (Scipio's sister),[44] while Cato himself, being a widower, started an affair with a prostitute, who would come to his house in secret. Naturally, in a small house inhabited by a new bride, it was impossible for this to go unnoticed. At some point, the harlot swept past the young man's room too boldly for his taste; although he said nothing, Cato's son shot her a dirty look and turned away—and Cato saw him do it. He realized that his son and daughter-in-law were disgusted with his affair, but he did not criticize or fault them on the spot, but merely went on with his daily routine. He walked down to the Forum with his clients, one of whom was named Salonius, who did some clerical work for him. He called out to this man in a loud voice, asking him if he had married his young daughter off to a man yet. When Salonius replied that he would not dare think of doing that without consulting his patron first, Cato remarked, "Excellent! I think I've found just the man for you, unless, by Zeus, you object on the grounds of age. You couldn't find a single fault with him, except that he is quite old." When Salonius told him to go ahead and take care of the arrangements and give the girl to whatever man he selected since she was, after all, his dependent and relied on his guardianship, Cato could not bear it any longer and revealed that he wanted the girl for himself. At first the man was floored by Cato's revelation, as one might imagine. He regarded Cato as well past the age to marry, and himself well beneath a union with a family decorated by a consulship and triumph. But when he realized that Cato was entirely serious, he eagerly accepted the proposal, and when they reached the Forum, they made the engagement official in front of witnesses.

While wedding preparations were underway, Cato's son approached him with some friends along for support, and asked if Cato was bringing a step-mother into the house because he had done something to upset or annoy him. Cato cried out, "Perish the thought, my boy! I'm proud of everything you've done and I have no complaint. I'm doing this because I want to magnify my legacy to my household and to the state—that is, produce more sons and citizens like *you*." They say, however, that Cato was not the first to put forth such a sentiment. That distinction goes to Pisistratus, the tyrant of the Athenians, who said it when he was foisting a step-mother upon his already grown-up

---

44. See above, ch. 20.

sons (she was Timonassa of Argos, who bore Iophon and Thessalus to him). Cato's marriage did produce a son, whom he gave the nickname Salonius after his mother.[45]

Cato's elder son died while serving as praetor, and Cato refers to him several times in his books as a good, brave man. They say that he endured the loss with a composed and philosophical spirit, and that his passion for politics was not diminished at all because of it. He did not, like Lucius Lucullus and Metellus Pius after him, grow weary of public service because of his age, or ever think that service to the state was some burdensome obligation. He also did not, like Scipio Africanus before him, turn his back on the people when his reputation was under siege by envious men, and decide to live out the rest of his life in easy retirement. No, Cato was different. Just as Dionysius was persuaded that tyranny was the best death shroud one could have, Cato believed that public service was the best possible way to grow old.

Whenever he had some free time, he turned for recreation and amusement to writing and farming. [25] He composed not only speeches on all sorts of subjects but historical treatises as well. As for farming, he devoted himself to it wholeheartedly while he was still young and had no choice in the matter (for he says that he had two ways to make a living: farming and being frugal). Now, however, life on the farm held a more theoretical and recreational interest for him. Indeed, he wrote a book about farming, in which he was so anxious to display his thoroughness and originality that he even included instructions for the making of flat cakes and the preserving of fruit.[46] Dinner in the country, too, was for him a rather extravagant affair. Without fail he would invite his friends from neighboring farms and the surrounding areas and spend the evening in cheer and joviality. And it wasn't just the old folks who wanted—no, *yearned*—to spend time with him. The young men also found his company riveting since Cato had been a part of many important events, had read many books, and had heard many speeches—all of which were worth listening to. He thought that the dinner table was the best place to make friends. Conversation frequently turned to the praise of noble and honorable citizens, but there was no talk of wicked, worthless men. These men Cato would not allow to make any sort of appearance at his dinner party, either through blame or praise.

[26] The destruction of Carthage can be thought of as the last of Cato's political projects. Although Scipio the Younger[47] was the one to complete the deed in the field, it was through Cato's advice and prodding that the Romans decided to embark upon the war in the first place. Here's how it happened. The Carthaginians and the Numidians under Massinissa were at war with each other. Cato was dispatched by the Romans to investigate the reasons behind their dispute. From the very beginning Massinissa had been a loyal ally of the Romans, while the Carthaginians had been subject to the terms of a treaty ever since their defeat at the hands of Scipio the Elder[48]—a

---

45. His full name was M. Porcius Cato Salonianus. Her name would have been Salonia after her father.

46. *De Agricultura*, the only work of his that survives complete.

47. Scipio Aemilianus, born of Aemilius Paullus but adopted into the family of the Scipios.

48. After the Second Punic War (202 BC), Carthage was sanctioned with severe penalties: their navy was limited to ten ships, they could not declare war without Rome's approval, and they

defeat that had deprived them of their empire and curtailed their power continually by imposing upon them a heavy indemnity. When Cato got there he discovered that the city of Carthage was not, as the Romans believed, in a wretched, depleted state, but was teeming with young, strong men, overflowing with wealth, and filled with all sorts of weapons and preparations for war. Worst of all, the Carthaginians' confidence was brimming because of their prosperity. This was not the time, Cato thought, for the Romans to resolve the immediate problem and simply put the affairs of Massinissa and the Numidians in order. No, if the Romans did not crush the city, one that had always been hostile and recalcitrant but had now grown implausibly powerful, they would again find themselves in a situation no less dangerous than before.

So Cato quickly returned to Rome and reported his findings to the Senate, how the defeats and misfortunes that the Carthaginians suffered in the previous war did not so much sap their power as it did their ignorance—that is, their reversal had made them not weaker, but more experienced in war. The current war against the Numidians, Cato argued, was nothing more than a warm-up for a match with the Romans; "peace" and "treaty" were nothing more than a cover-up for the span of time that the Carthaginians were enduring until presented with the opportunity to strike.

[27] In addition, the story goes, Cato cunningly arranged to have a Libyan fig fall out of the folds of his toga when he was arranging it in the Senate. As the senators sat there astonished at its size and beauty, Cato pointed out that the country that produced such remarkable fruit was only three days' sail from Rome. Then there is that famous (but overly vehement) habit of his, how, whenever he was called upon to express his position on a matter before the Senate, he would add, regardless of the topic, "It is also my view that Carthage should not exist." In response to this, Publius Scipio (the one surnamed Nasica) would always state his position by saying: "It is my view that Carthage *should* exist." Scipio's reasoning was, it seems, the following. He saw that the people of Rome were at that time making a great many mistakes because of their arrogance, and it had become difficult for the Senate to control them since they had grown impudent through their earlier successes. They were forcibly dragging the whole city down, he thought, tossing it violently in whatever direction their whims took them. So Scipio thought it best that there be at least *one* threat to loom over the state, one that could, like a bridle, be imposed on the masses to serve as a corrective to their insolence. He thought that the Carthaginians were not strong enough to subdue the Romans, but were not so weak that they could be despised.

But this was exactly the thing that Cato feared. With the Roman masses totally drunk and staggering around beneath their great power, here was Carthage, a city that had always been great but was now sobered and chastened by their misfortunes, looming over them. External threats to Rome's supremacy had to be entirely eradicated, so that they could have the opportunity to correct their internal problems.

This is how Cato is said to have brought about the third and last war against the Carthaginians. He died just after hostilities commenced, but before he did, he foretold of the man who was destined to put an end to the war. He was but a young man

---

were fined the enormous amount of 10,000 talents over fifty years. Cato's visit to Africa occurred in 152 BC, the final year that Carthage had to pay a fine.

still, yet when he was on campaign as a military tribune, he displayed both excellent judgment and great boldness in battle. When reports of his feats arrived at Rome, they say that Cato, upon hearing them, declared, "This man alone has sense; the rest are but fluttering shadows."[49] In short order Scipio validated Cato's prediction with his accomplishments.

Cato was survived by one son from his second marriage, whose nickname was, as we noted above, Salonius, and one grandson by the son who predeceased him. Salonius died while serving as praetor, but his son, Marcus, reached the consulship.[50] Salonius was the grandfather of Cato the philosopher, who proved to be the most renowned man of his time in virtue and judgment.[51]

## The Life of Aemilius Paullus (chs. 26–34)

The greatest accomplishment of the Roman general L. Aemilius Paullus (consul in 182 and 168 BC, censor in 164) was his defeat of Perseus, the last of the Macedonian kings descended from Alexander the Great, at the battle near Pydna in 168 BC. This victory struck a great blow to the Greek city-states, who were deeply suspicious of the increasing power of Rome. The following excerpt from Plutarch's life describes the aftermath of this resounding victory—Livy (44.42) reports that over 20,000 Greeks died—including the massive three-day triumph celebrated in the following year. As usual, Plutarch weaves a philosophical reflection into the narrative, in this case one having to do with reversals of fortune.

[26] When Gnaeus Octavius, the admiral of Aemilius' fleet, dropped anchor off Samothrace, he gave the order that Perseus was not to be harmed out of respect for the gods, but he also took measures to prevent him from making an escape by boat. Despite these efforts Perseus somehow managed to persuade the owner of a small boat, a certain Cretan named Oroandes, to take him and his possessions on board. Oroandes, however, like all Cretans, was a swindler. He took on board all of Perseus' possessions, but told Perseus himself to gather up his children and whatever slaves he might need and meet him at the harbor at Demetrium at night. But just as evening turned to night, Oroandes sailed off.

Meanwhile, Perseus was having a miserable time of it. He had to squeeze through a narrow window in the wall, towing behind him his wife and children, who were completely unused to physical exertion and being on the run. How pitiful was the

---

49. Homer, *Odyssey* 10.495.

50. In fact, it was Salonius' other son, Lucius, who achieved the consulship.

51. This is Cato the Younger, "the philosopher," who gained this moniker from his dogged adherence to Stoicism. He was a determined proponent of senatorial rule in the final phase of the Roman Republic and gained prominence as an acrimonious opponent of Julius Caesar. He chose to fall on his sword rather than accept Caesar's clemency after the civil war in 46 BC.

howl Perseus raised when, as he was wandering along the shore, someone informed him that he had seen Oroandes already on the sea and racing away! Day was just starting to break; Perseus, with all hope gone, fled back to the city walls with his wife. The Romans caught sight of them, but they made it back before the Romans could do anything about it. But his children were seized and delivered to the Romans by Ion, once Perseus' young lover,[52] but now his betrayer. This forced his hand; like a wild animal whose cubs had been taken, he was compelled to give up and deliver himself into the hands of those who held his sons captive. Perseus trusted Nasica[53] most of all and called for him, but he was not present. Cursing his luck, Perseus considered the tight spot he was in and finally decided to deliver himself to Gnaeus.

It was then that he made it abundantly clear that there was a more disgraceful character flaw in him than love of money, that is, love of life, and it was through this that he robbed himself of the only thing that Fortune cannot take away from the downtrodden—pity. For when Aemilius asked Perseus to be brought to him, he, thinking that the king was a great man whose downfall was caused by divine retribution and his own bad luck, rose from his seat with tears in his eyes and went with his friends to greet him. But Perseus—what a disgraceful sight!—threw himself face forward onto the ground, clutched Aemilius' knees, and poured forth disgraceful pleas and entreaties that were beneath his kingly status. Aemilius would not allow him to do this, and he refused to listen to his captive's pleas. He looked at Perseus with a pained and aggrieved look on his face and said, "You pitiful man, why do you free Fortune from the greatest charge you can level against her by acting like this? People will think that your suffering is not unwarranted and that you deserved not your former prosperity, but your present misery! And why do you spoil my victory and minimize my success by showing yourself to be neither a noble nor even a fitting antagonist for the Romans? Be sure of this: courage evokes great respect for the unfortunate even from enemies, but cowardice—even if it brings success—is to the Romans wholly dishonorable."

[27] Even so, Aemilius lifted Perseus up, gave him his hand, and gave him to Tubero to take care of.[54] Meanwhile, he led into his tent his sons, his sons-in-law, and some of the officers, especially the younger ones. There he sat for a long time in silent reverie, so long that everyone started to wonder. Then he launched into a lecture concerning Fortune and the human condition:

"Is it right, really, for a human being to be emboldened when success has come his way, and to feel high and mighty because he has conquered a people, a city, or a whole kingdom? Or is it better to contemplate this reversal of fortune that sits before our very eyes, one that reminds soldiers of the frailty that all humans share and teaches them not to believe that anything is lasting or certain? Is there any occasion when humans should feel confident? Our mastery of others, after all, should give us every reason to fear Fortune, does it not? And doesn't the consideration of the fickle nature of Fate, how it stands now beside one, now beside another, cast a pall of melancholy upon us even in our hour of glory?

---

52. Greek *eromenos*, the young male "beloved" taken by an older Greek male.
53. Scipio Nasica (cos. 162 BC), the son-in-law of Scipio Africanus, one of Aemilius' lieutenants.
54. Aelius Tubero, Aemilius' son-in-law.

"Consider what has just happened. You have, in the space of a single hour, brought down and subjected to your control the line of Alexander, the man who rose to the pinnacle of power and acquired a vast and mighty kingdom. You now look upon kings, who were just recently protected by tens of thousands of soldiers and thousands of cavalry, taking from their enemy's hands their daily rations of bread and drink. So do you think our current prosperity has any guarantee of holding out against Fortune in the long run? Will you not, my young charges, rid yourselves of this empty sense of superiority? Do not exult in your victory, but remain humble and cautious toward the future. You must always be on the lookout for the moment when the god will unleash his retribution upon each of you for your present success."

My sources say that Aemilius said many things like this, then sent the young men away, their arrogance and insolence reined in by his stinging words, as if by a bridle.

[28] After this, he gave the troops a rest, while he took himself to tour Greece, passing his time in an admirable and compassionate way. On his tour he reinstated free states, established their governments, and bestowed upon them gifts, in some cases grain, in others olive oil, all from the king's storehouses. They say that so much was found stored up there that those requesting and receiving aid would have run out before the mass of supplies found there was exhausted. In Delphi he saw a large square pillar built of white stones on which a golden statue of Perseus was about to be erected. He ordered that a statue of himself be put there instead—it was fitting, after all, that the conquered give way to the conquerors. In Olympia, they say, he uttered that now well-worn saying, "Phidias molded the Zeus of Homer."

When the ten ambassadors arrived from Rome,[55] Aemilius restored the Macedonians' land and allowed them to govern their cities freely and without interference from Rome, but imposed on them sanctions in the amount of one hundred talents, which was less than half what they used to pay to their kings. He celebrated spectacles with all sorts of contests, performed sacrifices to the Greek gods, and hosted at his own expense banquets and feasts. He drew liberally from the royal treasury to pay for these, but he was so meticulous and precise in the preparation and arrangement of the feasts, so careful in greeting and seating his guests, and so attentive in giving each of them the honor and courtesy they deserved, that the Greeks were amazed. Here was a *Roman* showing great interest in their cultural practices, and, although he was a man of great accomplishments, was giving full consideration to even the smallest of matters.

He also took joy in the fact that even among all of the many and wonderful offerings at the banquet *he* was the sight that brought the most joy to those present. He used to say to those amazed at his diligence that organizing a symposium required the same mindset as marshaling an army—in the one case, to bring sheer panic to the enemy, the other to bring sheer joy to the guests. Above all people praised his generosity and magnanimity. Although a huge amount of silver and gold had been collected from the king's treasuries, he refused even to look at it; he merely delivered it to the quaestors in charge of the state treasury. There were only a few things he kept: first, he allowed his sons, who were voracious readers, to sort through the books of the king and select those they wanted. Second, when he was giving out awards for courage in battle, he

---

55. After a victory over a new people, the Romans would send an embassy of ten high-ranking men to help the general in organizing and governing the new territory.

gave to his son-in-law Aelius Tubero a silver bowl that weighed five pounds. This is the Tubero we mentioned earlier, the one who lived with fifteen of his family members, all of whom lived off the produce of a tiny farm. This, they say, was the very first piece of silver—conducted by courage and prestige—that ever entered the house of the Aelii. Up until then, neither they nor their wives had had any use for silver or gold.

[29] After he had put everything on good footing, Aemilius said goodbye to the Greeks and told the Macedonians to remember the freedom the Romans had bestowed upon them and to safeguard it by acting lawfully and harmoniously. Then he marched to Epirus. He had received orders from the Senate that the soldiers who had fought with him against Perseus were to profit by pillaging the cities there. He wanted to fall upon all of the cities at the same time without any of them suspecting an attack, so he summoned the ten most important men from each city and instructed them, on a specified day, to bring out all of the silver and gold that they had in their houses and temples. He sent with each group a garrison of soldiers and a centurion, ostensibly for the same purpose, and they pretended that they were searching for and collecting the gold. But when the appointed day arrived, at one and the same time all of his soldiers set out to raid and pillage the cities. It was so sudden that in a single hour 150,000 men were enslaved and seventy cities sacked. Even so, out of all this complete destruction each soldier got less than eleven drachmas as his share of the spoils. Everyone shuddered at the outcome of the war—a whole nation had been demolished and yet each soldier's profit turned out to be so meager.

[30] After fulfilling this horrific mission—one that was completely out character for Aemilius, who was a reasonable and good man—he headed for the port city of Oricus. From there he crossed over to Italy with his army and sailed up the Tiber River on a royal ship with sixteen banks of oars. The ship was decked out with captured arms and scarlet and crimson drapes—so splendid was it that the Romans came out in droves as if it were some triumphal procession, a foretaste of what was to come, and they followed the ship along the banks of the river as the plashing oars drove it slowly upstream.

Now, when the soldiers eyed the king's treasures, they grew angry and bore a silent grudge against Aemilius because they had not gotten the amount of spoils they thought they deserved. But they kept hidden the real reason. Instead, they publicly accused him of being an oppressive and despotic ruler, and they opposed him in his desire to celebrate a triumph. When Servius Galba, Aemilius' political enemy (even though he had been one of his military tribunes), got wind of this, he was emboldened enough to state openly that Aemilius should not be granted a triumph. He spread among the whole mass of soldiers many slanderous rumors against their general, fanning the flames of their already fiery anger. He also demanded from the tribunes of the people that he be granted a second day to denounce Aemilius; there were only four hours remaining in the current day, hardly enough, he said, to level his accusations against him. When the tribunes ordered him to speak his mind right there, he launched into a long speech, replete with all kinds of venomous slurs, and used up the remaining time of the day. When darkness fell, the tribunes adjourned the assembly. Aemilius' soldiers, encouraged by the day's events, swarmed to Galba's side. Just before daybreak, they reassembled and took control of the Capitoline, where the tribunes were going to bring the assembly together for the vote.

[31] Voting began when it was day. As the first tribe was casting its vote against granting Aemilius a triumph, news of what was transpiring reached the rest of the populace and the Senate. The multitude was beside itself with grief over the smear campaign against Aemilius, but could only voice their objections with useless shouts of protest. But the most illustrious of the senators loudly condemned the awful events that were unfolding and urged each other to take action against the insolent audacity of the soldiers. These men, they said, would stoop to every lawless and violent act unless someone did something to prevent them from depriving Aemilius Paullus of his victory honors. So they pushed through the crowd, went up to the Capitoline as a group, and told the tribunes to suspend the vote until they had spoken their mind to the people. When voting was suspended and the people grew silent, Marcus Servilius, an ex-consul who had killed twenty-three enemy combatants in single battle, mounted the podium and said that he knew then, more than ever, just how great a general Aemilius Paullus was, now that he had gotten a glimpse of the kind of army he had at his disposal. So disobedient, so craven! What he must have done to perform such glorious and mighty accomplishments! Servilius also said that he was surprised that the people of Rome, who were overjoyed at the triumphs over the Illyrians and the Ligurians, would begrudge themselves of looking upon the king of the Macedonians—the glory of Alexander and Philip—paraded as a prisoner of war. "How would it not appear strange," he asked, "if, when an unsubstantiated rumor came to the city announcing victory, you sacrificed to the gods, praying that you would quickly see confirmation of this report, but now, when the general has come home with a real victory, you were to deprive the gods of their tribute and yourselves of joy? Are you afraid to look upon the greatness of our accomplishments? Or are you just being merciful to our enemy? And yet it would be better to do away with the triumph out of pity for the enemy than out of resentment toward the general. But," he continued, "through your actions you are giving wickedness so much free reign that a man who has never been wounded, whose body gleams because of his easy and sedentary life, dares to speak about leadership and triumphs to us—to us!—even though *we* have been taught through our many wounds how to judge the virtues and vices of generals."

As he spoke he tore open his clothes and revealed the unbelievably large number of wounds on his chest. Then he spun around and uncovered some of the parts of the body that it is normally inappropriate to show in public, looked at Galba, and said, "Galba, you may laugh at these, but I wear them as badges of honor before my fellow citizens. It is for these men here that I got them as I rode continuously day and night. Well, go ahead and take these men to vote. I will come down and accompany them all. Then I will know the contemptible and thankless ingrates who want to be flattered rather than commanded in war."

[32] They say that Servilius' speech was so powerful that it put an end to the soldiers' opposition and changed their tune. Every tribe voted that a triumph be granted to Aemilius. The following is an account of the triumphal procession as my sources tell it. The people built stands in the viewing areas for chariot races (they call them "Circuses") and along the Forum. Spectators also occupied the other parts of the city that offered a good view of the procession. All of them were decked out in their finest clothes. All of the temples were open to the public and filled with garlands and incense. There were many attendants and lictors contending with the disorderly crowds flooding into the streets, trying to keep the parade route clear and clean.

The parade was divided into three days. The first barely sufficed for the captured sculptures, paintings, and colossal statues. It took 250 wagons to carry them. On the following day the most beautiful and costly of the Macedonian's arms were paraded on many carts. The bronze and silver, recently cleaned, sparkled. They had been artfully and carefully arranged so as to look as if they had been heaped up at random. Helmets lay next to shields, breast-plates next to greaves, Cretan light shields and their Gallic wicker counterparts and quivers were intermingled with bridles, with unsheathed swords projecting through them and Macedonian spears planted beside them. The arms were not packed too tightly so that they would knock against each other while they were being paraded and make harsh and fearsome sounds—though they had been captured from a conquered enemy, the sight of them still evoked fear. After the wagons carrying the arms there came 3,000 men carrying silver coins in 750 vessels measuring three talents each—so heavy that it took four men to carry one. Other men carried silver mixing bowls, drinking horns, bowls, and drinking cups. All of them, outstanding in their size and the depth of their carved reliefs, were properly arranged for display.

[33] Then there was the third day's parade. At daybreak trumpeters marched forth, playing not the kind of music fit for a procession or parade, but the kind the Romans use to get themselves psyched up for war. After these came 120 stall-fed oxen, all with gilded horns, festooned with garlands and flowing ribbons. They were led by young men wearing purple-bordered garments that wrapped around the waist, leaving their torsos bare.[56] These men were attended by boys carrying silver and golden sacrificial bowls used in libations. Following these paraded the men who carried the gold coins, divided up, like the silver, into vessels measuring three talents. There were seventy-seven vessels in total. Next came the men holding up the sacred bowl commissioned by Aemilius—it weighed ten talents and was inlaid with precious gems—then those displaying the Antigonid, Seleucid, and Thericleian bowls, and all the golden ware from Perseus' dining service. These were followed by Perseus' chariot, his arms and his crown, which lay atop the arms. After a short break in the action, the king's children were paraded as slaves. With them was a throng of their caretakers, teachers, and tutors, all crying and stretching out their hands to the spectators, all while instructing their charges to beg and entreat the Romans for mercy. There were two boys and one girl, but none of them quite comprehended the magnitude of their misfortunes because of their young age. Because of this failure to understand their own change in fortune, they evoked more sympathy from the spectators, such that Perseus himself went virtually unnoticed as he walked along. The Romans' gaze was locked on the children, pity in their hearts. Many wept, and there was not a single person there who did not feel at least a tinge of pain amidst their joy until the children had passed from view.

[34] Behind the children and their attendants came Perseus himself, wearing a somber grey cloak and the boots of his native country. Stricken by the magnitude of his misfortunes, he had a completely dumbfounded and disoriented look about him. A Greek chorus of friends and acquaintances followed him, their faces weighed down in grief. They kept looking at Perseus and crying, giving the spectators the impression that they were lamenting their king's fate and cared very little about their own misfortunes. They felt pity for him, and yet Perseus had earlier sent Aemilius a message

---

56. The bare torsos indicated slaves, those that would perform the more menial parts of the sacrifice.

begging him not to parade him in the triumph. Aemilius' retort was a not-so-subtle jab at the king's cowardice and love of life: "Well, it was in his power all along to avoid a triumph, and still is now, if he chooses," meaning that he could choose death over disgrace. But this the craven coward could not endure. No, he, soft like a woman, clung to the flimsiest hope and so became part of his own spoils.

Immediately after these were paraded 400 golden crowns, which delegations from cities brought to Aemilius as tribute in honor of his victory. Then the man of the hour himself arrived, perched on a fabulously decorated chariot. He was a sight to behold even apart from the surrounding trappings of power. He wore a purple robe decorated with gold and held out in his right hand a laurel branch. The whole army, too, carried laurel branches as they, arrayed by companies and divisions, followed their general's chariot. Song pervaded the ranks. Some sang traditional songs mixed with jests, while others belted out victory songs and hymns praising the accomplishments of Aemilius, who was the object of everyone's gaze and admiration. No one but the base felt spiteful jealousy.[57]

---

57. The account of Plutarch goes on to describe how Aemilius' successes were balanced by the deaths of his two young sons, one five days before the triumph, the other three days after the triumph. Aemilius' reversal of fortune is foreshadowed by his speech to the young men after his victory over Perseus (ch. 27).

# Polybius

(ca. 200–118 BC, wrote in Greek)

## Introduction

The Greek statesman and historian Polybius wrote a history of Rome's rise to a world power in forty books, essentially covering the period from the First Punic War to the 140s BC. About one-third of it survives. Polybius was among the 1,000 Greeks deported to Rome and detained there after the Roman victory over the Greek general Perseus at the battle of Pydna in 168 BC (see Plutarch, *Life of Cato* 9 and *Life of Aemilius Paullus*). The deportees were held in Rome without trial, but Polybius found a friend and patron there in the powerful Scipio Aemilianus. Under Scipio's patronage, Polybius received preferential treatment, and likely accompanied Scipio on his military campaigns in both Spain and North Africa, where he got a close look at the practices of the Roman army that he describes in his history (see below, sections B and C).

Despite having been on the losing side of a war against the Romans, Polybius became an ardent admirer of Roman institutions and attempted to explain their astonishing success to his Greek-speaking audience. One of his primary aims of writing, he says, was "so that my readers may understand how, and through what institutions, the whole world was conquered and became subject to Rome in less than fifty-three years" (6.1). He then breaks off his narrative in the sixth book in order to give an analysis of the Roman constitution and military practices, and this is the section included here. The Greek word for "constitution" (*politeia*) entails not just the form of government, but also the particular cultural institutions and practices of an individual city-state. Polybius sees Rome's success as the direct result of the competitive and patriotic nature of the Roman people. In the following passages Polybius describes the power-sharing arrangement of the Roman constitution (section A, chs. 11–18), the structure and discipline of the Roman army (sections B and C, chs. 19–42), and the funeral rites of elite Romans, with particular attention to the role they played in inspiring young citizens to excellence (section D, chs. 53–54).

---

## *Histories*

Polybius has just given an account of the three kinds of "unmixed" constitutions: monarchy, aristocracy, and democracy. Earlier Greek political writers often debated which was the best form of government. One of the keys to Rome's success, Polybius argues, was that their government was a blend of all three forms, or a "mixed constitution."

## A    The Roman Constitution (*Politeia*)

[11] The Roman government is broken into three branches, which control matters collectively. All of these are so fairly and equitably arranged and administered that no one—not even a native Roman—could say for certain whether their government is an aristocracy, democracy, or monarchy. This is completely understandable. If one only considers the power of the consuls, their government looks just like a monarchy or kingship. If one focuses on the Senate's power, it seems like an aristocracy. If you only consider the people's power, however, you would think it is a democracy. What follows is an account of the powers each of the branches had at the time of the Carthaginian conflict, powers that remain today, with a few exceptions.

## The Consuls

[12] The consuls, when not leading an army in the field, remain in Rome and have supreme authority over all domestic matters. All the other magistrates, except the tribunes of the people,[1] are subordinate to them and must follow their commands. The consuls are the ones who introduce ambassadors before the Senate, who convene that body when urgent matters are to be discussed, and who make sure that their decrees are carried out. Now, many affairs that concern the whole state must be carried through by a vote of the people; even so, it is the consuls' responsibility to consider these issues, to convene the popular assemblies, to introduce measures before them, and to carry out the decrees of the majority.

In the preparation for war—in fact, in the execution of the entire campaign—the consuls have nearly unlimited powers. They have the power to command the allies as they see fit, appoint military tribunes, levy troops, and select men who are suitable for service. They also have the authority, while on campaign, to inflict punishment on any subordinate they wish, and they can spend as much of the state's funds as they deem necessary (they have a quaestor on staff who readily performs their orders). So you can see why someone considering only this branch would think that the Roman government was a monarchy or a kingship. These institutions may undergo some changes now or in the future, but that would not alter the fundamental truth of what I am saying. The same goes for everything that follows.[2]

## The Senate

[13] First and foremost, the Senate manages the treasury. It controls revenue and expenditures alike. In fact, the quaestors cannot sign off on any expenditure without a decree of the Senate (though, as noted above, funds for consuls are an exception). The most massive outlay of funds, far surpassing the others, comes every five years,

---

1. See Appian, *Civil Wars* A (ch. 1) in this volume.

2. An acknowledgment that the Roman constitution was in fact unwritten and changed over time.

when the censors require giant appropriations for the repair and construction of public works. The Senate controls this, too, and alone grants the necessary funds. Likewise, all crimes throughout Italy requiring a public investigation—treason, conspiracy, poisoning, assassination—are the Senate's responsibility. In addition, whenever a private citizen or city in Italy is in need of mediation, formal reprimand, aid, or a garrison, it falls to the Senate to intervene. It is also responsible for sending embassies to peoples outside of Italy when there is need to settle some dispute, urge some course of action, impose orders, receive a people under Roman control, or announce a declaration of war. The Senate also decides how embassies that come to Rome are to be treated, and what response will be given to their requests. The people have no say in these matters. For all of these reasons, someone living in Rome when the consuls are absent would conclude that the government was completely aristocratic. As a matter of fact, many Greeks—and many kings among them—are convinced of this, since all business between them and Rome is handled by the Senate.

## The People

[14] Based on what I've just said, one might reasonably wonder what part of the government could be left for the people. After all, the Senate controls all the aspects I just mentioned, the greatest being that it manages all revenue and expenditures. And the consuls have unlimited powers when it comes to preparing for war and on campaign. There is a part, however, that remains for the people, and it is extremely important. For the people alone have the authority to confer honors or exact punishments, and it is only through these that kingdoms, states, and—let's face it—all human society are held together. Think about those occasions when no distinction between the two is made, or when one is made but ill applied. Can any business be properly conducted? How could it, when good people are esteemed as much as the bad?[3]

Back to my main point. It is the people that pass judgment in those many cases where wrongdoing carries a sentence of a fine, most importantly when the defendants are former public officials. And the people alone can decide capital cases. In this area the Romans have an exceptional practice that deserves special mention. People on trial for their lives have the opportunity, if the voting is going against them, of departing openly and going into a self-imposed exile. They can do so up until a tribe casts the decisive vote that would condemn them to death. Men have found safe havens in Naples, Praeneste, Tibur, and other cities bound to Rome by treaty.

It is the people who vote deserving men into public office, the greatest reward for virtuous conduct in a state. They also have the power to pass or reject laws, and what is more important, to decide on war and peace. As for alliances, termination of hostilities, and treaties, it is the people who ratify or reject them. So again, when one takes these factors into account, one might reasonably say that the people have the greatest share and that the government is a democracy.

---

3. As seen more clearly below (chs. 39 and 53–54), Polybius believes that the public honoring of excellence was central to Rome's success. See Cicero, *Letters* 23.3 in this volume.

## Checks and Balances

[15] Now that I have outlined what powers each individual branch has, I will turn to checks and balances, how each branch might cooperate with, or counteract, the others. First, the consuls. Whenever a consul, invested with the powers mentioned above, sets out with his army on campaign, one might think that he had absolute power to complete his objectives. In fact, he still needs the people and the Senate, and without them he is not capable of completing his mission. Don't the legions constantly need supplies? Without the Senate's approval, there would be no food, clothing, or pay. So the consul's objectives will remain unaccomplished so long as the Senate is disposed to be willfully negligent or actively obstructive. It also lies in the hands of the Senate whether a general's long-term plans are brought to completion or not. At the end of a year, the Senate may either allow an incumbent general to keep his command, or replace him with another.[4] Furthermore, the Senate has the power either to celebrate a general's accomplishments with great pomp and circumstance, or to downplay and minimize them instead. The Romans have marvelous parades which they call "triumphs," in which the accomplishments of the generals are vividly represented before the very eyes of the citizen body. But these cannot be properly celebrated—or celebrated at all—unless the Senate assents and supplies the necessary expense for them.[5]

The consuls absolutely must respect the people as well, no matter how far away from the city they happen to be. As I said above, it is the people who ratify or dissolve truces and treaties. Most importantly, when magistrates leave office, they must account for all their actions before the people. It is therefore dangerous for generals to treat the Senate or the people with contempt.

[16] To return to the Senate, despite its considerable powers it must nonetheless pay attention to the masses and have some consideration for the people in public affairs. It cannot carry out the most serious and important investigations into, and exact penalties for, crimes against the state, which are punishable by death, unless the people confirm their decree. The same goes for matters that pertain to the Senate itself. If someone introduces a law in an attempt to curtail the Senate's time-honored authority, eliminate privileges or honors, or—god forbid—put limitations on their private fortunes, only the people have the power to pass or reject it.[6] Most importantly, if any one of the tribunes intervenes and opposes a measure, not only does it prevent the Senate from putting their resolutions into action, it also stops them from holding any meetings or sessions at all. And the tribunes are always obliged to act on the people's behalf and to respect their wishes.[7] For all these reasons the Senate fears and pays attention to the mood of the people.

[17] By the same token the people are also beholden to the Senate and must respect that body in both their public and private lives. After all, the number of public works is

---

4. A magistrate with *imperium* (praetor or consul) could have his power extended, continually, if desired, past the one-year term of his office by vote of the Senate. This is called prorogation, and the former magistrates with this power were called *propraetors* or *proconsuls*.

5. See Plutarch's *Life of Aemilius Paulus* 30–32 for political obstruction of a triumph.

6. For an attempt to curtail conspicuous consumption among senators, see Plutarch, *Life of Cato* 18.

7. See Appian, *Civil Wars* B, ch. 12.

huge. The censors issue contracts for the repair of old or for the building of new infra-structure all over Italy—so many it would be difficult to count them all. Then there is the upkeep of all the many rivers, ports, gardens, mines, and public lands—in a word, everything that falls under Rome's dominion. All of these state projects are carried out by the people, and virtually everyone is dependent on the contracts and the jobs they entail in one way or another. Some, for instance, negotiate and purchase the con-tracts directly from the censors. Then there are their business partners, investors, and underwriters. The Senate oversees all of this. It can grant an extension of time, reduce the contractual obligation if some mishap occurs, or completely annul the contract if the situation becomes hopeless. There are indeed many areas in which the Senate can greatly harm or benefit those carrying out public projects, since it has the ultimate decision over all of the aspects I've mentioned above. Most importantly, judges for a great many civil trials, both public and private, are drawn from the members of the Senate when the stakes of the case are high. Since the people depend on the Senate for their own security and stand in constant fear that they may at some point need their help, they are hesitant to block or oppose the Senate's wishes. Likewise, the people will only with great reluctance oppose the designs of the consuls, since everyone, individu-ally and collectively, are under their authority when on military campaign.

### Effectiveness in a Crisis

[18] These are the powers that each branch can use to impede or cooperate with each of the others, and in fact the harmonious union of all three is sufficient to tackle any crisis, such that it is impossible to find a political system that is superior to this one. Whenever some external force threatens the whole state, all three parts are forced to unite and work together. When this happens, the state becomes so strong that it cannot fail to meet any need since everyone is competing to come up with ideas to meet the challenge, and all decisions will be implemented in a timely manner since everyone is working, both publicly and privately, toward a solution to the problem. This is why this particular form of government has proven to be an irresistible force, capable of meeting every one of its objectives.

On the other hand, once freed from external threats, they begin to become compla-cent because of the good fortune and affluence that come from success. The inevitable happens: as they enjoy their prosperity, they surrender to flattery and sloth, and become insolent and overbearing. On these occasions the Roman system is, because of its very structure, extremely beneficial in rectifying the situation. When one of the branches, swelling out of proportion, becomes contentious and gains more power than it should, it is checked by the others. As outlined above, none of the branches is self-sufficient, and the designs of any one branch can be blocked or impeded by the others, and it is for this reason that none of them grows out of proportion or ignores the others. All three parts remain in equilibrium, since any aggressive move will be blocked, and there is the ever-present threat that the other branches will interfere.

# B    The Roman Army

[19] The consuls, after taking office, appoint twenty-four military tribunes, fourteen with five years' military service, ten with ten years' service. The Romans have specific terms of compulsory service: a cavalryman must serve ten years before his forty-sixth birthday, an infantryman sixteen. There is an exception for citizens under the minimum census requirement of 400 drachmae,[8] who are employed in the navy. In times of crisis infantry are required to provide twenty years' service. No one may hold political office without having completed at least ten years in the military.

## Drafting Soldiers

When the consuls decide to draft soldiers, they make a public announcement as to the date by which men of military age must be at Rome. This is done annually. When the day arrives and the men have assembled on the Capitoline Hill in Rome, the junior tribunes divide up into four groups to represent the four "legions"—that being the principal organizational unit for the army. The division of the tribunes follows the order in which they were appointed by the people or generals: the first four go to the first legion, the next three to the second, the next four to the third, and the last three to the fourth. The senior tribunes are likewise divided: the first two to the first legion, the next three to the second, the next two to the third, and the last three to the fourth.

[20] Once the tribunes are divided into equal numbers per legion, they break up into four groups and station themselves in separate locations. They then determine by lot the order of the tribes and call them forth one by one. From the first tribe they select four young men that are more or less alike in age and physique. When these are brought forth, the tribunes of the first legion get first choice, those of the second legion get second choice, and so on down the line. Then another group of four young men is brought forth, but this time the tribunes of the second legion get first choice, while those of the first legion get the last choice. A third group is brought forth, and the third legion gets the first choice, while the second legion gets the last. By staggering the order, the Romans ensure that each legion gets men of the same quality. They continue in this manner until they get to their predetermined number: forty-two hundred infantry during normal operations, or five thousand in times of great danger.

After this, they select the cavalry—well, that was the old system. Now they select the cavalry before the infantry, based on their wealth as determined by the censor in the last census. They outfit each legion with three hundred cavalry.

## Oath

[21] After the selection process is complete, the recruits of each legion are assembled by the tribunes in charge of administering the oath. Out of the whole group, they select a single man whom they believe is the most suitable and make him take the full oath: "I swear that I will obey my superiors and carry out the commands of my leaders to the

---

8. The fifth class according to the "Servian" requirements; see Livy chs. 42–43.

best of my ability." The others then come forward one by one and take the oath simply by declaring that they will do likewise.

## Allies

At the same time the consuls determine which allied towns will provide allies and send instructions to their leaders. The consuls determine the number, the day, and the place that the conscripted men are to muster in Rome. The cities draft their troops and administer the oath just as those in Rome do, supply them with their own general and paymaster, and dispatch them to Rome.

## Allocating Troops to Divisions

Back in Rome, after they administer the oath, the tribunes announce the time and place that the legions are to muster without arms, and then dismiss the troops. When they reassemble on the appointed day, the tribunes assign the youngest (and poorest) to the light-armed skirmishers (*velites*). The next older group is assigned to the so-called *hastati* ("armed with a spear"); those in the primes of their lives to the *principes* ("leaders"); and the oldest of all to the *triarii* ("third rankers"). These are the main divisions of the Roman army in terms of age, equipment and designation. Here are the numbers of each group: the eldest (the *triarii*), 600; the *principes*, 1,200; the *hastati*, 1,200; the youngest (the *velites*) make up the remainder. If a legion has more than 4,000 men, they distribute the extra men into all of the categories, except for the *triarii*, whose numbers always remain the same.

## Velites

[22] They require the youngest to carry a short sword, light javelin, and light shield. The shield is durable in construction, and its size offers a fair amount of protection. It is round and three feet in diameter. They also wear a simple helmet. Sometimes they put a wolf's skin or some other distinguishing feature over it, both as extra protection and to be more conspicuous—so that it will be easier for the subordinate officers to tell which of the *velites* bravely face danger and which don't. The javelin of the *velites* has a wooden shaft two cubits long (three feet) and about a finger thick; its head measures a span in length (eight inches) and is hammered down into such a fine and sharp blade that it crumples on first impact, which prevents the enemy from re-using it. Otherwise, the javelin could be employed by both sides.

## Armament of the *Hastati*, *Principes*, and *Triarii*

[23] The next oldest group, those called the *hastati*, are required to wear a complete set of armor. A full set of armor for the Roman solider begins with an oblong shield (*scutum*). Its width is two and a half feet and it is slightly convex; its length runs four feet. Its edges curve back from the center about a palm's width. It has a double frame, with

two planks tightly joined by glue, and its surface is covered first by canvas and then by calf's hide. It has an iron rim running along the top and the bottom, which protects it from sword-blows from above and from damage when resting on the ground. It also has an iron boss affixed to it; the function of this is to deflect the heaviest blows from stones, pikes, and basically any forceful projectile. They also have a short sword, carried on the right hip; this is also called a Spanish sword.[9] It has a fine point for thrusting, but its cutting edge can deliver a strong blow on both sides when slashing, because the blade, shaped like an obelisk, is strong and sturdy. In addition to these items, they also carry two spears (*pila*), a bronze helmet, and shin guards.

There are two types of spears: thick and slender. Of the former, there are ones with round shafts about a palm's width in diameter, and others with square shafts, a palm's width square. The slender spears are similar to medium-sized hunting spears. The Roman soldier carries one of each type. The wooden shaft of both types runs about three cubits in length; at the end it is fitted with a barbed iron head that is about the same length as the wooden shaft. They make doubly sure that the head is securely fastened to the shaft and retains its usefulness, fitting it halfway down the shaft and bolting it with numerous rivets. The result is that during battle the iron will break before it becomes separated from the shaft, even though the width at the bottom (where it is fastened to the shaft) is only one and a half fingers thick—so careful are the Romans in fastening the head to the shaft.

In addition to all these items, they adorn themselves with a crown of feathers, with three purple or black feathers standing upright about a cubit high. With these rising from the helmet and towering over the rest of the arms, a man effectively looks about twice as tall as he really is. The majority of soldiers also wear a bronze plate, about a span square, that covers the chest. It is also called a "heart-protector." That is the final piece of their armament. Citizens with an estate valued at more than ten thousand drachmae,[10] however, wear a breastplate consisting of chain-mail rather than a "heart-protector." The armament of the *principes* and the *triarii* are the same, except that the *triarii* carry long thrusting spears (*hastae*) instead of throwing spears.

### Organization: Subordinate Officers

[24] From each of the main divisions, except the youngest, they appoint ten company commanders based on merit. Then they make another selection of another ten from each. All of these receive the title "centurion."[11] The first man chosen also becomes a member of the military council.[12] The centurions themselves select an equal number

---

9. The Romans probably adopted the use of the famous *gladius* from Spanish mercenaries fighting for Carthage in the First Punic War (264–241 BC), although Polybius elsewhere dates it to the time of Hannibal.

10. Members of the first, or highest, Servian class. See Livy chs. 42–43.

11. The term "centurion" refers etymologically to the fact that this officer originally commanded one hundred (*cent-*) soldiers, which comprised a "century."

12. This is the senior centurion who led the first maniple of the *triarii*, also called *primus pilus* ("first spear").

of *optiones*.[13] These officers, in consultation with the centurions, divide each class, with the exception of the *velites*, into ten units, and assign two centurions and two *optiones* to each company. This unit is called by various names: *ordo* ("company"), *manipulus* ("maniple"), or *vexillum* ("flag-unit"); officers in charge of these units are called company commanders or centurions. These officers select the two bravest and most energetic men from the remaining troops of each maniple to be standard-bearers. The Romans are smart to choose two centurions for each maniple. One simply cannot know how a leader will act or what will befall him, and because war allows no room for excuses, the Romans want to make sure no maniple is without a leader and commander. When both centurions are present, the first chosen is the superior officer and commands the right half of the maniple, the second the left half. If either one is absent, the other is commander of the whole.

The Romans do not want their centurions to be overly bold or big risk-takers, but rather to be decisive, steady, and rather stoic emotionally. In other words, they do not want them to make attacks or initiate hostilities as much as to be ready and willing, when the battle is going against them and they are being hard pressed, to stand their ground and die on behalf of their country.

## Cavalry

[25] The cavalry is also divided up into ten squadrons, and they select three squadron commanders from each.[14] They, in turn, select three *optiones*. The first squadron commander chosen leads the whole squadron, while the other two are called "leaders of ten" (*decuriones*). In fact all three have this title, *decurion*. If the head officer is absent, the second is in charge of the squadron. The armament of the cavalry is now very similar to that of their Greek counterparts. In the old days they did not fight protected by a breastplate, but clothed in a light tunic, a dangerous practice. In terms of dismounting and mounting the horses, they were outfitted to do so quickly and effectively, but in close combat they were put in great peril since they were fighting essentially naked. Their lances too were impractical for two reasons. First, they were too slender and pliant, which made them hard to aim properly, and before the iron head of the lance could pierce anything, a great many of them shattered due to the vibrations caused by the motion of the horses. Second, they did not make them with spikes at the butt end, and they could only deliver a blow with the tip of the lance. If this was broken, the lance was useless. The shields they used to have were made out of ox-hide and were shaped like the cakes that are presented as offerings at sacrifices, the ones whose tops curve down to the sides. They were not effective against incoming missiles since they simply weren't strong enough. And if the leather covering came off and they got wet in a storm, they became not just problematic as before, but completely unusable.

---

13. An *optio* was second-in-command to a centurion, and had both administrative and tactical responsibilities, the latter as commander in the rear guard. The centurion would be in the front of his troops.

14. With thirty men in each squadron—Polybius assumes a notional strength of 300. See above, ch. 20.

When they realized that this armament was impractical from experience, they quickly changed to the equipment of the Greeks. Their lances are made such that the initial blow of the tip can be both well aimed and forceful. They are constructed as to be rigid and steady, and now the lance can be turned around and still deliver an effective blow with the butt end. It's the same with their shields. They are made sturdy and durable and can be used against incoming missiles and in hand-to-hand combat. When the Romans recognized the value in this, they quickly imitated the Greek way. They, more than any other nation, are good at adopting new practices and emulating other people who do something better.

## Mobilization of Troops

[26] When the tribunes have divided up the troops and given them their orders concerning armament, they send them back to their homes. When they are required to reassemble at the time and place determined by the consuls (each consul assembles his troops, that is, a part of the allies and two Roman legions, in a different place), all the enlisted men show up without fail. They promised to be there, and there is no excuse for absence except for adverse omens or complete debilitation. The allies assemble in the same place as the Roman soldiers. Their organization and administration are managed by the leaders, twelve in number, appointed by the consuls and bearing the name "prefects of the allies" (*praefecti sociorum*). The first thing the prefects do is select from the assembled allied forces the troops best prepared for special service. These men are called *extraordinarii*, or "elite" when translated into our language. The number of allied infantry is more or less equal to that of the Romans, but their cavalry is three times as large. They choose about a third of the cavalry and about a fifth of the infantry for the elite corps. The remainder are broken up into two units, one called the right wing, the other the left.

## C    The Roman Camp

When the army has been organized, the tribunes take both the Romans and allied forces and set up camp. They have a single plan for their camps, which they use no matter the place or situation. This seems to be the right occasion for me to try to describe the arrangement of their forces while on march, in camp, and on the battlefield. It is, of course, difficult to render a clear picture in the minds of my audience with mere words, but I will try my best to do so. After all, everyone who is drawn to excellence and splendid deeds will surely want to hear a bit of detail on the Romans' practices in this area, and a single reading will acquaint a person with a subject that deserves to be studied and understood.

[27] Here is how the Romans arrange and organize their camp. The first thing they do after choosing a site is to find the place in it that has the most commanding view and is best suited for issuing orders. This is where the *praetorium* ("general's tent") is positioned. They place a flag on the spot and measure out a square 200 feet by 200 feet around it, giving it a total area of four *plethra* (= 40,000 feet square). Then they determine which direction from this space will afford them the best access to water supply

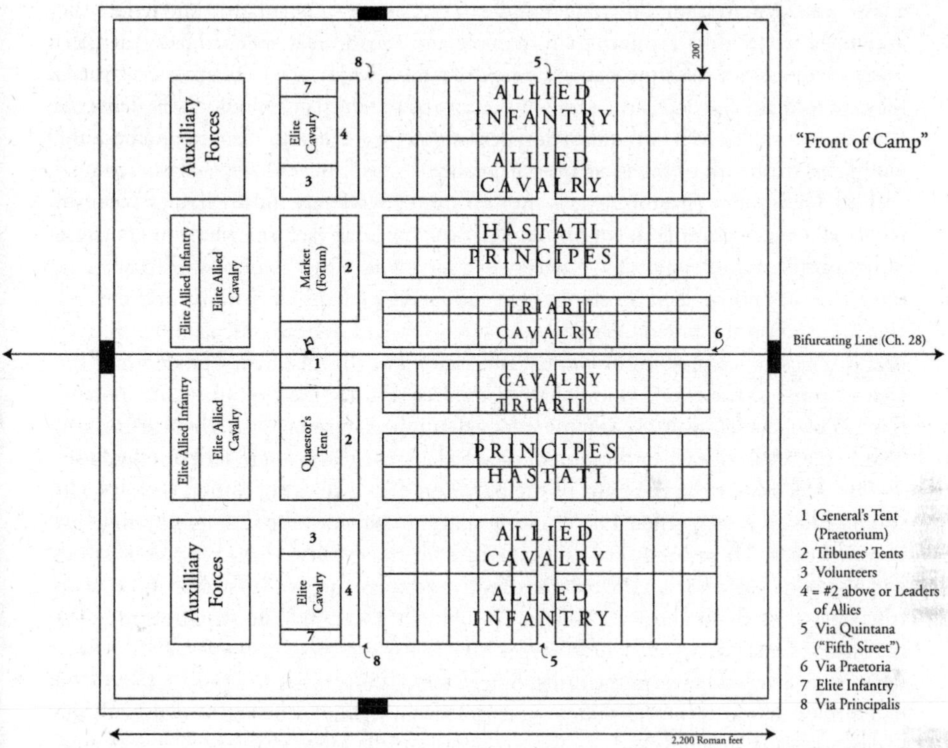
200'
8
5
Auxiliary Forces
7
Elite Cavalry
4
3
ALLIED INFANTRY
ALLIED CAVALRY
"Front of Camp"
Elite Allied Infantry
Elite Allied Cavalry
Market (Forum)
2
HASTATI PRINCIPES
TRIARII CAVALRY
6
Bifurcating Line (Ch. 28)
1
CAVALRY TRIARII
Elite Allied Infantry
Elite Allied Cavalry
Quaestor's Tent
2
PRINCIPES HASTATI
3
Auxilliary Forces
Elite Cavalry
4
7
ALLIED CAVALRY
ALLIED INFANTRY
8
5
1 General's Tent (Praetorium)
2 Tribunes' Tents
3 Volunteers
4 = #2 above or Leaders of Allies
5 Via Quintana ("Fifth Street")
6 Via Praetoria
7 Elite Infantry
8 Via Principalis
2,200 Roman feet

and foraging opportunities, and it is here that the Roman legions encamp. They are organized in a specific way. You'll remember that I said there were six military tribunes for each legion, and that each consul commands two Roman legions, so there will be a total of twelve tribunes for each consular army. Their tents are set up in a straight line, parallel to that side of the square mentioned above and set fifty feet away from it so that there is space for horses, beasts of burden, and all the other gear that the tribunes have in tow. The tribunes' tents face away from the *praetorium*, and the direction that they face will hereafter be referred to as the "front" of the camp. The tribunes' tents are equally spaced from each other such that they extend over the entire width of the camp.

[28] They then measure another hundred feet from the tribunes' tents and form another parallel line directly across from them, and it is here that the soldiers' quarters begin.[15] Let me explain how they divide up the space. First, they bisect the line in a perpendicular fashion, splitting the space in two halves. Then, they arrange the cavalry of each legion in right angles off this perpendicular line such that they face each other and leave a space of fifty feet in between the rows. The perpendicular line mentioned

15. This space between the tribunes' tents and the general encampment is called the *Via Principalis* ("Main Road").

above should run straight down the middle of this space.[16] The infantry and cavalry are encamped in a similar fashion; each maniple and squadron is assigned a square plot. Each square faces a road and has a frontage of a fixed width of a hundred feet. Usually they try to make the depth the same in the case of the Roman legions (for the allies, it is a different story). When the situation demands a bigger legion, they expand both the width and the depth of the plots proportionally.

[29] The cavalry encampment is thus set up perpendicular to the line of tribunes' tents like a street running down from it at a right angle. In fact, the whole road-system of the camp resembles a series of streets in a city, with either maniples of infantry or squadrons of cavalry lined up along them and facing each other. Now, behind the cavalry they station the *triarii* of both legions in a similar arrangement, each maniple set back-to-back to a squadron of cavalry and facing away from them. The depth of the area assigned to the *triarii* is only half of the length since their numbers are more or less half of the other units. Given the unequal numbers in some units, the Romans will change the depth of each encampment so as to keep the width a standard hundred feet.

Fifty feet away from the tents of the *triarii* on each side they position the *principes* so that they face each other. The resulting spaces in between the facing encampments become roads. These begin, just as is the case for the cavalry, at the road opposite to and one hundred feet from the tribunes' tents, and terminate at the far side of the camp (the area we decided above to call the "front" of the camp). The *hastati* occupy the next lines of encampments, which are set back to back to those of the *principes*. Again, there is no space in between the units. Since each of these three groups of soldiers—as determined at the very beginning—consists of ten maniples, it happens that all the streets are equal in length and terminate similarly at the camp wall toward the front of the camp. The last maniple in each line faces the wall and not the road it abuts.

[30] Across from the *hastati* and facing them are stationed the allied cavalry, with another fifty feet in between them. Their ranks begin and end at the same point as the others. You will recall from my earlier discussion that the number of allied infantry is roughly the same as the Romans', minus the elite units, while the number of cavalry is double, again subtracting that third of them that serve as elite soldiers. Again, in their attempt to maintain a standard width for each unit, they extend the depth of their encampments proportionally in accordance with their larger numbers. Now five streets have been created. Back to back with the squadrons of allied cavalry are stationed the maniples of allied infantry, again adjusting the depth of their encampment proportionally to their size. These face the outer walls of the camp.

The first tent at either end of each maniple's encampment is occupied by a centurion. Now, as they arrange their encampment in the way just mentioned, they also leave fifty feet unoccupied between the fifth and sixth units of infantry and cavalry alike, so as to produce another road through the encampment, running perpendicular to the five streets mentioned above and parallel to the tribunes' tents. They call this "fifth street" (*quintana*) since it runs along the fifth set of maniple and squadron encampments.

[31] Let us turn to the space behind the tribunes' tents. The areas adjacent to the *praetorium* are occupied by the marketplace to one side, and by the quaestor's tent

---

16. This space running down from the *praetorium* and between the cavalry is called the *Via Praetoria* ("Praetorian Road").

(*quaestorium*) and the equipment necessary to carry out his tasks on the other side. Behind the outermost tribunes' tents and essentially forming a wing behind them are stationed the elite cavalry chosen from the elite corps and some of the volunteers who re-enlisted out of a sense of duty to the consuls. All of these are quartered along the sides of the camp, and face either the marketplace or the *quaestorium*. These men, generally speaking, are not only encamped near the consuls, but also serve as the consul's and quaestor's bodyguard while on the march and during other military engagements. Set back to back with them and facing the outer wall are the elite infantry who serve the consul and quaestor in a similar fashion to the aforementioned cavalry.

Behind the marketplace, the *praetorium*, and the *quaestorium* they leave unoccupied a space one hundred feet wide and running parallel to the tribunes' tents. It runs the entire width of the camp. On the far side of this road are quartered the elite allied cavalry, facing toward the marketplace, the *praetorium*, and the *quaestorium*. Straight through the ranks of the cavalry is a road fifty feet wide that leads away from the general's tent to the back wall of the camp. The elite allied infantry are set back to back with the cavalry, thus facing the back wall which forms the outer limit of the whole camp. The remaining empty space along the outer flanks of the wall are reserved for foreign soldiers and any allies that happen to join after the campaign is underway.

The result of all of this is that the camp is laid out in a perfect square, and the road-system and general organization makes it look like a city. The soldiers' quarters are in all directions 200 feet from the wall. This open space is quite beneficial in many respects:

- When the legions are being led out or brought back into the camp, each unit filters into this empty space via their own roads, and so they do not crash into or get in each other's way, as would happen if they had to fall in along a single road.

- They can bring here all of the animals and war-booty taken from the enemy and easily watch over it at night.

- Most importantly, during attacks at night neither fire nor missiles can reach the soldiers' tents, and when on the rare occasion a projectile does make it to the tents, it is usually harmless because of the distance from the wall.

[32] Now that you know the number of infantry and cavalry (it doesn't matter if you use the 4,000 or 5,000 figure), as well as the width, depth, and number of individual encampments, and also the width of the roads and streets, it is possible for you, with a little concentration, to calculate the size of the space and the perimeter of the whole. But suppose there is a surplus of allies, whether from the beginning or through later addition while on campaign. In the latter case, they use the space next to the *praetorium*, reducing the area of the marketplace and *quaestorium*, to a bare minimum if need be. If from the very beginning there is a substantial number of extra allies, they will add another road on either side of the Roman soldiers' encampment.

What happens when both consuls are campaigning together and all four legions are camped within one wall? Easy. Just imagine the two armies joined back to back at the place where the elite infantry are stationed (this is the "back" of the camp we mentioned above). When this happens the camp's shape becomes an elongated rectangle. The area is doubled and the perimeter is one and a half times longer than before. This is the arrangement when the two consuls camp together. When they camp apart, it's the same as I described above, but they set up the *praetorium*, marketplace, and *quaestorium* in between.

[33] After the camp is set up, the tribunes meet and administer the oath to everyone in the camp, free and slave alike. Each man takes the oath separately: "I shall not steal anything from the camp, and if I find something I shall bring it directly to the tribunes." They then set the maniples of *principes* and *hastati* to their tasks. Two maniples are assigned to care for the area in front of the tribunes' tents. The majority of Roman soldiers spend their time during the day along this street, so they are always very concerned with washing and sweeping this area with meticulous care. As for the other eighteen maniples, each of the six tribunes (recall my earlier discussion about their numbers) are assigned three by lot. Each of these maniples takes a turn in performing necessary tasks for the tribunes. Here's what they have to do:

- When the army pitches camp, these men set up the tribunes' tent and level the ground around it.

- If certain supplies need extra protection, they take care to fence them off.

- They provide two sets of guards (one set equals four men), one posted in front of the tent, the other behind the tent next to the horses.

Since each tribune is assigned three maniples, and since the available men in each number over a hundred—not counting the *triarii* and the *velites* who are exempt from this service—the responsibility is actually quite light. Each maniple is called upon only every third day. In the process of performing the necessary day-to-day tasks they also magnify the dignity of, and show respect for, the tribunes' rank and authority. The *triarii* are freed from directly serving the tribunes, but each of their units must provide a set of guards to watch over the neighboring squadron of cavalry stationed behind them. These guards are generally responsible for the whole area, but they are particularly concerned with the horses. They make sure that the horses do not get tangled up in their ropes, hurt themselves, and become useless, or else get loose and cause a great disturbance in the camp when they encounter other horses.

Each day a single maniple out of all those in the camp attends to the general's tent. They offer him protection against plots on his life while enhancing the dignity of his rank and position.

[34] The allies are responsible for building two walls and digging the trenches in front of them—the two side walls next to which they are encamped. The Romans are responsible for the other two, with each legion taking one. Each maniple is assigned to the construction of one part of the wall, supervised by their centurions, who personally oversee the process. The whole operation is managed by two tribunes who ensure the quality of the work. The tribunes are also responsible for running the day-to-day business in the camp. They divide themselves into groups of two and are in charge of overall operations for two months out of a six-month period. The prefects of the allies also have the same kind of responsibilities.

Each day at dawn the cavalry and centurions assemble at the tribunes' tents, while the tribunes meet with the consul. The latter issues his orders to the tribunes, who relate them to the cavalry and centurions. They, in turn, communicate the orders to the rank and file at the appropriate time and place.

## The Watchword

Here is how the Romans maintain security when passing along the night watchword. A man is chosen from the tenth maniple (the one camped at the far end of the street) of each class, cavalry and infantry alike. This man is freed from guard duty and proceeds, when the sun is starting to set, to his tribune's tent, where he receives the watchword—actually a wooden tablet with the watchword inscribed on it. He then returns to his maniple with the tablet. Then he hands over the tablet, in the presence of witnesses, to the leader of the next maniple, who likewise passes it on to the leader of the maniple next to him. They keep doing this until the tablet reaches the first maniple, which is encamped nearest to the tribune. They are required to bring the tablet back to the tribune before dark. If the tribune gets back all of the tablets he sent out, he knows that everyone under his command got the watchword, since the tablet had to go through all of the maniples to get back to him. If one is missing, he investigates at once to find out what happened. Since each tablet has a distinguishing mark, he can easily determine which group has not returned the tablet.

## Night Watch

[35] Here is how they organize the night watch. The general and his tent are guarded by the maniple assigned to him. The tribunes and the cavalry are guarded by the men from the designated maniple, as I described above. Each unit also designates a guard for itself. The consul assigns all of the remaining duties. Normally, three sets of guards are posted at the *quaestorium*, while at the tent of each legate and council member there stand two sets of guards. The outer perimeter is manned by the *velites*, who are stationed each day along the wall—this is the specific duty designated for this class of soldier. These men also stand guard at the gates, ten at each.

Each evening one of the *optiones* brings all of his men who are slated to stand first watch to the tribune. The tribune gives each of them a small wooden token, one for each post, each of which has a specific mark. The guards take these and head out for their assigned posts. The cavalry has the responsibility of conducting rounds: In the morning, the leader of the first squadron in each legion is required to order one of his *optiones* to select four men and charge them with carrying out rounds in the evening. The selection is to take place before breakfast. By nightfall, the squadron leader must also inform the leader of the next squadron that it will be his responsibility to make arrangements for rounds on the following day. And this next officer will do the same the next day, and so on down the line.

The four men chosen by the *optiones* from the first squadron draw lots to determine for which watch they will conduct rounds. They then proceed to the tribune, where they get written orders as to which posts they must visit and at what time. Then they retire to the staging area next to the first maniple of *triarii*. They go here because the centurion of that maniple is responsible for announcing the change of watch with a trumpet blast. [36] When the appropriate time comes, the man who drew first watch conducts his rounds, taking with him some of his comrades as witnesses. He proceeds to his assigned posts; these are not just those posts on the perimeter, but include all of those posts among the maniples of infantry and squadrons of cavalry. If he finds those on duty awake, he takes the token away from them and moves to his next post. If, however, he finds someone sleeping or away from his post, he calls his comrades to witness that fact and departs. The men who conduct the rounds in the other three watches follow a similar procedure. The trumpet calls announce the change in watch, so that all of those going on rounds to the various posts do so at the same time. As I mentioned just a bit above, the centurions of the first maniple of *triarii* in each legion is responsible for ensuring the trumpet call to announce the watch and they take turns daily doing so.

Each of the men who go on rounds brings the tokens to the tribune at daybreak. If none are missing, they depart without any trouble. But if one of them brings fewer tokens than posts they visited, the tribunes inquire by examining the distinguishing marks on the tokens to determine which station's token is missing. Once the tribune has determined this, he calls upon the centurion, who in turn produces the men assigned to said post. These men are asked to respond to the report of the man who went on rounds. If the fault lies with the guards, the man on patrol immediately corroborates that fact by calling upon the witnesses who went with him. He is required to do this. If the guards had done nothing wrong, the blame falls on the man making the rounds.

[37] The tribunes assemble at once in order to try the accused. If he is judged guilty, he is punished with a clubbing. The procedure for this punishment is as follows. The tribune takes a club and lightly touches the guilty man with it. After this act, all of the soldiers in the camp commence striking the man with clubs and stones. The vast majority of the condemned are killed right there in the camp. But even if someone happens to escape, he has lost all hope of salvation. He's doomed. After all, he cannot return to his own home, and none of his kin would dare to shelter such a disgrace inside their house. Given all of this, once a soldier runs afoul of the rules of the camp he is completely and utterly ruined. The same punishment is reserved for the *optio* and the squadron commander if they fail to issue their orders in a timely fashion—that is, if the former does not assign men to conduct the rounds or if the latter fails to pass the baton to the leader of the next unit. Because the penalty is so severe and always enforced, the Romans conduct their night watches with great care and exactitude.

Just as the soldiers answer to the tribunes, the tribunes have to answer to the consul. Now, the tribune (or in the case of the allies, the prefect) has the power to assess fines, confiscate possessions as a penalty, and punish a wrongdoer with a flogging. Specific transgressions are punished by clubbing: if someone commits a theft, provides false testimony, is caught committing an immoral sexual act (if he is of mature age), or has been sanctioned three times for the same transgression. These offenses are categorized as willful crimes. Other offenses they assign to another category: that of cowardice and actions unbecoming of a Roman soldier. Among these are: providing an embellished report to the tribunes about one's bravery in combat in order to receive honors, or leaving one's assigned ranks in a covering force out of fear, or discarding any part of one's arms during the battle itself out of fear.

Therefore the men in covering forces often choose certain death, refusing to leave their ranks even when vastly outnumbered, owing to dread of the punishment they would later face. Some men who have lost a shield or sword or any other weapon in battle will often, against all rational thought, rush into the middle of the enemy in the hopes of recovering what they have left behind, or else escape by death the inevitable disgrace and derision they would receive from their own family.[17]

[38] Whenever these same disgraceful acts occur on a large scale—for instance, when whole units break ranks when the enemy bears down hard on them—the Roman leaders are reluctant to punish all of them with clubbing or execution. Instead, they have a solution to this problem, one that offers a terrifying deterrent while not weakening the army. Here is what they do. The tribune assembles the whole legion and brings forward into the middle of them the men who deserted their posts. The tribune first bitterly denounces them, then randomly chooses by lot five, eight, or twenty of the offenders—whatever number approximates one-tenth (*decimus*) of the total number of cowards. Those chosen are subjected to a clubbing in the manner described above.[18] There is no appeal. As for the rest, they receive a ration of barley instead of wheat and are forced to encamp outside of the safety of the camp. Since the danger and fear of being chosen for punishment hangs over every soldier equally, and since everyone fears being made a public example of cowardice by having to eat barley, these customs have proven powerfully effective ways of inspiring terror and fixing the immediate problem.

[39] The Romans also have a superb way of inspiring young men to risk their lives in battle. Whenever someone displays excellence on the battlefield, the general assembles the army and presents the men that in his judgment have accomplished some outstanding feat. He then gives a speech praising not only the soldiers' recent acts of courage but also any other meritorious actions from their previous service that is worthy of mention. Then the general bestows upon this man an award. A man who wounds an enemy receives a wooden spear; a man who kills and despoils the enemy gets an honorary plaque if an infantryman, or a harness-medallion if a cavalryman (although the award was originally a wooden spear). Now, they bestow these awards not on those who perform these feats in the normal course of battle or while storming a city, but in a skirmish or some other occasion when a soldier chooses on his own to engage in single combat without any compelling reason to do so. They award a golden crown to the man who first scales the walls of a city. Similarly, the general bestows awards to soldiers who defend or save the life of a Roman legionnaire or ally. Those saved may willingly agree to crown their rescuers. On other occasions the tribunes may deem that such an award is warranted and require those who owed their lives to do so. For the rest of their lives, the men who were saved revere their rescuers like fathers and feel obliged to serve them in every way, as a son would a father. These incentives inspire not only those present in the ranks but also those back home to strive to outdo each other on the battlefield.

The soldiers who receive these awards benefit greatly from them. First, they enjoy fame and glory inside the camp, and word immediately gets passed on back home about their fine deeds. Second, when the army has returned home and is celebrating a triumphal parade, those who have received an award stand out from the rest, since only those who have been honored by the general for bravery can wear their decorations. Third, these men hang their war-spoils in the most conspicuous place in their houses,

---

17. For an example, see Plutarch, *Life of Cato* ch. 20.

18. This process is the original meaning of our word "decimation."

serving as a monument and memorial to their bravery in war. Since the Romans are so concerned about the honors and punishments within the army, there is little surprise that their military campaigns turn out to be so brilliantly successful.

## Pay and Rations

Infantry receive as pay two obols per day, centurions four, while cavalrymen receive six.[19] In terms of rations, each month an infantryman receives approximately two-thirds of a *medimnus*[20] of wheat, cavalry get seven *med.* of barley and two *med.* of wheat. As for the allies, their infantry receives an amount equal to that of his Roman counterpart, while the cavalry get one and two-thirds *med.* of wheat and five *med.* of barley. These rations the Romans provide free to the allies.[21] As for the Romans, they have to pay the established price for rations, clothing, or any other equipment they need. The quaestor deducts the amount from their pay.

[40] Here is the procedure for breaking camp. When the first signal is given, the men take down their tents and pack their gear (though no one can take down, or set up, his own tent before those of the tribunes and general). At the second signal they load the baggage on the pack animals. On the third signal the first units head out, setting the whole camp in motion. At the head of the marching column they generally station the elite corps. Falling in behind them is the right wing of the allies, followed by their own pack animals. Marching behind them is the first Roman legion, likewise followed by its own baggage train. Then comes the second legion with its baggage train and that of the left wing of the allies. The left wing is positioned at the end of the marching column. As for the cavalry, their placement is flexible. Sometimes they cover the rear of their respective units, at other times they flank the pack animals, keeping them together and offering them protection. If trouble is expected to come from behind, they keep the order the same but move the elite allies to the rear rather than the front. The legions alternate their positions daily, as do the allied wings, so that each group has an equal chance of watering and foraging on fresh resources. This is made possible because they continually invert the order of march.

They deploy themselves differently when marching amidst possible danger over open ground. They create three parallel columns: one consisting of *hastati*, one of *principes*, and one of *triarii*. They position the pack animals of the first maniple *in front* of their unit, the pack animals of the second maniple behind the first maniple, the pack animals of the third maniple behind the second, and so on down the line, alternating animals and troops. By arranging the march in such a way, if some threat materializes, they can shift the maniples either to the right or left, converting the formation into a line positioned in front of the pack animals and facing the enemy. At a moment's

---

19. If Polybius is using the common equivalencies of one (Greek) *drachma* = one (Roman) *denarius*, the legionary at this point earned 3 1/3 asses, centurions twice that much, and cavalry one full *denarius* per day. See Appendix "Roman Currency, Weights, and Measures."

20. A *medimnus* was approximately three *modii*, the standard measure of volume (so the infantryman got 2 *modii* per month); see Appendix "Roman Currency, Weights, and Measures."

21. This may be inaccurate. The allied cities probably made a blanket payment to the Roman treasury for each campaign.

notice and in one movement the infantry is brought into battle formation (though the *hastati* sometimes have to wheel around the formation) and the baggage train is placed in a protected position during the encounter under the cover of the troops in battle array.

[41] When the army is approaching the place where the camp will be erected, the tribune and centurions assigned to the task head to that place in advance. After they have scouted out the whole area, the first thing they do (as I describe above) is decide where they will put the *praetorium,* and determine in what direction the legions will encamp. When these matters are settled, they measure out the space from the tent and mark the line where the tribunes' tents will be set up. Next they mark out the line parallel to this where the legions' quarters begin. Similarly they mark out the area on the other side of the *praetorium*—again, I described all of this in detail above.

All of this can be done in a short period of time. The measuring out of the area is easy since the distances and dimensions are predetermined and familiar to all. They mark out the area with flags, the first marking out the *praetorium*, the second the direction of the camp, the third the middle point along the line of tribunes' tents, and the fourth the point at which the soldiers' encampment begins. The flag for the *praetorium* is white, the rest red. They mark out the area behind the *praetorium* with simple spears or flags of colors other than white and red. They then measure out the streets, planting spears along each. It is fair to say that when the legions approach the site and get a good look at it, everyone immediately understands the whole arrangement from these markings, since they can figure out the whole camp based on the position of the flag marking the *praetorium*. Everyone knows the street and the exact spot along that street that he is to pitch his tent since he always occupies the same place in camp. It's no different from when soldiers return to their home towns. Once inside the gates each man turns and goes immediately to his own home without the slightest confusion. After all, each person knows the neighborhood and exact location of his own home! The Roman camp operates the same way.

[42] By placing so much emphasis on the convenience that this arrangement affords, the Romans are, as I see it, following a set of principles that are completely opposite to those of the Greeks. In setting up their camps, Greeks are guided primarily by the belief that one should take advantage of the natural defenses afforded by the land. This is partly because they are adverse to the hard labor required for building the walls and digging the ditches, and partly because they are convinced that artificial fortifications are inferior to those offered by nature herself. Thus the Greeks have to adjust their overall scheme of encampment, adapting it to the specific location. Sometimes that means shifting some of the parts to other, less suitable locations. The result of this is that a Greek soldier is never certain of his position, general or specific, within the camp. The Romans, on the other hand, choose to undergo the hard work of entrenchment because of the convenience of having a single scheme which is the same in every situation, and which everyone knows.

There you have it—the most important aspects of Roman military science, especially their ideas about encampment.

## D    Roman Funerals

[As an illustration of the sorts of Roman institutions that inspire its citizens to endure hardships and hazard their lives on the battlefield, Polybius describes the funeral customs of elite Romans.]

[53] Whenever a man of distinction passes away, at the conclusion of his funeral he is carried in decorated procession into the Forum and to the speaker's platform they call "The Beaks."[22] Most of the time he is seated in an upright position and visible for all to see, but on rare occasions he is brought in lying down. The whole community gathers around as the man's son—or another male relative if there is no male heir, if that heir is out of town, or if he is not old enough—mounts the platform and delivers a funeral speech in which he enumerates the deceased man's virtues and accomplishments in life. The result of this is that the multitude is reminded of the man's achievements and can survey them, and that everyone, both those who were personally involved in his life's work and those who were not, is so moved that the loss is felt not just by the family, but shared by the whole community.

Then, after they lay the man to rest and perform the customary last rites, they place the image of the man in the most conspicuous part of his home, housing it in a little wooden shrine. The image is a mask of the man's face, carefully rendered in form and detail to resemble the man in real life. During public festivals and sacrifices they display these images, decorating them with great reverence. When a distinguished family member passes away, they bring the masks to the funeral, putting them on those family members that most resemble the deceased in size and stature. These men also don a toga with a purple border if the deceased was a consul or praetor; a completely purple one if a censor; and one embroidered in gold if the deceased had celebrated a triumph or had achieved some other similar distinction. These same men ride in a chariot preceded by the *fasces* and any other regalia associated with magistracies, each in accordance with the highest honors he had achieved during his life. When they reach the Rostra, they get off and take their seats in a row of ivory chairs.[23] You would be hard pressed to find a more inspiring sight for an ambitious and public-spirited young man. Who would fail to be inspired by the seemingly living and breathing images of those men renowned for their excellence? What could be a more edifying sight?

[54] We should also remember that when the man delivering the funeral oration finishes speaking about the deceased, he turns to the other family members present and recounts their successes and achievements, starting with the oldest. Because noble men's deeds are continually brought to mind and their reputation for excellence rehearsed, the glory of men who have accomplished some noble deed never dies, and the fame of those who have served their country is known to the whole people and is continually passed down to the next generation. But most importantly, young men will go through every hardship in the common defense of their country to earn the glory that accrues to good men.

---

22. Latin *Rostra*, after ships' beaks placed on the speakers' platform in the Roman Forum after a naval victory over the Latins in 338 BC.

23. Curule chairs. See Glossary.

For proof that what I say is true, consider the following. Many Romans have willingly fought an enemy in single combat in order to settle a war. Many have chosen certain death, some to preserve the life of their comrades in war, others to safeguard the safety of their country in peace. But that's not all. Some magistrates have even put their own sons to death, contrary to the custom and norms of nature, in the conviction that the interests of their own country are more important than the natural ties with their blood relatives.

The Romans have many stories of this, but the story of one such individual will suffice to serve as an example and proof of my argument. It is the story of Horatius, the one nicknamed Cocles ("One-Eye"). He was fighting against two enemies on the far side of the bridge over the Tiber, the one right outside the city. When he saw a mass of enemy soldiers advancing in support of his opponents, he was afraid that they would force their way past him and fall upon the city. So he turned and shouted to his comrades behind him to retreat as quickly as possible and cut the bridge. They followed his command, while he held off the enemy's onslaught, suffering numerous wounds, until they could finish the job of cutting the bridge. The enemy was awestruck, not so much by his physical prowess, as by his courage and tenacity. When the bridge was cut, the enemy's attack was foiled, but Cocles jumped from the bridge in full armor, choosing death willingly, since he valued the safety of his country and everlasting fame more than the few years that remained of his life.

There you have it. The story, I think, captures in a nutshell the way that the traditions of the Romans inspire their young men to pursue, in eager rivalry, glorious achievements.

# QUINTILIAN

(ca. AD 40–100, wrote in Latin)

## Introduction

Quintilian was the star professor of what was by far the most important academic subject in the ancient Roman world, public speaking. His major treatise on education and literary culture, of which excerpts are given here, is a summation of Roman views and ideals on these subjects. It was highly influential throughout the Renaissance and early modern period, alongside the works of Cicero, to which it is complementary. *The Instruction of an Orator*, written in retirement in the 90s AD, is the product of Quintilian's long experience as a lawyer and a classroom teacher, and also of his wide reading. Quintilian, like Cicero, makes it clear that achieving the title of "orator" is no easy task. It requires talent, broad culture, an ethical way of life, and rigorous training from early youth. Underlying the entire discussion is the basic assumption that the purpose of education is not so much to allow each individual to find his or her own way, or to advance knowledge and research, but to train effective public speakers who would go on to positions of leadership and social prominence as lawyers and magistrates in their communities. Quintilian was training the elite, and *The Instruction of an Orator* is fascinating for what it reveals about the intellectual priorities of that elite, as well as the nuts and bolts of Roman educational practices and curriculum. His own views are sometimes unorthodox (for example, his rejection of corporal punishment), but they often shed light on the more common practices that he criticizes. Quintilian is not concerned with the education of girls, though that did not stop later writers from applying his principles to female education, as did the humanist Juan Luis Vives in his influential *Instruction of the Christian Woman* (1524). Nowadays Quintilian is looked at as the founder of the philosophy of education.

The selections below give an overview of the four principal levels of Roman education:

1) Preschool, overseen by nannies and *paedagogi*

2) Basic reading and writing with a primary school teacher (*litterator* or *magister ludi*, roughly ages six through ten)

3) The study of the correct literary language and all things discussed by the poets, under a "grammarian" (*grammaticus*, roughly ages ten through sixteen)

4) Public speaking and argumentation under a teacher of rhetoric (*rhetor*).

"Grammarians" taught far more than just grammar and correct speech. They dealt with reading, recitation, and interpretation of poetry, knowledge of the mythology and history contained in it, and even some philosophy, music, and astronomy—that is, the "liberal arts" (see Seneca, *Letters* 10 in this volume). Rhetoric teachers functioned mainly by teaching their students to deliver various kinds of practice speeches, called "declamations," and to master standard types of arguments or "commonplaces" (*loci communes*).

---

# The Instruction of an Orator

## Letter to the Bookseller

M. Fabius Quintilianus sends greetings to Trypho. Every single day you demand that I start sending you the books that I wrote on *The Instruction of an Orator* and dedicated to my friend Marcellus. Well, for a long while I myself was of the opinion that they were not yet ready for the public. As you well know, it took me a little more than two years to compose them, distracted as I was by so many other responsibilities. The majority of that time, moreover, was not spent in writing, but in research for this monumental work and reading through all the countless authors on the subject. So I followed Horace's advice in the *Art of Poetry* not to rush to publish, but "keep it under wraps until the ninth year." I was letting the work sit fallow for a while so that, after the enthusiasm for my creation had died down, I could judge it from a distance as a mere reader. But if, as you suggest, there is such an incredible demand, let us launch the ship and pray for fair sailing as we leave the shore. I leave my work to your care and diligence. I only ask you that you correct it so that buyers will have as clean a copy as possible. Best wishes, Quintilian.

## A    Intellectual Capacity (1.1.1–3)

When a son is born, a father should from the outset have the highest hopes for him. That way, the father will be more attentive to his son's upbringing from the start. Now, as for the common complaint that only a very few people are born with the ability to learn fully what they are taught, that's simply untrue. On the contrary, you'll find that the majority of people have no trouble figuring things out and are quick learners. In fact, humans are naturally gifted in this area. Aren't birds born to fly? Horses to run? Beasts to be ferocious? It's no different for us humans, who are naturally born for contemplation and ingenuity, and that's why people believe that the human mind's origins are in heaven. When a dim-witted person who is unable to learn is born, it is no more natural than when a child is born deformed or disfigured. These occasions are indeed rare. My proof lies in the fact that young boys show promise in all sorts of areas. If that promise disappears as they grow older, clearly the fault lies not with nature but with our own lack of attention.

"But some people are just plain smarter than others," you object? Of course that's true. But it is not a matter of *whether*, but *how much* one can learn. You won't find anyone who cannot achieve something through study. Whoever grasps this basic fact will, as soon as he becomes a parent, apply as much effort as is humanly possible to bring his son's promise to fruition and make an orator out of him.

**B**      **First Instruction** (1.1.4–14)

First of all, nannies should speak properly. If we follow Chrysippus' advice, nannies should be philosophers,[1] but at the very least we should choose the best available under the circumstances. Without a doubt, we should consider their character first and foremost, but we should also expect them to speak correctly. These are the first people a boy will hear speak, and it will be their words that he will try to reproduce in imitation, and we humans naturally cling to those habits we learn at a tender age. Think of how the first liquid you put into a new pot leaves a flavor that never quite goes away, or how you can't wash out the dye that you first used to color plain white wool. Furthermore, the worse the habits, the more persistent they are. Good things easily change for the worse. When will you find time to change your vices into virtues? This is why it is absolutely imperative that no one—least of all a young child—should learn a manner of speaking that will have to be unlearned.

As for parents, in a perfect world they would be extremely educated, and I do not just mean fathers. They say the eloquence of the Gracchi owed quite a bit to their mother Cornelia, whose extremely learned manner of speaking is clear from her surviving letters. And then there's Laelia, the daughter of Gaius Laelius, who is said to have had her father's eloquence when speaking. The speech that Hortensia, daughter of Quintus Hortensius, delivered in front of the triumvirs is still read, and not just because she was a woman.[2] Even those parents who have not received an education should not pay less attention to teaching their children. In fact, because of this they should be even more careful in attending to their child's every need. The same thing that I said about nannies above goes for the other children that will be educated alongside the child who is destined to become an orator. Concerning *paedagogi* I have a bit more to say.[3] They should either be clearly educated (this is the best case, of course), or else they should admit that they are not. There is nothing worse than those people who, with only a little more than the bare rudiments of education, have convinced themselves that they possess real knowledge. These are the kind of people who indignantly refuse to give up the role of instructor and, as if they've been officially vested with some power (the kind that makes this sort of person swell with arrogance), teach their own brand of stupidity with an imperious and sometimes brutal hand. Their mistaken beliefs also harm their charges' morals. Consider what Diogenes of Babylon tells us about Leonidas, Alexander the Great's *paedagogus*, who infected his charge with certain bad habits in his childhood that stayed with him even after he had become an adult and the greatest of kings.[4]

---

1. A Stoic philosopher (ca. 289–204 BC), whose work on education, now lost, is often praised by Quintilian.

2. In 42 BC the triumvirs Antonius, Octavian, and Lepidus took measures to tax the wealthiest women in Rome in order to pay for their large armies. Hortensia, the daughter of the eminent orator Q. Hortensius, and other women appealed to the wives of the triumvirs, but Fulvia, Antonius' wife, treated them with contempt, so Hortensia took to the speaker's platform and made an impassioned (and successful) speech.

3. A *paedagogus* was the slave responsible for supervising a boy in his daily routine. See Glossary.

4. Quintilian is unique in casting Leonidas in a poor light. In other accounts Leonidas instilled in Alexander a disciplined, frugal lifestyle.

If you think that I'm being very demanding, keep in mind that we're training an *orator*, a difficult task even when conditions are perfect, and that this is only the first step in a long series of rather difficult stages. What I mean is that he will have to study constantly under the most outstanding instructors and in a great number of different fields. Therefore, his early instruction has to be the very best. If a student doesn't take to it, it will be the fault not of the method, but of the person. Still, if someone isn't fortunate enough to have the outstanding nannies, slaves, and *paedagogi* that I prefer, then the child should be attended by at least one person somewhat knowledgeable about language who can immediately correct the faulty speech of those around him and make sure that it does not become ingrained. Just know that this is nothing more than a stop-gap measure; the best course of action is what I laid out earlier.

I prefer that a boy learn Greek first. Why? Because he's going to soak up Latin, which is spoken by the majority, whether we want him to or not. Furthermore, he should be instructed in Greek learning first because our learning derives from that of the Greeks. We should not, however, make this such a hard and fast rule that the child *only* speaks and learns in Greek for an extended period of time, as happens in many families today. This leads to a great many flaws both in pronunciation, which becomes infected with a foreign sound, and in speech patterns, which retain Greek idioms, ingrained through constant use, even when speaking another language. So we should begin to teach Latin soon after Greek, and then they should proceed side by side. That way, since both languages are given equal attention, neither gets in the way of the other.

## C    The Alphabet (1.1.24–29)

I am not pleased with the practice—which I see has become common—of teaching children the names and order of the letters before their forms. This gets in the way of learning to *recognize* the letters. Since children are working only from rote memory, they do not fix their attention on the forms of the letters themselves. This is the reason why teachers, even when they are convinced that their young students have firmly grasped the letters in their customary order, make them write the letters out again backwards, or otherwise disrupt the order of the letters. This ensures that the students know the letters by shape and not just by their place in the alphabet. Name and shape are best learned together—just like when we meet a new person. (Incidentally, the practice of learning sounds without seeing the forms, although harmful to letter acquisition, is perfectly fine for sound-combinations.) I am also not opposed to the well-known practice of encouraging babies to learn by giving them letters to play with made of ivory—or of any other thing one can find that children of that age would delight in handling, looking at, and naming.

Once a child begins to trace the letters, it will be helpful to have these letter shapes carved properly into a wooden tablet, so that a stylus can be led through them as if they were furrows cut by a plow. The child won't be able to make a mistake, like he would on a wax tablet, because the stylus will be held in by the edges of the carved letters and can't stray. By following these fixed traces of the letters quickly and frequently he will strengthen his fingers and eliminate the need of a guiding hand placed on top of his hand. The art of writing correctly and quickly—a skill that is, by and large, ignored by respectable people today—is important for the orator. Writing, in fact, is the *most* important skill in studies, since it is through this alone that true progress based on solid foundations is secured. A slow stylus slows our thoughts; clumsy and messy writing can't be read. The latter problem leads to a duplication of effort, when we have to dictate our work to a copyist. Given these potential problems, you will always be glad that you did not ignore this skill, especially when writing personal letters to family and friends.

## D    Home-Schooling vs. "Public" Education (1.2.1–29)

By now our boy has started to grow a bit, has left his nanny's lap, and is beginning to learn in earnest. Here we must consider the question whether it is preferable to keep our student within the walls of his own home, or to entrust him to the crowded schools and what we may call "public" instructors.[5] I know that the latter view has been held by distinguished authorities on the subject, and also by those who established the customs of the most famous and successful nations. Still, we must admit that some disagree with this "public" way due to a certain prejudice toward the private option. Their conviction seems based on two factors. The first is that it is better for their children's character if they avoid the mass of young people who are at an age that is particularly prone to bad habits. They claim, in essence, that many disgraceful acts arise from such an association. I wish I could say that they are wrong, but I cannot. Their second reason is that a single instructor will give more attention to a single pupil than he would if his attention were divided among many.

The first objection is far more serious than the second. If we were to grant that schools, although benefiting studies, also harm character, I think that it would be preferable to live virtuously than even to speak more persuasively than everyone else. But in my own opinion, these two things—living virtuously and speaking expertly—are linked and inseparable. I do not think it possible for anyone but a good man to be an orator, and if it is possible, I would rather not see it happen. So I'll speak to this objection first.

People think that character is ruined in schools. It's true that this does happen from time to time, but it happens at home, too. I could give you many examples of this, just as I could give you many instances where schools and at-home teachers maintain a spotless reputation. What matters is a child's natural disposition and the attention he receives. Suppose you're dealing with a mind that's naturally inclined toward misbehavior. Now suppose his teachers are lax in forming and reinforcing his sense of right and wrong while he is still young. Do you really think that private studies wouldn't offer the same opportunity for disgraceful behavior? After all, a private tutor can be a degenerate as well, and it is no safer to spend time with good-for-nothing slaves than with immoral free men.[6] On the other hand, if the young man's character is upright, and if his parents are neither blind nor lazy, then it is possible to select teachers with impeccable morals (smart parents are particularly concerned with this) and to assign

---

5. That is, teachers available to the public for a fee—not public in our sense of state- or community-supported schools. Quintilian himself was a public teacher in this sense.

6. An underlying concern here is sexual abuse by teachers, a commonly expressed anxiety. See Horace, *Satires* 1.6 in this volume.

an extremely rigorous course of instruction. And at the same time they should choose a serious friend[7] or faithful freedman to accompany their son at all times—such constant companionship may even improve the character of the kinds of boys one worries about.

We could have easily prevented them from becoming worrisome—if only we did not ruin the character of our children ourselves! From the moment of birth we coddle them with our pampering. There's a name for that soft upbringing—indulgence— and it serves only to weaken the toughness of our mind and body. If someone crawls around on purple as a baby, won't he as an adult want the whole world and more? The child hasn't formed his first words yet, but he already understands "crimson" and is fussy about "scarlet." We have taught them stylish taste before speech! They grow up in litters. If they touch the ground, they are supported by people holding them up on both sides. We are delighted when they say something naughty, and we laugh and kiss them when they utter something we would never accept even from our darling slaves from Alexandria. We shouldn't be surprised. We taught them this. They heard it from us. They see our girlfriends, our male prostitutes. Every dinner-party resounds with obscene songs. They see things it is shameful to talk about. Their habits and disposition are formed surrounded by such behavior. Our poor children learn these vices before they even know what vices are. And so, arriving depraved and undisciplined, they do not get these ills from schools. No, they bring them *into* the schools.

[2.9] The other objection is this: "one-on-one instruction allows the teacher to focus on just one student." First of all, there's no reason why individual and public education cannot be combined. But let's suppose it cannot. I would still prefer the bright openness of a school (provided it is upstanding) to shadows and solitude. After all, every outstanding teacher rejoices in a crowd of students and believes himself deserving of a greater theater in which to teach. Mediocre teachers, because they know they are inferior, consciously choose to attach themselves to an individual student and function as a sort of glorified *paedagogus*. But let us suppose parents have the influence, the money, or the connections to keep a highly learned and accomplished teacher in their home—is he really going to spend the whole day on one student? Can the student continue to focus the whole time? After all, the mind, like the eyes, grows weary of continual use.

And what about the fact that learning requires much more time in private than merely the time spent on instruction? A teacher isn't going to stand over a student as he writes, memorizes, and thinks, is he? When a student is engaged in study, any interruption will break his concentration. The same goes for reading; not all of it needs to be done with a teacher guiding or interpreting the text. How else is the student to become acquainted with the vast number of important writers if not by reading on his own? Not much time is required to give purpose and structure to a whole day's work, as it were. This is why even subjects that must be handled one-on-one can still be taught to several people at once. There are, however, a great many subjects that can be communicated simultaneously to all present. I don't mean just the outlines and the model speeches of the rhetoricians. Certainly in that case, no matter how many are present, each person gets the full lesson. The teacher's voice is not like a dinner party, where a

---

7. That is, a freeborn client.

person gets less when more people show up. Like the sun, it lavishes the same amount of light and warmth on one and all. The same is true for the language and literature teacher (*grammaticus*): if he discusses the proper use of language, explains a disputed point, elucidates a story, or interprets a poem, doesn't everyone in the audience learn the same things?

[2.15] Someone will object, "A large group gets in the way of correcting mistakes and teaching students to read out loud." For argument's sake, let's grant that this is an inconvenience (nothing can please everyone all the time). In a moment, we will counter this negative with all the benefits.

"Still, I refuse to send my boy to a place where he'll be neglected." Now, a good instructor would never burden himself with a crowd of students that is too big for him to handle. And what is more, *we* must take great pains to ensure that he is on completely friendly terms with us. That way, he will not approach teaching out of a sense of obligation, but out of affection, and we will never be "one of the crowd." And you will discover that no remotely scholarly person would refuse to foster a student who has demonstrated outstanding ability and an industrious work ethic. After all, a student's excellence would add to the instructor's reputation as well. Even if giant schools were to be avoided—and, to be clear, I do *not* concede this point if the great crowd has flocked to some deserving teacher—this still does not mean that *all* schools must be avoided. It is one thing to avoid them, another to choose from among them.

Now that I've countered other people's criticisms of education outside the home, let me explain my own views. Since an orator by his very nature must live surrounded by crowds and in the public eye, we must socialize them early on so that they do not dread contact with other people or choose to live the pale scholar's life, a recluse, as it were, in the shadows. His mind must be constantly exercised and stimulated. If he were to be cloistered away, his mind would either languish and start to rot (as if it never received any light), or swell up under the false belief of self-importance. After all, people start to think they are better than they really are if they do not have someone to compare themselves to. And when they are forced to show the fruits of their studies to the public, they are blinded by the sun. Everything is unfamiliar, and it upsets them. Why? Because they learned in solitude what one must do in a crowd.

I'll only briefly mention the friendships that the student will make, unshakeable friendships that will last into old age because they are created with bonds of a hallowed sort. Initiation into the same studies forms no less a sacred attachment among the participants than being initiated into the same sacred rites. And where is our student to acquire "social skills,"[8] as they are called, if he removes himself from the interaction with others? Isn't interaction a natural impulse found not only in humans, but even in mute beasts?

And then there's this: a home-schooled student will learn only the instruction given to him, whereas one taught in the schools will also learn from instruction given to other students. Every day he will hear many things approved of, and many corrected, and will benefit from seeing one student's laziness criticized or another's hard work praised. A desire for praise will kindle a competitive spirit in him. He will think it disgraceful to be outdone by one of his peers and glorious to surpass older classmates. All

---

8. Literally "common sense" (*sensus communis*).

of this will light the mind on fire, and although ambition itself is a fault, it frequently can produce virtues.

A practice that my own instructors followed is, in my mind, extremely effective: once they had distributed the boys into classes, they determined the order of speaking based on ability—the more progress a student made, the higher he would sit in the rankings. We were judged based on our speeches. Winning was quite a big deal to us, and the greatest honor by far was being head of the class in speaking. This position was not permanent, either; every thirty days a defeated student had the opportunity to try again. That way, the superior student would not slack off because of his success, while the loser was driven by the pain of his disgrace to wipe it away. I would even go so far to say that it was this more than anything else that kindled our desire to study public speaking—more than the urging of our teachers, the watchfulness of our *paedagogi*, or the prayers of our parents.

Just as rivalry promotes better progress in advanced studies, younger students beginning their studies will find it more agreeable to imitate their fellow students than their teacher, because it is easier. Students learning the basics can scarcely hope to produce what they consider the pinnacle of eloquence. But what they can do is grab hold of what's right next to them and, like vines growing around a tree, reach the top by always grasping the next higher branch.

The consequence of this is that the teacher who prefers practical steps to showmanship has the duty, when dealing with unshaped minds, not to overburden his students' weak minds, but to moderate his own powers and come down to the student's intellectual level. Think about it: if you tried to pour a lot of liquid into a small vessel with a narrow opening, wouldn't it all splash out over the sides? But if you poured it in little by little, or even by drops, you would fill it with ease. The same goes with young minds. You must know how much they can take in. Big, sophisticated ideas will simply not flow into minds whose openings are, if you will, too small to understand them. This is why it is helpful for students to have classmates whom they can first imitate, then try to surpass. In this way he will continually have hopes of achieving the next level.

# E    Classroom Management (1.3.6–13)

Once a teacher has determined the personalities of his students, he must figure out the best way to handle their dispositions. Some are lazy unless you keep on them. Others take commands poorly. Threats keep some on the straight and narrow but paralyze others. Some students have to pound away at their craft; others achieve more in short, concentrated bursts. In my experience, I prefer a student who is incited by praise, revels in glory, and cries when outperformed. Competition will nourish his mind. He will chomp at the bit when criticized. I would never have to worry about his drive for success.

Everyone needs some kind of relaxation, for two reasons. First, there is nothing on earth that can withstand the strain of continual hard work, and even plants and inanimate objects needs periods of relaxation, as it were, in order to rebound and maintain their strength. Second, you cannot force someone to learn; students must come to the table willingly. And so if you give them time to refresh themselves, they will bring to their studies more energy and sharper minds, which as a general rule resist tasks forced upon them. As for playing, I think it is perfectly fine for young boys—this, too, is a sign of liveliness. As for those students who are always downcast and gloomy, why would I expect them to exhibit an alert mind during their studies when they show no signs of the vitality that is so natural for that age?

Still, make sure that you find the right balance between work and relaxation. If you deny them free time, they will hate their studies; if you give them too much, they will get used to leisure. There are some very useful games you can employ to sharpen the minds of your young students—for instance, a competition in which they ask trivia questions back and forth. An added bonus: you can more clearly see your students' character while at play—that is, so long as we do not believe that there is any period of life so tender that it cannot instantly learn the difference between right and wrong, and so long as we realize that a boy's character is best molded when he is ignorant of deceit and is most ready to comply with his instructors. Think about it. You would more easily break a piece of wood that had warped than you would straighten it out. So a student must be reminded immediately not to steal, misbehave, or act with violence. We must always keep Vergil's well-known words in mind: "Such is the power of habit early formed."

# F    Corporal Punishment (1.3.14–18)

Should students be beaten? It is commonly done, and Chrysippus does not condemn the practice, but I wholly reject it. First of all, it is a disgraceful custom fit for slaves, and really it rises to the level of assault (which would be clear if you changed the age of the victim). Second, if your student's behavior is so recalcitrant that it cannot be corrected by scolding, then he will become hardened to blows, just like the lowliest of slaves. Finally, you wouldn't even need this kind of punishment if he had consistent supervision of his studies. Isn't it the negligence of the *paedagogi* that we're punishing?[9] Rather than forcing the boys to act correctly, we punish them for not having done so. And if you punish a child with blows, what are you going to do when he becomes a young man, immune to such intimidation and in need of learning even more important lessons?

Let's not forget that when children are flogged many things happen, whether because of pain or fear, that are too disgraceful to mention and inevitably lead to embarrassment. This shame breaks their spirit, leads to depression, teaches them to abhor and loathe the very light of day. And if someone takes too little care in choosing guardians and teachers with proper character, I blush to say to what horrific extremes these scoundrels go in abusing this so-called "right" to beat a child, and how others too might sometimes take advantage of these poor kids' fears. I won't dwell on this subject; everyone understands this all too well. So I think it's enough to say this: no one should have too much power over students of an age that is powerless and easily victimized.

---

9. Theon, a late antique writer on education, tells the story that Diogenes the Cynic, whenever he encountered a misbehaving son, struck the *paedagogus* instead of the boy (*Progymnasmata* 98.34).

Now I shall turn to the kinds of skills that a young man must acquire if he is to become an orator, and at what age each of them should be started.

## G   Language Study under the *Grammaticus* (1.4.1–5)

Once a boy has learned to read and write, the next step is to be placed under a grammarian. (I am speaking equally about both Latin and Greek studies, although I prefer Greek to come first. But it is the same path for both.) To simplify, the business of the grammarian is twofold: knowledge of speaking correctly, and exposition of the poets. But a great deal lies behind this rather simple façade, since linked with the business of speaking correctly is the task of learning how to write well. Prior to exposition of the poets comes the ability to read them out loud correctly. And mixed in with all of these are matters of taste and judgment (something so sternly employed by the grammarians of old that they gave themselves free rein to identify with a kind of censorial mark specific verses and books which they regarded as inauthentic, as if they were removing false sons from a family, as well as to draw up a canonical list of authors to the exclusion of others). And it is not enough simply to be familiar with the poets; one has to examine every kind of writer, not just for their stories, but for their vocabulary, since words often gain currency because of the author who uses them. Language studies must also include explication of music to be complete, since a student must be able to speak about meter and rhythm. He also cannot understand the poets unless he understands astronomy; to cite but one example of many, poets frequently use the rising and setting of the constellations to indicate the time of year. This period of study cannot ignore philosophy, either, since a great many passages (and in nearly every poem) are derived from sophisticated knowledge of the natural world. And then there are Greek writers like Empedocles and Latin writers like Varro and Lucretius, who wrote down philosophical ideas in verse form. Furthermore, it requires no small amount of eloquence to speak correctly and at length about each one of these subjects just mentioned. This is why we must not put up with those detractors who criticize the art of the grammarian as trivial and unproductive.[10] If we do not securely plant these foundations for our future orators, everything else we teach them—the whole superstructure—will come crashing down. The study of literature is a necessity for boys, a delight for old men, and a pleasant companion for our private moments. It is perhaps the only kind of study that has more substance than flash.

## H   Training under the Teacher of Public Speaking (*Rhetor*) (2.1.1–13)

There is a disturbing trend—one that keeps growing by the day—that students are being put under teachers of eloquence much later than is reasonable. This is a constant problem in the case of Latin training, but also sometimes for Greek as well. There are two related reasons for it: rhetoric teachers, especially those for Latin, have relinquished some of their responsibilities, while the language teachers have usurped

---

10. As does Seneca, for example (*Letters* 10 in this volume).

instruction that once belonged to the more advanced teachers. What I mean is that rhetoric teachers now believe that their only responsibility resides in public speaking itself and in the transmission of the theory and practice of delivering a speech. What's more, they focus only on deliberative and judicial subjects;[11] everything else, they feel, is beneath their profession. Language teachers, by contrast, have not only taken on the responsibility for the tasks the teachers of public speaking have given up (for which we should be thankful), but they have also appropriated for themselves the task of teaching character speeches,[12] which place extremely great demands upon the student. What has happened, in effect, is that the tasks assigned at the beginning of the more advanced course of study have now become the last tasks completed at the lower level. Students old enough to be studying loftier subjects end up languishing in a lower school and practicing public speaking under grammarians. The result is simply absurd: a boy is not deemed fit to learn from a teacher of public speaking until he already knows how to deliver public speeches.

We must assign each of these fields its proper place. *Grammatica*, which we translate into Latin as "literature" (*litteratura*), must keep within its own bounds—especially because it has strayed greatly from the moderate compass indicated by its very name, within which its first teachers stayed.[13] Once but a trickle from a spring, it has gained strength and now flows like a river nearly overflowing its banks. No longer content just with the theory and practice of speaking correctly (as if this wasn't expansive enough!), the grammarians have claimed for themselves nearly every other advanced subject.

By the same token, the field of rhetoric—the word itself signifies the power of speaking eloquently[14]—should not surrender what is rightfully its own responsibility or be happy that others are appropriating tasks that pertain to its mission. After all, since they have let others shoulder the work, they can barely make the claim that it still belongs to the realm of rhetoric. Now, I would never claim that language teachers *cannot* acquire enough knowledge to be able to pass on the skills adequately—he should simply acknowledge the fact that, while he does it, he is performing the role of a rhetoric teacher, not his own.

The next point is determining when a boy is ready to learn the lessons taught under a teacher of rhetoric. To my mind it is not a matter of the age of the student, but how much progress he has made in his studies. There's no need to go on at length about when a student should start studying with a rhetoric teacher, so I'll cut to the chase: as soon as he is ready. But all of this depends on our discussion above. If language teachers appropriate every subject up to *suasoriae*,[15] the need for a rhetoric teacher is postponed; if rhetoric teachers deign to take on the responsibility of basic rhetorical education, then their care will be needed from the moment students compose narratives[16] and

---

11. This refers to *controversiae*, practice speeches on legal matters, and *suasoriae*, practice speeches of persuasion (for example, "Should Cicero Criticize Antonius?").

12. *Prosopopoeia*, a speech put in the mouth of a historical personage or a fictional character.

13. Greek *grammaticē* = literally "the study of writing."

14. That is, in Greek (*rhetor*, "one who speaks").

15. See above, note 11.

16. These are basic assignments leading up to more advanced rhetorical exercises. At 2.4.1–17 Quintilian discusses the three kinds of narrative: fictitious ones based on tragedies and poems,

speeches of praise and blame.[17] Have we forgotten the kinds of practice that our fore-fathers used to improve their eloquence: the practicing of *theses*, standard arguments, and other speeches that concern both real and invented disputes (without reference to modern events or people)?[18] It is clear from this how shameful it is that rhetors have given up that kind of training that they originally provided and was for a long time their only task.

Yet is it not true that all these exercises that I've just outlined come into play in the rest of rhetoric properly speaking, as well as in actual legal cases? Don't we have to narrate the facts in the Forum? This may well be the most important part of rhetoric in actual practice. Praise and blame of individuals often plays a part in actual cases, does it not? And what about standard arguments? Aren't they at the very heart of litigation, whether they are the kind that are directed at vices, such as those penned by Cicero, or those which deal with more general topics, such as those published by Quintus Hortensius on topics like "how much should we rely on small details?" or "for and against the credibility of witnesses."

These are the weapons we must somehow develop and put in our arsenal so that they are available when the situation demands. If someone believes that these exercises have nothing to do with oratory, he would no doubt deny that a statue was being created when its limbs were being cast. Some may think that I'm being hasty and criticize me on the mistaken grounds that I believe that a student who is entrusted to the care of a rhetoric teacher should be immediately removed from the grammarian. I do not believe this. Each of the teachers will have his own time allotted to him, and there should be no fear that a boy will be overburdened by having two teachers at the same time. It will be the same amount of work; the tasks that were jumbled together under one teacher will now be divided between two. What's more, each teacher will be better at his own subject matter. The Greeks still adopt this division of labor, but Latin teachers of rhetoric have given it up. We think it excusable only because there have been other teachers to pick up the slack.

---

realistic narratives akin to those found in comedy, and factual accounts about historical events. Only the last properly belongs to the teacher of rhetoric.

17. That is, of famous people (see Quintilian, 2.4.20–21).

18. A *thesis* involved a comparison, such as "which is preferable, city or country life?" (2.4.24–25). A standard argument (literally "commonplace") was a denunciation of some vice, such as adultery or gambling, without naming a person (2.4.22–23).

# SENECA THE YOUNGER

(ca. 4 BC–AD 65, wrote in Latin)

## General Introduction

L. Annaeus Seneca is best known for his role as the Emperor Nero's tutor and adviser. It is unlikely that Seneca's father—the writer known as Seneca the Elder to distinguish him from his more famous son—could have foreseen the younger Seneca's prominence in the political arena when he sent him from his home in Spain to Rome at an early age to be educated. But by the reign of Caligula (AD 37–41), Seneca had become one of the most famous public speakers in the city. Exiled by the next emperor, Claudius (AD 41–54), Seneca was recalled by the emperor's wife, Agrippina the Younger, in AD 49 to train her eleven-year-old son Nero for the throne. When in AD 54 Agrippina hastened Claudius' death (see *The Ascension of the Pumpkinhead Claudius into Heaven* below), Seneca suddenly changed from a prince's tutor to the main adviser to the most powerful man in the empire. Seneca's life would be bound to the emperor's until AD 65, when Nero, suspecting him of complicity in an assassination plot, ordered Seneca to commit suicide.

Seneca wrote widely on a number of topics. In addition to his *Philosophical Letters*, generally regarded today as his greatest achievement (ten of which are translated below), Seneca wrote treatises on the nature of and therapy for anger, the tranquility of the mind, withdrawal from politics, the composure of the Stoic Wise Man, and the shortness of life. He was a committed, but not dogmatic, adherent of Stoic philosophy (see Epictetus, *A Handbook of Stoic Philosophy* in this volume). His terse, energetic prose style is something of a reaction against the more leisurely, balanced approach of writers like Cicero. He was also a fine satirist, a strain present even in his more serious works. Ten tragedies on mythological themes are also attributed to Seneca, although some scholars remain unconvinced that they are by Seneca. Below we provide translations of a selection of his philosophical letters, as well as the satirical *The Ascension of the Pumpkinhead Claudius into Heaven*.

---

### Introduction to *Philosophical Letters*

One hundred twenty-four letters survive from Seneca's correspondence with Lucilius (Latin title *Epistulae Morales*, abbreviated *EM*). Lucilius was a well-to-do member of the equestrian class, a mid-level imperial official, a literary talent, and a follower of Epicureanism. Although Seneca refers to Lucilius' letters, none of these have survived. Our picture of their relationship is thus one-sided: Seneca, the philosophical mentor, guides Lucilius through the thorny and often counterintuitive process of living his life according to philosophical principles. He deals with such subjects as the superiority of the mind over the body, the proper evaluation of possessions, the evils of luxury and low pleasures, the praise of philosophy as a guide to life, and the necessity of self-examination and action in self-improvement. These we might call Seneca's themes, but he takes advantage of the letter format to adopt various approaches to them. Seneca speaks now as a kindly counselor, now as an irate mentor, now as a neurotic fellow patient, now as an aloof social critic. The epistolary format also allowed Seneca to emphasize daily progress: the series of letters that arrive on Lucilius' doorstep, so to speak, would be a constant reminder of his commitment to philosophy.

The letters likely date to the end of Seneca's life, when he was becoming increasingly removed from imperial politics (see letter 2, below). A date of AD 62–64 is probable, based on the few personal details and historical events that Seneca mentions in the letters. A central question remains whether, or to what degree, the letters represent a genuine correspondence. Did Seneca really live above a bathhouse (letter 7, below)? Did he really jump out of a boat during a storm, as we read in another letter not translated here (*EM* 53)? Or are these and other events fictionalized vehicles for Seneca's broader philosophical message? Scholars disagree on this question, but a comparison of Seneca's letters to those of Cicero and Pliny included in this volume will reveal very different aims and goals.

## *Philosophical Letters*

## 1    What Matters Is on the Inside (*EM* 5)

I hear you're studying philosophy intensely and focused entirely on making yourself better every single day, letting nothing distract you. I commend you for this, and it brings me joy. I urge you—no, beg you—to keep it up. But let me give you one piece of advice. Don't act like those people who aren't so much interested in making progress as they are in getting noticed. Don't dress or act so as to catch people's attention. [2] That's right—no ragged clothes, no long, disheveled hair, no unkempt beard, no diatribes against silver, no sleeping on the hard ground—nothing that perversely aims at getting attention. Just the word "philosophy," even if we practice it unpretentiously, is enough to rouse other people's suspicions. What would happen if we started to remove ourselves from the ways of our fellow humans? We should be completely different on the inside, but our exteriors should match everyone else's. [3] Our togas shouldn't sparkle; but they shouldn't be filthy, either. We shouldn't have silver with solid gold inlay, but we also shouldn't think that not having silver and gold is proof of frugality. Bottom line: we should aim to pursue a better life than the common crowd, not a different one. Otherwise, we'll end up driving away and chasing off those very same people we want to reform. We'll also end up achieving this: they will not want to emulate *anything* we do, if they think they have to emulate *everything* we do.

[4] What is philosophy's primary promise? A sense of belonging, humanity, togetherness. Acting different will keep us from that promise. Of course we want people to admire us. But we have to make sure that the things we do to produce that admiration

are not laughable and hateful. Isn't the Stoic code "to live according to nature"? And isn't it against nature to torture one's own body, to reject simple luxuries when they are right at hand, to seek out squalor and eat food that's not only cheap, but foul and nasty as well? [5] It may be a sign of rank luxury to desire fine things, but to avoid commonplace and easily available items—that's lunacy. Philosophy demands frugality, not self-torment, but frugality doesn't have to be uncivilized. What kind of life do I advocate? One that is somewhere between perfection and the way the common people live. We want everyone to admire our way of life, but they must also relate to it as well.

[6] "What?" you say, "Are we really to act the same as the rest? Will there be no difference between us and them?" A great deal, Lucilius. But only those who get a close look at us will know that we are completely different from the common crowd. We want those who enter our house to admire us more than our furniture. Great is the person who enjoys clay table settings as much as silver; no less great is the person who enjoys silver table settings as much as clay. You know you are dealing with a small-minded person if he isn't able to deal with wealth.

[7] But it's time for me to share with you the gem of the day.[1] I read in our Stoic predecessor Hecato[2] that the elimination of desire helps to eliminate fear. "You cease to fear," he says, "if you cease to hope." Now, you'll say to me, "How is it possible that those completely opposite things go hand in hand?" Well, it's the truth, my dear Lucilius. Though they seem to go in opposite directions, they are in fact joined. Just as the same chain binds both prisoner and the soldier who guards him, so, too, do those two things travel together despite their great dissimilarity. Fear follows upon hope. [8] I for my part am not surprised that they go hand in hand. After all, both come from a mind in suspense. Both look anxiously toward the future. Add the fact that both arise primarily because we don't adapt ourselves to the present situation, but send our thoughts far into the future. The result? Foresight, the greatest boon to the human condition, has been converted into its bane. [9] Wild beasts flee when they see danger, but once safe, they relax. We torture ourselves over both the future and the past. Our blessings are often our own undoing. Hindsight recalls the anguish caused by fear, while foresight anticipates it. No one's misery is caused only by the present. Farewell.

## 2    Avoid the Crowd (*EM* 7)

You ask me what I think you should avoid above all else? Crowds of people. You cannot safely entrust yourself to them, not yet. I'm not afraid to admit my own weakness: I never come home as good a person as I was when I left. Some defect of mine that I thought I'd settled gets unsettled, some vice that I thought I'd escaped returns. The same thing happens to sick people who have been so ill for so long that they can't recover from the illness without some setback. We're the same, only it is our minds that are convalescing from a long illness. [2] Associating with the multitude is detrimental

---

1. Seneca often ends his letters to Lucilius with a quotation (or quotations) from other philosophical writers, mainly Epicurus. Seneca's focus in the letters—and perhaps the primary reason for choosing this form to deliver his philosophical message—is daily improvement.

2. Hecato was a Stoic philosopher of the 2nd–1st century BC who wrote a treatise on ethical responsibilities.

to our mental health. There's always going to be someone who will tempt us into vice, or stamp it on us, or smear it on us without our knowledge. And be sure about this: the bigger the group you associate with, the greater the danger will be.

But nothing is more detrimental to good character than whiling away the hours at some public games. While you're enjoying the show, vices will more easily creep into you. [3] What do you think I mean? That I come home more avaricious, more vain, more decadent? All true, but I also come home crueler and less humane. After all, I spent time with humans.

I happened to catch a midday show, where I expected to see some light entertainment, comedy, or some such relaxing break from the spectacle of human bloodshed. How wrong I was! All the fighting that took place earlier was an act of mercy. This? Murder, pure and simple. The victims had nothing to protect themselves; their whole bodies were exposed to blows, and never did one miss.[3] [4] A great many people prefer this kind of spectacle to the ordinary pairing of gladiators or even special events. Of course they do! There's no helmet, no shield to deflect the sword. Who needs armor? Or skill and technique? All those things simply delay death. Men are thrown to lions and bears in the morning, to their own spectators at noon! They demand that killers be thrown to their own executioners. Winners are kept in the arena for yet more slaughter. The only way out for the combatants is death. The action's kept going with spears and fire—and all this is happening at intermission!

[5] "But one of them is a cutthroat robber!" So what? "But he killed a man!" Fine, because he killed a man, he deserves this punishment. But what about you, my poor man? What have you done that you have to watch this?

"Strike 'em, beat 'em, burn 'em! Why does he meet the sword so meekly? Why does he strike so timidly? Why is he so unwilling to die? Why must he be driven by blows to meet his wounds? They should stand face to face and hack at each other's bare chests!" The show's at intermission: "Let some throats be cut in the meantime so that *something's* going on." Tell me, people, do you not even realize that bad behavior often comes back to haunt the one who sets the example? Give thanks to the immortal gods that you are teaching cruelty to someone who cannot learn that behavior!

[6] An impressionable mind, one that's not completely set on doing right, must be saved from the crowd. It easily bends to peer pressure. Even Socrates, Cato, or Laelius[4] would have lost their moral compass if they associated with a crowd so unlike them. As for us, we have just now started to bring our mind into harmony, so we certainly cannot withstand the onslaught of vices, accompanied as they are with such an entourage. [7] A single example of decadence or greed causes great damage. A luxury-loving housemate gradually weakens our resolve and makes us soft. A wealthy neighbor stirs our cravings. A spiteful acquaintance rubs off some of his nastiness even on someone who is earnest and pure. So what do you think happens to one's character when attacked from every direction? [8] You must either imitate them or hate them. But

---

3. In a typical day at the arena one would see beast hunts in the morning and gladiatorial combat in the afternoon, both of which require great skill and training. The "intermission" at noon would feature combat between condemned criminals or the exposure of those criminals to wild beasts.

4. Socrates (469–399 BC, Greek), Cato the Younger (95–46 BC, Roman), and C. Laelius (ca. 190–ca. 128 BC, Roman) were all considered persons who had made great philosophical progress.

you must avoid both; don't be like the vicious crowd because they are many, and don't become their enemy because they are nothing like you.

Focus on yourself as much as possible. Associate with those who will make you better; let in those people whom you can make better. It's a reciprocal process: people learn while they teach.

[9] There's no reason for you to be lured into the public eye in search of the glory that will come from broadcasting your considerable talents, no reason to give public lectures or engage in debates. Sure, I'd be happy for you to do this if you had a commodity that the common crowd could appreciate. But the fact is, not a single one of them could possibly understand you. Well, maybe you'll meet one here, one there, but even these you must mold and train in order for them to understand you. "So," you ask, "for whom did I learn all of this philosophy?" Don't worry, you haven't squandered all your hard work—that is, if you learned for yourself.

[10] Well, to prove to you that I haven't learned for myself alone today, I will share with you three splendid quotes that I found, all containing pretty much the same message. Take one of these and credit it to this letter; consider the other two as payment in advance.[5]

Democritus says, "To me, one person is worth as much as the whole population, the population as much as one."

[11] The following, too, is well said, although the speaker's name is uncertain. When he was asked by someone why he had put so much effort into acquiring his skill if only a few could appreciate it, he responded, "A few is enough for me, one is enough, none is enough."

The third is the fine saying of Epicurus, who wrote to one of his fellow students, "These words are meant not for many, but for you; we are a big enough audience for each other."

[12] My dear Lucilius, you should store these deep in your mind so that you can disdain the pleasure that comes from the admiration of the majority. Many praise you. But what reason do you have to pat yourself on the back if you're the kind of person the crowd understands? Your good qualities should look inward. Farewell.


3    **Self-Examination** (*EM* 27)

You say to me, "You're giving *me* advice? Why, have you already advised yourself? Have you fixed yourself, and so have time to work on correcting others?" I'm not so shameless, Lucilius, as to try to heal others while I am sick. No, think of it this way: you and I are lying in the same hospital room, and I'm conversing with you about our common illness and sharing my own attempts at a cure. So listen to me as if I were speaking with myself. I've let you into my private thoughts, and with your help I'm conducting a self-examination.

[2] I cry out to myself, "Count your years! Aren't you ashamed that you have the same desires as you did when a child, that you are pursuing the same old things? Offer yourself this gift on your dying day, that your vices die before you do." Rid yourself of those pleasures that disrupt your life and come at such a high cost—not just those in

---

5. For the "Gem of the Day," see above, note 1.

your future, but also those in your past. Both are harmful. Think about it this way: if someone committed a crime but wasn't caught red-handed, will he stop worrying once he's away from the scene? No. The same is true for immoderate pleasures: even afterwards, the guilt stays with you. These pleasures are insubstantial; you cannot depend on them. Even if they do not bring you harm, they evaporate. [3] Look around you for some lasting asset: there is none, except what your mind discovers for itself within itself. Virtue alone offers joy that is perpetual and unshakeable. And if something does try to blot out your joy, it's only a cloud that drifts beneath the sun but never overcomes it.

[4] When will you reach this everlasting joy? Even though you haven't been slack up to this point, you must still pick up the pace. There is much work still to be done, work that will cost you many sleepless nights and a great deal of sweat if you desire to reach the goal. This is a job you must do yourself; no one can stand in for you. [5] Other ordinary kinds of pursuits allow for assistance. Remember Calvisius Sabinus, that wealthy fellow a few years back? He had a freedman's wealth and a freedman's wits:[6] never in my life have I seen a well-to-do person act more disgracefully. His memory was so poor that he would often forget the name of Ulysses, or Achilles, or Priam—people we know as well as our own teachers. Think of all the old, doddering *nomenclatores*[7] who are so senile that they have to make up names for people because they can't recall them. Not a single one of them mistakenly names his master's thousands of clients more than our friend Sabinus does the Trojans and Greeks.

[6] Still, Sabinus wanted to appear learned, so he concocted the following shortcut. He spent a great sum on slaves, one who would know Homer by heart, another Hesiod, and he assigned individual slaves to each of the nine lyric poets! You shouldn't be surprised that it cost him so much to buy them. If he was not able to find slaves already learned, he had them made to order. After he had procured this mighty band of slaves, he started annoying his dinner guests. He kept these slaves at hand so that they could repeatedly feed him verses to quote, and even then, he'd frequently drop them mid-line.

[7] Satellius "the Freeloader" Quadratus used to egg him on. This fellow used to mooch off of dim-witted rich men, then (as inevitably happens in such cases) poke fun at them, and eventually (this is linked to the other two) openly mock them.[8] He told Sabinus that he should buy some grammarians to pick up the lines he dropped.[9] When Sabinus said each slave cost him a hundred thousand sesterces, Quadratus quipped, "You could have bought just as many bookcases full of books for less." Yet the mighty Sabinus was firmly convinced that he knew everything that his household knew. [8] So Satellius started urging him to take up wrestling, sick, pale, and gaunt though he was. When Sabinus responded, "How could I do that? I'm barely alive as

---

6. That is, very wealthy but uncultured, like Trimalchio in Petronius' *Trimalchio's Dinner Party* in this volume.

7. Slaves whose job it was to remind their masters of the names (*nomina*) of men calling upon them during the *salutatio*; see Glossary.

8. Evidently a *scurra* (see Pliny, *Letters* 24, with note, and Glossary).

9. *Grammatici*, elementary teachers of language and literature, who had their pupils memorize large amounts of poetry. See Quintilian section G in this volume.

it is!" Quadratus said, "Now, now, don't say that. Don't you see how many strapping, healthy slaves you own?"

A good mind is neither bestowed nor bought. Even if it were for sale, I'd wager that it would not find a buyer. Yet shabby minds are bought every day.

[9] But here, before I say goodbye, I give you the gem of the day. "Simple living according to the laws of nature is wealth." Epicurus frequently said as much in one way or another; but it can never be said too often, for people never take it completely to heart. Some people need remedies shown to them; others need them dinned into their heads. Farewell.

## 4    On the Humane Treatment of Slaves (*EM* 47)

I was glad to learn from those whom you sent to me that you are living on friendly terms with your slaves. This befits a man of good sense and erudition like yourself. "But they are slaves," people say. No, fellow human beings. "They are slaves." No, tentmates. "They are slaves." No, friends down on their luck. "They are slaves." No, fellow slaves, if you consider how much power fortune has over free and slave alike.

[2] This is why I laugh at those who believe that it is disgraceful to dine with one's slave. How is it disgraceful, except for the extremely arrogant custom that keeps a crowd of slaves standing around their master as he dines, to be at his beck and call? He eats more than he can hold, loading his stomach with his awe-inspiring gluttony until it is distended and forgets what its job is, such that it takes far more work to evacuate the mass than it did to ingest it! [3] As for his slaves, well, those sorry souls are not permitted to open their mouths, not even to speak. Every murmur is checked by the rod; even things they can't control—coughs, sneezes, and hiccups—are met with a beating. Any noise that interrupts the master's silence is paid for by great punishment. The whole night through they stand there, suffering, hungry, mute. [4] And so it happens that those who cannot talk in front of their master talk about their master behind his back. Yet slaves of olden times, slaves who were allowed to speak not only in front of their masters but even with them, slaves whose mouths were not sewn shut—these were prepared to stick their necks out for their masters and take on incoming threats on their behalf. They spoke at banquets, but said nothing on the rack.[10]

[5] That same arrogance I mentioned above gave rise to the widespread proverb "you have as many enemies as slaves." But we don't *have* them, we *make* them. For the moment I'll pass over other cruel and inhumane treatment, how we do not treat our slaves like human beings, but abuse them like beasts of burden, how [*gap in the text*. Instead, I'll focus on our treatment of them at dinners.][11]

When we've reclined to eat, one slave wipes up our spittle, another sits beneath the table and picks up what the drunken guests drop, [6] while yet another carves up expensive fowl. This last slave expertly guides his hand through the breast and haunches as he pulls out the morsels. I would pity the poor fool who lives for the sole purpose of

---

10. Slaves routinely gave evidence at trials under torture, on the assumption that otherwise they would lie.

11. A clause (or more) concerning the general maltreatment of slaves has dropped out of the text. We have supplied a transition that is not in the text.

carving up winged creatures properly, except that the person who teaches someone this skill for the sake of pleasure is to be pitied more than the person who learns it because he is forced to. [7] Another slave plays the wine-attendant, dressed up as a woman, fighting against his age. He is not allowed to escape his boyhood, always hauled back. Although he's got a soldier's physique, he's kept smooth-chinned, hair abraded away or plucked out completely, and stays up the entire night split between his master's drunkenness and lust, a man in the bedroom, a boy at the banquet.[12]

[8] Yet another slave has the task of sizing up the guests, standing there miserably and watching to determine which ones' fawning repartee or gluttony will get them invited back the next day. Let's not forget the shoppers, who have learned their master's tastes with exact precision. They know what foods have the flavor that will excite him and the presentation that will delight him, what novelties will revive his flagging appetite, what bores him with over-familiarity, and what he craves that day. But he would never dine with these kinds of people, believing that it would diminish his importance if he were to deign to join his slave at the same table. God forbid!

And yet, such men as these have their own masters, too. [9] I saw Callistus'[13] former owner waiting at his old slave's door. The man who had once pegged a price tag on Callistus and put him up for sale among the other reject slaves was kept from entering with the rest of the clients. The slave who had been tossed into the first items up for sale (this is when the crier is just warming his voice) repaid his master in kind: he rejected his master in turn and judged him unworthy of his own house. Callistus' owner sold him. But how much that sale cost the owner![14]

[10] You should reflect on the fact that the person you call a slave arose from the same origins, looks upon the same skies, breathes the same air, and lives the same and dies the same as we do. You are just as capable of looking at him as a freeborn person as he is of looking at you as a slave. Remember the Varian disaster?[15] So many young men of the highest rank, beginning their climb to the senatorial rank through military service—Fortune turned their lives upside down. One she made a lowly shepherd, another a lowly house attendant. As you think about that, go ahead and scorn the man of humble fortune, into which *you* may pass while you scorn him!

[11] I don't want to delve into the massive debate about the proper use of slaves, whom we treat with outrageous arrogance, cruelty, and contempt. This is the primary point of my lesson: you should treat your inferior as you would want your superior to treat you. Whenever you consider how much power you have over your slave, keep in mind that your master has just as much power over you. [12] "But I have no master," you say? You're young; perhaps you will one day. Do you remember at what age

---

12. Evidently a *cinaedus*; see Glossary and Pliny, *Letters* 24 in this volume.

13. Callistus was an influential freedman under the Emperor Claudius (reigned AD 41–54) who rose to the position of oversecretary for the emperor's petitions (*a libellis*).

14. The story is especially scandalous because of the normally warm ties between freedmen and their former masters, and the expectation that slaves would continue to perform some services even after manumission.

15. In AD 9 three legions were lost in the disastrous battle of the Teutoberg Forest in Germany under Augustus' legate P. Quinctilius Varus. Although our sources indicate that the legions were completely annihilated, Seneca adopts the (not unreasonable) rhetorical position that the soldiers suffered captivity.

Hecuba became a slave? Croesus? Darius' mother? Plato? Diogenes?[16] [13] Treat your slave like a fellow human, like a friend, even. Admit him into your conversations, into your deliberations, into your life.

[14] At this point I can just hear that whole band of pampered folk crying out, "Nothing's more shameful than this, nothing more disgraceful!" Yet these are the very same people that I catch kissing the hands of other people's slaves.[17] Don't you people see how our fathers kept slaves from loathing their masters, masters from abusing their slaves? They used to call masters the "fathers of the family"[18] and slaves "family members," a practice that endures today in mime.[19] They established a holiday on which masters and slaves were to dine together;[20] it was not the only day they would do so, but a special day on which they would particularly celebrate that practice. They allowed slaves to wield offices and pass laws inside the house, and they considered the house to be a miniature state.

[15] "Well then," you reply, "am I really to invite *every* slave to my table?" Not any more than you would invite every free person. You'd be mistaken to think that I would banish from my table certain slaves on the grounds that they perform the dirty jobs, for instance, mule-drivers or plowmen. I do not judge them by their jobs, but by their character. Character is up to us;[21] jobs are owed to chance. Some slaves should dine with you because they are worthy, others so that they become worthy. Whatever servile characteristics have developed in them from their lowly associations will be driven out of them by interaction with more respectable people.

[16] My dear Lucilius, there is no reason why you should look for friends only in the Forum and Senate House. If you look carefully, you will also find them at home. Good raw material often lies fallow without an artist to shape it: test it and see for yourself. If someone was about to purchase a horse and inspected not the horse itself but only its saddle and other gear, would he not be foolish? Likewise, it is completely foolish to judge a person by his clothing or his circumstances, which are wrapped around us just like clothing. [17] "He is a slave." But perhaps free in spirit. "He is a slave." How will this impair him? Show me someone who is not a slave. One's a slave to pleasure, one to greed, one to ambition; everyone's a slave to hope and fear. I can give you examples: an ex-consul enslaved to an old hag, a rich man to his slave girl, whole bands of the most genteel young men nothing more than slaves to pantomime-dancers.[22] No servitude is more disgraceful than the voluntary kind. Don't be deterred by those snobbish fools

---

16. Mythical and historical figures who were enslaved late in life.

17. Slaves of powerful people, such as the emperor.

18. The Latin term *familia* originally included all members of the household, including slaves; see Glossary, "*familia*."

19. A kind of popular stage comedy; see Glossary.

20. The Saturnalia was a festival in December which featured, among much else, the temporary dissolution of cultural norms; slaves would wear a freedman's cap and be on equal terms with their masters. See Glossary.

21. The phrase "what is up to us" is reminiscent of the position taken by Epictetus in the *Handbook of Stoic Philosophy* (see ch. 1).

22. Pantomime: a dramatic performance through dance; see Glossary.

from offering a pleasant attitude to your slaves. Though you are their superior, you do not have to be condescending. They should revere you, not fear you.

[18] Someone will now say that I'm calling for slaves to be freed and knocking their masters down from their lofty perch when I say that they should revere you rather than fear you. "Is this how it will be?" someone will say. "Are they to cultivate us like our clients, like our early morning callers?" Whoever says this is forgetting that whatever is sufficient for a god cannot be too little for a master. Whoever is revered is also loved. Love cannot involve fear. [19] So I judge you to be entirely correct because you do not wish your slaves to fear you and because you chastise them with nothing more than a tongue-lashing. Whippings are for beasts of burden. What annoys us does not always harm us as well. But our pampered way of life has driven us to such a point of madness that we fly into a rage if things don't turn out according to our wishes. [20] We have assumed the disposition of kings. They, too, forgetful of their own power and their subjects' weakness, seethe and burn white hot in anger when they think they've suffered some harm—as if this were possible, given that their lofty position keeps them entirely protected even from the *threat* of harm from their inferiors. They are perfectly aware of this fact, and yet they protest anyway and seize upon the opportunity for doing harm: they believe that they've been harmed so that they may harm others.

[21] I do not wish to detain you any longer, for *you* do not need any encouraging. Good character has, among many others, this quality: it is content with itself and permanent. Vice is fickle and changes often, not into something better, but merely into something else. Farewell.

## 5    Sin City: Baiae and Its Harmful Ways (*EM* 51)

We all must do with what we've got, Lucilius. You have Mt. Aetna over there, the most renowned mountain in Sicily (why Messalla and Valgius call it "one of a kind" in their works, I have no idea. They both use this term. But fiery lava comes out of the earth in many places, not just mountain tops—though that is more common, no doubt because fire rises—but also in low-lying ground). As for me, I must somehow make do with Baiae, however I can. You should avoid this place. It has some natural advantages, to be sure, but Extravagance has taken it over and made it her own personal resort.

[2] "What are you saying? Are we to be sworn enemies of any one place?" Not at all. But some clothing is more suitable than others for a virtuous Wise Man;[23] he may not hate any particular color, but think that one might be too showy for someone committed to the simple life. So, too, there are regions that a Wise Man, or someone making progress toward wisdom, will avoid as adverse to good character. [3] A Wise Man thinking about a retreat will never choose Canopus,[24] even though Canopus does not prevent a person from living simply. Nor will he choose Baiae, which has become one big resort of vice. In Canopus Extravagance runs riot; Baiae, as if granted some kind of special

23. See Glossary.

24. Canopus was a city in Egypt renowned for its party-going atmosphere, a sort of Mediterranean New Orleans.

dispensation by its geography, is even more dissolute.[25] [4] We ought to choose a place that is just as healthy for our character as for our bodies. Just as I would not want to live among torturers, I wouldn't want to live among bars and taverns, either. [5] Imagine the scene: drunk people wandering along the beaches, sailors carousing, the bays filled with the raucous songs of noisy partiers, and all the other kinds of corrupt behavior Extravagance, as if unbound by any law, both produces and promotes. Why put up with all that? [6] We should try to keep the stimuli to vice as far away from us as possible. The mind must be toughened and torn away from enticements to pleasure.

Consider Hannibal. A single winter in camp unstrung him. Yes, the man who overcame the frigid snows of the Alps was emasculated by the warm embraces of Campania. Behold, a conqueror in arms conquered by vice![26] We too must fight a war, but ours is the kind of war that allows no rest, no respite. We must first and foremost vanquish pleasures, which, as you see, have taken even the most savage characters prisoner. If you consider how great a task we have set for ourselves, you will realize that not one of our actions can be weak or soft. What do I care about those heated pools? Or those sweat-baths, into which hot dry air is pumped to drain the body? All sweat should come from hard work.

[7] Imagine if we were to do what Hannibal did, break off in the middle of our progress and leave the war behind so that we can coddle our bodies. Who would not be completely justified in criticizing our ill-timed idleness, idleness that is hazardous for one who has already claimed victory, but even more so for one who is still striving for victory. And we have even less margin of error than those following the Carthaginian standards. Our danger is greater if we retreat, our toil greater even if we press on.

[8] Fortune is waging war against me. I will not do her bidding. I will not wear her yoke—rather, I will shake it off, which requires even more courage. My mind must not become soft. If I surrender to pleasure, I must also surrender to pain, to toil, to poverty. Both ambition and anger will want the same control over me. I'll be drawn in different directions by so many emotions—or rather torn apart by them. [9] Freedom, yes, freedom is our objective. That's the reward for our hard work. What is freedom, you ask? To be a slave to no thing, no circumstance, no outcome, and to bring Fortune down to equal terms with you. The day that I realize her power is greater, she will have no power over me. Why must I put up with her, when death is firmly in my control?[27]

[10] Someone who is focused on these kinds of deliberations should choose for himself a sober, pure locale. Too much pleasantness makes the mind effeminate, and

---

25. Baiae, with its natural hot springs, was frequented for its restorative properties. By the 1st century BC elite Romans had built extensive villas in and around Baiae.

26. After a series of stunning victories against the Romans in 217–216 BC, Hannibal took up winter quarters in Capua in the heart of Campania. Livy (23.18.9–16) records the luxurious lifestyle of the soldiers amidst "sleep and wine, banquets and prostitutes, baths and idleness," and, like Seneca, finds it paradoxical: "those men who had never been conquered by any hardship were undone by excessive comforts and immoderate pleasures."

27. In Stoic philosophy, suicide was allowed when circumstances made taking one's life a rational decision. These included failing health, remaining loyal to friends and family, and avoiding being compelled to act against one's Stoic principles. In other words, suicide allowed the Stoic to remain independent of external compulsion.

one's surroundings certainly contribute to weakening its vigor. Beasts of burden will endure any path if their hooves have been hardened on rough ground. Those fattened on soft, marshy pasturage quickly get footsore. Tough soldiers, too, come from rough country. Those raised in the city in comfortable houses are sluggish. No one who takes up the sword after working the plow refuses hard work. Dapper folks with their hair slicked back, however, balk at the first sign of dust. [11] The severe training one receives from living in rough country toughens one's character and prepares it for great undertakings.

Scipio spent his years of exile more respectably in Liternum than he could have done in Baiae.[28] A downfall like his did not deserve such a soft landing. The men who first received into their own hands massive public funds from the successes of the Roman people—Marius, Pompeius, Caesar—indeed constructed villas near Baiae, but they built them on high hilltops. This gave their villas a more military look, as if surveying the sprawling lowlands from up on high. Consider the position they chose, the places where they erected their edifices, and what kind of buildings they were. You will realize they were not villas, but fortresses!

[12] Do you think M. Cato would have ever lived in Baiae?[29] Would he have wanted to count up the vast number of adulterous women sailing by, the countless kinds of boats painted in all kinds of colors, all the roses floating over the whole lake, or to hear the noisy nighttime songs of partiers? Wouldn't he rather have stayed behind the defensive wall that he had dug with his own hands for a single night?[30] Who wouldn't, provided that he's a real man? Who wouldn't rather have his sleep be interrupted by a war trumpet than by a chorus of revelers?

[13] Well, enough of our litigation against Baiae. But we should never stop putting our vices on trial. I beg you, Lucilius, prosecute them continually, ceaselessly. For they will ceaselessly and continually haunt you. Cast out all those vices that rend your heart; if they cannot be removed separately, then you must rip out your very heart and cast it out with them. You should especially expel pleasures. Consider them the most dangerous. They are just like those highway robbers, the ones the Egyptians call *philetai* ("lovers"):[31] they embrace us so that they may strangle us. Farewell.

## 6    Vatia's Villa, or, A Life Not Worth Living (*EM* 55)

I just got back from being carried around in a litter, no less tired than if I had walked the whole way instead of sitting. Being carried for a long time is also hard work, perhaps even harder work because it is contrary to Nature, who gave us feet so we could

---

28. P. Cornelius Scipio Africanus Maior, consul in 205 BC, conqueror of Hannibal in the Second Punic War. Despite his fame and despite attaining the highest public offices (censor in 199 BC, consul again in 194), he was later accused of bribery and embezzlement. He avoided a trial by retiring to a small, unassuming villa in Campania in 184 BC, where he would die the following year.

29. The ascetic Cato the Younger was a notorious critic of extravagance and luxurious living.

30. For soldiers building their own fortifications see Polybius ch. 34 in this volume.

31. A pun. The Greek word for "robber" was *phelétes*, which differed from the Greek word for lover (*philetés*) only in one letter and its accent.

walk on our own, eyes so we could see for ourselves. Easy living has crippled us. What we have refused to do for so long, we are no longer capable of doing.

[2] Still, I did it for my health, to dislodge the phlegm that had built up in my chest, and to alleviate my congested breathing by being jostled a little. I felt it was helping, so I endured riding around longer than usual. The beach itself was inviting, the one that curves between Cumae and the villa of Servilius Vatia,[32] hemmed in on one side by the sea, on the other by a lake, forming a narrow path. It was packed hard after a recent storm. (As you know, a beach is leveled out by frequent and vigorous waves, while a long period of calm will loosen it, when the sand loses the moisture that holds it together.)

[3] Be that as it may, I began to look around, as is my custom, to see whether I might find something there that would prove useful to me. I cast my gaze on the villa that once belonged to Vatia. Here is where that billionaire former praetor grew old, known only for his life of leisure, and for this one reason considered a blessed man. For every time one of his peers would get killed—some for being a friend of Asinius Gallus, others victims of Sejanus' hatred, then later of Sejanus' love (it was just as dangerous to have offended him as it was to have loved him)[33]—men would exclaim "Vatia, only you know how to live!"

[4] Live? No, he knew how to hide. There is a big difference between a life of leisure and a life of mere sloth. Whenever I would pass by Vatia's villa when he was still alive I would say, "here lies Vatia."[34] Yet, my Lucilius, philosophy is such a sacred business and has such a revered status that even what falsely passes for it finds favor. The common crowd believes that a person who has merely withdrawn lives a life of leisure, is carefree, is happy with himself, lives for himself. But no one can achieve any of this except a Wise Man. Only the Wise Man knows how to live for himself. After all—and this must come first—he knows how to live. [5] Consider the person who runs from problems and people, or who exiles himself because his own desires have been frustrated, or who cannot bear to see others more well-off than he, or who has burrowed himself out of the public eye because of fear like some timorous, petrified animal. Does he live for himself? No! Rather, he lives—and this is the most disgraceful thing of all—only for his belly, sleep, and lust. The person who lives for no one cannot live for himself. And yet, consistency in one's life, that is, always sticking to one's principles, is considered such a great achievement that even sloth, if steadfast, is considered impressive.

[6] Turning to the villa, I cannot give you much definite information, since I am familiar only with the facade and the exterior areas that are visible to passersby. There

---

32. Servilius Vatia achieved the rank of praetor in 25 BC, but seems to have immediately retired to the privacy of his family villa, where he would live into old age—at least the 30s AD, the period of political turmoil that Seneca refers to in this letter.

33. C. Asinius Gallus, consul in 8 BC and an influential senator. Judged "eager for the throne but not equal to it" by Augustus (Tacitus, *Annals* 1.13.2), he was later (AD 30) arrested by Tiberius. His associates were killed "for no other reason than that Tiberius said that [they] were friends of Gallus" (Dio 58.3.3). Aelius Sejanus was praetorian prefect under Tiberius. When the emperor retired to Capri in AD 26, Sejanus became the de facto ruler of Rome and set upon a number of prosecutions to eliminate his political opponents. When Tiberius realized his ambitions in AD 31, he had Sejanus killed and purged Rome of all of his supporters.

34. *Hic situs est*, a formulaic expression found on Roman gravestones.

are two manmade grottoes, a massive construction requiring great labor, equal in size to the biggest *atria* you've ever seen. One does not get any sun; the other gets sunshine the whole day through, even into evening. There's a grove of plane trees, and through the middle of it there flows a rivulet, which extends from the Acherusian lake to the sea, in the form of a canal, designed to furnish a steady supply of fish even if it were to be continually tapped. As long as the sea is calm, no one uses the rivulet. It's only when bad weather forces fishermen into a holiday that people thrust their hands into these well-stocked waters. [7] But the biggest advantage of the villa is that Baiae lies just past its walls, so it lacks all the inconveniences of that place while enjoying its pleasures.[35] These features I am familiar with myself; and I believe it's just as pleasant the whole year through. It is exposed to the westerly winds, and it captures the winds in such a way that they never reach Baiae. Vatia, it seems, was not foolish to choose this place for him to spend his retirement, slothful and decrepit as it was.

[8] Still, one's surroundings do not contribute much to one's peace of mind. No, it is the mind itself that makes all surroundings pleasant. I have seen gloomy expressions in a cheerful and pleasant villa, and people who appear busy in the middle of nowhere. So there's no reason to suppose that you are troubled in mind simply because you are not in Campania.

But you in fact *can* be here. Just send all your thoughts this way. [9] You can converse with absent friends however often and for however long you wish. This, the greatest of all pleasures, we enjoy even more when we are apart. The presence of friends spoils us, in fact. Since we can talk, take a walk, or sit and chat whenever we want, when we go our separate ways we do not give the slightest thought about the people whom we had just seen. [10] We should endure the absence of a friend without a fuss. After all, isn't every single one of us quite absent from those who are present? Consider the nights that separate us, our various engagements, the studies that require privacy, and the trips outside of the city. So you see that there's not all that much that a trip abroad steals from us.

[11] A friend should be embraced with the mind, which of course is never absent and can see whomever it wants on any given day. So study with me, dine with me, walk with me. Our lives would be narrow indeed if we were prevented from doing something in our thoughts. I gaze upon you, my Lucilius. I'm listening to you right this second. I am with you, such that I wonder if I should start writing you not full-blown letters, but notes on wax![36] Farewell.


7     **Living above a Bathhouse** (*EM* 56)

Well, I'll be damned if silence is really as important as it seems for a person studying in private. Just listen to that racket, all those noises echoing around me—I'm living right over a bathhouse! Imagine every kind of human sound that can grate on one's ears. Whenever the muscle men are working out, throwing punches weighed down with lead, when they are exerting themselves (or pretending to), I hear grunting. Whenever they release their held-in breaths, I hear hissing exhalations. When it comes to a lazy

---

35. See letter 5 above.

36. That is, wooden tablets with a reusable wax writing surface.

person who is content to have an ordinary rubdown, I hear the smack of hands striking shoulders, the sound varying whether the hand lands flat or cupped. But if a ballplayer arrives on the scene and starts counting the balls, well, I'm a goner! [2] Add to the mix hot-tempered blowhards, thieves caught in the act, and all the people who just like to hear themselves sing in the baths. Oh, and don't forget all those who jump into the pool just to see how loud a sound they can make when they hit the water!

In addition to these—who, if nothing else, are using their normal voices—imagine the hair-plucker who continually squeezes out a shrill, high-pitched voice to get more business. He never shuts up except when he's plucking someone's armpits. Then he forces someone else to shout in his place. Then there are the various cries of drink-sellers, sausage-makers, pastry-bakers, and tavern-keepers hawking their wares with their own peculiar—and unmistakable—inflections.

[3] "How iron-like," you say, "or deaf you must be, if your mind is at peace amidst so many and such jarring noises! Even our Chrysippus was nearly sent to his grave from hearing 'hello' constantly." But I swear by Hercules that I'm no more bothered by that hubbub than waves or a waterfall, although I hear that a certain people moved their city because they could not put up with the din caused by the Nile waterfall. [4] To me, a single voice is more distracting than background noise. The former diverts the mind, the latter merely fills and strikes the ears. Among those noises that do not distract me I count carriages racing by, a tenant carpenter, a neighboring sawyer plying his trade, and those who test horns and trumpets by the Meta Sudans,[37] not so much playing them as blaring into them. [5] Even now a sound which is intermittent is more bothersome to me than one which is continual. But I've now hardened myself against all those sorts of things such that I can even listen to a coxswain calling out "stroke! stroke!" to rowers in the harshest voice. I've compelled my mind to focus on itself and not to be distracted by external noises. Everything on the outside can resound so long as there is no uproar inside, so long as desire and fear do not quarrel amongst themselves, so long as greed and luxury do not wrangle with or incite each other. After all, what good does complete silence do if one's emotions rage?

[6] Varro writes, "All of night was settled beneath a peaceful calm."

Not true: there is no peaceful calm except that created by our rational minds. Night does not remove vexation, but produces it. Night merely changes the reasons for our worry. After all, when we fall asleep, our dreams are as upsetting as the light of day. Real tranquility is the expansive, unruffled calm of a philosophical mind.

[7] Consider the man who tries to find sleep in the complete silence of a spacious house. No sound strikes his ears. His slaves, the whole troop of them, are mute, and if they happen to pass close by his room, they walk on tiptoe. Of course, he tosses and turns, snatching a wink or two amidst his grief. He complains about the noises he did not hear. What do you think the reason is? His *mind* is in an uproar. [8] It is the mind that must be calmed. It is the mutiny of the mind that must be suppressed. Do not make the mistake of thinking that the mind is calm just because the body is still. Sometimes rest is restless. It is for this reason that we must rouse ourselves to action

---

37. The Meta Sudans ("Sweating Post") was a monumental fountain in Rome erected by Augustus at the bottom of the northeast slope of the Palatine Hill. Based on inscriptions nearby, the area was frequented by musicians and may have been a meeting place for their guild (see Glossary, "*collegium*").

and busy ourselves by engaging in beneficial study whenever restless inactivity has got us in a bad way.

[9] Why, don't great generals, when they see a soldier slacking off, check that behavior by giving him some task that requires hard work or occupy him with forced marches? People engrossed in an activity do not have time to grow dissolute, and there is nothing truer in the world than this old saw: the vices of leisure are dispelled by hard work.

Many of us, it seems, have gone into retirement because of the ennui that arises from political life or out of displeasure for a miserable and thankless post. Yet, in that hiding place, into which we were driven by fear or exhaustion, our ambition sometimes breaks out again. Our ambition disappeared not because we cut it out like diseased flesh, but because it had grown weary or even angry because things simply weren't going our way. [10] The same is true about luxury. Sometimes it seems to leave us, but then, when we have committed to a life of frugality, luxury pokes us and, amidst our simple life, yearns for its old pleasures, which were not condemned for good but only temporarily abandoned. And what is more, the more deeply they are buried, the more vehemently luxury wants them back.

[11] The vices that lie out in the open are milder, as are those bodily diseases, which are closer to the cure when they have broken out into the open and have revealed their true nature. Know this: greed, ambition, and all the other maladies of the human mind are most dangerous when they lurk beneath the pretense of good health. We think we're at peace, but we are not. For if we are truly at peace, if we have sounded the retreat, if we have wholly spurned attractive but empty honors, as I said before, *nothing* will distract us. No chorus of men or birds will interrupt our thoughts, since they will be healthy, solid, and unshakeable.

[12] The mind that is still stirred by voices and random noises is inconstant and has not yet focused itself inward. Some turmoil still resides inside, some nagging trepidation that makes it curious. As our Vergil puts it:

> As for me, who but moments ago stood undaunted
> amidst speeding weapons and hordes of hostile Greeks,
> now every breeze spooked me, every sound startled me,
> uneasy, fearful for both my companion and my cargo.[38]

[13] That earlier Aeneas was a Wise Man, the one who was frightened neither by flashing missiles, nor by the clash of men and steel, nor by the crash of his falling city. The other Aeneas was a fool,[39] fearing for his own possessions, dreading every noise, a man who took every voice as a great uproar and lost his composure, a man who felt dread at the slightest movement. His cargo made him fearful.

[14] So choose any of those blessed folks you wish, those who are hauling around their many possessions, who are carrying their many assets. He, too, is "fearful for both his companion and his cargo." Know that you have achieved a peaceful state of mind when no uproar bothers you, when no voice distracts you from yourself, be it charming or threatening or just meaningless chatter.

---

38. These lines come from Vergil, *Aeneid* 2.726–29, where Aeneas is escaping Troy with his son Ascanius at his side (his "companion") and his father Anchises on his back (his "cargo").

39. In Stoic philosophy, only two categories of people existed: the perfect Wise Man and everyone else, who were called collectively, regardless of their philosophical progress, "fools."

[15] "Well," you counter, "is it not sometimes more advantageous to be free of all the hubbub?" Of course. That's why I'll be leaving this place. I was trying an experiment to test myself. Why should I torture myself any longer, when Ulysses found such an easy remedy for his men even against the sweet-sounding Sirens?[40] Farewell.

## 8    Nature Requires Little, Humans Much (*EM* 60)

I've got a bone to pick with you, a complaint. I'm hopping mad. Do you still, even now, wish for the same things that your nanny, *paedagogus*, and mother wished for you? Do you not understand how much harm they were wishing on you? Our family's prayers are so detrimental to us. And the more they come true, the more detrimental they are. I'm no longer surprised that our maladies have stayed with us since our early years— we've grown up surrounded by our parents' curses! At some point the gods must hear *our* voice, made on our own behalf, one that asks for nothing in return. [2] Will there ever be a time we don't ask the gods for some favor? Are we not yet capable of supporting ourselves? How long will we sow the fields of great cities, how long will their citizens harvest them for us? How long will fleets of ships transport the supplies for a single meal (and not from just one sea, mind you)? A bull's appetite is satisfied by a few acres of pasturage. Several elephants subsist on a single forest. Humans? They feed on both land and sea. What? Could it be that Nature, though giving us such modest bodies, endowed us with such insatiable bellies that we surpass the appetites of the hugest and most gluttonous animals? Hardly. How little of what we ingest is given to Nature! It only takes a little to send her packing. No, it's not the natural hunger of our bellies, but rather our never-ending quest for more that is so costly to us. We should therefore classify those people that Sallust calls "slaves to their stomachs"[41] not as human beings, but as animals, and some we shouldn't even classify as animals, but dead. Who is really living? The person who benefits many. Who is really living? Those who put themselves to good use. But those who lie hidden in their house, sluggish and indolent—they might as well be in a tomb! You could well carve an inscription into the marble on the doorways of these peoples' homes: THOSE INSIDE HAVE ANTICIPATED THEIR OWN DEATHS. Farewell.

## 9    Stop Wasting Time (*EM* 62)

All those people who want you to think their numerous occupations are keeping them away from pursuing philosophy—they're not telling the truth. All they're doing is pretending to be busy, adding to their busy schedule, or making themselves busy. I'm free, Lucilius, yes, free, and wherever I happen to be, I'm all my own. Why? I do not consign myself to affairs—I merely lend myself to them, and I do not seek out excuses for wasting time. Wherever I am located I turn to my thoughts and contemplate something that will benefit my soul. [2] When I give myself to my friends, I do not leave

---

40. In Homer's *Odyssey* (book 12) Odysseus ordered his men to plug their ears with wax and to bind him securely to the mast so that he could safely listen to the Sirens' song.

41. Sallust, *War with Catiline* 1.

my own company, and I refuse to linger with those whose company I owe to some chance occasion or some social obligation. I associate only with the best people. I direct my thoughts to them, no matter where or when they lived. [3] In fact, I take my Demetrius, the best of men, around with me, and, leaving behind all those clothed in purple, I converse with this half-clothed man. I admire him.[42] And why shouldn't I? I have come to see that he lacks nothing. A person can reject everything, but no one can have everything. The shortest path to riches is to reject them. Our friend Demetrius lives not as though he has rejected everything, but as though he has consented to let others have it all. Farewell.

## 10    On the Liberal Arts (*EM* 88)

You desire to know my opinion of the liberal arts?[43] I do not respect any pursuit, or count it among our useful possessions, if its goal is monetary gain. They are nothing more than money-making devices, useful only if they prepare our minds and do not detain them.[44] One should only be occupied in these studies when the mind is not able to perform some greater task. These are our ABCs, so to speak, not our *magnum opus*.

[2] Surely you see why they are called "liberal" arts. They are worthy of a free (*liber*) man. Yet there is but one pursuit that is truly "liberal"—because it makes a man free—and that is the pursuit of philosophy. This will lift him up, make him brave, and strengthen his soul. All the other pursuits? Trifling and childish distractions. How can you believe that there is anything profitable in those pursuits? Isn't it obvious that those who practice them are the most disgraceful and shameful of all people? Now's not the time to learn the liberal arts. We ought to have mastered them long ago.

Some believe that the crucial question about liberal arts is whether they make a man good. But liberal arts do not promise nor do they even strive to achieve knowledge in this matter. [3] Language Arts? They deal with correctness of speech and, if you want to define it a bit more broadly, with historical and mythical stories and, when carried to its outer limits, with poetry. Do any of these pave the path toward virtue? No. The enunciation of syllables, attentiveness to words, the memorization of stories, the rules of versification and scansion—which of these removes our fears, banishes our desires, reins in our lust? [4] Let us turn to geometry and music. You will discover that those studies do nothing to eliminate one's fears and desires. If you don't know how to achieve this, everything else you learn is pointless.

[There is no reason to ask whether those people who teach liberal arts][45] teach virtue or not. If they do not teach it, they cannot impart it. If they do teach it, they are

---

42. Demetrius was a Cynic philosopher who adopted an ascetic lifestyle.

43. That is, the ordinary upper-class educational curriculum focused on grammar, literature, and public speaking (see Quintilian, *On the Training of an Orator* in this volume), but also included some geometry, mathematics, and natural science. The liberal arts in Seneca's day generally did not include philosophy, and this is his main complaint against them.

44. Quintilian also complains about students who were overly focused on the financial gain to be had through the study of rhetoric (1.12.17).

45. The transition is rather abrupt and there is something missing here. There is a change of topic from geometry and music to those who teach liberal arts in general.

philosophers. And if you want to know how far removed from teaching philosophy those professors really are, just take a look at how much their pursuits differ from one another! And yet, their lessons would be similar if they were teaching the same things.

[5] Suppose they try to convince you that Homer was a philosopher—still, the evidence they use to prove that is suspect at best, contradictory at worst. After all, they sometimes make him a Stoic, who approves only virtue, flees from pleasures, and departs from the honorable course not even at the price of immortality. At other times they make him an Epicurean who praises a community that is at peace and spends its days among banquets and songs. After that they make him a Peripatetic who puts forward the three kinds of goods, and finally an Academic who says that nothing is knowable.[46] Clearly, Homer espouses none of these philosophies if he contains them all. They are, in fact, mutually exclusive. But let us grant them their position that Homer was a philosopher. Surely he was wise before he learned any of those poems, correct? So let us learn instead what it was that made Homer wise.

[6] But to research which of the two authors, Homer or Hesiod, was older is no more helpful to our ultimate pursuit of virtue than to know why Hecuba, although she was younger than Helen, looked so old. What, I ask you, is the point of investigating the ages of Patroclus and Achilles? [7] Why are you researching where Ulysses wandered, rather than making sure you do not wander for the rest of your life? You simply do not have time to listen to a lecture on whether he was buffeted between Italy and Sicily or in a part of the world beyond our knowledge (in fact, so long a wandering could not have occurred over so narrow a space). Why? Because storms of the mind buffet us every day, and our own indifference drives us into every trial and tribulation Ulysses endured. We have plenty of beauties right here that tempt the eyes and there are plenty of enemies around us. Right here we face savage monsters that rejoice in human blood, treacherous songs to beguile the ears, shipwrecks and disasters of a thousand kinds. Teach me instead how to love my country, my wife, my father, and how I might sail to these most honorable destinations even after I've been shipwrecked. [8] What's the point of inquiring whether Penelope was actually unfaithful and pulled the wool over all her contemporaries' eyes? Or whether she suspected that the man that she saw was Ulysses before she really knew? Teach me rather what faithfulness is, how important it is, and whether it is a virtue of the body or of the mind.

[9] Now on to the music teacher. He may teach me how high and low notes can complement each other, how strings of different notes can produce harmony. Rather, make it that my mind is always in harmony with itself, that my goals are never out of tune. You may show me the proper chords for a song of lament; show me instead how to hold back my laments when I am in the grip of misfortune.

[10] A surveyor teaches me how to compute the size of my giant estates, rather than how I might compute how much is sufficient for a person. He teaches me how to count and how to use my fingers for greed, but he does not teach me that all those calculations do not matter in the end. After all, someone is not more fortunate because his accountants can't keep up with all his holdings! In point of fact, you possess far too

---

46. The Peripatetics, the philosophical school descended from Aristotle, divided human "goods" into three parts: 1) those of the soul; 2) those of the body; and 3) the external (e.g., money and distinction). The Academic school, which originated with Plato, by this time had adopted a rigorous kind of skepticism.

many unnecessary items if calculating your massive assets all by yourself causes you misery! [11] What good does it do me to know how to divide a small plot of land into parts, if I do not know how to share it with my brother? What good does it do me to measure the acreage of my fields with precision, so much so that I know if it is off even by a couple of feet, if an insolent neighbor makes me unhappy by pinching off some of my land? The surveyor teaches me how I might not lose any of my property, but what I want to learn is how I can lose it all and still remain cheerful.

[12] "But I'm being banished," you say, "from the land of my father, of my grand-father!" Ask yourself this: before your grandfather, who held that land? Can you tell me to whom it belonged? And I don't mean which person, but which nation. You did not enter that land as a master, but as a tenant. And whose tenant are you? If you are lucky, your heir's. The legal experts say that no one can claim ownership of public land merely by occupation. This land which you hold, which you call yours, is not just public, but belongs to the whole human race.

[13] What an outstanding skill! You know how to measure circles and reduce every-thing into square units, no matter what shape you found it in. You can tell the distance between stars. There is nothing you can't measure. If you are truly a master at your skill, measure the human mind, tell us how great or tiny it is. You know when a line is straight and true. How does this help you, if you don't know how to keep your life on the straight and narrow?

[14] I now turn to the man who boasts of his knowledge of the heavens,

> where the icy star of Saturn retires,
> in what orbits Mercury's heavenly fire drifts.[47]

In what way will it benefit me to know this? So that I can be worried when Saturn and Mars stand in opposition? Or when Mercury sets in the evening as Saturn watches on? Isn't it better that I learn that, wherever those celestial bodies are, they are always propi-tious and cannot change?[48] [15] They are impelled on their paths by the uninterrupted chain of fate, a predetermined course. They come and go at regular intervals, and they either determine or herald the outcome of all things. Even if they do cause every event, what good does that knowledge do since you could not change it if you wanted? And if they only signify what is going to happen, what's the point of having foreknowledge if you can't avoid the outcome? Whether you know or don't know, it's going to happen.

> [16] But if you pay attention to the ferocious sun and the stars
> that follow in order, never will tomorrow's hour fool you
> nor will you be caught by the tricks of a cloudless night.[49]

I've taken plenty of precautions to protect myself from trickery without their help. [17] "But won't I be fooled by tomorrow's hour?" you say? "After all, everything that happens to an ignorant person fools him." I for my part do not know what will hap-pen, but I know what sorts of things can happen. Because of this I won't try to ward

---

47. Vergil, *Georgics* 1.336–37.

48. The regular movements of celestial bodies were, according to Stoic cosmology, a sign of an orderly universe under the guidance of an intelligent and benevolent deity.

49. Vergil, *Georgics* 1.424–26.

anything off by prayer; I expect it all. If something awful *doesn't* happen, I chalk it up to the good. The hour fools me if it spares me, and even then I'm not really fooled. Just as I know that anything can happen, I also know that it's no guarantee that anything will happen. So I anticipate success, but I'm prepared for adversity.

[18] You're going to have to bear with me since I'm not following the script. I'm simply not convinced that I should, like others, include painters in the ranks of the liberal arts. The same goes for statue-makers, marble-sculptors, and all the other artists who make our luxurious lifestyles possible. I'm also kicking out of the liberal arts wrestlers and that whole "science" of theirs that consists of oil and mud—otherwise, I'd have to include perfumers, cooks, and all the other types who apply their considerable talents for our pleasure. [19] I ask you, what is "liberal" about those fasting binge-drinkers? Their bodies are completely stuffed and fat, their minds are emaciated and lethargic. Are we to believe that *this* is a liberal pursuit for our young men, whom our elders used to whip into shape by making them throw spears, drive stakes into the ground, ride horses, and learn to handle their arms? Nothing that they taught their sons (*liberi*) could be learned while reclining on a couch.

But neither the ways of our ancestors nor the contemporary liberal arts teach or foster virtue. What good does it do to be able to control a horse or guide his course with bit and bridle when you're being drawn off course by the most unbridled emotions? What good is it to conquer many opponents in a wrestling or boxing match when you're being conquered by your angry temper?

[20] "What's that you say? Liberal pursuits don't do anything for us?" In other respects, they do quite a lot; in terms of virtue, nothing. Even those openly humble trades—the ones where people use their hands—contribute quite a bit to the furtherance of life, yet they have nothing to do with virtue. "So why do we teach our sons the liberal arts?" It's not because they are able to bestow virtue on them, but because they prepare the minds so that they can obtain wisdom. Those first lessons (called "grammar" in the olden days), during which boys learn the rudiments, do not teach the liberal arts but pave the way for the next step, comprehension. Likewise, the liberal arts do not lead the mind to virtue but merely make it possible.

[21] Posidonius[50] states that there are four kinds of "arts": 1) the vulgar and lowly; 2) those pertaining to spectacle; 3) the youthful; and 4) the liberal. The "vulgar" arts belong to tradesmen who use their hands and who are engaged in providing the necessities of life; in these there is not even the pretense of something honorable or noble. [22] The "spectacular" arts are those that aim at pleasing our eyes and ears; you can count among their practitioners the engineers who contrive scaffolding that rises on its own and platforms that seem to levitate into the sky. There are all kinds of other surprising devices, too: objects that were once closed suddenly gape open, others that were separate join together on their own, and still others that were once raised slowly come back down to earth. The eyes of the naive are star-struck by these things; they marvel at everything unexpected because they do not know what causes it.

[23] The "youthful arts"—and these have something akin to the liberal arts—the Greeks call "general education" (*encyclios paideia*) whereas we Romans dub them "lib-

---

50. Posidonius (ca. 135–ca. 50 BC) was an important Stoic philosopher who wrote on a vast number of subjects, from astronomy and physics to history and geography.

eral arts." But the term "liberal arts" ought to be restricted to those that are truly liberating, that is, those concerned with virtue.

[24] "But," you object, "just as one part of philosophy deals with physics, another ethics, another logic, so, too, does this mass of liberal studies claim a place within philosophy. When it comes to the investigation of nature, the philosopher depends on the evidence of geometry." [25] To respond: many things aid us but are not necessarily part of us. In fact, if they were part of us, they would not aid us. For example, food is an aid to the body, but it is still not part of it. Geometry offers us a useful tool, and it is as indispensable to philosophy as a carpenter is to geometry itself. But neither is a carpenter part of geometry nor is geometry a part of philosophy. [26] Besides, each field has its own boundaries. The Wise Man investigates and understands the causes of natural phenomena; the surveyor gives a complete reckoning and computation of them. The Wise Man knows the principles guiding the celestial bodies, what their powers are, what their nature is. As for their comings and goings and those laws that determine their setting or rising or even those occasions they seem to be standing still (although no celestial body can stand still)—all of that data the astronomer collects. [27] The Wise Man will know what causes a reflection in a mirror; the mathematician can tell you how far the object is from the reflection, and what kind of reflection any given shape of mirror will produce. The philosopher will prove that the sun is big. How big? The astronomer, who advances knowledge though a certain trial and error and continual attention, will prove that. But in order for the astronomer to advance in his craft, he has to acquire certain fundamental principles. So here's the rub: a field of study is not independent if its foundation is on loan from another.

[28] Philosophy by contrast needs nothing from any other field. It constructs its whole edifice from the ground up, on its own soil. Astronomy is, so to speak, built on someone else's property, a tenant on someone else's land. It borrowed its basic principles so that with their help it could reach greater heights. If it reached the truth, if it were able to comprehend the nature of the whole universe on its own, I would freely admit that it could contribute a great deal to our minds. After all, as we reflect upon the heavens our minds grow and soak in something of the divine from on high.

[29] The mind is perfected by one thing and one thing only, the unshakeable knowledge of what is good and what is not[51]—and there is no other pursuit besides philosophy that inquires into good and evil. Let us take a tour of the individual virtues. Courage is the scorner of terrifying things. It sneers at, challenges, and breaks whatever frightens us and aims to subject our freedom to its control. Well now, can liberal arts give us more courage? Loyalty is the most revered asset in the human heart. No situation, no matter how dire, will compel it to be unfaithful. It cannot be broken by bribes, at any price. "Burn me," it says, "flog me, kill me. I will not speak. No, the more pain you apply to extract my secrets, the deeper I will bury them in my heart." Can liberal arts produce this kind of loyalty? Moderation controls our desires; it loathes and drives away some, others it regulates and reduces to a healthy level, but never does it approach desires for their own sake. Moderation knows that the best measure for our cravings is not how much we want to take, but how much we should take. [30] Kindness toward

---

51. Seneca here refers to the evaluation of what is truly good (virtue, the perfection of reason), what is evil (vice, lack of correct reasoning), and what is neither (called "indifferents," such as money, fame, bodily health, even life).

our fellow man forbids us from being arrogant toward our associates, forbids us from being disagreeable. In everything it says, does, and feels, it presents itself as obliging and ready to help everyone. It looks upon every other person's problems as its own, and it loves its own success for the sole reason that it may help someone in the future. Do liberal studies instill this kind of character? No, no more than it does honesty, temperance and discretion, thrift and frugality, or mercy, which is as sparing of other people's blood as it is of its own and knows that people should not be wasteful of other people's lives.

[31] "So," someone might object, "although you Stoics state that one cannot attain virtue without liberal studies, how can you deny that they contribute positively to virtue?" Simple: you also cannot reach virtue without food, yet food has nothing to do with virtue. Wood doesn't contribute positively to a ship, although you can't have a ship without it. I state it firmly: do not imagine for a moment that something is created through the assistance of that without which it cannot exist.

[32] In fact, this, too, can be said: someone can attain wisdom without liberal studies. Although virtue must be taught, one does not learn it through these pursuits. Why should I suppose that an illiterate person would not become a Wise Man? Wisdom does not reside in letters! Wisdom is a matter of content, not words, and it's certainly possible that one's memory would be better if it did not have an external crutch to rely on. [33] Wisdom is a great and far-reaching possession. It requires empty space. One must learn about matters divine and human, about the past and future, about the transitory and the eternal, and about time itself. Consider just how many questions there are about that last item. Is time something in and of itself? Was there something before time, without time? Did it begin alongside the cosmos, or did it exist before the cosmos—that is, if something else existed, did time also exist?

[34] There are also countless questions just about the mind. Where does it come from? What is it made of? When does it begin to exist? How long does it survive? Does it pass from one being to the next and change habitats, implanted into other forms of living beings continually? Or is it enslaved to a body just once and, once freed, does it drift back into the whole? Is it corporeal or not? What will it do once it has stopped acting through our agency, and how will it use its freedom when it has escaped from this cage? Does it forget its prior existence and only then begin to know itself after it has been separated from the body and retreated to the heavens?

[35] No matter what small aspect of the human and divine realms you choose, you will be worn out by the sheer mass of questions to answer, things to learn. In order to furnish a place in your mind to dwell on such massive questions, all the other pointless rubbish must be cleared out. Virtue will not put up with such narrow confines. A great thing, virtue. It yearns for space to unfurl. Let everything else be purged. Let your heart be open for its arrival.

[36] "But knowledge of many things is satisfying." Fine. But let us retain only what is necessary. We criticize the person who collects unnecessary possessions for their enjoyment and puts on a parade of precious objects in their palatial homes. Should we not also criticize the person who is absorbed in furnishing his mind with an unnecessary array of literature? It is a kind of overindulgence to want to know more than is enough. [37] And don't forget that excessive pursuit of liberal studies turns people into troublesome, wordy, tactless, self-satisfied bores. And don't forget that they are not learning what is necessary because they've learned what is useless.

Didymus the scholar[52] wrote four thousand books. I'd pity him if he only had to *read* that many pointless texts. In these books he researched many questions: from what land Homer hailed, who the real mother of Aeneas was, whether Anacreon was more lustful or drunk, whether Sappho was a whore—the kind of trivia that, if you had learned it, you'd be better off unlearning at once. Go on now and tell me that life isn't long!

[38] But even when you come to Latin literature, I'll show you how much excess foliage ought to be pruned, and how it should be pruned—with an axe! It comes at a great cost of time and great annoyance to other people's ears, this reputation: "What an educated person!" We should be content with this less sophisticated title: "What a good person!"

[39] Is this how it's going to be? Am I to wade through the annals of every nation to investigate who was the first to write a poem? Am I to calculate how much time intervened between Orpheus and Homer, even though I don't have any official records? Am I to examine Aristarchus' notations, by which he denoted which verses were inauthentic, and to wear my life away in the examination of syllables? Am I to linger in the dust of geometry?[53] Have I lost sight of that most beneficial precept, "Be sparing of time"? Are these the things I should know? And what should I not know? [40] Do you remember the scholar Apion, who in the reign of Caligula was all the rage in Greece, always surrounded by flocks of people and adopted by every city in the name of Homer? He used to assert that Homer, after completing both of his masterpieces, the *Odyssey* and *Iliad*, added a prequel to his work that encompassed the entire Trojan War.[54] His proof? He claimed that Homer had deliberately planted two letters in the first verse indicating the total number of his books. [41] This is exactly the sort of thing a person should know—if that person's desire is simply to know a lot of stuff.

Wouldn't you rather want to know how much time you have lost because of bad health, because of public engagements, because of private engagements, because of daily engagements, because of sleep? [42] Count how many years you have left. There's just not enough time for many things.

So far I've been talking about liberal pursuits. Philosophers, too, pursue countless unnecessary activities, many without any real use. They, too, have stooped to examining the divisions of syllables and the peculiar uses of conjunctions and prepositions. They must be jealous of literary scholars and mathematicians. Whatever pointless pursuits they found in those fields they've transferred to their own. The result? They know how to speak correctly, but not how to live correctly.

[43] Listen, and you'll know how much nonsense their excessive ingenuity has created and how hostile it is to the truth:

Protagoras says that one can argue, with equal success, on both sides of every question—even on that very issue, whether all questions can be argued on both sides.

---

52. A 1st-century BC scholar of relentless industry who compiled a vast number of books on numerous subjects—he earned the nickname "Brazen-guts" because of his stamina.

53. Mathematicians and other related professions often drew their computations in the sand or in dust.

54. The *Iliad* recounts only a few weeks of the Trojan War, while the *Odyssey* covers the ten years after the war's conclusion. We have preserved summaries of the other epics (attributed sometimes to Homer, sometimes to other writers) of the so-called "Epic Cycle."

Nausiphanes maintains that, of all things that appear to exist, nothing exists more than it does not exist.

Parmenides holds that, of all things that appear to exist, there is nothing except the whole.

Zeno of Elea eliminated all difficulties from the issue: he says that nothing exists. Pretty much the same thing is held by the Pyrrhonian, Megarian, Eretrian, and Academic schools. They've introduced a fancy new kind of knowledge, one where knowledge is knowing nothing!

Throw all these nonsensical beauties into that useless heap of liberal studies. While teachers of the liberal arts pass on knowledge that won't help me, those philosophers snatch away all hope of acquiring any knowledge. It's better, of course, to know unnecessary facts than to know nothing at all. One set of philosophers provides no light that would guide my eyes to the truth, but the others dig out my eyes and leave me blind. If I believe Protagoras, there is nothing in the world but doubt. If Nausiphanes, this is the only certainty, that nothing is certain. If Parmenides, there is nothing except the whole. If Zeno, there is not even that. What, then, are we? What are those things that surround us, nourish us, and sustain us? I don't know what makes me angrier, those who do not want us to know anything, or those who do not even leave us the option of knowing nothing. Farewell.

## Introduction to *The Ascension of the Pumpkinhead Claudius into Heaven*

After thirteen years in power, the Emperor Claudius died in October AD 54 under suspicious circumstances, and was succeeded by Nero, who would reign until 68. Shortly after Claudius' death, Seneca wrote the following satire, which mocks the emperor's shortcomings and, by extension, the senatorial vote that decreed his deification. Seneca had every right to despise Claudius, who had exiled him to Corsica in 41 on a trumped-up charge of adultery. All of that emperor's faults, both physical and moral, are on satiric display: his limp, his slurred speech, his chronic illnesses, his general lack of awareness, his predilection for gambling, his meddling with the justice system, the wide extension of citizenship rights, his over-reliance on his freedmen, and his capricious executions. The work is, however, not only a condemnation of Claudius as a ridiculous emperor but also an exaltation of the new emperor, Nero, as the great hope for a renewal of good government in Rome—a hope that would soon be crushed.

The work is a unique Latin example of Menippean satire. Named after its most noted practitioner, Menippus of Gadara (early 200s BC), the genre featured a mixture of styles and forms, and an alternation between prose and verse. Seneca's satire fits the template well: alongside proverbs, colloquial speech, and vigorous narrative, we find learned allusions to Homer, Vergil, and other poets, a mixture of Greek and Latin, and frequent puns. A journey to heaven and a meeting of the gods are also found in other examples of the genre.

The exact meaning of the title is debated. It is a pun on the Greek word *apotheosis* ("making into a god") in which the element *-colocynth* ("gourd") replaces *-the* ("god"), but since there is no transmutation of Claudius into a gourd in the work (as the word would imply) and since gourds were synonymous for "blockheads," the title is probably nothing more than a loose pun implying just what is found in the work: an unsuccessful attempt of a failed (blockhead) emperor to rise into heaven.

## The Ascension of the Pumpkinhead Claudius into Heaven

I would like to set down for the record the events that took place in heaven on the 13th of October in that year which ushered in a new era of unprecedented good fortune. My account will not be biased by old grudges or favors. It's the whole truth—I swear. If someone asks me where I got all this from, well, in the first place I don't have to answer if I don't want to. Who's going to force me? I know I can say whatever I want now, ever since the day *he* passed away—you know, the one who proved the proverb true, that one ought to be born either a king or a clown. And if I *do* feel like answering, I'll just say whatever pops into my head. I mean, who in the world has ever demanded that a historian produce sworn testimonials?

Fine. If you insist that I produce my source, go ask the man who saw Drusilla going up to heaven.[55] That same man will say that he also saw Claudius making the journey, as Vergil puts it, limping along behind "with uneven steps." He gets to see everything that goes to heaven, whether he wants to or not. He's the supervisor of the Appian Way, after all. As you well know, that's the way deified Augustus and Tiberius Caesar made their way to join the gods. He'll talk to you if you go alone and ask him. But he won't make any statement at all if there's more than one person present. Remember the time when he swore in front of the Senate that he had seen Drusilla rising into heaven, and all he got for such excellent news was total disbelief? After that, he pledged with binding words that he'd never testify again, even if he saw a man murdered smack in the middle of the Forum. As for me, I'm only reporting what I heard from him with my own ears, plain and simple. I swear. I swear on *his* life.

[2] Now the Sungod had narrowed his orbit and arc,[56]
and the hours of shadowy Sleep were increasing,
as the Moon-goddess stole away hours from day,
and foul Winter devoured the splendor and grace
of fair Autumn's abundance, and vintners were picking
the last grapes of the season to age into Bacchus . . .

Perhaps you'll understand better if I put it this way: it was October, the 13th to be exact. The precise time I really can't tell you—our clocks agree about as often as our

---

55. Livius Geminus, a senator who swore he saw the ascension of Julia Drusilla, the Emperor Caligula's sister, into heaven. She was formally deified by the Senate after her death in AD 38 to flatter the emperor, who was said to have had a long sexual relationship with her (Suetonius, *Life of Caligula* 24.1).

56. The indented portions of this text are poetic interludes.

philosophers do—but it was just after the sixth hour ended.[57] "Oh, come *on*, you hillbilly, that's *so* unsophisticated. Poets aren't content to describe only sunrises and sunsets—they even harass noontime as well. They just can't help it. Are you just going to let such a promising hour pass you by?"

> Now the Sun god had passed through mid-sky with his team
> and, now closer to Night, was inciting his steeds,
> as he guided his torch on a down-slanting course

and Claudius began to hack and wheeze, trying to gasp out his life, but he could not give up his ghost.

[3] Then Mercury, who had always been a big fan of the man's talent,[58] pulled aside Clotho, one of the three Fates, and said, "Cruel, cruel woman, why do you let this pitiful man agonize so? Tortured for so long, will he never find rest? He's been struggling to breathe for sixty-four years, for Hercules' sake! What do you have against him? Or his country? You should let the astrologers be right at some point. They've been trying to bury him every month of every year since he became emperor![59] Then again, it's no wonder that they keep making mistakes and no one can predict when he's going to go. I mean, no one even noticed he'd been born. Go do what must be done. As the poet says,

> Yield him unto death; let a better man rule in his stead.

But Clotho objected, "For Hercules' sake! I was just trying to give him just a teensy bit more time so that he could bestow Roman citizenship onto those dozen or so folks still without it. He was *so* determined to see every Greek, Gaul, Spaniard, and Briton wearing a toga. But since you're resolved to keep some foreigners around to sow a new crop, and since you command it so, it shall be done." She opened up a small chest and pulled out three spindles: the first was Augurinus', the next was Baba's, and the third Claudius'.[60] "These three men," she said, "I will order to meet their deaths in the same year, only a short time apart; I will not send that man of yours to death unaccompanied. It just isn't right for a man who but moments ago saw so many thousands of people following him, so many preceding him, and so many swarming about him, to suddenly be left on his own. But for the time being he'll have to content himself with these companions."

> [4] With these words did she twirl in his hideous spindle,
> and she severed the threads of his dull-witted life.
> But Lachesis,[61] her tresses and temples adorned,
> with Pierian laurel upon her fair brow,

---

57. The seventh hour began at noon. See Appendix "Roman Time Reckoning."

58. Ironic, since Hermes the messenger god was the patron of eloquent speakers, whereas Claudius' stammering was infamous.

59. A rival or enemy of the emperor might have his horoscope cast to predict the day of his death, in order to capitalize on it politically, a punishable offense (Tacitus, *Annals* 12.52.1). To cast a horoscope, however, one needed to know the precise day and hour of birth.

60. The names are alphabetic, perhaps indicative of a nursery rhyme.

61. Another of the Fates.

took shining wool from a snow-white fleece
and began to work it with her magical touch. When spun,
it took on a new, marvelous color. Her sisters
were amazed as the colorless wool turned to gold.
Golden, the Age that spun down on those threads,[62]
and the threads kept on spinning; the Fates, overjoyed,
filled their hands with lovely, miraculous wool.
Of its own did the work hasten on, unceasing,
as the delicate threads spun down on the spindle.
They surpassed the long years of Tithonus and Nestor.[63]

Look, Lord Phoebus[64] is here to entertain them with song,
glad and joyous at the dawn of the new age.
Now he strums his lyre, now he helps with the wool,
enchanting the Fates as they work to his song.
While enrapt with the musical strains of their brother,
their quick hands spun prodigious amounts, and their work,
a spectacular effort, surpassed human years.
"Go, Fates," Phoebus commanded, "take naught from his life,
but allow this good soul to exceed human years.
He resembles me so, in fair beauty and grace
and in his honey-sweet voice. He will bring the weary world
a great age of abundance and reverence for law.
Picture the Morning Star, who puts constellations to flight,
or the Evening Star, rising as the star lights return,
or the Sun, when rosy-cheeked Dawn first dispels
the dark shadows of night and restores the bright day,
when he gazes on earth, a great luminous orb,
and incites his swift team from the gates of the morn.
So bright will our new sun, Caesar, rise,
so resplendent will Nero shine as Rome looks on.
On his countenance blazes a splendor serene,
and beneath flowing tresses his shapely neck gleams."

So Apollo spoke. Now Lachesis, because she was well disposed toward such a good-looking man, was generous and gave Nero many years from her own stockpile. As for Claudius? They ordered everyone "to conduct the poor man from his house in great joy."[65]

And gurgle out his life he did. From that moment he stopped appearing to be alive. He expired while listening to some comic actors—now I hope you'll see that my fear of those types is entirely justified! His last utterance among the living was heard right after

---

62. Representing Nero's life and reign.
63. Famously long-lived men of mythology; the allusion predicts a long life for Nero.
64. Apollo, the young, musically gifted god, favored by the young, musically gifted Nero.
65. A quotation of a line from a lost play of Euripides.

he sent forth a rather loud noise from that channel of the body through which he used to more easily converse: "Good lord, I think I've shit myself!" Whether he did or not, I can't say for sure, but I wouldn't be surprised. He certainly shat on everything else.

[5] No need to report what happened on earth after that. You all know it perfectly well, and there's no risk of forgetting events stamped on the brain because they brought the people joy. No one forgets his own good luck. So listen instead to what happened in heaven. My source—he'll vouch for my account. A messenger brought Jupiter word that someone of good build and very white hair had arrived in heaven. To judge by the constant shaking of his head, the man, he said, was making some kind of threat, and he was dragging his right leg behind him. When asked about his nationality, the man made a reply, but the sound was all confused and his voice was garbled. The messenger said that he couldn't understand the man's language. He wasn't Greek, or Roman, or any other known nationality.

So Jupiter ordered Hercules, who had traveled across the whole of the earth and seemed to be familiar with every nation, to go find out where he was from. When Hercules first set eyes on him, he was visibly shaken; it seemed that he hadn't faced off against every monster yet! When he saw Claudius' strange appearance and weird gait, and heard his voice, which was nothing like any terrestrial animal's, but rough and indistinct like some sea monster's, he thought that he had just met his thirteenth labor. But when he looked closer, it appeared to be something approximating a man. And so Hercules eased toward him and, in the kind of Homeric speech that comes quite easily to those Greekish types, said:

Who are you, and from where? What city and parents are yours?

Claudius was overjoyed to find that there were some scholars in heaven (he hoped that maybe there would be some place for his histories there).[66] So as to indicate that he was Caesar, he, too, employed a Homeric verse:

"From great Troy I was borne by the wind to the land of the Cicones. . . ."

It would have been more accurate if he had chosen the *next* verse from Homer:

". . . where I pillaged their city and destroyed the people."[67]

[6] Claudius would have pulled the wool over Hercules' eyes—you see, Hercules isn't the sharpest knife in the drawer—if the goddess Malaria hadn't been on the scene.[68] She had left her shrine behind to accompany the man; all the other gods had stayed behind in Rome. "Oh, no you don't," she said, "this guy's not from Troy; he's feeding you a line. Let me give you the real story. I've lived with this guy for years. He was

---

66. Hercules addressed Claudius with a Homeric question, a sign of learning. Claudius was well educated in Greek—Suetonius (*Claudius* 41–42) reports that he often recited Homeric verses in court—and wrote several histories on Roman, Etruscan, and Carthaginian affairs. See also Inscriptions no. 59, the text of one of Claudius' speeches.

67. These three Homeric lines are from *Odyssey* 1.170, 9.39, and 9.40.

68. *Febris* ("[Malarial] Fever") had a shrine on the Palatine Hill, near Claudius' residence. Claudius' various physical and psychological peculiarities (chronic ailments, poor hearing, limping, speech defect, absent-mindedness, irascibility) have been attributed by some scholars to chronic malarial fever, and by others to brain damage resulting in cerebral palsy of the spastic variety.

born in Lyons. That's right—you're looking at a native of Munatius' town.[69] I tell you, he was born sixteen miles from Vienne. He's a true son of Gaul. And he did what any blue-blooded Gaul would do: he captured Rome![70] You have my word that he was born in Lyons, where Licinus played king for all those years.[71] You of all people should know, as someone who's set foot in more places than any veteran long-distance mule driver, that there are hundreds of miles between the Xanthus[72] and the Rhône rivers."

At this point you could see the steam coming out of Claudius' ears. He was white hot and vented his rage with as mighty a muttering as he could muster. What he was trying to say, though, no one knew. As it turns out, he was trying to order someone to take Malaria away and execute her. He was using the gesture he commonly used to have people beheaded (only then did his hands stop shaking). But from the way no one paid him even the slightest attention, you would have thought they all were his freedmen.

[7] Then Hercules said, "Listen up, you, and stop your clowning around. You've come to a place where the *mice* gnaw through iron. The truth *now*, or I'll shake this nonsensicalness out of you." To appear even more frightening, he spoke with the bravado of tragedy:

> Reveal at once the place that saw your birth,
> else taste my club and fall upon the earth—
> this club has often smitten savage kings.
> Fool, put aside this incoherent babble!
> What land, what nation reared your bobbing head?
> Speak out at once! Upon my travels west,
> to reach the triple-bodied king's[73] domain,
> that distant land, from which I drove to Greece
> that noble herd, I saw a ridge[74] that looms
> above two streams and faces Phoebus' orb
> at sunrise. Here the mighty Rhône did surge,
> a rushing river; hard by the placid flow
> of the Saône, which seemed in doubt which way
> it would flow, so gentle was its course
> as it glided by with silent majesty.
> Is this the land that fed and raised you? Speak!

---

69. L. Munatius Plancus (87–15 BC), officer of Julius Caesar and later under Marcus Antonius, founded Lyons (Lugdunum), in southern France, in 44 or 43 BC (see Inscriptions no. 3 in this volume).

70. The Gauls sacked Rome in 390 BC.

71. Licinus, a Gallic slave and later freedman of Julius Caesar, was appointed procurator of Lyons by Augustus and held office from 16–15 BC, during which time he unscrupulously amassed great riches.

72. A river in Troy.

73. The mythical monster Geryon, who owned a herd of fabulous cattle in the far west. Hercules led the cattle back by land to Greece.

74. The site of Lugdunum (modern Lyons).

This was all bold and brave enough, but still, like the mad Hercules of tragedy, he seemed to cringe in fear of a bolt out of the . . . *buffoon*. Well, when Claudius saw Hercules' massive mightiness, he stopped messing around. He realized that although he might have been the biggest cheese in Rome, he didn't have nearly the same prestige up here: a rooster is king only of his own dung-castle. As far as we could tell, this was Claudius' response: "It was my hope that you, Hercules, mightiest of the gods, would support my case in court, and if someone asked me to produce a sponsor, I was planning on naming you. You know me best, after all. Think back: wasn't it I who spent entire days trying law-cases in front of *your* temple during the hottest months of the year? You know what awful misery I suffered there, having to listen to those god-awful lawyers day and night.[75] If you had had to face that crap, no matter how brave you may think you are, you would have preferred to clean out Augeas' muck. I unclogged far more shit there than you ever did. Now, because I was planning . . ."

[*several pages missing*][76]

[8] ". . . I'm not surprised that you, Hercules, came barging into the Senate house here. I mean, *nothing's* closed off to you. But come on, tell us what sort of god you want your friend here to be. An Epicurean god? Nope, not possible. They're neither troubled nor cause others trouble. Stoic? In what way is this fellow 'spherical,' to use Varro's words, 'without a head, without foreskin'? Wait, I see it now: there *is* something of a Stoic god in him: he's got neither heart nor head!

"For Hercules' sake, even if he had asked this favor from Saturn—and you know how our Saturnalian[77] emperor here celebrated that god's month all year round—well, he would not have received it even from him! So what makes you think that *Jupiter* would install him as a god? After all, Claudius essentially convicted him of incest when he killed his son-in-law Silanus!"[78]

Hercules broke in, "Why'd he go and do that?"

"Because that most delightful of all girls—you know, his own sister, the one everyone else called Venus—well, Silanus preferred to call her *Juno*."

"I don't get it. His own sister?" Hercules inquired.

---

75. Claudius was famously overzealous in judging legal cases that were brought to him on appeal. He carried on even during holidays and festivals (Suetonius, *Claudius* 14). Official business was often done in the porticoes surrounding temple precincts, such as that of Hercules, who in myth was said to have cleaned out Augeas' stables.

76. There is a considerable gap in the text, during which Claudius apparently won Hercules over; they barged into the palace of Jupiter (here conceived of as the Curia, or Senate house), and Hercules pleaded on behalf of Claudius, who may have also delivered a speech in his own defense. The text resumes with a response from one of the gods.

77. The Saturnalia festival included (among much else; see Glossary) the appointing, by a throw of the dice, of a Saturnalian king, who could order all other members of the party to perform whatever absurdity he wanted.

78. L. Junius Silanus Torquatus was a descendant of Augustus. He was forced, as the result of an imperial court intrigue, to commit suicide, thanks to a trumped-up charge of incest with his sister (AD 48). The joke here is that by condemning Silanus to death for incest Claudius also condemned Jupiter, who was married to his sister Juno.

"Study up, stupid. You can go halfway in Athens and all the way in Alexandria, but in Rome, no way. Strictly taboo.[79] Look, is this really the man who will straighten out the crooked? He doesn't even have the first clue what's going on in his own bedroom.[80] Look, he's already got that vacant look on his face as he 'gazes out at the swath of heaven.' And this guy wants to become a god? Isn't it enough that he's got a temple in Britain?[81] Or that barbarians now worship him as if a god, praying that the Moron might look down graciously upon them?"

[9] Finally it occurred to Jupiter that if members of the general public were within the Senate house, no formal business could be conducted: no making of motions or debate was allowed. "Distinguished Colleagues," Jupiter said, "I had graciously allowed you to question this man, but you—you've turned this Senate house into a shack of squabblers. Must I remind you to follow the procedural rules of the Senate? What must this man think of us, whatever his standing?"

So Claudius was dismissed, and Father Janus was called upon to give his opinion first. He had just been appointed as the afternoon consul for July 1 of the following year. This clever chap could see both in front and behind him, at least as far as his own street goes.[82] From his time living in the Forum he had gained a great gift of gab, so he spoke eloquently and at great length; the stenographer, in fact, couldn't keep up and so I won't relate it all—I wouldn't want to misquote him, you know. He spoke on and on about the majesty of the gods: he didn't want this distinction to be handed out to just any jerk in a toga. "There was once a time," he said, "that becoming a god was a momentous occasion. Now you've gone and made it into a farce. But since I don't want you to think that I'm personally attacking this man instead of simply sticking to the principle of the matter, I move that henceforth not one of those who, as the poet says, 'eat the fruit of the earth' or whom the 'grain-giving earth' nourishes, be made a god. And anyone who is made, said to be, or depicted as a god in contravention of this senatorial decree is to be handed over to torturers and to receive a cane-thrashing alongside the fresh crop of gladiators at the next set of games."

Next Diespiter, Vica Pota's boy,[83] was asked to give his recommendation. He, too, was consul-elect and a small-time wheeler-dealer, eking out a living by selling citizenship rights. Hercules approached Diespiter politely and reminded him of a favor he owed him by touching his earlobe. So Diespiter made a motion with the following words: "Whereas the deified Claudius is related by blood not only to the deified Augustus, but equally to the deified Augusta,[84] his grandmother, whom Claudius himself ordered

---

79. Classical Athenian law permitted marriage between children of the same father, but not of the same mother; the Ptolemaic dynasty of Alexandria in Egypt practiced full brother-sister marriage. Roman law permitted neither. Claudius, by marrying his niece Agrippina the Younger, flouted Roman practice.

80. A jab at his wife Messalina's notorious and numerous sexual affairs.

81. A temple to Claudius existed at Camulodunum (Colchester), the scene of Claudius' military victory in Britain.

82. The god Janus, whose temple was located on the northern edge of the Roman Forum, is represented as looking both forward and backward.

83. Diespiter was a native Italian sky god, Vica Pota an obscure deity, also native Italian.

84. Livia, Augustus' wife.

to be deified; whereas he far outstrips all other mortals in wisdom; and whereas it is in the best interest of the Republic that there be someone up here who can 'devour hot turnips'[85] with Romulus, I move that from this day forward the deified Claudius be made a god, just as all those others before him who had impeccable qualifications, and that these proceedings be appended to the end of Ovid's *Metamorphoses*."[86]

The gods' opinions differed widely, but the vote seemed to be swinging in Claudius' favor. Hercules, who saw that his own irons were in the fire, as they say, was doing all he could to help by making the rounds and saying, "Don't snub me. My reputation's on the line here, too. And if you need a favor in the future, you can count on me. One hand washes the other, you know."

[10] Then it was the deified Augustus' turn to state his opinion. He rose and spoke with the greatest of eloquence. "Distinguished Senators," he said, "you are my witnesses that ever since I was made a god, I have said not a single thing. I've always minded my own business. But now, now I can no longer hide my feelings or contain my grief, grief that has been exacerbated by shame. Was it for this that I forged peace on land and sea? Was it for this that I quelled our civil wars? Was it for this that I stabilized Rome with solid laws and adorned the city with magnificent buildings, so that—I'm sorry, my distinguished colleagues, I just don't have the words. Nothing can adequately express my indignation. So I must fall back on that famous remark of that most skillful speaker, Messala Corvinus: 'I'm ashamed of my power.'

"This man, distinguished colleagues, who might seem to you incapable of bothering a fly, used to kill men as readily as a dog sits on its haunches. But why speak about the deaths of so many distinguished men? There's no time to weep over public massacres when you consider the calamity of my own house. So you'll have to forgive me when I pass over the former to discuss the latter—I know that the knee is closer than the shin, even if my ankle doesn't. That man standing there before your eyes, who hid beneath *my* name for countless years, repaid my favor how? Yes, that's right, by killing my two great-granddaughters named Julia—one by the sword, the other by starvation—not to mention one of my great-great-grandsons, Silanus. Jupiter, you will determine whether he was justified or not in Silanus' case—it's similar to your own case, if you are objective and fair about the matter.

"Now tell us, my 'deified' Claudius: why did you condemn all those men and women to execution before you found out the facts, before you tried them in court? Where is this the way things are done? I'll tell you one thing: it doesn't happen here in heaven. [11] Consider Jupiter, who's been king for untold years—he only broke one god's legs, Vulcan's, whom, as Homer says,

he seized by the foot and hurled down from heaven,

and when he got angry at his wife he only hung her up.[87] But he certainly didn't *kill* anyone. But you did kill your wife, Messalina, and I was her great-great uncle just as much as I was yours. Did I just hear you mumble 'I don't know'? May the gods damn you, man! That you 'don't know' is more reprehensible than having killed her!

---

85. The end of a verse by an unknown poet.

86. Ovid's epic poem about mythical transformations ends with the deification of Julius Caesar and a forecast of that of Augustus.

87. See Homer, *Iliad* 1.586 ff., 15.18 ff.

"Claudius also didn't stop trying to one-up his predecessor, Caligula, even after he died. Caligula killed his own father-in-law; Claudius saw that and raised him a dead son-in-law.[88] Caligula forbade Crassus' son to call himself 'the Great'; Claudius restored his name but took away his head. From this one family he killed not only Crassus, but Magnus and Scribonia, too. We may not be talking about the bloodline of Assaracus[89] here, but they were distinguished people all the same, and Crassus was such a clown that he even could have been king.

"This man . . . do you really want to make him a god? Just look at his body. So deformed! The gods must have been angry on the day it was made. To put it bluntly, if you can get him to say three words in a row quickly, well, you can haul me off as your slave. Who'd worship him as a god? Who'd believe it? If these are the kind of gods you make, no one would believe that *you* were gods. In short, my distinguished colleagues: if I've always acted honorably among you and never responded offensively to any of your opinions, avenge the wrongs he perpetrated against me.

"The following, then, after careful consideration, is my formal motion." He pulled out a tablet and read aloud, "Whereas the deified Claudius killed his father-in-law Appius Silanus; his two sons-in-law, Magnus Pompeius and Lucius Silanus; the father-in-law of his own daughter, Crassus Frugi, a man as similar to himself as two eggs are to each other; Scribonia, his own daughter's mother-in-law; his own wife Messalina; and countless others whose number cannot be calculated, it is my proposal that he be subjected to severe punishment, that he have no recourse to appeal this verdict, that he be deported as soon as possible, and that he be given no more than thirty days to leave heaven and no more than three to leave Olympus."

The gods all moved away from Claudius to Augustus' side—the vote had swung decisively toward Augustus' proposal. Vote passed. No delay. Mercury grabbed Claudius, twisting his neck, and hauled him out of heaven and down to hell, "whence," as the poet says, "naught may return."

[12] As they headed down along the Sacred Way,[90] Mercury asked what the huge crowds of people were for. Was it Claudius' funeral? It was an exquisite ceremony, with attention to every detail. From the pomp and circumstance you could not imagine that anyone *but* a god was being given the last rites. There was such a massive ensemble of trumpeters, horn-players, and every other kind of brass instrument that even Claudius could hear it. And what's more, everyone was bright and cheerful. The Roman people walked around like they were free, free at last.

Well, Agatho and a few shady litigator types were wailing loudly, and they weren't faking their grief.[91] Well-respected jurists were emerging from the shadows, pale, undernourished, and barely alive, as though they had at just this moment come back to life.

---

88. The father-in-law was C. Appius Iunius Silanus, executed by Claudius in AD 42; the son-in-law is either L. Silanus or Cn. Pompeius Magnus (see below).

89. Assaracus was a mythical king Troy of distinguished lineage.

90. A street in the center of Rome.

91. Though by law Roman trial lawyers (*causidici*, "litigators") were not supposed to be paid by their clients, this rule was often ignored. Jurists or legal scholars (*iurisconsulti*) were highly respected under the Republic. But Claudius took to ignoring them and interpreting the law himself, often idiosyncratically (Suetonius, *Claudius* 14).

When one of them saw the litigators wallowing together and lamenting their rotten fortune, he approached them and scolded them: "I always told you that the Saturnalia wouldn't last forever!"

When Claudius saw his own funeral, he realized that he was dead. For they were singing a dirge for him with a chorus *très grand*:

> Pour out your tears and beat your breasts,
> let streets resound with mournful cries:
> a fine and gifted man has fallen!
> His bravery and fortitude
> no other man on earth could match.
> His was the speed and agility
> to overtake swift Parthians,
> rebels along the empire's fringe,
> and rout insurgent Eastern foes,
> to harry Persia with light arms,
> to zing with sure and steady hand
> shrill singing arrows, planting them
> into the painted backs of Medes,
> Medes hurtling in hasty flight—
> a wound so small, but deadly still.[92]
> He forced the Britons, a distant race
> beyond yon seas, beyond our ken,
> and the Brigantes, painted men
> whose bodies bear the stain of blue,
> to bow their heads beneath Rome's yoke.
> Wide Ocean, vanquished, trembled at
> its Roman master and the rule
> imposed beneath its iron axes.[93]
> Weep for the man who ran a trial
> more swiftly than all other men –
> for only one side would he hear,
> and often neither. Now what judge
> will hear our lawsuits all year through?
> Now Minos, lord of Crete and its
> one hundred towns, who renders firm
> judgments among the silent dead,
> will yield his seat to you forthwith.
> Lawyers, you venal race of men,
> lash your breasts with blows of mourning!
> Mourn, all you poetasters, mourn!

---

92. Heavily ironic, because Claudius had done nothing to check the rapid advance of Rome's historic eastern rival, the Parthian empire, based in what is now Iran.

93. Claudius' campaign in Britain in AD 43 was brief and overblown. He had himself proclaimed *imperator* several times, and celebrated a triumph, after spending only sixteen days there. Still, it marked the beginning of the successful Romanization of Britain.

> Mourn, all you gamblers who've amassed
> a mighty fortune throwing dice![94]

[13] Now Claudius was simply delighted with all this praise and wanted to watch longer. But Mercury grabbed him and hauled him off, covering his head so that no one would recognize him. They passed through the Field of Mars and headed down to the underworld between the Tiber and the Covered Road. Claudius' freedman Narcissus had already beaten him there by taking a shortcut in order to greet his patron,[95] and as Claudius approached, that dapper man—he looked like he had just come from the baths—ran up to them and said unctuously, "And what brings gods here to us mortals?"

"No time for niceties," Mercury said, "go and announce that we're on our way." Before he finished speaking, Narcissus sped off. Descent's easy—the whole way runs downhill. So, although Narcissus was all gouty, he arrived in no time at Death's Door, where Cerberus, or as Horace calls him, "the Hundred-Headed Behemoth," was lying in wait. At first Narcissus jumped back a bit at the sight. His pets had always been froufrou little females of the whitish sort, but here was this big, black, shaggy hound, the kind of thing you really, really don't want to meet in a dark place. When Narcissus got himself together, he cried out in a loud voice, "Claudius is on his way!"

Throngs of Claudius' victims began to come forth, applauding and singing like initiates of Isis, "Hooray! We have found him at last!"[96] Among them were the consul-elect C. Silius (dead because of Claudius), the ex-praetor Iuncus (dead because of Claudius), and Sextus Traulus, Marcus Helvius, Trogus, Cotta, Vettius Valens, Fabius—the last six members of the class of Roman *equites* whom Narcissus had ordered to be executed. Right in the middle of this chorus of happy singers was the handsome pantomime-dancer Mnester, who put his head where it didn't belong (if you know what I mean), and lost it because of Messalina.[97]

Word of Claudius' arrival spread as quickly as wildfire. A massive group flocked together. First came all of Claudius' freedmen: Polybius, Myron, Arpocras, Ampheus, Pheronaotus—all of whom Claudius had sent ahead to hell, no doubt so that he would be suitably attended when he arrived. Following these were the two Prefects of the Praetorian Guard: Iustus Catonius and Rufrius Pollio. Then came his trusty advisers Saturninus Lusius, Pedo Pompeius, Lupus, and Celer Asinius—all ex-consuls. Bringing up the rear were his brother's daughter and his sister's, too, his sons-in-law, fathers-in-law, mothers-in-law—damn near every relative he ever had. They all ran up

94. The laws against gambling were often ignored. Claudius did so conspicuously (Suetonius, *Claudius* 5, 33.2).

95. Narcissus, one of Claudius' freedmen, committed suicide shortly after the emperor's death but before his deification. One of the most common complaints against the Julio-Claudian emperors, and Claudius in particular, was the influence wielded by imperial freedmen. By assisting the emperors, these ex-slaves gained substantial power over the careers, property, and even the lives of Roman senators and *equites*.

96. The rites of Isis included a ritual search and discovery of Isis' dead husband Osiris. It was a time of great celebration because it marked renewal and life.

97. A star pantomime dancer, Mnester had sex with Messalina. It was at her insistence, but he was executed nonetheless.

to meet Claudius *en masse*. When he saw the huge crowd, he cried out, "The whole place, full of my friends! How did *you* get down here?" Pedo Pompeius burst out, "What's that you say, you callous son of a bitch? Are you really asking how? Who else sent us here but you, you executioner of all your friends? Off to court we go; I'll show you the judges' benches down *here*."

[14] Pedo led him at once to the tribunal of Aeacus,[98] who heard cases under the Cornelian law concerning murder. He had him arraigned on this indictment: "Executions: senators, 35; *equites*, 321; others, 'as many as there are grains of sand or specks of dust.'" No one wanted to serve in Claudius' defense. At last Publius Petronius, one of his old buddies, a speaker as *un*gifted in speech as Claudius was, stepped forward and demanded a recess. Denied. Pedo presented the prosecution's case amid great shouts. Then the defense was just about to put their case forward, but Aeacus, fairest of the fair, put a stop to it and declared Claudius guilty after only one side was heard, saying: "If you suffer what you have wrought, justice would straightway be done."

It was so silent you could hear a pin drop. Everyone was struck dumb, stunned by the unusual events unfolding before them, and they kept saying that the verdict was unprecedented. Claudius had seen this type of justice many times before, but thought it unfair in *his* case. They discussed for a long time what punishment would be most appropriate. Some said Sisyphus had carried his burden long enough, or that Tantalus would die of thirst if someone did not take his place, or that at some point poor Ixion's wheel would have to put on the brakes. But no one thought it a good idea to give any of the old-timers reprieve from their punishments, else Claudius, too, might hope for something similar down the line. So it was decided that some new punishment had to be found, some futile task devised in which Claudius might continually hope for something but never get it. Aeacus handed down the sentence: he was to play dice using a dice-box with a hole in it. Hardly a moment had passed and already Claudius was chasing after the ever-escaping dice, getting nowhere with his task.

> When the man shook the dice-box, preparing to throw,
> the two dice did escape through a hole down below.
> When he'd gathered the courage to gather and toss
> those slick bones once again, always yearning to play,
> always chasing them down, they deceive him once more.
> The two dice just continually slip from his hands,
> a deceitful device, always crushing his hopes.
> Just so Sisyphus' task: when he's all but arrived
> at the top of the mountain, the load in his arms
> rolls away, down the hill, his hard labor is squandered.

All of a sudden Caligula appeared on the scene and demanded that Claudius be restored to him as his slave. He produced witnesses who testified that they had once seen him beating Claudius to a pulp with whips, canes, and blows with his fists. Judgment was rendered. Aeacus awarded him to Caligula. The latter then just handed him off to his own freedman Menander—to serve as his clerk in judicial matters.

---

98. Aeacus, king of Aegina, became one of the three judges in the underworld after his death.

# SULPICIA

(late 1st century BC, wrote in Latin)

## Introduction

A collection of eighteen short and medium length Latin poems survives, attached in medieval manuscripts to the collected works of the love elegist Albius Tibullus (ca. 55–19 BC). These poems, all in elegiac couplets, seem to come from the circle of literary friends and relations surrounding Tibullus' patron, the prominent statesman and general Messalla (M. Valerius Messalla Corvinus, 64 BC–AD 8). Among them are the six short poems translated here, a rare example of the survival of Latin poetry composed by a woman. The speaker says she is named Sulpicia, daughter of Servius; to her lover she gives the name Cerinthus, a Greek pseudonym of the type normally used by male Latin love poets to camouflage the identity of the beloved. By contrast she is quite forthcoming about herself. In the space of forty lines she informs us that she is young (3.18.3), the daughter of a man named Servius (3.16.4), with property in Etruria (3.14.4), and that a Messalla is her kinsman and, in some manner, guardian (3.14.5–6). This Servius has been identified as a son of Cicero's friend Servius Sulpicius Rufus, who married Messalla's sister Valeria, which would make Sulpicia herself a niece of Messalla. She would therefore count as a member of the highest Roman nobility of the Augustan period.

---

## *Elegies*

**1      A Love That Should Be Talked About** (*Corpus Tibullianum* 3.13)

Love has come (at last!)—such a love that to hide it out of shame
    rather than expose it to someone would bring
more shame upon me. In my poetry I begged Venus to bring him,
    and she did, set him right down in my lap.
Venus has done as she promised: if someone is said not to have
    joys of her own, she can tell of *my* joys.
I use sealed tablets for my messages to him, for fear that someone else
    might read them first—but I'd rather not.
I'm happy in my disobedience. Putting on a false front to avoid
    the rumors is tiresome. People would say we're perfect.      10

## 2    A Rotten Birthday in the Country (3.14)

My birthday is coming, but I hate it. I'll have to spend it in the stupid
    countryside, and without my love Cerinthus.
What is more delicious than being in Rome? A country villa's no place
    for a girl, nor rural Arretium with its freezing streams.
Messala, you're my kin, but please stop. You are too attentive to my needs.
    Your trips all too often come at a very bad time.
When I leave here, abducted, I leave my mind and heart behind,
    all because you won't let me have my way.

## 3    An Unexpected Surprise (3.15)

Have you heard? That dreary trip has been lifted off your girl's mind,
    canceled. Now I can spend my birthday in Rome.
Let's celebrate the day together with all our friends, a day that
    arrives for you as such a delightful surprise.

## 4    A Cheating Lover (3.16)

Thank you for allowing yourself to be completely unconcerned for me.
    This way, I won't suddenly make an awful fool of myself.
Go ahead, think more about that cheap toga-wearing whore,[1] wool-basket
    in tow, than about Sulpicia, the daughter of Servius.
There are people who care about me. And their main cause for worry
    is that I not end up with a worthless man like you.

## 5    A Hard-Hearted Lover (3.17)

Cerinthus, do you care at all for your girl? Any devotion to me,
    now that fever torments and wears out my body?
Ah! I wouldn't want to be cured of this grim affliction
    if I didn't think *you* desired it, too.
But what good does it do me to overcome my malady, if you
    can look upon my sufferings with a cold heart?

## 6    A Lover's Mistake (3.18)

My light, I swear: May I no longer be the object of your fiery love
    (as I seem to have been a few days ago)

---

1. Female prostitutes were the only Roman women who wore the toga, a formal garment otherwise only permitted to male citizens.

if I have ever done *anything* as foolish in my whole foolish youth,
   anything I have regretted half as much,
as when I left you alone last night in a misguided attempt
   to conceal from others my passion for you.

# Valerius Maximus

(1st century AD, wrote in Latin)

## Introduction

Valerius Maximus' background is unknown, but he was attached to a very prominent patron, Sextus Pompeius, a relative of Augustus who was consul in AD 14 when the emperor died, and was close to his successor Tiberius. Valerius accompanied his patron, who was serving as governor of the province of Asia in the mid-20s AD, and around that time began a large collection of anecdotes and sayings of famous Romans, along with similar items from foreign nations (Latin title *Facta et Dicta Memorabilia*, "Memorable Deeds and Sayings"). He dedicated the original ten books to the Emperor Tiberius in the early 30s AD.

The collection is loosely structured by topic. It is not history proper, even by Roman standards for the genre. Rather, it is a more highly styled version of the informal "commonplace books," compilations of excerpts one kept on a certain subject as one read, such as were made by Pliny the Younger and his uncle, and no doubt by many other educated Romans as well (see Pliny, *Letters* 8 and 15 in this volume). Like one of his main sources, Livy, Valerius' main focus is moralistic, with examples of virtues, vices, and cautionary tales, but it also includes sections on religion, political institutions, and much else. Its main practical use would have been to supply historical examples for persuasive use in speeches, and as such it was used and excerpted in late antiquity, and was enormously popular in Europe in the Renaissance. We offer below a modest selection of stories, with a focus on Roman religion. Valerius is prone to errors of detail, and we have pointed those out in the notes whenever possible.

---

## Memorable Deeds and Sayings

### Preface

[To the Emperor Tiberius]

Many of the deeds and sayings from the city of Rome and from foreign nations are well worth recording. Other authors have dealt with these stories at great length, but this makes it impossible to learn about them in a short period of time, so I have decided to make a selection of them from the most famous writers. I have arranged the stories in such a way that readers who want to find historical precedents would be spared the trouble of spending a lot of time on research. I had no desire to include everything.

434

Who could collect the achievements of all time within a modest number of volumes? What person in his right mind would hope that he could record the course of Roman and foreign history, which has been treated by previous writers in an elegant style, and do so either with greater attention to detail or with more striking eloquence?

To sanctify this work, therefore, I call upon you, our emperor, the true savior of our country. Both gods and men are united in their wish that every sea and land should be under your control. With heavenly foresight, you kindly nourish the virtues that I shall speak of, and you severely punish every vice. In the old days public speakers quite rightly began their speeches with a prayer to Jupiter Best and Greatest, and the most outstanding poets started off with a prayer to some god. I am only a minor writer, so I am even more justified in seeking the protection of your favor. Our faith in the other gods derives from popular belief, but our faith in your divinity comes from your living presence and is as sound as our faith in the stars of your father and your grandfather.[1] The extraordinary brightness of those stars has added a glorious brilliance to our religion. The other gods came to us from heaven, but the Caesars are our gift to heaven. And since it is my intention to start off with the worship of the gods, I shall briefly discuss its nature.

## A     General Organization of Roman Religion (1.1)

Our ancestors organized the regular annual festivals by means of the traditional science of the pontiffs; they guaranteed success in public affairs through the observations of the augurs; they interpreted the predictions of Apollo from the books of the seers; and they averted evil portents by the rites of the Etruscans.[2] It has been our ancient custom to resort to religious rites such as prayer when we want to entrust some matter to the gods; a religious vow when we have to request something;[3] a formal thanksgiving when we have to repay the gods; a search for favorable signs, either from animal organs or from lots, when the future has to be ascertained; and sacrifice when we want to perform a solemn rite. We also use sacrifice to avert evil when portents are reported or places are struck by lightning.

Our ancestors were very eager not just to preserve religious observance but even to expand it, so when the state was already very powerful and prosperous, the Senate

---

1. The Emperor Augustus adopted Tiberius as his son, which would make Julius Caesar his grandfather by adoption. Comets had appeared in the sky after the deaths of Caesar and Augustus and were interpreted as signs of their divinity. Caesar was declared a god in 42 BC, and Augustus in AD 14.

2. The pontiffs supervised the national religion and organized the religious calendar; the augurs observed the behavior of birds to determine the future; the books of the seers were the Sibylline Books, and the "rites of the Etruscans" were the rites of the Etruscan diviners, who predicted the will of the gods through the examination of animal entrails. See Glossary for more on pontiffs, augurs, sibyls, and divination.

3. By means of a "religious vow" (*votum*), a Roman would promise some offering to a god or goddess in exchange for some favor. As soon as the favor was granted, he had to present the gift. Such gifts are known as votive offerings. See Inscriptions no. 92 in this volume.

voted to send ten sons from their foremost families to the various peoples of Etruria, so that the young men might learn the Etruscan science of ritual.

Our ancestors had from the very beginning worshiped Ceres in the Greek manner, so in choosing a priestess of Ceres, they brought Calliphana in from Velia,[4] even though that city had not yet obtained the right of Roman citizenship. They wanted the goddess to have a priestess trained in her ancient rituals.

Our ancestors had a very beautiful temple for this goddess in the city, but when, during the Gracchan troubles, they were warned by the Sibylline Books to placate Most Ancient Ceres, they sent the committee of ten to propitiate her at Henna, since they believed that this place was the origin of her cult.[5]

Our generals likewise often went all the way to Pessinus after gaining a victory so as to fulfill their religious vows to the Mother of the Gods.[6]

## B    Religious Procedure (1.3–4, 1.6, 1.8, 1.10)

We must praise the religious respect shown by his twelve fasces, but we must praise even more the obedience of twenty-four fasces in a similar matter.[7] In a letter sent from his province to the college of augurs, Tiberius Gracchus[8] told them that he had been reading books about public sacrifices. These books made him aware that the augural tent had been wrongly set up during the consular elections, which he himself had organized. When the augurs reported this matter to the Senate, the Senate ordered Gaius Figulus to return to Rome from Gaul and Scipio Nasica to return to Rome from Corsica. Both men had to resign their consulships.

(1.4) Similarly, during periods when very different wars were going on, Publius Cloelius Siculus, Marcus Cornelius Cethegus, and Gaius Claudius were ordered, and indeed forced, to resign their priesthoods, because they had carried the animal organs toward the altars of the immortal gods in a careless manner.

(1.6) To these cases we must add the following story. The chief pontiff, Publius Licinius, decided to have a vestal virgin flogged to punish her for being careless in watching over the eternal fire one night.

(1.8) It is not surprising that the gods have constantly watched over us, and have had the kindness to protect and expand our empire, since we seem to pay careful attention to the tiniest details of religious observance. It must not be imagined that our state

---

4. A Greek city in southern Italy.

5. Henna was located in central Sicily; for the Gracchan troubles (in 133 BC), see Appian, *Civil Wars* section A in this volume.

6. In 205 BC the Romans, in the midst of the Hannabalic War, consulted the Sibylline Books, which commanded them to bring back the cult of the Great Mother of the Gods from Pessinus in Asia Minor to Rome. On the Great Mother, see Lucretius, *On the Nature of Things* section C in this volume.

7. The twelve *fasces* (see Glossary) refer to the consul in the previous story (not translated here). The twenty-four *fasces* refer to the two consuls of 162 BC, C. Marcius Figulus and P. Cornelius Scipio Nasica Corculum.

8. Ti. Sempronius Gracchus, consul in 177 BC, father of the tribune Ti. Gracchus (see below, section E).

ever allowed its eyes to wander from the strictest observance of religious ceremonies. After Marcus Marcellus had conquered Clastidium and later Syracuse, he held his fifth consulship and wanted to consecrate a temple to Honor and Courage in fulfillment of religious vows he had made in public.[9] The college of pontiffs forbade this, and ruled that a single temple could not properly be dedicated to two gods. They argued that if some portent occurred in the temple, it would be impossible to distinguish which of the two gods would have to be placated by a sacrifice. They also pointed out that it was not the custom for sacrifices to be offered to two gods, except in the case of some well-established divine pairs. As a result of this ruling by the pontiffs, Marcellus had to set up statues of Honor and Courage in separate temples. The prestige of this very distinguished man did not deter the college of pontiffs, nor did the additional expense incurred deter Marcellus—he followed the proper procedure in his religious observances.

(1.10) The same sentiments were also to be found in the hearts of private citizens. When our city was captured by the Gauls, the flamen of Quirinus and the vestal virgins were carrying sacred objects, sharing the burden among them. They crossed the Wooden Bridge and were beginning to go up the hill that leads to the Janiculum, when they were spotted by Lucius Albanius, who was bringing his wife and children in a wagon. The religion of the state meant more to him than his personal feelings for his family, so he ordered them to get off the wagon. He put the virgins and their sacred objects on the wagon, abandoned his previous journey, and brought them all the way to the town of Caere. The people there welcomed the sacred objects with the greatest veneration. A testimony of our gratitude for their hospitality and kindness survives to this very day: we adopted the term "ceremonies" (_caerimoniae_) for sacred rites at that time, because the people of Caere had faithfully honored our rites when the Republic was shattered, just as they had done when it was flourishing. That dirty farmyard wagon had come just in time to carry our sacred objects, and its glory equals and perhaps surpasses the glory of our most brilliant triumphal chariot.[10]

## C    The Retribution of the Gods (1.14, 1.19)

But in these matters that relate to the maintenance of religious belief, I suspect that Marcus Atilius Regulus[11] surpassed everyone. He had been brilliantly victorious, but had been reduced to the wretched status of prisoner of war by the treacherous tactics of Hasdrubal and the Spartan commander Xanthippus. Regulus was sent as a messenger to the Roman Senate and People to ask that several young Carthaginians be released in exchange for him, just one elderly man. Instead, he advised the Romans against the exchange and went back to Carthage, though he was quite aware that he was returning to a cruel people who were understandably antagonistic to him. He did so because he had sworn to the Carthaginians that he would go back to them if their prisoners of

---

9. M. Claudius Marcellus had conquered Clastidium during his first consulship in 222 BC, and Syracuse when he was governor of Sicily in 211 BC. He held his fifth consulship in 208 BC.

10. The Gauls captured Rome in 390 BC. The seaport of Caere in Etruria had always been friendly to Rome.

11. M. Atilius Regulus was tortured to death in 255 BC during the First Punic War.

war were not released. Certainly, the immortal gods could have curtailed the ferocious savagery of the Carthaginians, but the gods allowed them to behave in their usual manner so that the glory of Atilius would be all the more conspicuous. In the Third Punic War the gods would exact a just revenge for the cruel torture of this most religious soul by wiping out their city.

(1.19) Apollo's son, Aesculapius,[12] was just as effective in avenging himself when his cult was insulted. Turullius, Antony's prefect, cut down a large part of a sacred grove belonging to his temple in order to build ships for Antony. While Turullius was performing this wicked task, Antony's forces were utterly defeated.[13] Augustus commanded that Turullius be put to death, and the god revealed his divine powers by having him dragged into the very place he had desecrated. The god made sure that Augustus' soldiers killed him there rather than anywhere else. By his death, Turullius paid the penalty for those trees he had already cut down and guaranteed that the trees still standing would be protected from such a violation. The god thereby increased the extraordinary devotion that his worshipers had always felt for him.

### D    Foreign Superstitions (3.3)

Story as recorded by Julius Paris:[14] During the consulship of M. Popillius Laenas and Cn. Calpurnius (139 BC), the praetor for foreigners, Cn. Cornelius Hispanus, issued an edict ordering the Chaldaeans to leave the city and Italy within ten days. The praetor felt that they deceived frivolous and silly people with their dishonest interpretation of the stars, and cultivated a money-making air of obscurity with their lies. The Jews had tried to corrupt Roman values with their cult of Jupiter Sabazius, so the praetor forced them to go back to their home.

### E    The Importance of the Auspices[15] (4.2, 4.3, 4.6)

Story as recorded by Nepotianus: When Tiberius Gracchus was going up for election as tribune, he consulted the sacred chickens at his home, and they opposed his going to the Campus Martius. When he went on obstinately, he soon knocked his foot outside the door so badly that he broke a joint. Then three crows flew in his face with ill-omened caws, started fighting among themselves, and in doing so knocked a tile down before his feet. When he consulted the gods on the Capitol he received similar auspices. He had behaved badly as a tribune, so he was killed by Scipio Nasica: first he was struck with a piece of a bench, then he was killed with a wooden club. The plebeian aedile, Lucretius, ordered that his body, and the bodies of those who were killed with him, be left unburied and thrown into the Tiber.[16]

---

12. Aesculapius was the god of medicine.

13. Antonius lost to Octavian (later Augustus) at the battle of Actium in 31 BC.

14. This and the next three stories are not found in the manuscripts of Valerius Maximus, but come from two later epitomes.

15. See Glossary, auspices.

16. Compare Appian's account of Gracchus' death (133 BC) in *Civil Wars* section B in this volume.

(4.3) Story as recorded by Nepotianus: During the First Punic War, Publius Claudius, a headstrong man, consulted the sacred chickens. When someone said that the chickens were not eating, which was a bad omen, he replied, "Let them drink!" and ordered that they be thrown into the sea. Shortly after that, he lost his fleet off the Aegates Islands. This was a great disaster for our Republic and for Claudius himself.[17]

(4.6) Story as recorded by Nepotianus: Our own Cicero, after he had been put on the death list, was hiding in the region of Caieta, and Antony was hunting him down. A crow knocked the iron pointer that shows the hours so hard with his beak that he broke it off; then the crow grabbed Cicero's toga and pulled at it. At that very moment, his assassins rushed toward him.[18]

## F    Omens (Chance Utterances) (5.1, 5.3, 5.7)

The observation of omens has some connection with religion since people believe that these things do not happen by chance but are caused by divine providence.

Omens had an important effect when the city had been devastated by the Gauls.[19] The Conscript Fathers were deliberating whether they should move to Veii or rebuild our city walls. At that moment, some cohorts were returning from guard duty, and their centurion happened to shout in the assembly place, "Standard-bearer, set up the standard; this is the best place for us to stay." When it heard these words, the Senate declared that it accepted the omen, and it removed all traces of its plan to move to Veii.[20] These few words determined their choice of a home for what would eventually be the greatest of empires! I think the gods must have felt it was not right that the Roman nation, which had begun with the most favorable auspices, should change its name and turn into the city of Veii; or that the glory of their famous victory should be granted to the ruined city recently defeated by them.

(5.3) And what of the memorable omen that came to the Consul Lucius Paullus! It fell to him by lot to wage war against King Perseus.[21] He went back home from the Senate house and kissed his little daughter Tertia, who was a very small girl at that time. He noticed that she was sad, and he asked her why she had that face on her. She answered that Persa was dead. A puppy that the girl adored had died, and its name was indeed Persa. Paullus seized the omen and from that chance statement he acquired almost certain hope of a very glorious triumph.[22]

(5.7) Marcus Brutus, after carrying out the assassination,[23] was warned by an omen

---

17. P. Claudius Pulcher suffered a disastrous defeat at Drepanum (modern Trapani on the west coast of Sicily) while consul in 249 BC.

18. Cicero was murdered by order of Antonius in 43 BC when the triumvirs massacred their political opponents.

19. The Gauls captured Rome in 390 BC.

20. A flourishing southern Etruscan town taken by Rome in 396 BC.

21. The Senate would cast lots to decide which consul would command the army. The lots supposedly revealed the will of the gods.

22. L. Aemilius Paullus defeated King Perseus at Pydna in 168 BC and celebrated a triumph over him in 167 BC. See the excerpt of Plutarch's *Life of Paullus* in this volume.

23. Of Julius Caesar in 44 BC.

of the predestined end he richly deserved. After that evil deed he was celebrating his birthday, and when he wanted to recite some Greek poetry, his mind led him to recite this particular Homeric line:

But dreadful fate and the son of Leto killed me.

At the battle of Philippi, that very god, chosen by Augustus and Antony as their watchword, turned his weapons against Brutus.[24]

## G    Prodigies (Unnatural Events) (6.1, 6.9, 6.11–13)

When Servius Tullius[25] was just a little boy, the people in his household saw with their very own eyes a flame flickering around his head as he was sleeping. Tanaquil, the wife of king Ancus Marcius, was amazed at this prodigy, and although Servius was the son of a slave woman, Tanaquil brought him up as her own son and raised him to the glory of royal power.[26]

(6.9) The fact that they were both consuls in the same year, made similar mistakes, and died in the same way, brings me from Tiberius Gracchus to a story about Marcellus.[27] He was inflamed with pride because he had captured Syracuse and had been the first to force Hannibal to flee (in front of the walls of Nola).[28] He worked very hard to destroy the Carthaginian army in Italy or to expel it from Italy, and by means of a solemn sacrifice, he tried to ascertain the will of the gods. The first victim that fell before the brazier was found to have no lobe on its liver; the next had a double lobe on its liver. After inspecting them, the diviner reported with a sad face that he did not like the look of these organs since the propitious one only appeared after the defective one. Although he was warned in this way not to attempt anything risky, Marcus Marcellus dared to go out on the following night with a few men to reconnoiter. He was surrounded by a large number of enemy soldiers in Bruttium, and the grief caused by his death was as great as the loss inflicted on his country.[29]

(6.11) At this point we cannot get away with passing over in silence the case of Marcus Crassus, which must be counted among the most serious defeats of the Roman Empire.[30] Before this great disaster he was bombarded by a large number of very obvious portents. When he was about to lead his army out of Carrhae against the Parthians,

---

24. M. Junius Brutus (tyrannicide, 44 BC) was defeated at Philippi by Augustus and Antonius in 42 BC. Brutus committed suicide after the battle. Apollo, the son of Leto, was the patron god of the triumvirs, who chose the god's name as their watchword.

25. The sixth king of Rome (578–535 BC). See Livy ch. 39 in this volume.

26. Tanaquil was actually the wife of the fifth king, Tarquin the Elder (616–579 BC), not of the fourth king, Ancus Marcius (640–617 BC).

27. Gracchus and M. Claudius Marcellus were consuls together in 215 BC. The story of Tiberius Gracchus is not included here.

28. Marcellus captured Syracuse in 212 BC and drove the Carthaginians away from Nola in 216 BC, thus raising morale after the devastating defeat at Cannae earlier that year.

29. In 208 BC in his fifth consulship.

30. M. Licinius Crassus Dives, the triumvir, launched a disastrous campaign against the Parthian empire in 53 BC.

he was given a black cloak, although it is customary to give a white or purple cloak to those going off to battle. The soldiers gathered sadly and silently at his headquarters, though they should have been running and shouting eagerly, in accordance with the old custom. One of the eagle-standards could hardly be pulled up by the senior centurion; the other was extracted with great difficulty, and then as it was being carried it turned of its own accord in the opposite direction. These prodigies were considerable but that defeat was even more so: all those beautiful legions were destroyed, all the standards were captured by the enemy, and the great glory of the Roman army was trampled underfoot by the cavalry of the barbarians; the father's face was spattered with the blood of his son, who was a young man of excellent character; among the corpses piled up in random heaps lay the body of the general, left there to be torn apart by birds and beasts. I should have liked to speak more calmly, but what I have recorded is the truth. This is how the gods flare up when their warnings have been ignored; this is how human plans are reproved when they exalt themselves over the plans of the gods.

(6.12) Pompey had also been warned abundantly by almighty Jupiter not to go ahead and face the ultimate risk of a war with Caesar.[31] When he marched out from Dyrrachium, Jupiter threw thunderbolts against his army, swarms of bees concealed his standards, a sudden sadness afflicted the spirits of his soldiers, the entire army panicked at night, and sacrificial victims fled from the very altars. But the invincible laws of destiny did not allow his mind to judge those prodigies correctly, although in general he was far removed from any folly. He made light of them, and thus in the space of one day he lost his great prestige, his wealth, which was greater than that of the highest ranking private person, and all those honors that starting as a young man he had accumulated to the envy of others.

It is widely known that on that day statues of their own accord turned their backs in the temples of the gods; war cries and the clanging of weapons were heard in Antioch and Ptolemais, and the sound was loud enough to make everybody run to the city walls; the sacred drums sounded out from the inner sanctuaries of the temples in Pergamum; a green palm tree shot up to its full height from the cracks of the pavement under Caesar's statue in the temple of Victory at Tralles. It is clear from these things that the power of the gods favored the glory of Caesar and wanted to end the errors of Pompey.

(6.13) In veneration of your altars and your most holy temples, o divine Caesar, I pray that your spirit will be propitious and favorable, and that your caring protection will allow the misfortunes of these great men to disappear from view behind the precedent set by your own misfortunes. For we have all heard of that day when you sat on a golden throne, wrapped in a purple robe, because you did not want people to think you were rejecting this honor that the Senate had created and was bestowing upon you with so much enthusiasm. Before you presented yourself to the view of the eager and expectant citizens, you devoted some time to that supernatural world you were soon to join. After sacrificing a choice bull, you did not find a heart among its organs, and Spurinna the diviner replied that this sign concerned your life and plans, since both of these were contained in the heart. Then suddenly, those men burst forth to assassinate you, but although they wanted to remove you from among the living, they actually added you to the company of the gods.

---

31. Pompey led the armies of the Republic against Caesar in 48 BC, losing at Pharsalus, Greece.

## H    Dreams (7.2, 7.3, 7.5)

The mind of Augustus was naturally quick and subtle in judging every situation, but he paid particular attention to the dream of Artorius because of what had happened recently in his own family. He heard how Calpurnia, the wife of his father, the divine Caesar, had seen a vision in her sleep during the last night that he had spent on this earth.[32] She had seen him lying in her bosom, covered with wounds, and she was really terrified by this frightful dream. She begged him continually to keep away from the Senate house on the following day. But he did not want people to think that he would base his actions on a woman's dream, so he went off to hold that Senate meeting during which those murderers laid their violent hands on him.

It is not right to compare a father and a son in any matter, especially when they have both attained the rank of gods, but Caesar had already won the path to heaven by his achievements, whereas Augustus still had a long series of good deeds to perform on this earth. The gods wanted Caesar simply to know about the transformation he would soon undergo, but they wanted Augustus to delay his transformation into that higher status; in this way, the heavens would have a new glory in Caesar and the promise of another in Augustus.

(7.3) Here is another dream that was quite amazing and had a glorious outcome. On the same night, the two consuls, P. Decius and T. Manlius Torquatus (340 BC), had this dream during the Latin War, which was a serious and dangerous war.[33] They were in their camp not far from the foot of Mount Vesuvius when a vision appeared to each of them in his sleep. It predicted that one side had to yield its commander to the gods of the Underworld and to Mother Earth, whereas the other side had to yield its army to them. If the leader of one side dedicated the enemy forces and also himself to those gods his side would win.[34] On the following day, the consuls tried to appease the gods by sacrifice to see whether the prediction could be evaded, but they promised to obey it if it proved to be a genuine warning from the gods. The organs of the sacrificial victims confirmed the dream. The consuls arranged it between themselves that if one wing of the army began to experience difficulties, its commander would save our country from its fate by sacrificing his own life. Neither commander shrank back from this arrangement, but fate demanded the life of Decius.

(7.5) We should not cover up the following story in silence either. Cicero was expelled from the city through the schemes of his enemies.[35] He was staying at a country house in the plain of Atina,[36] and when his mind was deep in sleep, he dreamt that he was wandering through a deserted region that had no roads. Marius came up to him dressed in the outfit of a consul and asked him why he was going around aimlessly with such a sad face. When Marius heard of the misfortune that was afflicting Cicero, he

---

32. On the night before Caesar's death on March 15, 44 BC; see G (6.13) above.

33. Against the peoples of Latium and Campania; the Romans claimed victory in 338 BC.

34. This ritual dedication of oneself as a sacrifice to the gods of the earth and the underworld was called a *devotio*.

35. P. Clodius Pulcher (aedile 56 BC) engineered Cicero's exile in 58 BC. See Cicero, *Letters* 6–9 in this volume.

36. Atina was in Lucania (southern Italy). Cicero stayed there before going into exile in Macedonia.

took Cicero's right hand, presented him to his nearest lictor, and had the lictor escort Cicero to the monument built by Marius himself, explaining that Cicero would find hopes of a happier fortune there. And that is how things turned out, for it was in the temple of Jupiter built by Marius that the Senate decree allowing Cicero to return was passed.[37]

# I    Miracles (8.1–3)

The Roman dictator, Aulus Postumius, and the Tusculan leader, Mamilius Octavius, were fighting fiercely at Lake Regillus, and for a long time neither army was retreating.[38] Then Castor and Pollux appeared as champions of the Roman side and completely routed the enemy forces.

A similar thing happened in the Macedonian War.[39] Publius Vatinius, a citizen of Reate, was going to Rome at night, and he thought he saw two very handsome young men come toward him riding on white horses. They announced that on the previous day, King Perseus had been captured by Paullus. He revealed this to the Senate and was thrown into jail for insulting the majesty and dignity of the Senate with such a silly story. But a letter from Paullus revealed that Perseus had indeed been captured on that day, so Vatinius was released from prison, and on top of that he was rewarded with a plot of land and exempted from military service.

There was yet another time when people realized that Castor and Pollux had been watching out for the empire of the Roman people. They were seen washing off sweat from themselves and from their horses at the pool of Juturna, and their temple near this stream was unlocked and opened, by no human hand.[40]

(8.2) But let us continue with other gods who also favored this city with their divine power. Our citizens had been devastated by a plague for three years in a row, and we saw that neither divine mercy nor human devices would put an end to this great and lasting misfortune. But by carefully inspecting the Sibylline Books, the priests discovered that we could not recover our usual health unless Aesculapius were brought here from Epidaurus.[41] Since this was the only remedy that was destined to help us, we sent envoys there, confident that our request would be granted since our prestige was already very great throughout the world.

We were not deceived in our expectation. We were offered assistance as eagerly as we had requested it. The Epidaurians immediately led the Roman envoys to the temple of Aesculapius, which is five miles outside their city, and they very kindly invited the envoys to feel free to take anything from the temple that they thought might be

---

37. Cicero was recalled in 57 BC after a year of exile. The Senate often met in temples, but Marius built the temple of Courage, not the temple of Jupiter.

38. The Romans defeated the Latins at the battle of Lake Regillus in 499 or 496 BC.

39. The Romans fought Perseus in the Third Macedonian War from 172 to 167 BC; see Plutarch, *Life of Paullus* in this volume.

40. The temple of Castor and Pollux and the pool of Juturna are located in the Roman Forum.

41. The chief temple of Aesculapius (the most prominent god of healing in the Greco-Roman world) was in Epidaurus at southern Greece. The cult of Aesculapius was brought to Rome in 292 BC.

beneficial to our country. The god himself went along with their ready kindness, and he gave his divine approval to the words of these mortals, as we can see from what ensued.

There is a snake that the Epidaurians rarely saw, but whenever they did, it always brought some great blessing upon them and they worshiped it as a form of Aesculapius. It started to slide through the most crowded parts of the city with kindly eyes and in a gentle manner, and for three days everyone saw it and devoutly admired it. Then the snake clearly revealed its eager longing for a more glorious home, because it made its way to the Roman trireme. The sailors were terrified at this unusual sight, but the snake continued on its way up to the place where the tent of the envoy, Quintus Ogulnius, was located, and there it very calmly curled itself up into several coils. At this, the envoys felt they had achieved what they had hoped for, so they expressed their gratitude, learned about the cult of the snake from local experts, and joyfully set sail.

After a safe voyage, they landed at Antium.[42] The snake, which had stayed still on the ship up until now, slid forward to the entrance of the temple of Aesculapius, and curled itself around a very tall palm tree that stood over a myrtle bush with lots of spreading branches. For three days it was given its customary food, and the envoys were very worried that it might refuse to go back onto the ship. But after enjoying the hospitality of the temple at Antium, the snake allowed itself to be brought to our city. When the envoys landed on the banks of the Tiber, the snake swam across to the island where the temple was dedicated.[43] As soon as it arrived, it put an end to the crisis that it had been brought here to remedy.

(8.3) Juno was equally glad to move to our city. When Furius Camillus captured the city of Veii, he ordered some soldiers under his command to remove the statue of Juno Moneta, which was venerated with extraordinary devotion in that place, and bring it to our city.[44] As the soldiers were trying to remove the statue from its temple, one of them jokingly asked the goddess whether she wanted to go to Rome, and she replied that she did. When they heard these words the soldiers were astounded and put an end to their joking. They now believed that they were not just carrying a statue but bringing the goddess Juno herself from heaven. They joyfully placed her in that part of the Aventine hill where we can still see her temple today.

---

42. Antium was south of Rome on the coast of Latium.

43. The temple of Aesculapius was located on Tiber Island in Rome.

44. The dictator Camillus captured Veii in 396 BC and brought this statue of Juno Regina (not Juno Moneta) to Rome; the Romans built a temple to her on the Aventine Hill in 392 BC.

# VERGIL

(70–19 BC, wrote in Latin)

## Introduction

P. Vergilius Maro was born in 70 BC in Mantua in northern Italy and died in 19 BC in Brundisium. He had personal contacts with the Emperor Augustus through Augustus' close advisor Maecenas; the poet Horace was also a close friend (see Horace, *Satires* 1.5 in this volume). Vergil was the author of three highly influential works, a collection of ten pastoral poems called *Eclogues*, four books on farming entitled *Georgics*, and the *Aeneid*, an epic of twelve books on the journey of Aeneas and his companions from Troy to a new settlement in Italy, which is generally regarded as the greatest literary masterpiece in Latin. Two of his earlier poems are translated here, the first and fourth *Eclogues*.

Pastoral is a Greek genre of poetry, best represented in the extant poems of Theocritus (flourished in the early 3rd century BC), in which shepherds sing to each other in an idyllic countryside, trading and capping each other's verses with improbable sophistication. Vergil took up the form in Latin but altered in *Eclogue* 1 the idyllic quality of the setting, putting his shepherds in the middle of the turmoil of the Roman civil wars, with its widespread land confiscations. In 42 BC, after the battle of Philippi, the members of the Second Triumvirate (Antonius, Octavian, and Lepidus) confiscated for distribution to their veterans many estates in Cisalpine Gaul—including, according to some sources, that of Vergil's family. *Eclogue* 1 describes the unhappy state of those who were deprived of their possessions, in the person of the shepherd Meliboeus. The recently freed slave shepherd Tityrus represents one who was so fortunate as to have his farm restored to him by the favor of Octavian (the "god" and "young man" mentioned in lines 6 and 42). Tityrus employs his pastoral eloquence to praise Octavian as a deity for his munificence. Traditionally Tityrus has been read as a stand-in for Vergil himself (though the shepherd is old, and Vergil was about thirty at the time the poem is set), and the poem as an expression of gratitude to Octavian. But by capturing the woeful consequences of civil war for the people of rural Italy, Vergil gave the poem a resonance beyond his own personal situation.

*Eclogue* 4 is also highly unorthodox as pastoral. In it Vergil adopts a lofty, prophetic, and somewhat riddling style to announce the birth of a prominent person's son, a son who will usher in a new Golden Age of peace and contentment. Here again the trauma of the civil wars lies in the background. Taking up the motif of the succession of the ages, with its long roots in Greek literature and mythology, Vergil optimistically imagines that a new Golden Age will replace the current Age of Iron. The identities of this new baby and his father, however, are unclear. The poem itself is dedicated to C. Asinius Pollio, whose consulship in 40 BC is mentioned as marking the beginning of the new age. Pollio's brokering of a peace agreement between the feuding triumvirs Antony and Octavian may account for some of the optimism, though the truce did not last long. Because of the poem's prophetic nature, some Christians in late antiquity put forward the interpretation that the child was Jesus Christ, hence the common name that has attached itself to the poem, the "Messianic Eclogue."

---

## Eclogues

### 1    A God Gave Us These Carefree Days

*Meliboeus*
>Tityrus! You lie there beneath the shelter of a sprawling beech tree,
>piping a woodland tune on a slender flute, thinking of music.
>We must abandon our home and cherished farmlands.
>We are exiled from our homeland! But you, Tityrus, laze about
>in the shade, making the woods sing "winsome Amaryllis."

*Tityrus*
>Good Meliboeus, a *god* gave us these carefree days.
>Yes, that man will always be a god to us; the blood of
>a tender sacrificial lamb from our folds will often stain
>his altar. It's thanks to him my cows roam free
>and I play whatever songs I want on a woodland flute.                    10

*Meliboeus*
>I don't begrudge you, just surprised. Throughout the countryside
>there is nothing but upheaval. Look at me, driving these goats
>onward, distraught. Tityrus, this one here can barely keep up.
>Poor girl, she just gave birth here amidst the dense shrubs to twins—
>the flock's great hope!—but birthed on hard rock they died.
>The signs of this disaster were there, I remember—oaks
>touched by lightning—if only my mind had understood!
>No matter. Tell us, Tityrus: just who *is* that god of yours?

*Tityrus*
>Do you know the city they call Rome, Meliboeus?
>Fool that I was, I thought it like the city here,                       20
>where we shepherds bring our baby lambs to market.
>I've seen puppies turn into dogs, and baby goats grow to look
>like their mothers, and that's how I compared small and great.
>But how wrong I was! That city towers over all the others
>as lofty cypresses soar over pliant rose shrubs.

*Meliboeus*
> Well, what was so important that you had to visit Rome?

*Tityrus*
> Freedom! I was lazy and slow to earn it,[1] but it smiled on me
> now that my beard shows grey when it's trimmed.
> Yes, freedom arrived, though it took its time, and came
> only after Galatea left me and Amaryllis took her place.          30
> I confess, so long as Galatea had me in her grips,
> I had no hope of freedom or concern for money.
> Though I took to town many a fat sacrificial lamb,
> and pressed cheese for those cheapskate city folk,
> I never came back home with a hand full of coins.

*Meliboeus*
> Amaryillis,[2] I was wondering why you were calling on the gods
> in sadness, why you let your fruit hang on the trees
> unpicked. Your Tityrus was away! Tityrus, these very pines,
> these springs, these woods kept crying out to you.[3]

*Tityrus*
> What else could I do? I could not slough off my slavery           40
> or find such helpful gods anywhere but Rome.
> It was there, Meliboeus, that I met that young man. I will
> honor him twelve days every year with the smoke of sacrifice.
> For he was the first to respond to my petition:
> "Slaves, pasture your cows as before, and rear your bulls."

*Meliboeus*
> How lucky you are, old man. You will keep your land.
> Not much, but enough for you, though it's all
> bare rocks or reedy, swampy marsh instead of pasture.
> But your ewes won't fall ill from unfamiliar fodder,
> and no foreign neighbor's flock will give them disease.           50
> How lucky you are, old man. You will enjoy the cool shade
> here, among familiar streams and sacred springs.
> Here you will often drift to sleep, lulled by the gentle buzz
> of Sicilian bees as they feed on the flowers of willows
> along the neighbor's hedges, as you've always done.
> You'll hear the songs of the woodsmen echoing

---

1. Slaves saved their money (*peculium*) to buy their freedom, and the thriftier and more industrious they were the sooner they could get it. Tityrus, a farm-slave, having saved enough, goes up to buy his freedom from his owner, and the owner of the estate, who is living at Rome.

2. This is Tityrus' new, thriftier girlfriend, conceived of as present alongside Tityrus.

3. That is, Amaryllis' laments could be heard throughout the countryside.

in the hills. You'll hear your pets, the cooing wood-pigeons,
and the gentle moan of the turtle doves up in the elms.

*Tityrus*

Meliboeus, fleet-footed stags will pasture in the sky,
disappearing seas will leave fish bare on the sands,                    60
the Parthians and Germans will switch their homes
and drink from each other's rivers, the Arar and Tigris,
before the countenance of that god ever slips from my mind.

*Meliboeus*

Well, *we* will all be leaving here. Some will go to parched Libya,
others to Scythia and the surging river Oaxes,
others to Britain, cut off from the rest of the world.[4]
Will I ever again see these lands where I was born,
my humble cabin, roofed in sod? Will I ever, on some distant day,
gaze upon the marvelous wheat-fields of my little kingdom?
No, some wicked soldier will possess these fields that *I* tended.      70
Some foreigner will reap these crops. Look at the misery
our civil wars have produced—I planted these fields for *them*?
Sure, Meliboeus, graft your pears and arrange your vines.
Go on now, my goats. Move along, you once thriving flock.
I used to lie in a mossy cave and watch from afar
as you pastured on bramble-covered crags. No more.
No more will I sing songs. No more will I watch over you,
my goats, as you nibble on blooming clover or bitter willow.

*Tityrus*

Still, you could rest here this one night, with me,
upon a soft pallet of leaves. I have ripe fruit,                       80
soft chestnuts, and a great store of cheese. Look,
see how the smoke rises from distant villa rooftops?
The lofty mountains are casting longer shadows upon the earth.

## 4    This Glorious New Era Will Begin

Sicilian Muses, we must now sing of more lofty subjects!
Not everyone is fond of groves and lowly tamarisks.
If we are to sing of trees, let them be worthy of a consul![5]

---

4. Meliboeus rather melodramatically imagines himself wandering to the ends of the earth.

5. The lofty, prophetic tone of this poem was not typical of the pastoral genre. The consul honored here is C. Asinius Pollio (see introduction and below, note 9).

The last age of the Cumaean prophecy is upon us,
and the great progression of ages is being born anew.[6]
Soon the Virgin will return, soon the reign of Saturn,
soon a new line will be sent down from lofty heaven.[7]
Chaste Lucina,[8] look kindly upon the birth of this child;
with him the Age of Iron will cease and the Age of Gold
will rise over all the earth. May your brother Apollo reign!    10

This glorious new era will begin with you as consul, Pollio,[9]
yes, with you: the great months will begin their march.
Under your guidance, all remaining traces of our sins
will be erased, freeing the world of its endless fear.
That child will receive a life of the gods. He will see
heroes mixed with gods, and will be seen by them. His father
pacified the globe, and he will rule it with his father's virtues.

Tiny babe, for you the earth will provide your first gifts,
untilled, pouring forth creeping ivy, spikenard,
and lily-beans, together with laughing acanthus.    20
She-goats will return home with udders taut with milk.
Livestock will feel no fear of mighty lions.
As you lie upon the earth she will send up fair flowers,
your cradle. Serpents will perish. So, too, plants veiling
their poisons. Assyrian balsam will grow aplenty.

As soon as you can read the praises of heroes and the deeds
of your father, and can start learning the meaning of virtue,
the fields will begin to grow tawny with soft grains,
the ruddy grape will hang on vines untended,
and hard oaks will weep dew-like honey.    30
Even so, a few traces of our old wicked ways will return,
driving us to put ships on Thetis' sea, raise walls
around our cities, and cleave furrows into the earth.
In that age another Tiphys will emerge, another Argo
to convey chosen heroes. There will be a second war,
and again a great Achilles will be sent to Troy.

Then, when you have become a man and strong,
seafarers will retire from the sea, and no ship of pine

---

6. Presumably from the Sibylline Books. See Glossary.

7. All of these are markers of the Golden Age. The Virgin is Dike ("Justice"), who left earth when morals had degenerated.

8. Goddess of childbirth, identified here with Diana, sister of Apollo.

9. C. Asinius Pollio (76 BC–AD 4) was consul in 40 BC, an influential statesman with literary interests and author of a history of the civil wars.

will traffic its wares. Every country will yield everything.
No plowshare will sting the soil, no pruning hook the vine.                    40
Even the hardy plowman will unyoke his bulls.
There will be no need to teach wool how to take on artificial colors.
No, as the ram pastures in the meadows his fleece
will turn now sweet blushing crimson, now saffron yellow,
and lambs will be cloaked in vermillion as they graze.
"Run on, you blessed ages," the Fates said to their spindles,
in harmony with the unyielding will of destiny.[10]

Beloved offspring of the gods, Jupiter's great adjutant,
the time draws near—enter upon your high honors!
Behold, the world with its curved mass assents to your coming;            50
so, too, the lands, the sweeping seas, and heaven's vast dome.
Behold, everything is overjoyed at the coming age!

How I hope that my life lingers long into that age,
and that I have enough breath to sing your deeds:
neither Thracian Orpheus nor Linus could rival my songs,
though one has his mother, the other his father, by their sides:
Calliope beside Orpheus, comely Apollo beside Linus.
Pan, too, if he were to vie with me with Arcadia as judge,
Pan, too, would admit defeat with Arcadia as judge.[11]

No delay, small boy! Learn your mother's face with a smile—                60
for nine long months your mother endured loathsome trials.
No delay, small boy! If you do not smile upon your mother,
no god will honor you at his table nor goddess in her bed.

---

10. The Fates were envisaged as three old women who spun the threads of time and life on their spindles, as if working wool.

11. Orpheus, Linus, and Pan were all famous singers. Calliope was one of the Muses, while Apollo was the god of song. Pan, a rustic god originating in rural Arcadia, was expert at the pan-pipes.

# INSCRIPTIONS

(2nd century BC–4th century AD)

## Introduction

This selection of one hundred documents from the Roman period is meant to illustrate some of the types of texts written on stone and other objects, and to shed light on some important aspects of Roman civilization, such as the class structure, patron–client relationships, urbanism, religion, euergetism, entertainments, family, and marriage ideals. Preference was given to documents that are vivid and tell some kind of story, or evoke the world of the Romans in a memorable way. The function of any such small selection as this, after all, is not simply to compile facts and documents, but to catch the imagination and spur the reader to investigate further. To that end we have mentioned some publications where more examples and details about particular types of documents can be found. We give dates when they are mentioned in the document itself or are reasonably secure from other data, but it is often difficult or impossible to assign a precise date.

Some of the sources from which the original texts of these documents are drawn, especially *Inscriptiones Latinae Selectae* (*ILS*) and *Carmina Latina Epigraphica* (*CLE*), are in the public domain and freely available online. The sources are indicated after each document, using abbreviations that are explained on p. 502. Editorial supplements are given in brackets, as follows:

(text): words not present in the document, but clearly implied.

[text]: words likely in the original document, but lost because of damage

[ . . . ]: unknown words lost because of damage

The material has been organized as follows:

I. Epitaphs and other documents about individuals (nos. 1–56)
   a.   persons of senatorial status
   b.   persons of equestrian status
   c.   town councilors (decurions)
   d.   soldiers
   e.   persons certainly or likely freeborn
   f.   persons of unknown status
   g.   persons of freed status
   h.   slaves
   i.   slave collars

II. Proclamations by and for emperors (nos. 57–63)

III. Inscriptions relating to public works (nos. 64–71)

IV. Documents relating to festivals, games, and shows (nos. 72–88)

# I. Epitaphs and Other Documents about Individuals

Because of the tendency to place tombs along well-traveled roads leading into and out of towns, epitaphs in the Roman world were more public and accessible than is usual now. Besides the expected references to family affection, we often find messages directed to passers-by. Those epitaphs honoring persons of high status routinely list offices held and distinctions conferred. The large majority of those commemorated in stone are not aristocrats, however, but from a servile background: ex-slaves and their children. Most elite literary sources have nothing but disdain for freedmen, especially those involved in trade, so epitaphs are valuable in expressing the dignified self-image of members of this class. Slaves themselves are also often commemorated when close to the master's family. Nor are all commemorators rich, or even highly literate. Many soldiers' epitaphs are preserved from around the empire, and they give valuable evidence for varied military careers. Since the intent of this section is to exemplify some of the various classes of Romans, a few honorary inscriptions are included that, while not strictly epitaphs, are similar in content. The famous *Laudatio Turiae* ("Praise of Turia") is not a true epitaph, either, but an inscribed version of a funeral speech about a wife, given by her husband.

## Persons of Senatorial Status

1        ### The So-Called *Praise of Turia*

The *Laudatio Turiae*, or "Praise of Turia," is an inscription from the 1st century BC that records the funerary speech of a husband for his wife after a marriage of forty years that spanned the extremely turbulent times of the civil wars of the late Republic. This provides the background for the most famous event in the *Laudatio*, namely the wife's saving of her husband from death and subsequent securing of his recall from exile and reinstatement as a citizen. Since later writers preserve an anecdote about a woman named Turia who saved her husband by hiding him in their house during this same period, many scholars once believed that this inscription was about her. Although almost none continue to make this identification, the name has stuck. The only person related to the speaker that is named in the inscription is a brother-in-law, C. Cluvius, who is otherwise unknown, so we are at a dead end in tracing the people involved. The *Laudatio* is remarkable for several reasons, including its length (even though we are missing much of it, it is still among the longest non-official Latin inscriptions ever found) and its intensely personal nature, but it is perhaps most interesting as a document that gives us insight into the nature of marriage and expectations about gender roles in the late Republic and early Empire.

## Left-Hand Column

[1] [ . . . ] through the uprightness of your character [ . . . ] [ . . . ] you remained up[right. . . ]
You were unexpectedly orphaned before our wedding day when both of your parents were killed together when they were alone in the countryside. You are the one most responsible for ensuring that your parents' deaths were not left unavenged—I had gone off to Macedonia, and your sister's husband Cluvius to the province of Africa.[1] You discharged your familial duty by making demands and pursuing justice with so much dedication that, even if we had been present, we could not have presented a better case than you did. Moreover, you have this in common with your sister, who was just as devoted. While you were busy with this, to protect your modesty, once you had demanded that the criminals be punished, without further ado you went from your family home to that of my mother, where you waited for me to return.

[13] Then they tried to get the two of you to agree that the will of your father, in which we were named heirs, should be declared null and void because he had entered into a *coemptio*[2] with his wife. If the verdict turned out against you, you and all your father's possessions by law would have had to revert to the guardianship of those who were behind the legal action; your sister, too, would have had no legal standing as his heir because she had been transferred to Cluvius' authority.

Even though I was not there, I have come to know on good authority the incredible courage and resolution you showed in enduring and resisting these sham proceedings. You defended our common cause with the truth: the will had not been invalidated, you said, so both of us should be heirs rather than you alone getting everything. What is more, so fixed was your resolve to defend the written testament of your father that you declared that if you did not prevail you would still give your sister her share. You said that you would not submit to their legal guardianship; they had no authority over you under the law since it could not be proved that your family was part of any *gens* that could legally force you to do so. For even if your father's will had been invalidated, those who were behind this suit had no legal standing because they belonged to a different *gens*. They yielded to your steadfastness and dropped the suit altogether. As a result, you had succeeded in the task you had taken entirely upon yourself, namely to defend your obligation to your father, your familial duty to your sister, and your loyalty to me.

[27] Marriages as long as ours, which are ended by death instead of being broken apart by divorce, are not common. It was our lot that our marriage lasted until its fortieth year without any friction between us. If only our long partnership had ended with something happening to me instead! It would have been more just for the older of us to give in to fate.

---

1. The husband evidently left Italy to join Pompeius' forces in Macedonia when Julius Caesar led his troops into Italy and initiated the civil wars in 49–48 BC.

2. A form of marriage that involved the fictitious "purchase" (*emptio*) of the wife by the husband with certain implications for inheritance.

[30] Your domestic virtues—modesty, obedience, kindness, even temper, eagerness for working wool, religious reverence free of superstition, humbleness in your use of adornment, modesty in your style of dress—why should I mention them? Why should I speak of your affection toward your friends or your devotion to your family, as when you cared for my mother the same way you did for your parents, when you took the trouble to provide her with the same easy life as you did them, and when you have countless other qualities in common with all married women who care for their good reputation? The virtues that I claim here for you are those that you alone possess. Very few women experience events like those that happened to you, which would make them suffer so greatly and distinguish themselves so much, since Fortune makes sure these are rare for women.

[37] Through our joint efforts we have kept intact the whole inheritance we got from your parents. You had no interest in acquiring for yourself what you had entrusted to me completely. We divided our responsibilities in such a way that I acted as the guardian of your property and you kept watch on mine. I will skip over a lot about this topic so that I don't claim a share of credit for what is yours alone. Let it be enough for me to have given this hint about what you were really like.

[42] You demonstrated your generosity not only to a great many friends but especially to your immediate family. One could also bring up other praiseworthy women, but you had only one equal to you in this regard [ . . . ] your sister. For the two of you raised, as part of our households, the girls in your family that deserved [ . . . ] such acts of kindness in your houses. So that these same women could secure matches worthy of your family, you provided dowries. Once the two of you had decided on these, Cluvius and I jointly assumed responsibility for them. Admiring your generosity, we substituted our own property and gave estates of our own as dowries so that you and your sister would not have your inheritance penalized. I bring this up not so we can congratulate ourselves but so that it will be known that those plans of yours, motivated by devoted generosity, led us to make them a reality from our own resources as a matter of honor.

[52] I have decided to pass over your many other acts of kindness [*several lines missing*]

## Right-Hand Column

[2a] You more than took care of my needs when I was in exile. You even arranged for me to lead a comfortable life by removing all the gold and pearls from your own body and sending them to me, and you always kept me well supplied while I was away with slaves, money, and provisions, which you cleverly got to me by deceiving the spies set by our enemies. You pleaded for my life while I was gone, a courageous act prompted by your virtue. You won over the men you were trying to convince and I was kept safe through their mercy. Nevertheless, you always maintained your strength of mind when you spoke.

[9a] In the midst of all this, Milo,[3] whose house I had purchased when he was in exile, organized a gang of men, and when they took the opportunity offered by the civil

---

3. T. Annius Milo was a leading politician in Rome who killed his rival, Clodius, in an incident of factional violence in 52 BC and went into exile, returning to Italy to fight against Julius Caesar in 48, when he was killed. See Cicero, *Letters* 9 in this volume.

wars to attack and plunder, you successfully fought them off and defended our house. [*several lines missing*]
[ . . . ] to exist [ . . . ]
[1] [ . . . ] that I was returned to my country by him,[4] for if you had not looked out for my welfare and made sure that there was something—me—for him to save, the promise of his assistance would have done no good. So I owe my life to your devotion as much as to Caesar.

[4] Why should I now make public our personal and secret plans and our private conversations? Why should I tell how, when I was called by unexpected news to face imminent and threatening danger, I was saved by your advice? Why tell how you did not allow me to rashly undergo danger too recklessly and how, once I was thinking more sensibly, you arranged a safe hiding place for me and took your sister and her husband, C. Cluvius, as partners in your plan to save me—putting all our lives in the same danger? It would take me years to tell the story even if I tried to summarize it. All that matters for the two of us is that I hid safely.

[11] For all that, I confess that the most painful experience of my life was what happened to you. It was after I had regained my status as a citizen of my country through the kindness and judgment of Caesar Augustus, who was abroad. His colleague Marcus Lepidus,[5] who was in Rome, grew annoyed at you because you brought up the matter of my recall. You fell to his feet and begged him, but not only did they not help you up, they dragged and carried you off like a slave. Your body was covered in bruises, but your spirit was absolutely firm as you reminded him of Caesar's edict and his congratulations on my restoration. Although you were the target of abusive language and received cruel wounds, you kept talking about the decree in public so that people would know who was responsible for the danger I was in. This incident soon came to hurt him. What could have been more effective than this act of bravery? You gave Caesar the chance to show his mercy and to rebuke Lepidus' savage cruelty—while still saving my life—through your exceptional endurance.

[22] Why say more? Let me not belabor the point. My speech can and should be brief. I would not want, in addressing your most noble deeds, to fail to do them justice. Let me instead publicly declare that, in return for the great services you rendered me, you are my official "savior."

[25] With the whole world at peace and the Republic restored, we finally got to enjoy quiet and happy times. Children were our dream, which Fate had begrudged us for so long. If Fortune, who was usually on our side, had allowed that to happen, what would either of us have lacked in life? But she took a different path and was killing our hopes. What you did because of this, and the actions you proposed to take, would perhaps be remarkable and wonderful in other women, but in you they are hardly astonishing when set alongside your other virtues, so I won't go into detail about them. When you despaired of conceiving and were pained that I had no children, so

---

4. The emperor Augustus (earlier Octavian), who is called Caesar in this inscription because he was adopted by his great-uncle Julius Caesar.

5. Octavian (later Augustus), Marcus Antonius (Mark Antony), and Lepidus were the three members of the Second Triumvirate, the coalition that led Rome in the aftermath of Julius Caesar's assassination in 44 BC. As time went on, Lepidus was marginalized by his colleagues and in 36 BC was removed as a triumvir by Octavian.

that I would not lose hope of having children by staying married to you and become unhappy because of it, you raised the subject of divorce. You said you would hand over our empty house to another woman's fertility. Your only motivation was for you yourself, based on our well-known harmony of opinion, to find and secure a worthy and suitable match for me. You insisted that you would consider any future children as communal offspring and like your own. You declared that you would not divide up our inheritance, which until then we had held as communal property, but that it would be under my authority and, if I wished it, under your management. You would hold no part separate that had been divided off, but you would afterward assume the duties and devotion of a sister or mother-in-law.

[40] I must admit that I got so angry that I went out of my mind. I was so horrified by what you were proposing that I barely regained my senses. As if it were possible that a divorce between us could be contemplated before Fate made its decree! As if it were possible for you to conceive of some plan by which you would stop being my wife while I was still alive! After you had stayed absolutely faithful to me when I had nearly been exiled from life itself! What great desire or need to have children could I have had to make me cast aside loyalty and exchange the certain for the uncertain? Why say more? You stayed with me as my wife. I could not have agreed to your proposal without shaming myself and making us both miserable. But what other quality is more worth celebrating than how dedicated you were to working it out so that when I could not have children with you, I could nevertheless have them through your efforts, and when you had no hope of giving birth, you could provide me with the possibility of having children through marriage to another woman.

[51] How I wish that both our ages had allowed our marriage to continue until I, as the older, could have been buried first and—what would have been more just—you could have paid your last respects to me. Then I could have died while you lived on, standing in for the daughter I never had. But you were fated to go before me. You have guaranteed me the sorrow that comes from missing you, and you have left me miserable without the comfort of children. I for my part will bend my thoughts to your judgment and follow your principles. But all your carefully considered precepts should give way to the praises you deserve so that I may be comforted by them and won't miss too much what has been consecrated to immortality to be remembered forever.

[58] The good things that came from your life won't desert me. I find strength of mind when I think of your fame and I have learned from your actions, and so I will resist Fortune, who has not deprived me of everything since she has allowed your memory to grow greater with praise. But when I lost you, I also lost the condition of tranquility that used to be mine. When I think about how you could spot the dangers I was in and defend me against them, I am crushed by the disaster and I cannot keep to my promise. My natural grief tears away my powers of self-control. I am overwhelmed by sorrow. I lose my resolve in the face of both the grief and fear that torture me. When I go back over in my mind the dangers I faced in the past and fear what will happen in the future, I lose my strength. I have been deprived of your help, which was so powerful and extraordinary, and so, although I contemplate your fame, I no longer feel up to the task of enduring these things—I feel more like I've been kept alive to grieve and mourn.

[67] This is the last thing I will say in my speech: you deserved everything, but it

wasn't in my power to give you everything. I have followed your last wishes as if they were law. If there is anything else that I will be able to do, I will do it.

[69] I pray that your *Di Manes* grant you rest and watch over you.[6]

*Source: CIL* 6.1527, E. Wistrand, *The So-called Laudatio Turiae* (Berlingska Boktryckeriet, 1976). Translation by Stephen M. Trzaskoma.

## 2    An Aide to Augustus

Memmius helped Octavian, the future Augustus, in the delicate task of settling veterans on Italian land after the battle of Philippi in 41 BC. He also helped (after 22 BC) to oversee another potentially explosive political process, the distribution of free grain to about 200,000 citizens in the city of Rome.

L. Memmius, son of Gaius, voting tribe Galeria, quaestor, tribune of the plebs,[7] member of the senatorial board for distributing grain rations, prefect in charge of distributing lands at Luca among legions XXVI and VII, Alban priest. Memmia, his daughter, had this made in accordance with the terms of his will.

*Source: ILS* 887, in the vicinity of Rome.

## 3    A Member of Julius Caesar's and Augustus' Inner Circle

Munatius Plancus, who survived the civil wars by changing allegiance, ultimately had a successful career under Augustus. The division of land in Beneventum and foundation of colonies in Gaul took place in 43–42 BC (see also Seneca, *The Ascension of the Pumpkinhead Claudius into Heaven* ch. 6).

L. Munatius Plancus, son of Lucius, grandson of Lucius, great-grandson of Lucius, consul, censor, twice hailed Imperator, member of the Board of Seven priests for banquets (in honor of Jupiter). Celebrated a triumph over the Raetians, rebuilt the temple of Saturn from the spoils of that war. In Italy he divided the lands at Beneventum, and in Gaul founded colonies at Lugdunum (Lyons) and Augusta Raurica.

*Source: ILS* 886; on his mausoleum in Gaeta, Italy.

## 4    A Paelignian Senator

The Paeligni were an Italian people from the Abruzzo, in the Apennines in central Italy. Ovid came from the same region, but chose not to pursue a senatorial career (see Ovid, *Tristia* 4.10 in this volume). Varius Geminus is a

---

6. *Di Manes* were spirits of the dead, sometimes conceived of as the spirits of the departed, sometimes as the guardian spirits of the dead.

7. It is unclear whether the stone originally mentioned a praetorship after "tribune of the plebs."

good example of how men from remoter regions of Italy made their way into the mainstream under Augustus. For addition of other ethnicities to the Senate, see the Lyons Tablet below (no. 59).

In honor of Q. Varius Geminus, son of Quintus, legate of deified Augustus on two occasions, proconsul, praetor, tribune of the plebs, quaestor, judicial examiner, supervisor of the distribution of grain rations, member of the Board of Ten for deciding disputes, superintendent for the maintenance of public temples and sacred monuments. He was the first Paelignian man to become a senator and hold these offices. The people of Superaequum set this up at public expense, to their patron.

*Source: ILS* 932; from Castelvecchio Subequo, Italy.

## 5    A Lady of the Highest Nobility

Of the ancient family of the Cornelii Scipiones, Licinia Cornelia Volusia Torquata is mentioned by Pliny the Elder for having given birth at age sixty-two (*Natural History*, 7.62). Her husband was consul in AD 3. The son she bore at an advanced age went on to become consul.

Licinia Cornelia Volusia Torquata, daughter of Marcus, wife of Lucius Volusius, consul, augur.

*Source: ILS* 924; from Rome.

## 6    A Brother and Sister from the Age of Trajan

The first inscription, found in Sarmizegetusa (near Hateg, Romania) but subsequently lost, outlines the career of an illustrious senator and consul (AD 116) in the reigns of Trajan (AD 98–117) and Hadrian (AD 117–138). The second inscription, composed by his sister, was found on a (now lost) stone facing of the Great Pyramid in the Giza necropolis outside Cairo, Egypt.

(*inscription* 1) To [D. Ter]entius Gentianus, military tribune, quaestor, tribune of the plebs, legate of the emperor, consul, *pontifex*, census officer for the province of Macedonia. The colonies Ulpia Traiana and Augusta Dacica Sarmizegetusa set this up for their patron.

(*inscription* 2, *in verse*) I saw the pyramids without you, dearest brother, and here I grieve and shed tears—which is all I could do for you—and I inscribe this lament in memory of my grief. So now, on the lofty pyramid will be read the name of Decimus Gentianus, *pontifex*, consul and censor before the age of thirty, a man who was, Emperor Trajan, comrade in your military triumphs.

*Source: ILS* 1046 and 1046a = *CLE* 270.

7    **The Death of a Young Girl**

See Pliny the Younger, *Letters* 13 in this volume, which tells us much more about this young girl. *Di Manes* refers to the semi-divinized souls of the departed, and is a very frequent phrase in Roman epitaphs.

To the *Di Manes* of Minucia Marcella, the daughter of Fundanus. She lived twelve years, eleven months, seven days.

*Source: ILS* 1030; Monte Mario in Rome.

## Persons of Equestrian Status

8    **A Young Equestrian**

Proculus participated in the parade of selected youth of equestrian status which passed before the censor every July 15, ending at the temple of Castor in the Roman Forum. He possessed a horse provided to him at state expense, a distinction granted to the elite within the equestrian order.

To the *Di Manes* of Sextus Gavius Proculus, son of Sextus. He lived sixteen years. He rode in the procession on a publicly provided horse.

*Source: ILS* 1313; from Montefiascone, Italy.

9    **Graffito Mocking an Equestrian**

The cognomen Ventrio ("The Gut") is evidently made up. Saying that he was born among the beets and cabbages is a way of mocking his rural origins.

C. Hadius Ventrio, Roman equestrian, was born among the beets and cabbages.

*Source: ILS* 1319; from the wall of a house in Pompeii.

10    **A Military Tribune**

This soldier served with one of the legions wiped out with its commander Varus in AD 9, and if he perished in that campaign, his tomb in Rome would have been a cenotaph (a tomb without a body). His role as "supervisor of the equestrians" meant that he oversaw the yearly parade of equestrians (see no. 8 above).

C. Pompeius Proculus, son of Gaius, voting tribe Teretina, military tribune of the 18th legion, supervisor of the engineers, one of the six supervisors of the equestrian squadrons, is buried here.

*Source: ILS* 1314; from Rome.

## 11    An Imperial Procurator

Equestrian procurators like Valerius Proculus were important in provincial administration under the emperors. Drusus, the son of the Emperor Tiberius, was in overall charge of the Balkans in the years AD 17–20.

The council and people honored T. Valerius Proculus, procurator of Drusus Caesar. He purged the Hellespont of piracy, and kept the city free of oppression in every way.

> *Source: IMT* 313; inscribed in Greek on a column of the temple of Apollo Thymbraeus, near the plain of Troy.

## 12    A Businessman and His Wife Who Achieved Equestrian Status

This inscription from North Africa describes a man who, through hard work, made enough money to be counted among the equestrian class. One might compare the freedmen in Petronius' *Trimalchio's Dinner Party* in this volume.

Stranger, perhaps you ask whose shade it is that this large monument covers. Pause briefly and learn. Here lies buried Laelius Timminus, a hard-working, frugal man, sober and alert, who made a not inconsiderable fortune for his family, and raised his family from humble status to equestrian rank. Joined with him is his wife Calpurnia Victoria, a woman of spotless character and modesty. They lie here together, at rest. Their grieving children erected this monument as an offering to the *Di Manes*.

> *Source: CLE* 1868 (in verse); from M'Daourouch, Algeria (Madauros).

# Town Councilors (Decurions)

## 13    Election Notices from Pompeii

In municipalities the town council of around one hundred members was sometimes referred to as a Senate, but the term "Order of Decurions" (*ordo decurionum*) was more frequent. As at Rome magistrates came from the body of the Senate, so in the municipalities local magistrates were elected from among the decurions. At Pompeii every March elections were held for the four senior magistracies: two town aediles and two judicial *duumvirs* ("Board of Two Men"). The aediles were junior officials, with similar responsibilities to the aediles in Rome, and the *duumviri* were the executive magistrates, analogous to the consuls in Rome. Elections at Pompeii were vigorously contested, to judge from the roughly 2,800 examples of painted election notices found on the outside walls of houses and public buildings, and even on graves along the roads into town. Most were written by professional sign-painters, and sponsored by trade associations, neighborhoods, and individuals, including many women (who were not themselves allowed to vote). The offices involved were annual.

6400 I urge you to make L. Rusticelius Celer judicial *duumvir* again. He is worthy of the community. | 6401 I, Vesonius Primus, urge you to make C. Gavius Rufus *duumvir*. He is helpful to the community. | 6404b I urge you to make L. Ceius Secundus *duumvir*. Elpis Afra supports him. | 6404c L. Ceius Secundus for judicial *duumvir*. Primus the fuller supports him. | 6405 Bruttius Balbus for *duumvir*. Genialis supports him. He will conserve the treasury. | 6409 Neighbors urge you to elect L. Statius Receptus judicial *duumvir*, a worthy man. Aemilius Celer wrote this, a neighbor. Jealous man, if you erase this, I pray you fall ill. | 6411a M. Holconius Priscus for judicial *duumvir*. All the fruit sellers along with Helvius Vestalis support him. | 6412a C. Julius Polybius for *duumvir*, supported by the mule-drivers | 6412e I urge you to make C. Julius Polybius aedile. He brings good bread. | 6419a I urge you to make Cuspius Pansa aedile. He is a good young man, and worthy of the community. | 6422b (*in verse*) If a decent life does a person any good, then Lucretius Fronto here is well worthy of office. | 6430a A. Vettius Caprasius Felix for aedile in charge of streets, sacred and public buildings. His neighbors support him. | 6431d A. Vettius Firmus for aedile. He is worthy of the community. The ball-players urge you to elect him.

> **Source:** A small selection is given here, with their numbers in *ILS*.
> For more, see Alison E. Cooley and M.G.L. Cooley, *Pompeii:*
> *A Sourcebook* (London: Routledge, 2004), ch. 6.

## 14    A Patron and Official from Ostia

> The person honored in this inscription was by far the greatest patron of guilds and associations that we know of, but many decurions were adopted as patrons in a similar way by merchants' associations, professional guilds, and religious groups of all kinds.

In honor of Cn. Sentius Felix, son of Gnaeus, grandson of Gnaeus, voting tribe Teretina, by decree of the decurions admitted to the rank of an aedile, by decree of the decurions admitted as a decurion, quaestor of the treasury of Ostia, *duumvir*,[8] quaestor of the company of young men. He was the first man ever to be designated *duumvir* for the following year in the same year he was adlected into the order of the decurions and appointed quaestor of the treasury.[9] He was chief officer of the board overseeing seafaring ships. He was admitted without payment into the guild of the Adriatic shippers and the guild that meets at the statue of the chariot in the wine-merchants' forum. He was patron of the association of secretaries, letter-writers, book-keepers, lictors, and messengers; likewise patron of the town criers, the bankers, the wine-dealers from the city of Rome, the grain-measurers of Ceres Augusta, the corporation of boatmen and ferrymen at Lucullus' crossing, the officials of Cybele's cult, the toga-wearers from the forum, those in charge of weights and measures, and the freedmen, the public slaves, and the olive oil merchants, and the young carriage-drivers, the veterans of Augustus,

---

8. See introduction to no. 13 above.

9. The term "adlection" refers to a special appointment to a position without having achieved the qualifications of the office on one's own.

the staff of the procurators of Augustus, and the fishermen and fishmongers. He was in charge of the official parade of the young men. His son, Cn. Sentius Lucilius Gamala Clodianus, dedicates this to his most indulgent father.

*Source: ILS* 6146; from Ostia, the port of Rome.

## 15     A Priest and Patron from Spain

This and the next inscription indicate how wealthy citizens contributed to their towns, and how the townspeople honored their benefactors.

To C. Julius Pedo, son of Gaius, voting tribe Galeria, priest (*flamen*) of the gods, in return for governing the community well and for assisting the grain supply with contributions of money. The people (set this up), having taken up a collection.

*Source: ILS* 6897; from Bejar, western Spain.

## 16     A Priestess and Patron from Spain

To Licinia Rufina, daughter of Quintus, lifetime priestess in the colony of Ucubi, in the municipality of Ipsca, and in the municipality of Iliberri, most beloved by her fellow-citizens. The community of Ipsca gave this statue to her as a gift, having taken up a collection, in recognition of her services. Licinia Quinta Rufina, daughter of Quintus, accepted the honor but remitted the expense.

*Source: ILS* 6909; from Baen, Spain.

## 17     A Kind Official from a Village in Gaul

For Sex. Julius Senior, voting tribe Voltinia, prefect of the village of Valeria, and judicial *duumvir*. Sextus Masuinnius Verinus (put this up) for his excellent guardian. He supported me in place of my parents for fourteen years and guided me to a certain independence. He was a most holy and deserving man.

*Source: ILS* 7001; from Vienne, France.

## 18     An Aedile and *Duumvir* from Germany

To the *Di Manes* of Masclinius Maternus, decurion of Colonia Agrippinensis (Cologne), aedile, *duumvir*, supervisor, priest (*sacerdos*), member of the council. Masclinius Leo made this for his deserving father, in the consulship of Decentius Caesar and Paulus.

*Source: ILS* 7069; from Zülpich, Germany, AD 352.

# Soldiers

## 19    A Legionary Soldier Serving in Britain

Flaminius was from Faventia in northern Italy and died at Wroxeter (Viroco-nium), a legionary camp laid out around AD 55 during the invasion of what is now Wales. Abandoned by the army in around AD 74, it developed into a civilian settlement. Above the inscription stood a sculpted relief of a soldier wearing sandals and carrying a staff.

[T. Fl]aminius, son of Titus, voting tribe Pollia, from Fa[ventia], forty-five years old, with twenty-two years' service, soldier of Legion XIV Gemina. I served as a soldier and now here I am. (*in verse*) Read this and be blessed in life (more than I was). When you enter Tartarus the gods keep you from the wine-grape and water. While the star of your life grants you time, live decently.

*Source: RIB* 292; from Wroxeter, England (Viroconium).

## 20    An Aged Legionary Soldier

Legion II Augusta was stationed at Caerleon, one of three permanent military fortresses in Britain. Martinus also set up an inscribed tomb for his mother, who lived seventy-five years (*RIB* 737). Soldiers and their families stayed after the end of service, and Caerleon, like other such bases (see no. 19 above), became the nucleus of a town.

To the *Di Manes*. Julius Valens, veteran of Legion II Augusta, lived 100 years. Julia Secundina, his wife, and Julius Martinus, his son, had this made.

*Source: RIB* 363; from Caerleon, South Wales (Isca).

## 21    A Legionary Trumpeter

A relief above this inscription shows Surus holding his *bucina*, or trumpet, and surrounded by arms.

To the *Di Manes*, in honor of Aurelius Surus, ex-trumpeter of Legion I Adiutrix Loyal and Faithful, served eighteen years, lived forty years. From Syria. Septimius Vibianus his heir and colleague had this constructed for a well-deserving man.

*Source: AE* 1976, no. 642; from Byzantium, Bithynia, 200s AD.

## 22    A Legionary Standard-Bearer

To the *Di Manes* in honor of T. Flavius Surillio, standard-bearer of Legion II Adiutrix Loyal and Faithful, served eighteen years, lived forty years. Aurelius Zanax, standard-bearer of the same legion, erected this in honor of his well-deserving colleague.

*Source: AE* 1976, no. 641; from Byzantium, Bithynia, 200s AD.

## 23    A Legionary Cavalryman, the Captor of Decebalus

This inscription, which came to light in Macedonia in 1965, represents one of the most detailed career descriptions of a Roman soldier so far known. Its hero is the captor of one of imperial Rome's great antagonists, Decebalus, the extraordinary king of the Thracian tribes in Dacia, beyond the Danube frontier, from AD 87–106. The historian Dio confirms that Decebalus killed himself to avoid being captured alive (68.14.3). A relief at the top of this monument shows Maximus, on horseback, looking over Decebalus, who sits on the ground, having just slit his throat. Trajan paraded Decebalus' head before the troops, then sent it to Rome where it was thrown down the Gemonian Steps. Maximus was decorated twice in the Dacian wars, and once in the Parthian war, which makes him one of the most decorated Roman soldiers known.

Ti. Claudius Maximus, veteran, had this monument made while he was still alive. He served as a cavalryman in Legion VII Claudia Loyal and Faithful, was appointed quaestor of the legionary cavalry, guard of the commander of the same legion and standard-bearer of the cavalry. In the Dacian war he was awarded military decorations for bravery by the Emperor Domitian. He was promoted to double-pay soldier in the second auxiliary cavalry unit of Pannonians by the deified Trajan, by whom he was also appointed to the position of scout in the Dacian war. He was twice awarded military decorations for bravery in the Dacian and Parthian wars, and was promoted to squad-commander in the same cavalry unit by the same emperor because he had captured Decebalus and brought his head back to him at Ranisstorum. After voluntarily serving beyond his time, he was honorably discharged by Terentius Scaurianus, commander with consular rank of the army in the new province of [Mesopotamia (?) . . . ].

*Source:* AE 1969/70, no. 583, from Macedonia; see also M. Speidel, *Journal of Roman Studies* 60 (1970), 142–53.

## 24    A Gallic Cavalryman

The Petrocorii were a Celtic people of Gaul (capital Péigueux, France).

Adbogius, son of Coinagus, Petrocorian by birth, cavalryman of the auxiliary unit of Ruso, twenty-eight years old, with ten years' service, lies here. His freedman set this up in accordance with his will.

*Source:* ILS 2500; from Mainz, Germany, early 1st century AD.

## 25    An Archer from Sidon Serving in Germany

Abdes received Roman citizenship under the Emperor Tiberius. His nickname was evidently "the leopard" (*Pantera*).

Ti. Julius Abdes Pantera, from Sidon, sixty-two years old, with forty years' service, soldier from the first cohort of archers, is buried here.

*Source:* ILS 2571; from Bingen, Germany, 1st century AD.

## 26     A Soldier in the Imperial Fleet

This inscription, which comes from a well-preserved tomb in Aquileia, shows the connection between a simple sailor and his commander-in-chief, the emperor.

L. Trebius, son of Titus, the father. L. Trebius Ruso, son of Lucius, had this monument made.
(*in verse*) I was born in extreme poverty, later served as a soldier in the fleet at the side of the emperor for seventeen years without malice, without giving offense, and was honorably discharged.
(*in prose*) The plot is sixteen feet square.

**Source:** *CLE* 372; from Aquileia, Italy.

## 27     A Centurion Who Came up Through the Ranks

Over his fifty years in the army Fortunatus served in thirteen different legions and crisscrossed the empire from Britain, Lower Germany, on the Danube, in the eastern provinces, and Africa, his final resting place and perhaps also place of origin. There were several routes to a post as a centurion, of which promotion from the ranks was the slowest and rarest of all, requiring, as Fortunatus' career shows, promotion through many clerical or junior officer posts.

[ . . . Petronius Fortunatus] served for fifty years, four in legion I Italica as a clerk, officer in charge of watchword, deputy centurion, standard-bearer; he was promoted to centurion by the vote of the [same] legion. He served as centurion of Legion I Italica, centurion of Legion VII [Ferrata], centurion of Legion I Minervia, centurion of Legion X Gemina, centurion of Legion II A[ugusta], centurion of Legion III Augusta, centurion of Legion III Gallica, centurion of Legion XXX Ulpia, centurion of Legion VI Victrix, centurion of Legion III Cyrenaica, centurion of Legion XV Apollinaris, centurion of Legion II Parthica, centurion of Legion I Adiutrix. In the Parthian expedition he was decorated for bravery with a *corona muralis* and *corona vallaris*[10] and with honorary torques and medallions. He was in his eightieth year at the completion of this monument for himself and for Claudia Marcia Capitolina, his beloved wife, who was in her sixty-fifth year at the time of the completion of this monument, and for his son M. Petronius Fortunatus, who served in the army for six years, centurion of Legion XXII Primigenia, centurion of Legion II Augusta, who died at age thirty-five; for their beloved son, Fortunatus and Marcia, his parents, built this as a memorial.

**Source:** *CIL* 8.217; from Kasserine, Tunisia.

---

10. Golden crowns with different decorations were awarded to a soldier who first mounts an enemy wall (*muralis*) or camp fortification (*vallaris*).

**28     A Centurion on the Danube Frontier**

Oescus (Gigen, Bulgaria) was one of a number of bases in the defensive system on the lower Danube (Moesia), at first a garrison town but later an important crossroads for trade and agriculture, as well as wood and ore processing. In the 1st century AD the Romans brought 100,000 settlers from the region beyond the Danube south to Moesia. By the early 3rd century, the date of this inscription, the population of Oescus was Romanized but ethnically mixed, with individual immigrant communities evidently retaining autonomy and self-government, under the watchful eye of prominent Romans like Flavinus and his friend Nicomedes. Caracalla reigned from AD 198–217.

To T. Aurelius Flavinus, son of Titus, voting tribe Papiria, chief centurion and president of the magistrates of the colony of Oescus, town councilor of the communities of the Tyrani, Dionysiopolitani, Marcianopolitani, Tungri, and the Aquincenses, patron of the guild of engineers, honored by the deified Great Emperor Antoninus (Caracalla) with 50,000 sesterces and 25,000 sesterces and promotion because of his dashing bravery against the enemy forces of the [*name illegible*], and exploits successfully and bravely accomplished. Claudius Nicomedes, town councilor of the community of the Tyrani, (set this up) to his very worthy friend. This site was granted by decree of the town councilors.

> **Source:** *ILS* 7178 = *AE* 1961, no. 208; from Gigen, Bulgaria.

**29     A Praetorian Guardsman**

Augustus created a standing corps of "praetorian" soldiers (from *praetorium*, "general's quarters") who held elite status with better pay, a shorter period of service (normally sixteen years), and were personally responsible to the emperor. In AD 14 there were at least nine praetorian cohorts, and soon there were twelve, each probably at 500 men. Some were stationed in Rome, and others in neighboring cities, like Ostia.

[ . . . ], soldier of the sixth praetorian cohort. The people of Ostia granted a place for his burial and decreed that he should be buried with a public funeral because he was killed while extinguishing a fire. Frontage twelve feet, twenty-five feet back.

> **Source:** *ILS* 9494; from Ostia, early 1st century AD.

**30     A Decorated Praetorian Guardsman**

This inscription honors the patron of a town northeast of Rome. His status and presumably wealth came from his exceptional service in the army and as personal guard of the emperor.

To C. Arrius Clemens, son of Gaius, voting tribe Cornelia, soldier of the ninth praetorian cohort, a cavalryman of the same cohort, decorated by Emperor Trajan with honorary torques, armbands, and medallions for service in the Dacian War, aide of the praetorian prefects, officer in charge of the watchword, deputy centurion, clerk in charge of the treasury, chief clerk of a military tribune, reservist of the emperor, centurion of the first cohort of fire brigade, centurion of the imperial messengers, centurion of fourteenth urban cohort, centurion of the seventh praetorian cohort, *trecenarius*,[11] decorated by Emperor Hadrian with a *hasta pura* and a *corona aurea*,[12] centurion of Legion III Augusta, chief centurion, one of the *duumviri quinquennales*,[13] patron of the municipality, guardian of the community. The town councilors, the board of six *Augustales*, and the citizens of the municipality of Matilica (set this up).

*Source: ILS* 2081; from Matilica in Umbria, Italy.

## 31    A Reservist of the Emperor

Augustus created a special unit of *evocati*, who carried a staff like the centurions, but were beneath them in rank. They were soldiers who stayed on in the army after the completion of their regular service, either as volunteers or on order of the emperor.[14] Many, like Paullinus, came from the praetorian units.

To the *Di Manes* of Lucius Naevius Paullinus, son of Lucius, voting tribe Camilia, reservist of the emperor. Served as a cavalryman in the first praetorian cohort, second in command of the cavalry, chief clerk of a tribune, was on active service for sixteen years, was a reservist for three years. Lucius Pessedius Agilis, reservist of the emperor, set this up for his outstanding friend.

*Source: ILS* 2077; from Rome.

## 32    A Member of the First Urban Cohort

Augustus established three cohorts of about 500 men each modeled on military units for the purpose of "policing" Rome. These "urban cohorts" were closely connected with the praetorian guard, but had as their primary function the maintenance of peace in the city. This custom spread to other cities, and Rome itself later had four cohorts. It was not unusual for men of distinguished military career to go on to become town councilors (decurions) in their local communities, as Sabinus did in Beneventum.

C. Luccius Sabinus, son of Gaius, voting tribe Stellatina, town councilor at Beneventum, in his lifetime constructed this for himself and Ofillia Parata, his wife, and Luccius

---

11. An obscure title that probably indicates a person who has held the centurion positions in all three urban units (fire brigade, urban cohort, praetorian cohort).

12. The "pure spear" (that is, untipped) and "golden crown" were bestowed upon soldiers for gallantry on the battlefield; the former was restricted to centurion-level soldiers and above.

13. A town magistracy elected every five years (*quinqu-*), with powers similar to censors in Rome (also elected every five years).

14. In the Republic the *evocatus* was a soldier who had served the minimum requirement but who had been "called back" for the maximum of sixteen years.

Verecundus, his brother, and his descendants. He served in the first urban cohort, was an attendant to the tribunes, supervisor of the hospital, supervisor of the prison, aide, clerk to the tribune, put in charge of the examination of witnesses by Annius Verus prefect of the city, also officer in charge of the watchword, deputy centurion, standard-bearer, clerk of the treasury, supervisor in charge of records, senior clerk of a tribune, clerk of Valerius Asiaticus prefect of the city. He was discharged by Emperor Hadrian Augustus in the consulship of Servianus for the third time and Vibius Varus (AD 134), [ . . . ] 22 April(?), in the consulship of Erucius Clarus for the second time (AD 146). Frontage, twenty feet, twenty feet back.

*Source: ILS* 2117; from Beneventum, Italy, AD 146.

### 33    A Mounted Guardsman from the Reign of Hadrian

The author, whose name is uncertain, seems to have belonged to the thousand-strong corps of *equites singulares*, a mounted guard popularly called Batavi ("Dutchmen," as the Batavi were a Gallic tribe from what is now Holland). "Pannonian shores" in this poem refers to the Roman province of Pannonia, roughly modern Hungary, on the frontier formed by the Danube river, a hotspot of conflict with neighboring peoples. The historian Dio Cassius (69.9.6) also reports that the Batavians crossed the Danube in full armor, to the terror of the enemy.

(*in verse*) It is I, once the most famous soldier on Pannonia's shores, foremost champion of the many thousands of Batavians. The Emperor Hadrian himself was present as judge when I swam the vast breadth of the deep Danube in full armor. When a missile had been fired from a bow I pierced and broke it in midair with another arrow—a feat never equaled by Roman or barbarian. No legionary with his spear could do it, no Parthian with his bow. Here I lie, having consigned my deeds to stone, my memorial. Good luck, posterity, in attempting to equal my deeds: I am my own precedent, the first to accomplish such deeds.

*Source: CLE* 427 = *ML* 126, around AD 130; text known only indirectly from medieval manuscripts.

# Persons Certainly or Probably Freeborn

### 34    A Man Who Enjoyed His Wine

The monument to which the inscription was attached showed Flavius reclining, as if at a feast, with a libation dish (*patera*) in one hand—a common type of representation on tombstones. Despite a few references to an afterlife, the more common view in epitaphs is the one expressed here, that nothing survives the grave. Agricola's home, the modern Tivoli, is eighteen miles east of Rome.

(*in verse*) Tibur is my fatherland, Flavius Agricola I was called. I am the one you see reclining before you. This is just how I enjoyed my short life in the world above for the years that Fate granted to me—I was never caught without a cup of wine. My most pleasing wife Primitiva predeceased me—her family name was Flavia, too—a chaste and attentive worshipper of Isis, full of grace and beauty. I spent thirty sweet years with her. For consolation she left her own offspring, Aurelius Primitivus, to tend and keep our home faithfully. He has preserved this safe and eternal resting place for me. Friends, if you read this, heed my warning: mix the wine, put a garland of flowers round your head, and drink away. And don't deny the pretty girls the pleasures of sex. When death comes, everything will be consumed by earth and fire.

*Source: CLE* 856 = *BNP* ii.236; from Rome, around AD 160.

## 35    A Father's Love for His Daughter

Sacred to the *Di Manes.* (*in verse*) You excelled all in beauty and learning, Julia, dear girl, taken away because of your father's destiny. Nothing is more precious than gold and gems, nothing more beautiful than cloth dyed in Tyrian or Spartan purple, nothing more resplendent than marble from Paros or Carystos. Nothing could be better or fairer than your beauty. No Arachne could rival you in wool-spinning. In singing you surpassed the Sirens and the daughters of Pandion,[15] and in beauty you surpassed all those mentioned above, you who were born of a Greek father, Heros, grown to the age of sixteen and then snatched away by cruel death. I, Julia Paula, now lie buried in this tomb.

*Source: CLE* 1996 = *ML* 189; from Haïdra, Tunisia.

## 36    An Exemplary Mother

> Compare the values in this inscription with those espoused in Inscription no. 1 above, the so-called "Praise of Turia."

(*in verse*) Here lies Sabina. She was praised by all and declared to possess every quality for which women are admired: she spoke the truth, revered the gods, had good sense, and was a fertile bearer of excellent children. Because of her good character the gods granted that she die shortly after her husband, the only one she had known. She lived to the threshold of old age.

*Source: CLE* 1872; from Dougga, Tunisia.

## 37    A Musician

> The Sabina in this inscription is not to be confused with the one in no. 36 above.

T. Aelius Justus, salaried water-organ player attached to the Legion II Adiutrix, had this made for his wife. (*in verse*) Sabina, cherished and loyal wife, lies here enclosed in

---

15. The mythical daughters of Pandion were Procne and Philomela, who were turned into a swallow and a nightingale, two musical birds.

stone. She was the only one to surpass her husband in her training in the arts. She had a lovely voice, and plucked with her thumb the lyre's strings. But now she is silent, stolen away too soon. Alas, she lived only twenty-five years, three months, and fourteen days. She herself, while she lived, played the water organ pleasingly and to popular acclaim. Be fortunate, all you who read this, may the divine powers preserve you, and sing with pious voice: "Farewell, Aelia Sabina."

*Source:* *CLE* 489; from Aquincum, now Budapest, Hungary, in the frontier province of Pannonia.

### 38    Graveside Banquets in Honor of a Mother

Graveside meals were a common feature of popular culture and religious observance, both pagan and early Christian (see Catullus, poem 101 in this volume). This stone tablet from the north African province of Mauretania Sitifensis contains an acrostic poem, the first and last letters of each line spelling out "the children to their sweetest mother."

To the memory of Aelia Secundula. (*in verse*) Now we all have sent many offerings for her burial, as she deserved. In addition, we decided to add a stone table to the altar of our departed mother Secundula. We place upon it a cloth and food and drinking cups, and around it we recall her many great deeds, as a way of healing the terrible wound of grief that gnaws at our hearts. As we delight in telling stories about her late into the night, praising our good and chaste mother, the dear old lady herself sleeps. O nourishing mother, you lie now at rest, forever sober and sensible. She lived seventy-five years. Julia Statulenia made this (monument) in the year of the province 260 (AD 299).

*Source:* *CLE* 1977; from Aïn El Kabira (Satafis), Algeria, AD 299.

### 39    A Mother Who Lost Her Children

Despite the opening, it is Parpiria Tertia who speaks, regretting in her grief that she ever had children.

T. Truppicus, son of Titus, and Papiria Tertia, daughter of Titus. (*in verse*) Stranger, you can see how I, bereft of my children, have placed this monument here, and how I miss my children, now a pitiable and gloomy old woman. My lonely old age should go to prove the point that sterile wives can count their lucky stars. T. Truppicus, son of Titus, built this.

*Source:* *CLE* 369; from Ferrara, Italy.

### 40    A Young Wife

This inscription expresses love between a wife and her husband, one of the many tender statements found on Roman tombstones.

To the soul of Rubria Tertulla. She lived twenty years, four months, four days. C. Refanius Macrinus made this for his excellent wife. (*in verse*) My twin sister and I were raised in Forum Livi, born from an excellent father and a devout mother. I was dear to my faithful husband, well-married and chaste, but the hateful law of Fate rendered my prayers useless. The only consolation to this poor loving wife was to be able to die in the arms of her husband.

**Source:** *CLE* 386; from Galeata, Italy.

## 41    A Loving Couple

The *Di Manes* were sometimes thought to perceive the offerings and honors paid to them at their tombs, and even to take on body and face, appearing to loved ones in dreams, and giving them nocturnal advice. See also the end of Inscription no. 1.

An offering to the *Di Manes* for tending to the reverend soul. I, Furia Spes, made this for my beloved husband, L. Sempronius Firmus. We met as boy and girl and were bound by mutual love. I lived with him for only a very short time. At a time when we should have been living together we were ripped apart by an evil hand. And so I ask of you, most reverend *Manes*, treat my dear Firmus well and be most kind to him so that I might see him during the nighttime hours. I also pray that he ask the Fates to allow me to come to his side quickly and sweetly.

**Source:** *ILS* 8006; from Rome.

## 42    A Wife and Business Partner

Here lies Urbanilla, my wife, a woman of complete modesty, a partner and ally in my business dealings at Rome, a remarkably thrifty woman. When all our ventures had prospered she returned with me to our fatherland. But, alas, Carthage stole my ill-starred partner from me. Such a wife was she, I have no hope of living without her. She it was who kept my house safe, she it was who helped me with her advice. Pitifully deprived of the light, she now lies enclosed in a marble tomb. I, your husband Lucius, covered you over with marble in this place. This is the fate that destiny allotted us all at birth.

**Source:** *CLE* 516; from Al Amra, Algeria, 200s AD.

## 43    An Avid Ball Player

This thought-provoking inscription describes a ball-game that employs a glass ball, an otherwise unattested sport in antiquity. Ball games were very popular pastimes at the baths (as attested by special areas or rooms devoted to them, called *sphaeristeria*; see also Petronius, ch. 27 in this volume). One interesting (but not certain) interpretation of this inscription is that the "glass ballgame" is a metaphor for the vicissitudes of campaigning for political office.

I am Ursus, the first toga-wearing Roman, if you will believe me, to play elegantly with glass throwing-balls along with my fellow players, to the loud applause of the people in the Baths of Trajan, Agrippa, and Titus, and often also in the Baths of Nero. You ball-players, come together in joy and load the statue of your friend with flowers, violets and roses, and with much foliage and luscious perfumes. Go to the imperial cellar, bring out the wine—dark Falernian, or Setine, or Caecuban—while I am still alive and willing, and pour it out unmixed. Sing in harmony to celebrate Ursus the merry, witty, ball-playing, scholarly old fellow, the one who surpassed all his predecessors in tact, grace, and refined skill. Now, aged friends, our verses must confess some truth: I admit it, I was beaten by my patron Verus, thrice consul—not once, but repeatedly. To him I am glad to play second fiddle.

*Source: CLE* 29 = *ML* 124; from Rome.

### 44    A Wife Who Died in Childbirth

The wife's name VETURIA GRATA appears in acrostic in the first letter of each line.

(*in verse*) Pause and rest now, hurried traveler, and read of a painful misfortune. I am a grieving husband, Trebius Basileus, and I wrote this so you might know the words of my heart from what is written below. This woman was endowed with all good qualities, gentle, genuine, a stranger to deceit. She lived twenty-one years, seven months. She bore to me three children; these were still little when she died, and her womb was full with a fourth, in her eighth month. Look now at the initial letters of each line and marvel: be willing to read all the way down, I beg you, and find the dedication. Recognize the name of a deserving woman, my beloved wife.

*Source: CLE* 108; from Rome.

# Persons of Unknown Status

### 45    An Anonymous Infant

(*in verse*) Here lies a pitiable infant stolen from her mother's arms before she had lived nine full circuits of the moon. Her grieving mother and father weep for her as she lies, little body enclosed in a marble tomb.

*Source: CLE* 397; from Rome, 1st century AD.

### 46    An Anonymous Foster-Son

A foster-child (*alumnus* or *alumna*) was typically either a slave, an abandoned child, or perhaps the child of another family member who could not raise it. Although one would expect foster-children to have a second-class status within the family, the sources show the opposite, that *alumni* were favored and sometimes doted on. Spedia Prisca's husband was somehow attached to the imperial fleet at Ravenna. It is the deceased child who speaks in verse.

[ . . . *man's name*] of the fleet mentioned above and Spedia Prisca made this for their dear and much deserving foster-son. (*in verse*) O Fates, you were all too brief and hostile to me. You relieved me of my tiny life and sent me here, fully eleven years of age. My foster-parents did all they could for me.

Source: *CLE* 102; from Ravenna.

# Persons of Freed Status

### 47    The Family of a Swine Dealer

The Syneros in this inscription was an *Augustalis,* one of a small group of distinguished freedmen in each city responsible for the imperial cult. It was the highest public distinction to which a freedman might aspire. The other offices mentioned are important municipal posts at Beneventum held by Syneros' son, Vementius. The sons of freedmen were citizens in full.

C. Acellius Syneros, the freedman of Gaius and Lucius, an *Augustalis* and swine dealer, made this for himself, for his wife Calpurnia Phyllis, daughter of Spurius, and for his son C. Acellius Vementius, son of Gaius, of the Falernian voting tribe. His son was aedile, *praefectus, duumvir, quinquennalis,* and *praefectus fabrum.*[16] (*in verse*) You are human: stop and consider my grave. As a young man I set out to make money I could live on (when old). I injured no one, and helped a great many. Don't wait to live well: this is where you are headed.

Source: *CLE* 83; from Benevento, Italy.

### 48    A Seller of Goat-Skins

Like Syneros in the previous example, this person, too, is proud of his profession. The name L. Nerusius Mithres is spelled out in the acrostic formed by the first letter of each line.

To the *Di Manes.* He whose name is revealed in the initial letters of the lines made this monument while still alive, for himself and for all his freedmen and freedwomen, and for their descendants. (*in verse*) I am now free from cares. Reader, learn who I was. Well-known in the Sacred City as a seller of goat-skins, I set out merchandise that was useful to the people. My honesty was matched by few and was praised by absolutely everyone. My life was prosperous, I built a marble tomb for myself, I lived carefree, and as a contractor I always paid my taxes. I was open in all my dealings, fair to everyone

---

16. *Quinquennalis* refers to the office in towns that had powers similar to those of censors in Rome and were, like censors, chosen every five years. *Praefectus fabrum* was the captain of military engineers.

so far as it lay in my power, and often came to the aid of people who asked, and was always respectful and generous to my friends. That I built this safe resting place for my body is an even greater and better tribute of honor than all the rest, since I did this not thinking only of myself, but I was also concerned about my heirs. Whoever lies buried on his own property has everything with him. Fame will speak of me. I lived a life of exemplary good repute every day I breathed the air. And I was concerned to provide a resting place after death for many others as well.

*Source:* CLE 437 = ML 128; from Magliano, Italy.

## 49    Freedman of a Slave Dealer

The freedman in this inscription, Valerius Aries, shows his literary interests by quoting Ovid at the beginning of his epitaph (*Tristia* 1.11.11–12).

L. Valerius Aries, freedman of the slave-dealer Zabda. (*in verse*) "Call it madness, call it a mind gone numb, but all my cares have been lightened by taking care of this." I have completed this monument at my own expense, so that friendly Earth might provide lodging for my bones, a thing that all ask for but only the fortunate obtain. For what is finer or more desirable than to breathe the last weary breath of your old age in the place where you first received the light of freedom? That is the greatest mark of an honest life.

*Source:* CLE 89; from Rome.

## 50    A Freedman Murdered by His Slave

Below the inscription is a relief sculpture depicting a man tending cattle. For other slaves who killed their masters, see Pliny, *Letters* 3.14 (Larcius Macedo); Tacitus, *Annals* 14.42–45 (Pedanius Secundus), not included in this volume.

For Jucundus, freedman of M. Terentius, and a cattle-breeder. (*in verse*) Traveler, whoever you are who read this as you pass by, stop and learn how I was wrongfully murdered, now an empty complaint. I did not make it past thirty years, because my life was stolen by a slave, who then cast himself into the river. The Main River took from him what he took from his master. Jucundus' patron set up this monument and paid for it.

*Source:* CLE 1007 = ML 193; from Mainz, Germany.

# Slaves

## 51    A Favorite Slave Girl

The stone is heavily damaged, and it is uncertain whether the inscription mentions the name of the girl. In any case, the relationship between slaves and their owners was not necessarily one full of tension and scorn.

(*in verse*) Here lies a girl of outstanding character, who was Vettia's favorite slave girl and his darling. Though she has died, they still cherish her, and fill her grave monument with tears and funeral gifts, and lament also for themselves, that they have been deprived of the life of a slave girl whom the gods preferred to have as their favorite.

**Source:** *CLE* 1867; from Rome.


**52    A Fourteen-Year-Old Slave Who Died after Giving Birth**

The girl's name, Calliste, means "most beautiful" in Greek. Childbirth was the leading cause of death for adult females. Of note is the "omniscient" speaker, who, though dead, knows the rumors about her death.

(*in verse*) My name was Calliste, a name borne out by my beauty. As for my age, I was in my fifteenth year. I was pleasing to my master, and beloved by both my parents. When I grew ill, the seventh day of the sickness was my last. The cause of my death is unknown—though people say it was childbirth. Whatever it was, I did not deserve to die so soon.

**Source:** *CLE* 1035; from the Appian Way near Rome.


**53    A Short-Hand Writer**

Xanthias was a *notarius*, a stenographer who took dictation from his master. A very efficient form of short-hand was said to have been invented by Tiro, Cicero's freedman (see Cicero, *Letters* 12 in this volume, first note). For another *notarius* see Seneca, *The Ascension of the Pumpkinhead Claudius into Heaven* 9 in this volume.

This epitaph, this altar, these ashes comprise the tomb of the slave-boy Xanthias, who was snatched away by a bitter death. He was already skilled at short-hand, his speeding stylus capable of taking down letters and words as fast as the speedy tongue could utter them. Soon he was unsurpassed in reading, and soon the man who sped to take his master's dictation became his master's confidante. Alas, he who would have become the sole sharer of his master's secrets has fallen in speedy death.

**Source:** *CLE* 219 = *ML* 131; from Cologne, Germany.


**54    A Scholarly Slave Boy**

The slave Antigenes was the son of his owner, Hilarus, and a slave woman. The poem implies that Hilarus would have given him his freedom and thus become his *patronus* as well, if the boy had not died prematurely. Acheron was a river in the underworld, here named as Tartarus.

To the *Di Manes* of Petronius Antigenides. (*in verse*) You, traveler, making your way with your boot laced up, halt, I ask you, and please do not refuse to read my epitaph.

Delicately nurtured and loved, I lived on earth for ten years, two months, two days. I memorized the doctrines of Pythagoras and the sayings of the Sages. And I read the lyric poets and the holy epics of Homer. I knew what Euclid had laid down on his abacus. Still, I had fun and enjoyed high-spirited play. All this my father[17] Hilarus had bestowed upon me, and he would have become my patron as well, had not I, unlucky that I was, encountered the hostility of Fate. I have escaped tempestuous life. Now I dwell in the underworld by the waters of Acheron beneath the foul stars of Tartarus. Hope and Fortune, goodbye. You don't have anything more to do to me, so go cheat others, please. This is my eternal home, here I lie, here I shall stay forever.

*Source:* *CLE* 434 = *ML* 70; from Pesaro, Italy, around AD 200.

## 55     A Twelve-Year-Old Gold Worker

Urban slaves performed a huge variety of tasks, including highly skilled labor and craft work. Children were often trained in crafts from a young age. For legal purposes slave children like Pagus were reckoned to be productive from the age of five (*Digest of Roman Law*, 7.7.6). The final line includes a quotation of Vergil's *Aeneid* (2.558), which describes the death of the great king of Troy, Priam.

To the *Di Manes*. (*in verse*) Traveler, whoever you are, shed a tear. One lies here who lived only twelve years of his blooming youth. He was his master's favorite, the fond hope of his parents, whom he left to lasting grief after his death. He knew how to make necklaces with skillful hands, and to set gems of many colors in pliable gold. The boy's name was Pagus, but now he lies in his tomb, a bitter death, ash, "a corpse without a name." (*in prose*) He lived twelve years, nine months, thirteen days, eight hours.

*Source:* *CLE* 403; from Rome.

## 56     Collars Worn by Recaptured Fugitive Slaves

Recaptured fugitive slaves were typically given as punishment a tattoo that signaled their propensity to run away. In some cases, however, they were given a necklace or collar that conveyed the same message. This item gives all known slave collars with words on them, based on the comprehensive catalogue of D.L. Thurmond, plus one that emerged on the antiquities market after Thurmond wrote. The use of collars to identify slaves with a propensity to run away long predates the triumph of Christianity, but for some reason of the thirty-eight collars and pendants that happen to survive from antiquity virtually all come from the 300s AD, when Christianity became dominant, and many include Christian symbols. Some of the collars may be modern forgeries (esp. nos. 19 and 23).

---

17. Although slaves were defined by law as having no father, they would use the expression for their masters.

1 Arrest me, I have fled. When you have returned me to my master Zoninus you receive one *solidus*[18] | 2 Bulla (is my name). Arrest me so I do not flee | 3 Patronia (is my name). Arrest me because I have fled and bring me back to the House of Theodotenis to my master Vitalio | 4 I am a slave of my master Scholasticus, *vir spectabilis*. Arrest me so I do not flee from the House Pulverata[19] | 5 Adulteress. Whore. Arrest me, because I have fled from Bulla Regia | 6 Fugitive (slave) of Deuterius, *beneficarius*. Arrest me[20] | 7 Minervinus. Fugitive (slave) of Italicus, officer in charge of the watchword of the twelfth urban cohort | 8 Slave of God, fugitive[21] | 9 I am a slave of V.D. Arrest [ . . . ] because I am fleeing[22] | 10 Arrest me and return me to Apronianus, *palatinus*, near the Golden Napkin on the Aventine, because I have fled[23] | 11 Arrest me because I have fled and return me to my master Bonifatius, linen-worker[24] | 12 Arrest me. I have fled. I am (the slave) of Concessus, owner of the Gemellian (House) near the Hill of Paullus | 13 [ . . . ] to my master [ . . . ] | 14 Arrest me. I am fleeing. Return me in the Graecostadium to Eusebius the merchant[25] | 15 Arrest me so I do not flee. I am fleeing | 16 I am (the slave) of the veteran centurion, from the office of the governor of the province Valeria Byzacena. Arrest me, but (treat me) well | 17 I am the slave of Felix, archdeacon. Arrest me so I do not flee | 18 By order of our three lords, let no one take in another's slave[26] | 19 Asellus, slave of Praeiectus of the office of the prefect of the grain supply. I have gone beyond the walls. Arrest me because I have fled. Return me to the barbers' shops near the temple of Flora | 20 I am called Januarius. I am the slave of Dextrus, short-hand writer of the Senate, who lives in region V in Macarius square | 21 I am the slave of Leontius, Senate archivist. Arrest me so I do not flee, and bring me back to the Triarian Hill | 22 I am a fugitive. Return me to the Aventine, to the house of Potitus, senator, near (the baths) of Decius | 23 Arrest me so I do not flee. Bring me back to Aurelius, Region I | 24 Arrest me because I am fleeing, and bring me back to my master Flavius on the Via Lata | 25 Arrest me because I have fled and bring me back to Gemellinus, physician, on the Via Lata | 26 I am (the

---

18. The main coin of Roman currency in late antiquity, made of gold. For legal purposes Constantine designated the value of an ordinary slave at twenty *solidi* (*Codex Iustinianus*, 6.1.4).

19. *Vir spectabilis* ("admirable man") was a rank used to distinguish holders of high office in late 4th century Rome. It is not clear to what the "House Pulverata" refers.

20. *Beneficarius* is a military rank (clerk or quartermaster), which suggests that the master was attached to the legion stationed at Lambaesis (see Hadrian's speech to soldiers at Lambaesis, no. 63 below).

21. From a slave belonging to a church.

22. V.D. may represent a name, or a rank (*vir devotissimus*) from after AD 350. The collar is broken in half.

23. A *palatinus* was a government official in 4th and 5th century Rome. The "Golden Napkin" is a place also known from 4th-century regionary catalogues of the city of Rome, perhaps a tavern.

24. The words are followed by Christian symbols, including the Chi Rho (*monogramma Christi*), the exact form of which dates this to the age of Constantine.

25. Literally "middle-man." Eusebius was evidently some kind of wholesale merchant or intermediary operating from a market-like area in Rome known as the Graecostadium.

26. The three lords are Valentinian, Valens, and Gratian, who ruled the empire jointly in the 360s and 370s AD.

slave) of Hilario. Arrest me and return me because I have fled from Region XII near the bath of Scriboniolus, Rome[27] | 27 Arrest me because I have fled and return me to Leo in the basilica of Paullus | 28 (*side a*) Arrest me and bring me back to the Forum of Mars to Maximianus, the official archivist. (*side b*) Arrest me because I have fled, and bring me back to Bonosus at the house of Senator Elpidius on the Caelian Hill[28] | 29 Arrest me so I do not flee and bring me back to my master Pascasius in the Forum of Trajan in the Porphyry Portico | 30 (*side a*) Arrest me because I have fled and bring me back to Victor, acolyte at the Basilica of Clemens. (*side b*) I have fled. (Return me to) Euplogius from the office of the Urban Prefect[29] | 31 Arrest me so I do not flee, and return me to my master Euviventius in Callistus Square | 32 Arrest me because I am fleeing and bring be back to the Saepta[30] | 33 Arrest me so I do not flee and bring me back to the house of [ . . . ] | 34 Arrest me so I do not flee [ . . . ] | 35 (*side a*) I am (the slave) of Clodius Hermogenianus, senator, former prefect of the city, from his own gardens. (*side b*) I am from the garden of Olibrius, senator, praetorian prefect. Do not arrest me. It will not be advantageous to you[31] | 36 (*side a*) I am (the slave) of Clodius Hermogenianus, senator, former prefect of the city, from his own gardens. (*side b*) I am from the garden of Olibrius, senator, praetorian prefect. Do not arrest me. It will not be advantageous to you | 37 Arrest me because I have fled, and return me to my master Cethegus, senator, in the market of Libanius, Region III[32] | 38 Arrest me so I do not flee. (I came) from the house of Tertius.[33]

*Source:* D.L. Thurmond, "Some Roman Slave Collars in CIL," *Athenaeum* 82 (1994), 459–93.

# II. Proclamations by and for Emperors

The inscriptional record preserves a number of interesting texts relating to emperors, from loyalty oaths taken by provincial citizens, to senatorial grants of powers, to speeches and letters of the emperors themselves, put up locally

---

27. Below the words are the Christian symbols alpha and omega.

28. Side a dates to the age of Constantine. The piece of metal was re-used in the late 4th or early 5th century, judging by the form of the Christian symbol on side b.

29. Side a is from the age of Constantine, judging from the form of the Christian monogram that accompanies it; side b is later, probably the mid- or late 4th century.

30. The Saepta was a public space in Rome, originally used for voting, but later for gladiatorial fights, and, by the time of this document (4th century AD), as a market.

31. Q. Clodius Hermogenianus Olybrius was urban prefect in AD 369–370, praetorian prefect of the East in AD 378–79, consul in 379. He was Christian. This and the following item evidently belonged to his gardeners, and exceptionally instruct the reader not to detain the slave. The reason for this is not clear.

32. Cethegus was beheaded at Rome for adultery in about AD 370 (Ammianus Marcellinus, 28.1.16).

33. Unpublished. Auctioned by Michael Malter Galleries (Fresno, California) in 2003 (www .liveauctioneers.com/item/49355).

by groups who were honored with an imperial visit or communication. Most people in the provinces and even in the city of Rome would probably never see the emperor or even deal with the relatively limited imperial bureaucracy. But from such documents as these, and from Augustus' *Accomplishments* (in this volume, also set up as an inscription in the provinces), one can get some idea of how the person and image of the emperor was presented and seen around the empire. Because of the complicated nature of imperial titulature, we have highlighted in bold the name of the emperor as he is commonly called today.

### 57     Oath of Loyalty to Augustus and His Family

Paphlagonia, the central section of northern Anatolia (Turkey), became a Roman province in 6 BC. This loyalty oath was administered in the whole province three years later, and it shows that, however much Augustus presented himself in Rome as the first among equals, in the eastern provinces he was effectively viewed as a king. The cultic worship of the emperor during his lifetime represents the Roman imperial version of ruler cult already commonly practiced among the Hellenistic kings in the Greek East. From the perspective of the towns, which offered sacrifices, prayers, and hymns (often within the setting of a city festival), ruler cult was an expression of political ties and political self-definition. From the ruler's point of view, it was a means of safeguarding his power symbolically. The reference here to "the temples of Augustus and the altars of Augustus in the several districts" shows that Augustus was inserted seamlessly into this tradition. Later emperors followed suit.

Dated after the twelfth consulship of Caesar **Augustus**, son of the deified (Julius Caesar), in the third year of the province (3 BC), March 6. Gangra, in [the assembly]. The oath sworn by the people of Paphlagonia, and by the Romans engaged in business among them:

"I swear by Zeus, Earth, Sun, and all the gods and goddesses, and by Augustus himself, that I will be devoted to Caesar **Augustus**, to his children, and to his descendants forever, in word and deed and thought. I will consider their friends my friends and their enemies my enemies; I will spare neither my body nor my soul nor my life nor my children for their interests, but in every way I will undergo every danger for their interests; if I learn or hear that something is said, plotted, or being done against them, I will report it and will hold as a personal enemy the man who says, does, or plots any of these things; (I swear that) whoever they deem are enemies, these persons I will pursue by land and sea and will punish with all arms and sword. If I do anything contrary to or inconsistent with this oath as I have sworn it, I will myself call down a curse of utter and complete destruction upon myself, my own body, my soul, my life, my children, and all my people and interests, down every generation from me and all my descendants, and may neither earth nor sea receive my body or those of my descendants, nor bring them fruit or profit."

All persons [in the province] swore this same oath in the temples of Augustus at the altars of Augustus [in the several districts]. Likewise all the citizens of Phazimon, living in the city now called Neapolis, swore the oath at the altar of Augustus in the temple of Augustus.

*Source: ILS* 8781= Peter Herrmann, *Der Römische Kaisereid*
(Göttingen: Vanderhoeck and Ruprecht, 1968), no. 4, 123–4; from
Çankırı, Turkey (Gangra in Paphlagonia).

## 58    Oath of Loyalty to Caligula Sworn by Residents of Aritium, Spain

This oath from the western part of the empire invokes as the highest deity Jupiter Optimus Maximus, rather than "Zeus, Earth, and Sun," as in the previous item. In the western part of the empire the ruler cult was somewhat slower to catch on than in the East. Augustus at first took into consideration the sensitivity of the city of Rome and allowed his cult only if it was combined with that of the goddess Roma, and even that was rare in the west until under Claudius and Vespasian. Note the lack of reference here to any temples or altars of the living emperor. Augustus, however, is spoken of as a god. He had been deified as *divus Augustus* by the Senate shortly after his death, and his divine power (*numen*) and personal spirit (*genius*) received cult (see below, no. 72). For a satirical treatment of the consecration of dead emperors, see Seneca's *The Ascension of the Pumpkinhead Claudius into Heaven* in this volume.

To C. Ummidius Durmius Quadratus, legate of Gaius Caesar Germanicus Imperator (**Caligula**) with propraetorian power. Oath of the Aritiensians:

"I solemnly swear that I will be an enemy to those who I know are enemies of Gaius Caesar Germanicus, and if someone threatens him or his welfare, I will never cease to pursue him with armed might and war of extermination on land and sea until he pays the penalty he owes to him. I will consider neither myself nor my children dearer than his welfare, and I will consider those with hostile intentions toward him my enemies; if I knowingly break my oath, may Jupiter Best and Greatest and the deified Augustus and all the other immortal gods deprive me and my children of our homeland, our safety, and all our fortunes."

Sworn the fifth day before the Ides of May (May 11) in the town of Aritium when Cn. Acerronius Proclus and C. Petronius Pontius Nigrinus were consuls (AD 37) when the (local) magistrates were Vegetus son of Tallicus and [ . . . ].

*Source: ILS* 190 = Peter Herrmann, *Der Römische Kaisereid*, no. 1, 123;
from near Mação, Portugal (Aritium).

## 59    Claudius' Speech to the Senate Concerning Admission of Gauls to the Senate

Acting as censor in AD 48, Claudius, always eager to raise the status of provincials (see Seneca, *Ascension of the Pumpkinhead Claudius into Heaven*

ch. 3 in this volume), delivered this speech to the Senate in which he proposed to fill vacancies in the Senate with dignitaries from Gallia Comata
("Long-Haired Gaul"). This speech is, with differing details and emphasis,
also reported by Tacitus, *Annals* 11.23–25, who informs us that after Claudius'
speech the Senate passed a resolution granting the Aedui, longstanding allies
of Rome, the right to serve in the Roman Senate—thus setting the precedent for the inclusion of *all* non-Italian provincials from all over the empire.
Historically, the Senate had been reserved first for elite Romans and later
elite Italians—a manifestation of the deep-seated conservative Roman view
of "us vs. them." A scholar of Roman and Etruscan history, Claudius produces a counter-argument to this conservative view by depicting a state that
has always been inclusive of outsiders and ready to adopt new traditions.
This particular inscription was set up by the citizens of Lugdunum (Lyons), a
city located in Gallia Comata, a region that stood to benefit from Claudius'
patronage. It not only commemorates the inclusion of Gauls in the Roman
Senate but also honors its hometown hero, Claudius, who happened to be
born there while his father Drusus was on campaign.

## Column 1

[*The upper part of the column is lost.*]

Right at the outset I want to anticipate your initial reaction to my request, a natural
one to be sure, but one that I foresee as being my biggest obstacle. Do not, gentlemen,
reject my proposal for fear that it is something revolutionary. No, I would ask you to
consider all of the innovations that have occurred in this state and all of the various
changes to the form and constitution of our nation, starting from the very beginning
of our city's existence.

Once kings controlled this city, but even so they did not pass this control on
to members of their own families. They were succeeded by outsiders, and some of
them were complete strangers. For instance, Romulus was succeeded by Numa, who
hailed from Sabine country. That made him a neighbor, true, but an outsider still.
Ancus Marcius was succeeded by Tarquinius Priscus. His father, Demaratus, was a
Corinthian, his mother a well-born woman from Tarquinia, but poor, which is why
she was forced to marry such a husband. Because Tarquinius' blood was impure, then,
he was prevented from holding office at home, and so he migrated to Rome, where
he became king. Between him and his son, or possibly grandson—there is a debate
among historians—came Servius Tullius. He, if we are to believe our own version, was
born of the captive slave Ocresia. But the Etruscan version tells a different story—that
he was the loyal supporter of Caelius Vibenna, who faithfully stood at his side in
times good and bad. When Caelius' fortune changed, he was driven into exile and left
Etruria with all of Caelius' remaining forces. He occupied the Caelian Hill in Rome,
which he named after his own leader, Caelius. He changed his original Etruscan name,
Mastarna, to the name I mentioned above, Servius, and ruled as king, to the greatest
benefit of the whole state. Later, after the behavior of Tarquinius Superbus became
hateful to our people—well, not only his, but also his sons'—we tired of being subject to the whims of kings, and so the administration of the state fell to yearly-elected
magistrates, the consuls.

Need I mention the dictatorship and its great power, which exceeds that of the
consuls? Our ancestors created this position so that they could effectively deal with

difficult wars or civil disturbances that got out of hand. What about the creation of the tribunes of the people in order to protect the common people? Or the time when power shifted from the consuls to the *decemviri* and back again after the latter's reign of power was dissolved?[34] Or what about the period when the consular power was divided among several men, called "military tribunes with consular power," sometimes six in number, more often eight? And what about the change that happened when plebeians were allowed a share of power, not only political offices, but also the priesthoods?

Now, if I were to recount the wars started by our ancestors and how far we've come, I'm afraid that you might think that I was being overly presumptuous and looking for an occasion to boast about having extended the Roman Empire beyond Ocean.[35] So I will return to my main thread. Citizenship [*Some text is lost.*]

## Column 2

[*The upper part of the column is lost*] it is possible. Was it not revolutionary that the deified Augustus, my uncle, and **Tiberius** Caesar decided to add to this Senate the flower of each and every colony (*colonia*) and town (*municipium*) with Roman citizenship? All of them, of course, were upstanding and decent men. What's that? You say that an Italian senator is preferable to one from the provinces? I'll give you my general thoughts about that issue and offer some specifics in a moment, when I turn to explaining that aspect of my censorship. For now I'll say this: not even provincials, provided that they add luster to this body in some way, should be rejected outright.

Consider the illustrious and flourishing Roman colony of Vienne: it has been providing senators to this body for quite a long time. From this colony comes Lucius Vestinus, a luminous star of the equestrian order with few peers, an extremely close friend of mine and now a member of my private council. I pray that his children enjoy the highest grade of priesthood and then, as the years advance, continually add to their rank and achievements. I will not mention the fell name of that brigand, that monster of the wrestling yard that I loathe, who brought home the consulship even before his colony had received the full benefits of Roman citizenship.[36] I can say the same of his brother, who is so pathetic and unworthy because of his family's downfall that he could not be a senator of any use to you.

It is now time, Tiberius Caesar Germanicus (**Claudius**) to disclose your hand to the senators and tell them the point of your speech. After all, you're already at the end of Gallia Narbonensis!

Look at all these outstanding men that stand before my eyes. Should we be ashamed of having these serve as senators any more than Persicus, a most noble man and a friend of mine, when he reads the name of Allobrogicus among the images of his ancestors? No! Now, if you agree that this is correct, what more do you need than for me to point

---

34. The *decemviri* ("Board of Ten Men") were put in power in 451 BC to write the Twelve Tables (see translation in this volume). They were forced out in 449 BC.

35. Under Claudius' rule the Romans conquered the island of Britain (AD 43). See Seneca, *The Ascension of the Pumpkinhead Claudius into Heaven* ch. 12 in this volume.

36. Valerius Asiaticus, a native also of Vienne (and a fan of wrestling), was consul in AD 35 (suffect) and again in 46, and a commander of Claudius' forces in Britain. Condemned on a possibly trumped-up charge of conspiracy against Claudius by the latter's wife Messalina, he was killed in AD 47.

out with my finger those senators that hail from beyond the province of Narbonensis? That land already sends you senators, and we are not ashamed of having men of our rank from Lugdunum!

Only with trepidation have I gone past the comfortable borders of the provinces that are familiar to you, but now I must make the case for Gallia Comata in earnest. If you remember the ten years of warfare that they waged against deified Caesar, you should balance against that the hundred years of unshakeable loyalty and allegiance to Rome since then—loyalty that has passed muster countless times when Rome found herself in doubtful circumstances.

When my father Drusus was subjugating Germany, those men provided him secure and peaceful conditions behind him as he campaigned. And what is more, Drusus had been called away to war while in the middle of taking a census—at that time a strange and unfamiliar process to the Gauls—and we know from experience how hard a task that is even for us (and now more than ever), although nothing more is demanded of us than a public recording of our resources. [*The surviving inscription ends here, but doubtlessly would have continued on another tablet now lost.*]

> **Source:** *ILS* 212; from Lyons (Lugdunum), AD 48. Translation by R. Scott Smith.

## 60     Senatorial Resolution Ratifying the Powers of the Emperor Vespasian

This bronze tablet preserves most of a decree of the Senate passed in AD 69 or 70, recognizing and legally empowering Vespasian, who emerged as the ultimate victor in a period of civil war from 68–69 after the death of Nero. It represents a codification and statement of the extraordinary legal powers that the Roman emperors had been accumulating since the rise of Augustus a century earlier. Augustus and his successors Tiberius and Claudius are mentioned here as precedents, but Caligula and Nero are passed over in silence.

[1] [ . . . ] that he be permitted to conclude a treaty with whomever he wishes, just as it was permitted to the deified Augustus, to **Tiberius** Julius Caesar Augustus, and to Tiberius **Claudius** Caesar Augustus Germanicus; [2] and that it be permitted for him to convene the Senate, to propose a matter for discussion, to send any matter back for reconsideration, to procure a decree of the Senate by the proposing of a motion and calling for a vote, just as it was permitted to the deified Augustus, to **Tiberius** Julius Caesar Augustus, Tiberius **Claudius** Caesar Augustus Germanicus; [3] and that whenever a Senate meeting is held at his pleasure or by his authority, order, or directive, or in his presence, all proceedings at such a meeting shall be accounted valid, and observance shall be given to them just as if the meeting of the Senate had been announced and held in accordance with ordinary procedure; [4] that whatever candidates he recommends to the Senate and Roman people and to whom he has given or promised his electoral support for any magistracy, special power, military command, or supervisory authority over anything, those candidates shall be given special preference at their various elections; [5] that it be permitted for him to extend the boundaries of the *pomerium* whenever he will judge it to be in the public interest, just as it was permitted to Tiberius **Claudius** Caesar Augustus Germanicus; [6] that he will have full

right and authority to do and execute whatever he will judge to be consistent with the interests of the state and the dignity of matters divine and human, public and private, just as it was permitted to the deified Augustus, to **Tiberius** Julius Caesar Augustus, and to Tiberius **Claudius** Caesar Augustus Germanicus; [7] that Imperator Caesar **Vespasianus** will be exempt from all laws and plebiscites from which it was written that the deified Augustus, or **Tiberius** Julius Caesar Augustus, and Tiberius **Claudius** Caesar Augustus Germanicus should be exempt, and that whatever it was lawful for the deified Augustus, or **Tiberius** Julius Caesar Augustus, or Tiberius **Claudius** Caesar Augustus Germanicus to do on the basis of any law or bill, all these things Imperator Caesar **Vespasianus** Augustus shall have the right to do; [8] that whatever has been done, accomplished, decreed, or ordered by Imperator Caesar **Vespasianus** Augustus before the proposal of this law, or has been done by anyone at his command or directive, those things should be considered lawful and valid, just as if they had been done by order of the people or the plebs.

Oath:

> If any person has taken or will take any action because of this law that is contrary to other laws, bills, plebiscites, or resolutions of the Senate, or if because of this law he has failed to take any action that is required by a law, bill, plebiscite, or resolution of the Senate, it shall not be a crime on his part, nor shall he be liable to pay any penalty to the people on that account, nor shall anyone bring suit or conduct an investigation concerning that matter, nor shall anyone permit a legal process to be carried out before him concerning that matter.

> **Source:** *ILS* 244, with P.A. Brunt, *Journal of Roman Studies* 67 (1977), 96–116; from Rome.

### 61    Vespasian's Letter to the Town Councilors of Sabora

Cities of the Roman empire were responsible for maintaining, improving, and administering their own infrastructure with local tax revenue, but had to get permission to levy new taxes. The people of Sabora now enjoyed Latin rights, a preferential status. The town councilors here ask for permission to remove their administrative center and public buildings from a typical hilltop site to one in the plain, and to rename their city Flavia Sabora, after Vespasian's family name, Flavius.

Imperator Caesar **Vespasianus** Augustus, *pontifex maximus*, in his ninth year of tribunician power (AD 77/78), hailed Imperator for the eighteenth time, consul eight times, Father of the Fatherland, sends greetings to the Board of Four and the councilors of Sabora. Since you indicate you are in an unsatisfactory condition and laboring under many difficulties, I give you permission to construct a town center on level ground, bearing my name as you wish. The tax revenue which you say you were granted by Augustus, I leave unchanged; if you want to add any new taxes you will have to take the matter up with the governor, for I cannot make any determination without hearing from the other side of the case. I received your decree on July 25, and gave your envoys permission to leave on the twenty-ninth day of the same month.

Farewell. C. Cornelius Severus and M. Septimius Severus had this inscribed on bronze using public funds.

> **Source:** *ILS* 6092; from Cañete la Real, Spain (Sabora), AD 77/78.

## 62    Inscription on a Triumphal Arch in the Circus Maximus, Honoring Titus

The Senate and people of Rome (set this up) for Imperator **Titus** Caesar, son of the deified **Vespasianus** Augustus, *pontifex maximus*, in his tenth year of tribunician power (AD 80/81), hailed Imperator for the seventeenth time, consul for the eighth time, Father of the Fatherland, their own leader, because, by the instructions and advice and under the auspices of his father, he conquered the race of the Jews, and destroyed the city of Jerusalem, a feat that all previous generals, kings, and races either tried in vain, or did not attempt at all.

> **Source:** *ILS* 264; the inscription was seen in the Circus Maximus in the 9th century, copied down, and is preserved in a 9th-century manuscript. This arch is not to be confused with the surviving arch between the Colosseum and the Roman Forum.

## 63    Hadrian's Address to the Army at Lambaesis

The Emperor Hadrian (reigned AD 117–138) went to Numidia in North Africa in 128 to review the effectiveness of Rome's army there. His evaluation of this army's preparation was part of an empire-wide review of the legions, and he offered his praise and critique in a set of speeches after the maneuvers. This is consistent with the report of the historian Dio Cassius (69.9.6), who states that "Hadrian drilled his men in every kind of combat, praising some and criticizing others, and he taught them what he expected from them." The army in Lambaesis later had the speeches carved into a massive inscription on the base of a monument on the parade ground at Lambaesis. Though fragmentary, the text is valuable in showing Hadrian's lively interest in military training, and it is the only surviving instance of an address by an emperor to the troops. We have translated only the portions of the inscription that are generally intact.

Emperor Caesar Trajan **Hadrian** Augustus addressed Legion III Augusta as follows, after observing its maneuvers, in the consulship of Torquatus (for the second time) and Libo, July 1.

To the chief centurions: My legate Catullinus is an ardent supporter of you. In fact, he has told me himself on your behalf everything you might have had to put before me: that a cohort is absent because one is sent in turn every year to the staff of the Proconsul (of Africa); that two years ago you gave a cohort and five men from each century to the fellow third legion (III Cyrenaica); that many distant outposts keep you scattered; that twice in living memory you have not only changed camp but even built new ones. Because of all this I would have forgiven you if you have relaxed somewhat in your training. But neither do you seem to have relaxed in any way, nor is there any reason why you should need my forgiving [ . . . ]

To the cavalry of the legion: Military maneuvers have their own rules, so to speak, and if anything is added or taken away, the exercise becomes either less effective or more difficult. Indeed, the more complications are added, the less impressive it appears. Of the difficult maneuvers, you have completed the most difficult of all by throwing javelins while wearing metal corselets [ . . . ] a loss [ . . . ] on the contrary, I applaud your spirit [ . . . ]

To the *principes*:[37] Work that others would have divided over many days, you completed in one day. You have built a lengthy wall, the kind of wall that is made for permanent winter quarters, in nearly as short a time as if it were built from cut turf, which is easily carried and handled and laid without difficulty, since it is naturally smooth and flat. But you built with big, heavy, uneven stones that no one can carry, lift, or lay without their unevenness becoming evident. You dug a ditch through hard and rough gravel, keeping it straight, and leveled it by raking it. When your work had been approved, you came back into the camp quickly, ate, took up your arms, and followed the cavalry that had been sent out, and hailed them with a great shout as they were coming back [ . . . ]

To the auxiliary infantry: [ . . . ] and you did this with hands not slack. And so, since you did not fire at the command, given because the enemy was in range, the prefect fired you up to release your arrows oftener and more urgently, so that among the many arrows the enemy would not dare to lift his head above his shield. [ . . . ] You were slow to close ranks [ . . . ] you will break out more briskly [ . . . ] my Catullinus, the legate [ . . . ] the prefect [ . . . ].

To a cavalry unit: I praise him for directing you toward this maneuver that has the aspect of real fighting, and for training you like this [ . . . ] that I can praise you. Your prefect Cornelianus has fulfilled his duty fearlessly. I am not fond of wheeling attacks, nor was the deified Trajan, my model. A horseman should ride out from cover and [ . . . ]. If he does not see where he is going, or cannot rein in his horse when he wishes, he is certainly at risk of falling into hidden pits and trenches that he does not see. If you want to attack, you must charge across the middle of the field. Just as when facing the enemy, everything must be done with forethought.

**Source:** Michael P. Speidel, *Emperor Hadrian's Speeches to the African Army—A New Text* (Mainz: Verlag des Römisch-Germanischen Zentralmuseums, 2006); from Lambaesis, near Batna, Algeria.

## III. Inscriptions Relating to Public Works

The spirit of civic generosity was very pronounced in the Greco-Roman world, so pervasive that the phenomenon has earned its own term, "euergetism," derived from the Greek for "to do good." These "good works" were expected and urged on the wealthy of a community by their fellow citizens, and also

---

37. One of the main infantry units, which formed a single battle line.

stimulated by their own ambitions. It was often these funds that came from personal estates, rather than official tax revenue, that built temples, basilicas, city squares, roads, sidewalks, aqueducts, and all the amenities for public use that we associate with Greco-Roman urbanism. And these benefactions were duly commemorated in inscriptions. Freedmen participated, as did women— seemingly anyone who had the money. The emperors continued this project on a large scale, founding and equipping cities around the empire.

## 64    An Aqueduct and Other Amenities for Aletrium

Local magnate Betilienus Varus spent a fortune refurbishing the urban infrastructure of Aletrium, about forty miles east of Rome. The aqueduct he financed is an excellent early example, carrying water 7.5 miles from the source north of town, over the deep gorge of the river Cosa on a bridge with two tiers of arches. The reference to "solid pipes" perhaps refers to the fact that it used an inverted siphon, made out of lead pipes, to carry the water back uphill.

L. Betilienus Varus, son of Lucius, commissioned the construction of the following, in accordance with the will of the Senate (of Aletrium): all the sidewalks in the town, the covered walkway that goes to the citadel, the playing field, the sundial, the market, the stucco on the basilica, the benches, a bathing pool, a fountain at the gate. He constructed an aqueduct into the town, with arches 340 feet in height, and solid pipes. For these things he was twice made censor, the Senate decreed that his son be excused from military service, and the people set up a statue to him under the name Censorinus.

*Source: ILS* 5348; from Alatri, Italy, around 120 BC.

## 65    Walls and Towers Repaired at Private Expense

Imperator Caesar **Augustus**, son of the deified (Julius Caesar), father of the *colonia*, gave the wall and towers. T. Julius Optatus, at his own expense, restored the towers that had collapsed with age.

*Source: ILS* 5336; from Zadar, Croatia.

## 66    Wall for a City Square Financed by a Freedman

In the fourth consulship of Imperator Gaius Caesar (**Caligula**), L. Pomponius Malcius, freedman of Lucius, *duumvir*, commissioned the construction of the whole wall of the city from square cut stone.

*Source: ILS* 5320; from Korba, Tunisia, AD 41.

## 67    Streets Financed by a Governor

C. Asinius Tucurianus, proconsul, paved the street which had been unpaved.

*Source: ILS* 5352; from Sulci, Sardinia.

## 68    Streets Financed By a Group of Freedmen

In honor of Imperator Caesar **Augustus**, son of the deified (Julius Caesar), *pontifex maximus*, Father of the Fatherland and the town, the chief officers of the *Augustales*: C. Egnatius Glyco freedman of Marcus, C. Egnatius Musicus freedman of Gaius, C. Julius Isochrysus freedman of Caesar, Q. Floronius Princeps freedman of Quintus, commissioned the paving of the Augustan Way with stone, from the Via Annia beyond the gate as far as the temple of Ceres, at their own expense, in place of games.

*Source: ILS* 5373; from Falerii in Etruria.

## 69    A Playing Field Financed by a Local Magistrate

C. Catius, son of Marcus, member of the Board of Four, oversaw the leveling of the playing field at public expense, and at his own expense oversaw the construction of the surrounding wall, the lounge areas, the solarium, and the sidewalk. To the Genius of the *colonia*, and in honor of the colonists, may they prosper and enjoy the use of it forever.

*Source: ILS* 5392; from Nola, Italy.

## 70    A Temple of Apollo Restored by a Local Magistrate

L. Aninius Capra, son of Lucius, member of the Board of Four for a second time, commissioned the restoration at his own expense of the temple of Apollo and the surrounding wall.

*Source: ILS* 5397; from at Setia, forty miles south of Rome.

## 71    Wall around a Shrine Financed by a Woman

Ansia Rufa, daughter of Tarvus, in accordance with a decree of the decurions, commissioned the construction at her own expense of the inner wall around the sacred grove, the outer wall, and the doorway.

*Source: ILS* 5430; from Padula, southern Italy.

# IV. Documents Relating to Festivals, Games, and Shows

A number of inscriptions relate to the financing of theater, games, and shows of various kinds, and reveal how fully entertainment was enmeshed in the networks of local government, patronage, and religious observances. Epitaphs of gladiators are important evidence for the fact that arena fatalities of well-trained gladiators were relatively rare, that most gladiators fought no more than twice per year, and that many gladiators enjoyed a strong sense of camaraderie and had wives and families. Inscriptions honoring charioteers bear witness to the fabulous amounts of prize money that successful jockeys could earn. And the epitaphs of mime and pantomime actors give a small window into these very popular but now rather neglected forms of Roman entertainment.

## 72    Decree of Town Councilors Sponsoring Public Events as Part of Imperial Cult

Starting with Augustus, the emperor became identified with the Roman empire itself and was gradually incorporated into religious rites. Local governments took responsibility for celebrating the elaborate festivals, which included sacrifices, prayers, and games, on important days for the imperial family. (For the imperial household's presence in the calendar, see also "A Roman Calendar" in this volume.) This inscription commemorates the creation of new festivals, including games, in honor of the Emperor Tiberius at Forum Clodii, a town in Etruria.

In the third consulship of **Tiberius** Caesar, the second of Germanicus Caesar (AD 18), when the *duumvirs* were Cn. Acceius Rufus Lutatius, son of Gnaeus, voting tribe Arnensis, and T. Petillius, son of Publius, voting tribe Quirina, the following were decreed:

- The shrine and these statues, and the victim for the dedication.
- The usual two victims sacrificed on September 24, the birthday of Augustus, at the altar of the divine power (*numen*) of Augustus, shall be sacrificed on both September 23 and 24.
- Likewise, that on the birthday of Tiberius Caesar (Nov. 16) the decurions and the people shall have a (free) dinner, and shall do so every year in perpetuity—thanks to the generosity of Q. Cascellius Labeo, who promised to bear the expense in perpetuity—and that a calf be sacrificed every year on that same day.
- And that, on the birthdays of Emperors Augustus and Tiberius, before the decurions go to eat, the spirits (*genii*) of those emperors shall be invited with (offerings of) incense and wine to dine at the altar of the divine power (*numen*) of Augustus.

At our own expense we provided:

- the altar to the divine power of Augustus
- games (*ludi*) for six days, beginning August 13
- honey-wine and a cake for the women of the community in the Bona Dea district on the birthday of Augusta (Livia)
- honey-wine and cakes for the decurions and the people on the occasion of the dedication of the statues of the emperors and of Augusta. And we declared that we would do the same in perpetuity on the day of that dedication, and,

so that each year the festival will be better attended, we will keep it on March 10, the day that Tiberius Caesar was most happily made *pontifex maximus*.

*Source: ILS* 154, with Duncan Fishwick, *Zeitschrift für Papyrologie und Epigraphik* 160 (2007), 247–55; from Forum Clodii, Etruria, AD 18.

## 73     A Sponsor from Pompeii

One of the obligations upon entering office as a local magistrate (or when admitted into the decurions) was to donate, either in cash or public games, a certain sum of money to the town. Clodius was *duumvir* for the third time in 2/1 BC. In most towns the forum, with its wide, open rectangular space, was the main arena for shows, including gladiatorial combat. The forum in Pompeii was abutted by a temple of Apollo.

A. Clodius Flaccus, son of Aulus, voting tribe Menenia, judicial *duumvir* three times, *quinquennalis*, tribune of the soldiers by popular vote. In his first term as *duumvir* at the games of Apollo he gave in the forum a procession, bulls, bull-fighters, *succursores*,[38] three pairs of bridge fighters, team boxers and fighters, games with every musical entertainment and with all the pantomimes, and Pylades,[39] and a payment to the public of 10,000 sesterces in honor of his duumvirate. In his second duumvirate, as *quinquennalis* at the Games of Apollo in the forum (he gave) a procession, bulls, bull-fighters, *succursores*, team boxers; on the following day (he presented) in the amphitheater entirely on his own thirty pairs of athletes, five pairs of gladiators, then with his colleague (he presented) thirty-five pairs of gladiators, and a hunt, with bulls, bull-fighters, boars, bears, and various other wild animals. In his third duumvirate he presented games (*ludi*) as he did the first time, but adding musical entertainments, with a colleague.

*Source: ILS* 5053; from Pompeii.

## 74     A Sponsor from Alife

For the responsibility of a new *decurio* to repay the city with cash or games, see previous inscription.

To L. Fadius Pierus, *duumvir*, most generous citizen, who in return for the honor of the decurionate put on a show of thirty pairs of gladiators and a hunt of African beasts, and a few months later, still during his term as *duumvir*, having received 13,000 sesterces from the community, gave full hunts and twenty-one pairs of gladiators, and likewise a year later put on theatrical shows at his own expense. The *Augustales* (set this up) in space granted by a decree of the decurions.

*Source: ILS* 5059; from Alife, Italy.

---

38. An obscure term that occurs only here. The element *cursor* suggests running of some sort.

39. The most popular interpretative dancer (pantomimist) in the Roman world in the Augustan Age.

## 75    A Producer and Head of the Guild of Latin Mime Actors

The emperors mentioned are probably Marcus Aurelius and Marcus Annius Verus, who ruled jointly AD 161–169. The actors in question were certainly mime actors (see Glossary). Guilds of actors were important intermediaries between those who sponsored games and shows and those who performed in them. Plebeius was an impresario who managed actors' contracts, and his status as an imperial freedman meant valuable personal connections with imperial house.

For M. Aurelius Plebeius, freedman of the emperors, appointed manager on a permanent salary, secretary and magister for life of the guild of Latin actors, managing the affairs of the above-mentioned guild with incomparable honesty [ . . . ]

*Source: ILS* 5206, with W.J. Slater, *Phoenix* 59 (2005), 316–23;
from the country around Alba, near Rome.

## 76    A Star Mime Actor

Eutyches was evidently a "common" mime in the employment of a city, as opposed to those owned, rented, and loaned by a private person, or those obliged to travel and accept irregular work. As "archmime" of such a group he will have been one of the great stars of the period. The "Parasites of Apollo" was another elite group of citizen mime and pantomime performers. Eutyches was an evidently wealthy decurion at Bovillae, ten miles from Rome.

For L. Acilius Eutyches, son of Lucius, voting tribe Pomptina, elite archmime of the public mime actors, board member with full salary, Parasite of Apollo, honored by tragic, comic, and all corporations to do with the stage, decurion at Bovillae. He was the first man to be named "Father" by the theater artists' executive board. The theater artists' executive board (set this up) after taking up a collection, because of his services and devotion to that body. In honor of the dedication (of this monument) he gave to the members a donation of twenty-five denarii each, to the decurions of Bovillae a gift of five denarii each, to the *Augustales* three denarii each, to the honored women and to the people a denarius each. Dedicated August 11, in the consulship of Sossius Priscus and Coelius Apollinaris (AD 169). [*There follows a list of sixty members of the board, not translated here.*]

*Source: ILS* 5196, with W.J. Slater, *Phoenix* 56 (2002), 315–29;
from Bovillae, Italy.

## 77    Epitaph of a Pantomime Dancer

Several very young pantomime (see Glossary) performers are known, one even as young as five, but Pylades the great pantomime performer mentioned above (in Inscription no. 73), was very old at the time of that performance.

To the *Di Manes* of the boy Septentrio, aged twelve, who danced in the theater at Antipolis on two successive days, to acclaim.

*Source: ILS* 5258; from Nice, France (Antipolis).

## 78    Epitaph of a Pantomime Dancer

Thyas, dancer, (in the troupe) of Metilia Rufina. She lived fourteen years. Thalamus put this up for his fiancée.

*Source: ILS* 5260; from Carthage.

## 79    Epitaph of the Gladiator Flamma

Even if death was a fair and accepted result of gladiatorial fights, a variety of non-lethal outcomes were possible. There were draws, as Flamma's career shows, and gladiators who fought well but lost due to injury or to an opponent's superior skills could appeal and be spared. On draws and reprieves for gladiators, see Martial, *Epigrams* 8 in this volume, with note.

Flamma, *secutor*. He lived thirty years, fought thirty-four times, won twenty-one times, and fought to a draw nine times. He lost four times, but was spared. Syrian by birth. Delicatus erected this for his worthy comrade-at-arms.

*Source: ILS* 5113; from Sicily.

## 80    Epitaph of the Gladiator Ajax

According to Homer there were two Greek heroes named Ajax that fought in the Trojan War, and this epitaph contains poetic echoes of Homeric language, indicating a high degree of learning for the person who composed the lines—probably not Ajax or his wife, but someone else connected with creating the inscription. Several tombstones in Greece (where gladiatorial combat was no less embraced than in the West) exhibit the peculiar boast of not having hurt anyone or of having saved lives, as here, suggesting that on some occasions gladiators (and not the producer of the games or the crowd) had the power over a defeated opponent.

(*in verse*) You are looking at Ajax—not the one from Locris or even Telamon's son, but the one who pleased spectators in the stands in warlike battles. I resolutely spared many souls when they were at my mercy in the hope that I would receive the same treatment from others. I was not slain by an opponent, but I died my own death. My dear wife laid me to rest here, in the holy fields of Thasos. Kalligeneia erected this monument in memory of her husband Ajax.

*Source: IG XII Suppl.* 479; from Thasos, Greece.

## 81 Epitaph of the Gladiator Exochus

Whereas plays and circus races were connected with the regular sacred festival calendar (and called *ludi*, "games"), gladiatorial fights (*munera*, lit. "gifts") were not. They were occasional, as in the case of Exochus' finest hour, the *munera* given in connection with Trajan's posthumous triumph over the Parthians in AD 117. The existence of freeborn gladiators (like the Fimbria mentioned here) is also well attested. Below the first line there is a picture of Exochus holding his armed right hand to his head and a palm in his left.

M. Antonius Exochus, *thraex*. M. Antonius Exochus, by birth Alexandrian. (In the shows given) at Rome on account of the triumph of deified Trajan, on the second day, as a beginner, he fought to a draw with Araxes, imperial slave. At Rome on the ninth day of the same games he defeated Fimbria, a freeborn gladiator with nine fights under his belt, and sent him away spared. At Rome, in the same games [ . . . ]

*Source: ILS* 5088; from Rome.

## 82 Epitaph of the Gladiator Niger

The following inscription highlights how few times a gladiator might be expected to fight over a career. See also no. 79 above.

To the *Di Manes* of M. Antonius Niger, veteran *thraex*, who lived thirty-eight years, fought eighteen times. Flavia Diogenis had this made at her own expense for her well-deserving husband.

*Source: ILS* 5090; from Rome.

## 83 Epitaph of the Gladiator Volusenus

For the liberation of gladiators after a fight, see Martial, *Epigrams* 8 in this volume.

To the *Di Manes* of Volusenus, *thraex*. His friends set this up. He was liberated after his eighth fight.

*Source: ILS* 5086; from Rome.

## 84 Epitaph of the Gladiator Felix

The Tungri mentioned below were from Lower Germany, near Liège, Belgium.

To the *Di Manes* of M. Ulpius Felix, veteran *myrmillo*. He lived forty-five years. Tungrian by birth. His wife Ulpia Syntyche, freedwoman, had this made for her most sweet and well-deserving husband, as did their son Justus.

*Source: ILS* 5104; from Rome.

## 85    Epitaph of the Gladiator Amabilis

For Amabilis, *secutor*, Dacian by birth, fought thirteen times, deceived by Fate, not man.

**Source:** *ILS* 5111; from Stobreč, Croatia.

## 86    Epitaph for Two Gladiators Who Killed Each Other

There is wordplay on the word *munus*, the general word for gift but also for "gladiatorial show" as well as "funeral offering." It was probably rare that the sponsor of the show would pay out the funds to bury a gladiator, and the fight between Decoratus and Caeruleus must have been a remarkable fight that brought Constantius great popularity. It was clearly exceptional for both combatants to die in a single gladiatorial bout.

Constantius, sponsor (*munerarius*), because of the great popular acclaim of his gladiator show (*munus*), has given the gift (*munus*) of a tomb to his gladiators: to Decoratus, who killed the *retiarius* Caeruleus and then fell, himself killed. The trainer's rod killed them both, the funeral pyre covers them both. Decoratus, the *secutor*, veteran of nine fights, bequeathed primarily grief to his wife Valeria.

**Source:** *ILS* 5123; from Trieste (Tergeste), northeastern Italy.

## 87    Inscription Honoring Polynices the Charioteer

Most performers in ancient Rome were from distant provinces, but Polynices is identified as "of domestic origin," or "a home-born slave" (*verna*). In contrast to gladiators, charioteers competed frequently, often many times in one day.

M. Aurelius Polynices, of domestic origin, lived twenty-nine years, nine months, and five days. He won 739 races, receiving the palm of victory. Of these victories, 655 came with the Red Team, fifty-five with the Green, twelve with the Blue, and seventeen with the White. He won a 40,000-sestertius purse three times, a 30,000-purse twenty-six times, and exhibitions with no prize purse eleven times. He raced in an eight-horse chariot eight times, in a ten-horse chariot nine times, and in a six-horse chariot three times.

**Source:** *ILS* 5286.1; from near Rome.

## 88    Inscription Honoring Diocles the Charioteer

The following is the most extensive surviving inscription about a charioteer's career. It informs us about prize purses, the kinds of races one might compete in, and the strategy involved in winning a race. Diocles raced for three teams, won a great deal of money, and finally retired as a member of the Red Team after a staggering 4,257 races and a thirty-four percent winning percentage. The latter, largely obscure portion of this long inscription has been omitted.

Gaius Appuleius Diocles, driver for the Red Team. Spaniard by birth, from Lusitania, aged forty-two years, seven months, twenty-two days. He first drove for the White Team in the consulship of Acilius Aviola and Corellius Pansa (AD 122), and won his first victory for that same team in the consulship of M. Acilius Glabrio and C. Bellicus Torquatus (AD 124). He started driving for the Green Team in the consulship of Torquatus Asprenas (for the second time) and Annius Libo (AD 128). His first victory for the Red Team occurred in the consulship of Laenas Pontianus and Antonius Rufinus (AD 131).

Career statistics: He drove a four-horse chariot for twenty-four years, had 4,257 starts, and came in first place 1,462 times, with 110 of those coming in the opening race.[40] In single-entry races he won 1,064 times.[41] Earnings: He won major purses ninety-two times: 30,000 sestertii: thirty-two times (three of these on six-horse chariots); 40,000 sestertii: twenty-eight times (two on six-horse chariots); 50,000 sestertii: twenty-nine times (once on a seven-horse chariot); 60,000 sestertii: three times. In double-entry races he had 347 victories, four of them on three-horse chariots with a first place prize of 15,000 sestertii. In triple-entry races he had fifty-one victories. All told, he took home prizes 2,900 times: he took second 861 times, third 576 times, and fourth once when it carried a prize of 1,000 sestertii. He had 1,351 finishes out of the money. When allied with the Blue Team he had ten victories, and eighty-nine more victories when allied with the White Team, two of which carried a prize of 30,000 sestertii. His lifetime earnings were 35,863,120 sestertii. In addition, he secured three victories over charioteers with a thousand wins under their belts in two-horse chariot events, once against a thousander from the White Team, twice against one from the Green Team. He sprinted out to the lead and won 815 times, and came from last place for sixty-seven victories. On thirty-six other occasions he won [ . . . ]. He won thirty-two times with using various techniques. 502 times he snatched victory from an opponent in the last moments of the race, 216 times from the Green Team, 205 from the Blue Team, and 81 times from the White Team. He rode nine horses to 100 victories, and one to 200.

*Source: ILS* 5287; from Rome. Translation by R. Scott Smith.

# V. Prayers and Dedications to Gods

A large category of documents relates to humans' dealings with the gods. Inscribed texts of regulations (*leges*) relating to sacrifice at altars suggest the legalism of Roman state cults, and incidentally illustrate how divine honors for emperors slotted in comfortably with honors for the more traditional deities. A sense of the sheer diversity of gods available comes from a set of

---

40. Unlike modern practice, the first and not the last race was the featured matchup.

41. That is, with four chariots, one from each team. A double-entry race, as mentioned below, would have eight chariots on the track at once.

altars excavated in the multi-ethnic milieu of the Roman frontier, with its contingents of soldiers from all over the empire. For more sources on religion see the superb *Religions of Rome* (two volumes, vol. 2 comprising translated sources) by Mary Beard, John North, and Simon Price (Cambridge: Cambridge University Press, 1998).

## 89    Dedication of an Altar to Jupiter Optimus Maximus

The regulations of this particular altar are keyed to those of an altar in Rome, a symbolic link of the religious practices in this Roman colony in the Greek East with those of the imperial center. An introductory sentence, not printed here, identifies the consular date, AD 137, and the day, October 9. The day of dedication of an altar or temple was often celebrated with special events on the annual anniversary.

C. Domitius Valens, judicial *duumvir*, established the regulations (for the altar) in the words given below, as dictated by the *pontifex* C. Julius Severus: Jupiter Optimus Maximus: I will give and dedicate this altar to you today, and will give and dedicate it under those regulations and within those boundaries which I will here openly declare today, here at the foundation surrounding this altar, as follows: If anyone makes an animal sacrifice here, even if he does not expose the entrails, still it will count as correctly done. The other regulations governing this altar shall be the same as those laid out for the altar of Diana on the Aventine Hill (in Rome). Under these regulations and within these boundaries as I have said, I give, declare, and dedicate this altar to you, Jupiter Optimus Maximus, so that you might be well disposed and propitious to me, my colleagues, the town councilors, the citizens, the inhabitants of the *colonia* Martia Julia Salona, and to our wives and children.

*Source: ILS* 4907 = *BNP* 10.1c; from Solin, Croatia
(Salona in Dalmatia).

## 90    Dedication of an Altar to the *Numen* of Augustus

In AD 11 the citizens of Narbo, Gaul (modern Narbonne, France) decided to erect an altar to the *numen* ("divine presence or power") of Augustus in response to his settlement of a class dispute in the city. Unlike in the East, where the Emperor Augustus was himself treated as a divine figure (see no. 57 above), in the West the idea of a divine living emperor took more time to take hold. Instead of worshipping Augustus himself, the citizens set up an altar to the emperor's divine powers, which forged a connection between the emperor and citizens—many of whom would never see the emperor himself. The regulations of this altar resemble those in the preceding item.

Divine power (*numen*) of Caesar Augustus, Father of the Fatherland: I will give and dedicate this altar to you today, and will give and dedicate it to you under these regulations and within those boundaries which I will here openly declare today, at the foundation surrounding this altar and these inscriptions: if anyone wishes to clean, decorate, or repair (the altar), provided he does it with helpful intent, let it be lawful and right. Or if anyone makes an animal sacrifice, even if he does not expose the entrails, still it will count as correctly done. If anyone wishes to give a gift to this altar and enlarge it, let it be permitted, and let the same regulations apply to this gift as apply to the altar. The other regulations for this altar and its inscriptions shall be the same as those that apply to the altar of Diana on the Aventine Hill (in Rome). Under these regulations and within these boundaries as I have said, on behalf of Emperor Caesar Augustus Father of the Fatherland, *pontifex maximus*, in the thirty-fifth year of his tribunician power (AD 12/13), on behalf of his wife and children and family, the Senate and the people of Rome, and the citizens and inhabitants of the *colonia* Julia Paterna Narbo Martius, who have bound themselves to the worship of his divine power (*numen*) forever, I give and dedicate this altar to you, so that you might be well disposed and propitious.

*Source: ILS* 112, second half; from Narbonne, France (Narbo).

## 91    Prayer of Married Women to Juno

The following is a prayer offered by Roman matrons at the Temple of Juno Regina ("Queen Juno") on the occasion of the Secular Games, a festival held periodically to herald the beginning of a new era. This prayer comes from the Secular Games under Septimius Severus in AD 204, but it is nearly identical in wording to the prayer offered in 17 BC (*ILS* 5050, verses 125 ff.), when Augustus first held such a festival. The monumental inscription from which this comes tells us that the emperor's wife, Julia Domna, and the two chief Vestal Virgins accompanied 110 leading women to the temple.

Queen Juno, for the [greater benefit] of the citizens of Rome, [permit us, the 110 mothers of families], the brides of Roman citizens, to pray to you and beseech you to grant increase to the empire and the maje[sty of the Roman people] at war and at home, and that you always [protect the Latin name, favor] the people and the legions of Rome, and keep the state of the Roman people safe. And may you be well disposed and propitious to [the Board of Fifteen for Performing Sacrifices of the Roman people, to us, our homes, and to our households. These things we, the 110 mothers of families,] wives of Roman citizens, on our knees, pray, beg, and beseech. [*A list of the women follows.*]

*Source: CIL* 6.32329, verses 10ff.; from Rome, around AD 204.

## 92    Votive Offering to Bona Dea

A votive offering is a type of gift to a divinity which is common all over the world. Placed in a shrine in fulfillment of a vow (*votum*) as a gesture of thanks, it also serves as a testimony to the power of the deity. Inscribed examples often include stories of miraculous cures. Bona Dea ("Good Goddess") was an important Roman deity associated with fertility, healing, and the protection of the Roman state (see Cicero, *Letters* 3 in this volume).

Felix Asinianus, a public slave of the priests (*pontifices*) fulfills his vow to the Bona Dea of the fields, called "blessed," by sacrificing a white heifer—gladly, because his eyesight has been restored, though the doctors had given up on him. After ten months he was cured by her, thanks to our Lady's remedies. Cannia Fortunata had the entire monument restored.

> **Source:** *ILS* 3513; from near Rome, on the Via Ostiense. The final sentence is a later addition.

## 93    Altars near a Fort on Hadrian's Wall

This item translates all the altars found at one site on Hadrian's Wall (Carvoran) and published in *Roman Inscriptions in Britain* (references to that publication are given before each item). It gives a representative picture of the kinds of altars found, and gods worshipped, in this period among Latin speakers in Britain.

1775 To the god Baliticaurus,[42] a vow | 1776 To the god Blatucadrus, the vow was paid | 1777 To the goddess Epona,[43] P[ . . . ] So[ . . . ] (set this up) | 1778 To the Emperor's Fortune, for the welfare of L. Aelius Caesar. Titus Flavius Secundus, prefect of the First Cohort of Hamian Archers, because of a vision, willingly fulfilled his vow as was right | 1779 To Fortune. Audacilius Romanus, centurion of the VI, XX, and (II) Augusta Legions, (set this up) | 1780 To the goddess Hammia. Sabinus made this | 1781 To the god Hercules [ . . . ] | 1782 To Jupiter Best and Greatest of Doliche [ . . . ] | 1783 To Jupiter Best and Greatest of Heliopolis, Julius Pollio [ . . . ] (set this up) | 1784 To the god Mars Belatucairus | 1785 To the Mother Goddesses [ . . . ] | 1786 To the god M[ . . . ] and to the *numina* of the emperors, Julius Pacatus and [ . . . ] Pacutius C[ . . . ] built this building from ground-level, willingly fulfilling their vow as was right | 1787 To the deity M[ . . . ] | 1788 [ . . . ] to Minerva [ . . . ] | 1789 To the goddesses the Nymphs. Vettia Mansueta and Claudia Turianilla, her daughter, willingly fulfilled their vow as was right | 1790 To Silvanus. Vellaeus [ . . . ] | 1791 (*in verse*) The Virgin Goddess in her heavenly place hovers over the Lion, holding stalks of wheat: the inventor of Justice, founder of cities, by whose gifts it is mankind's good fortune to know the gods. Therefore the same goddess is Mother of the Gods. She is Peace, Virtue, Ceres, and the Syrian Goddess, weighing life and laws on her scale. Syria has sent the constellation seen in the heavens to Libya to be worshipped. That is where we all learned of her. M. Caecilianus Donatianus came to this understanding led by your divine power, serving as tribune in the post of prefect

---

42. A war god. The different spellings likely indicate Latin speakers trying to spell out the name of a Celtic deity that they had only heard orally.

43. A Celtic goddess of horses.

by the emperor's gift.[44] | 1792 To the Syrian Goddess. Licinius Clemens, prefect of the First Cohort of Hamians (set this up) under Calpurnius Agricola, the emperor's propraetorian legate | 1793 To the god Veteris.[45] Necalames willingly fulfilled his vow as was right | 1794 To the god Veteris, Necalames willingly fulfilled his vow | 1795 To the holy god Veteris. Julius Pastor, *imaginifer*[46] of the Second Cohort of Dalmatians, willingly fulfilled his vow as was right | 1796 To the holy god Vetiris. Andiatis on the fulfillment of the vow willingly and deservedly set this up. | 1797 To the god Veteris, a vow | 1798 To the god Viteris | 1799 To the god Vitiris, Menius Dada willingly fulfilled his vow as was right | 1800 To the god Vitiris. Milus and Aurides willingly fulfilled their vow as was right | 1801 To the god Vitiris. Necalimes [ . . . ] willingly set up his vow as was right | 1802 To the Veteres [ . . . ] | 1804 To the gods the Veteres [ . . . ] willingly fulfilled the vow as was right | 1805 To the gods the Vitires, Deccius willingly fulfilled his vow as was right | 1806 To the god, Binius (gave) this bracelet, willingly and deservedly fulfilling his vow.

*Source: RIB* 1775–1806, various dates in the 100s and 200s AD.

# VI. Curse Tablets (*Defixiones*)

More than 1,500 curse tablets and binding spells survive from the ancient world, which were usually inscribed on thin metal sheets, folded up, pierced in ritual fashion, and buried or otherwise dedicated to chthonic deities, such as Pluto and Persephone. Most of these have been found by archaeologists where they were placed by religious professionals or their clients, often in graves or wells. They reveal attempts to use the techniques of magic to influence the outcomes of various risk-filled endeavors, including lawsuits, horse races, and love affairs. Many include phrases that are not any known language, so are probably magic formulas provided by the magic expert to the one cursing his enemies (printed in *italics* in our translations below). For more, see John G. Gager, *Curse Tablets and Binding Spells from the Ancient World* (Oxford: Oxford University Press, 1992).

---

44. A dedicatory poem inscribed to go with a statue of the goddess Virgo-Caelestis ("Heavenly Virgin") from around AD 200. The Virgin is the constellation Virgo, which is near the constellation Leo, and was taken by the ancients to represent the female personification of Justice or Ceres, and seen as holding shafts of wheat. She was also identified with other powerful goddesses, such as Cybele and Atargatis, the chief goddess of northern Syria, whom the Romans called "the Syrian Goddess." The poem also honors Julia Domna, the Syrian wife of the Libyan or African emperor Septimius Severus (reigned AD 193–211), who was well loved by soldiers and often called the "Camp Mother." Julia Domna was identified with the Virgin, and coins from the reign of Severus show Julia Domna riding on the Lion. Donatianus was promoted to a tribune's rank while serving as a *praefectus cohortis. CIL* 7.759 = *CLE* 24 = *RIB* 1791.

45. The god Veteris (spelled variously) was a Celtic war god attested from many inscriptions in Roman Britain. The dedicants were exclusively male. During the 200s AD the cult was evidently popular in the ranks of the Roman army.

46. One who carries the image of the emperor as a standard.

## 94    Lead Curse Tablet from Chagnon, France

This curse tablet consisted of two lead plaques joined together and pierced with a nail. A coin of Marcus Aurelius (AD 172) was found next to it. The occasion of this curse was a trial.

I denounce the persons written below, Lentinus and Tasgillus, so that they may leave here and go to Pluto and to Persephone. Just as this puppy harmed no one . . . and let them not prevail in this lawsuit. Just as the mother of this puppy could not protect it, so may their advocates not be able to protect them, so let these enemies be beaten in the lawsuit. *Atracatetracati gallara precata egdarata hehes celata mentis ablata.* Just as this puppy was destroyed and cannot get up, so let it be for them. Let them be pierced through, just as it was. Just as all the living beings in this tomb have gone silent and cannot get up, nor can they [. . .] *Atracatetracati gallara precata egdarata hehes celata mentis ablata.*

*Source:* Audollent, *Defixionum Tabellae,* nos. 111 and 112;
found near Chagnon, France (Aquitania, Gaul).

## 95    Lead Curse Tablet from Minturno, Italy

Found in a tomb made from roof tiles, placed under the skull of the deceased; with it was found a marble statue of elegant workmanship representing a woman with elaborate hairstyle, eleven centimeters tall.

Gods of the underworld, if you have any sanctity, I consign and hand over to you Tychene the wife of Carisius. Whatever she does, whatever happens to her, let all go against her. Gods of the underworld, to you I consign her limbs, her color, her figure, head, hair, shadow, brain, forehead, eyebrows, mouth, nose, chin, cheeks, lips, [word,] visage, neck, liver, shoulders, heart, lungs, intestines, belly, arms, fingers, hands, navel, bladder, woman parts, knees, shins, heels, feet, toes. Gods of the underworld, if I see her wasting away (I vow to) dedicate to you the annual sacrifice to her parents' *Manes,* willingly [ . . . ] let her waste away.

*Source:* Audollent, *Defixionum Tabellae,* no. 190.

## 96    Lead Curse Tablet from Carthage

Clodia Helena, Clodia Successa, Clodia Stertia, Clodius Fortunatus, Clodius Romanus, Murcius Crim [ . . . ]enius, Servilius Faustus, Valerius Extricatus. Just as (I have listed) these names [ . . . ] against me, let them fall silent [ . . . ] just as this rooster (cannot) speak, just as I have torn out its tongue while it was still alive, and pierced it, so let the tongues of my enemies who slander me fall silent [ . . . ]

*Source:* Audollent, *Defixionum Tabellae,* no. 222;
found on a farm near Carthage.

**97    Illustrated Lead Curse Tablet from Carthage**

(*side a*) *Cuigeu censeu cinbeu perfleu diarunco deasta bescu berbescu arurara bazagra* (on the chest of the demon:) *Animo arait to* (on the boat:) Nightwandering Ocean of the Tiber

(*side b*) I conjure you, demon, whoever you may be, and order you to torture and kill, from this hour, this day, this moment, the horses of the Green and White teams; kill and smash the charioteers Clarus, Felix, Primulus, Romanus; do not leave a breath in them. I conjure you by him who has delivered you, at the time, the god of the sea and air: *Iao, Iasdao, Oorio, Aeia.*

> **Source:** Audollent, *Defixionum Tabellae*, no. 286; found in a grave near Carthage. Illustrated in Audollent, p. 397.

# VII. Certificates of Sacrifice from the Decian Persecution

In late AD 249 or early 250 the Emperor Decius, in an attempt to reunify the empire, issued an edict commanding all inhabitants of the empire, citizen or non-citizen alike, male or female, adult or child, to sacrifice to the gods. Although as far as we know the gods were not specified, state gods (including the emperor) were clearly indicated. In these sacrifices we know of offerings to the deified emperors, to Jupiter, to the triple cult of Jupiter, Juno and Minerva, to the *genius* of the living emperor, to Apollo, Diana, and Venus. The documents below are from Egypt and are known as *libelli*. A *libellus* was a written petition of an inhabitant of the empire addressed to the local authorities requesting that they countersign a declaration of pagan religious loyalty, and give written testimony of sacrifice performed in their presence. Forty-six of these formulaic but personalized documents are known, preserved thanks to the dry conditions hospitable to the survival of papyrus in Egypt. The ones known up to 1923 were collected and translated by J.R. Knipfing, on whose work this selection of three is based. **Source:** J.R. Knipfing, "The *libelli* of the Decian Persecution," *Harvard Theological Review* 16 (1923), 345–90, nos. 2, 3 and 35.

**98    Two Brothers and Their Wives**

*First Hand*: To the commission of the village of Philadelphia chosen to superintend the sacrifices. From Aurelius Syrus and Aurelius Pasbeius, his brother, and Demetria and Sarapias, our wives, dwelling beyond the town gates. We have always and without interruption sacrificed to the gods, and now in your presence in accordance with the edict's decree we have poured a libation, and partaken of the sacred victims. We request you to certify this for us below. *Second Hand*: We, Aurelius Syrus and Aurelius Pasbeius, presented this petition. I, Isidorus, wrote on their behalf, as they are illiterate.

## 99    A Priestess of the God Petesouchos

To the commission chosen to superintend the sacrifices. From Aurelia Ammonous, daughter of Mystes, priestess of the god Petesouchos, the great, the mighty, the immortal, and of the gods of the Moeris quarter. I have sacrificed to the gods all my life and without interruption, and now again, in accordance with the decree and in your presence, I have made sacrifice, and poured a libation, and partaken of the sacred victims. I request that you certify this below.

## 100    Inaris and Her Children

*First Hand:* To the commission chosen to superintend the sacrifices. From Inaris, daughter of Akios of the village of Theoxenis, together with her children, Ajax and Hera, all residing in the village of Theadelphia. We have always and without interruption sacrificed to the gods, and now in your presence in accordance with the edict's decree we have made sacrifice, and poured libations, and partaken of the sacred victims. We request that you certify this below. Farewell. *Second Hand:* We, Aurelius Serenus and Aurelius Hermas, saw you sacrificing. *First Hand*: The year one of the Emperor C. Messius Quintus Trajanus Decius Pius Felix Augustus, Pauni 23 (June 17, AD 250).

Abbreviations used in this section:

| | |
|---|---|
| *AE* | *L'Année Épigraphique, 1888–*. Paris: Presses Universitaires de France. |
| Audollent | Audollent, A. 1904. *Defixionum Tabellae*. Paris: A. Fontemoing. |
| *BNP* | Beard, M., J. North, and S. Price, 1998. *Religions of Rome*, 2 vols. Cambridge: Cambridge University Press. |
| *CGL* | Goetz, G. 1888–1923. *Corpus Glossariorum Latinorum*. 7 vols. Leipzig and Berlin: Teubner. |
| *CIL* | *Corpus Inscriptionum Latinarum*, 1863–. 17 vols. Berlin: Walter de Gruyter. |
| *CLE* | Bücheler, F., and E. Lommatzsch, eds. 1895–1926. *Carmina Latina Epigraphica*. Stuttgart: Teubner. |
| *IG XII Suppl.* | von Gaertringen, H., and F. Friedrich, eds. 1939. *Inscriptiones Graecae: Supplementum*. Berlin: Walter de Gruyter. |
| *ILS* | Dessau, H. 1892, repr. 1975. *Inscriptiones Latinae Selectae*. 3 vols. in 5. Chicago: Ares. |
| *IMT* | Barth, M., and J. Stauber, 1993. *Inschriften Mysia und Troas*. Munich: Leopold Wenger-Institut. |
| *ML* | Courtney, E. 1995. *Musa Lapidaria: A Selection of Latin Verse Inscriptions*. Atlanta: Scholars Press. |
| *RIB* | Collingwood, R. G., and R. P. Wright, 1965. *Roman Inscriptions of Britain*. Oxford: Clarendon. |

# LAWS OF THE
# TWELVE TABLES

(5th century BC, written in Latin)

## Introduction

The Twelve Tables are so named because they were said to have been first written down and displayed publicly on twelve oak tablets. They represent the first known set of codified laws in Rome. According to tradition (see Livy 3.33–34, not in this volume) they were created in 451–450 BC by a committee of ten men (*decemviri*) that was established in response to the plebeians' protests of the unrestricted powers and abuses of the patrician class, which had exclusive access to the major magistracies and priesthoods. The laws promulgated in the Twelve Tables, no doubt based on long-established customary practices, cover a range of subjects concerning mainly private law: legal procedure, debts, family law, inheritance, contracts and sales, land disputes, as well as crimes against both state and gods. They represent the first attempt to establish, in written form, the entirety of the rights, responsibilities, and duties of a Roman citizen. As such, they were central to Roman society—Cicero recalled having learned them by heart by chanting them—and continued to be respected long after their specific provisions had lost all relevance as they were replaced by other forms of legislation.

The laws have not survived in their entirety, but are transmitted only in fragmentary form by later authors, who often paraphrase rather than quote them verbatim. Some of the laws, therefore, will look incomplete or inconsistent in terms of length, form, and language, and unavoidably contain material from a later date. We are also ill-informed about the order and arrangement of these laws, and so reconstructions, including the one followed below, are partly conjectural. Scholars have generally arranged the laws into groups of related material; we have added titles to the individual tables below to indicate the contents of each. When only part of the law is known, we use angle brackets ("< >") to indicate either lost material or our reconstruction based on other evidence. Explanatory material will be found in parentheses or in the notes.

# Laws of the Twelve Tables

## Table 1: Procedure

1.1 If a defendant is called to court, he shall go. If he does not, the plaintiff shall summon witnesses and only then take hold of the defendant.

1.2 If a defendant goes into hiding or takes to flight, the plaintiff shall lay his hands upon the defendant.

1.3 If a defendant is impeded by disease or age, the plaintiff shall provide him an animal for transportation, but is not obliged to provide a carriage.

1.4 For a land-owning defendant another landowner shall act as representative; for a landless defendant anyone who so chooses may act as his representative.

1.5 Allies, whether steadfast or reinstated, <shall have the same right to make contracts and conduct business with the Roman people>.

1.6 If disputing parties reach a settlement, an official shall announce it publicly.

1.7 If there is no settlement, the parties shall present their cases in the Comitium or Forum in the morning.

1.8 The two parties shall present their cases together in each other's presence. If only one is present at midday, the judge shall award the case to that party.

1.9 If both are present, the trial is to be concluded by sundown.

1.10 <. . .> bail-bonds and sureties for appearance in court <. . .>

## Table 2: Procedure (Continued)

2.1 Legal action involving oaths:[1] for possessions valued at 1,000 *asses* or more, parties shall deposit 500 *asses*; if less, the deposit shall be 50 *asses*. If the suit concerns the freedom of a person, the deposit shall be 50 *asses*.

2.2 Unless serious disease is at hand, the appointed trial date with a foreigner shall be kept. If judge, arbitrator, plaintiff or defendant is stricken, the day of the trial shall be put off.

2.3 If someone requires a witness' testimony, he shall go every other day to the witness' door to proclaim his request aloud.

## Table 3: Debt

3.1–6 Regarding an acknowledged debt: when the matter has been formally adjudicated, the law provides a grace of thirty days to make good. Afterward, one shall arrest the debtor. The plaintiff shall bring the debtor to court. If the latter does

---

1. This seems to be an early form of civil case whereby both parties swore oaths that they were telling the truth and deposited goods (later money) in good faith for their claim. The loser of the case forfeited his deposit, which would be transferred into the state treasury.

not discharge his debt, and no one else assumes responsibility at trial, the plaintiff shall take the debtor with him and bind him either in stocks or fetters weighing no less than 15 pounds, but may be more, if the plaintiff wishes. The debtor may decide to live on his own means; if not, the plaintiff is to provide a pound of wheat every day, but may give more if he wishes. If no settlement is reached, the debtor shall be held in chains for 60 days. During this period the debtor shall be brought to the Comitium on three consecutive Market Days,[2] and the amount for which he was legally judged responsible shall be publicly announced. On the third Market Day, however, he shall be put to death or sent across the Tiber and sold in a foreign land. <If more than one plaintiff is owed money,> on the third Market Day the multiple plaintiffs shall cut the debtor into pieces.[3] If one cuts more or less than their share, there shall be no penalty.

3.7 Against a foreigner, the right of ownership shall be valid in perpetuity.[4]

## Table 4: Rights of Fathers (*Patria Potestas*)

4.1 If a father refuses to acknowledge a visibly deformed child as his own, there shall be no penalty.[5]

4.2 If a father sells his son three times, the son shall be emancipated from his father.[6]

4.3 A husband renouncing his wife shall take away her keys and order her to keep her possessions.

4.4 A child who was in the womb at the time of his father's death shall be considered a legal heir. A child born more than nine months after his father's death shall have no legal claim.

## Table 5: Inheritance and Guardianship

5.1 Females, even those of mature age, are to remain under guardianship,[7] except for the Vestal Virgins, who shall remain free.

---

2. See Appendix "A Roman Calendar: April" in this volume.

3. This provision has been variously explained, but it is highly unlikely that the body alone is meant here (though later Romans interpreted it literally). More probably the assets are divided up.

4. This presumably exerts the rights of a Roman citizen against those of a non-citizen in regard to ownership, even in the case where the non-citizen has "continuous use" of an article (see Table 6.3).

5. Failure to acknowledge a child amounted to death by exposure, except in the unlikely circumstance that another took the child in.

6. A father was allowed to sell his son into slavery to another party to pay off debts he could not otherwise repay. If the buyer later freed the son, the son would automatically return to the power (*manus*) of his father. Freeborn adults too, if heavily in debt, could be reduced to slavery in lieu of repayment.

7. The source citing this statute notes "because of the fickleness of their minds," but this seems to be a later addition.

5.2 The transferable property of a woman under the guardianship of her male paternal relatives[8] cannot be acquired through continuous use[9] unless the transfer was
authorized by her guardian.

5.3 Whatever provisions one makes in his will concerning his household, his property
or the guardianship of his estate shall be law.

5.4 If a person dies intestate and has no natural heirs, the closest male paternal relative
shall take possession of the household.

5.5 If no male paternal relative exists, possession shall fall to the deceased's clan.[10]

5.6 Male paternal relatives shall act as guardians of persons who are not appointed a
guardian by will.

5.7 If a person is insane or profligate, control over his person and possessions shall
belong to his male paternal relatives or his clansmen.

5.8 The inheritance of a Roman citizen's freedman falls to his patron, if the freedman
dies intestate and has no natural heir <. . .> from said household to said household <. . .>

5.9 Outstanding debts owed to the deceased are not subject to division when they
have been divided among the heirs by law. Debts that the deceased owed are
divided among the heirs by law, in proportion to the share each heir receives.

5.10 In regard to division of an estate: if one seeks separation, let him demand a judge
or arbitrator.

## Table 6: Acquisition and Possession

6.1 When someone makes an agreement[11] or sale, an oral contract shall have the force
of law. <*unclear language*> A buyer acquires an article through purchase or in bar-
ter only when buyer has made payment to the seller or satisfies him in some other
way, either by providing a guarantor or collateral. If a slave be proclaimed a free
man on the condition that he pay a fixed amount to the heir, even if he has been
sold by the heir to another party, he shall attain freedom by paying the sum to said
party.

6.2 It is sufficient that a vendor make good on defects that are explicitly noted; he
shall pay double damages for defects he withholds.

6.3 One shall have permanent possession of moveable items after a year of continuous
use; in the case of estates or buildings, the process requires two years.

---

8. In normal cases, the woman was under the *manus* of her father or husband; in the event she
had neither, she would be assigned to one or more of her *agnati* (male relatives on her father's
side) who would act as guardian(s).

9. See Table 6.3 for possession by continuous use.

10. "Clan" here translates the word *gens*, which refers to the extended familial group (see
Glossary).

11. There is little certainty concerning the Latin term *nexus*, which is translated here as "agreement." It may refer generally to a contract or more specifically to debt-slavery, whereby a free
person would serve the lender until the debt is paid off.

6.4 If a woman does not wish to become subject to a husband's *manus* through continuous habitation,[12] she shall spend three consecutive nights away from him each year, thus interrupting the continuous habitation for each year.

6.5 If the two parties lay their hands on an item before an official <. . .>[13]

6.6 A magistrate shall release a defendant according to the principle of freedom<. . .>

6.7 One shall not remove a beam that is integral to a building or a vineyard.

6.8 The person who has been convicted of knowingly stealing and affixing a stolen beam is liable for double damages.

6.9 <. . .> from the time of pruning until the fruit has been removed <. . .>

## Table 7: Land Rights

7.1 One cannot take possession of the required boundary space of five feet between property through continuous use.

7.2 The boundary space extending from a wall shall be 2 1/2 feet.

7.3 If a person erects a stone wall abutting someone else's land, he shall not cross the boundary; if a fence, he must leave a foot to spare; if a building, he must leave two feet; if a trench or a pit, the space must be equal to its depth; if a well, six feet. An olive tree or fig tree must be nine feet away from the other person's property; any other fruit tree must be five feet away.[14]

7.4 The word *villa* ("farm estate") is nowhere mentioned in the Twelve Tables, with *hortus* ("enclosure") bearing that meaning. Instead of our modern word *hortus* ("garden") the laws used *heredium* ("large plot").

7.5 If there is a disagreement <. . .> three arbitrators shall determine the boundaries.

7.6 The width of a road is to be eight feet along straight portions, but sixteen feet at sharp curves.

7.7 Property owners shall maintain the road. If they do not pave it with stones, a person may drive his yoked team wherever he wishes.

7.8 If rain water does damage <. . .> an arbitrator shall order that it be contained. If a watercourse running through a public place does damage to a private person, said person shall have the right to file suit to have the damage repaired.

7.9 If a tree from a neighbor's farm is bent such that it leans over another's property, branches of the tree that extend 15 feet from the ground may be cut back <. . .> that property owner shall have the right to sue for its removal.

---

12. The source of this law notes that this process is similar to "continuous use" described in Table 6.3. This statute does not concern divorce, but rather the process for allowing a woman to remain under the *manus* of her father.

13. This either describes the procedure for resolving a disputed claim over an item or one of many processes for a transfer of ownership.

14. The source of this statute is describing Solon's Athenian laws, which, as he informs us, were regarded as the basis for many laws in the Twelve Tables. Even so, we cannot be sure whether or how closely these Athenian laws concerning boundaries reflect those in the Twelve Tables.

7.10 An owner may collect any nuts or fruit that have fallen into his property from someone else's tree.

## Table 8: Crimes

8.1 If a person casts a spell <. . .> or composes a malicious poem or song that brings disgrace or shame on another, he shall be beaten to death with clubs.

8.2 If a person maims the limb of another, he shall receive punishment in kind, unless the parties reach an agreement on compensation.

8.3 If someone breaks a bone of another,[15] he shall be penalized 300 *asses* in the case of a free person, but 150 *asses* in the case of a slave.

8.4 If someone injures another, he shall be penalized 25 *asses*.

8.5 <. . .> maim <. . .>

8.6 If an animal is determined to have caused damage, whatever caused the damage shall be awarded to the victim, or else the value of the damage shall be paid.

8.7 If an animal pastures on fruit from another person's tree, the tree's owner shall have no right to file suit for compensation if that fruit has fallen into the adjacent property.[16]

8.8 If a person puts a hex on someone else's crops or enchants his harvests <. . .>

8.9 If a person secretly and under the cover of night pastures on or harvests a crop that has been acquired by farming, the punishment shall be death by hanging as a sacrifice to Ceres, if the perpetrator was an adult; if a minor, at the discretion of the magistrate he shall be punished by public flogging or payment of double the damage.

8.10 If a person burns down a building or a mound of grain next to a house, he shall be bound, beaten, and killed by fire, provided that he acted knowingly and willingly. If the act was accidental, he shall repair the damage, unless he does not have sufficient funds, in which case he shall receive a lighter sentence.

8.11 If a person cuts down a living, productive tree of another, the transgressor shall pay 25 *asses* for each tree.

8.12 If a person commits a theft at night, and the owner kills him, the killing shall be considered lawful.

8.13 A thief shall not be killed in the light of day, unless he brandishes a weapon in his defense <. . .> and one shall call out <. . .>[17]

8.14 In the case of other thieves caught in the act, if freeborn they shall be flogged and awarded to the victim of the theft, provided that they committed the crime in the light the day and did not resist with a weapon. If slaves, they shall be bound,

---

15. The Latin word *os* can mean "bone" or "face." Later legal writers interpreted this as "bone," but there are provisions in Hittite laws that concern the disfigurement of the face.

16. See Table 7.10.

17. That is, to call the attention of witnesses who would testify that the killing was justifiable.

flogged and thrown from the Tarpeian Rock. If minors, at the discretion of the magistrate they shall be flogged and ordered to compensate for the loss.

8.15 A search may be conducted with tray and loin-cloth;[18] if a theft is discovered in this manner, it shall be considered as if caught in the act.

8.16 Punishment for theft that was not detected in the act shall be to pay double the damages.

8.17 Stolen articles are not subject to acquisition by continuous use; possession of a stolen item shall belong to the original owner in perpetuity.

8.18 No one may lend out money at a rate more than 1/12th;[19] a person in violation of this rule is assessed a penalty of four times the amount.

8.19 Embezzlement carries a penalty of double damages.

8.20 Guardians and caretakers who have defrauded their wards shall pay double damages.

8.21 A patron that defrauds his client shall forfeit his life to the gods.

8.22 If someone commits to testifying, or was a witness to a sale, if he does not state his testimony in court he shall be considered disgraced and disqualified as a witness.

8.23 A person who has been convicted of providing false testimony shall be thrown from the Tarpeian Rock.

8.24 If a weapon has escaped one's hand rather than being aimed, a ram is to be offered as a substitute <. . .>

8.25 <. . .> harmful drug <. . .>

8.26 No person shall hold nighttime assemblies within the city.

8.27 Members of *collegia* have the power to impose on themselves whatever rules they wish, provided that none violate public law.[20]

## Table 9: Public Law

9.1 Laws pertaining to one citizen or group shall not be enacted.

9.2 Measures involving the life or death of a Roman citizen shall not be passed except by the greatest assembly[21] and those who are enrolled as Roman citizens.

9.3 If a judge or arbiter appointed by law is convicted of bribery in rendering a verdict, he shall be punished with death.

9.4 <. . .> investigators of murder cases <. . .>

---

18. The phrase *lanx et licium*, translated here as "tray and loin-cloth," is an archaic phrase and has been variously interpreted. This type of search was evidently conducted formally in front of witnesses and with the plaintiff lightly clothed so as not to be able to plant an item in the house of the accused thief.

19. It is unclear whether this is compounded yearly (= twelve percent interest) or monthly (= one hundred percent interest).

20. A *collegium* was a formal organization of people with shared interests (see Glossary).

21. The *Comitia Centuriata*.

9.5 A person who incites the enemy or delivers a citizen into their hands shall be punished with death.

9.6 No person shall be put to death without being found guilty in court.

## Table 10: Funeral Law

10.1 One shall not bury or burn a dead person in the city.

10.2–7 One shall not do more than the following.[22] One shall not smooth a pyre with a hatchet or have more than three shawls, one small purple tunic, and ten flute-players. Women shall not tear at their cheeks nor wail in lamentation because of the death. One shall not collect the remains of a dead man in order to hold the burial later,[23] with the exception of a death in a war or when abroad. Ritual anointing by slaves and celebrations around the corpse are not permitted. There shall be no extravagant sprinkling, no long garlands, no incense boxes. If a person has earned a crown of bravery it is permitted to place it on his own pyre or that of a parent.

10.8 It is forbidden to have more than one funeral or to have more than one bier for a single person.

10.9 One shall not add gold; but if someone has teeth bound with gold, and he is buried or burned with it, it shall remain free from sanction.

10.10 A new pyre or burning mound shall not be built closer than 60 feet from another person's buildings without his consent.

10.11 The entrance court or the burning chamber of the tomb may not be acquired by continuous possession.

## Table 11: Supplementary Laws I[24]

11.1 Marriages shall not take place between patricians and plebeians.

11.2 <. . .> regarding the intercalation of the calendar <. . .>[25]

11.3 <. . .> calendar <. . .> business days <. . .>

## Table 12: Supplementary Laws II

12.1 The seizure of collateral is sanctioned against the person who purchases a sacrificial victim but who does not pay in full, and against the person who does not pay

---

22. This whole set of provisions is an example of sumptuary laws, those which aimed limited private expenditure and luxurious living. See Plutarch, *Life of Cato the Elder*, ch. 16.

23. Presumably this provision was aimed at limiting the period of mourning over the body.

24. According to tradition, after the original promulgation of the Ten Tables, a second commission of ten men produced two additional sets of laws.

25. Every other year an intercalary month was inserted after February 23 to bring the lunar calendar in line with the solar year. See Appendix "Roman Time Reckoning."

the required amount for an animal he has leased so as to make the necessary funds to put on a sacred banquet.

12.2 If a slave commits a theft or causes damage with his master's knowledge, the suit shall be held against the master in the slave's name. In regard to crimes committed by children or slaves in a household, suits are transferred onto the father of the household, such that as father or master he may either assume the assessment for damages, or hand over the offending party for punishment.

12.3 If a person has made a false claim on an item, if the owner should wish <. . .> a <magis>trate shall provide three arbitrators; if they render judgment in favor of the owner, the false claimant is to pay double the amount.

12.4 One shall not dedicate for sacred use any item that is under dispute; if one does so, he shall pay double the value of the item.

12.5 The most recent resolution of the people shall have the force of law.

# A ROMAN CALENDAR: APRIL

(The *Fasti Praenestini*, erected around AD 9, written in Latin)

This calendar (*fasti*) was inscribed on stone and set up in the forum of Praeneste, an important city east of Rome, around AD 9. Its author was the freedman Verrius Flaccus (60 BC to after AD 14), a native of that city and one of the leading scholars of his day. Flaccus was highly regarded enough that the Emperor Augustus employed him as tutor of his beloved grandsons, Gaius and Lucius (see Augustus' *Accomplishments*, ch. 14 in this volume). Flaccus later turned to composing a calendar that combined traditional religious festivals (most related to agriculture) with important events in the lives of the imperial household. This calendar, one of many from the imperial period, offers us insight into the rhythm of the Roman year in the 1st century AD, and shows how the imperial family, as the center of the empire, emerges to rival the state traditions of great antiquity (see April 23 and 24 below, and Inscription no. 72 in this volume). The calendar of Flaccus, probably in a more extensive written form, was used by the poet Ovid, who set the first six months into verse, expanding it with legendary and mythological stories, as well as descriptions of some of the festivals (see the excerpt from Ovid's *Fasti* in this volume).

The Praeneste calendar is fragmentary, but from other calendars of the early empire we can reconstruct a substantial part of what is missing. These sections are marked in brackets, e.g., "[*two lines lost*]". Material that we add for clarity is placed in parentheses. Below is a key to symbols and notation used in the calendar:

Column I: The day of the "week," actually an eight-day market cycle, counting A through H.

Column II: The date, counting inclusively up to next crucial date (Kalends, Nones, Ides), thus:

- Kalends = First of month; the next day (April 2) in April is marked IIII = "four days before the Nones" (counting inclusively); then III = "three days before the Nones," etc. PR = "the day before (*pridie*) the Nones."

- Nones = Fifth of the month (in other months the seventh[1]), followed by VIII = "eight days before the Ides." PR = "the day before the Ides."

- Ides = Thirteenth of the month (in other months the fifteenth), followed in April by XIIX = "eighteen days before the Kalends of the next month (May)." PR = "the day before the Kalends of the next month (May)."

---

1. In March, July, October, and May, the Nones fall on the seventh day (so Ides on the fifteenth). In all other months including April (the month given here) the Nones fall on the fifth, the Ides on the thirteenth.

Column III: The Types of day

- F *Dies Fasti* ("permitted days"), normal business days: assemblies (*comitia*) cannot meet.
- C *Dies Comitiales* ("assembly days"): similar to *Dies Fasti*, but assemblies could be called.
- N *Dies Nefasti* ("impermissible days"): assemblies cannot meet, and *curule* magistrates cannot exercise powers.
- NP The exact meaning of this mark is unknown; probably *dies nefastus* with additional prohibitions.

Column IV: Festivals and other significant events.

## The Praeneste Calendar: April

[The name APRIL is derived from] Venus[2] because she was [by Anchises the mother of Aene]as, king of the [Lat]ins and progenitor of the Roman people. [Others say that the name is derived from the adjec]tive *aperilis*, because it is in this month that crops, flowers, animals, and the seas open up (*aperiuntur*).

| C | Kalends | F | Women in great numbers pray to Fortuna Virilis ("Masculine Fortune"); lower-class women even go to the baths to do so, because there men reveal exactly that part of the body that inspires the favor of women. |
|---|---------|---|---|
| D | IIII | F | |
| E | III | C | |
| F | PR | C | Games to the Great Idean Goddess, Mother of the Gods. These games are called the Megalensia, because this goddess is called Megale ("Great"). Elite Romans in great numbers host feasts, because the Great Mother, in accordance with the Sibylline Books, was summoned from Phrygia to Rome, where she took up her new seat.[3] |
| G | Nones | N | Games. Sacrifice to Fortuna Publica on the Quirinal Hill. |

---

2. That is, from Venus' Greek name Ap(h)rodite; the cluster "ph" (φ) in Greek was pronounced closer to our "p" sound than "f."

3. In 205 BC, during a crisis in the second Punic War, the Romans consulted the sacred Sibylline Books (see Glossary), which advised them to bring the cult statue of the Great Mother (Cybele, Magna Mater)—an aniconic stone, perhaps a meteorite—to Rome. The Megalensia, which featured dramatic performances, ran until April 10, the anniversary of the dedication of the temple of Magna Mater in 191 BC.

| | | | |
|---|---|---|---|
| H | VIII | NP | Games. A holiday, because on this day Gaius Caesar son of Gaius defeated [king Juba in Africa.][4] |

*[inscription lost for the next three days, 7–9 April]*

| | | | |
|---|---|---|---|
| D | IIII | N | [For two days a very large sac]rifice [is made] to Fortuna Primigenia;[5] on each day her oracle is open and the *duumviri* sacrifice a calf. There are games in the Circus for the Great Idean Goddess, Mother of the Gods, because on this day her temple was dedicated. |
| E | III | N | |
| F | PR | N | [Games for Ceres.[6]] |
| G | Ides | NP | [Games.] |
| H | XIIX | N | [Games.] |
| A | XVII | NP | Ford[icidia.][7] Games [. . .] Oscan and Sabine. Aulus Hirtius, supported by Gaius Caesar, his colle[ague with *imperium*, claimed victory at Mutina.][8] For this reason the populace, [even to o]ur day, [still prays to Victoria Augusta.] |
| B | XVI | N | Games. |
| C | XV | N | Games. |
| D | XIIII | N | Games. |
| E | XIII | NP | Festival to Ceres. Games held in the Circus. |
| F | XII | N | |
| G | XII | NP | Festival to Pales. [Shepherds(?)] leap over fires. The beginning of the [shepherd's ye]ar [. . .] is driven back (?).[9] |
| H | X | N | |
| A | VIIII | F | Festival of Wine (*Vinalia*). To Jupiter [*2 lines lost*. A libation of every new wine is] consecrated [to Jupiter] because [when the Latins were] in trouble against the Rutulians, Mezentius, the king of the Etruscans, promised to help only on the condition that he receive the first-fruits of each year's vintage. Julia |

---

4. This commemorates Julius Caesar's victory at Thapsus in 46 BC.

5. This is part of the local color of the calendar. The vast complex of Fortuna Primigenia was located in Praeneste (the grand architecture is still worth a visit today).

6. The cult of Ceres, goddess of grain, was brought to Rome in 493 BC; her festival lasted eight days from April 12–19.

7. On this day a pregnant (*forda*) cow was sacrificed along with the unborn calf. Ovid informs us that the sacrifice was originally made to avert a famine in King Numa's reign and that the ashes would be used to purify the people during the Parilia (April 21).

8. In 43 BC, Octavian/Augustus (here called Gaius Caesar), with proconsular powers, aided the consul Hirtius against Antony's forces. See M. Cicero, *Letters* 22–23.

9. The 21st of April was the sacred day of the pastoral god Pales and the traditional date of the foundation of Rome. See the excerpt from Ovid, *Fasti* in this volume.

|   |   |   | Augusta[10] and Tiberius Augustus dedicated a statue to their father, the deified Augustus at the Theater of Marcellus. |
|---|---|---|---|
| B | VIII | C | Tiberius Caesar donned the toga of manhood during the consulship of Imperator Caesar for the seventh time and M. Agrippa for the third.[11] |
| C | VII | NP | Festival of Robigus.[12] Holiday. At the fifth milestone on the Via Claudia they sacrifice to Robigus to prevent him from harming the grain crop. They hold games consisting of older and younger racers. It is also a holiday for gigolos, because the day before was a holiday for prostitutes. |
| D | VI | F | Deified Caesar added this day to the calendar. |
| E | V | C |  |
| F | IIII | NP | Games for Flora. Holiday, authorized by vote of the Senate, because on this day the shrine and altar of Vesta was dedicated in the house of Imperator Caesar Augustus, Pontifex Maximus, in the consulship of Quirinius and Valgius (12 BC). On the same day the temple to Flora, who controls the growth of things, was dedicated because of a drought.[13] |
| G | III | C | Games. |
| H | PR | C | Games. |

XXX Days.

---

10. Augustus' daughter, who in 11 BC married Tiberius, who would be adopted by Augustus in AD 4 after the death of Augustus' grandson Gaius.

11. 27 BC. Tiberius was born on November 16, 42 BC, making him fifteen when he donned the *toga virilis* and was entered into the rolls of adult male citizens in Rome.

12. *Robigus* was the deity that prevented *robigo* ("rust"), or a reddish mildew that attacked grain and vines.

13. In either 241 or 238 BC a temple to Flora, ordered by the Sibylline books, was dedicated following a long drought.

# A ROMAN SCHOOLBOOK

(*Colloquia Monacensia*, late 3rd century AD?)

## Introduction

This elementary school book is a bilingual set of model sentences and short dialogues on topics from daily life, meant, as the text itself tells us, to be memorized and repeated back to a teacher. It could thus be used as an aid to learn either of the two dominant languages of the Roman empire, Greek or Latin. It resembles closely the model dialogues familiar to anyone who has studied a modern foreign language, except that here the sentences are given in both the target language and the primary language (it is in fact unclear which is which).

The scenes are arranged from morning to bedtime, so they provide an interesting sketch, albeit stereotyped in the stilted manner of such works, of what went on in a typical Roman day. There is a morning scene, in which the young protagonist gets dressed with the help of his *paedagogus* and nurse, greets his parents, and goes off to school. The school scene gives a vivid impression of the ancient classroom. He learns to read and write, and also studies grammar and elementary literary analysis. He comes home for lunch, and goes back to school. Then there are scenes from adult life, as the father goes about his legal business with the various officials of the (unidentified) province. There is a visit to a friend who turns out to be sick, but on the mend; some shopping and preparations for dinner; a visit to the bath; a dinner party; and a tongue-lashing for some less than efficient slaves as the boy prepares for bed.

The exact date and place of origin of this and similar texts, found in manuscripts from the 9th to 15th centuries, are unclear. Teachers probably felt free to update, change, add, and excerpt, and did so to an extent that is impossible to determine. On the other hand, parallels with the vocabulary in dated Greek papyri, and the presence of pagan and the lack of Christian elements, suggest that in the main the dialogues and accompanying glossaries (not included here) can reasonably be treated as belonging to the 3rd to 4th centuries AD. They seem to reflect the common urbanized culture of the Roman empire, with its courtrooms and officials, its large public bath complexes, its dinner parties in *triclinia* ("dining rooms," see Glossary), and its multi-story apartment buildings (called *insulae*).

---

# *Colloquia Monacensia*[1]

## Preface

[1] Greetings. May you have good fortune. I see that many students desire to converse in Latin as well as Greek but cannot, due to the difficulty of the language and the size of the vocabulary. So I decided to spare no effort and care on my part in making it possible to collect all the necessary words into three books of *Translations*. For I see that many authors have undertaken the task, not in the worthy manner which the subject demands, but just on a whim or as an exercise. From this they have garnered an altogether undeserved acclaim. That is why, to be absolutely frank, I wish to make it clear to everyone that nobody has yet done translations better or more carefully than I have in the three books which I have composed. The first volume of our *Translations* includes all the words, arranged alphabetically. Now, therefore, I begin to write, since I have observed that it is essential for young boys[2] just beginning their education to hear translations about everyday life, in order to make easier progress in speaking Latin and Greek. This is why I have written the following brief exercises about everyday life.

## Getting up and Going to School

[2] I awoke at dawn. I got up from my bed, I sat on the chair, I picked up my socks, my shoes. I put them on. I asked for water for my face. I washed my hands first, then I washed my face. I dried off. I put away my sleeping clothes. I put my tunic on my body. I put on my belt. I anointed my hair and combed it. I put a cloak around my shoulders. I put on my white upper garment;[3] over it I put on my overcoat.[4] I left my bedroom with my *paedagogus* and with my nurse to say good morning to my mother and father. I embraced and kissed them both. And thus I left the house. I go to school. I went in. I said: "Greetings, teacher." And he greeted me in turn. The slave who holds my book case gave me my writing tablet, my stylus box, and my ruler. Sitting in my place, I erase. I copy out the model sentence. After finishing I show it to my teacher. He corrected it, he marked it; he asks me to read it aloud. When asked to do so I gave the model sentence to another student. I learn translations[5] by heart; I recited them from memory. But immediately a fellow student dictated a text to me. You, too, dictate to me, he said. I said to him: First, you must recite from memory. And he said: Didn't you see when I was reciting from memory before you? You are lying; you did

---

1. This set of dialogues (*colloquia*) derives its name from the place where the manuscript resides, Munich.

2. The students here are assumed to be boys, but one of the other colloquia mentions girls specifically, so we should probably not assume that these texts were exclusively aimed at boys.

3. Presumably a toga, though not called that.

4. There is of course no suggestion that one went out wearing this much clothing; the author is simply trying to use all the main words for different types of garments.

5. That is, model sentences and dialogues like these, and also bilingual word lists in Greek and Latin.

not recite. I am not lying. If you're telling the truth, I will dictate to you. Meanwhile, at the request of the teacher, the smaller boys got up in two groups. One of the older boys gave one group of them syllables to spell; the others recited word lists in order to the assistant teacher. They print the words; they wrote lines of verse; and I, who am in the advanced class, was given a dictation exercise. When we sat down I went through my word lists and my notes on grammar and style. Called up by the head teacher to read aloud, I listened to his comments on narration, speech, and characterization. I was questioned about grammar; I gave my answers. "To whom?" he said. "What part of speech?" I declined the different types of nouns; I analyzed a line of verse. When we had done these things, he let us out for lunch. Having been let out, we go back home. I change; I take fresh bread, olives, cheese, dried figs, nuts. I drink cold water. After lunch I go back to school. I find the teacher re-reading lessons. And he said: Begin from the beginning.[6]

## Father at Work

[4] And my father went out and met his friend, and said: Hello, Gaius. And he kissed him. And he greeted him in turn, saying: I hope you are doing well, Lucius. Good to see you, finally. What are you up to? Everything is good. How are you doing? I congratulate you just as I do myself [*gap in text*] a case. Before whom? Before the quaestor? Not there. But where? Before the proconsul? Not there, either, but before the magistrates in charge of record keeping for the provincial governor. What sort of case is it? Not very important, since it is essentially a financial matter. Come along and assist, if you have the time. The judges picked today as the day to render their verdict, and so I want to consider the case with the attorneys while you are present. Did you call witnesses? I called witnesses. Whom? Your friends. Well done. Did you make an appointment? At what hour? In what place? In the forum; in the portico, next to the stoa of Victory. I'll be there in a little while. But please, don't forget. Don't worry; I'll remember. Let's go to the banker; let's get a hundred denarii from him. Let's give an honorarium to the advocate and to the prosecuting attorneys and to the lawyers so they will defend us more energetically.[7] Here he is. Take the money from him and follow me. Here is Gaius, just as we agreed. Let us call him into the defense council. Here we have the documents and supporting evidence. Did you take his testimony? I took his testimony. Did you testify? I testified. Get ready. I am ready. The opposing counsel would also like to make a motion. Silence. I am silent. Be silent; let's listen to the verdict. Gaius, did you hear? We won.

## A Visit to the Moneylender

[5] Sir, how can I help you? Do you have any cash available for loan? How much do you need to borrow? If you have it, loan me 5,000 sesterces. Even if I did not have

---

6. Section 3, an almost exact repetition of the beginning of section 2, is omitted.

7. Note the inclusion of various substitute terms for language practice; this is not a fully realistic narrative.

them on hand, I would have found them for you from somewhere. Do you want collateral? No, thank you. No need. Sign here for me, indicating that you have received it. What is the interest rate? Whatever you think is fair. I signed. I thank you. Affix your seal. I affixed my seal. Count it out. I counted it. Test the purity. I tested it. Please return the same purity you have received. When I pay you back I will make sure it is right. [6] Good day. Have you arrived? I have arrived. Did you get it? Did you give it to him? I gave it. Have you paid it back? Is there anything else you need? Have a nice day.

## Checking up on a Friend

Come with me, if you want. Where? To visit our friend Lucius. Oh, how is he doing? He is sick. Since when? It started a few days ago. Where does he live? Not far away. If you want, we can walk there. This is his house, I think. This is it. Here is the doorman. Ask him if we can come in and see his master. And he said: Who are you looking for? Your master. We have come to inquire after his health. Come up. How many flights? Two. Knock on the door at the right and see if he is back; he had gone out. Let's knock. Look who it is. Hello, everyone. We want to visit with your master. If he is awake, let me know. And he said: He is not here. What do you mean? Where is he? He went down to the laurel grove to take a walk. Good for him! When he returns, tell him we stopped by to say hello and to look after his health, and that everything is fine. I will do so.

## An Invitation to Lunch

[7] Where are you off to? I am in a hurry to get home. Why do you ask? If you like, why not come over today for a light lunch? We can have some good house wine. Ok. Come on over, and be on time. Send a message over to me when you are ready. I'm at home. Very good.

## Shopping

[8] You, boy,[8] follow me to the meat market; let's buy something for lunch. Ask how much the fish costs. Ten denarii. You, boy, go home, so we can go to the vegetable market and buy some vegetables, as much as we need, and some fruit, some mulberries, figs, peaches, pears, crab apples.[9] There, you have everything we bought. Go home.

## Preparing for Dinner

[9] Someone call the cook. Where is he? He went back up. And what does he want? Get him down here. Take this meat and cook it carefully. Make it into a good accompaniment with bread. Bring me the key. Open the strong box and take out the key to

---

8. Latin *puer* (Greek *paidarion*), a common type of address to a slave.

9. Greek *trikokkon*, "three-seeded fruit" from the *mespilon* (tansy-leaved thorn), a small tree of the rose family native to Turkey, whose fruit resembles the crab apple.

the storeroom. Bring out what is needed: the salt, the Spanish olive oil, and oil for the lamps, garum (first and second class),[10] sour vinegar, white and red wine, aged unfermented wine, dry wood, charcoal, hot coals, an axe, vessels, plates, an earthenware pot, a kettle, a brazier, a lid, mortar and pestle, a knife. What else do you want? Just these, boy. Go to Gaius and say to him: Come, let's go to the baths. Go, run, do it quickly. Not slowly, but with haste. Were you with him? I was. Where was he? He was sitting at home. And what was he doing? He was studying. And what did he say? He said: I'm coming, but I'm waiting for my people. Go back and say to him: Everybody is here. Come with him. In the meantime, you lot put out the glassware and copperware carefully. Set up the dining room and throw out the water. I want to see everything looking like new. We have already set it up. Everything is ready. He hasn't come yet? Go and tell him: You're making us dine late. Look, there he is. Go meet him. He was coming here. Go ask him: Why are you standing outside?

## A Visit to the Baths

[10] Get out your bath towels, the strigil,[11] face cloth, foot cloth, oil flask, bath salts. Go ahead; you all choose the place. Where do you suggest we go? To the *thermae*,[12] or to a privately run establishment? Wherever you suggest. Just go ahead of us. Yes, I'm talking to you there. Let's visit the hot room. When we leave, I'll let you know. Get up, let's go. Do you want to go for a walk through the portico next? Does anyone want to come to the latrine? Good idea; I feel the urge. Let's go now. Get my clothes off, undo my shoes, put away the clothing, cover it up, guard it closely, do not doze off, because of the thieves. Get us a ball. Let's play in the ball court. I want to work out on the exercise floor. Let's wrestle there in a bit, one round. I don't know, maybe. I haven't wrestled in a long time. Still, maybe I'll give it a try. I am a bit tired. Let's go into the first sauna room.[13] Give the money to the bath attendant. Take back the change. Anoint me. I anointed you. I anoint myself. Give me a rub down. Go to the sweat room. Are you sweating? I am sweating. I am worn out. Let's go to the bathing tub. Get in. Let's go sunbathe, and then get into the bathing tub. Get in. Pour over me. Get out now. Jump into the outdoor swimming pool. Swim. I swam. Come into the washing tub. Pour water over yourself. I poured water over myself. I picked it up. Hand over the strigil. Towel me off. Wrap the towels around me. Dry off my head and my feet. Give me my sandals. Tie them up. Give me my robe, my cloak, my *dalmatica*.[14] Collect my clothing and all my things. Follow me home and buy us some small seeds, lupines, bean salad from the bath. Did you have a good bath? Take care.

---

10. *Garum*, also called *liquamen*, was a fermented fish sauce much loved by the Romans and widely used in cooking.

11. A curved metal scraper used for cleaning off the skin.

12. Large, publicly financed bath complexes.

13. Evidently distinct from the hot room mentioned before. The Greek name suggests stifling heat, hence "sauna."

14. A type of tunic with long wide sleeves, popularized by the Emperor Commodus (reigned AD 180–192).

## A Dinner Party

[11] Put the chairs here, the seats, the bench, the chaise-lounge, the pillow. Sit down. I am sitting. Why are you standing? Wash the cup with hot water. Mix a drink, for I am very thirsty. Mix for everybody. Who wants what? Seasoned wine, or mulled wine?[15] Mix that for him. You, what do you want? Rinse the cup, mix hot wine for me, not boiling hot, and not lukewarm, but just right, and pour out a little from there. Put in some fresh water. Add some unmixed wine. Why are you standing? Be seated. Let's recline, if you want. Where do you suggest? Recline in the place of honor. Give us some water-garum. Let us taste the hot mallow. Hand me a napkin. Bring it. Pour some olive-oil-garum into the saucer. Divide the pigs' feet. Chop up the tripe, the octopus tentacles. Look and see if you have any pepper sauce. Dip. I'm having some. Have some. Give me the tender fig-fed pork, thrushes, sweetbreads, lettuces. One of you, break the bread and put it into the basket. Pass it around. Break up the pieces. Bon appétit. That fellow is quite a worthy dining companion. Pass the cured meat, anchovies, pea pods, sprouts with garum and Spanish olive oil, *rapatus* (?), roasted chicken, bits-in-broth, sliced meat, roasted pork. Put down the platter with the crudités, radishes, mint, white olives, and cottage cheese, truffles, mushrooms. Let the servers have dinner, and the cook—give them dessert, too, since they have served well. Give me water for hand washing. Wipe off the table. Give me new wine. Give me pure wine. Give me unmixed wine. Let us drink fresh wine from the cooling jar. Mix in warm wine. Would you like some in this larger cup? Thank you, in the smaller one, for I hope to keep drinking. If you don't mind, I will drink a toast to you. Would you receive it? From you, with pleasure.[16] Why aren't you drinking? Drink, sir. I asked, and no one gave me a drink. Give us sweet flat-cakes. That's enough for us. Let's go now. Light the lamp. Take it. You have entertained us well.

## Bedtime and Admonishing the Slaves

[12] Boy, come here, gather up these things and put them all away in their proper places. Carefully make the bed. We have made it. Oh, is that why it is so hard? We have shaken it out and fluffed up the pillow. Still, because you have done your job so poorly, no one is going out tonight and fooling around. If I hear a single word, I won't hold back! Now get out, go to sleep, and wake me up at cock crow, so I can go out.

---

15. Sweet wine boiled down.

16. This is the *propinatio*, in which one proposes a toast to someone else, drinks, then hands that person the cup.

# Appendices

# Roman Naming Conventions

## Male Citizens

Male citizens typically had three names:

1.  The *praenomen* (forename), like Gaius, Lucius, Marcus, Publius or Quintus. This was probably used within the family and among close associates like our first name. These gradually fell out of use altogether, and are often abbreviated or not mentioned in texts. Only about seventeen were in use, of which the most common are listed below, with their ancient abbreviations.

2.  The *nomen* or *gentilicum* ("the" name, also called the gentile name), like Julius, Claudius, Cornelius, Aemilius, or Antonius. This indicates membership, passed down on the male side, in an extended clan or *gens*, possibly one with many branches. Romans wanted very much to preserve this either by having or adopting children. A few powerful *gentes* tended to dominate Roman politics and priesthoods in the Roman Republic.

3.  The *cognomen* (surname). At first used to indicate branches of larger clans, later (1st centuries BC/AD) it became the main name by which a person was known (Caesar, Cicero, Sulla). About 2,000 are recorded, many of which mean something, or are based on physical deformities or characteristics. For instance, Cicero means "chickpea," probably first given as a nickname to one of his ancestors who had a cleft in his nose that resembled the bean.

The *cognomen* was originally optional, but became nearly universal in the 1st century AD. Much later, people stopped using names one and two above and reverted to a system of one man, one name. In Christian times the tendency to revert to single names strengthened, except among aristocrats.

Here is a list of army recruits, Egypt, AD 103 (*P. Oxy.* 1022):

| | |
|---|---|
| Gaius Veturius Gemellus, age 21 | [Gemellus = "twin"] |
| Gaius Longinus Priscus, age 22 | [Priscus = "ancient"] |
| Gaius Julius Maximus, age 25 | [Maximus = "very big"] |
| [ ] Julius Secundus, age 20 | [Secundus = "second"] |
| Gaius Julius Saturninus, age 23 | [Saturninus = "favorite of Saturn?"] |
| Marcus Antonius Valens, age 22 | [Valens = "strong"] |

Note the lack of variety in *praenomina* and gentile names, contrasted with the variation in *cognomina*. This made the *cognomen* a more useful thing to call someone.

## Freeborn Women

Normally a Roman girl was given only the feminine form of her father's gentile name (*nomen*). The daughter of P. Cornelius Scipio, therefore, would be known simply as Cornelia, and the daughter of C. Julius Caesar was Julia. Daughters of the same man might be differentiated by a *cognomen* denoting birth order (Maior or "Elder," Minor or "Younger," Tertia or "Third"). By the late Republic, the daughter might bear the feminine forms of both her father's *nomen* and *cognomen*, such as Caecilia Metella, who was daughter of Q. Caecilius Metellus Creticus. On marriage a woman did not take her husband's name, but kept her original family name, which was in fact her main name, though in inscriptions the husband's name (and/or that of her father) would normally be prominently displayed.

## Slaves

One name. Probably the most common was "Lucky:" Felix, Faustus, and Fausta. Many were "wish names" that expressed the hopes of the owner for what the slave might be like: Hilarus ("Happy"), Fidus ("Trusty"), Vitalis ("Healthy"), Celer ("Swifty"). Many were Greek: Eutychus and Eutyches ("Lucky" again), Nicephorus ("Victory Bringer"), Pamphilus and Pamphila ("Dear to All"), and some bore mythological names, such as Ajax, Polyphemus, and Scylla.

## Freedmen

On gaining freedom and citizen status male slaves needed a full three-part citizen name, so they took the *praenomen* and gentile name of the former master, but kept the slave name as a *cognomen*. For example, upon manumission by his master M. Tullius Cicero, the slave Tiro became M. Tullius Tiro. If the former owner was a woman, the freedman lacked a praenomen.

## Multiple Names

*Cognomina* helped to differentiate branches of a single large extended family. But they started to lose their usefulness when one branch reached large dimensions. There were many Cornelii Scipiones in the 2nd century BC, for example. And so at this time fourth and even fifth names (still termed *cognomina*) were added: e.g., P. Cornelius Scipio Nasica, his son P. Cornelius Scipio Nasica Corculum, and his son P. Cornelius Scipio Nasica Serapio. Note that the gentile name and the original *cognomen* (Cornelius

Scipio) stay the same. In some cases, an additional name came from success in war. Thus, P. Cornelius Scipio was called Africanus because of his victories in the Second Punic War, and L. Aemilius Paullus gained the name Macedonicus from his victories in Greece in the 2nd century BC.

# Adoption

When a male was adopted, he would take on the full name of his adoptive father but retain his original *nomen* in a modified form (in *-anus*) as a *cognomen*. Thus, when L. Aemilius Paullus was adopted by Scipio Africanus, his adopted name became P. Cornelius Scipio Aemilianus. When C. Octavius was adopted by C. Julius Caesar in the latter's will, he became C. Julius Caesar Octavianus, hence our modern designation "Octavian."

# Abbreviations of Praenomina

| | |
|---|---|
| A. | Aulus |
| Ap(p). | Appius |
| C. | Gaius |
| Cn. | Gnaeus |
| D. | Decimus |
| L. | Lucius |
| M. | Marcus |
| M'. | Manius |
| N. | Numerius |
| P. | Publius |
| Q. | Quintus |
| Ser. | Servius |
| Sex. | Sextus |
| Sp. | Spurius |
| T. | Titus |
| Ti(b). | Tiberius |
| V. | Vibius |

# Anglicized Names

A few famous names have become thoroughly Anglicized over time: Marcus Antonius is now normally known as "(Mark) Antony," Gnaeus Pompeius Magnus as "Pompey," Gaius Julius Caesar Octavianus (the dictator's adopted son, later the emperor Augustus) as "Octavian." Likewise many Latin authors: Horace (Horatius), Vergil (Vergilius), Ovid (Ovidius), etc.

# Emperors

"Caesar" was the *cognomen* of the ill-fated dictator, C. Julius Caesar, who was killed at the height of his power by a group of senators in 44 BC. Octavian, his adopted heir, kept the *cognomen* when he became the first emperor, Augustus. Because of the latter's role in creating the principate, both his adoptive name "Caesar" and his honorary title "Augustus" came to mean essentially "emperor." For its part, the word "emperor," which we use for the monarch of the Roman empire, comes from the adoption of the title *imperator* ("successful general") as a *praenomen*; every *princeps* from Nero on used *imperator* in their official titles. As time went on emperors developed a profusion of names and honorary titles, but are conventionally known in English by single names, occasionally by two names. Here are the full titles of the first five emperors (27 BC–AD 68) and of Septimius Severus (reigned AD 193–211), with their conventional names in bold:

Imperator Caesar Divi Filius **Augustus**

Imperator **Tiberius** Caesar Augustus

**Gaius** Caesar Augustus Germanicus (a.k.a., **Caligula**)

Tiberius **Claudius** Caesar Augustus Germanicus

Imperator **Nero** Claudius Caesar Augustus Germanicus

Imperator Caesar Lucius **Septimius Severus** Pius Pertinax Augustus

See also Inscriptions nos. 57–63.

# ROMAN TIME RECKONING

**Years**. Roman sources normally identify a certain year by naming the two consuls of that year. Valerius Maximus, for example, begins a story, "During the consulship of M. Popillius Laenas and Cn. Calpurnius . . . ," meaning 139 BC. Lists of consuls were kept as public records, and most of these names survive, so there is normally no trouble in converting consular dates to modern dates.

**Months**. The Roman year was originally organized by months based on the lunar cycle with a total of 355 days. Governance of the calendar and its festivals was overseen by the *pontifices*, one of whose jobs was to add extra days in February (a so-called "intercalary month") from time to time to bring the lunar calendar into sync with the solar year. Still, the calendar fell more and more out of sync with the solar year, until Julius Caesar in 46 BC mandated an overhaul so that the calendar followed the solar year (with 365 days with a leap year every four years). The Julian calendar is the basis of our current calendar, with some important modifications made by Pope Gregory in 1582, the so-called Gregorian calendar, which omits a leap year three times every four hundred years.

The names of our months come from the ones employed by the Romans. Originally, it seems, there were only ten months, as evidenced by the fact that the last month, December, comes from the Latin word for "tenth" (*decim-*). Likewise, "September" comes from the Latin word for "seventh" (*septim-*). At some point two months were added to the calendar (January and February), but these were placed originally at the end of the year. This is why the Roman priests inserted the extra days at the end of February (and why we add a leap day in the same month). At some point later the "new year" was moved to January 1st, and by 153 BC, the new consuls took office on that day. The months July and August, originally Quintilis ("the fifth month") and Sextilis ("the sixth month"), were named after Julius Caesar and his adopted son Augustus because of their exceptional careers.

A more detailed discussion of how the Romans reckoned time within a month—they had no concept of the seven-day week until very late—can be found in "A Roman Calendar" in the documentary section of this volume.

**Days**. The Romans broke a day into twelve hours beginning at sunrise and ending at sunset. Because the length of a day varied greatly from winter to summer, an hour was about 44.5 minutes at the winter solstice, but about 75.5 minutes in high summer. Night, like day, could be broken into twelve equal hours, or, under the influence of the military system, into four watches. When the Romans wanted to measure out certain lengths of time, such as in trials where an attorney had a specific allotment of time to speak, they could employ a water clock (*clepsydra*).

526

# ROMAN CURRENCY, WEIGHTS, AND MEASURES

## Currency

After the Second Punic War, Roman money became the currency of the whole Mediterranean world. Only Egypt remained somewhat isolated, with its own system of currency. Unlike our current system, ancient coinage was based on the intrinsic value, that is, coins were made of precious metal. The units of Roman money around the time of Augustus are as follows:

*as* (pl. *asses*). A bronze coin, originally weighing about a Roman pound, but later reduced to 1/24 lb. A *quadrans* (a "fourther"), a small copper coin, was one-fourth the value (and weight) of an *as*.

*sestertius* (pl. *sestertii*, English "sesterces"). Originally a small silver coin, later a larger brass coin. All significant values were computed in sesterces, abbreviated *HS*.

*denarius* (pl. *denarii*). The standard silver coin, struck eighty-four to a Roman pound. Originally equivalent to ten asses (hence the name; *den-* = "ten"), it came to be worth sixteen asses, and was of roughly the same value as the Greek *drachma*, on which it was modeled.

*aureus* (pl. *aurei*). A gold coin, struck forty (forty-five from Nero's time) to a Roman pound, equivalent to twenty-five *denarii*. Not frequently minted or used as currency, the *aureus* was used primarily for large money transfers.

1 *aureus* = 25 *denarii* = 100 *sestertii* = 400 *asses*

Information from Pompeii indicates that wages for skilled laborers were typically between five and sixteen asses a day. From 46 BC to AD 84 Roman legionaries received a daily wage of ten *asses* (compare the lower figures for 2nd century BC in Polybius, ch. 39), which came to 225 denarii a year. Members of the elite praetorian guard received two *denarii* a day (= 730 *denarii* a year).

## Weights and Measures

Weight. A Roman pound was broken down into twelve ounces ("ounce," in fact, comes from Latin *uncia*, "one-twelfth"). A talent was a large unit of weight, equivalent to about eighty Roman pounds.

Volume. The basic unit was a *modius*, which is equivalent to about 8.75 liters or 1 peck. In shops and markets, liquids were usually marketed by the *sextarius* ("one sixther"), which was slightly more our pint. 16 *sextarii* = 1 *modius*; 3 *modii* = 1 *amphora*.

Distance. The Roman *pes* ("foot") was slightly shorter than our modern foot, about 11.65 inches. Our word "mile" comes from the Roman phrase *mille passuum* ("a thousand steps") which, with five Roman feet to a step, came out to about 4,854 feet (compare to our mile of 5,280 feet).

Land Area. The *iugerum* (pl. *iugera*) was a plot of land 240 by 120 Roman feet (about .625 acre), or the amount of land that the Romans thought a pair of oxen could plow in a single day.

# A LIST OF ROMAN EMPERORS TO AD 337

| | | | |
|---|---|---|---|
| Augustus | 27 BC–AD 14 | Elegabalus | 218–222 |
| Tiberius | 14–37 | Severus Alexander | 222–235 |
| Caligula | 37–41 | Maximinus | 235–238 |
| Claudius | 41–54 | Gordian I & II | 238 |
| Nero | 54–68 | Pupienus & Balbinus | 238 |
| Galba | 68–69 | Gordian III | 238–244 |
| Otho | 69 | Philip | 244–249 |
| Vitellius | 69 | Decius | 249–251 |
| Vespasian | 69–79 | Trebonianus Gallus | 251–253 |
| Titus | 79–81 | Valerian | 253–260 |
| Domitian | 81–96 | Gallienus | 253–268 |
| Nerva | 96–98 | Claudius II | 268–270 |
| Trajan | 98–117 | Aurelian | 270–275 |
| Hadrian | 117–138 | Tacitus | 275–276 |
| Antoninus Pius | 138–161 | Probus | 276–282 |
| Marcus Aurelius | 161–180 | Carus | 282–283 |
| Commodus | 180–192 | Numerian | 283–284 |
| Pertinax | 193 | Carinus | 283–285 |
| Didius Julianus | 193 | Diocletian | 284–305 |
| Septimius Severus | 193–211 | Maximian | 286–305 |
| Caracalla | 211–217 | Maxentius | 306–312 |
| Macrinus | 217–218 | Constantine | 306–337 |

# NOTES ON THE TEXTS AND TRANSLATIONS

The following list indicates the editions of the Greek and Latin texts used to produce the translations, along with some other commentaries and scholarly works that we employed. The principal translator, if one of the editors, is indicated in parentheses, though the work of each was thoroughly vetted by the other and can reasonably be said to be the product of both. In those cases where we reprint another scholar's translation, no initials appear and the citation indicates the source. This list does not include the sources for the documents in the Documentary section, which are indicated along with the translations themselves.

## Authors

| | |
|---|---|
| Appian (RSS) | Mendelssohn, L., and P. Viereck. 1905. *Appiani Historia Romana.* Leipzig: Teubner. |
| Augustus (RSS) | Brunt, P. A., and J. M. Moore. 1967. *Res Gestae Divi Augusti The Achievements of the Divine Augustus.* Oxford, UK: Oxford University Press. |
| Catullus (CF) | Quinn, K. 1973. *Catullus: The Poems.* 2nd ed. London: Macmillan. Commentary: Fordyce, C. J. 1961. *Catullus: A Commentary.* Oxford, UK: Clarendon Press. |
| Cicero, M., *Archias* (CF) | Clark, A. C. 1911. *M. Tulli Ciceronis Orationes.* Oxford, UK: Oxford University Press. Commentary: West, G. S. 1987. *Cicero: Pro Archia.* Bryn Mawr, PA: Bryn Mawr Latin Commentaries. |
| Cicero, M., *Letters* (CF) | Shackleton Bailey, D. R. 1965–7. *Cicero's Letters to Atticus.* 6 vols. Cambridge, UK: Cambridge University Press; Shackleton Bailey, D. R. 1977. *Cicero: Epistulae ad Familiares.* 2 vols. Cambridge, UK: Cambridge University Press; and Shackleton Bailey, D. R. 1980. *Cicero: Epistulae ad Quintum Fratrem et M. Brutum.* Cambridge, UK: Cambridge University Press. Our notes are indebted to these works, as well as to Walsh, P. G. 2008. *Cicero: Selected Letters.* Oxford, UK: Oxford University Press. |
| Cicero, Q. (CF) | Shackleton Bailey, D. R. 1988. *M. Tullius Cicero, Epistulae ad Quintum Fratrem.* Stuttgart: Teubner, 142–64. Commentary: Laser, G. 2001. *Quintus Tullius Cicero Commentariolum Petitionis.* Darmstadt: Wissenschaftliche Buchgesellschaft. |

Epictetus (RSS)    Boter, G. J. 2007. *Epictetus Encheiridion.* Berlin and New York: De Gruyter.

Horace (CF)    Wickham, E. C., and H. W. Garrod, eds. 1912. *Q. Horati Flacci Opera.* 2nd ed. Oxford, UK: Oxford University Press.

Juvenal (CF)    Braund, S. M. 1996. *Juvenal: Satires Book I.* Cambridge, UK: Cambridge University Press.

Livy    From: Warrior, V. 2006. *Livy: The History of Rome, Books 1–5.* Indianapolis: Hackett. Reprinted by permission of Hackett Publishing Company, Inc. All rights reserved. The notes and section headings to Livy and the added Eutropius excerpts are our own.

Lucretius    From: Smith, M. F. 2001. *Lucretius: On the Nature of Things.* Indianapolis: Hackett. Reprinted by permission of Hackett Publishing Company, Inc. All rights reserved. We have adapted the notes to fit the new context.

Martial (CF)    Shackleton Bailey, D. R. 1993. *Martial: Epigrams.* 3 vols. Cambridge, MA: Harvard University Press.

Novatian (CF)    Saggioro, A. 2001. *Novaziano: Gli Spettacoli.* Bologna: Centro Editoriale Dehoniano.

Ovid, *Ars* (CF)    Kenny, E. J. 1994. *P. Ovidi Nasonis: Amores, Medicamina Faciei Femineae, Ars Amatoria, Remedia Amoris.* Oxford, UK: Oxford University Press. Commentary: Hollis, A. S. 1977. *Ovid: Ars Amatoria, Book 1.* Oxford, UK: Oxford University Press.

Ovid, *Fasti* (RSS)    Fantham, E. 1998. *Ovid Fasti Book IV.* Cambridge, UK: Cambridge University Press.

Ovid, *Tristia* (CF)    Owen, S. G. 1915. *P. Ovidi Nasonis Tristium libri.* Oxford, UK: Oxford University Press.

Perpetua (CF)    Halporn, J. W. 1984. *Passio Sanctarum Perpetuae et Felicitatis.* Bryn Mawr: Bryn Mawr Latin Commentaries.

Petronius    From: Ruden, S. 2000. *Petronius Satyricon.* Indianapolis/Cambridge, MA: Hackett Publishing Company. Reprinted by permission of Hackett Publishing Company, Inc. All rights reserved. We have adapted the notes to fit the new context.

Pliny (CF)    Mynors, R. A. B. 1963. *C. Plini Secundi Epistularum libri decem.* Oxford, UK: Oxford University Press. Commentary: Sherwin-White, A. N. 1966. *The Letters of Pliny: A Historical and Social Commentary.* Oxford, UK: Oxford University Press.

Plutarch (RSS)    Perrin, B. 1914, 1918. *Plutarch's Lives.* Vols. 2 & 6. Cambridge, MA: Loeb Classical Library. Commentary: Sansone, D. 1989. *Plutarch: The Lives of Aristeides and Cato.* Warminster, UK: Aris & Phillips.

Polybius (RSS)    Walbank, F. W., and C. Habicht, eds. 2011. *Polybius: The Histories, Books 5–8.* Trans. W. R. Paton. Cambridge, MA:

|  | Harvard University Press. Commentary: Walbank, F. W. 1957. *A Historical Commentary on Polybius*. Vol. 1. Oxford, UK: Clarendon Press. |
|---|---|
| Quintilian (RSS) | Winterbottom, M., ed. 1970. *M. Fabi Quintiliani Institutionis Oratoriae Libri Duodecim*. Oxford, UK: Oxford University Press. |
| Seneca, *Apoc.* (RSS) | Eden, P. T. 1984. *Seneca: Apocolocyntosis*. Cambridge,UK: Cambridge University Press. |
| Seneca, *Letters* (RSS) | Reynolds, L. D. 1965. *L. Annaei Senecae ad Lucilium Epistulae Morales*. Oxford, UK: Clarendon Press. |
| Sulpicia (CF) | Lowe, N. J. 1988. "The Syntax of Sulpicia." *Classical Quarterly* 38: 193–205. |
| Valerius Maximus | From: Walker, H. J. 2004. *Valerius Maximus, Memorable Deeds and Sayings: One Thousand Tales from Ancient Rome*. Indianapolis: Hackett. Reprinted by permission of Hackett Publishing Company, Inc. All rights reserved. We have adapted the notes to fit the new context. |
| Vergil (RSS) | Mynors, R. A. B. 1972. *P. Vergili Maronis Opera*. Oxford, UK: Oxford University Press. |

# Documentary Section

| Inscriptions (CF) | The source of each inscription is provided after the translation; a list of abbreviations is provided on p. 502. |
|---|---|
| Twelve Tables (RSS) | We follow the order and text of Warmington, E. H. 1967. *Remains of Old Latin*. Vol. 3. Cambridge, MA: Harvard University Press, with minor modifications based on Crawford, M. H. 1996. *Roman Statutes*. Vol. 2. London: Institute of Classical Studies. |
| The Praeneste Calendar (RSS) | Degrassi, A. 1963. *Inscriptiones Italiae*. Vol. 13.2. Rome: Libreria dello Stato. |
| A Roman Schoolbook (CF) | *Colloquia Monacensia*, in Goetz, G. 1892. *Hermeneumata Pseudodositheana. Corpus Glossariorum Latinorum*. Vol. 3. Leipzig: Teubner, 644–54. |

# GLOSSARY

Latin and Greek terms are printed in italics, except for those that have been naturalized into English by long use.

**academic:** member of a school of philosophy (based originally in a public gymnasium in Athens sacred to the hero Academus) associated with a rigorous skepticism that denied the possibility of knowledge and enjoined the suspension of judgment.

**aedile:** a magistrate, elected annually, in charge of streets, sacred and public buildings, and weights and measures; this office was found in *municipia* in addition to Rome.

**amphitheater:** an enclosed oval area used for gladiatorial games and other public spectacles.

**Appian Way:** the principal route from the city of Rome to Capua, and later to Brundisium, paved in the 3rd and 2nd centuries BC.

**Aqua Marcia:** an important aqueduct built in the 140s BC that brought the coolest and purest water of all Roman city aqueducts directly to the Capitol.

**Arval Brother:** member of a prestigious board of twelve priests, the *fratres Arvales*, whose main ritual obligations were the festival of the goddess Dea Dia and later the annual vows for the safety of the reigning emperor.

*as* (pl. *asses*): a bronze coin; see Appendix "Roman Currency, Weights, and Measures."

**Asia:** Roman province organized in 133 BC in what is now northwestern Turkey, home to several prosperous Greek-speaking cities.

**atrium** (pl. atria): front room of a Roman house, where the master of the house would receive his visitors in the morning (see *salutatio*).

*auctoritas*: influence, clout (as opposed to formal authority), a type of power typically ascribed to the Senate, which had mainly advisory powers. Augustus later claimed that it was a major part of his success.

*augur*: a diviner or priest whose task it was to take the auspices before the beginning of any public business (*see* auspices).

*Augustalis* (or *sevir Augustalis*): priests, usually freedmen, who were responsible for maintaining the imperial cult both in Rome and in towns throughout the empire.

**auspices:** observation of the flight, feeding, or other behavior of birds (believed to indicate the approval or disapproval of the gods) prior to taking some important action.

**basilica:** a general term for the long, rectangular administrative buildings normally abutting the forum of a town or city.

**Board of Fifteen:** a priestly college of the city of Rome that performed sacred rites for the gods of the Roman state religion, and were in charge of the interpretation of the prophetic Sibylline Books, consulted in times of crisis (*see* Sybilline Books).

Board of Seven: one of the priestly colleges of the city of Rome, responsible for organizing the annual sacrificial banquet in honor of Jupiter, Juno, and Minerva during the Plebeian Games in November.

Board of Three: the name of several committees in Rome; one had oversight of the
mint, while another was in charge of supervising the distribution of land during
the Gracchan reforms.

Campus Martius: the "Field of Mars," an open area in the center of Rome along the
Tiber, used for the gathering of armies and, at other times, for recreation.

censor: an officer in charge of the census, and of reviewing the moral conduct of senators and *equites*.

census: a periodic counting (normally every five years) of the number of Roman citizens, whom two elected senior magistrates, called censors (see above), ranked
according to the amount of property they possessed.

centurion: the principal professional officer of the Roman army, of which the standard
legion had sixty, six for each of ten cohorts.

*cinaedus*: a male prostitute or slave concubine.

circus: a Roman racetrack for chariot racing, the most famous being the Circus Maximus in the heart of Rome.

cognomen: see Appendix "Roman Naming Conventions."

*collegium*: a formal organization of people with shared interests, whether religious,
professional, or social.

*colonia*: a settlement or colony of citizens sent from Rome.

Comitium: central public meeting space in the Roman Forum; the plural (*comitia*)
refers to an assembly of the Roman people for electing magistrates or passing laws.
For the various *comitia*, see the introduction to Q. Cicero, *Running for Office: A
Handbook*.

consul: the highest political office at Rome during the Republic, held annually by two
men, who gave their names to the year.

*contio*: an (often raucous) mass meeting of the people summoned to the Forum by a
magistrate to address them on matters of policy or politics—to be distinguished
from the more orderly *comitia*, or voting assemblies, in which the people were
divided up into categories for voting purposes.

*cursus honorum*: a mostly standardized career path followed by public office holders,
including the various magistracies, such as quaestor, aedile, praetor, and consul, to
be held in sequence and only after certain minimum ages.

curule chair: an ornate ivory folding seat used by higher Roman magistrates, who were
called "curule" magistrates.

decimation: a punishment inflicted on undisciplined military units by selecting one-
tenth (*decima*) of the men to be put to death.

decurion: a member of a town council or municipal senate outside Rome, typically
composed of ten (*dec-*) divisions of ten men each. They had various responsibilities, including collecting taxes; successful decurions could have access to higher
posts in the Roman imperial administration.

denarius: a silver Roman coin; see Appendix "Roman Currency, Weights, and Measures."

*devotio*: the devotion by a general of himself and his army to the infernal gods on his country's behalf.

*Di Manes*: the spirits of the dead, often conceived of as underworld gods.

dictator: a magistrate of the Roman Republic with temporary (maximum of six months) but absolute powers, appointed in times of emergency.

*dignitas*: excellence, dignity, honor; rank, status, or, alternatively, a public office conferring such rank and status.

divination: the gaining of insight or discovery of the unknown or the future (that is, the will of the gods) by observation of the supernatural or by magical means.

dole: see *sportula*.

donative: a donation or gift, especially one given formally or officially by a general or later the emperor.

*duumvir* (pl. *duumviri*): the two senior annually-elected magistrates at Pompeii and other towns, roughly equivalent to the consuls in Rome.

*encyclios paideia*: general education, intended to train the intellect and form the character of a youth through a general study of grammar, rhetoric, dialectics, arithmetic, geometry, astronomy, and music.

Epicureans: followers of the moral and natural philosopher Epicurus (341–270 BC), who pursued contentment by secluding themselves from the affairs of the city and living a simple lifestyle; Epicurus' philosophical ideas are particularly known via the Roman poet Lucretius' *On the Nature of Things* (*De rerum natura*).

equestrian class: see *equites*.

*equites*: translated in English as "the knights," or "equestrians," these men comprised a small but politically influential class of the non-senatorial rich, numbering perhaps 5,000 men in the reign of Augustus, so called because in the early period they were classed together in voting assemblies based on service in the cavalry. They wore an identifying gold ring and dress, served as the primary jury pool, appeared together in an annual parade on horseback (July 15), and sat together in the first fourteen rows at the theater.

*fasces*: bundles of rods, usually including an axe, given to senior magistrates and carried by attendants called lictors.

*fasti*: the list of festivals and other significant events recurring annually that represents the Roman calendar; also the name of a poem by Ovid.

fetial priest: see *fetiales*.

*fetiales*: a college of twenty priests who were consulted by the Senate in matters of war and peace and international relations.

*flamen*: a priest assigned to carry out the rituals associated with a particular deity.

forum: a town square and associated public buildings, the center of public and political life, devoted especially to legal business, banking, and assemblies; the main one in Rome was the Forum Romanum, often referred to as "the Forum."

Galli: eunuch priests of the goddess Cybele.

*gens*: a Roman clan or group of families sharing the same *nomen*, whose lines led back to a putative "first" ancestor. See more in Appendix "Roman Naming Conventions."

*haruspex* (pl. *haruspices*): a priest who, when consulted by the Senate or a private individual, interpreted signs from the gods observed in thunderbolts, unusual or unnatural events, or in the entrails of sacrificial animals.

*imaginēs*: wax portrait-masks of distinguished ancestors displayed by Roman nobles in the atrium of the house, and brought out to be paraded at the funerals of family members.

*imperator*: the term for "victorious general," later used as a title of the *princeps* (our word "emperor" comes from *imperator*).

*imperium*: in the Republic, the power to lead an army through the offices of consul and praetor (and proconsul and propraetor); later, the power exercised by Roman emperors (hence our word "empire").

insula: a large, multi-story apartment complex that usually occupied a whole city block (hence the name "island").

intercalary month: extra days in February added by the *pontifices* every other year (or so) to bring the lunar calendar into sync with the solar year.

*iugerum* (pl. *iugera*): a Roman unit of area, roughly .625 acre. See Appendix "Roman Currency, Weights, and Measures."

Julian Laws on Marriage: a series of laws passed in 18 BC which punished adultery, laid down penalties for those who were unmarried, and offered privileges for those with three children.

Lares (sing. Lar): Roman spirits that were worshipped in houses, on streets, and at crossroads, and were conceived of as the guardians of houses, city quarters, or villages.

Latium: the region of central Italy where Rome was located, and where Latin was originally spoken.

*latus clavus*: the broad purple stripe stitched on the tunic (not the toga), the wearing of which was the first step in the promotion of a man of equestrian rank to the Senate; *equites* wore a narrower stripe than men of senatorial status.

Leaders of the Youth: young members of the equestrian order, including senators' sons who had not yet started serving in public office, took part in an organization known as *iuvenes* ("young men"). Augustus named his two grandsons as "Leaders" of this group, establishing the precedent of the emperor naming his future heir(s) in such a fashion.

*legatus*: "legate," a deputy assistant to a general, provincial governor, or the emperor.

lictor: an attendant of senior magistrates who carried bundled wooden rods (*fasces*), symbolic of the magistrate's authority to punish.

*lituus*: curved staff used for taking the auspices (see *augur*).

Lupercalia: a ritual celebrated in Rome on February 15, which included the sacrifice of a goat and a running through the center of the city by the "Luperci," men naked except for a pelt loincloth. These men would hit the bystanders, particularly the women, with goatskin straps, an action which was considered to be fertility-promoting.

*lustrum*: a special purification ceremony conducted by the censors after the taking of the census every five years.

*Manes*: see *Di Manes*.

*medimnos*: a Greek dry measure of about 50 liters or 11.5 gallons, used to express amounts of grain given as military and other rations.

military tribune: *see* tribune (military).

mime: a leading genre of comic theater in the late Republic and imperial periods (along with "pantomime"). Mostly improvisational and cruder than comedy proper, it featured colorful interplay of speech, song, dance, and clowning; adultery and seduction plots; intrigues and deceptions of all kinds; gross obscenity; and riotous action.

*municipium* (pl. *municipia*): a self-governing town or community in Italy (under the empire, applied to similar communities outside Italy).

*myrmillo*: a type of heavily armed gladiator.

New Man (Lat. *novus homo*): the first man in his family to reach political distinction in Rome; "upstart."

*nomen*: the Roman name indicating one's *gens*: see Appendix "Roman Naming Conventions."

*nomenclator*: a slave kept by Roman politicians, charged with accompanying his master and informing him of the names of those he met.

*obol*: a Greek coin, six to the *drachma*, and so roughly 1/6 of a Roman denarius.

*optimates*: politicians who favored the interests of the *optimi* or "best men" (their own flattering term) and upheld the authority of the Senate. They opposed the distributions of wealth and property made to citizens by their opponents, the *populares*.

ovation (*ovatio*): a minor triumph, granted to a general whose success in war was considerable but did not meet the standards for a full triumph.

*paedagogus*: a child-minder, usually an older and trusted male slave, charged with monitoring a youth's public behavior in the streets, at meals, etc., and escorting him to and from school.

pantomime: a kind of (primarily mythological) drama performed by masked, sinuously-moving dancers to the accompaniment of music, extremely popular in the Roman empire of the 1st century AD and later.

*paterfamilias*: the "father of the family," the male Roman head of a household, usually a father or grandfather, who held *patria potestas* ("fatherly power") over his descendants and household slaves.

patrician: member of a privileged class of Roman citizens, an aristocracy of birth especially important in early Roman history, but mainly an honorific title by the late Republic.

plebeian: *see* plebs.

plebs (adj. plebeian): the general body of Roman citizens, as distinct from the patricians; the common people, the rank and file (plebs is a singular noun, referring to the group as a whole).

*pomerium*: the sacred boundary of the city; burial was not permitted within it, and soldiers under arms could not enter except during a triumph.

*pontifex* (pl. *pontifices*): member of the most important board of priests in the city of Rome (there were fifteen in the late Republic), whose main duty was to advise the Senate on religious matters, and which was led by the chief priest or Pontifex Maximus.

pontiff: see *pontifex*.

*populares*: politicians who claimed to represent the interests of the people, as opposed to the Senate and the upper orders generally, stressing the sovereignty of the popular assemblies and the importance of the office of tribune of the people, and advocating economic and social reforms to help the poor (see *optimates*).

*praenomen*: the first name of a Roman citizen; see Appendix "Roman Naming Conventions."

praetor: the second most important of the annually elected magistrates after the consuls, the praetors (eight in the late Republic, twelve in the principate) held *imperium* and were in charge of the legal system and served as provincial governors after their terms of office.

praetorian prefect: commanding officer of the Praetorian Guard, an elite army unit that, beginning with Augustus, served in Rome, and protected the person of the emperor.

prefect: an appointed administrator or supervisor.

*princeps*: "first man," the title preferred by Augustus to describe his anomalous position in the Roman constitution (as opposed to king or dictator); it became a synonym for "emperor," and the origin of the modern term for Augustus' refashioned constitution, the "principate."

principate: the regime established by Augustus, who called himself *princeps*; also, the period of Roman history between Augustus and the late 3rd century AD.

proconsul: *see* propraetor.

procurator: manager, keeper, superintendent; also a title used for several posts in the imperial civil administration.

propraetor (proconsul): an official who exercised the responsibilities and competencies of a praetor (or consul) through a process called prorogation, whereby a praetor's (or consul's) powers, most importantly *imperium*, were extended beyond their term of office.

proscription: publication of a list of Roman citizens who were declared outlaws and whose property was confiscated, a technique occasionally used for the purging of enemies by victors in the Roman civil wars, especially under Sulla and the Second Triumvirate.

*publicani*: companies of private businessmen who were contracted to perform various functions for the Roman government, such as building projects, but especially tax collection.

Punic Wars: a series of three wars between Rome and Carthage (the Latin word for Carthaginians is *Poeni*), that took place between 264 and 146 BC, starting over control of Sicily and ending with the complete destruction of Carthage, whose territory became the Roman province of Africa.

quaestor: a magistrate who performed mainly financial duties as an assistant to higher magistrates or provincial governors; it was the first step of the *cursus honorum*.

Quirinus: a god worshipped on the Quirinal Hill in Rome, commonly identified with the deified Romulus.

Quirites: a formal name for the citizens of Rome collectively in their peacetime functions, often used in direct addresses and appeals.

*relegatio*: a relatively mild form of exile, in which the offender was removed from Italy but retained basic civil rights such as citizenship and the right of making a legally valid will.

Republic: government by elected magistrates and popular assemblies; also, the period of Roman history between the fall of the kings in 509 BC and the rise of Augustus (*see* principate).

*retiarius*: a gladiator who carried a net (*rete*) for entangling his opponent.

Rostra: the platform from which speakers addressed the people of Rome in the Forum, adorned with the ramming beaks (*rostra*) of ships captured at Antium in 338 BC.

Salian Priests: an ancient priesthood devoted to Mars, noted for their sacred dances and a special hymn, the *Carmen Saliare*.

Salii: *see* Salian Priests.

*salutatio*: "morning greeting," the formal reception in the atrium of the house; here great Roman patrons and statesmen met their clients and friends who came en masse in the morning to pay their respects.

Saturnalia: a popular Roman festival, lasting between three and seven days in December, at which gifts were exchanged, and the social distinction between masters and slaves was set aside, with slaves dining with their masters.

*scurra*: an entertainer, professional or non-professional, who specialized in calling out and humorously criticizing those he saw as falling short of community standards, a sort of insult comic.

Secular games: theatrical games and sacrifices held by the Roman state to commemorate the end of one era (*saeculum*) and the beginning of another—notionally every 100 or 110 years, but the timing was sometimes adjusted.

*secutor*: "pursuer," a type of gladiator who was typically matched with a retiarius.

sesterce: see Appendix "Roman Currency, Weights, and Measures."

*seviri*: see *Augustalis*.

Sibylline Books: secret, prophetic books associated with a priestess or Sibyl based at Cumae on the Bay of Naples, a collection of cryptic texts in Greek hexameters believed to be relevant to the fate of Rome and consulted in times of crisis (*see* Board of Fifteen).

Social War: a war within an existing group of allies (*socii*), especially the struggle between Rome and her Italian allies (91–88 BC) that resulted in the full inclusion in Roman citizenship of all Italy south of the Po River.

*sportula*: a gift of food or money given in Rome by patrons to clients, notionally a basket (*sportula*) of food given in lieu of the old-fashioned invitation to a proper dinner (*cena recta*), but in the 1st century AD more often a money dole of 100 *quadrantes*.

strigil: a curved metal instrument used to scrape off the oil, sweat, and grime after exercise and a visit to the baths.

suffect consul: a man appointed to the consulship to replace (*sufficio*) either a consul who had died, or (from the time of Julius Caesar) one who was still living, in order to increase the number of consulars; the first consuls of the year were then styled "ordinary" (*ordinarii*).

talent: see Appendix "Roman Currency, Weights, and Measures."

Tarpeian Rock: a precipitous cliff on the Capitoline Hill in Rome off which murderers and traitors were thrown, named after the famous mythical traitor of the time of Romulus, Tarpeia.

Tartarus: in Greek mythology, the name of the deepest region of the underworld, a place of punishment.

Temple of Janus: a double gate and shrine to Janus in the Roman Forum, with one door facing east and one to the west, the directions into which the two bearded faces of the statue looked; the double doors were shut during periods of peace in the entire empire, a gesture that goes back to King Numa and was revived later by Augustus.

*thraex*: a kind of gladiator armed like a Thracian, with a sabre and short shield.

toga: a woolen robe that was worn only by Roman citizens; for two specific types, see next entries.

*toga praetexta*: a toga that was edged (*praetexta*) with an ornamental border of purple, worn as the formal dress of magistrates and priests, but also by boys before the donning of the *toga virilis*.

*toga virilis*: the toga of manhood, the plain, adult's toga made from undyed wool, whose ceremonial donning marked at one and the same time the attainment of adulthood and of legal competency (see *toga praetexta*).

tribe: a division of the Roman people, initially based on kinship, but in the later Republic based on place of residence.

tribune (military): military officers of equestrian status (see *equites*), of lower rank than the consul or praetor but higher than centurions.

tribune of the people (*tribunus plebis*): Roman magistrate traditionally appointed first in 494 BC to protect the plebs from patrician oppression, and continuing through the Republic and principate with varying duties.

*triclinium*: the dining room of a house, where "three couches" (*tri* + *klinai*) would have been set out for diners, who ate reclining on them.

trireme: the primary Greek warship of the classical period, having three (*tri-*) banks of oars (*remi*).

triumph: a victory procession through the city of Rome developed in the period of the Republic; voted on by the Senate, it was a thanksgiving service for a decisive victory, a military parade, and a widely enjoyed public spectacle. *See also* ovation.

triumvirate: a term used to designate the "rule of three men"; the first triumvirate (60 BC) consisted of Pompeius, Crassus, and Caesar, while the second (43 BC) was composed of Marcus Antonius, Octavian, and Lepidus.

Vestal Virgin: member of the order of six priestesses in Rome dedicated to the service of Vesta, chosen from the aristocracy and sworn to a lifetime of celibacy and chastity.

villa: a country estate, originally a working plantation, but later also a lavish rural retreat for wealthy city dwellers.

Wise Man: the Stoic term (Latin *sapiens*) for a human of perfected reason, one who does not experience any troublesome emotions (such as the canonical four: fear, grief, hope, or overexcitement) because he properly evaluates what is good (virtue) and what is not (everything else, including money, fame, public office, and even one's bodily health).

# INDEX